"Melissa has ⟨...⟩ creating a profitable practice. We don't learn this in graduate school and Melissa has structured advice and tips to help you grow faster. We all need guides and coaches, and Melissa is clearly adding her voice to the conversation. I couldn't be more impressed!"

— *Joe Sanok, Private Practice Consultant and #1 Podcaster*

"If there's one thing I know, it's the power of working with people who truly know their craft. Melissa is one of those people. Not only does she share incredible, experience-based wisdom and thought-provoking ideas and concepts in this book, but she does so with an empathy that most don't possess. A true leader in her field, this book is going to help thousands of other like-minded professionals do what Melissa does daily: help people."

— *Chris Ducker, Best-Selling Author, Podcaster, and Entrepreneur*

"The Profitable Private Practice is an honest exploration of everything a therapist in private practice wishes they knew when starting a business. There are many pitfalls that therapists run into when starting and maintaining a private practice. Melissa tackles them all in this book! In my own experience, I wish I had such a thoughtful book that navigated me through the maze of business development in mental health. I'm so glad that therapists have Melissa's book as a valuable resource. I will be recommending this book to everyone."

—Ernesto Segismundo Jr., M.S. Licensed Marriage & Family Therapist (LMFT); Professor; Founder and Owner of www.FYLMIT.com

"Melissa DaSilva is ON FIRE in her industry. If you have a private practice or plan on starting one, read this book. She discusses the ins-and-outs of running a therapy business that most people take years to learn. Take my advice, and read this book!"

—John Lee Dumas, Founder and Host of the Podcast "Entrepreneurs on Fire"

"Authentic and transparent, Melissa DaSilva delivers her step-by-step strategies for building a profitable private practice. Melissa is magical; her enthusiastic personality, relentless drive, unstoppable passion and 'There's Always a Way' attitude makes her THE PERSON to model after if you want to build a profitable private practice. I am consistently amazed at Melissa's optimism — when it appears all roads are closed, she finds a way! She never gives up. I highly recommend this book to anyone staring a private practice. Melissa shares her strategies and problem-solving skills to running a *successful private practice.*"

–*Jax Anderson, The Psyko Therapist*

The Profitable
Private Practice

by Melissa DaSilva, LICSW

First Edition, 2018

ISBN 9781731332851

Indie Published by Melissa DaSilva

Contents

Acknowledgements..................................11

Foreword..13

Introduction..16

Chapter 1: Why Start a Private Practice?.....28

Chapter 2: What's Your Niche?....................45

Chapter 3: Branding................................56

Chapter 4: Your Office Space...................60

Chapter 5: Money Mindset....................67

Chapter 6: Naming Your Business............76

Chapter 7: HIPAA and More...................87

Chapter 8: Your Website.......................100

Chapter 9: Email Marketing..................119

Chapter 10: Online Marketing................128

Chapter 11: Community Marketing............151

Chapter 12: Networking.........................159

Chapter 13: Making the Money..............173

Chapter 14: Becoming an In-Network
    Provider..191

Chapter 15: Your First Client Session.........198

Chapter 16: Assessments, Progress Notes
    & Treatment Plans..........................208

Chapter 17: Filling Out Claims...............212

Chapter 18: What to Do With All That Cash ..236

Chapter 19: Taking Care of Yourself So You
    Can Take Care of Business…………………...240

References…………………………………………..250

About the Author…………………………..…..252

by Melissa DaSilva

Dedication

———

To my husband, for keeping me grounded but
never holding me back.

The
Profitable
Private
Practice

How to Start, Run, and
Grow a Therapy Practice

By Melissa DaSilva, LICSW

Acknowledgements

———

There are so many people I need to acknowledge for helping me grow as a person and as a successful entrepreneur. First, I need to thank my mother for teaching me how to be creative and teaching me that if there is a will then there is a way. I also want to acknowledge my father. Even though he isn't with me in this life any longer, I know he has had a hand in my success from the other side. I need to thank my fourth-grade teacher and lifelong friend Sandra Lamb for all her support and for editing all my college papers for me. She was also the one to introduce me to the idea of someday being an author.

My business would not be as successful as it is if it wasn't for my amazing assistant and "Lady Sitter" Selena Ainzuain. I am always impressed by her intelligence, skill and her ability to keep up with me. She always makes me feel like the funniest person in the world. I wish everyone could have a Selena.

Thank you to my Mother-in-Law, Dottie Jean DaSilva. She has been my sounding board, my audience and emotional support on really tough days.

I need to thank John Lee Dumas for teaching me so much about business through his podcasts, books and words of wisdom. His positivity and drive have been infectious. I hope to someday follow in his footsteps to Puerto Rico.

Chris Ducker: as promised, his Tropical Think Tank event was life changing. He opened my world to online business and changed the way I think about entrepreneurship. I am still striving to be the Chris Ducker of the therapy world.

Thank you to Joe Sanok, my first business coach. Without him and his podcast, I would have never realized that I could live the lifestyle I deserve as well as be a social worker.

Last but not least, I want to thank my book coach Dallas Woodburn. Without her, I would still be writing random thoughts in a notebook labeled "Future Book." Thank you for finding me and being such a support through this process.

Forward

———

When I was five, I had a Kool-Aid stand. I had a little brown table, cups, and sugar water with hints of strawberry. Of the few days I grew the business to employ seven other children. I didn't have to work as hard by doing this. People bought a cup and seven little kids said, "Thank you!"

At the end of one day, I counted the money with my mom. After paying the other kids a portion and set aside money for sugar and Kool-Aid, I had only a few coins left. I had worked all day to make less than my child labor "employees." I gave up on the business.

As a five year old, I had no sense of profit, margins, or an owner's cut. But, when I launched my practice I knew I couldn't run it like a Kool-Aid stand. But, I never took a business class in college. The business guys were usually cocky, smarmy, and just plain weird. I once had a roommate, who was a business major. He wrote an entire paper about the economics of canned soup compared to the "just add water" soup. To me, business had no heart.

But that changed when I launched my practice. I noticed that as I grew, so did my impact on my clients. As I added clinicians, more people experienced impact. Then, I started teaching what I learned on a podcast. More practices helped more people through more therapy and better living for the owner and clinicians.

But that transition and learning wasn't fast. I listened to business podcasts, read books, and got my own consultant. It took years of diligent work and consulting to distil how to run a successful practice.

Most people still run their practices like a Kool-Aid stand. They don't know their numbers. They aren't sure where referrals come from. They put a website up and hope it works. Like a five year old who works all day only to have nothing at the end, most private practice owners are burned out and unsure if they'll be open in a few years.

In a world of lowering insurance rates, while people need more help than ever, we need to have a strong private practice!

Our practices need to be strong financially.
Our marketing needs to be on point.
Our vision for change needs to be clear.

As you pick up Melissa's book, I want you to ask yourself, "Am I creating a Kool-Aid stand?" There is no need to do that, Melissa has distilled the essentials of private practice into this book. So leave behind the Kool-Aid stand approach and get started on building a dynamic practice!

Joe Sanok
Podcaster + Private Practice Consultant
Traverse City, MI
November 2018

Introduction

———

It was a warm Tuesday afternoon, and I was writing this book while sitting outside on my deck with my two dogs. Earlier in that day, I was at my therapy office when I decided that it was way too nice outside to be working inside all day. That was when I decided that as the boss that I am, I am going to go home to take a nap, conduct a phone meeting and relax on my deck to start working on writing this book, which treats various steps on how to create and run a profitable practice, so that you can live the lifestyle you have always wanted.

At the time of writing this book, I had 14 office spaces, a smooth running six-figure therapy business and a successful coaching business. By the time you will be reading this, who knows where I'll be. Maybe I will be speaking on different stages all over the world, or hosting a retreat at my winter home in Puerto Rico which I currently don't own yet, but this is why I am writing this book. I do not only want to give you the step-by-step procedure on how to create and run a successful practice but also to teach you that when you share your dreams with the universe and work your ass off to achieve them, great things will surely happen. Not just for you, but for the others around you as well.

In 2015 I decided to start my own business. Even though I never studied business in school, yet there has always been an entrepreneurial spirit inside of me. I first became aware of this when I was 15. I started working at a beach store on the shores of Westerly, Rhode Island. I fell in love with the challenge of selling the most thong bikinis and temporary tattoos each season. I was good at this. I learned the importance of marketing and branding. This was when I learned that if people know, love and trust you, they are willing to buy from you. This is very important, especially when you're selling bikinis, one of the most dreaded clothing purchases people engage in. I loved the job so much that I had dreamt of one day moving to Florida where it's summer every day, and getting open my resort shop. But that dream never came to be. I think part of me was not wanting to leave my family, while the other part of me was thinking I couldn't have my own business since I didn't have any money. I also felt that a resort wear shop wouldn't make the impact in the world I was hoping to build.

Later, after graduating high school, I decided to pursue the dream of wanting to help others, besides encouraging people to throw caution to the wind and strut their stuff in a Brazilian-cut two-piece. I wanted to become a social worker, to help adolescents who are struggling in life as I had once done. I specifically wanted to be a school social worker.

College was a struggle every step of the way. I have always had challenges with Spelling and grammar. I had an undiagnosed learning disability, which teachers said would be corrected with a new invention called "spellcheck." Because I was born in the 80's so spellcheck was new at that time. However, spellcheck did not help me with my grammar or knowing that three words that sound the same can have three different meanings such as there, their and they're. Don't even get me started on the whole "I before E except after C" bullshit! I learned to work around my spelling and grammar difficulties. Which made writing this book an amazing accomplishment on it's own. I once heard that people who have difficulty with grammar, usually have an easier time with math. Nope, I must be the outlier on that theory since I was also horrible with numbers. I have a tendency to flip them around or just completely forget to add them into equations.

Some might say that these weaknesses are all reinforced by my mindset and belief system. That if I tell myself that I am good with numbers and writing and try hard, I could be much better in these areas. Although this could be true, instead I have learned to accept my weaknesses for what they are and take pride in finding ways to work around them. I can even find humor in them at times. If it wasn't for my inability to write well, I might not have the same strong bond with my fourth-grade teacher as I still do today. If it wasn't for Mrs. Lamb editing all my graduate papers, I may not have gotten through college in the short amount of time that I did. Notice I didn't say: "I probably wouldn't have graduated without her." I know that that would never have happened. I am a hustler and would have found one way or another to get through school. I refuse to fail at anything, especially that which I put my mind to. I think this is one of my favorite qualities I like about myself. Recently a close friend of mine said, "If Melissa had a motto it would be; there is more than one way to skin a cat." I guess that would be a perfect sum up of myself. I also believe that if there is a will, there's a way and that most things in life can be fixed. Maybe not the way you planned it, but the way it was meant to be.

After graduating, advanced standing I might add, I did some work at a couple of nonprofit organizations, doing home-based therapeutic services. After 5 years I finally found my dream job as a social worker at a charter school. I loved this job. I was able to work with adolescents, get summers off, eat tater tots on a regular basis and fulfill my dream of performing "All That Jazz" from the musical Chicago on a big stage in front of the real audience. Believe me it's a true story, it's also on YouTube. Being a school social worker was amazing until my circumstances changed.

School policy changed so I was no longer getting paid through the summer and my physical health started to decline. To this day, I still believe I was suffering from Sick Building Syndrome. I was working in a building built over 100 years ago. I kept experiencing symptoms that resembled carbon monoxide poisoning. However, after testing the air and installing alarms, there was no evidence of carbon monoxide.

The school's idea of dealing with this issue was to try convincing me that I was having anxiety attacks. They moved me to the third floor of our ancient school building, into a larger room without any windows, heat or AC. I had one outlet for everything that needed electricity. This included my overhead lighting, which was in fact a string of Christmas lights. I named my new office The Bat Cave. I felt that this was appropriately named since there was a hatch in my new office to the attic where bats lived. I also received 8 rabies shots after stepping on a bat in this same building. On top of all of these concerns, I had reached the top level of our school's pay scale. At 33 years old I was already making the most of what this position would allow me to make. If I wanted to make more money to live the lifestyle I wanted to live, I would have to get a second job. I knew that this wouldn't work for me. I am an introvert, and I need a lot of time to myself to reset and re-charge to be the best version of myself.

After 8 years of working in this profession, I knew I could not continue at this pace. I began contemplating a career change. Becoming a plumber seemed like a reasonable change. Fixing toilets would help families in a time of need, as well as meet my needs for problem solving. I thought of naming my company Ms. Melissa's Plumbing Company. I would love to do headshots for that profession. Hmm... I may do it for the back cover of this book.

Instead of adding to my school debt and doing a profession change, I took the scary leap of faith and started my own private practice. I was going to take control of my life and my income. I wanted a situation were I would be able to take a nap when I wanted, travel at any time of the year and no longer trade hours for dollars. Working for my own private practice allows me to be happy and still help others.

Although I would have loved to quit the school job completely and just jump into private practice immediately, I realized that this wouldn't have been a good decision. I didn't have any money to start this business. I basically purchased what I needed most on my personal credit card when I started. When I began this business, it was during that first summer where I wasn't receiving a paycheck. I quickly realized I didn't know the basics of starting or running a business. This was not a skill that I had learned in graduate school. So I had to figure it out.

Graduate school teaches us the very important skills of being a therapist such as active listening, specific therapeutic techniques, the code of ethics and how to write effective treatment plans. What they don't teach us is how to make a living as a therapist. They don't teach how to file claims, create a HIPAA compliant office or marketing and branding. I believe that some of the reasons that schools don't teach us the particulars of running a business is because we would have to discuss the topic of money. So many times I've heard, "You don't get into this business for the money." Therapists have been programmed to believe that we shouldn't want to make a lot of money. Wanting to do that would mean that we are selfish and that we are in the wrong profession. I feel that in all entirety, this type of language implies that we shouldn't "want" anything. It goes further to imply that a good therapist is someone who gives of themselves selflessly until there isn't anything left of them. This is a badge of honor.

Have you ever thought about who would show up at your funeral service, and wonder what people would say about you and how you lived your life? I have. I think about how people will be all lined up around the block at my funeral to thank me for all the support and care I had given them at one point in their life. I see them talking to the person behind them in line with how I would have given the shirt off my back if I knew someone needed it. How they are impressed with how many hours I worked a day and all the organizations I helped, yet I always had time to spend with my family. This fantasy then turns into a frightening reality check when I realize that the reason I am dead at 50 is because I worked myself into dying from a stress-induced heart attack!

I believe that this mindset of giving until we can't give anymore needs to change. What we do as a profession is different than what most people think we do. Most people believe that therapists sit in a chair and just listen to people complain all day and get paid a lot of money for it. If you are a therapist, definitely you will know that this is far from the truth. We work extremely hard at creating and holding space for individuals who have experienced life events that no human should have to experience. We remember years of personal stories for each of our clients, as well as change our approach and demeanor with each client depending on what they need as a part of their treatment. Some therapists experience vicarious trauma from listening and experience the pain, fear and terror our clients have experienced. We experience hours and hours of this mentally and physically draining work, while most of us only get 2 weeks of vacation a year.

This is no way to live our lives.

I don't want therapists to burn themselves out trying to live the lifestyle they desire and never getting the opportunity to do so.

I don't want you to think that this process was easy for me. I wasted a lot of time and money trying things that didn't work. I didn't have a specific resource that showed me step-by-step how to start a private practice and make it successful. That is why I am writing this book for you. I am going to walk you through the steps of creating a private practice and how to make it profitable.

I want to warn you: private practice is not for everyone, but we will discuss that more in a little bit. I will also help you with getting on insurance panels, creating intake paperwork, developing a website and how to get your clients. Throughout the book, I will give you suggestion of services you may consider using to help create a successful practice. I may be an affiliate for these services, and if I am it's only because I use or honestly believe they are a good product or service. Although I am not an affiliate for some of the services and products I will suggest, I know they are useful because I have either tried them out myself or I have confidence in the product because of the creator or author. Many of the templates I will discuss in this book will be located on my website, and if you ever need more assistance, I am available for you. Just email me at hello@MsMelissaDaSilva.com.

I suggest that you read through this entire book before implementing the steps right away. It's a good idea to get an overview of the business process before diving into it yourself. A practice can be started on very little money, and I will teach you how this can be done. Creating your own business can be both rewarding and taxing. Remember to take some time for yourself and take it one step at a time.

Chapter 1:
Why Start a Private Practice?

———

In this chapter, we are going to start exploring your "why." In the introduction I discussed my "why." Just in case you skipped the intro, my "why" had to do with wanting more flexibility with my time and more control over my finances. But what I haven't discussed is why I created the particular business model that I created.

When I started my company East Coast Mental Wellness, I knew that I wanted to create a place that therapists would be happy to work. I wanted therapists to be happy, because when they are happy, they do a better job with their clients. The tagline for my company is: "Therapy with results." Fulfilled therapists have more energy to help clients get the results they desire. I started my business with the LGBTQ community in mind. I saw that there was a need for this service and made sure that my practice was known as the place to go no matter what your orientation is. I created a therapeutic environment that is more relaxing than your traditional therapy offices. I offer cold and hot beverages to all clients, comfortable seating and soothing music. Clients should feel safe and comfortable when coming to their appointments.

Another component about my practice that is different than many other therapy practices around me is that I want the client to have more control over who they wanted to see as a therapist. Based on the therapist's profiles describing their ideal client, clients can pick who they feel would best fit their needs. They no longer have to just see the person who has the next opening. We encourage clients to set up consultation calls with their prospective therapist to see if they feel that there is a connection. If there isn't a connection, clients are free to pick another therapist.

This approach has worked well for me. I have created a multiple six-figure business in less than 3 years. I found that it's important to put the people first and the rest will follow. When I think about the future for myself and my business, I like to think about the next 3-5 years. Where I will be and how my business will be different and the same. When I think about the future, I see myself traveling around the world teaching others how to create a successful private practice. My business will be running itself for the most part, and I will still be receiving passive income (passive income will be discussed further in the book). Meanwhile, my practice will continue to offer outpatient services in the office and schools, hopefully in several different states as well.

Since my client base has always been the LGBTQ community, I will continue to give back in different forms. I currently have a seat on the board of Rhode Island's only LGBTQ magazine, and I regularly participate in fundraisers and events that bring attention to the needs of the community. I hope that in the next five years I can start my own non-profit organization that will include a thrift shop for transgender and non-binary individuals. We can raise money for homeless transgender individuals, as well as help with securing access for medical needs such as hormones and surgery.

Now that I have laid out all my "why's" and my future business goals, start thinking about your plans around your private practice.

1. How will it benefit the community you want to serve?
2. How will it enhance your lifestyle and your family?
3. What do you hope your practice will achieve, or what legacy do you hope to leave when you are done with this chapter of your life?

Don't stop yourself from thinking big because you don't believe your dreams are possible for one reason or another. If you want to move to Japan and work with military personnel, then put that out there. Don't let anyone, even yourself, slow you down. To help you out with this a little more, I have created a worksheet for you with specific questions to get you thinking more about your "why's" and where you want to go in the next 3-10 years. This worksheet can be found at TheProfitablePrivatePractice.com

One thing that I did to help me out when I was first starting was to create a vision board. I used a book called *The Right-Brain Business Plan: A Creative, Visual Map for Success* (Lee, 2014). I highly recommend this book if you are like me and need to see things in pictures to fully understand it. I got very specific with my vision board, right down to the colors of my offices. I must warn you, this is not the type of business plan you will want to bring to a bank if you are seeking out loans. They don't seem to understand us artsy right-brain thinkers. Once you have created your vision board, make sure you put it someplace you will see it every day. If you decide to add to your future vision or change a part of it, that's okay. The point is to keep your vision at the top of your mind, so that you know where you are going. I have also found out that it makes a great conversation piece when visitors come into your house.

When creating your vision board, be very specific around not only your business, but what you will be able to do with your time and money when your business is successful. Do you want to travel, have kids, raise puppies or paint murals? Take some time to sit and think about what you really want in your future and get it down someplace—if not on a board, then in a journal or record yourself talking about your future dreams.

Now that you have a vision of what you want out of your life, we need to discuss if private practice is actually for you. If not, it's okay. You can reach your lifestyle goals in other ways, just not by running your own therapy business. Here is what you need to know about getting into this wonderful, yet also frightening, world of running your very own private practice.

The good stuff:

- The sky is your limit in regards to when you want to work, how much you want to make, when you want to take a vacation and who you want to work with when you have your own private practice.
- You can work towards goals that you want to achieve related to the mission of your practice: for example, what causes you want to donate to and the impact you want your practice to make on the world.
- You will decide how you want your company to run.
- You don't have a boss above you who dictates what you do and how you do it.
- You get the opportunity to create something from nothing.
- You can create an office environment that suits your needs as well as the needs of your clients. (I always have a couch for napping in my office.)
- You could create jobs for others if you decided to hire assistants, consultants or clinicians.

Here are some of the not-so-great parts of running your practice:

- If you are sick or need to take time off, you don't make any money.
- You need to create all the systems and processes for intake, payment, scheduling, emergency calls, HIPAA, marketing, website, paying bills, filing and don't forget cleaning. If any of these systems fail, you are the only one responsible for it.
- You have to pay your own taxes quarterly or at the end of the year (this adds up to a lot!)
- Your business will be on your mind all the time, even when you are sleeping. Most likely when you start out, you will be working more than 40 hours a week.
- You are accountable for holding yourself accountable. It's pretty easy to push things until tomorrow when nobody is keeping you to a deadline.
- You need to figure out how you are going to get health insurance.

- You are the only one who makes the big decisions about your business, such as expanding your practice, adding another clinician, or taking out a loan. This means you, and only you, are responsible for the outcome.

I know that there seems like a lot of negative aspects to running your own practice, but they are things you need to know about before starting. As you go through this book, I am going to teach you how to address these issues, but you need to be honest with yourself about whether you really want to jump into this venture and hustle to make it work. Many practices failed in the first year due to the lack of understanding and planning on how to get over the hurdles of starting on your own. Just in case you don't know of anyone who has had a private practice fail, let me give you an example of how easily it can happen.

Meet Chad. He is a clinician who has spent the last 3 years working for a non-profit. Chad loves helping the clients he sees every week, but he feels overworked, underpaid and undervalued by the company. After a long day at work, he goes to his favorite pub and runs into an old grad school classmate. While discussing what life has been like since graduation, Chad learns that his old classmate has started her own private practice. She can't stop talking about all the benefits there are in running your own business. The flexibility, the chance to work with your ideal clients, not having to answer to anyone else, and making some decent money. Chad loves what he hears and decides that maybe he would like to start his own practice.

After leaving his friend that evening, he is so excited about the idea of having his own private practice. He can't sleep so he decides to do some internet research about how much a therapist in private practice can make, how he can start a private practice—if he was smart he would have read this book!—and even starts looking into postings of available office spaces in the area. He researches how much insurance companies will reimburse for sessions; although he doesn't get an exact rate, he rounds it up to around $60 per session.

He pulls out his calculator and does the math.

If Chad sees 40 clients a week at $60 a session, he could make $2,400 a week! If he works 50 weeks out of the year, he could make $120,000!! This is double what he makes at the non-profit. Chad starts thinking that it would be stupid if he didn't start his own practice at once. (Some of you may be thinking that there is no possible way anyone could think this way, but it happens, and I know from my own experience *hanging my head in shame.*) Chad decides that he is going to give his boss at the non-profit a month's notice that he will be leaving the company and begins spending hours looking at possible offices to rent, creating his business cards and setting up his Google Voice account.

Now let's fast forward a month, as we now find Chad in his newly furnished office space waiting for his first client to call. But he isn't getting the clients he thought he would be getting. He has started the process of getting on some insurance panels, but he has learned that it can take up to 120 business days to be approved — that is if they don't lose your application in the process. Even if Chad does get a call from a prospective client, if they want to use their insurance, he won't be able to take them unless they have the insurance plan that allows them to make an out-of-network payment. He could offer to take clients for an out-of-pocket fee, but most people who have insurance will want to use it unless you are offering a service they can't get anywhere else.

While Chad is still waiting for his first clients to call him, he begins to create some intake paperwork and create a Psychology Today profile. He starts looking into creating his website, and learns that websites cost money if you want them to look professional and be found on Google. Chad keeps calling the insurance companies every week to check on his application. He spends hours upon hours waiting on hold for simple answers such as, "It's still in process" or the dreaded, "I don't see your paperwork on file." Chad is starting to feel the stress of a lot of money and time being spent without anything coming back in.

Finally, Chad gets the email that tells him that he has been approved to be paneled on one of the health insurances he applied for. His Psychology Today profile brings him his first client. Things are going well. He completes the first session, gets all the insurance information, which is just a card with a name and a long identification number. He takes a copy of the front and back (because that's what he has seen at his own personal doctor appointments) and creates his first client file. Chad fills out his first claim forms. He doesn't know what all the codes are asking, but he looks them up online and fills it in as well as he can. He slaps a stamp on the envelope and sends it off to the address that was on the back of the client's insurance card.

Three weeks later, he receives an envelope in the mail. It must be the check for the sessions he has had with his client. He opens it up to find that there is no check, just a piece of paper with some codes on it. After looking it over, he realizes that there is a deductible the client needs to meet before the insurance company pays for the sessions. This means that Chad has been seeing this client for four consecutive weeks and was supposed to get full payment for each session from the client. The client owes Chad $240. How is he going to ask that of his client when one of the issues the client talks about in session is the lack of money and how it causes stress in his life. Chad decided that he can't, and that he will just eat the cost and ask the client to pay the cost of the session from here on out.

Although Chad feels uncomfortable talking about money with his client, he explains the situation. The client says that he understands, and then pays for that day's session and leaves. The following week, the client doesn't show up for his session. No call, no show. Chad can't charge for a no show according to his insurance company, so again he has lost money. Let's hope for Chad's sake that he has had some more clients during this time who have been able to pay him. Even if he has had more than this one client, I can guarantee he has spent a lot of time and lost a of money trying to create this practice that he thought would be extremely lucrative. Chad has realized that he spent more time on the phone with the insurance companies and tracking his reimbursements down in the past four months than he has with clients.

The issues that Chad has experienced are issues that aren't normally discussed in graduate school. It's the business side that is usually left out. Chad and many others found that they don't like the business portion of having their own private practice. At this point in his business, Chad can decide if he wants to learn how to create a practice that runs smoothly and make money, or close his doors. (Hopefully he doesn't have a year lease on that great office space!) If he had known a little more about what it takes to run a therapy business, he may have made some different decisions. He might have decided to start his practice on a part-time basis instead of going into it full-time right away. He could have subleased a space for 1 or 2 days a week and slowly built up his business.

Another option would have been to work as an independent contractor under someone else or as part of a group practice. This option is great for those who want more control over how they conduct their therapeutic process and who they want to treat without the hassles of the business side of having your own practice. Typically, all the therapist has to do is show up for sessions and do what they do best, help clients. It's helpful if they try to recruit new clients to the practice, but not always a requirement. Group practices do take a percentage of the therapists' reimbursements that are brought in to cover overhead such as rent, billing, scheduling and marketing. If you're the kind of clinician that doesn't like the business aspect of running your own practice, this percentage is definitely worth it. I have seen clinicians receive between 40-70% of their reimbursements after the group practice takes their cut. Just make sure this agreement is in the contract you sign before you join a group practice.

If I were coaching Chad, I would have suggested that he keep his full-time job, join a group practice and see clients for a few hours a week. Yes, he would have been working a lot of hours a week between the two jobs, but if private practice is what he really wants to do, he will need to work hard at the beginning. Taking this route instead of jumping into private practice right away would have given him the chance to get on insurance panels, get his name out there, provide therapy to the clients he enjoys working with and still have a steady income.

If Chad's story hasn't scared you off yet, I am glad. This means that you have the drive to start your own business and create a profitable private practice.

Don't worry; you won't have to do this all on your own. I am going to teach you the steps you should take when starting out on your own. My way isn't the only way to do this, and I can't guarantee anything, but I am going to share everything I learned from the mistakes I have made and also the successes I have accomplished. I must have done something right since my business hit six-figures in less than 2 ½ years after starting my practice.

Remember, if you have any additional questions you can always find me and other resources on my website aprivatepracticemadeeasy.com. In the next chapter, we are going to start to get into the nitty-gritty of starting your practice. Before anything else, you need to figure out who your client avatar is. We will dive into that much more in Chapter 2.

Let's recap this chapter:

- Decide if Private Practice is for you.
- Create a vision board or a business plan.
- Create a plan of how to responsibly get into the business.

Chapter 2:
What's Your Niche?

One mistake I often see therapists make when they first set out on starting up their own private practice is that they want to be the best therapist to everyone. They want to throw a broad net out there so that they can get as many clients no matter who the client is or what issues they are struggling with. When you try this route, you don't end up getting the clients you love to work with, or who you may not be an excellent match for you.

I know you must be thinking that there is no way that you will want to work with one type of issue day in and day out for the rest of your career. The truth is that you will get clients who are not only your identified client. They will come, you don't have to worry about that. You need to decide what your niche will be, and I am going to help you do that by walking you through the means of identifying what your niche will be so that you can create your client avatar. You can also download the Client Avatar PDF worksheet from this site: TheProfitablePrivatePractice.com

First, take a moment to think about three types of issues or populations you enjoy working with currently or in the past. For example, I enjoy working with angry adolescent boys, individuals struggling with obsessive-compulsive disorder and members of the LGBTQ+ community. Once you have your three groups in mind, think about the group you wouldn't mind spending a majority of your therapeutic hours helping.

- Out of these three groups, who do you feel you are most knowledgeable about?
- Out of the three, who do you have the most connections with personally or in the community? You may have to get creative in this area. For example, do you have a friend who works in the schools system or do you have a history of being a foster parent?
- Who do you know that would have access to the clients you would want referrals from?
- Also, think about people or organizations you have worked with in the past who would be

excited to send referrals your way.

- When you are thinking about what niche you want to work with, what group are you an advocate for or would like to advocate more for?
- What group would need your services in your area?

The goal is to figure out where your low-hanging fruit is, in regards to where you can get referrals of clients you want to work with quickly.

I am going to take you through my process. My three identified groups are angry adolescent boys, clients who struggle with obsessive-compulsive disorder, and members of the LGBTQ+ community.

Angry adolescent boys:

I have a history of working with this population in schools and the community. I have also had lots of success with these clients and it's fun working with them. They seem to connect well with my type of therapy. I would be able to get a lot of referrals from local school since I have worked with them in the past.

Although, thinking about having angry boys as the majority of my clientele—at first instance, the thought wasn't appealing to me. Yes, I was awesome with a couple of angry adolescent boys on my caseload, but to have more than that would be overwhelming and I knew I would burn out quickly. Another negative aspect of working with this population for me is the amount of family work that is involved with the treatment. Although I can work with families, I know that it's not my strong suit. So I don't think that this would be the best population for my identified niche.

Individuals who are dealing with obsessive-compulsive disorder:

This population has always fascinated me. I have been known to binge-watch shows such as Hoarders and My Strange Addiction. Some of my favorite clients have been ones who are struggling with OCD. I am amazed by the way the disorder makes up stories for these clients and can gain control over their lives and the ones around them. I enjoy working on these issues with some of my clients;

however, I know that I don't have the specialized training to help people with severe OCD diagnoses. I also don't have a connection to some sort of referral source specifically for clients with these issues. Another factor is that we already have a great OCD program at our local inpatient hospital. My services would not be in high demand.

Members of the LGBTQ+ Community:

This is the niche that I targeted when I began my private practice. I am passionate about helping people in the LGBTQ community and want to create a safe place for them to receive mental health services. I specifically enjoy working with transgender and non-binary young adults. I know that my services are in need in my area since it was challenging finding a therapist for one of my transgender students while I was working at a school.

I had a good referral opportunity since my husband and I are a part of the community and we are strong advocates too. He plays on the only LGBTQ softball league in our state, and we have family members who also identify as LGBTQ. When I think about helping clients in this niche for the majority of my therapeutic hours, I feel like I would stay energized and not burn out. I am knowledgeable about this area and also excited to learn more about how to help my clients.

When you finally figure out your niche, you need to become even more specific about who your ideal client would be. You want to create a Client Avatar. This is very important, especially when you start to market and brand yourself and when you need to make decisions about your company. Here is an example of my Client Avatar, Taylor.

Taylor is 24 years old and identifies as non-binary. They have recently graduated from college and has been trying to figure out what they would like to do for the rest of their life. They have a full-time job, but is not completely happy with it. Taylor has been in a long-term relationship with this woman but still has questions about their own sexual identity. They are pretty sure that they would like "top surgery" and to legally change their name. They are not sure about having children in the future and has had some trauma in the past.

See how specific I got with my ideal client? Don't forget Taylor, because I am going to refer to them again in the future.

Not all my clients are going to be like Taylor, not even half, but it's important to be that specific so that you know where to start when marketing for clients. When you market to this particular avatar, you will also attract other individuals who may have some qualities as your avatar. Even though I market toward individuals like Taylor, I also get clients who are married and are coming out as transgender, plus clients who are confused about their sexual orientation.

Remember that you can't be the best fit for everyone, but you can be the most awesome therapist for your niche. A part of getting these referrals is making sure that you are offering something to your clients that another therapist may not be offering. You want to be the "it" therapist for your niche. If you are having a difficult time buying into this idea of being, then this look at it this way...

One day you are out shopping, and you have an unfortunate fall in the frozen food aisle. You hurt your back badly and you will have to sue to get some money to cover your medical bills and time you lost not being able to work. You are going to need a lawyer. Your cousin Benny is a lawyer and has done a little work in helping clients with these issues, but it was mostly around car accidents, and that was when he was back in law school. Then there is the lawyer in town who specifically handles personal injury law. You know of her because you have seen her commercials and billboards as well as heard testimonials from people who have worked with her. Wouldn't you want to go to the lawyer who specializes in the area of expertise you need?

You need to think of your practice as you would if you were going to a lawyer or doctor. You don't want a generalist: you want a specialist. As I had stated before, you need to have this niche identified before you start marketing yourself.

Another aspect of getting your name out there is to get people to know, love and trust you. Getting the world to know, love and trust you sounds like a big job and I am not going to lie—it can actually be a big job. But if you want your practice to be successful, people have to know who you are and how amazing you are. You also want people who make an appointment with you to return over and over again. So how do you do this? Some of it has to do with your marketing, but the other part has to do with you and how you present yourself and your business even before you open your doors to the world.

Remember the last time you needed to make a decision about a purchase. It could have been a new gym membership, a phone plan, a doctor or even a restaurant. You will be more likely to choose the person or place you know from experience or from the recommendation from someone else that you trust. This is true for clients when they are looking for a clinician. If people know you and what you do, they will refer to you. If your private practice comes up on a Google search, they are going to click on your website first. A lot of this online marketing stuff will be explained later in the book, but I want to make sure that before you head into getting involved with clients, you need to get the word out about your new practice and what you will be offering that is different from other therapists in your area. You need to start thinking about this even before you leave your full-time job, because the people you are making connections with there may be the people who want to send you clients in the future. Always keep those business cards and get out there and do some socializing.

I have a feeling that a majority of therapists are introverts and the thought of socializing and talking about your future business scares the crap out of you. I know that it did for me when I started. Since most therapists are introverts, you pushing yourself to get out there puts you "ahead of the therapist pack" from the start. You need to be where either your potential clients are or where people who can refer to you are. Another tip for when you are out and about trying to socialize with others in the least awkward way is to use the skills you know best, your therapist skills. You should know how to actively listen by asking others open-ended questions about themselves and how to reflect. It's almost like giving them a sample of what you do for a living. Remember not to go "full therapist" on them, because that wouldn't be ethical, but just be yourself.

Once you get that first client, you are going to want to figure out your style of interaction. I want to warn you that it can be tough at the beginning. I remember when my first private practice client was scheduled to see me. I was so nervous that I was actually praying that she wouldn't show up. She did, and I survived. We had a great therapeutic relationship with a lot of learning on both parts.

So, think of places you can be where people get to know, trust and love you. Will it be at PTA meetings, a friend's picnic, a hair salon? Get creative and get out there. Start letting others know that you are amazing at what you do and that you are creating something great!

Let's Recap:

- Who are your ideal clients? Complete the Avatar Worksheet found here TheProfitablePrivatePractice.com Where are you going to be so that you have contact with your ideal clients?
- Figure out your style of client interaction.
- Get people to know, love and trust you.

Chapter 3:
Branding

———

Discussing branding may seem a little soon in your journey, but it's something that you need to keep in the back of your mind as you start taking more steps in creating your business. Understand that you are creating a product where you are the brand. You embody the practice you are creating with everything you put out there. I feel that branding and mindset can go hand-in-hand. If you want your business to be taken seriously and you want to make six figures, you will need to start thinking about how you exude this.

I tell clinicians all the time, "Clients can smell the lack of self-confidence all over you." Who wants a therapist who isn't a good role model or confident in what they are creating? Clients and non-clients will take your lead in how seriously you take yourself, the services you provide and the business you run by the way you present yourself, your office space and your online marketing.

I realized this when I first started my private

practice. I knew that I want my business to be taken seriously because even if it is just you sharing one office space with two other clinicians part-time, you are running a real business and you need to show that to the world. So this is where you may need to kick the Imposter Syndrome right in the ass, because this is definitely where it's going to start rearing its ugly head. Here are some of the things Imposter Syndrome might try to tell you:

- "A solo practice isn't a real business."
- "Nobody is going to take you seriously."
- "You can't make real money doing this."
- "You don't know what you're talking about with your clients."

If you want a business where you are making six figures, dress and act like you already have a six-figure business. One of the first things I did to help me with this was buy myself a beautiful light blue suede Coach bag. A real one, not off the streets of New York. When I walked around with that purse on my wrist, I felt like a six-figure business owner. I called it my "Six-figure Bitch Bag." Okay, so the truth is, it was purchased at an upscale thrift shop, but I loved it and the way I felt walking into a networking meeting with it.

You don't have to spend a lot of money to appear confident and in charge. Things such as making sure your feet look good if you are wearing open-toed shoes (this goes for men too), having a clean office space, offering water in your waiting area and arriving at session on time are crucial to your branding. Even if you are a hot mess — and let's face it, most of us have stuff we are dealing with in our real lives — you need to check it at the door before you walk into your office. This is another reason why it's good to have your own therapist to check in with you on a regular basis.

Think about how you want people to see you and your business and make sure that the theme or brand is cohesive. Try using a similar color scheme in your logo, website and office space. Sometimes I go as far as matching my clothes to my brand colors. You want to try and use the same type of font on your website, marketing materials and office signage. I use the same headshot on my website, online profiles and business cards. This way, people start to recognize you when they see your face over and over again.

Branding can be a book all on its own, but if you want to learn how to brand yourself and your business, take a look at Marissa Lawton's website http://www.risslawton.com/cathartic-marketing. She teaches techniques specifically geared towards private practitioners.

Now that you have a little understanding about branding yourself and your business, let's start creating your office space in the next chapter.

Let's Recap:
- You are your business and the brand.
- Act the way you want others to see you and your business.
- Keep everything as uniform as possible.

Chapter 4:
Your Office Space

Now you have now figured out who you are specifically going to work with, which would be the avatar you created in Chapter 2, it's time to take that knowledge and use it for the next few steps. You are going to need to think about where the location of your office is going to be. You need to get this information so that you will have an address to put on all of your marketing materials and application for insurance panels if you've decided that you want to take clients who will use their health insurance.

Some things to think about are:

- Where does your avatar live?
- Are they on college campuses, in a remote location or in a specific community?
- Do they have specific need such as access to public transportation, access to an elevator or free off-street parking?
- What will you as the therapist need in your new office location?

- Do you need to be close to home or near childcare?
- Does your office space need to have a window? (This was very important to me after working in my Batcave office.)
- Do you have a certified therapy animal that will be accompanying you?

Another thing to think about is sound in your office space. Spend some time in the potential new space and see if you can hear through the walls or heating vents. This has been an issue for me in the past. I once had an office next door to a therapist that had clients engage in "primal yelling." It was a bit shocking for myself and the client I was having a session with. I have come up with some clever ways to addressing sound issues, which I will share with you in another section of this book.

Another aspect you may want to consider is what population are the people around you serving? Are you going to need a space that caters to children, and will this disturb others around you?

Once you have a general idea of what you are

looking for, you need to think about the amount of time you will be using the space/office. I know you will probably want to get an office that you can use whenever you want, but I advise against this when you are just getting started.

Remember the story I told you about Chad? You are more likely to succeed if you continue your day job and build a practice on your off-hours. This will also help decrease your overhead. As I see it, there are two ways you can go about doing this.

1. You and another clinician, someone you know and trust, can rent a space together. You can split the cost of the rent, utilities, furniture and hours you occupy the space. This can be tricky if you two are not on the same page with how you want the room to work or if one feels that the other is getting prime office hours or you can't agree on the location. There is always the concern that one person may not pay their portion of the rent. That's when you would want to draw up a contract that both of you can agree upon.

2. The other option is to sublease on your own from someone who has office space they aren't using on specific days. Usually, these spaces are already furnished, include utilities and might even possess a great referral source. The downsides can be that the furniture isn't your style and you may not be able to increase your amount of time to include more days if they are renting to other people the days you are not using it.

Another suggestion is to see if you can plan to start renting your desired location a month or two in the future and not right away. This could be beneficial for both of you. If they have someone in a space they know will be leaving in a month or two, they may be willing to agree to have you move right in after they leave. This would also give you some time to get your practice ready and not have to worry about paying rent for a place you're not using because you don't have clients yet. Most landlords would want a security deposit for an agreement such as this.

Once you have decided on the office, you will

need to sign a sublease agreement. Many landlords don't require a full year, so you can negotiate it for six months or a month-to-month basis. If you decide to do a month-to-month agreement, there is usually a clause in the document about giving 30 or more days' notice if you plan on leaving.

If you are having a difficult time finding a place, I suggest you post on your social media pages. If you decide to set up a profile on Psychology Today, you can post on their PeerCast section. And there is always Craigslist: look for rentals in the commercial section. If there is a building you know that you would like to rent in, call the business management office. Sometimes they will be able to help you by letting you know if there is going to be space available or if they know of someone looking to sublease.

The amount you should be paying in rent will be dictated by the location of the market you are in, so I can't give you an exact number on what to expect, but generally, you will only want to spend 30% of your income on rent. You will need to do a little math to figure out what you can afford for a given space. You will need to have a general idea of how much you will be charging for a session; or take a look at what others are charging to get an idea; or, if you plan to get on insurance panels, try to find out how much you might get for reimbursements. Many insurance companies won't tell you what the reimbursement rate is unless you credential with them. You can ask other therapist friends what they get reimbursed.

For the sake of this equation, let's pretend you get $60 for a 45-minute session. You would like to rent an office space for 1 day a week. Your rent would be $150 a month. This means you would need to see 3 clients a month to cover your rent. That's not too bad. If you get one client who sees you weekly, your rent would be covered. Even though you wouldn't be able to pay yourself yet, you would have succeeded in taking care of the rent. That's why you would still be working in your day job from the start.

Don't forget that rent isn't going to be the only expenses you are going to have each month. You will probably want an Electronic Health Record system, a HIPAA-compliant phone system and a website which all cost money each month. Each of those average around $20 a month. See if that will work in your budget to start. You may need to reconsider the amount you are charging (if you are on insurance panels this isn't very negotiable), how many clients you will see and how much the rent is.

This budget doesn't have to be set in stone, and it shouldn't be. It will change as you grow your practice. Speaking of growing and money, let's explore that more in the next chapter!

Let's Recap:
- Decide the best location for your office.
- Decide what the best renting options are.
- Figure out your budget by figuring out how many clients you will need to see to cover your overhead.

Chapter 5:
Money Mindset

————

Before we go any further into the business aspects of opening your own private practice, I want to discuss the importance of mindset (belief). Most therapists I have coached have difficulty with the money mindset in business and life. Many people believe that this business isn't for making a lot of money, and that if you want to make a lot of money, you will be viewed as being "selfish" and not in the field for the "right" reason. A lot of people fear making a lot of money because it could disappear at any moment: they are always waiting for the bottom to fall out. This was my block around money and it took me a long time to realize this. It comes from the stories that we have created from things we have seen while growing up.

My mother and father were married until I was 10 years old. Up until then, we lived a very nice lifestyle. My birthdays and Christmases were filled with lots of joy and presents. Sometimes when my mom and I came home my dad would have surprised us with a new entertainment center or living room set. I do have a memory of hiding in the bathroom from the oil man when we didn't have enough to pay him. We went on one family vacation, and I remember there was a fight about the amount of money it was going to cost to get back home. Even when things seemed good, there was still an underlying fear of running out of money. This continued, especially after the divorce. My mother and I ended up moving to an apartment in a tenement house, in an area that was embarrassing to say one lived in. Our apartment was so small that my mother and I had to share a bedroom. At least it was a big bedroom where we could both have our own area, but we still didn't have the privacy we both needed. We had a lot of great times in that apartment, and my mother taught me how to be a strong woman who never gives up and always finds a way. My mom worked really hard to keep us afloat and refused to receive state assistance. She is a self-proclaimed Coupon Queen, even still today.

During this time in my life, I knew never how to ask for anything in fear of being told, "No, we don't have the money." Eventually, my mom was able to get a loan for a house, and things started to get better, but there was always still this cloud of worry that something was going to go wrong and we would have a big bill to pay, which we wouldn't have the savings for.

I carried this mindset into my adulthood. So even at a point when my business was doing well, I would always have the fear that something bad was around the corner. I was of the mindset that "nothing good can last forever." The other factor that played in my negative money mindset was that nobody in my family had ever had a successful business. My dad did try to start a business once, but it never got off the ground. I was the first one in my immediate family to go to college and graduate from college. I didn't have a role model on how to have a positive money mindset and how to create the lifestyle that I wanted to live. Although I still have these thoughts on occasion, I have been able to let go of this way of thinking, which has helped with my massive success.

A lot of therapists have the scarcity mindset. This is the feeling or thought that there isn't enough.

This could be there isn't enough money, clients, time or talent. I have experienced therapists who refuse to help other therapists out with referrals even if they think they would be a good fit for a particular client in fear of losing business. You cannot run a successful business in any industry with this mindset. You need to believe from the start that you will succeed. Put all of the "I will give private practice a try, and if it doesn't work then I will go back to my old job" aside. Believe me when I say this, because my experience has proven that there are enough clients to go around. There are so many agencies with waiting lists. There aren't enough therapists to go around, so don't think you will lose business to a fellow therapist.

One thing that I wish I did when I started out was to have a good grip on my finances. So I would suggest that you start your business off with an understanding of where every dollar is going and coming in right from the start. It's a good habit to get into. You can start doing this in a spreadsheet at first or invest in accounting software such as Quickbooks or Freshbooks. You may think that you are too small to worry about this part of the business already, but if you follow the steps in this book you are going to grow pretty fast. If you are expanding your practice to include passive income, which I highly suggest you do in the future if you haven't already, you are going to need to know what parts of your business are making you money and what isn't.

The other mindset monster that I want to warn you about is Imposter Syndrome, which we touched upon briefly in Chapter Three. This is the fear that you aren't qualified to be doing what you are doing either as a therapist or as a business owner. This can be hard because you will rarely see other therapists share their mistakes and doubts in fear that others will think that they are less qualified. This will make it feel like you are the only one who is feeling this way. Also, social media can cause an increased feeling of Imposter Syndrome. We see other therapists with their cool posts about all the great things going on in their practice, or you see snarky remarks in Facebook groups by other therapists when someone asks a legitimate question. Yes, there is no doubt that running your own practice can be scary and lonely.

So my suggestion is that you get yourself into

a peer supervision group. This would be a group made up of other therapists, counselors, psychologists and psychiatrists who get together on a regular basis to help work out difficult cases, brainstorm ideas and give feedback. If you can't find one that has already been established, you can create one yourself. This can be beneficial in several ways, because by engaging in interactions like this...

1. You don't feel so isolated when you have a group of peers meeting on a regular basis.

2. It's a great way to establish relationships so that you have someone to contact when you have questions between meetings. A good way to do this is to use Slack, Facebook message groups, Google Hangouts or Yahoo Groups. It can be a very comfortable support system.

3. It's a nice place to share referral opportunities. This is great if the other therapists work in the same niche as you. If you are promoting a group or have opening, you can share that with your peer supervision group.

4. The group gives you a place to discuss difficult cases and get some professional suggestions.

I know that some people charge other therapists to join their peer supervision group. I have found it to be more beneficial if you hold a group without asking people to pay. More therapists will want to join, which means more people will get to know, love and trust you.

Another way to beat the feeling of isolation is to join an online or in-person mastermind. One of the most life-changing masterminds that I went to was Chris Ducker's Tropical Think Tank located in Cebu, Philippines. The many friends I made there and the connections that were created are still going strong to this day. Spending five days with these entrepreneurs opened my mind to a different way of thinking about my business, in real life and online. There are a variety of masterminds available; you will want to do a little research to find which one would be the best fit for you.

I have discovered that masterminds can be very useful in the business side of things. If you don't know already, masterminds are typically a small group of individuals at varying levels of business.

by Melissa DaSilva

Some masterminds only have individuals that are in the same type of business, while others can include a wide variety of experience and areas of expertise. The group will meet on a regularly scheduled basis. This could be either in person or online. Each session, one or two individuals are in the "hot seat." They discuss their business and ask for help. One of the most important aspects of being on the "hot seat" is not to shut down any suggestions and to listen to others.

Masterminds will also open up doors to peer support between sessions. These groups tend to grow a strong bond and become a significant part of a business owner's success. This has been true for me when I joined a mastermind, and this is why I created my own mastermind that focuses on the business aspect of private practice. It has been beneficial for everyone who has been a part of it. If you are interested in learning more about my mastermind, you can find more information at my website, MsMelissaDaSilva.com.

In the next chapter, we are going to start creating your business by picking the best name for your practice. There is so much more to picking a name than you might think!

Let's Recap:

- You need to have an abundance mindset from the start, not one of scarcity.
- You will feel like an imposter at one time or another (but I can help you through that).
- Make time to be with others in your field.
- Consider joining a mastermind group.

Chapter 6:
Naming Your Business

———

This part of starting a business can be both fun and frustrating. This is where you will have to decide on a name that people understand, connect with and know what you are selling. You will want to pick a name that you can buy a website domain for. You should also include some key terms that people may be looking up in your business name such as: therapy, counseling, mental health, etc. You can look at domains that are still available on sites such as Whoeis.com. You can see if your domain name is available or not. If there is a domain you want, such as your name, you can place an offer for it if you don't like the price the current owner is selling it for. I just looked up my name, MelissaDaSilva.com, and it is being sold for $688 by the current owner, whose name probably isn't Melissa DaSilva.

Another aspect to consider is if you plan on growing your practice in the future to include more people than just yourself at your practice? If so, you may not want to name the business after yourself, such as MelissaDaSilvaTherapySoluions.com. If you did start your business with it named after yourself, you can decide to change it in the future if you want by filing a DBA (Doing Business As). I ended up having to this because the original name that I created for my business caused a lot of confusion.

The name of my business was one of the first mistakes I made when I started out. Today my therapy practice is Doing Business as East Coast Mental Wellness, but the original name that my LLC filed with was "OM" Therapy. I thought this was such a clever name. I am a trained yoga instructor and have always dreamt of someday having a practice that included mind-body integration. Now if you are not familiar with the concept of "OM," it is usually the last sound that is chanted together in a yoga class. It has a bunch of spiritual meanings in Buddhism and many Indian religions. Most people who know what the "OM" symbol is would understand that I integrate mind, body, and spirituality in my therapy practice. The other aspect to this was the use of rainbows in the yoga world. If my client understands

"OM" they will most likely know what chakras are, and that together their colors make a rainbow. You know what else uses a rainbow? The LGBTQ+ community!

I thought this name was great. It embodied everything I ever wanted in private practice. Unfortunately, if my clients didn't have any experience with yoga, they had no idea what the name of my business meant or symbolized. I would have to spell out O-M when people asked me what my name was. Many people would ask me who O.M. was, as if it was the initials of a distant relative. For about a year I tried to make this name work. I even attempted getting a small yoga class stared in a little studio in the small office next to mine with no success. I had three yoga teachers and not one paying student.

When I decided that I want to bring on my first clinician, I took the opportunity to change the name and lose the yoga stuff. I then filled a DBA to change my business name to East Coast Mental Wellness. Doing so didn't cost much at all. There are several reasons why I chose this name for the practice. I chose East Coast since we are located on the east coast of the U.S., and maybe someday I could open up another location on the East Coast on Puerto Rico. This is a dream of mine, so why not prepare for it from the start? "Mental" is a keyword that is used a lot since people use the phrase Mental Health a lot in their searches. I like the word "Wellness" in the name because it sounds more holistic and not so clinical. When I put all these words together and looked to see if the domain was available, it all came together.

When starting your business, you may want to consider filing as a Limit Liability Company or a Corporation. You want to make sure you protect the business that you are building, as well as protect your home and family. I am not an attorney, so here is Legalzoom's explanation of the difference between the two:

A limited liability company, or LLC, is a business entity created under state law that combines characteristics of both a corporation and a partnership. Like a corporation, the owners of an LLC are generally not personally liable for company debts. Like a sole proprietorship or a partnership, an LLC has operating flexibility and is, by default, a "pass-through" entity for tax purposes. This means that the LLC does not pay taxes on its profits, but instead, profits and losses are "passed through" to the owners, who must then pay tax on their share of LLC income.

What are the differences between an LLC and a corporation?

Although an S corporation shares many of the same tax characteristics just as an LLC does, an LLC has more flexibility and fewer restrictions on ownership than does an S corporation. An S corporation must not have more than 100 shareholders, all of whom must be U.S. citizens or legal residents. An S corporation is also subject to more formalities, such as holding annual meetings and keeping corporate minutes. On the other hand, LLCs generally are not required to hold formal meetings, but an LLC owner may be subject to higher self-employment taxes than a comparable S corporation owner. That is because an S corporation owner is required to pay self-employment tax only on salary, but not on dividends from the corporation.

I decided right off to do an LLC. I didn't want to risk my family's financial future if something happened with the company. I also suggest that you create a relationship with an accountant. Someone you can call when you have any questions throughout the year. Remember when I suggested getting bookkeeping software? Well, this is helpful for your accountant. They can have easy, and secure, online access to help you whenever you have a question, instead of you having to figure out what the heck they are asking you for, such as a PnL.

Back to picking a name. You may want to take a little time to explore and compare terms in your industry that are being used. For example, my private practice is marketed towards members of the LGBTQ+ community. I would think that they would look up "LGBTQ therapist" in a Google search to find a therapist. I soon learned that in fact, "gay therapist" is the term that is looked up over "LGBTQ therapist." You can do some exploring yourself on Google Trends. It also allows you to locate a specific area where the terms are being used more, which is helpful if you are just marketing to individuals in your state.

You will want a name that also has a website domain available. This way, it will be easy for people to find you if they type your business in the search bar. You can use a service such as Godaddy.com to try out some names and see if they are already purchased or not. You can also see if people are selling the domain you really want. It's interesting to look at the prices of some of these domains. Someone owns my name MelissaDaSilva.com and is willing to sell it for $688. You do not have to purchase the domain from Godaddy.com; I have discovered that it's just a good search tool.

Once you have decided on some names, I suggest you now ask others what their opinions are. You can also use this opportunity to drum up some chatter about your new business by taking a poll on Facebook. Ask people what business name they like best. You can then make an announcement once you have decided on the name. You can use this as an opportunity to keep friends and family updated on the progress of your new business.

Now that you have decided on the name, you may want to start thinking about a logo for the business. You will be able to get people used to the logo right from the start if you do this now. You can try and design it on your own if you have those skills or you can use a logo design website. I enjoy Freelogodesign.net. The other option is hiring someone else to create your logo for you. Someone for 99designs.com, Fiverr.com and Upwork.com could be an option. The cost of logos can range from $5 and up. If you have a logo, it will make you appear more professional and keep you above the rest of the pack.

When thinking about a logo, you will want a design that looks good in color and in black and white, with simple clean lines. You can also take this opportunity to decide on a color scheme you will want to use on all your marketing materials, such as business cards, letter heads and brochures. If this isn't your area of expertise or of interest to you, then you can hire someone to create an entire branding package for you. This can be a bit expensive, unless you can find a college student who needs to do a project for school, who will create one for you for free!

Creating the business name, logo and color scheme can be fun and overwhelming. Don't allow this step to be the reason you get stuck and don't continue with the next steps of creating your practice.

Having something that isn't perfect is better than not having anything at all.

Buying your domain (website address) will be the next step you will want to take. This is where you buy the address where your website will be found. Depending on where you buy this address, the price may be different. You can purchase the domain for one year or for multiple years at a time. I do suggest that you purchase the privacy protection they offer at check out. If you don't purchase this protection, you will soon be flooded by phone calls and emails from people who want to help you build your website or help you with marketing.

Next, you will want to decide on what platform you will be hosting your website on. The hosting site is where you will create your website that everyone will see. Some programs allow you to purchase and host your website in the same place as well as get your personalized email address. On the hosting site, you will be able to create and customize your web pages to give potential clients a taste of who you are and what it will be like to work with you. If you purchase a domain on a different site than where you are going to host it, you are able to transfer it to your hosting site when you are ready to do so. A couple of places where you can buy your domain are Godaddy.com and Bluehost.com. Some sites that allow you to purchase your domain and host in it the same place include Squarespace.com, Wix.com, Weebly.com, and Wordpress.com.

You should try several of these platforms out before committing to one. They all have their pros and cons, and you want to give them a trial before you start creating the website. It can be very unpleasant to create your website and then learn that you don't understand the platform or that you don't like the way it works. I had this experience myself with Wordpress. I still use the platform for my private practice, but I have hired someone who understands it better than myself to make changes to my website.

Now that you have a name for your practice and website, in the next chapter we are going to start discussing how people are going to contact you and what you will need to do when your first clients make their appointments with you.

Let's Recap:

- Choose a name with keywords for your practice.
- Make sure the domain is available.
- Create a logo or have one made for you with clean, simple lines that will look good in black and white and color.
- Choose two or three colors that you will be using throughout your marketing materials and possibly your office.

Chapter 7:
HIPAA and More

So far, you have started to let people know that you are starting your private practice. You have gotten yourself in the right mindset. You have also started your online presence by securing your domain name and launching your website. However, we haven't yet discussed how exactly your new potential clients will be contacting you and scheduling their first appointments. Both of these things need to be done in a private, confidential and HIPAA-compliant manner.

If you are like me, the word "HIPAA" sends a bit of a shiver down your spine. I use to have this fear that HIPAA ninjas would come out of nowhere and cite me for all my violations. I would then be put on a "bad clinician" list and lose my practice. It can be so overwhelming to think about all the things that need to be protected just to abide by the HIPAA laws. However, if you start your practice thinking about making it HIPAA compliant from the start, it will be easier than trying to change things a year or two in the future after you have many clients and different systems and processes you've gotten thrown together. I am going to help you out by taking things one step at a time.

First, I want to let you know that HIPAA compliant, patient privacy and confidentiality do not mean the same thing. HIPAA may not actually apply to you if you are not a "covered entity."

*HIPAA stands for the <u>Health Insurance Portability and Accountability Act</u>. This is a U.S. law designed to provide privacy standards to protect patients' medical records and other health information provided to health plans, doctors, hospitals and other healthcare providers. Developed by the <u>Department of Health and Human Services</u>, these new standards provide patients with access to their medical records and more control over how their personal health information is used and disclosed. They represent a uniform, federal floor of privacy protections for consumers across the country. State laws providing additional protections to consumers are not affected by this new rule. HIPAA took effect on April 14, 2003. *1*

HIPAA defines a covered entity as 1) a health care

provider that conducts certain standard of administrative and financial transactions in electronic form; 2) a health care clearinghouse; or 3) a health plan.

A therapist is a "covered entity" if they conduct transactions that are electronic exchanges involving the transfer of healthcare information between two parties for specific purposes such as the following:

- claims and encounter information
- payment and remittance advice
- claims status
- eligibility
- enrollment and disenrollment
- requests to obtain referral certifications and authorizations
- coordination of benefits
- premium payment

Under HIPAA, if a therapist conducts one of the adopted transactions electronically, they must use the approved standard.

(Medical Definition Of HIPAA, n.d.).

by Melissa DaSilva

Protected Health Information

The HIPAA Privacy Rule protects most "individually identifiable health information" held or transmitted by a covered entity or its business associate, in any form or medium, whether electronic, on paper, or oral. The Privacy Rule calls this information protected health information (PHI). Protected health information is information, including demographic information, which relates to:

- the individual's past, present, or future physical or mental health or condition,
- the provision of health care to the individual, or
- the past, present, or future payment for the provision of health care to the individual, and that which identifies the individual or for which there is a reasonable basis to believe can be used to identify the individual.

Protected health information includes many common identifiers (e.g., name, address, birth date, Social Security Number) when they can be associated with the health information listed above.

For example, a medical record, laboratory report, or

hospital bill would be PHI because each document would contain a patient's name and/or other identifying information associated with the health data content.

By contrast, a health plan report that only noted the average age of health plan members was 45 years would not be PHI because that information, although developed by aggregating information from individual plan member records, does not identify any individual plan members and there is no reasonable basis to believe that it could be used to identify an individual.

The relationship with health information is fundamental. Identifying information alone, such as personal names, residential addresses, or phone numbers, would not necessarily be designated as PHI. For instance, if such information was reported as part of a publicly accessible data source, such as a phone book, then this information would not be PHI because it is not related to health data (see above). If such information was listed with health condition, healthcare provision or payment data, such as an indication that the individual was treated at a certain clinic, then this information would be PHI. (Office of Civil Rights, 2015)

If you are a "covered entity" you will need a HIPAA-compliant phone line. Even if you are not considered a "covered entity" you will still want a line that allows the keeping of your voicemails confidential. You do not want to use your cell phone number as your business number for several reasons such as:

1. You will not want clients and potential clients having access to your personal number. Even though you can have a talk with them about the appropriate times to call you, new clients aren't going to know that they are calling your cell phone at 9 pm, leaving you a message to see if you are taking new clients.

2. Your regular cell phone service is most likely not going to be HIPAA-compliant. If you want to make sure of this, ask them about HIPAA and if they have a BAA for you to sign. Most of the time if you ask the representative these questions they don't know what you are referring to, which is a good indication that they aren't going to meet your HIPAA needs.

3. You will want to have a line that you can forward over for your off-hours or when you are going away. This could be a single person or services such as a Virtual Assistant. (I recommend AssistantToTheTherapist.com) This is key to prevent burnout when running your business and a necessity if you are going to be on insurance panels.

You are probably wondering, What makes a phone line HIPAA-compliant? It has to do with the VoIP which stands for Voice Over Internet Protocols and the method of using the internet to make calls using Wi-Fi, 3G or a cellular connection. Unlike the old days where a person sits at a desk and answers the phone that is connected to a landline, most of us have mobile devices that we use in running our businesses. We need to make sure that if someone calls, faxes or emails us, that their information is being protected. All this information is being turned into data and stored for a long period of time. We need to be sure that the services we use is protecting this data and not giving access to unauthorized individuals or services.

One of the keys to knowing if a service is HIPAA-compliant is to request a Business Associate Agreement to protect Personal Health Information (PHI). Any third-party service provider you work with should have a BAA signed or you have one that they sign.

For a phone service to be HIPAA-compliant it must have the following:

- The phones have to be authenticated with a certificate which gives the phone a "unique user ID."
- Data must be encrypted.
- Access controls must be in place so that different categories of users can use the system.
- Logs should be maintained of all call data.
- A HIPAA Business Associate Agreement must be offered by a cloud-based VoIP service provider.

(Georgetti, 2016)

Many therapists start out using Google Voice; it's free and super easy to use. Unfortunately, it isn't

HIPAA-complaint. It may also be difficult to be positive that the information is kept confidential. Grasshopper.com is another great platform that isn't HIPAA-complaint but is a bit closer to the standards that are needed. If you are using either one of these services or your own cell phone service, I would highly recommend switching to a HIPAA-compliant platform, such as Phone.com. I have tried several platforms, and I have found this one to be easy to use and customer friendly. Whatever number you are currently using, it can easily be transferred to their platform. You can pay a flat fee each month or choose one of their many other package options. I have an affiliate code in my resource guide that you are welcome to use if you would like to use this platform. I have been really pleased with this service and find them to be very affordable.

Another HIPAA-compliant platform you need to consider when starting your practice is your Electronic Health Record (EHR) system. Some therapists decide to continue to keep notes and records on paper only, and this can be an excellent option. If this is your mode of record-keeping, then you want to make sure you have a good system for keeping all the records securely locked. I recommend that if you do keep your charts in paper format, you hand write notes instead of typing notes on the computer and printing them out to put in the chart, unless you create a secure system with your computer and where your records are stored.

If you decide to use online platforms, there are plenty to choose from. Most of them give you a trial period to get a feel for the platform. If you decide to try some out, use your own information or made-up information. Don't start using it for clients before committing to the platform. Most platforms will offer you the ability to keep your schedule, keep client charts, send out intake paperwork on a secure client portal, take payments online and send out reminders to clients. Many platforms will offer you the ability to submit claims through their system. From my personal experience, this can be helpful but it depends on the insurance company. Some companies will reimburse faster if you send your requests through the mail in paper form, or submit them on their billing platform.

I enjoy SimplePractice.com. I have a link for $50 off if you are interested in signing up for this platform. I have used it for years and it has grown with me from a solo practice to a group practice of 13. One of the features that I have found most useful is their customer service. They are very quick to respond to your questions as well as take your suggestions into consideration to improve their platform.

The third platform you need to decide on will be your email provider. It may seem like a no-brainer, but you actually need to put some thought into this one too. Many people will use their Gmail email when starting out. A lot of times when you purchase a domain, the hosting site will offer you an email box at a discounted rate with your domain at the end of it, such as Melissa@eastcoastmentalwellness.com. If you want your email to be HIPAA-compliant and keep your information confidential, which I know you do, you will need to take another step and have your fancy new email with your domain at the end forward to a HIPAA-compliant email service. This service will not be free. Protecting this information from hackers takes a lot of work, so there has to be a fee for services such as this. Your email accounts should be password protected with the ability to encrypt your emails. These emails will require the client to have a password to unencrypt the information. Just like the phone data, encryptions prevents hackers from being able to grab information without your consent.

I have used Hushmail.com from the start of my business without any issues. Clients get to pick their password the first email they receive from you. Most of the time they will forget it, but you can always reset it for them. Some other HIPAA-complaint emails include Paubox.com, Entrvst.com and G Suite (this is a paid option for Google).

Now that you have your HIPAA-compliant platforms, you need to hang your HIPAA laws and Privacy Policies in your office for your clients to see. It should also be included in your paperwork and on your website so clients can always access it. I also want to let you know that Google Office Suites does give you a BAA to sign so that you can use Google Drive. It doesn't encrypt the information, so be aware of the identifying information being included in the documents that are being saved on the drive.

Make sure that any third-party service provider signs a Business Associates Agreement (BAA). This means parties that are also required to follow HIPAA laws if they are working with you as a service provider. This can include your phone system, your billing clearing house, and virtual assistant agencies.

Let's Recap:

- HIPAA, Confidentiality and Patient Privacy does not all mean the same.
- Not everyone needs to abide by HIPAA laws. If you are not a covered entity, then you don't need to worry.
- So that there is no breach of information, you should invest in the appropriate phone system, email service, and electronic health records.
- You should have your own BAA for third parties to sign if they don't have one already.

Chapter 8:
Your Website

———

Setting up a website for your practice can be another daunting task if you don't have any experience. The truth is that your website is going to be one of the #1 ways people would find you. Research has shown that 75%-96% of new clients looks online for their new therapist. Besides your website, I would say the second most common ways clients will find you is through Psychology Today profiles. Before you set up a Psychology Today profile, you will need to have a place to send potential clients if they want more information about you.

You picked out your domain name and the

platform you are going to build the site on. Now it's time to put some information on the site. You don't have to do this yourself. You can always decide to have someone create it for you. This is especially when you are starting out, you don't have to have a fancy site. Having something imperfect is better than having nothing at all. I went through many versions of my site. I can guarantee your first site isn't going to be as great as your 5th version, but that is okay. Once you make some money, you can always hire someone to beef up your site later.

There are a few items you need to have on your website, and I suggest you place them "above the fold." Just in case you don't know what that means, it refers to the area on the website you see when you first land on it before you scroll down. You want some specific information seen right away, so people don't need to scroll down to look for it.

1. The name of your practice
   a. This may seem like a no-brainer, but sometimes people place it too far down on the home page.
2. Your phone number

    a. This is why it's one of the first things I suggested for you to get in place. See how it's all coming together? You want to make sure that your phone number can be found in two spots on your website above the fold: in the corner of the header, and in the center of your page. Don't make them search for your phone number.

3. "Accepting New Clients"

    a. Let them know right away that you have openings. Put in bold red type if you need to.

Another thing you should add to your home page, but not necessarily above the fold, is a beautiful picture of you or your practice space. I need to digress a little and talk to you about photos.

Do not—and I repeat, do not!—use a selfie of you in a car, a bathroom mirror or with your pet as your professional headshot. Believe me, I love my dog Brutus like he is my child. He is even a certified Pet Assisted Therapy dog at my practice, but I don't have him sitting on my lap for my professional headshots. If you do this, then you are risking being added to one of those "Awkward Photos" books.

highly suggest you spend a little money on a professional headshot. It makes a difference to hire someone who understands lighting, angles and can touch up some of those little rough spots through the magic of Photoshop. If you want to try and give it a shot on your own, I suggest heading over to jaxandersonmedia.com. She is a therapist who knows her way around a camera. She has trainings on how to take a good photo of yourself for your website. I also think that it's good idea to take some nicely lit photos of your office space inside and out. Give your client the feel of what it is going to feel like when walking in for their first appointment.

Now that you have these great photos for your website, how have you started saving them on your computer? This surely matters for your online search ranking. We will talk more about that later. For now, save your photos using some of those keywords you looked up back when you were trying to figure out your domain name. For example, if you are a play therapist by the name of Dave Smith practicing in Groton, CT, you may want to save your headshot as "Groton CT Play Therapist David Smith." How you saved your file on your computer will show up on your website as the name you saved it as.

Let me show you what I mean. Go to any website and hover your mouse over an image. Now right click the image and click "Save As." Your Save As box will show up and now look at the file name that automatically appears. Is it something that makes sense, or does it look like garbled words and numbers such as 0148_orig? If the photo was saved by the author using some of their keywords for Google and other search engines, these would show up on the photo file.

I also want to warn you, do not copy and save images and then use them on your site without the author's/owner's permission. Doing this can put you at risk of violating copyright law. There are sites where you can purchase stock photos that you can use however you want, for the most part. Sites like Fivrr.com, istock.com and shutterstock.com are great.

Sometimes adding a little filter to your pictures is needed to make them website worthy. When this is needed I like to use Canva.com. I call it "Photoshop for people who can't figure out

Photoshop." I also use the ColorStory App. You can purchase different filter packages if you want, but the basic free level is also good.

Okay now back to the website itself. I know some of the basics of building a website, but to get a better understanding of what you should know about creating your website, I decided to ask my own Website designer C.T. some questions.

What are four important things a therapist should keep in mind when creating their first website?

1. Responsive Design

Responsive design means that your website will "flex," or adjust, to the width of the device your visitor is using. Two or three years ago, this was "nice to have"... not anymore. It's mandatory in 2018 if you want your business to be taken seriously. What good is it to have a great looking desktop site if it breaks when users try to navigate on tablets or mobile devices? When your website is being built, you also want to continually ask, "How will this look on smaller screen sizes?" and/or "How will users interact with this element/section on smaller screen sizes?"

2. Contact Information

I always talk about making the website experience "frictionless." You want it to be frictionless for prospective clients to do business with you. This couldn't be more true with listing vital contact information on your site (such as phone numbers, emails, hours, etc). I would place this information up in the header, as well as the footer (bottom of the website). This should allow any visitor to access your prominent information quickly, from any device, on any page.

3. Consistent CTA's (Call To Actions)

What is the main action you want your visitors to take when they land on your website? Is it book a free consultation with you? Is it to sign up for your latest ebook download? Is it to simply learn more about you and your practice? Whatever it is that you want them to do, you want to make that prominent and clear on every page. I would consider calling it out two or three times on the homepage (for example: above the fold, middle of the page and near footer), as well as once on each internal page.

4. Online Scheduling

Remember when I said that we want to eliminate friction? Scheduling is a *big* area of friction, in my opinion. Whether someone is viewing your site while at work, on the go or after hours, you want to make sure that they have a great experience. So, instead of having to message/email you (and wait for your reply) or call you (and wait for your call back) they can simply book their appointment online.

There are plenty of online scheduling services that can streamline this process for you. I use Calendly for all of my business' scheduling needs. I'm not affiliated with them by any means but absolutely love their service. All I have to do, is simply send my customer's a link and they pick the day/time that works best for them. If you're in practice with one (or just a few therapists), Calendly would be a great fit.

What are three mistakes you see people make when starting a website?

1) Too Much Content

At some point while surfing the Internet, you may have come across a site that had so much content staring at you, you didn't last more than five seconds. You see paragraphs upon paragraphs of text, along with a bunch of images, and video that's too big, therefore taking up the full width of your computer screen. It's like sensory overload — on steroids.

When your visitors land on your homepage, you want to give them "a hook," a teaser, a reason to stick around, to keep browsing your site, and not a bunch of Discovery Channel.

2) An Empty Blog

Creating a blog is an outstanding idea but make sure it's not live until you're ready to run with it. I have seen numerous businesses with a "coming soon" message on their blog page for weeks or months on end. This is not a good look. I would wait until you have at least 4-6 blog posts in the hopper so you can publish them on a regular basis & kickstart your efforts.

PRO TIP: When you create a blog post, also record a video for it. That video could just be a 30-60 second summary of that particular post (you already have the script/content written up) or you could go into greater detail with it. It's totally up to you. This allows you to offer your visitors another way to consume your content, as well as provide another way for prospective clients to find you (YouTube).

3) Too Many Distractions

When a prospective or current client lands on your website, what do you want them to do? Let's say the main thing you want them to do is book a free consultation. You obviously want to make that prominent, but more importantly than that, you need to get rid of any distractions. I often see websites that are cluttered and confusing. They are asking the visitor to do five different things all at once... and when/if that happens, how many things do you think the user will accomplish? If you guessed zero, you're correct. So make sure you keep it simple!

Another term I have used several times in the book so far is "SEO." SEO stands for Search Engine Optimization which is the process of maximizing the number of visitors to your website by ensuring that the site appears high on the list of results returned by a search engine such as Google, Yahoo and Bing. I envision the internet crawlers looking like digital spiders that could be from the movie "The Matrix," which comb through all the information in cyber-space to see what people are looking at, and that's the process of getting traffic. If web pages are updated regularly, what's the quality of the traffic to a website, what keywords are used, and how readable are the sites? The crawlers bring all those 1s and 0s back to the search engine to build an index. That index is then fed through an algorithm that tries to match all that data with the query of your potential clients (*What is SEO?*" n.d.).

I asked my SEO guy, John, some questions about this topic, since I am not the expert, and here is what he had to say.

Why is SEO so important for therapists to know about?

If you build it, they will not come... until you do SEO! In general, sites don't show up high in search results without SEO. If you are hoping to grow your business through your website, there needs to be an ongoing investment made into learning SEO. If your competition is making the investment and you're not, you will slowly slip further and further behind in rankings.

What are the three most important things therapists should know about SEO?

1. SEO is a marathon, not a sprint, and it should never end. There are no "winners"; there are only temporary leaders of the pack. Search results can change quickly. Make sure to stay in the race.

2. It's much more effective to make continuous slow improvements to a website instead of making a one-time investment and not touching it again.

3. When hiring an SEO partner, do your homework. The industry has some shady players, so you need to be careful. Some good questions to ask before hiring include:

- What is your strategy for my business?
- Will you provide me with information about what you've done monthly?
- Will you provide me reports?
- Can you guarantee me a #1 ranking on Google? (If they answer yes to this question, you should not use them as no one can guarantee this.)

What are some mistakes you see people making in regards to SEO?

I have seen many mistakes! Some examples are:

- Businesses paying for an SEO package without fully understanding what SEO is or what the package includes. There are many providers offering automated SEO packages where a human being never touches your site. Hosting providers are known for selling these types of packages.

- Agreeing to an SEO and website package from an overly aggressive salesperson from a "Yellow Page" type company. Clients have come to me with these contracts to find out that the "Yellow Page" company owns the rights to their website and URL. They must then start over.

- Working with a company that sent a spammy email solicitation promising "page 1 search results" at a low price. Good SEO companies aren't desperate for new clients, and they don't send spammy emails. Many of these companies are overseas and won't do much of anything to help your rankings.

What are some tips you can give for ranking higher on search platforms?

- Your website is very important, so make an investment in building a good site.

- Content is king. Well, I should say: *quality* content is king. Make sure you have a robust site with an individual page for each of your services. If you do individual therapy and group therapy, you should have two pages.

- Your digital footprint is important. When search engines crawl the internet, do they find information about your company in places other than your website? Having online profiles on other sites is the way to achieve this.

- Links are important. Getting links from other quality (not spammy) sites will help with rankings.

- Dedicate part of your marketing budget to finding a good SEO specialist or SEO company. SEO is a discipline that people spend their full-time jobs working on week in and week out. Although you can DIY, you'll be much more successful if you find someone you can trust. The fees you pay with will be well worth it.

John mentioned online content being one of the biggest components to having good SEO. Blogs, Vlogs, and links back to different parts of your site are good starts on starting your SEO game. Blogs—some people refer to these as "Copy"—should be added to your site on a consistent basis. A lot of therapists get hung up on, "What could I possibly write about on a consistent basis?" or "I am a terrible writer, I can't have that on my website." As a therapist, you will have a ton of things to write about. Think about the common issues you see in your office. Write a blog post about anxiety, depression grief or relationships. Think about your Ideal Client Avatar. What would they want to read about?

Some people discovered creating a monthly theme as an easy way to coming up with ideas. For example, August could be about kids and school anxiety. If this is your ideal client, you can easily write four blogs for the month and post them on your website every week.

If the fact that you aren't the best writer is stopping you, there are plenty of ways to get around this. Trust me, this is coming from the woman who has a learning disorder, and who is constantly in an argument with her spellcheck because it has no idea what she is attempting to spell out. "Sound it out

Spellcheck!" Look at me now: I have written a book!

One way I have found useful with dealing with writer's block is creating Vlogs. Vlogs are videos of you discussing a particular topic: a video blog. These can be added to your website with some notes containing some of the keywords that are touched upon during your video. I do have such a difficult time with writing, which makes me sometimes resort to video instead of sending a written email.

Other ways to get around the writing block could be having someone read your copy and make edits for you. For me, this was my fourth grade teacher, whom I am still very close to. When I felt that I was overwhelming her with all my blogs, I then hired a copy editor on Fivrr.com. It may take a couple of trials to find the editor who works best for you, but it's definitely worth it. Upwork.com is another great resource for finding an editor. For everyday types of editing, I will have one of my Virtual Assistants take a look at what I have written and make some edits to it. You can find yourself your own Virtual Assistant at AssistantToTheTherapist.com.

When you do write your blog or record your

blog, you will want to refer back to some information located on another page of your website. If you have an anxiety group running soon for anxious kids, you can link to this page in your copy. You want to provide as much quality information as possible when adding content to your website. If you are interested in working with C.T. and/or John for website and/or SEO, you can find more information about them both on my resource page.

Your website and SEO are only a small part of your online marketing. In the next chapter, I will discuss other ways to market yourself online.

Let's recap:

- Having a "just okay" website to start is better than not having a website at all.
- Specific pieces of information should be right on top of your homepage: your name, the name of your practice, your phone number, and that you are taking on new clients.
- SEO is a long game.
- Post new content consistently on your site.

Chapter 9:
Email Marketing

———

Before I go any more into the specifics about online marketing, I need to discuss the importance of getting a potential client's email. In the online world, an email that you receive from a potential customer is like receiving a piece of gold. As soon as you create your website and start seeing clients, you need to start building your email list. One easy way of doing this is to include it in your intake form. Ask for permission to send clients future emails about updates in your practice.

There are many different platforms you can use for email marketing. I have used MailChimp for many years. It is a free service until your email list is over 2,000 contacts. After that, you have to pay for the subscription. (Although this is not a terrible problem to have—if you have to pay for the subscription, you know you are doing some good email list creating.) Besides MailChimp, there are many other platforms you can try out before committing to the service. These include Drip, Aweber and Hubspot.

Why is gathering clients' email addresses so important? Emails can be used to inform current and past clients and referral sources about what is happening at your practice. You can send out emails with helpful information and spreading the word if you have openings for new clients. Emails are a great way to share your latest blog or Vlog. By sending out consistent and useful emails to your referral sources and potential clients, you build trust with them that you are an expert in your niche. Send out updates on programs you are running or information on a specific topic that is beneficial to your niche. I recommend that when you are collecting your emails, you only request the person's first name and email. There is no need to ask for more than this, and it helps you with HIPAA compliance and confidentiality.

I do need to give you a warning though, which is even if you have asked for permission for these emails and you are providing nothing but useful information, they may still unsubscribe from your list. Many email platforms will give you the option of getting a daily update on how many people opened your email, clicked any links and unsubscribed. I turned this feature off. I don't like knowing how many people are rejecting a piece of work I put time and effort into. It creates a feeling of rejection when I see this number. I probably should speak to a professional about this reaction, but until then I will spare my therapist's time and not pay attention to the daily unsubscribe number. Instead, I focus on offering great content.

The other reason why emails are so important is that you can use this information to target new customers in your online marketing strategies through platforms like Facebook, Instagram, Google Adwords and Twitter. You can create custom audiences with these emails when you run an ad on these sites and also create a look-alike audience with the emails you already have. This will target new people who have similar qualities to the customers on your email list. I am not going to give you the logistics of how to specifically create these ads since I am in no way an expert in that area. There are many great online trainings out there that help you do this task on your own. If you do decide to take one of these trainings, make sure that it's the most current version. Online platforms change their algorithms all the time, and you want to be sure that you are choosing a training that is up-to-date. I also recommend that you choose one platform to start your learning from, and do all you can to learn it well, before trying out a new platform. This will prevent you from throwing away money trying to figure them all out at the same time. The other option is that you can decide to hire someone who does this as a job. You will get much better results, but it's not a cheap service.

Another way to gather emails is to have a pop-up box on your website. When people come to your site, a box will pop up and ask if they want to join your mailing list. This is a feature that can be added to most website platforms. If you decide that you will be using these emails to send out newsletters, make sure you are consistent with sending them out, whether it's one time a month, every other week, or weekly. Remember to include a link on the newsletter that links back to your website. This is great for SEO. Sending out newsletters keeps people up-to-date on what you are doing in your practice and is an opportunity to let them know about upcoming programs you are holding. Even if people don't open your emails, just seeing your name on a regular basis keeps you in the back of their minds for the time they may need a therapist or if they know someone else who is in need of therapy.

Creating consistent content is one of the steps in the Sales Progression Process. David P. Dana explains this well in his book *Marketing for the Mental Health Professional*. Here is what it looks like:

The first step is building trust. You do this by creating and offering something of value to your ideal client. This builds your credibility in your niche. Once a potential client has trust in you, the next step is to take customer actions. This may be joining your email list or following you on social media. You then reward them by offering more valuable resources. You are not attempting to have them make an appointment with you yet. By offering more value without asking for something in return, you build further trust, which then turns into people starting to spread the word about you and your practice. You are now getting word-of-mouth marketing.

When it's time for you to offer a group or let people know you have limited spots available for new clients, you can announce it to your email list and on social media. Because of the trust that has been built, you are more likely to get people to join your group or call for an appointment.

Another aspect of building trust has to do with your customer service. How fast are you at answering a call from new clients? How long does it take for you to return a call or email? If you are not the right fit for the potential client, do you go out of your way to offer other referral options? Do you offer free phone consultations? How well you do these tasks can make or break the trust that a new client has in you.

You may be asking yourself, "How am I supposed to answer my phone or respond to emails quickly if I am in session?" This is why I highly recommend hiring a Virtual Assistant, even if it's for just two hours a week. I don't know how many times I have sent clients to other providers who come back to me to say, "I left a message and never got a call back." I don't want you to be that provider who is too overwhelmed and busy to take a possible referral call or answer an email. Having someone help you in this area can set you so far above other providers in your area. You will appear professional and organized to your referral sources and future clients. And who doesn't want to be able to say, "I will get my assistant on that"?

If you do not have a system set in place for your phone or emails to be answered quickly, the next person on that potential client's Google search list is going to end up with that client. We have all done it. You search for a massage therapist or a plumber — the first one who answers that phone will most likely get your business. Spending $50 a week on a Virtual Assistant is well worth the money. If you get one new client a month because your VA was able to provide great customer service, it has paid for itself. If you are interested in stepping up your customer service game and want to add a VA to your practice, check out my website database with trained Virtual Assistants at AssistantToTheTherapist.com

A lot of people in private practice don't think about these important steps such as collecting emails and providing exceptional customer service. Most are just thinking about getting clients in the office and doing therapy for 45 minutes, and that's it. You should know that there is so much more to building a thriving practice! If you continue to follow the steps in this book, you are going to grow your business so much faster than other therapists in your niche.

Let's Recap:
- Start collecting emails ASAP!
- Ask for permission to send emails during the intake paperwork process.
- Use emails in your sales process and future online ads.
- Create and share useful content consistently.
- Offer amazing customer service to increase trust in potential clients. This might require hiring a Virtual Assistant.

Chapter 10:
Online Marketing

There are so many ways to market yourself online. It can be very overwhelming when you think of all the ways you can do this, such as Facebook, Facebook Ads, Google Ads, Podcasts, Instagram, Twitter, Yelp, local online magazines and so on and so on...

Without a clear vision of what you want to achieve with this marketing, you can easily spend hundreds of dollars and not get anywhere. So, always have it in mind that the first place to start is your website, and if you haven't done that yet make sure you do before going any further with your marketing efforts. The next step is to get yourself on Psychology Today. They always rank high with their SEO, so it's good to link back to your website from your Psychology Today profile. There is a fee of $29 a month, but if you can get one new client a month, it pays for itself. I have an affiliate code I can share with you so you can get six months free if you are signing up for the first time. All you need to do is email me at hello@msmelissadasilva.com letting me know you would like to open a new Psychology Today account, then I can hook you up.

The next place you may want to market yourself is on social media. You need to decide if this is an area you want to get promoted on, because you need to know how often are you willing to stay dedicated to social media and if it's the best option for your business. Some therapists don't want to step into this territory at all. Some therapists are concerned about confidentiality (therapist and client) and ethics when it comes to social media. If you are deciding to use social media in your practice, I highly suggest that you include a social media policy in your intake paperwork. Also post it in your office as well as on your website. Do not friend or follow any of your clients. If a client attempts to friend you, you will need to have a discussion about your social media policy. Warning: putting yourself out there on social media can open you up to negative public feedback. So this is something you need to decide if you're willing to deal with or not.

If you have decided that you are willing to take the risks along with the positive aspects of online marketing, here are some of the first steps you will want to take.

Think about your Ideal Client Avatar again. Where are they hanging out on social media? Are they on Twitter, Pinterest or Facebook? There are so many social media options, but it's best to only focus on one or two social media platforms—otherwise you are going to feel overwhelmed real quick. You will also need to think about how the content you are using on different platforms will funnel clients into your practice. This is why it's important to choose one or two platforms instead of trying to do all of them and not know how it is going to benefit your business.

I have to admit that I made this mistake when I first started. I wanted to try everything. I even started a podcast that cost me $400 a month, yet it didn't bring me any return on this investment in regards to new clients. My Ideal Client Avatar didn't even listen to podcasts! It did open some doors to other opportunities, but not to achieving my original goal of funneling clients to my practice. I also started a Twitter account for my private practice, but I didn't even know how to tweet. I just don't get the platform, and I didn't want to waste my time trying to figure that one out.

Currently, for my private practice I focus a lot on my Facebook and Instagram platforms. I enjoy these two because I know this is where my ideal clients are, I have some understanding of how to use them for marketing (after a ton of reading, taking online classes and trial and error) and they are good platforms to use for repurposing content you create. Here are some examples of content that can be used in your social media marketing.

Blogs:

We learned in a previous chapter how blogs are important. They are great for your website and your social media platforms. Don't forget to link the social media posts back to your website. I hear people often say that they don't blog because they "don't know what to write about." Yes, it can be very overwhelming if you are planning on writing a new blog post every single week. One suggestion is to create a social media theme calendar. For each month, create a theme that is relevant to the time of year and your ideal client. If you plan on releasing a blog every week, you can then come up with four topic ideas that correlate with your theme of the month. For example, August is when kids go back to school. If you work with kids, you may want to create a blog for parents with topics such as:

- 5 signs your child is experiencing anxiety about school
- How to get your child into a good routine for a successful school year
- How to know if your child is being bullied or is a bully
- How to deal with the end-of-summer blues

See how easy that can be? All you need is a little creativity and some planning. Some people go as far as planning out their entire year, so they don't have to come up with topics at the last minute.

Vlogs:

Another way to create material for social media is by vlogging. Vlogging is just like blogging, but instead of the information being in written format, it is presented in a video format. I know that most people don't like being on video, but the fact is that this is how a lot of people are consuming content today. This is especially true for the younger generation. We have clients come to our office all the time telling us they found our video on Youtube and decided that they wanted to make an appointment. It really seems to build trust for potential clients. You can do vlogs on Youtube, Facebook and Instagram.

If you have a smartphone and know how to point it at yourself to take a video, you can vlog. Don't overly think about what you look like and what you're saying. Just be natural. People connect better with the genuine side of you more than the scripted version of you. If you are really having a difficult time with the live video idea, you can always record yourself on Zoom, edit it a little and post it on your social media. It takes more time and you have to be okay with looking at your own video and listening to your own voice. I personally don't like doing either of these; that's why I pay an editor to do this part.

We talked about social media platforms earlier: how you can use them with your email list and repurpose the content you created. I want to discuss some of the platforms in a little more detail and how they can be useful to your practice.

Facebook:

You will want to create a Facebook businesses page. Include your practice's contact information and your website. This is the place you can share your blog posts, inspirational quotes and pictures you think your audience would enjoy. Make sure to invite friends to like your business page and encourage them to share it.

Facebook also gives you the option to advertise on their platform. You can target specific areas, ages, gender and topics that your potential clients may be interested in. Keep in mind: Facebook doesn't show your posts to everyone in your friend group every time you post something. This is especially true if you are an inconsistent poster.

Facebook rewards you with more exposure if you are consistent with your posts and if you are getting traffic on the posts. Then they do share with your friends. At the time of writing this book, Facebook was giving more value to live videos over other types of posts.

One important suggestion I will make is that you do a weekly video or vlog that you post on your Facebook business page. This can be about anything you think your ideal client can benefit from. Here is another pro tip: Facebook doesn't particularly like YouTube videos. If you post a video from YouTube on your Facebook page, you may not get as many views as you would if you did a video directly on Facebook. If you have a YouTube channel, you can always upload video from Facebook to the channel. I do this with my Facebook Lives "Chit Chat with a Therapist." I do a Facebook Live, repurpose it to YouTube, and then do a podcast version. This is a great way to increase your SEO.

Facebook has a lot of great features to help you market your business. There are entire books and courses written about the best way to go about using ads to get traffic to your site, convert ads into sales and engagement with your audience. Some of these in resources are free, while others will cost you. If you are interested in a course and an online community that can help you with Facebook ads, I suggest taking a look at my friend Andy Bengal and his course at www.theadviking.com.

Instagram:

In case you didn't know already, Facebook owns Instagram. You can post items on either account, and it will automatically appear on the other platform. I like to think of Instagram as an online scrapbook. You post a picture and then add a caption. It can be a little story, a thought or just a simple comment. Then you can add hashtags (#) to the descriptions. Here is a secret: you don't have to hashtag specifically what the picture is about. If you are trying to get followers for your practice, you will want to use hashtags that will attract people to your post, even if they aren't looking for therapy. For example, hashtag the name of the city, state, and topics your ideal client may be interested in. For me, it would be #LGBT #LBGTQ #Pride #Providence #RI. If a new college kid has just moved to Rhode Island and looks up #RI on the Instagram search, they will see tons of images that have also been tagged with #RI in the description. Your post will be included in this search result. If this person decides to follow #RI, anytime you create a post with this hashtag, they will see it in their feed.

You can have up to 40 hashtags, and I suggest you use as close to 40 as you can with each post. You don't need to create a new list of 40 posts every time you create a new post. The trick is to have a premade list of hashtags saved on your phone in the Notes app. Copy and paste the list to the post you are creating.

Instagram is also offering InstaStories and Instagram Live. Stories are short videos and pictures that are recorded and only available to your audience for 24 hours. Instagram Live is very similar to Facebook Live; the difference between the two is that Instagram deletes your live video after 24 hours, while Facebook keeps the live video as a video on your page. Just like Facebook, Instagram allows you to have a personal account as well as a business account. You can toggle back and forth between your Instagram accounts as needed. They don't share the same followers.

Pinterest:

Pinterest is a platform that uses visual aids to get you interested in a topic that the picture is linked to. Once you click on the picture, you may be sent to a piece of content that is linked to the photo. If you are planning on using Pinterest for marketing, you want to make sure that your niche or ideal clients are woman between their late 20's and 45 years of age. This age group tends to be the highest number of users for this platform. A lot of people like to use Pinterest to find inspirational quotes, tips on dealing with day-to-day issues and creating projects.

Pinterest can be fun to use for marketing if you are a visually creative person. Before you use this platform, I suggest that you spend some time consuming the information on the platform to get a feel of what it is like. If you enjoy using Pinterest as a consumer, you may find it a useful tool for marketing your practice.

LinkedIn:

LinkedIn has a reputation for being the platform for job seekers. However, LinkedIn can be leveraged for marketing your practice and getting the word out about what services you provide. Here is a way of doing just that. If you already have a LinkedIn profile, you can add that you have a new position at your company: private practice. People who are linked with you will get this notification, and some may send you congratulations on the new position. At that point you can engage them in a conversation if you think they may be a good referral opportunity.

In the past, I have used LinkedIn to connect with other therapists in the area who may want to get together for coffee. I have made some great connections this way. If your ideal clients are people who use LinkedIn, you may want to post some of your content on your feed as a way of getting more exposure.

Twitter:

I need to let you in on a secret: I don't use Twitter. I don't completely understand it or how to use it effectively. To me, Twitter is like shouting a short statement out into the world, and maybe someone might hear it. If you @ someone in your statement, then you know they will hear it. If you add a hashtag (such as in Instagram) people who follow that hashtag will also be informed about your tweet. Unlike Facebook or Instagram Twitter only allows you to post a message with 140 characters or less. You can add a photo to your posts and links back to your website. Some would say that Twitter is a cross between micro-blogging and a messenger board. You can update people on your life and intimate thoughts, inform people about your business and coordinate meet-ups.

Since I don't use Twitter myself, I reached out to my Facebook group, A Private Practice Made Easy (if you are not a member yet, please request to join) to see if any therapists have used Twitter to market their practice and had success from it. That's when I met psychotherapist Lena Hilder McCain who was kind enough to let me interview her about her Twitter skills.

Do you use Twitter for marketing your private practice?

Yes, I use it to advertise the groups I run for teens. I know that they are my niche and that Twitter is a platform they use a lot. My groups are reasonably priced so teens might be more willing sign up.

How else do you use Twitter?

We use it to create connections, for networking and to share information about other topics our clients would find interesting.

Are you afraid of client confidentiality?

We have a policy that all our new clients receive about our social media. They can decide to engage in it or not. Marketing isn't like it used to be. Social media plays a big role nowadays.

Are you nervous about negative feedback possibly going viral?

We had an incident recently where I posted something that had two red X's in the comment. I did not realize that they were symbolic of something opposite of what we stand for. We made another post explaining our mistake and moved on.

Lena seems to have a good understanding of using social media for her practice and has a great website you should take a look. You can find her practice at https://interfaithbridge.com. Her logo is an excellent example of what I discussed in a previous chapter.

Podcasts:

I love podcasts because you can find one on almost any topic. A lot of what I learned about business came from the podcasts that I listen to, which includes EO Fire, Youprenuer, Practice of the Practice, Selling the Couch, Online Marketing Made Easy, and The Speaker Lab. I am also crazy about The Model Health Show, because without the health, you don't make the wealth.

Podcasts can be used to market your practice. Podcasting may be something you want to do down the road, after you have made some income. Until then, you may be interested in being a guest on other podcasts that targets your ideal clients. Being on a podcast helps build your creditability in your niche, as well as gives you exposure by promoting your practice. It's always nice to get links back to your website from the podcast website. The other great part of being on the podcast is that you are able to have a place on your webpage that says: *As Featured On.* You can link your episode to an image of the podcast's logo that you posted on your *As Featured On* section.

Getting on podcasts isn't very difficult. If you are strong in regards to your expertise, and have a decent website with a nice bio of yourself, you should be able to get on some shows. Reach out and ask to be a guest on a podcast that you think would be a good match. Remember the saying: "Ask not, get not." You can't get on if you don't ask. When you ask to be on a show, make sure you have listened to a few episodes of the show first. There is nothing worse in podcasting then having someone request to be on your show and not have a clue what it's about or know the show's tone. You want to make sure you are of service to the show and its listeners, not just thinking about how the show can help you. Sometimes you will hit it off with a show, and they may ask you to be a returning guest. This was the case for me with "Interview with Exes." The creator sought me out, and now I am a regular on the show. (It's an awesome podcast—I suggest you listen to it.)

Side note: While I was writing this chapter, I decided to take some of my own advice. I have always wanted to be a guest on Chris Ducker's podcast "Youprenuer." I have been a huge fan for a couple of years and have attended several of his conferences. I have never had the guts to ask if I could be a guest, until today. I sent him a message, and he said, "Yes." Chris has helped my business grow so much over the past three years, and I look forward to talking about this with his audience. If I didn't ask, I wouldn't have gotten the opportunity.

You are probably wondering, "How much time do I need to dedicate to social media to promote my business?" Have you ever noticed that some people post multiple times a day? They may have an inspirational quote in the morning and then a nice infographic at 2pm and then maybe a video of a great thing they saw on their evening walk. It appears that social media is on their mind all the time and they are always on their smartphone. I know that when I first started, I couldn't figure out how people were able to dedicate so much time and brain space to this task.

Eventually, I figured out that there are apps to help you with scheduling your social media posts, such as Later.com and Hootsuite.com. I like to use Later.com. You dedicate one or two times a week to creating social media content for your platforms. You then load everything up on Later.com, and then it will post the content for you on several media platforms when you schedule them to do so. Instagram does make you approve the post before you automatically post, but it only takes a second to open the app and have it approved: much less time than trying to create a post on the spot and add your 40 hashtags. Having systems like this can make your business run so much smoother. I will talk more about helpful systems later in the book.

Online question-and-answer boards:

These can be helpful with marketing, since it will help increase your credibility. Some of these platforms include Reddit and Query. Typically people will ask a question, and you can help them out by answering the question and directing them to a piece of your content you have created in the past that may be of help to them. I suggest you take a look at these platforms and see what they are like before starting to use them as a marketing tool. Even if you decide that it isn't the platform for you, you could still use it as a place to get ideas for content topics. You know it's something people need information on since they are already asking the questions.

Help A Reporter Out (HARO)

Help A Reporter Out is a site that I have used many times to get my expertise out into the online world. You sign up to receive three emails a day that include requests from a variety of news outlets. They may be looking for help with very specific topics. This may include quotes, stories, articles, interviews and live appearances. You may not always know what news outlet will be looking for a contributor.

They have the option of stating who they are or be anonymous. The news outlet could be a small or large magazine, an online outlet, a podcast or even a television show. When you receive the emails, you can browse through the lists and see if you would be a good match for any of the requests. You can send in your submission and that requestor may want to use your expertise to assist them in their application. You won't get chosen every time, but it's worth a try. If your submission doesn't get selected, you can use what you created on your own site. I had one of my articles posted on headspace.com, and it has definitely helped with my creditability and SEO.

Downside: the three emails a day, five days a week, can be overwhelming, especially since most of the outlets have a tight schedule. My suggestion is for you to only open the emails if you have a little time dedicated to them each week to submit to these requests.

Guest Blogging

If there is a blog you follow that you think you could offer your expertise on, don't be afraid to ask to be a guest blogger on the site. You can offer to write them a piece that they can post on their site. This helps them get some SEO, and gives you the opportunity to get some traffic back to your site. Even if the traffic doesn't pull in potential clients, understand that because the blog you are guest posting on is read all over the world, it will no doubt help bring legitimate traffic to your website, which is what those SEO crawlers like to see.

TV and Radio

Most local TV stations and radio stations can now be found online, so I will add this to the online marketing section of this book. Advertising on TV and radio can be expensive. I once inquired about an ad on my local NPR station. They quoted me $60 for a 10-second ad at the peak of commute hours. On the other hand, a local Latino station gave me a quote of $500 for two weeks of several promotions throughout the day. If you are going to invest in TV or radio ads, you will need to consider the return on investment (ROI) and if your ideal client will be listening to your ad on this particular TV or radio station.

TV can also be expensive. You may be able to get around this high cost by offering to do a segment on your local news show on a topic that you are an expert on that is relevant to your local news station. For example, during the "back to school" time of year, you might want to offer a group to help teens with school anxiety. You can pitch an idea to your local news show about school anxiety and discuss the signs parents may want to look out for. At the end of the discussion, you can make an offer about the group that you are starting to help teens and parents. If you are offering information that is beneficial to the audience and the news station, then you are likely to be invited on the show. You could also use this tactic to get on local radio shows. Doing this could get you more clients and may also open doors to more networking opportunities.

Let's Recap:

- There are a lot of options for marketing on social media! Pick one or two platforms and learn them well before trying other social media platforms. Using a scheduling app helps too.

- Psychology Today is a great way to get clients. Email me at <u>Hello@msMelissaDaSilva.com</u> for an invitation to six months free.
- Online question-and-answer boards, HARO and guest blogging can help you get exposure and create new content.
- Radio and TV ads can be expensive, but you can be creative and get yourself on local programs to share your expertise.

Chapter 11:
Community Marketing

A lot of people like online marketing because they feel less "sales-y" and don't have to be face-to-face with other providers and potential clients to market and network. Unfortunately, marketing in the community with humans is something you will need to do if you want clients to find you. We will talk more about networking in the next chapter but for now, let me give you some ideas on how to go about marketing in your community.

First, think of your ideal client.

- Where do they hang out?
- What are they reading?
- What are they buying?
- What type of life transitions are they going through?

Let's look at my Ideal Client Avatar again so you can see some of the community marketing ideas I have used to get more clients to my practice.

First, I published an ad in our local LGBTQ+ magazine. I purchased a business card sized ad with my practice information and my amazing headshot. I ran the ad for 12 months. I got a deal for signing up for a recurring ad every month instead of just doing it for a couple of months at a time. I also offered to write articles for the magazine about mental health. At the end of each article, I cited my practice and offered free 15-minute phone consultations. I am currently a on the board of this magazine due to being so involved in promoting the magazine and being a part of the community.

Another community marketing opportunity I took advantage of was purchasing a booth at our local Gay Pride event. I created a wellness basket that I raffled off, and handed out marketing materials for the practice. I had people put their email address on tickets for the raffle. After the event, I added their emails to my email list so that I could send them updates of services we were providing at my practice.

As a vendor at the event, I also got promoted through their event guides.

Another community marketing tactic I used was dropping my business cards at shops that my ideal clients may shop at. I would spend a little time chatting with the shop owner or salesperson about my practice. Many times, this would open conversations about what the owner thinks the community could benefit from. This is a fantastic way to open up communication and start getting members in the community to learn who you are and start to trust you. I also hung flyers on community bulletin boards at libraries and shopping centers.

Supporting local charities that also serve your clientele is a great way to not only market your practice, but also to help populations in need. Many times, the charities will announce that you are a sponsor, which can create referrals to your practice. It shows others that you are knowledgeable and that you have invested in the community. One charity that my practice sponsors is Aids Care Ocean State (ACOS). They hold a monthly Drag Bingo event. Every month I get the opportunity to get on stage, talk about my practice and describe the services I am offering. I get to speak to hundreds of potential clients every month. My practice information is included in all informational flyers sent out to ACOS supporters.

This sponsorship has recently opened up a new opportunity for my practice to partner with ACOS by offering one of my offices to be an Aids/HIV testing site. This means a new stream of potential clients will be coming to my office on a weekly basis. We have also donated to a new organization in our area called "Project Fearless." They help connect LGBTQ+ individuals who don't have access to mental health services due to lack of insurance to providers who will see them at a lower fee or for free.

I continue to be creative in some of my community marketing by wearing T-shirts that grab people's attention and make them want to talk about the shirt or share their opinion. I have two shirts that I wear on a regular basis. One says "Self-Care is Sexy" and another that says "Proud Therapist" with a rainbow heart in place of the "O." If you are crafty, you can make your own shirts. Jax Anderson of

JaxAndersonMedia.com recently created two shirts herself that say: "My Therapist Says Relax, It's Just Neurons Firing" and "My Therapist Says Everyone is Diagnosable." If you are interested in making your own attention-grabbing T-shirt, you can create a design and have shirts printed on Vistaprint.com.

In the past, I had a car magnet made with my logo and business number on it. I liked the idea, but it didn't get me much business, so I got rid of it. You can make car magnets, T-shirts, business cards and a host of other products containing your logo and info at Vistaprint. They usually have a sale on different items every month. If you are just starting out, you can get a ton of business cards at a low price. I went through several different designs of business cards when I started, and you may too, so starting with a cheap option is a good idea.

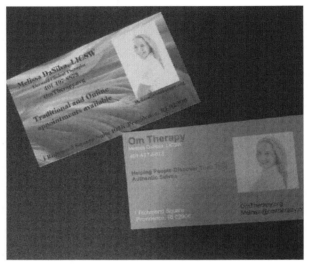

(My first business cards)

If you are ready to have a business card that stands out for marketing purposes, you can get yourself some Moo.com business cards. They offer a wide variety of cards with different shapes, weight, embossing and photos. Like they say in their own marketing: "You know when you have a Moo card in your hand." They are pretty high-class cards and don't get lost in the shuffle of the other business cards your potential client may find.

Another way to market in the community is to be a speaker at an event or hold your own event. You can offer to speak at places such as a school, PTO or PTA meetings, business bureaus, local business groups, and libraries. Become known as an expert in your niche by offering free speaking engagements. Have a topic in mind of what you want to talk about before pitching your talk to your potential host. Remember that your discussion needs to be beneficial to the host and the potential attendants of the event.

Finally, create a list of other therapists, doctors, and community organizations you know from your past that you may have worked with who also work with your ideal clients. These people already know who you are, and hopefully, trust you so they will be willing to share information about your practice. Create an information packet that includes your business cards, flyers of upcoming groups and postcards of the services that you are providing at your practice. These are items they can hand to clients if they feel clients could benefit from having a session with you. If you find that you are getting referrals from these people, make sure that you continue to send them information. A one-and-done approach is not how you go about keeping this flow of referrals coming.

This last suggestion was a little mixture of marketing and networking, so let's dive more into networking in the next chapter!

Let's Recap:
- You need to get out of your office and talk to people.
- Find businesses, providers and organizations that work with your ideal clients and share your information with them.
- Partner up and sponsor organizations that serve the same population you do. Remember if they are non-profit, you can write your donation off on your taxes at the end of the year.
- Be creative and be bold to grab the attention of potential clients.
- **Give, Give, Give** before asking in return.

Chapter 12:
Networking

―――

If someone told me five years ago that I would love networking, I wouldn't have believed them. How could I? I mean, a shy introvert love networking? For heaven's sake, I have a therapy dog to address my own social anxiety issues. Low and behold, because of my networking skills I created a six-figure business in less than two years. I am going to let you in on some of the secrets.

1. Fake it and perform, baby

I love singing karaoke. Weird for an introvert, right? But I love it. I get up there and sing from my heart. I like to control the stage. Yup, sometimes I embarrass myself doing Cher's "If I could Turn back Time" but I roll with it. I act like I am okay with messing up or mumbling the words. Nobody really knows or cares if you don't.

Likewise, when I am planning to go to a meeting or a networking event, I put on my "business woman" persona and perform from my heart. I am so passionate about my business and what I am offering, so people want to know more. I walk up to strangers and ask what they do, and in turn, they eventually ask me the same. That's when I share what I do and how I help people in my specific niche.

You need to be proud of what you are doing and the practice you are building. People will pick up on your energy and will want to continue to engage with your enthusiasm. You are in control of the show you are performing while you are at these events. Don't ever forget to have your business cards and a pen on you. You want to give the appearance that you are organized and professional; having cards on hand really helps with this.

2. Network at non-therapeutic events

Yes, you will want other therapists to know you have openings at your practice and that you specialize in a specific area, but I haven't found many therapists who are willing to refer to another therapist they met at a networking event. Usually, you aren't the only therapist trying to spread the word at these events that you have immediate openings.

I have found business networking events to be a great place to spread the word about your practice. Everyone knows of someone, if not themselves, who needs a therapist. So never fail to make sure you have those business cards with your picture on them to share with your new business friends. Remember to get their cards too. Write a little something on the back of their card as a way to remember who they are and what you discussed. Within the next day or two, send a follow-up email about what you discussed. Try to meet face-to-face to create a stronger connection. If it was someone looking for therapy, see if they are interested in setting up an appointment.

3.   Find your Golden Goose

You only need to find that one provider who sees your ideal client and laser focus on this provider. This may be a doctor or a psychiatrist or maybe even a school. Find out how you can contact them. This might be done through an email or a phone call. Next, try to take them out to have coffee or lunch. If they say they can't leave work to meet you, offer to go to them with a coffee or lunch. Most therapists don't attempt this approach. So the provider you are trying to connect with may be surprised at first, but if they understand that you want to collaborate on how you and they can help your clients better, they tend to open up more about meeting with you. This is the #1 way I was able to grow my business so fast.

Here is what I did: I identified one of the only doctors in my area who works with the same clients as I do. I work with transgender individuals, and she is one of the only endocrinologists who works with transgender adolescents and young adults in my state. The first thing I did was send her a notecard with my logo on it (created at Vistaprint.com). Inside I wrote:

Dear Dr. F,

My name is Melissa DaSilva, and I recently opened a private therapy practice in Providence. I specialize in working with individuals who identify as transgender. I would love to meet you for coffee sometime to discuss how I can be of more service to you and the clients we see. I know that you are a very busy person but until we can get together, please have a coffee on me. I look forward to hearing from you.

    -Melissa

I included a $5 coffee gift card in the note. I put this notecard with my business cards and postcard in a shiny mailing envelope and sent it to her office. I put this stuff in a very obvious package so that it was not going to get lost in a pile of papers. There was no way she was going to miss my letter.

A few weeks went by, and lo and behold she contacted me by phone. We had a mutual client, and since she was aware of me because of my package, she reached out to me. During our conversation, I offered to meet her for coffee and she agreed. We set a time and place for the coffee date, but unfortunately, we ended up canceling due to her busy schedule. That's when I offered to bring lunch to her office. She let me know that she would want to eat lunch in front of her staff and not offer them anything. So I offered to bring them all lunch. She agreed. I was not going to let this meeting slip through my hands. I was determined to be on this doctor's radar. I can almost guarantee that no other therapist has gone this far to meet with this doctor.

I ordered Panera Bread catering for about 10 people. The total came to about $60. This may seem like an expensive lunch, but I knew if I got one client from this practice, my return on investment would have been made, and I would still make a profit.

On the day of the lunch appointment, I lugged all the food to the office. Of course, it was 90 degrees out and I parked in the wrong lot, so I had to walk all the way around the medical building to get to the office. Once I found my way to the office, I was a huge hit. I spent time with the staff and a few minutes with the doctor, eating and chatting. I gave everyone my business cards and talked about what I could offer their clients as a therapist. Nobody had ever done this for them before, and they were so grateful.

Now that the doctor got to meet me, she felt comfortable referring her clients to me. She has a sense of who I am and what my personality is like. When a client tells her that they are working with me, they are always excited that their doctor knows their therapist and feels confident in my work. I continue to see this doctor often at community events. We greet each other with a hug and check in on how we are doing. I regularly send her office information about my practice, and she is very accessible for when I need to get my clients in to see her sooner that the waiting list would allow.

If you do this with at least one provider a month, you won't believe how fast your practice will grow.

4. Offer Before Asking

When I first started, I tried to meet as many people as possible who worked with my ideal client. I searched on Psychology Today for psychiatrists who worked with my client. I would send them a message via their profile or website, typically something like this:

Dear_____,

I want to introduce myself. My name is Melissa DaSilva, and I am a therapist with a new practice in the area. It appears that we work with the same population. I would love to meet for coffee and discuss how I can be of service to our clients. Please let me know if you would be interested. My treat.

   -Melissa

If I didn't hear a response back after about two weeks, I would send one of my shiny information packages. At this point they would have heard about me twice: once through email and another time through my information package. So even if they didn't schedule to have a meeting with me, they had the stuff to give their clients if they were in need of a therapist. Sometimes they would call to set up a time to meet or just to thank me for the gift card and information. My goal is to get stuck in their subconscious. This is another reason I put my photo on my business cards.

   If you get the opportunity to meet with one of the providers, make sure you meet them at a nice café. Ask them about themselves, their work and how you can help their clients. Again, most therapists don't go out of their way to do this type of stuff because they are too nervous to get out there and meet people as a

A Profitable Private Practice

means to networking. If you do take this opportunity, you are surely ahead of your colleagues.

5. Don't send cold intro letters

I often get these letters in the mail. A new therapist that I have never heard of is in town, has availability for new clients, and is hoping I will send my overflow referrals to them. This letter usually includes a bunch of plain white business cards for me to hand out to potential clients. I will give you a guess where those cards and letters go, and it's not on top of my desk. It's the trash can.

I want to make sure that you know that I am not throwing them out because I think they are my competition—although many people may feel this way. I throw them out because I don't know who this new person is and they aren't trying to get to know who I am. I am not going to hand out business cards for a therapist I don't know and haven't had the opportunity to gain trust in. They are just sending out cards, asking for some business.

Don't waste your money on stamps and business cards by taking this approach. Be very deliberate in who you send your letters to and make sure you are offering before asking. Attempt to create a situation to build trust in each other.

6. Create a list of people you want to network with

Create a list of 30 people you want to network with. Attempt to connect with one person a day by either email or phone. Yes, you might need to get on the phone and call people you want to network with. I did this when I first started out and it was kind of scary. However, I ended up getting some good leads and making some good connections doing so.

If contacting one person a day for 30 days seems like a lot of work, you can always decide to batch the people you are reaching out to. Reach out to seven people one day a week if that works better for you. The goal is to try and get 30 connections in one month. You won't get a response from all of the people you reach out to. Some will have wanted to respond to your email, but it got lost in the shuffle. Or you may even need to play a little phone tag with providers if you leave them messages and they decide to call you back. For emails, I like to use the Google application Boomerang. It allows you to schedule emails, reminds you of emails you haven't responded to, and "boomerangs" mail back to you that hasn't been opened yet. When you do get a response to your outreach attempts, try to meet them for coffee or even just get them on the phone to chat.

7. Hold an event

Offer to have a small get-together with other providers in your area. Take those 30 people you have attempted to reach and invite them to your little meet and greet. This invite can be a second attempt to connect with them. Create a list of other providers you would like to connect with from Psychology Today. If your office isn't big enough to hold something like this, you can look into other options such as a local tavern, a conference room or a shared workspace. I would suggest you use the Everbrite ticket platform to have people RSVP. This will be helpful so that you have an idea of how many people to expect. Offering hors d'oeurves and drinks can also be a way to persuade people to come to your event. Just make sure that if you are offering an alcoholic beverage, that it's okay with the facility.

You don't need to spend much on this event. Just consider the ROI. How many referrals will you need to cover the cost of putting on the event?

There is something to be said about a therapist who is willing to put something like this together. You will come across as a confident therapist who is not afraid to share clients and is also an available go-to person in your field.

If this is your first event, make sure you give yourself some time to put this together. I would suggest at least one month of preparation. After the first event, coordinating more in the future will be easier for you.

8. Talk Talk Talk

This probably sounds pretty obvious, but to network in the community make sure you talk about your business to anyone who will listen — after you ask them about themselves first, of course. Talk to people everywhere: in line at a store, on an airplane, at the coffee shop, at family get-togethers and at children's sports events. You never know when you will meet someone who you want to connect with. If this seems like it will be difficult for you because you are shy, start off with just saying hello to strangers when you pass them in the hall of your office building or in the community. Practice talking to people when you are not in-session. You will eventually start feeling comfortable chatting about your business with strangers.

As you can see, there are many ways to get out there and network. Meet as many people as you can and ask how you can help them. You may need to be creative. If you try any of these suggestions, you will be ahead of the pack in growing your profitable private practice.

Let's Recap:
- Fake it and perform from your heart until you are no longer scared to network.
- Reach out to non-therapists. Your services could be of use to their clientele.

- Find that one "golden goose" provider and try hard to connect with them. Just do whatever it takes.
- Talk to anyone who will listen.
- Create networking goals.
- Ask how you can help other providers before asking if they can help you.

Chapter 13:
Making the Money

It's now time to decide how you are going to make the money. There are several options available to bring money into your business. You can be a managed-care organization, which means you panel with insurance companies, health care organizations, or provider panels/insurance panels. These are typically the plans that employers choose to offer to their employees. You can be an out-of-network provider, a cash-only practice or a mixture of all three.

Even if you don't plan on taking insurance, knowing the difference between plans and commonly used terms will be very important for you and your clients. Honestly, I think this information should be taught in high school as a part of a life skills course. I didn't have a good understanding of this information until I started my private practice at the age of 34. I am going to assume that you might not either, so I am going to take some time and explain some of these terms for you.

Managed Care Plans/Insurances (private programs)

Managed Care Plans or Managed Care Insurance are programs that contract with health care providers, therapists and medical facilities to provide care for members at reduced costs. These providers make up the plan's network. How much you get reimbursed for the services you provide will depend on the plans' rules, which all differ across plans. Generally, there are two types of plans that are available in the managed care world: PPO plans (Preferred Provider Organizations' plans) and HMO plans (Health Maintenance Organizations' plans).

HMO (Health Maintenance Organization)

- When signing up for HMO plans, clients are asked to identify a primary care physician who will help determine what treatments a client might need.
- Clients with HMO plans will need to get referrals for their primary care physician in order to see a specialist, such as a mental

health provider.

- Therapists will only be able to receive referrals for these clients if you are also on the same network (paneled on their specific insurance plan) as the referring physician.

- If a client decides that they want to see a specialist outside of the network plan, the client will need to pay the entire medical cost.

- HMO plans are typically more restrictive in regards to the number of visits, tests and treatments they will cover.

- Premiums (the recurring amount of money the client will pay on a monthly basis, even if they aren't seeing a specialist) are generally lower for HMO plans and there is usually no deductible (the lump of money that needs to be paid at the start of every yearly billing cycle before the insurance will begin to cover the costs) or a low deductable.

PPO (Preferred Provider Organization)

- PPO plans are more flexible than HMO plans. They have in-network providers but there are fewer restrictions.
- They do not ask primary care physicians to make referrals for treatment.
- If a client decides to see an out-of-network provider, the PPO may pay part of or all of the fee depending on the plan. Clients get a better deal if they stay with in-network providers.
- Premiums tend to be higher, and there is usually a deductible.

EPO (Exclusive Provider Organization)
- EPO plans are a mixture of HMO and PPO programs.
- Clients will be covered for in-network provider visits, but will need to pay co-payments at sessions and in-network provider discount during the deductible period.
- Here, a clinician files the claim to the insurance company.
- EPOs do not typically require a preauthorization to see clients.

POS (Point-of-Service Plan)

- This type of plan is also a mixture of HMO and PPO programs.
- These plans typically offer the client a 3-tiered system so that they can choose the number of benefits and out-of-pocket fees they would like to participate in.
- Clients will get a discount if they stay with in-network providers, but do have the option to choose an out-of-network providers.
- Claims are also filed by the clinician.

In summary, HMOs tend to be more affordable but with less coverage and more restrictives. PPOs are more flexible and offer more coverage, but are more expensive and usually have a deductible. EPO and POS programs are a mixture of the first two programs, and they offer more flexibility to the client. The more flexibility and access to providers, the more money the client will have to pay in premiums and deductibles.

It may not be clear from the client's insurance

card if your services will be covered. This is why it is suggested that you call the insurance company before the first session to make sure you will get paid. Some clinicians require the client to look into the insurance coverage before the first visit, but I have found that clients either won't find out if they will be covered or don't understand the plan coverage before the initial session. You may be stuck with an unpaid bill if you don't look into this information yourself before your session.

If you decide to take insurance, these will typically be the four types you will come into contact with most. I will explain how to credential with these plans a little later in the chapter.

Third-Party Payers

Employee Assistance Programs

Some employers offer this program to their employees. It will usually be in addition to the health coverage that they provide. The program provides a specific number of counseling sessions a year to their employees and dependents (spouse, children) with a particular provider. The contracted provider will offer therapy sessions, assessments and referrals. Many employees will use the free session with the EAP and then use their insurance to continue the service with the same provider. Research has shown that EAPs help increase job satisfaction and productivity while decreasing absences, which in turn helps companies make more money.

- For a client to use their EAP benefits, you will need to be an in-network provider for their company.
- You will need to get pre-authorization to see the client. The client will need to call the program to get this.
- EAP may offer to contract with you at a lower price than your set rate.
- Review your EAP contract to learn about how to file claims with the program, charge missed appointment fees, the number of sessions allowed and follow-up expectations.

Medicaid, Medicare and TRICARE (Government Programs)

The following definitions are adapted from the website:

by Melissa DaSilva

https://www.hhs.gov

Medicare

Medicare is a federal insurance program. Medical bills are paid from trust funds that those covered have paid into. It serves people who are primarily over 65, whatever their income; and serves younger disabled people and dialysis patients. Clients pay part of costs through deductibles for hospital and other expenses. Small monthly premiums are required for non-hospital coverage. It is basically the same everywhere in the United States and is being run by the Center for Medicare & Medicaid Services, an agency of the federal government.

Medicaid

Medicaid is a federal-state assistance program. It serves low-income people of every age. Clients usually pay no part of costs for covered medical expenses. A small co-payment is sometimes required. It also varies from state to state. It is operated by state and local governments within federal guidelines.

These programs run similarly to the private insurance plans we discussed previously, but are offered by the government to help individuals who are over 65, disabled or with very low income who cannot afford the private insurance plans. I have found that these programs reimburse close to what the private insurance companies reimburse, but do tend to be lower.

TRICARE

TRICARE is a program designed to provide health care and mental health services to people associated with the United States military in various capacities.

Out-of-Network Providers/Cash Only Providers

Another option to make money in private practice is to be an out-of-network provider. This means that you are not paneled with an insurance company. Sometimes, depending on the insurance plan a client has, they may be able to get some reimbursement for the session they have with you as an out-of-network provider. They would need to have

PPO or POS out-of-network benefits. Being an out-of-network provider frees you from having to submit claims and chase down reimbursements, and allows you to charge the session fee you want to set for yourself. Many clinicians offer to create an invoice or a "superbill" for clients so that they can submit it to their insurance company for possible reimbursements. Some clinicians will offer to send the invoice out for the client, but this is not required. I have included a downloadable superbill template for you on my website. www.TheProfitablePrivatePractice.com

How do you know what to choose?

There are some misconceptions about whether you should try to panel on all insurances, be an out-of-network provider or a cash-only practice. The truth is, it's up to you on what you want to do to bring money into your business. You don't need to be on all insurance panels if you don't want to. You can choose what panels are good for you and your practice and credential with them. You can also decide to be an out-of-network provider for the insurance companies that you don't panel with. Another choice is to not deal with insurance at all and just create a cash-only practice. Although small, there are individuals out there who prefer not to use their insurance for confidentiality reasons. There are pros and cons to taking insurance, being in contract with a third-party payer or just being an out-of-network provider. Here are some examples:

Pros of being an out-of-network or cash-only practice:

1. You can make more money per session, since you get to set your fee independently.
2. There is less paperwork.
3. You don't have to submit claims and track down payments.
4. You don't have to request prior authorizations before seeing clients.
5. You don't need to spend a lot of time on the phone with insurance companies.
6. You have more freedom in treatment modalities.

Cons of being an out-of-network or cash-only

practice:

1. You will receive fewer referrals compared to being on an insurance panel. Other providers may also be hesitant to send clients to you.
2. It can take up to one year to get a full caseload.
3. You will need to market yourself to potential clients who will be able to afford your fees. Your services may not be accessible to all populations unless you would like to implement a sliding scale.

Pros of being on insurance panels:

1. Being on insurance panels gives you access to more referral opportunities, either from the insurance company themselves or other providers.
2. You make mental health services available to more diverse populations.
3. You can have a full caseload in an average of six months.

Cons of being on insurance panels:

1. It can take up to 6 months to get on the insurance panel after they receive your applications.
2. You agree to a lower price for your service fees when you agree to take insurance.
3. You will have to spend a lot of time on the phone trying to locate payments.
4. You will need to spend time finding out information on each client's benefits.
5. Insurance companies can change their reimbursement rates or a diagnosis that they cover at any time, sometimes without warning.
6. You will need to learn a lot about managed care that you most likely have never had to think about before.

If you decide to take insurance, I need to give you some warnings I have learned along the way:

Warning #1

Managed care was not created to make you wealthy. Insurance companies make a lot of money, and I am convinced that they have so much because they don't pay their providers. They purposefully make it extremely difficult to get the money you are owed. I once met someone who worked in managed care for 15 years who is also convinced of this. She said that each insurance company is tangled and you need to be able to dedicate a lot of time, energy and patience if you want to completely understand the ins and outs. Managed care companies purposely don't tell you all the information you need to maximize your reimbursements. Many times you need to specifically request part of your contract to know about the important information. I find this ironic since you need to know what to actually request to get specific information. How are you supposed to know what you don't know?

This happened to me. I didn't realize that one of the companies I was credentialed with didn't cover all the plans with the name of the client' insurance card. Let's call the insurance Blue Ocean Insurance. Several times we were declined on claims that we thought we were going to get payments for, since a specific type of Blue Ocean Insurance wasn't a part of the panel we were credentialed on. I asked the rep, "How am I supposed to know this?" She said it was on my fee schedule and that I needed to request it on a specific form. So I went ahead and completed the form, and then received my 40-page fee schedule ten days later. Why didn't the company have this attached to my contract when I signed it so I would be fully aware of the client insurance I was able to take? This type of situation can happen with all types of insurances and with a host of different kinds of information.

Warning #2

Fifty percent of the time, parts of your application—and sometimes even your entire credential packet—may become lost after you send it out. From the time the insurance companies receive your application, they have 120 days to process your application. What happens if they don't process your application within 120 days? From my experience, nothing. There are no consequences for the company for not keeping their end of the bargain. Insurance companies regularly lose applications. One insurance company took over a year to credential one of my clinicians. They lost parts of the application several times and closed her case. I can't express this enough: always make a copy of your application before sending it out.

Warning #3

If you call the provider relations line three times with the same question, you will likely get three different answers. Nobody is accountable for giving you the right or wrong answers to your questions. Although they do record the calls, it doesn't do you as the provider any good. They are not going to review your call for some claims or credentialing issues. You can request to speak to a manager, but they can take up to 30 days to respond, and this will usually be through email. If you have a follow-up question to that email, it could take another 30 days for the answers to come.

If you ever get lucky enough to get a direct line to a provider relations representative, keep that number in a safe place. You may be able to contact them in the future with other questions and start creating a personal connection with them. I have a place in my Credentialing Tool Kit for you to keep all this important information properly organized.

In summary, there are several options to choose from when thinking about how you are going to bring in income to your practice. If you decide that you want to panel with some insurance companies, I will give you some tips on how to do this in the next chapter. You will always have the option to decide not to be on insurance panels in the future. Some clinicians make this decision when they have a better understanding of what insurance companies pay better than others, who will pay easily and who makes submitting claims easy. If you decide to come off an insurance panel, make sure to read over your contract first to find the requirements for canceling your contract.

If I haven't scared you off with my warnings about paneling with insurance companies, then continue onto the next chapter where I will give you a step-by-step guide on how to start the process. If you plan on being an out-of-network or cash-only provider, you may want to just skip over to the section on invoices and superbills. You will still need to know about these even if you don't panel with an insurance company.

Let's Recap:

- You can bring in money to your practice by paneling with managed care organizations, third-party payers and being an out-of-network provider.
- There are pros and cons to paneling with insurance, being an out-of-network provider or a cash-only practice. Some clinicians are a mixture of in-network and out-of-network.
- If you panel with insurance, you can always decide to cancel a contract in the future.
- Do your homework and ask around to learn what other local clinicians have experienced with specific insurance companies.
- Start off organized and stay organized to maximize your reimbursements and payments.

Chapter 14:
Becoming an In-Network Provider

———

I know that in the last chapter I gave you some scary warnings about credentialing with insurance panels. But it isn't so bad if you go into it knowing what to expect and how to address the issues before they turn into some annoying problems. I hope that this next chapter and the template I offer you will help in having a good experience with managed care companies.

Step 1:

You need to decide what insurance panels you want to get on. You may want to get on all of them, or just a few. For some time at my practice, I only paneled with one insurance company, and took other clients as an out-of-network provider. I chose to be on our state-issued insurance so that my services were accessible to low-income populations. As I grew my solo practice into a group practice (I will discuss how to do this in a future book) I decided to panel with other companies.

You will want to decide how you want to set up your practice. Ask around to see what other colleague have experienced with specific companies. Due to Anti-Trust laws, we are not supposed to ask other clinicians what insurance companies are reimbursing them. You can find more about this at FTC Antitrust Law Guide (https://www.ftc.gov/tips-advice/competition-guidance/guide-antitrust-laws) or you can call some of the companies you may panel with to see if they will give you an idea of what their reimbursement rates for the following CPT (Common Procedural Technology) codes:

90791   Initial Assessment
90834   45-52 Minute Follow-up Session
90837   53-60 Minute Follow-up Session
90847   Couple/Family Therapy Session
90853   Group Therapy Session

When asking them for the reimbursement rate for

these codes, be sure to let them know what licensure level you're inquiring about. There may be a difference between Social Workers, Mental Health Counselors, and Psychologists. This is referred to as the HCPCS Code.

Step 2:

Once you have gathered this information and have decided that you want to panel with insurances, then you will need to complete a CAQH profile. You can find this at https://proview.caqh.org. Once you fill this profile out, you will be given a CAQH number that many insurance panels will ask for during the application process.

CAQH is a free online platform where insurance companies can locate all your professional information. I like to think of it as your professional resume for insurance companies. It does take several hours to complete, since they will ask you for a lot of information about past education, job positions, licenses and liability insurance. CAQH will contact you via email every 180 days to make sure all your information stays updated.

The insurance companies that you try to panel with will ask for your permission to access your account when they are reviewing your application. My understanding is that CAQH was created to help minimize duplication of paperwork. As you will soon see, there is still a lot of duplicate information you will be providing as you attempt to panel with insurance companies.

Step 3:

Contact the insurance company you want to panel with. You may want to start online to see if they have a provider portal. Some companies will have detailed steps and PDFs for you to download and complete to start the inquiry process. Some sites will have a number for you to call, while others might have you send a letter of interest to join their panel. Some companies will take up to three months to respond to your request. Be sure to document when you send out these letters and emails so that you know when to follow up on your request if you don't hear from them.

Not all insurance companies are accepting

new providers to their panels. This can be due to an oversaturation of providers already in your area, or they may not reimburse for your level of licensure. You can attempt to appeal this decision if you offer a special service or treatment or speak another language.

Step 4:

Now is the time to start completing the applications. Some of the companies will have the applications on their sites, but most of them will have to send you a copy via email for you to fill out and fax back. The application is going to ask you a lot of information about your practice, business, treatment modalities, specialties, education, office accessibility, hours of operation, vacation coverage and any history of complaints or licensing sanctions. Before sending the completed application in, make sure you make a copy of the entire application. I cannot stress this enough! (See Warning #2 in the last chapter.)

Step 5:

I also recommend checking the status of your

application about a month after sending it in. You will want to contact the provider relations department or the credentialing department of the insurance company when checking on the status. You will want to call to make sure that all parts of the application were received and that it is in the process of being reviewed. I suggest that you continue to call every other week after this to check on the processing status. Eventually, the applications will get to the medical director to be approved and signed. Once approved, you will be sent a copy to review, sign and send back. Read the contract carefully to make sure you agree with the terms.

To help you keep track of your credentialing process, I have created a template that you can download on my website. TheProfitablePrivatePractice.com

That's it: you are credentialed on insurance panels! Now you probably want to know what to do when you get your first client with insurance? That is covered in the next chapter, so read on!

Let's Recap:

- Do your homework and decide if and what insurance companies you would like to be paneled on.
- Complete your CAQH profile.
- Send a letter or email of interest to the insurance companies you want to work with.
- Once given the go-ahead, start completing the application.
- Make a copy of the application before sending or faxing it in.
- Call the company to check on the progress of your application.
- Review and sign the contract and return it to the insurance company.

Chapter 15:
Your First Client Session

Checking Client Eligibility

Finally, you have your first client asking you for an appointment! What are you going to do? First off, take a deep breath and ask the potential client what brings them to make the call today. They may go into some dialogue on what is bothering them. Asking this question starts to build a relationship with the potential client.

Next, you will want to see what their availability is and if it matches with yours. Moving on to the next step, some therapists sometimes have a hard time discussing payment with the potential client. Ask how they will be paying for the services. You can easily do this by asking, "Will you be using insurance for your sessions?" If yes, try to get that information right away so that you can check their eligibility and benefits before the first session. Get in the habit of doing this right away. It will help you avoid a lot of headaches in the future. You will want to ask them for:

- The name of their insurance company
- The name on their card
- Their date of birth
- Their member ID number
- The phone number on the back of the card

If you are like me when I first started, you probably won't know what any of the terms mean when you call up to find out what mental health benefits the potential client has. Let's explore some of these terms, so you feel a little more comfortable when making that call. Make sure that when you do call that number they gave you off the back of the card, you are connecting to the behavioral health line. Sometimes you will be connected to the medical benefits line if you don't realize you need the other line.

When you are given the option to check the

by Melissa DaSilva

benefits of the member, try to get a human on the phone. The automated benefits line isn't always accurate and won't be able to tell you how much of a deductible has been met, if there is one. The secret to getting a real person on the line is to press "0" or ask for "representative" when prompted to state your reason for the call.

Once you get the representative on the phone, ask of an explanation of client benefits. They will probably rattle off a bunch of terms you won't understand. Don't be afraid to ask the representative for some clarifying information. They are usually understanding and very happy to explain the benefits more in-depth with you. Here are some terms you will want to know before calling:

EIN or TIN: This is your Tax Identification number. If you haven't specifically applied for a tax ID, it will automatically be your social security number. This piece of information will be asked a lot, especially when dealing with claims. The government will want to know how much money to tax you at the end of the year for the reimbursements you receive from the insurance companies.

Deductible: This is the amount that the client will have to pay each year before the insurance will cover the services. You will only be able to charge the contracted rate, not your out-of-network rate, if the payments are going towards a deductible. Some people have no deductible, while others have very high deductibles.

Copayment/Co-insurance: This is the portion of the contracted rate that the client will be responsible for paying at the end of each session. Sometimes this kicks in after the deductible is met. Some insurance plans require the client to pay a percentage of the fee, instead of a flat rate.

Example: Contracted Rate for a session is $75

- *Plan A: Client is required to pay a $25 co-pay per session once the deductible is met. The insurance will reimburse you $50.*

- *Plan B: Client is covered 90% after the deductible is met. This means that the client would buy 10% of the contracted rate of $75. Client will owe you $7.50 per session. The insurance will reimburse* *you $67.50*

Client, Insured and Payee: It took me some time to figure out the difference between these terms, so I am going to make sure you know the difference.

- **Client:** This is the identified person that you will be seeing in session.
- **Insured:** This may be the client if the client is the primary insurance policy holder, or it could be another person in the family who is the policy holder. This happens especially when working with minors. The minor would be the client, while the parent will be the insured. If this is the case, make sure you get the date of birth of the parent.
- **Payer:** This term refers to the entity that is paying you the money.
- **Payee:** This refers to the person receiving the reimbursement.

Be aware that some clients will have two insurance plans. One is a primary, and then there is the secondary. What typically happens in this situation is that the primary will cover the percentage of the session that is agreed upon in the provider contract. After this, the secondary insurance may cover the rest. If you are not a provider for the primary insurance, the secondary insurance will not cover the entire fee of the service.

Another piece of information you will want to know is how many sessions a client is allowed in a year and if they have used any of them yet. Some plans will require a pre-authorization before you meet with the client. Sometimes when you call to check benefits, you may learn that the client doesn't have insurance coverage. The client may not realize this themselves. Some plans require members to re-enroll each year to keep coverage, or the client may be between jobs and the new coverage hasn't started yet.

So many obstacles can come in the way of you getting paid for your first session. If you can get in the habit of checking beforehand, you will be so grateful that you did.

Intake Paperwork

Many Electronic Health Record (EHR)

programs give you the option of sending intake paperwork out via email before the first session. Many allow you to create your own forms and add them to the EHR platform. If you choose this option, be sure to still review the paperwork at the start of the first session. You want to be sure that clients know:

- Your no-show policy (some insurance companies allow you to charge a fee, while others do not — review your contract)
- HIPAA
- Your social media policy
- Payment responsibilities
- What to expect when engaging in therapy

Be sure to document that you reviewed these forms with the client. I also recommend that you keep a copy of the policies and procedures on your website. If they do not want to complete the paperwork online, be sure to have hard copies in your office for them to complete upon arrival to the first session.

You can purchase my Intake Paperwork Packet at my website. This way you don't have to re-create your own paperwork when you start out.

The Initial Sessions

Your first and second session will typically include an assessment of what is causing the client distress, what their goals are and some history of their symptoms and life events that could cause distress. Before you can submit a claim for the first session, you will need to have an appropriate diagnosis identified for this client. During your assessment, you will need to make sure that the client meets medical necessity for receiving mental health services. Not all insurance companies reimburse for every diagnosis. You will want to ask each insurance provider if there are any specific diagnosis they do not cover. This can change periodically throughout the year. You will want to make sure you read those newsletters or bulletins they send you on a regular basis to see if there are any changes you need to be aware of.

At the initial session, you will also want to have clients sign all "release of information" forms you may need. I like to have clients/guardians sign a release to share information with the primary care physicians, the insurance company, any past and current mental health providers, and schools if it's a minor. Keep extra copies of these releases in your office. You never know if your client will mention another contact in a session that may be useful to coordinate with. Some insurance companies require that you have their members sign a specific release of information that they provide. They can be found on their website if this is the case.

I won't go into the therapeutic process of your practice. That is information that you learned in school, and that's not what this book is about. So, you go ahead and create the therapeutic magic you were trained to do. I will teach you what you need to do after your session in the next chapter: progress notes, treatment plans and biosocial assessments.

Let's Recap:
- Start creating a relationship during the first call by asking what brings them to make an appointment with a therapist today.
- Check insurance eligibility before the first session.

- Send out paperwork electronically or have them fill out hard copies at the first session.
- Review your policies and procedures at the first session.
- Be sure that client meets medical necessity to receive therapy services.

Chapter 16:
Assessments, Progress Notes
& Treatment Plans

——

If you are not working with insurance companies for reimbursement, you won't have to follow all the requirements I am going to discuss in this section. Do keep in mind that although you may not be a provider on a client's insurance plan, you will still want to stay very compliant to the case file if you are providing the client an invoice for reimbursement. Insurance companies may sequester files of out-of-network providers if the insurance company is being asked to reimburse their members for therapy sessions. The companies may want to be sure that their member is receiving services that are medically necessary and goal-driven. If your practice is cash-only and not providing invoices, you will still want files that are ethically and professionally appropriate.

Your first session with a client will typically be

a little longer than future sessions. The first and second sessions will usually include a biosocial assessment, creation of treatment goals and objectives. This is when you will start to assess if the client meets that criteria for any diagnosis in the DSM-V. When billing for the initial assessments, make sure to use the Initial Assessment Code 90791. Insurance companies reimburse slightly more for this session, since there is a lot that needs to be covered. I have included a Biosocial Assessment Template at my website TheProfitablePrivatePractice.com

Your progress notes will also need to include specific information that insurance companies may look out for if your files are audited. Each note will need to include:

- Client name (on every page)
- Date of Service
- Time of Service
- Diagnosis Code
- Type of service (initial assessment, individual, group, couples)
- Follow up for previous sessions
- Presenting problem and symptoms (as

evidenced by...)

- Focus of session (goals and objectives addressed)
- Progress towards goals
- Any risk factors, change in medication and mental status
- Plan for future session
- Clinician Signature and Date

Insurance companies will also want you to have a treatment plan for their members. They want to be sure that each session has goals that the client and therapist are working towards, along with ways to measure the success of treatment. Again, treatment plans are topics that you have learned in graduate school, so I will not explain in detail here how to create one. I have included a Treatment Plan Template in the paperwork packet located on my website. I have also included a list of great books dedicated to this topic in my resource guide at the end of this book.

There is a lot of paperwork and information that needs to be obtained, even before the therapeutic process begins. Once you create a system and work through it several times, it will become much easier as you grow. If you are utilizing an Electronic Health Record system, they may offer a template for your opening paperwork, progress notes, assessments and treatment plans. This may be something you will want to inquire about if you are looking for the best ERH system for your practice.

Let's Recap:
- Make sure your intake paperwork is completed and reviewed by the end of the first session.
- Complete assessments during the first couple of session and see if they meet medical necessity for mental health services.
- Keep progress notes and treatment plans compliant with insurance company requirements and professional ethics.
- Check out my website for a helpful paperwork packet to use for your new practice.

Chapter 17:
Filling Out Claims

—

Now that you have finished your initial assessments with your client and have checked to see if they are covered by benefits, it is time to complete your insurance claim. Your claims can be filled out by hand using CSM-1500 forms that can be purchased at Staples or on Amazon. You will have to send them by mail to the claims department of each insurance company to receive your reimbursements. Surprisingly, some companies reimburse faster if they get the claims by mail.

If you are using an Electronic Health Record platform, you may be able to use their platform to submit claims. They will usually charge a fee per claim submitted. Many clinicians find this feature helpful and very easy to understand. Another option is to hire a billing company that will take care all of your filing needs. They will usually charge a percentage of the reimbursement that they help bring in. You will need to decide what the best option for you will be. If you are not hiring a billing company, you will need to have some understanding of the CMS-1500 forms.

Here is what that form looks like. If you are printing the form out, make sure you use the required red ink, otherwise they will not process the claims.

by Melissa DaSilva

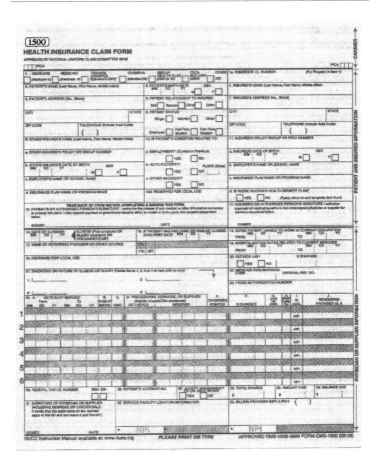

Here is an adapted guide on how to fill the form out. For more detailed instructions you can find an updated manual at http://www.nucc.org.

Item Number	Title	Instructions
1	Medicare, Medicaid, TRICARE, CHAMPVA, Group Health Plan, FECA, Black Lung, Other	Indicate the type of health insurance coverage applicable to this claim by placing an X in the appropriate box. Only one box can be marked.
1a	Insured's ID Number	Enter the insured's ID number as shown on insured's ID card for the payer to which the claim is being submitted. If the patient has a unique Member Identification Number assigned by the payer, then enter that number in this field.
2	Patient's Name	Enter the patient's full last name, first name, and middle initial. If the patient uses a last name suffix (e.g., Jr, Sr), enter it after the last name and before the first name. Titles (e.g., Sister, Capt, Dr) and professional suffixes (e.g., Ph.D, MD, Esq) should not be included with the name. Use commas to separate the last name, first name, and middle initial. A hyphen can be used for hyphenated names. Do not use periods within the name.

If the patient's name is the same as the insured's name (i.e., the patient is the insured), then it is not necessary to report the patient's name. |
| 3 | Patient's Birth Date, | Enter the patient's 8-digit birth |

	Sex	date (MM | DD | YYYY). Enter an X in the correct box to indicate sex (gender) of the patient. Only one box can be marked. If sex is unknown, leave blank.
4	Insured's Name	Enter the insured's full last name, first name, and middle initial. If the insured uses a last name suffix (e.g., Jr, Sr), enter it after the last name and before the first name. Titles (e.g., Sister, Capt, Dr) and professional suffixes (e.g., PhD, MD, Esq) should not be included with the name.
5	Patient's Address (multiple fields)	Enter the patient's address. The first line is for the street address; the second line, the city and state; the third line, the ZIP code
6	Patient Relationship to Insured	Enter an X in the correct box to indicate the patient's relationship to insured when Item Number 4 has beencompleted. Only one box can be marked. If the patient is a dependent, but has a unique Member Identification Number and the payer requires the identification number be reported on the claim, then report "Self", since the patient is reported as the insured.
7	Insured's Address (multiple fields)	Enter the insured's address. If Item Number 4 is completed, then this field should be completed. The first line is for the street address; the second line, the city and state; the third line, the ZIP

		code.
8	Reserved for NUCC Use	This field was previously used to report "Patient Status." "Patient Status" does not exist in 5010A1, so this field has been eliminated.
9	Other Insured's Name	If Item Number 11d is marked, complete fields 9, 9a, and 9d, otherwise leave blank. When additional group health coverage exists, enter other insured's full last name, first name, and middle initial of the enrollee in another health plan if it is different from that shown in Item Number 2. If the insured uses a last name suffix (e.g., Jr, Sr), enter it after the last name and before the first name. Titles (e.g., Sister, Capt, Dr) and professional suffixes (e.g., Ph.D, MD, Esq) should not be included with the name.
9a	Other Insured's Policy or Group Number	Enter the policy or group number of the other insured
9b	Reserved for NUCC Use	This field was previously used to report "Other Insured's Date of Birth, Sex." "Other Insured's Date of Birth, Sex" does not exist in 5010A1, so this field has been eliminated.
9c	Reserved for NUCC Use	This field was previously used to report "Employer's Name or School Name." "Employer's Name or School Name" does not exist in 5010A1, so this field has been eliminated
9d	Insurance Plan	Enter the other insured's

	Name or Program Name	insurance plan or program name
10a-10c	Is Patient's Condition Related To	When appropriate, enter an X in the correct box to indicate whether one or more of the services described in Item Number 24 are for a condition or injury that occurred on the job or as a result of an automobile or other accident. Only one box on each line can be marked. The state postal code where the accident occurred must be reported if "YES" is marked in 10b for "Auto Accident." Any item marked "YES" indicates there may be other applicable insurance coverage that would be primary, such as automobile liability insurance. Primary insurance information must then be shown in Item Number 11.
10d	Claim Codes (Designated by NUCC)	When applicable, use to report appropriate claim codes. Applicable claim codes are designated by the NUCC. Please refer to the most current instructions from the public or private payer regarding the need to report claim codes. When required by payers to provide the sub-set of Condition Codes approved by the NUCC, enter the Condition Code in this field. The Condition Codes approved for use on the 1500

		Claim Form are available at www.nucc.org under Code Sets. When reporting more than one code, enter three blank spaces and then the next code
11	Insured's Policy, Group, or FECA Number	Enter the insured's policy or group number as it appears on the insured's health care identification card. If Item Number 4 is completed, then this field should be completed. Do not use a hyphen or space as a separator within the policy or group number
11a	Insured's Date of Birth, Sex	Enter the 8-digit date of birth (MM│DD│YYYY) of the insured and an X to indicate the sex (gender) of the insured. Only one box can be marked. If gender is unknown, leave blank.
11b	Other Claim ID (Designated by NUCC)	Enter the "Other Claim ID." Applicable claim identifiers are designated by the NUCC. When submitting to Property and Casualty payers, e.g, Automobile, Homeowner's, or Workers' Compensation insurers and related entities, the following qualifier and accompanying identifier has been designated for use: Y4 Agency Claim Number (Property Casualty Claim

		Number)
		Enter the qualifier to the left of the vertical, dotted line. Enter the identifier number to the right of the vertical, dotted line.
11c	Insurance Plan Name or Program Name	Enter the name of the insurance plan or program of the insured. Some payers require an identification number of the primary insurer rather than the name in this field.
11d	Is there another Health Benefit Plan?	When appropriate, enter an X in the correct box. If marked "YES", complete 9, 9a, and 9d. Only one box can be marked.
12	Patient's or Authorized Person's Signature	Enter "Signature on File," "SOF," or legal signature. When legal signature, enter date signed in 6-digit (MM|DD|YY) or 8-digit format (MM|DD|YYYY) format. If there is no signature on file, leave blank or enter "No Signature on File."
13	Insured's or Authorized Person's Signature	Enter "Signature on File," "SOF," or legal signature. If there is no signature on file, leave blank or enter "No Signature on File."
14-33	Date of Current Illness, Injury, or Pregnancy (LMP)	Enter the 6-digit (MM|DD|YY) or 8-digit (MM|DD|YYYY) date of the first date of the present illness, injury, or pregnancy. For pregnancy, use the date of the last menstrual period (LMP) as the first date. Enter the applicable qualifier to

		identify which data is being reported. 431 Onset of Current Symptoms or Illness 484 Last Menstrual Period Enter the qualifier to the right of the vertical, dotted line.
15	Other Date	Enter another date related to the patient's condition or treatment. Enter the date in the 6-digit (MM DD YY) or 8-digit (MM DD YYYY) format
16	Dates Patient Unable to Work in Current Occupation	If the patient is employed and is unable to work in current occupation, a 6-digit (MM DD YY) or 8-digit (MM DD YYYY) date must be shown for the "form–to" dates that the patient is unable to work. An entry in this field may indicate employment-related insurance coverage.
17	Name of Referring Provider or Other Source	Enter the name (First Name, Middle Initial, Last Name) followed by the credentials of the professional who referred or ordered the service(s) or supply(is) on the claim. If multiple providers are involved, enter one provider using the following priority order: 1. Referring Provider 2. Ordering Provider 3. Supervising Provider
17a	Other ID#	The Other ID number of the

		referring, ordering, or supervising provider is reported in 17a in the shaded area. The qualifier indicating what the number represents is reported in the qualifier field to the immediate right of 17a. The NUCC defines the following qualifiers used in 5010A1: 0B State License Number 1G Provider UPIN Number G2 Provider Commercial Number LU Location Number (This qualifier is used for Supervising Provider only.)
18	Hospitalization Dates Related to Current Services	Enter the inpatient 6-digit (MM | DD | YY) or 8-digit (MM | DD | YYYY) hospital admission date followed by the discharge date (if discharge has occurred). If not discharged, leave discharge date blank. This date is when a medical service is furnished as a result of, or subsequent to, a related hospitalization.
19	Additional Claim Information (Designated by NUCC)	Please refer to the most current instructions from the public or private payer regarding the use of this field. Report the appropriate qualifier, when available, for the information being entered. Do not enter a space, hyphen, or other separator between the qualifier and the information.

20	Outside Lab Charges	Complete this field when billing for purchased services by entering an X in "YES." A "YES" mark indicates that the reported service was provided by an entity other than the billing provider (for example, services subject to Medicare's anti-markup rule). A "NO" mark or blank indicates that no purchased services are included on the claim.
21	Diagnosis or Nature of Illness or Injury	Enter the applicable ICD indicator to identify which version of ICD codes is being reported. 9 ICD-9-CM 0 ICD-10-CM Enter the indicator between the vertical, dotted lines in the upper right-hand area of the field. Enter the codes left justified on each line to identify the patient's diagnosis or condition. Do not include the decimal point in the diagnosis code, because it is implied. List no more than 12 ICD-10-CM or ICD-9CM diagnosis codes. Relate lines A - L to the lines of service in 24E by the letter of the line. Use the greatest level of specificity. Do not provide narrative description in this field.
22	Resubmission and/or Original Reference Number	List the original reference number for resubmitted claims. Please refer to the most current instructions from the public or private payer regarding the use of this field.

		When resubmitting a claim, enter the appropriate bill frequency code left justified in the left-hand side of the field. 7 Replacement of prior claim 8 Void/cancel of prior claim This Item Number is not intended for use for original claim submissions
23	Prior Authorization Number	Enter any of the following: prior authorization number, referral number, mammography pre-certification number, or Clinical Laboratory Improvement Amendments (CLIA) number, as assigned by the payer for the current service. Do not enter hyphens or spaces within the number.
24		Supplemental information can only be entered with a corresponding, completed service line. The six service lines in section 24 have been divided horizontally to accommodate submission of both the NPI and another/proprietary identifier and to accommodate the submission of supplemental information to support the billed service. The top area of the six service lines is shaded and is the location for reporting supplemental information. It is

		not intended to allow the billing of 12 lines of service. The supplemental information is to be placed in the shaded section of 24A through 24G as defined in each Item Number. Providers must verify requirements for this supplemental information with the payer.
24a	Date(s) of Service [lines 1–6]	Enter date(s) of service, both the "From" and "To" dates. If there is only one date of service, enter that date under "From." Leave "To" blank or re-enter "From" date. If grouping services, the place of service, procedure code, charges, and individual provider for each line must be identical for that service line. Grouping is allowed only for services on consecutive days. The number of days must correspond to the number of units in 24G.
24b	Place of Service [lines 1–6]	In 24B, enter the appropriate two-digit code from the Place of Service Code list for each item used or service performed. The Place of Service Codes are available at: www.cms.gov/Medicare/Coding/place-of-service-codes/Place_of_Service_Code_Set.html
24c	EMG [lines 1–6]	Check with payer to determine if this information (emergency indicator) is necessary. If required,

		enter Y for "YES" or leave blank if "NO" in the bottom, unshaded area of the field. The definition of emergency would be either defined by federal or state regulations or programs, payer contracts, or as defined in 5010A1.
24d	Procedures, Services, or Supplies [lines 1–6]	Enter the CPT or HCPCS code(s) and modifier(s) (if applicable) from the appropriate code set in effect on the date of service. This field accommodates the entry of up to four 2-character modifiers. The specific procedure code(s) must be shown without a narrative description.
24e	Diagnosis Pointer [lines 1–6]	In 24E, enter the diagnosis code reference letter (pointer) as shown in Item Number 21 to relate the date of service and the procedures performed to the primary diagnosis. When multiple services are performed, the primary reference letter for each service should be listed first, other applicable services should follow. The reference letter(s) should be A – L or multiple letters as applicable. ICD-10-CM or ICD-9-CM diagnosis codes must be entered in Item Number 21. Do not enter them in 24E.
24f	$Charges [lines 1–6]	Enter the charge amount for each listed service. Enter the number right justified in

		the left-hand area of the field. Do not use commas when reporting dollar amounts. Negative dollar amounts are not allowed. Dollar signs should not be entered. Enter 00 in the right-hand area of the field if the amount is a whole number.
24g	Days or Units [lines 1–6]	Enter the number of days or units. This field is most commonly used for multiple visits, units of supplies, anesthesia units or minutes, or oxygen volume. If only one service is performed, the numeral 1 must be entered
24h	EPSDT/Family Plan [lines 1–6]	For reporting of Early & Periodic Screening, Diagnosis, and Treatment (EPSDT) and Family Planning services, refer to specific payer instructions.
24i	ID Qualifier [lines 1–6]	Enter in the shaded area of 24I the qualifier identifying if the number is a non-NPI. The Other ID# of the rendering provider should be reported in 24J in the shaded area. The NUCC defines the following qualifiers used in 5010A1: 0B State License Number 1G Provider UPIN Number G2 Provider Commercial Number LU Location Number ZZ Provider Taxonomy (The qualifier in the 5010A1 for Provider Taxonomy is PXC, but ZZ will remain the qualifier for the 1500 Claim Form.)

24j	Rendering Provider ID # [lines 1–6]	The individual providing the service is reported in 24J. Enter the non-NPI ID number in the shaded area of the field. Enter the NPI number in the unshaded area of the field. The Rendering Provider is the person or company (laboratory or other facility) who rendered or supervised the care. In the case where a substitute provider (locum tenens) was used, enter that provider's information here. Report the Identification Number in Items 24I and 24J only when different from data recorded in items 33a and 33b.
25	Federal Tax ID Number	Enter the "Federal Tax ID Number" (employer ID number or SSN) of the Billing Provider identified in Item Number 33. This is the tax ID number intended to be used for 1099 reporting purposes. Enter an X in the appropriate box to indicate which number is being reported. Only one box can be marked.
26	Patient's Account Number	Enter the patient's account number assigned by the provider of service's or supplier's accounting system.
27	Accept Assignment?	Enter an X in the correct box. Only one box can be marked
28	Total Charge	Enter total charges for the services

		(i.e., a total of all charges in 24F).
29	Amount Paid	Enter total amount the patient and/or other payers paid on the covered services only.
30	Reserved for NUCC Use	This field was previously used to report "Balance Due." "Balance Due" does not exist in 5010A1, so this field has been eliminated.
31	Signature of Physician or Supplier Including Degrees or Credentials	INSTRUCTIONS: "Signature of Physician or Supplier Including Degrees or Credential" does not exist in 5010A1. Enter the legal signature of the practitioner or supplier, signature of the practitioner or supplier representative, "Signature on File," or "SOF." Enter either the 6-digit date (MM|DD|YY), 8-digit date (MM|DD|YYYY), or alphanumeric date (e.g., January 1, 2003) the form was signed.
32, 32a and 32b		
32	Service Facility Location Information	enter the name, address, city, state, and ZIP code of the location where the services were rendered. Providers of service (namely physicians) must identify the supplier's name, address, ZIP code, and NPI number when billing for purchased diagnostic tests. When more than one supplier is used, a separate 1500 Claim Form should be used to bill for each supplier

32a	NPI#	Enter the NPI number of the service facility location in 32a. Only report a Service Facility Location NPI when the NPI is different from the Billing Provider NPI.
32b	Other ID#	Enter the qualifier identifying the non-NPI number followed by the ID number. Do not enter a space, hyphen, or other separator between the qualifier and number.
33	Billing Provider Info & Ph #	Enter the provider's or supplier's billing name, address, ZIP code, and phone number. The phone number is to be entered in the area to the right of the field title. Enter the name and address information in the following format: 1st Line – Name 2nd Line – Address 3rd Line – City, State and ZIP code
33a	NPI#	Enter the NPI number of the billing provider in 33a
33b	Other ID#	Enter the qualifier identifying the non-NPI number followed by the ID number. Do not enter a space, hyphen, or another separator between the qualifier and number

It takes some practice to figure out how to fill these forms out. It takes time and several denials for you to learn how to complete these forms so that you can receive your reimbursements. If you are filling these out by hand and sending in the mail, make sure you have a copy of your completed form saved in your files. Sometimes they can get lost in the mail. It can take up to 45 days to receive a reimbursement. You can always call the company's claims department to check on your claims process if you feel that it is taking longer to receive payment than you think it should.

Claim Denials

There is truly nothing like opening a Reimbursement Advice (this is the Explanation of Benefits that is sent to the provider) hoping to see a big chunk of money, to then see a row of $0 for your reimbursement amounts. Each denial will come with a code that should have a definition at the end of the document. This will give you an idea of why your claim was not paid. Sometimes it will be vague, and you still won't have any idea to you why you didn't get paid and you will need to contact the claims department to get a better understanding. If you need to call the claims department, be sure to document the call, who you spoke with and what the outcome was. If you need to make an adjustment to the claim and resend it, be sure to document this as well. Let's look at what a Reimbursement Advice looks like. Reimbursements Advice look very similar to what clients receive in their Explanation of Benefits.

Not all RA will look the same from every insurance company, but they are pretty similar. Call the claims department if you have any questions about your reimbursements. I have found that if you are very nice to them, they will try and help you as much as they can. If you need to complete an appeal for a denial, you will also want to inquire how to go about doing this. Appeals will take several weeks to get processed. Document everything regarding your appeals so that you stay on top of the status.

Chasing claims and payments can be maddening. If you are doing this process yourself, give yourself plenty of time to be on the phone and keep your documentation organized.

Being an Out-of-Network or Cash-only Provider

There are many benefits to being a provider that doesn't panel with managed care organizations. Chasing down your money and filing claims is a huge plus. If you are an out-of-network provider, you will have the ability to set your fees to the price you feel is appropriate for your services. The client will be responsible for paying you your fee at the end of the session. Your client may want to try and get reimbursement by filing a claim on their own for the session with their insurance company. They may qualify for a partial reimbursement depending on their out-of-network benefits.

If this is the case, you will need to provide them with an invoice or superbill. An invoice is a bill that will include only one date of service at a time. It informs your client about payment due for services you have provided. If it was paid at the time of service, indicate that on the invoice. A superbill is a document that includes all dates of services, that you give to your clients at the end of the month so that they can submit for insurance reimbursement. Some of the information that you will include will be your practice information, date of services, NPI, client information, diagnosis code, service code and service fee. I have included a template in my paperwork packet available on my website.

Out of everything in starting out a private practice, this area tends to be the most difficult for clinicians. I hope that this chapter has helped clear up some of the confusion with how to get paid. Now that you are getting paid, what should you do with all that money? I will give you some suggestions in the next chapter.

Let's Recap:

- If you are on insurance panels, you will need to know how to fill out CSM-1500 forms.
- Make copies of the forms if you are sending them in by mail and save them in your file.
- Many Electronic Health Record platforms can help you submit your claims electronically.
- Don't be afraid to contact the claims department if you have a question about your reimbursement.
- You can file an appeal for denials.
- Out-of-network providers may need to give clients superbills to submit to their insurance company.

Chapter 18:
What to Do With All That Cash

———

Now that you are starting to get some money flowing into your practice, you are going to have to do something with it. If you haven't done so already, make sure you have a separate bank account for your business. Some of the insurance companies will offer you a direct deposit for your reimbursements. If you are interested in this service, you will want to get that set up even before you start applying to insurance panels. If you aren't making direct deposit, the companies will send you paper checks for your reimbursements. I will admit that this was super fun when I first started, but as I got busier, I started misplacing them before I got a chance to get to the bank. I quickly switched to the direct deposit option.

I would also suggest that you consider taking credit cards and debit cards as a form of payment. A lot of people will want to pay for their session with their cards, and you want to be able to accommodate them—especially if you are an out-of-network provider. Check with your bank and see if they have a merchant service option. You will be charged a fee for every transaction, but I believe this small fee, which is usually around 2%, is reasonable for accommodating your clients. You can also look into options such as Square, Paypal and Stripe.

One of the scariest things to think about when you are running your own business is having to deal with your own taxes and insurance. I know a lot of clinicians, including myself, who have at times felt overwhelmed by finances and have decided to address it by sticking our heads in the sand, and just not worry about it until there is an issue. Handling your finances in this way surely means that there will be future issues.

When thinking about your business finances, you want to have a clear understanding of what your overhead is and how much you need to make to survive. Also, start thinking about putting some money away for future taxes, retirement and insurance. You will want to at least put away 30% of what you pay yourself in a separate account so that you will be prepared to pay the IRS and state taxes.

Taxes aren't the only financial concerns you need to think about when working for yourself. You will also need to think about disability insurance, life insurance and planning your future retirement. You may not be able to do this right away when starting your practice, but you will want to keep these items on your radar for the near future when you start bringing in the big money.

You will need to find yourself a good tax person and a financial advisor. After I started bringing in some big revenue, I started attending a financial planning mastermind with Pam Prior. She taught us how to get a grip on our money, how to know what is making the most revenue in the practice and how to grow the business. I highly suggest you check out her mastermind at https://pamprior.com.

Creating and running your own business takes a lot of time and patience. It can be fun, but it can also be a cause for burnout. I want to touch on this topic in the next chapter. Having a thriving practice won't mean anything if you are not living a truly fulfilling life outside of your business.

Let's Recap:
- Don't ignore finances because you don't think you're good at them.
- Save at least 30% of your income for taxes.
- Find yourself a good accountant and financial advisor.

Chapter 19:
Taking Care of Yourself
So You Can Take Care of Business

———

Starting and running your own business is extremely hard. Not everyone wants to or can do it. It takes a special type of person to start their own private practice. You need to take a leap of faith and know that you will do what you need to do in order to make your practice successful.

I have found out through experience that it can be easy to lose yourself while creating your amazing business. At first, it may be not exercising or eating right because you are trying to get as many clients in as possible. You may start to notice that you don't have any hobbies because you feel guilty if you are not working on your business. It's so bad for some people that they even don't have anything to talk about with their loved ones besides the business, because that is all they are consumed with. All these scenarios have happened to me. If you do not build in self-care as a part of your business plan, you will crash and burn very fast. You will start making decisions out of frustration and exhaustion. You will start second-guessing yourself, and you will lose sight of what you started the business for to begin with.

I wrote the conclusion of this book in Las Vegas, Nevada. This trip was a decision I made one day before leaving. I booked myself a first-class ticket to a hotel with a pool. I had hit my breaking point at the practice. I couldn't make sound decisions anymore, and I was constantly feeling overwhelmed. I needed time to reboot on my own. That's what I did.

I have worked very hard at creating a business so that I can take these mental health trips as I need them. I also schedule a weekly head massage with my hair stylist. It helps relieve the tension I keep in my jaw. You will need to find the things that make you the fabulous therapist and the business owner you are. Create a safety plan for yourself for when things get to feel too much. I guarantee that at some point, it will. Who are the people you will be able to go to for support? Where are the safe quiet places you can rest your brain? Write this plan down.

Another phenomenon you may find yourself dealing with while you are building your business is the Imposter Syndrome. At some point that voice in the back of your head will yell out, "Hey! Who do you think you are to be starting your own business?" or "You are not good enough at this, just quit and go back to non-profit." Don't listen to that voice. We all have it. Things will not always turn out the way you plan, but things turn out the way they are supposed to. You will make mistakes and learn from them.

One way that I deal with Imposter Syndrome is to talk to other therapists who are entrepreneurs. This can be in real life or even in Facebook groups. The good thing about our field is that we are a bunch of helpers and always willing to support someone who is down. If you ever feel this way, make sure you join my Facebook group A Private Practice Made Easy. We are always there to support you and answer questions. Getting yourself a therapist can also be helpful: someone to brain dump everything on. Helpers need helpers too.

Some other ways that I have prevented

burnout for so long has been planning trips to business conferences. I have met a lot of great people during these types of events, and these are people who have turned into amazing sources of support in my business and life. We periodically meet throughout the year at different conferences and enjoy each other's company.

I have also gotten into the habit of saying "yes" to invitations that I would typically say "no" to, and vice versa. I need to push myself to get out into the world and be with people who do not have anything to do with work. This can be very uncomfortable for me since, I am an introvert. Talking to people about anything not related to business or therapy makes me feel overwhelmed and wanting to take a nap.

Naps are one of my other super powers. I call myself the professional napper. I could nap just about anywhere at any time. I have learned over the years that naps are a big part of being able to take care of myself. I have a nice couch in my office that I nap on regularly. Sometimes I need this break to reboot and get through the rest of the day.

Exercise has also become an important part of my week. I am at the gym about five days a week at around 5 am. I enjoy listening to my podcasts and getting my heart rate up a bit. I have found that my mood and productivity are off on days that I don't get to the gym. A lot of people are shocked when they hear what time I am up and moving in the morning. Most of the time it's around 4:30. This is just when my body is ready to take on the day. This may also be the reason I need to nap around 1 pm every day.

Likewise, I have a very strict bedtime. I am usually in bed at 9:15pm, no matter what day of the week it is. I get excited to crawl into bed and read a good book for about 45 minutes. If you haven't read the book *Sleep Smarter* by Shawn Stevenson, I highly recommend it. You won't look at sleep the same way. I go above and beyond to make sure that I have the best quality sleep experience every night. I have gone as far as not sleeping with the same blankets as my husband, just to prevent his movements from waking me up. I love my dogs, but they can't sleep on the bed. I am too busy preparing to take on a new day.

Creating and running your own business can

be overwhelming, especially if you haven't had this experience in the past. There are a lot of moving parts to get into place, and by now after reading this book you are probably bursting at the seams with information and wanting to implement it all. You may want to do all of the ideas and suggestions I have given you.

You may even start to experience Shinny Object Syndrome. This is when you are distracted from a current project by another project that you find newer and more appealing. I have to say that social media can be a huge culprit of this. If you follow other therapists, you might end up finding yourself feeling like you aren't doing things as well as the other person, or you should start doing what they are doing because it seems easy and is getting them more business. Don't believe everything you see.

Not having the daily structure of a typical 9-to-5 job is another thing that can be a challenge when running your own business. Before you know it, you are watching Netflix at noon with a bunch of case notes still waiting to be filled out from last week. I have found some tools that have been really helpful in this type of situation:

John Lee Dumas has created two helpful books that I have used in creating a structure to my days and my goals. They are The Freedom Journal and The Mastery Journal. John is a great example of what can be accomplished with structure and goal setting. He created one of the first daily business podcasts. I have learned a lot about running a business from JLD himself and the entrepreneurs he has interviewed on his show. If you want to see the power of great marketing and personal connection, take a look at his site EOFire.com.

Asana.com has been helpful for me in organizing all my tasks, big and little ideas. This is a workflow platform that can be used on your computer and your smartphone. It can help you map out your goals and integrates all your other platforms together, including emails and schedules. You can upload files, pictures and share tasks with your team. Asana is free, but if you would like some additional features, there is a small fee.

These next two items will seem trivial, but I use them on a daily basis: post-it notes and a journal. I am famous for having post-it notes on my wall when I am planning out a marketing strategy and on my computer with daily to-do lists and random thoughts. I have a huge post-it pad hanging in my office for when I need to visually see a plan.

I absolutely love journals. I use them during session to jot down words that will remind me of something I will need to write in my case note later on. I let my client know at the start that this is what I am doing. I know some of us were taught in school not to do this because it puts a barrier between yourself and the client. I show them what I have written and it's typically an illegible word or phrase. I like to think of myself as the Tyler Henry of the therapy world (if you don't know him, look up Hollywood Medium videos). I have even found my favorite type of pen and to date, I have refused to purchase any other for my office.

Amazon Prime has been a huge life saver on several occasions. (Warning, if you are like me, don't Amazon shop after 9pm. You end up with some things you might be able to live without.) The $100 a year fee is worth every penny in free 2-day shipping.

It will save you from wasting a ton of time surfing the internet for what you want to buy and the time it takes to drive to the store. I have found the return process to be really easy when I didn't like what I purchased.

I have also enjoy Audible. For $12 a month you get one credit for a book. I have been able to consume so many more books because I was able to listen to them on my phone. They will even allow you to return the book if you don't like it, no questions asked.

I can't go on enough on how much having a Virtual Assistant helped me grow my business. I currently have an in-person assistant who I call my Lady Sitter. She has been such an integral part of keeping my business growing and organized. She has also been a voice of reason when I want to do things such as hang a yoga swing in the center of my office, or rent more real estate. She and I created the site AssistantToTheTherapist.com so that we can offer assistance to other therapists, to help them stay organized and grow a profitable private practice.

These tools are just some of what I have been

using over the years. I will continue to share other books, tools and helpful platforms on my website MsMelissaDaSilva.com. You can also find additional resources and training on this site. I will keep this updated so you will always be in the know of the newest and best ways to run a successful private practice.

I hope that you have found this book to be helpful because starting and running your own business can be difficult. If it was easy, then everyone would be doing it. If you completed this book and you are feeling inspired and ready to take the leap of faith and start your own business, then you are going to be just fine.

Remember, failure is not an option. Live your life as if you have already achieved your dream of creating a practice that is already making an impact on the world. You will make mistakes no doubt, but you will learn from them, and you don't have to do it alone. You can always find me online at my website MsMelissaDaSilva.com or on my Facebook group A Private Practice Made Easy. Until then, keep being amazing.

References

_____

- Collins English Dictionary (2012). *SEO*. Retrieved from (https://www.dictionary.com/browse/search--engine--optimization?s=t

- Federal Trade Commission. (n.d.). *Guide to Antitrust Laws.* Retrieved from https://www.ftc.gov/tips-advice/competition-guidance/guide-antitrust-laws

- Georgetti, S. (2016, November). *Is Your Business VoIP Phone System HIPAA Compliant?* Retrieved from http://www.voiply.biz/voip/114-is-your-business-voip-phone-system-hipaa-compliant.html

- Lee, J. (2014) *The Right-Brain Business Plan: A Creative, Visual Map for Success.* San Francisco, CA : New World Library

  https://amzn.to/2FaKNdi

- Medical Definition Of HIPAA (n.d.). Retrieved from https://www.medicinenet.com/script/main/art.asp?article key=31785

- Moz.com (n.d.) *What is SEO?* Retrieved from https://moz.com/learn/seo/what-is-seo

- Office of Civil Rights (2015, November). *Guidance Regarding Methods for De-identification of Protected Health Information in Accordance with the Health Insurance Portability and Accountability Act (HIPAA)* Privacy Rule. Retrieved from https://www.hhs.gov/hipaa/for-professionals/privacy/special-topics/de-identification/index.html#protected

About the Author

————

Melissa DaSilva, LICSW, is a therapist, entrepreneur, podcaster, speaker, artistic up-cycler and self-proclaimed karaoke queen. She is the founder of the successful private practice East Coast Mental Wellness, the online Facebook community A Private Practice Made Easy and the resource-filled website AssistantToTheTherapist.com. Melissa enjoys teaching other therapists how to create a practice that gives them the freedom to live the lifestyle they choose. Melissa is a strong advocate for the LGBTQ+ community and sits on the board of Options Magazine. She is currently based in Providence, RI. Visit her at MsMelissaDaSilva.com.

Behavioral Psychology: Understanding Human Behavior

Behavioral Psychology: Understanding Human Behavior

Edited by Tom Eccleston

CLANRYE
INTERNATIONAL
www.clanryeinternational.com

Clanrye International,
750 Third Avenue, 9th Floor,
New York, NY 10017, USA

ISBN: 978-1-63240-721-4

Cataloging-in-Publication Data

Behavioral psychology : understanding human behavior / edited by Tom Eccleston.
    p. cm.
Includes bibliographical references and index.
ISBN 978-1-63240-721-4
1. Human behavior. 2. Behaviorism (Psychology). 3. Psychology. 4. Social psychology.
I . Eccleston, Tom.
BF199 .B44 2018
150.194 3--dc23

For information on all Clanrye International publications
visit our website at www.clanryeinternational.com

Contents

Preface..VII

Chapter 1   **Angry Facial Expressions Bias Gender Categorization in Children and Adults: Behavioral and Computational Evidence**..1
Laurie Bayet, Olivier Pascalis, Paul C. Quinn, Kang Lee, Édouard Gentaz and James W. Tanaka

Chapter 2   **Iconicity in the Lab: A Review of Behavioral, Developmental, and Neuroimaging Research into Sound-Symbolism**..16
Gwilym Lockwood and Mark Dingemanse

Chapter 3   **Drugs as Instruments: Describing and Testing a Behavioral Approach to the Study of Neuroenhancement**..30
Ralf Brand, Wanja Wolff and Matthias Ziegler

Chapter 4   **Introducing a Short Measure of Shared Servant Leadership Impacting Team Performance through Team Behavioral Integration**..41
Milton Sousa and Dirk Van Dierendonck

Chapter 5   **The Item versus the Object in Memory: On the Implausibility of Overwriting as a Mechanism for Forgetting in Short-Term Memory**..53
C. Philip Beaman and Dylan M. Jones

Chapter 6   **The Effect of Altruistic Tendency on Fairness in Third-Party Punishment**..67
Lu Sun, Peishan Tan, You Cheng, Jingwei Chen and Chen Qu

Chapter 7   **The Cognitive-Behavioral System of Leadership: Cognitive Antecedents of Active and Passive Leadership Behaviors**..78
Edina Dóci, Jeroen Stouten and Joeri Hofmans

Chapter 8   **Development of Visual Motion Perception for Prospective Control: Brain and Behavioral Studies in Infants**..93
Seth B. Agyei, F. R. (Ruud) van der Weel and Audrey L. H. van der Meer

Chapter 9   **Measuring Individual Differences in Decision Biases: Methodological Considerations**..107
Balazs Aczel, Bence Bago, Aba Szollosi, Andrei Foldes and Bence Lukacs

Chapter 10   **Cognitive Load does not Affect the Behavioral and Cognitive Foundations of Social Cooperation**..120
Laura Mieth, Raoul Bell and Axel Buchner

Chapter 11   **Assessing Anger Regulation in Middle Childhood: Development and Validation of a Behavioral Observation Measure**..134
Helena L. Rohlf and Barbara Krahé

Chapter 12   **Behavioral and Neurophysiological Signatures of Benzodiazepine-Related Driving Impairments**...**148**
Bradly T. Stone, Kelly A. Correa, Timothy L. Brown, Andrew L. Spurgin,
Maja Stikic, Robin R. Johnson and Chris Berka

Chapter 13   **Angels and Demons: Using Behavioral Types in a Real-Effort Moral Dilemma to Identify Expert Traits**..**162**
Hernán D. Bejarano, Ellen P. Green and Stephen J. Rassenti

Chapter 14   **Reminders of Behavioral Disinhibition Increase Public Conformity in the Asch Paradigm and Behavioral Affiliation with Ingroup Members**...**178**
Kees van den Bos, E. A. Lind, Jeroen Bommelé and Sebastian D. J. Vande Vondele

Chapter 15   **Deployment of Attention on Handshakes**..**193**
Mowei Shen, Jun Yin, Xiaowei Ding, Rende Shui and Jifan Zhou

Chapter 16   **Compulsive Buying Behavior: Clinical Comparison with other Behavioral Addictions**...**205**
Roser Granero, Fernando Fernández-Aranda, Gemma Mestre-Bach, Trevor Steward,
Marta Baño, Amparo del Pino-Gutiérrez, Laura Moragas, Núria Mallorquí-Bagué,
Neus Aymamí, Mónica Gómez-Peña, Salomé Tárrega, José M. Menchón and
Susana Jiménez-Murcia

Chapter 17   **Personalized Behavioral Feedback for Online Gamblers: A Real World Empirical Study**...**217**
Michael M. Auer and Mark D. Griffiths

              Permissions

              List of Contributors

              Index

Preface

This book aims to highlight the current researches and provides a platform to further the scope of innovations in this area. This book is a product of the combined efforts of many researchers and scientists, after going through thorough studies and analysis from different parts of the world. The objective of this book is to provide the readers with the latest information of the field.

Behavioral psychology is the scientific study of the behavior exhibited by humans. The behavior is mostly observed in reaction to specific situations. Behavioral psychology integrates principles of philosophy and psychology. This book presents the complex subject of behavioral psychology in the most comprehensible and easy to understand language. From theories to research to practical applications, case studies related to all contemporary topics of relevance to this field have been included herein. It will help the readers in keeping pace with the rapid changes in this field.

I would like to express my sincere thanks to the authors for their dedicated efforts in the completion of this book. I acknowledge the efforts of the publisher for providing constant support. Lastly, I would like to thank my family for their support in all academic endeavors.

Editor

1

Angry facial expressions bias gender categorization in children and adults: behavioral and computational evidence

Laurie Bayet[1,2]*, Olivier Pascalis[1,2], Paul C. Quinn[3], Kang Lee[4], Édouard Gentaz[1,2,5] and James W. Tanaka[6]

[1] Laboratoire de Psychologie et Neurocognition, University of Grenoble-Alps, Grenoble, France, [2] Laboratoire de Psychologie et Neurocognition, Centre National de la Recherche Scientifique, Grenoble, France, [3] Department of Psychological and Brain Sciences, University of Delaware, Newark, DE, USA, [4] Dr. Eric Jackman Institute of Child Study, University of Toronto, Toronto, ON, Canada, [5] Faculty of Psychology and Educational Sciences, University of Geneva, Geneva, Switzerland, [6] Department of Psychology, University of Victoria, Victoria, BC, Canada

Edited by:
Bozana Meinhardt-Injac,
Johannes Gutenberg University
Mainz, Germany

Reviewed by:
Irene Leo,
Università degli Studi di Padova, Italy
Elisabeth M. Whyte,
Pennsylvania State University, USA

*Correspondence:
Laurie Bayet,
Laboratoire de Psychologie et
Neurocognition, Centre National de la
Recherche Scientifique, UMR 5105,
Université Grenoble-Alpes, Bâtiment
Sciences de l'Homme et
Mathématiques, BP47, Grenoble
38040, France
laurie.bayet@upmf-grenoble.fr

Specialty section:
This article was submitted to
Perception Science, a section of the
journal Frontiers in Psychology

Angry faces are perceived as more masculine by adults. However, the developmental course and underlying mechanism (bottom-up stimulus driven or top-down belief driven) associated with the angry-male bias remain unclear. Here we report that anger biases face gender categorization toward "male" responding in children as young as 5–6 years. The bias is observed for both own- and other-race faces, and is remarkably unchanged across development (into adulthood) as revealed by signal detection analyses (Experiments 1–2). The developmental course of the angry-male bias, along with its extension to other-race faces, combine to suggest that it is not rooted in extensive experience, e.g., observing males engaging in aggressive acts during the school years. Based on several computational simulations of gender categorization (Experiment 3), we further conclude that (1) the angry-male bias results, at least partially, from a strategy of attending to facial features or their second-order relations when categorizing face gender, and (2) any single choice of computational representation (e.g., Principal Component Analysis) is insufficient to assess resemblances between face categories, as different representations of the very same faces suggest different bases for the angry-male bias. Our findings are thus consistent with stimulus-and stereotyped-belief driven accounts of the angry-male bias. Taken together, the evidence suggests considerable stability in the interaction between some facial dimensions in social categorization that is present prior to the onset of formal schooling.

Keywords: face, emotion, gender, children, representation, stereotype

Introduction

Models of face perception hypothesize an early separation of variant (gaze, expression, speech) and invariant (identity, gender, and race) dimensions of faces in a stage called structural encoding (Bruce and Young, 1986; Haxby et al., 2000). Structural encoding consists of the abstraction of an expression-independent representation of faces from pictorial encodings or "snapshots." This results in the extraction of variant and invariant dimensions that are then processed in a hierarchical arrangement where invariant dimensions are of a higher order than the variant ones (Bruce and Young, 1986).

Facial dimensions, however, interact during social perception. Such interactions may have multiple origins, with some but not all requiring a certain amount of experience to develop. First, they may be entirely stimulus-driven or based on the coding of conjunctions of dimensions at the level of single neurons (Morin et al., 2014). Second, the narrowing of one dimension (Kelly et al., 2007) may affect the processing of another. For example, O'Toole et al. (1996) found that Asian and Caucasian observers made more mistakes when categorizing the gender of other-race vs. own-race faces, indicating that experience affects not only the individual recognition of faces (as in the canonical other-race effect, Malpass and Kravitz, 1969), but a larger spectrum of face processing abilities. Third, perceptual inferences based on experience may cause one dimension to cue for another as smiling does for familiarity (Baudouin et al., 2000). Finally, it has been suggested that dimensions interact based on beliefs reflecting stereotypes, i.e., beliefs about the characteristics of other social groups. For example, Caucasian participants stereotypically associate anger with African ethnicity (Hehman et al., 2014). This latter, semantic kind of interaction was predicted by Bruce and Young (1986) who postulated that (1) semantic processes feedback to all stages of face perception, and (2) all invariant dimensions (such as race, gender) are extracted, i.e., "visually-derived," at this semantic level. More generally, prejudice and stereotyping may profoundly influence even basic social perception (Johnson et al., 2012; Amodio, 2014) and form deep roots in social cognition (Contreras et al., 2012). Data on the development of these processes have reported an onset of some stereotypical beliefs during toddlerhood (Dunham et al., 2013; Cogsdill et al., 2014) and an early onset of the other-race effect in the first year of life (Kelly et al., 2007, 2009).

One observation that has been interpreted as a top-down effect of stereotyping is the perception of angry faces as more masculine (Hess et al., 2004, 2005, 2009; Becker et al., 2007), possibly reflecting gender biases that associate affiliation with femininity and dominance with masculinity (Hess et al., 2007). Alternatively, cues for angry expressions and masculine gender may objectively overlap, biasing human perception at a bottom-up level. Using a forced-choice gender categorization task with signal detection analyses and emotional faces in adults (Experiment 1) and children (Experiment 2), and several computational models of gender categorization (Experiment 3), we aimed to (1) replicate the effect of anger on gender categorization in adults, (2) investigate its development in children, and (3) probe possible bases for the effect by comparing human performance with that of computational models. If the bias is purely driven by top-down beliefs, then computational models would not be sensitive to it. However, if the bias is driven by bottom-up stimulus-based cues, then we expect computational models to be sensitive to such objective cues. To investigate the impact of different facial dimensions on gender-categorization, both own-race and other-race faces were included as stimuli - the latter corresponding to a more difficult task condition (O'Toole et al., 1996).

Experiment 1: Gender Categorization by Adults

To assess whether emotional facial expressions bias gender categorization, adults categorized the gender of 120 faces depicting unique identities that varied in race (Caucasian, Chinese), gender (male, female), and facial expression (angry, smiling, neutral). We hypothesized that the angry expression would bias gender categorization toward "male," and that this effect might be different in other-race (i.e., Chinese in the present study) faces that are more difficult to categorize by gender (O'Toole et al., 1996).

Materials and Methods
Participants and Data Preprocessing
Twenty four adult participants (mean age: 20.27 years, range: 17–24 years, 4 men) from a predominantly Caucasian environment participated in the study. All gave informed consent and had normal or corrected-to-normal vision. The experiment was approved by the local ethics committee ("Comité d'éthique des center d'investigation clinique de l'inter-région Rhône-Alpes-Auvergne," Institutional Review Board). Two participants were excluded due to extremely long reaction times (mean reaction time further than 2 standard deviations from the group mean). Trials with a reaction time below 200 ms or above 2 standard deviations from each participant's mean were excluded, resulting in the exclusion of 4.70% of the data points.

Stimuli
One hundred twenty face stimuli depicting unique identities were selected from the Karolinska Directed Emotional Face database (Lundqvist et al., 1998; Calvo and Lundqvist, 2008), the Nim-Stim database (Tottenham et al., 2002, 2009), and the Chinese Affective Picture System (Lu et al., 2005) database in their frontal view versions. Faces were of different races (Caucasian, Chinese), genders (female, male), and expressions (angry, neutral, smiling). Faces were gray scaled and placed against a white background; external features were cropped using GIMP. Luminance, contrast, and placement of the eyes were matched using SHINE (Willenbockel et al., 2010) and the Psychomorph software (Tiddeman, 2005, 2011). Emotion intensity and recognition accuracy were matched across races and genders and are summarized in Supplementary Table 1. See **Figure 1A** for examples of the stimuli used. Selecting 120 emotional faces depicting unique identities for the high validity of their emotional expressions might lead to a potential selection bias, e.g., the female faces that would display anger most reliably might also be the most masculine female faces. To resolve this issue, a control study (Supplementary Material) was conducted in which gender typicality ratings were obtained for the neutral poses of the same 120 faces. See **Figure 1B** for examples of the stimuli used in the control study.

Procedure
Participants were seated 70 cm from the screen. Stimuli were presented using E-Prime 2.0 (Schneider et al., 2002).

A trial began with a 1000–1500 ms fixation cross, followed by a central face subtending a visual angle of about 7 by 7°. Participants completed a forced-choice gender-categorization task.

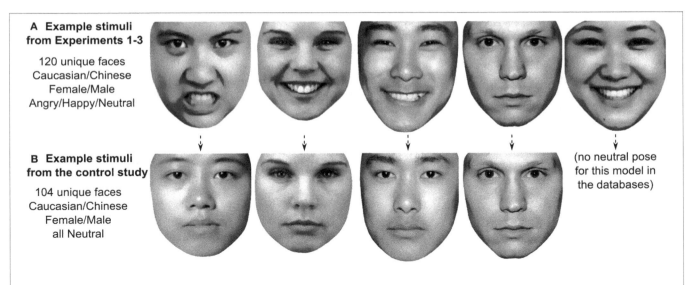

A Example stimuli from Experiments 1-3

120 unique faces
Caucasian/Chinese
Female/Male
Angry/Happy/Neutral

B Example stimuli from the control study

104 unique faces
Caucasian/Chinese
Female/Male
all Neutral

(no neutral pose for this model in the databases)

FIGURE 1 | Example stimuli used in Experiments 1–3 (A) and in the control study (B). The identity of the faces used in Experiments 1–3 and in the control study were identical, but in the control study all faces were in neutral expression while faces in Experiments 1–3 had either angry, smiling or neutral expressions. Sixteen of the 120 faces from Experiments 1–3 had no neutral pose in the database.

They categorized each face as either male or female using different keys, and which key was associated with which gender response was counterbalanced across participants. The face remained on the screen until the participant responded. Participant response time and accuracy were recorded for each trial.

Each session began with 16 training trials with 8 female and 8 male faces randomly selected from a different set of 26 neutral frontal view faces from the Karolinska Directed Emotional Face database (Lundqvist et al., 1998; Calvo and Lundqvist, 2008). Each training trial concluded with feedback on the participant's accuracy. Participants then performed 6 blocks of 20 experimental trials, identical to training trials without feedback. Half of the blocks included Caucasian faces and half included Chinese faces. Chinese and Caucasian faces were randomly ordered across those blocks. The blocks alternated (either as Caucasian-Chinese-Caucasian… or as Chinese-Caucasian-Chinese…, counterbalanced across participants), with 5 s mandatory rest periods between blocks.

Data Analysis

Analyses were conducted in Matlab 7.9.0529 and R 2.15.2. Accuracy was analyzed using a binomial Generalized Linear Mixed Model (GLMM) approach (Snijders and Bosker, 1999) provided by R packages lme4 1.0.4 (Bates et al., 2013) and afex 0.7.90 (Singmann, 2013). This approach is robust to missing (excluded) data points and is more suited to binomial data than the Analysis of Variance which assumes normality and homogeneity of the residuals. Accuracy results are presented in the Supplementary Material (Supplementary Figure 1, Supplementary Tables 2, 3). Inverted reaction times from correct trials were analyzed using a Linear Mixed Model (LMM) approach (Laird and Ware, 1982) with the R package nlme 3.1.105 (Pinheiro et al., 2012). Inversion

was chosen over logarithm as variance-stabilizing transformation because it led to better homogeneity of the residuals. Mean gender typicality ratings obtained in a control study (Supplementary Material) were included as a covariate in the analysis of both accuracy and reaction times. Finally, signal detection theory parameters (d', c-bias) were derived from the accuracies of each participant for each condition using the female faces as "signal" (Stanislaw and Todorov, 1999), and then analyzed using repeated measures ANOVAs. Because female faces were used as the "signal" category in the derivation, the conservative bias (c-bias) is equivalent to a male bias. Data and code are available online at http://dx.doi.org/10.6084/m9.figshare.1320891.

Results

Reaction Times

A Race-by-Gender-by-Emotion three-way interaction was significant in the best LMM of adult inverse reaction times (**Table 1**). It stemmed from (1) a significant Race-by-Emotion effect on male [$\chi^2_{(2)} = 6.48$, $p = 0.039$] but not female faces [$\chi^2_{(2)} = 4.20$, $p = 0.123$], due to an effect of Emotion on Chinese male faces [$\chi^2_{(2)} = 8.87$, $p = 0.012$] but not Caucasian male faces [$\chi^2_{(2)} = 2.49$, $p = 0.288$]; and (2) a significant Race-by-Gender effect on neutral [$\chi^2_{(1)} = 4.24$, $p = 0.039$] but not smiling [$\chi^2_{(1)} = 3.31$, $p = 0.069$] or angry [$\chi^2_{(1)} = 0.14$, $p = 0.706$] faces. The former Race-by-Emotion effect on male faces was expected and corresponds to a ceiling effect on the reaction times to Caucasian male faces. The latter Race-by-Gender effect on neutral faces was unexpected and stemmed from an effect of Race in female [$\chi^2_{(1)} = 7.91$, $p = 0.005$] but not male neutral faces [$\chi^2_{(1)} = 0.28$, $p = 0.600$] along with the converse effect of Gender on Chinese [$\chi^2_{(1)} = 5.16$, $p = 0.023$] but not Caucasian neutral faces [$\chi^2_{(1)} = 0.03$, $p = 0.872$]. Indeed, reaction time for neutral female

Chinese faces was relatively long, akin to that for angry female Chinese faces (**Figure 2B**) and unlike that for neutral female Caucasian faces (**Figure 2A**). Since there was no hypothesis regarding this effect, it will not be discussed further.

Importantly, the interaction of Gender and Emotion in reaction time was significant for both Caucasian [$\chi^2_{(2)} = 18.59$, $p < 0.001$] and Chinese [$\chi^2_{(2)} = 19.58$, $p < 0.001$] faces. However, further decomposition revealed that it had different roots in Caucasian and Chinese faces. In Caucasian faces, the interaction stemmed from an effect of Emotion on female [$\chi^2_{(2)} = 14.14$, $p = 0.001$] but not male faces [$\chi^2_{(2)} = 2.49$, $p = 0.288$]; in Chinese faces, the opposite was true [female faces: $\chi^2_{(2)} = 2.58$,

$p = 0.276$; male faces: $\chi^2_{(2)} = 8.87$, $p = 0.012$]. Moreover, in Caucasian faces, Gender only affected reaction time to angry faces [angry: $\chi^2_{(1)} = 11.44$, $p = 0.001$; smiling: $\chi^2_{(1)} = 0.59$, $p = 0.442$; neutral: $\chi^2_{(1)} = 0.03$, $p = 0.872$], whereas in Chinese faces, Gender affected reaction time regardless of Emotion [angry: $\chi^2_{(1)} = 25.90$, $p < 0.001$; smiling: $\chi^2_{(1)} = 7.46$, $p = 0.029$; neutral: $\chi^2_{(1)} = 5.16$, $p = 0.023$].

The impairing effect of an angry expression on female face categorization was clearest on the relatively easy Caucasian faces, while a converse facilitating effect on male face categorization was most evident for the relatively difficult Chinese faces. The effect of Gender was largest for the difficult Chinese faces. The angry expression increased reaction times for Caucasian female faces (**Figure 2A**) and conversely reduced them for Chinese male faces (**Figure 2D**).

Sensitivity and Male Bias

A repeated measures ANOVA showed a significant Race-by-Emotion effect on both d′ (**Table 2**) and male-bias (**Table 3**).

Sensitivity was greatly reduced in Chinese faces ($\eta^2 = 0.38$, i.e., a large effect), replicating the other-race effect for gender categorization (O'Toole et al., 1996). Angry expressions reduced sensitivity in Caucasian but not Chinese faces (**Figures 3A,B**). Male bias was high overall, also replicating the finding by O'Toole et al. (1996). Here, in addition, we found that (1) the male bias was significantly enhanced for Chinese faces ($\eta^2 = 0.35$, another large effect), and (2) angry expressions also enhanced the male bias, as predicted, in Caucasian and Chinese faces ($\eta^2 = 0.17$, a moderate effect)—although to a lesser extent in the

TABLE 1 | Best LMM of adult inverse reaction time from correct trials.

Effect	d.f.	χ^2	p
(Intercept)	1	334.15	<0.001
Race	1	2.95	0.086
Gender*	1	6.17	0.013
Emotion	2	0.07	0.967
Mean gender typicality rating*	1	25.97	<0.001
Gender-by-emotion*	2	32.13	<0.001
Race-by-emotion*	2	6.45	0.040
Race-by-gender	1	0.09	0.761
Race-by-gender-by-emotion*	2	7.56	0.023

The model also included a random intercept and slope for participants. Significant effects are marked by an asterisk.

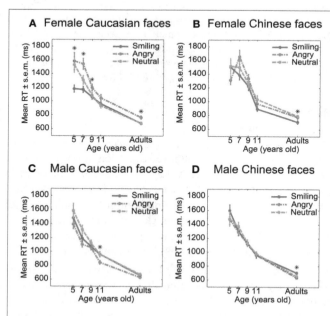

FIGURE 2 | Reaction times for gender categorization in Experiments 1 (adults) and 2 (children). Only reaction times from correct trials are included. Each star represents a significant difference between angry and smiling faces (paired Student t-tests, $p < 0.05$, uncorrected). **Top:** Caucasian **(A)** and Chinese **(B)** female faces. **Bottom:** Caucasian **(C)** and Chinese **(D)** male faces.

TABLE 2 | ANOVA of d-prime for adult gender categorization.

Fixed effects	SS	d.f.	MS	F	p	η^2
Race*	17.77	1	17.77	106.38	<0.001	0.38
Emotion*	5.91	2	2.96	22.24	<0.001	0.13
Race-by-emotion*	3.56	2	1.78	13.84	<0.001	0.08
Error	5.40	42				
Total	47.30	131				

The ANOVA also included a random factor for the participants, along with its interactions with both Race and Emotion. Significant effects are marked by an asterisk.

TABLE 3 | ANOVA of male-bias for adult gender categorization.

Fixed effects	SS	d.f.	MS	F	p	η^2
Race*	17.16	1	17.16	93.03	<0.001	0.35
Emotion*	8.24	2	4.12	40.57	<0.001	0.17
Race-by-emotion*	3.18	2	1.59	12.71	<0.001	0.06
Error	5.26	42	0.13			
Total	49.55	131				

The ANOVA also included a random factor for the participants, along with its interactions with both Race and Emotion. Significant effects are marked by an asterisk.

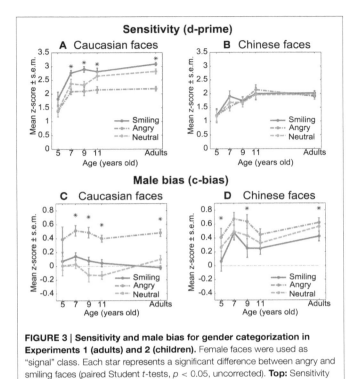

FIGURE 3 | Sensitivity and male bias for gender categorization in Experiments 1 (adults) and 2 (children). Female faces were used as "signal" class. Each star represents a significant difference between angry and smiling faces (paired Student t-tests, $p < 0.05$, uncorrected). **Top:** Sensitivity for Caucasian **(A)** and Chinese **(B)** faces. **Bottom:** Male bias for Caucasian **(C)** and Chinese **(D)** faces.

latter (**Figures 3C,D**). Since Emotion affects the male bias but not sensitivity in Chinese faces, it follows that the effect of Emotion on the male bias is not solely mediated by its effect on sensitivity.

Further inspection of the experimental effect on the hit rate (female trials) and false alarm rate (male trials) confirmed, however, that the overall performance was at ceiling on male faces, as repeated measures ANOVAs revealed a significant interactive effect of Race and Emotion on the hit rate [$F_{(2, 42)} = 12.71$, $p < 0.001$, $\eta^2 = 0.07$] but no significant effect of Race, Emotion, or their interaction on the false alarm rate (all $ps > 0.05$). In other words, the effects of Race and Emotion on d' and male bias were solely driven by performance on female faces. Accuracy results are presented in the Supplementary Material (Supplementary Figure 1, Supplementary Table 2).

Discussion

The effect of anger on gender categorization was evident on reaction time, as participants were (1) slower when categorizing the gender of angry Caucasian female faces, (2) slower with angry Chinese female faces, and (3) quicker with angry Chinese male faces. Interestingly, the angry expression reduced sensitivity (d') of gender categorization in own-race (Caucasian), but not in other-race (Chinese) faces. In other words, angry expressions had two dissociable effects on gender categorization: (1) they increased difficulty when categorizing own-race faces, and (2) they increased the overall bias to respond "male."

The results are consistent with the hypothesis of a biasing effect of anger that increases the tendency to categorize faces

as male. However, a ceiling effect on accuracy for male faces made it impossible to definitively support this idea. To firmly conclude in favor of a true bias, it should be observed that angry expressions both hinder female face categorization (as was observed) and enhance male face categorization (which was not observed). While a small but significant increase in accuracy for angry vs. happy Chinese male faces was observed (Supplementary Figure 1D), there was no significant effect on the false alarm rate (i.e., accuracy on male trials).

Different from the present results, O'Toole et al. (1996) did not report an enhanced male bias for other-race faces (Japanese or Caucasian) faces, although they did find an effect on d' that was replicated here, along with an overall male bias. The source of the difference is uncertain, one possibility being that the greater difficulty of the task used in O'Toole et al. (a 75 ms presentation of each face followed by a mask) caused a male bias for own-race faces, or that the enhanced male bias to other-race faces found in the present study does not generalize to all types of other-race faces. Finally, O'Toole et al. (1996) found that female participants had displayed higher accuracy on a gender categorization task than male participants. However, the sample for the current study did not include enough male participants to allow us to analyze this possible effect.

Experiment 2: Gender Categorization in Children

One way to understand the male bias is to investigate its development. There is a general consensus that during development we are "becoming face experts" (Carey, 1992) and the immature face processing system that is present at birth will develop with experience until early adolescence (Lee et al., 2013). If the angry male bias develops through extensive experience with peers observing male aggression during the school years, it follows that the angry male bias should be smaller in children than in adults and that the bias would increase during the school years, a time period when children observe classmates (mostly males) engaging in aggressive acts inclusive of fighting and bullying.

In Experiment 2, we conducted the same gender categorization task as in Experiment 1 with 64 children aged from 5 to 12. The inclusion of children in the age range from 5 to 6, as well the testing of 7–8, 9–10, and 11–12 year-olds, is important from a developmental perspective. Experiment 2 should additionally allow us to (1) overcome the ceiling effect on gender categorization for male faces that was observed in Experiment 1 (as children typically perform worse than adults in gender categorization tasks, e.g., Wild et al., 2000), and (2) determine the developmental trajectory of the biasing effect of anger in relation to increased experience with processing own-race (Caucasian) but not other-race (Chinese) faces. While facial expression perception also develops over childhood and even adolescence (Herba and Phillips, 2004), recognition performance for own-race expressions of happiness and anger have been reported to be at ceiling from 5 years of age (Gao and Maurer, 2010; Rodger et al., 2015).

Methods

Participants and Preprocessing

Thirteen 5–6 year-olds (9 boys), 16 7–8 year-olds (3 boys), 15 9–10 year-olds (9 boys), and 14 11–12 year-olds (3 boys) from a predominantly Caucasian environment were included in the final sample. These age groups were chosen a priori due to the minimal need to re-design the experiment: children from 5 to 6 years of age may complete computer tasks and follow directions. A range of age groups was then selected from 5 to 6 years old onwards, covering the developmental period from middle to late childhood, and the time when children begin formal schooling. The experiment was approved by the University of Victoria Human Research Ethics Board and informed parental consent was obtained. Six additional participants were excluded due to non-compliance ($n = 1$) or very slow reaction times for their age ($n = 5$). Additionally, trials from participants were excluded if their reaction times were extremely short (less than 600, 500, 400, or 300 ms for 5–6 year olds, 7–8 year olds, 9–10 year olds, or 11–12 year olds, respectively) or further than 2 standard deviations away from the participant's own distribution. Such invalid trials were handled as missing values, leading to the exclusion of 11.35% data points in the 5–6 years olds, 5.57% in the 7–8 year olds, 5.28% in the 9–10 year olds, and 4.88% in the 11–12 year olds. The cut-offs used to exclude trials with very short reaction times were selected graphically based on the distribution of reaction times within each age group.

Stimuli, Procedure, and Data Analysis

Stimuli, task, procedure, and data analysis methods were identical to that of Experiment 1 except for the following: Participants were seated 50 cm from the screen so that the faces subtended a visual angle of approximately 11 by 11°. Due to an imbalance in the gender ratio across age groups, the participant's gender was included as a between-subject factor in the analyses. Data and code are available online at http://dx.doi.org/10.6084/m9.figshare.1320891.

Results

Reaction Times

There was a significant Race-by-Gender-by-Emotion interaction in the best linear mixed model (LMM) of children's inverse reaction times from correct trials (**Table 4**), along with a three-way Age-by-Gender-by-Participant gender interaction, an Age-by-Race-by-Emotion interaction, and a Participant gender-by-Gender-by-Emotion interaction.

The interaction of Age, Gender, and Participant gender was due to a significant Gender-by-Participant gender interaction in the 11–12 year olds [$\chi^2_{(1)} = 6.19, p = 0.013$], with no significant sub-effects ($ps > 0.05$). The interaction of Gender, Emotion, and Participant gender was due to the effect of Gender on angry faces reaching significance in female (female faces, inverted RT: $9.35 \pm 3.67.10^{-4}\,\mathrm{ms}^{-1}$; male faces: $10.67 \pm 3.51.10^{-4}\,\mathrm{ms}^{-1}$) but not male participants (female faces, inverted RT: $8.88 \pm 3.24.10^{-4}\,\mathrm{ms}^{-1}$; male faces: $9.72 \pm 3.26.10^{-4}\,\mathrm{ms}^{-1}$), although the effect had the same direction in both populations. Importantly, however, the overall Gender-by-Emotion interaction was

TABLE 4 | Best LMM of children's inverted reaction times from correct trials.

Fixed effects	d.f.	χ^2	p
(Intercept)	1	113.97	<0.001
Race*	1	14.07	<0.001
Gender*	1	4.00	0.046
Emotion*	2	7.27	0.026
Age*	3	11.18	0.011
Participant gender	1	0.16	0.687
Mean gender typicality rating*	1	75.34	<0.001
Race-by-gender	1	0.38	0.539
Gender-by-emotion*	2	13.32	0.001
Race-by-emotion*	2	12.97	0.002
Age-by-race*	3	12.17	0.007
Age-by-gender*	3	8.80	0.032
Age-by-emotion	6	8.58	0.198
Participant gender-by-gender	1	0.50	0.480
Participant gender-by-emotion	2	3.45	0.179
Participant gender-by-age	3	3.21	0.360
Race-by-gender-by-emotion*	2	9.89	0.007
Age-by-race-by-emotion*	6	18.66	0.005
Age-by-gender-by-participant gender*	3	9.35	0.025
Participant gender-by-gender-by-emotion*	2	8.16	0.017

The model also included a random intercept and slope for the participants. Significant effects are marked by an asterisk.

significant in both male [$\chi^2_{(2)} = 7.44, p = 0.024$] and female participants [$\chi^2_{(2)} = 52.41, p < 0.001$]. The interaction of Race and Emotion with Age reflected the shorter reaction times of 5–6 year olds when categorizing the gender of Caucasian vs. Chinese smiling faces [$\chi^2_{(2)} = 7.40, p = 0.007$], also evidenced by a significant Race-by-Age interaction for smiling faces only [$\chi^2_{(3)} = 10.11, p = 0.018$]. Faster responses to smiling Caucasian faces by the youngest participants probably reflect the familiarity, or perception of familiarity in these stimuli.

Finally, the interactive effect of Gender and Emotion on reaction times was significant in Caucasian [$\chi^2_{(2)} = 49.81, p < 0.001$] but not Chinese faces [$\chi^2_{(2)} = 2.25, p = 0.325$] leading to a Race-by-Gender-by-Emotion interaction. Further decomposition confirmed this finding: Race significantly affected reaction times for male [$\chi^2_{(1)} = 19.52, p < 0.001$] but not female angry faces [$\chi^2_{(1)} = 1.86, p = 0.173$], Gender affected reaction times for Caucasian [$\chi^2_{(1)} = 17.01, p < 0.001$] but not Chinese angry faces [$\chi^2_{(1)} = 0.48, p = 0.489$], and Emotion significantly affected the reaction times for Caucasian female [$\chi^2_{(2)} = 29.88, p < 0.001$] but not Chinese female [$\chi^2_{(2)} = 3.82, p = 0.148$] or male faces [$\chi^2_{(2)} = 5.13, p = 0.077$].

Children were slower when categorizing the gender of angry vs. happy Caucasian female faces (**Figure 2A**), and slightly faster when categorizing the gender of angry vs. happy Caucasian male faces (**Figure 2C**). The interaction of Gender and Emotion was present in all participants but most evident in female participants. It was absent in Chinese faces. In other words, an angry expression slows gender categorization in own-race (Caucasian) but not in other-race (Chinese) faces.

Sensitivity and Male Bias

ANOVAs with participant as a random factor showed a small, but significant Race-by-Emotion interaction on sensitivity (d', **Table 5**, $\eta^2 = 0.02$) and male-bias (c-bias, **Table 6**, $\eta^2 = 0.03$). Neither for sensitivity nor for male-bias did the Race-by-Emotion interaction or its subcomponents interact with Age.

Two additional effects on sensitivity (d') can be noted (**Table 5**). First, there was a significant effect of Age as sensitivity increased with age ($\eta^2 = 0.09$). Second, there was an interactive effect of Emotion and Participant gender that stemmed from female participants having higher sensitivity than male participants on happy [$F_{(1, 114)} = 9.14, p = 0.003$] and neutral [$F_{(1, 114)} = 18.39, p < 0.001$] but not angry faces [$F_{(1, 114)} = 0.39, p = 0.533$]. Emotion affected the overall sensitivity of both female [$F_{(1, 102)} = 21.07, p < 0.001$] and male participants [$F_{(1, 72)} = 4.69, p = 0.014$].

The pattern of the interactive effect for Race and Emotion was identical to that found in adults: anger reduced children's sensitivity (d') to gender in Caucasian faces (**Figure 3A**), but not in the already difficult Chinese faces (**Figure 3B**). This pattern is remarkably similar to that found in reaction times. In contrast, anger increased the male-bias in Caucasian (**Figure 3C**) as well as Chinese faces (**Figure 3D**), although to a lesser extent in

TABLE 5 | ANOVA of d' for children's gender categorization.

Fixed effects	SS	d.f.	MS	F	p	η^2
Race*	28.32	1	28.32	80.59	<0.001	0.13
Emotion*	6.14	2	3.07	12.65	<0.001	0.03
Age*	21.04	3	7.01	6.40	0.001	0.09
Participant gender	4.15	1	4.15	3.79	0.057	0.02
Race-by-emotion*	4.55	2	2.27	8.58	<0.001	0.02
Age-by-race	2.56	3	0.85	2.42	0.076	0.01
Age-by-emotion	0.89	6	0.15	0.61	0.719	<0.01
Age-by-gender-by-emotion	1.12	6	0.19	0.71	0.644	0.01
Participant gender-by-race	0.83	1	0.83	2.35	0.131	<0.01
Participant gender-by-emotion*	3.99	2	1.99	8.21	0.001	0.02
Participant gender-by-gender-by-emotion	0.36	2	0.18	0.68	0.511	<0.01
Age-by-participant gender	3.63	3	1.21	1.10	0.356	0.02
Error	28.07	106	0.27			
Total	223.56	347				

The ANOVA also included a random factor for the participants along with its interactions with both Race and Emotion. Significant effects are marked by an asterisk.

TABLE 6 | ANOVA of male-bias for children's gender categorization.

Fixed effects	SS	d.f.	MS	F	p	η^2
Race*	4.88	1	4.88	53.50	<0.001	0.07
Emotion*	7.65	2	3.83	36.49	<0.001	0.12
Age	0.50	3	0.17	0.34	0.797	0.01
Participant gender	0.49	1	0.49	0.99	0.324	0.01
Race-by-emotion*	1.88	2	0.94	17.08	<0.001	0.03
Age-by-race	0.68	3	0.23	2.5	0.070	0.01
Age-by-emotion	0.44	6	0.07	0.7	0.654	0.01
Age-by-gender-by-emotion	0.12	6	0.02	0.35	0.909	<0.01
Participant gender-by-race	0.03	1	0.03	0.31	0.578	<0.01
Participant gender-by-emotion	0.26	2	0.13	1.25	0.290	<0.01
Participant gender-by-gender-by-emotion	0.27	2	0.13	2.42	0.093	<0.01
Age-by-participant gender	0.63	3	0.21	0.43	0.734	0.01
Error	5.80	106	0.06			
Total	66.35	347				

The ANOVA also included a random factor for participant, along with its interactions with both Race and Emotion. Significant effects are marked by an asterisk.

the latter category. In other words, the biasing effect of anger cannot be reduced to an effect of perceptual difficulty. Further analyses revealed that Race and Emotion affected the hit (female trials) and false alarm (male trials) rates equally, both as main and interactive effects [Race-by-Emotion effect on hit rate: $F_{(2, 106)} = 10.70, p < 0.001, \eta^2 = 0.02$; on false alarm rate: $F_{(2, 114)} = 13.48$, $p < 0.001, \eta^2 = 0.03$]. That is, the male-biasing effect of anger is evident by its interfering effect during female trials as well as by its converse facilitating effect during male trials. Accuracy results are presented in the Supplementary Material (Supplementary Figure 1, Supplementary Table 3).

These last observations are compatible with the idea that angry expressions bias gender categorization. The effect can be observed across all ages and even with unfamiliar Chinese faces, although in a diminished form. The biasing effect of anger toward "male" does not seem to depend solely on experience with a particular type of face and is already present at 5–6 years of age.

Discussion

The results are consistent with a male-biasing effect of anger that is in evidence as early as 5–6 years of age and that is present, but less pronounced in other-race (Chinese) than in own-race (Caucasian) faces. The ceiling effect observed in Experiment 1 on the gender categorization of male faces (i.e., the false alarm rate) was sufficiently overcome so that the male-biasing effect of anger could be observed in male as well as female trials.

Participant gender interacted with Emotion on sensitivity and with Emotion and Gender on the reaction times of children. This finding partly replicates the finding by O'Toole et al. (1996) that female participants present higher face gender categorization sensitivity (d') than male participants, particularly with female faces. Here, we further showed that in children, this effect is limited to neutral and happy faces, and does not generalize to angry faces.

It is perhaps surprising that anger was found to affect the male-bias on Chinese as well as Caucasian faces, but only affected sensitivity (d') and reaction times on Caucasian faces. Two dissociable and non-exclusive effects of angry expressions may explain this result. First, angry expressions may be less frequent (e.g., Malatesta and Haviland, 1982), which would generally slow down and complicate gender categorization decisions for familiar (Caucasian) but not for the already unfamiliar (Chinese) faces. This effect is not a bias and should only affect sensitivity and reaction time. Second, angry expressions may bias gender categorization toward the male response by either lowering the decision criterion for this response (e.g., as proposed by Miller et al., 2010) or adding evidence for it. It naturally follows that such an effect should be evident on the male-bias (c-bias), but not on sensitivity. Should it be evident in reaction time, as we initially predicted? Even if a bias does not affect the overall rate of evidence accumulation, it should provide a small advantage on reaction time for "male" decisions, and conversely result in a small delay on reaction time for "female" decisions. While this effect would theoretically not depend on whether the face is relatively easy (own-race) or difficult (other-race) to categorize, it is possible that it would be smaller in other-race faces for two reasons: (1) the extraction of the angry expression itself might be less efficient in other-race faces, leading to a smaller male-bias; and (2) the

small delaying or quickening effect of anger could be masked in the noisy and sluggish process of evidence accumulation for other-race faces.

Three possible mechanisms could explain the male-biasing effect of angry expressions: Angry faces could be categorized as "male" from the resemblance of cues for angry expressions and masculine gender, from experience-based (Bayesian-like) perceptual inferences, or from belief-based inferences (i.e., stereotype). Of interest is that the male-biasing effect of anger was fairly constant from 5 to 12 years of age. There are at least two reasons why the male-biasing effect of anger would already be present in adult form in 5–6 years olds: (1) the effect could develop even earlier than 5–6 years of age, or (2) be relatively independent of experience (age, race) and maturation (age). Unfortunately, our developmental findings neither refute nor confirm any of the potential mechanisms for a male-bias. Indeed, any kind of learning—whether belief-based or experience-based - may happen before the age of 5 years without further learning afterwards. For example, Dunham et al. (2013) evidenced racial stereotyping in children as young as 3 years of age using a race categorization task with ambiguous stimuli. Similar findings were reported on social judgments of character based on facial features (Cogsdill et al., 2014). Conversely, the resemblance of cues between male and angry faces would not necessarily predict a constant male-biasing effect of anger across all age groups: for example, the strategy used for categorizing faces based on gender may well vary with age so that the linking of cues happens at one age more than another because children use one type of cue more than another at some ages. For example, it has been established that compared to adults, children rely less on second-order relations between features for various face processing tasks, and more on individual features, external features, or irrelevant paraphernalia, with processing of external contour developing more quickly than processing of feature information (Mondloch et al., 2002, 2003). Holistic processing, however, appears adult-like from 6 years of age onwards (Carey and Diamond, 1994; Tanaka et al., 1998; Maurer et al., 2002). Therefore, each age group presents a unique set, or profile, of face processing strategies that may be more or less affected by the potential intersection of cues between male and angry faces. Whichever mechanism or mechanisms come to be embraced on the basis of subsequent investigations, what our developmental findings do indicate is that the angry-male bias is not dependent on peers observing an association between males and aggression during the school age years.

Experiment 3: Computational Models of Gender Categorization

To determine if the effect of anger on gender categorization could be stimulus driven, i.e., due to the resemblance of cues for angry expressions and masculine gender, machine learning algorithms were trained to categorize the gender of the faces used as stimuli in Experiments 1–2. If algorithms tend to categorize angry faces as being male, as humans do, then cues for anger and masculinity are conjoined in the faces themselves and there should be no need to invoke experience- or belief-based inferences to explain the human pattern of errors.

Methods

Stimuli

Stimuli were identical to those used in Experiments 1, 2.

Different Computational Models

Analyses were run in Matlab 7.9.0529. The raw stimuli were used to train different classifiers (**Figure 4A**). The stimuli were divided into a training set and a test set that were used separately to obtain different measures of gender categorization accuracy (**Figure 4B**). Several models and set partitions were implemented to explore different types of training and representations (**Table 7**; **Figure 4A**).

Different types of representations (Principal Component Analysis, Independent Components Analysis, Sparse Auto-encoder, and Hand-Engineered features; **Table 7**; **Figure 4A**) were used because each of them might make different kinds of information more accessible to the classifier; i.e., the cue-dimension relationship that drives human errors may be more easily accessible in one representation than another. Sparse auto-encoded representations are considered the most "objective" of these representations in contrast to other unsupervised representations (Principal Component Analysis, Independent Components Analysis) that use a specific, deterministic method for information compression. Conversely, hand engineered features are the most "human informed" representation, since they were defined in Burton et al. (1993) using human knowledge about what facial features are (eyes, brows, mouth) and about the assumed importance of these features for gender categorization and face recognition. The choice of Principal Component Analysis as an unsupervised representation method (used in models A–C, and as a preprocessing step in models D–F) was motivated by the knowledge that PCA relates reliably to human ratings and performance (O'Toole et al., 1994, 1998) and has been proposed as a statistical

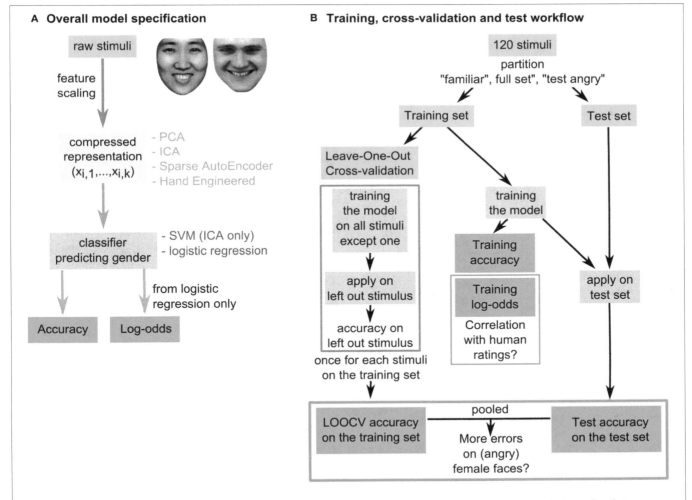

FIGURE 4 | Computational models. (A) Overall model specification. Each model had an unsupervised learning step (either PCA, ICA) followed by a supervised learning step (logistic regression or SVM). **(B)** Training, cross validation and test workflow. Stimuli were partitioned into a training set and a test set. Variables used in further analysis were the Leave-One-Out Cross-validation (LOOCV) accuracy, the test accuracy, and the log-odds at training. Human ratings were obtained in the control study (Supplementary Material).

TABLE 7 | Representations, classifiers, and face sets used in the computational models of gender categorization.

Representation	Classifier		Training and test faces			Sets size	
		Partition	Training set	Test set		Training	Test
Principal component analysis (PCA)	Logistic regression	A "Familiar"	Neutral and happy Caucasian	Angry and Chinese		$n = 40$	$n = 80$
		B "Full set"	All faces	–		$n = 120$	$n = 0$
		C "Test angry"	Neutral and happy	Angry		$n = 80$	$n = 40$
Independent component analysis (ICA)	Support vector machine (SVM)	D "Familiar"	Neutral and happy Caucasian	Angry and Chinese		$n = 40$	$n = 80$
		E "Full set"	All faces	–		$n = 120$	$n = 0$
		F "Test angry"	Neutral and happy	Angry		$n = 80$	$n = 40$
Sparse auto-encoder (SAE)	Logistic regression	G "Familiar"	Neutral and happy Caucasian	Angry and Chinese		$n = 40$	$n = 80$
		H "Full set"	All faces	–		$n = 120$	$n = 0$
		I "Test angry"	Neutral and happy	Angry		$n = 80$	$n = 40$
Hand-engineered features (HE)	Logistic regression	J "Familiar"	Neutral and happy Caucasian	Angry and Chinese		$n = 40$	$n = 80$
		K "Full set"	All faces	–		$n = 120$	$n = 0$
		L "Test angry"	Neutral and happy	Angry		$n = 80$	$n = 40$

analog of the human representation of faces (Calder and Young, 2005).

All models included feature scaling of raw pixels as a first preprocessing step. Models based on Principal Component Analysis (PCA, models A–C) used the first 16 principal components for prediction (75% of variance retained). Models based on Independent Components Analysis (ICA, models D–F) used the Fast-ICA implementation for Matlab (Gävert et al., 2005) that includes PCA and whitening as a preprocessing step. Sparse representations (models G–I) were obtained using the sparse auto-encoder neural network implemented in the NNSAE Matlab toolbox (Lemme et al., 2012). A sparse auto-encoder is a particular kind of neural network that aims to obtain a compressed representation of its input by trial and error. The hand-engineered features used in models J–L were the 11 full-face 2D-features and second-order relations identified in Burton et al. (1993) as conveying gender information (for example, eyebrow thickness, eyebrow to eye distance, etc.).

Most models used a logistic regression classifier because this method provides log-odds that were useful for human validation. Models D–F used the Support Vector Machine Classifier implementation from the SVM-KM toolbox for Matlab (Gaussian kernel, $h = 1000$, quadratic penalization; Canu et al., 2005) because in those models the problem was linearly separable (meaning that using logistic regression was inappropriate and would lead to poor performance).

Each model was trained on a set of faces (the training set, leading to the computation of training set accuracy), and then tested on a different set of faces (the test set, resulting in computation of test accuracy). Accuracy on the training sets was further evaluated using Leave-One-Out cross-validation (LOOCV), which is thought to reflect generalization performance more accurately than training accuracy. Accuracies at test and cross-validation (LOOCV) were pooled together for comparing the performance

on (angry) female vs. male faces. See **Figure 4B** for a schematic representation of this set up.

The partitioning of faces as training and test sets differed across the models (**Figure 4B**). The partitioning of models A, D, G, and J ("familiar") was designed to emulate the actual visual experience of human participants in Experiments 1–2. The partitioning for models B, E, H, and K ("full set") was designed to emphasize all resemblances and differences between faces equally without preconception. The partitioning for models C, F, I, and L ("test angry") was designed to maximize the classification difficulty of angry faces, enhancing the chance to observe an effect.

Human Validation

Gender typicality ratings from a control experiment (Supplementary Material) were used to determine how each model accurately captured the human perception of gender: the classifier should find the most gender-typical faces easiest to classify, and vice-versa. Ratings from male and female faces from the training sets were z-scored separately, and the Pearson's correlation between those z-scored ratings and the linear log-odds output from each model at training were computed. The log-odds represent the amount of evidence that the model linearly accumulated in favor of the female response (positive log-odds) or in favor of the male response (negative log-odds). The absolute value of the log-odds was used instead of raw log-odds so that the sign of the expected correlation with gender typicality was positive for both male and female faces and one single correlation coefficient could be computed for male and female faces together. Indeed, the faces with larger absolute log-odds are those that the model could classify with more certainty as male or female: if the model adequately emulated human perception, such faces should also be found more gender typical by humans.

Data and code are available online at http://dx.doi.org/10.6084/m9.figshare.1320891.

Results

Results are summarized in **Table 8** below.

Overall Classification Performance

Sparse-based models (**Table 8**, SAE, G–I) performed poorly (around 50% at test and cross-validation) and showed no correlation with human ratings, probably due to the difficulty of training this kind of network on relatively small training sets. Those models were therefore discarded from further discussion. PCA-based models (**Table 8**, PCA, A–C) on the other hand had satisfactory test (68.75–77.50%) and cross-validation (66.25–76.67%) accuracies, comparable to that of 5–6 year old children (Supplementary Figure 1). ICA- and SVM- based models (**Table 8**, ICA, D–F) performed, as expected, slightly better than models A-C at training (100%) and cross-validation (85%). However, performance at test (68.75–72.50%) was not better. Models based on hand-engineered features (**Table 8**, HE, J–L) had test and cross-validation performance in comparable ranges (62.50–76.67%), and their training accuracy (81.00–85.00%) was comparable to that of 85.5% reported by Burton et al. (1993) on a larger set of neutral Caucasian faces ($n = 179$). Most notably, the latter models all included eyebrow width and eye-to-eyebrow distance as significant predictors of gender.

Human Validation

Classification evidence (absolute log-odds) correlated with z-scored human ratings in 2 of the 3 models from the PCA based model family (**Table 8**, A,B) as well as in 2 of the 3 models based on hand-engineered features (**Table 8**, K,L). The highest correlation (Pearson $r = 0.46$, $p = 0.003$) was achieved in model A that used PCA and a training set designed to emulate the content of the participants' visual experience ("familiar").

PCA-based representations might dominate when rating the gender typicality of familiar faces, while a mixture of "implicit" PCA-based and "explicit" feature-based representations might be used when rating the gender typicality of unfamiliar faces.

Replication of Human Errors

Only one of the models (**Table 8**, D) exhibited an other-race effect, and this effect was only marginal [$\Delta = -15.00\%$, $p = 0.061$, $\chi^2_{(1)} = 3.52$]. Two models actually exhibited a reverse other-race effect, with better classification accuracy on Chinese than Caucasian faces [model C: $\Delta = 16.67\%$, $p = 0.046$, $\chi^2_{(1)} = 3.97$; model K: $\Delta = 16.67\%$, $p = 0.031$, $\chi^2_{(1)} = 4.66$]. Overall, the computational models failed to replicate the other-race effect for human gender categorization that was reported in Experiments 1–2 and in O'Toole et al. (1996).

The pattern of errors from PCA- or ICA-based models (**Table 8**, A–F) and feature-based models (**Table 8**, J–L) on female vs. male faces were in opposite directions. Four out of 6 PCA- and ICA- based models made significantly (**Table 8**, A,B,D) or marginally more mistakes (F) on male vs. female angry faces. Conversely, all 3 feature-based models (**Table 8**, J–L) made more mistakes on female vs. male angry faces, as did humans in Experiments 1–2. Similar patterns were found when comparing classification performance on all female vs. male faces, although the effect only reached significance in 2 out of 6 PCA- or ICA-based models (**Table 8**, A,D) and in 1 out of 3 feature-based models (**Table 8**, L). Hence, two different types of representations led to completely different predictions of human performance, only one of which replicated the actual data. Thus, the features of angry faces resemble that of male faces, potentially biasing gender categorization. However, this information is absent in

---

TABLE 8 | Accuracy, correlation with human ratings, and replication of experimental effects by different computational models of gender categorization.

		Accuracy (%)			Correlation with ratings		Female vs. male: Angry faces			Female vs. male: All faces		
		Training	CV	Test	r	p	$\Delta\%$	p	$\chi^2_{(1)}$	$\Delta\%$	p	$\chi^2_{(1)}$
PCA	A	82.50	72.50	68.75	0.46	0.003	45.00	0.001	10.16	30.00	<0.001	12.9
	B	92.50	76.67	–	0.23	0.019	35.00	0.013	6.14	6.67	0.388	0.75
	C	81.25	66.25	77.50	0.11	0.357	15.00	0.256	1.29	6.67	0.426	0.64
ICA	D	100.00	85.00	68.75	–	–	50.00	<0.001	10.99	35.00	<0.001	19.18
	E	100.00	85.00	–	–	–	15.00	0.256	1.29	3.33	0.609	0.26
	F	100.00	85.00	72.50	–	–	25.00	0.077	3.14	5.00	0.487	0.48
SAE	G	72.50	50.00	48.75	0.14	0.379	10.00	0.519	0.42	−18.33	0.045	4.03
	H	62.50	50.00	–	−0.05	0.587	−10.00	0.527	0.40	−6.67	0.465	0.53
	I	61.25	53.75	50.00	0.06	0.643	0.00	1.000	0.00	−1.67	0.855	0.03
HE	J	85.00	72.50	62.50	0.11	0.494	−45.00	0.004	8.29	−1.67	0.847	0.04
	K	81.67	76.67	–	0.25	0.012	−40.00	0.006	7.62	−3.33	0.666	0.19
	L	83.75	76.25	62.50	0.24	0.043	−75.00	<0.001	24.00	−30.00	<0.001	13.30

Models used either Principal Component Analysis (PCA, models A–C), Independent Component Analysis (ICA, models D–F), features generated by a sparse auto-encoder (SAE, models G–I), or hand-engineered features (HE, models J–L). Correlations with ratings are Pearson correlation coefficients between absolute log-odds at training and z-scored gender typicality ratings from humans. Results from the sparse auto-encoder vary at each implementation as the procedure is not entirely deterministic; a single implementation is reported here.

PCA and ICA representations that actually convey the reverse bias.

Absolute log-odds obtained by the feature-based model J on familiar (neutral and happy Caucasian) faces significantly correlated with mean human (children and adults) accuracy on these faces in Experiments 1–2 (Spearman $r = 0.39$, $p = 0.013$), while the absolute log-odds obtained by the PCA-based model A on those same faces correlated only marginally with human accuracy (Spearman's $r = 0.28$, $p = 0.077$). In other words, feature-based models also better replicated the human pattern of errors in categorizing the gender of familiar faces. See Supplementary Table 4 for a complete report of correlations with human accuracies for models A–C and J–L.

Discussion

Overall, the results support the idea that humans categorize the gender of faces based on facial features (and second-order relations) more than on a holistic, template-based representation captured by Principal Component Analysis (PCA). In contrast, human ratings of gender typicality tracked feature-based as well as PCA-based representations. This feature-based strategy for gender categorization leads to a confusion between the dimensions of gender and facial expression, at least when the faces are presented statically and in the absence of cues such as hairstyle, clothing, etc. In particular, angry faces tend to be mistaken for male faces (a male-biasing effect).

Several limitations should be noted, however. First, training sets were of relatively small size (40–120 faces), limiting the leeway for training more accurate models. Second, the ratings used for human validation were obtained from neutral poses (control study, Supplementary Material) and not from the actual faces used in Experiment 3, and there were several missing values. Thus, they do not capture all the variations between stimuli used in Experiment 3. While a larger set of faces could have been manufactured for use in Experiment 3, along with obtaining their gender typicality ratings, it was considered preferable to use the very same set of faces in Experiments 1–2. Indeed, it allowed a direct comparison between human and machine categorization accuracy. Finally, our analysis relied on correlations that certainly do not imply causation: for example, one could imagine that machine classification log-odds from feature-based models correlated with mean human classification accuracy not because humans actually relied on these features, but because those features are precisely tracking another component of interest in human perception—for example, perceived anger intensity. A more definitive conclusion would require a manipulation of featural cues (and second-order relations) as is usually done in studies with artificial faces (e.g., Oosterhof and Todorov, 2009). Here, we chose to use real faces: although they permit a more hypothesis-free investigation of facial representations, they do not allow for fine manipulations.

That a feature-based model successfully replicated the human pattern of errors does not imply that such errors were entirely stimulus driven. Indeed, a feature-based strategy may or may not be hypothesis-free: for example, it may directly reflect stereotypical or experiential beliefs about gender differences in facial features (e.g., that males have thicker eyebrows) so that participants would use their beliefs about what males and females look like to do the task—beliefs that are reinforced by cultural practices (e.g., eyebrow plucking in females). In fact, a feature-based strategy could be entirely explicit (Frith and Frith, 2008); anecdotally, one of the youngest child participants explicitly stated to his appointed research assistant that "the task was easy, because you just had to look at the eyebrows." On a similar note, it would be inappropriate to conclude that angry faces "objectively" resemble male faces as representations from Principal Component Analysis may be considered more objective than feature-based representations. Rather, it is the case that a specific, feature-based representation of angry faces resembles that of male faces. This point applies to other experiments in which a conjoinment of variant or invariant facial dimensions was explored computationally using human-defined features (e.g., Zebrowitz and Fellous, 2003; Zebrowitz et al., 2007, 2010). It appears then that the choice of a particular representation has profound consequences when assessing the conjoinment of facial dimensions. Restricting oneself to one particular representation of faces or facial dimensions with the goal of emulating an "objective" perception may not be realizable. Evaluating multiple potential representational models may thus be the more advisable strategy.

General Discussion

Overall, the results established the biasing effect of anger toward male gender categorization using signal detection analyses. The effect was present in adults as well as in children as young as 5–6 years of age, and was also evident with other-race faces for which anger had no effect on perceptual sensitivity.

The present results (1) are in accord with those of Becker et al. (2007) who reported that adults categorized the gender of artificial male vs. female faces more rapidly if they were angry, and female vs. male faces if they were smiling, and (2) replicate those of Hess et al. (2009) who reported that adults took longer to categorize the gender of real angry vs. smiling Caucasian female faces, but observed no such effect in Caucasian male faces. Similarly, Becker et al. (2007) found that adults were faster in detecting angry expressions on male vs. female faces, and in detecting smiling expressions on female vs. male faces. Conversely, Hess et al. (2004) found that expressions of anger in androgynous faces were rated as more intense when the face had a female rather than male hairline, a counter-intuitive finding that was explained as manifesting a violation of expectancy. Here, we complement the prior findings taken together by providing evidence for a male-biasing effect of anger using signal detection analyses, real faces, and a relatively high number of different stimuli.

We did not observe an opposing facilitation of gender categorization of female smiling faces, as could be expected from the results of Becker et al. (2007) and Hess et al. (2009), probably because in the present study, facial contours were partially affected by cropping. Furthermore, our results differ from those of Le Gal and Bruce (2002) who reported no effect of expression (anger, surprise) on gender categorization in 24 young adults, a null finding that was replicated by Karnadewi and Lipp (2011). The difference may originate from differences in experimental procedure or data analysis; both prior studies used a Gardner paradigm with a relatively low number of individual Caucasian models (10 and 8, respectively) and analyzed reaction times only, while reporting very high levels of accuracy suggestive of a ceiling effect [in fact, 22 participants from Le Gal and Bruce (2002) that had less than 50% accuracy in some conditions were excluded; not doing so would have violated assumptions for the ANOVAs on correct reaction times].

The findings yield important new information regarding the development of the angry-male bias. In particular, the male-biasing effect of anger was fairly constant from 5 to 6 years of age to young adulthood; the extensive social observation gained during schooling does not seem to impact the bias. This result is in accord with recent reports by Banaji and colleagues (Dunham et al., 2013; Cogsdill et al., 2014) showing that even belief-based interactions in the categorization of faces appear in their adult form much earlier than expected and do not appear to require extensive social experience. For example, Caucasian children as young as 3 years of age (the youngest age studied) were as biased as adults in categorizing racially ambiguous angry faces as Black rather than Caucasian (Dunham et al., 2013), an implicit association usually understood to reflect stereotyping (Hehman et al., 2014). Similarly, children aged from 3 to 5 stereotypically associated maleness with anger in cartoon faces (Birnbaum et al., 1980). Such biases may begin to develop in early infancy, a developmental period characterized by the emergence of gendered face representations rooted in visual experience (Quinn et al., 2002). Indeed, studies of racial prejudice have demonstrated a link between the other-race effect, a perceptual effect developing in infancy, and belief-based racial biases that are apparent from early childhood through adulthood such as associating other-race African faces with the angry expression (Xiao et al., 2015). It is possible that similar trajectories from perceptual to social representations may be found for gender. For example, a recent, unpublished study found that 3.5-month-old infants preferred a smiling to a neutral female expression, but preferred a neutral to a smiling male expression (Bayet et al., manuscript under review), suggesting an early association between female faces and positive emotions that results from differential perceptual or social experience with female caregivers. Such an early association could be a precursor to the increased performance of 5–6 year old children on smiling female faces that was observed in Experiment 2. Future studies on the developmental origins of stereotypes should focus on (1) finding precursors of stereotypes in infancy, and (2) bridging the gap between infancy and early childhood, thus providing a basis for early intervention that could curtail formation of socially harmful stereotypes.

Here, the male-biasing effect of anger appeared to be at least partially mediated by featural (e.g., brow thickness) and second-order (e.g., brow to eye distance) cues. While children have been reported to be less sensitive than adults to second-order relationships in some studies (e.g., Mondloch et al., 2002) and are less accurate in identifying facial emotional expressions (Chronaki et al., 2014), their encoding of featural information appears already mature at 6 years of age (Maurer et al., 2002) and they can recognize angry and smiling expressions most easily (Chronaki et al., 2014). Thus, the stability of the male-biasing effect of anger does not contradict current knowledge about children's face processing skills.

As discussed above, neither our behavioral nor our computational findings allowed us to embrace a particular mechanism for the male-biasing effect of anger, i.e., whether it was stimulus driven (an inherent conjoinment of dimensions) or stemmed from belief-based inferences. The findings are, however, relevant to the ongoing debate about the nature of face representations in the human brain. As stated by Marr (1982), any type of representation makes some kind of information evident while obscuring other kinds of information, so that studying the nature and origin of representational processes is at the heart of explaining low, middle, and high level vision. Various types of face representations have been proposed. For example, an important study in rhesus macaques found face-specific middle temporal neurons to be tuned to particular features or their combination while being affected by inversion (Freiwald et al., 2009). Other studies in humans have (1) emphasized the role of 2-D and 3-D second order relations in addition to features (Burton et al., 1993), and (2) argued for a double dissociation of featural and configural encoding (Renzi et al., 2013). An opposing line of argument has been advanced for a role of unsupervised representation analogs to Principal Component Analysis (Calder and Young, 2005) or Principal Component Analysis combined with multi-dimensional scaling (Gao and Wilson, 2013) or Gabor filters (Kaminski et al., 2011). All of those potential representations are fully compatible with the general idea of a face space (Valentine, 2001) since the face space may, in theory, present with any particular set of dimensions. Here, we provide additional evidence supporting the importance of features and second-order relations in the human processing of faces, and argue for the need to systematically consider various representational models of face processing when determining whether performance is stimulus driven, and to evaluate their respective contributions in perception depending on task, species, and developmental stage.

In conclusion, the present results indicate that the angry-male bias, whether stimulus- or belief- driven, does not require extensive social interaction with school-age peers to develop. It is in evidence as early as 5 years of age, and appears remarkably unaffected by experience during the primary grade levels, a developmental period that presumably includes observation of males engaging in aggressive acts.

Author Contributions

Study design was performed by LB, KL, OP, PQ, and JT. Data acquisition was conducted by LB, OP, and JT. Data analysis was performed by LB. All authors contributed to data interpretation, approved the final version of the article, revised it critically for intellectual content, and agree to be accountable for all aspects of the work.

Acknowledgments

This work was funded by the NIH Grant R01 HD-46526 to KL, OP, PQ, and JT, and a PhD scholarship from the French Department of Research and Higher Education to LB. The authors thank the families, adult participants, and research assistants that took part in these studies, and declare no conflict of interest.

References

Amodio, D. M. (2014). The neuroscience of prejudice and stereotyping. *Nat. Rev. Neurosci.* 15, 670–682. doi: 10.1038/nrn3800

Bates, D., Maechler, M., and Bolker, B. (2013). *lme4: Linear Mixed-Effects Models using S4 Classes.* R Packag. version 1.0.4.

Baudouin, J. Y., Gilibert, D., Sansone, S., and Tiberghien, G. (2000). When the smile is a cue to familiarity. *Memory* 8, 285–292. doi: 10.1080/09658210050117717

Becker, D. V., Kenrick, D. T., Neuberg, S. L., Blackwell, K. C., and Smith, D. M. (2007). The confounded nature of angry men and happy women. *J. Pers. Soc. Psychol.* 92, 179–190. doi: 10.1037/0022-3514.92.2.179

Birnbaum, D. W., Nosanchuk, T. A., and Croll, W. L. (1980). Children's stereotypes about sex differences in emotionality. *Sex Roles* 6, 435–443. doi: 10.1007/BF00287363

Bruce, V., and Young, A. (1986). Understanding face recognition. *Br. J. Psychol.* 77, 305–327. doi: 10.1111/j.2044-8295.1986.tb02199.x

Burton, A. M., Bruce, V., and Dench, N. (1993). What's the difference between men and women? Evidence from facial measurement. *Perception* 22:153. doi: 10.1068/p220153

Calder, A. J., and Young, A. W. (2005). Understanding the recognition of facial identity and facial expression. *Nat. Rev. Neurosci.* 6, 641–651. doi: 10.1038/nrn1724

Calvo, M. G., and Lundqvist, D. (2008). Facial expressions of emotion (KDEF): identification under different display-duration conditions. *Behav. Res. Methods* 40, 109–115. doi: 10.3758/BRM.40.1.109

Canu, S., Grandvalet, Y., Guigue, V., and Rakotomamonjy, A. (2005). *SVM-KMToolbox.*

Carey, S. (1992). Becoming a face expert. *Philos. Trans. R. Soc. Lond. B. Biol. Sci.* 335, 95–103. doi: 10.1098/rstb.1992.0012

Carey, S., and Diamond, R. (1994). Are faces perceived as configurations more by adults than by children? *Vis. Cogn.* 1, 253–274. doi: 10.1080/13506289408402302

Chronaki, G., Hadwin, J. A., Garner, M., Maurage, P., and Sonuga-Barke, E. J. S. (2014). The development of emotion recognition from facial expressions and non-linguistic vocalizations during childhood. *Br. J. Dev. Psychol.* doi: 10.1111/bjdp.12075. [Epub ahead of print].

Cogsdill, E. J., Todorov, A. T., Spelke, E. S., and Banaji, M. R. (2014). Inferring character from faces: a developmental study. *Psychol. Sci.* 25, 1132–1139. doi: 10.1177/0956797614523297

Contreras, J. M., Banaji, M. R., and Mitchell, J. P. (2012). Dissociable neural correlates of stereotypes and other forms of semantic knowledge. *Soc. Cogn. Affect. Neurosci.* 7, 764–770. doi: 10.1093/scan/nsr053

Dunham, Y., Chen, E. E., and Banaji, M. R. (2013). Two signatures of implicit intergroup attitudes: developmental invariance and early enculturation. *Psychol. Sci.* 24, 860–868. doi: 10.1177/0956797612463081

Freiwald, W. A., Tsao, D. Y., and Livingstone, M. S. (2009). A face feature space in the macaque temporal lobe. *Nat. Neurosci.* 12, 1187–1196. doi: 10.1038/nn.2363

Frith, C. D., and Frith, U. (2008). Implicit and explicit processes in social cognition. *Neuron* 60, 503–510. doi: 10.1016/j.neuron.2008.10.032

Gao, X., and Maurer, D. (2010). A happy story: developmental changes in children's sensitivity to facial expressions of varying intensities. *J. Exp. Child Psychol.* 107, 67–86. doi: 10.1016/j.jecp.2010.05.003

Gao, X., and Wilson, H. R. (2013). The neural representation of face space dimensions. *Neuropsychologia* 51, 1787–1793. doi: 10.1016/j.neuropsychologia.2013.07.001

Gävert, H., Hurri, J., Särelä, J., and Hyvärinen, A. (2005). *Fast ICA for Matlab.* version 2.5.

Haxby, J. V., Hoffman, E. A., and Gobbini, M. I. (2000). The distributed human neural system for face perception. *Trends Cogn. Sci.* 4, 223–233. doi: 10.1016/S1364-6613(00)01482-0

Hehman, E., Ingbretsen, Z. A., and Freeman, J. B. (2014). The neural basis of stereotypic impact on multiple social categorization. *Neuroimage* 101, 704–711. doi: 10.1016/j.neuroimage.2014.07.056

Herba, C., and Phillips, M. (2004). Annotation: development of facial expression recognition from childhood to adolescence: behavioural and neurological perspectives. *J. Child Psychol. Psychiatry* 45, 1185–1198. doi: 10.1111/j.1469-7610.2004.00316.x

Hess, U., Adams, R. B. Jr., Grammer, K., and Kleck, R. E. (2009). Face gender and emotion expression: are angry women more like men? *J. Vis.* 9, 1–8. doi: 10.1167/9.12.19

Hess, U., Adams, R. B. Jr., and Kleck, R. E. (2007). "When two do the same, it might not mean the same: the perception of emotional expressions shown by men and women," in *Group Dynamics and Emotional Expression. Studies in Emotion and Social Interaction, 2nd Series,* eds U. Hess and P. Philippot (New York, NY: Cambridge University Press), 33–50.

Hess, U., Adams, R. B. Jr., Kleck, R. E., and Adams, R. B. (2004). Facial appearance, gender, and emotion expression. *Emotion* 4, 378–388. doi: 10.1037/1528-3542.4.4.378

Hess, U., Adams, R., Kleck, R., and Adams, R. Jr. (2005). Who may frown and who should smile? Dominance, affiliation, and the display of happiness and anger. *Cogn. Emot.* 19, 515–536. doi: 10.1080/02699930441000364

Johnson, K. L., Freeman, J. B., and Pauker, K. (2012). Race is gendered: how covarying phenotypes and stereotypes bias sex categorization. *J. Pers. Soc. Psychol.* 102, 116–131. doi: 10.1037/a0025335

Kaminski, G., Méary, D., Mermillod, M., and Gentaz, E. (2011). Is it a he or a she? Behavioral and computational approaches to sex categorization. *Atten. Percept. Psychophys.* 73, 1344–1349. doi: 10.3758/s13414-011-0139-1

Karnadewi, F., and Lipp, O. V. (2011). The processing of invariant and variant face cues in the Garner Paradigm. *Emotion* 11, 563–571. doi: 10.1037/a0021333

Kelly, D. J., Quinn, P. C., Slater, A. M., Lee, K., Ge, L., and Pascalis, O. (2007). The other-race effect develops during infancy evidence of perceptual narrowing. *Psychol. Sci.* 18, 1084–1089. doi: 10.1111/j.1467-9280.2007.02029.x

Kelly, D. J., Liu, S., Lee, K., Quinn, P. C., Pascalis, O., Slater, A. M., et al. (2009). Development of the other-race effect during infancy: evidence toward universality? *J. Exp. Child Psychol.* 104, 105–114. doi: 10.1016/j.jecp.2009.01.006

Laird, N. M., and Ware, J. H. (1982). Random-effect models for longitudinal data. *Biometrics* 38, 963–974. doi: 10.2307/2529876

Lee, K., Quinn, P. C., Pascalis, O., and Slater, A. M. (2013). "Development of face-processing ability in childhood," in *The Oxford Handbook of Developmental Psychology, Vol. 1: Body and Mind,* ed P. D. Zelazo (New York, NY: Oxford University Press), 338–370.

Le Gal, P. M., and Bruce, V. (2002). Evaluating the independence of sex and expression in judgments of faces. *Percept. Psychophys.* 64, 230–243. doi: 10.3758/BF03195789

Lemme, A., Reinhart, R. F., and Steil, J. J. (2012). Online learning and generalization of parts-based image representations by non-negative sparse autoencoders. *Neural Netw.* 33, 194–203. doi: 10.1016/j.neunet.2012.05.003

Lu, B., Hui, M., and Yu-Xia, H. (2005). The development of native chinese affective picture system—a pretest in 46 college students. *Chinese Ment. Heal. J.* 19, 719–722.

Lundqvist, D., Flykt, A., and Öhman, A. (1998). *The Karolinska Directed Emotional Faces*. Stockholm: Sweden Karolinska Inst.

Malatesta, C., and Haviland, J. M. (1982). Learning display rules: the socialization of emotion expression in infancy. *Child Dev.* 53, 991–1003. doi: 10.2307/1129139

Malpass, R. S., and Kravitz, J. (1969). Recognition for faces of own and other race. *J. Pers. Soc. Psychol.* 13, 330–334. doi: 10.1037/h0028434

Marr, D. (1982). Vision: a computational investigation into the human representation and processing of visual information. *Phenomenol. Cogn. Sci.* 8, 397.

Maurer, D., Le Grand, R., and Mondloch, C. J. (2002). The many faces of configural processing. *Trends Cogn. Sci.* 6, 255–260. doi: 10.1016/S1364-6613(02)01903-4

Miller, S. L., Maner, J. K., and Becker, D. V. (2010). Self-protective biases in group categorization: threat cues shape the psychological boundary between "us" and "them." *J. Pers. Soc. Psychol.* 99, 62–77. doi: 10.1037/a0018086

Mondloch, C. J., Geldart, S., Maurer, D., and Grand, R. L. (2003). Developmental changes in face processing skills. *J. Exp. Child Psychol.* 86, 67–84. doi: 10.1016/S0022-0965(03)00102-4

Mondloch, C. J., Le Grand, R., Maurer, D., and Grand, R. L. (2002). Configural face processing develops more slowly than featural face processing. *Perception* 31, 553–566. doi: 10.1068/p3339

Morin, E. L., Hadj-Bouziane, F., Stokes, M., Ungerleider, L. G., and Bell, A. H. (2014). Hierarchical encoding of social cues in primate inferior temporal cortex. *Cereb. Cortex.* doi: 10.1093/cercor/bhu099. [Epub ahead of print].

O'Toole, A. J., Deffenbacher, K. A., Valentin, D., and Abdi, H. (1994). Structural aspects of face recognition and the other-race effect. *Mem. Cognit.* 22, 208–224.

O'Toole, A. J., Deffenbacher, K. A., Valentin, D., McKee, K., Huff, D., and Abdi, H. (1998). The perception of face gender: the role of stimulus structure in recognition and classification. *Mem. Cognit.* 26, 146–160.

O'Toole, A. J., Peterson, J., and Deffenbacher, K. A. (1996). An "other-race effect" for categorizing faces by sex. *Perception* 25, 669–676.

Oosterhof, N. N., and Todorov, A. (2009). Shared perceptual basis of emotional expressions and trustworthiness impressions from faces. *Emotion* 9, 128–133. doi: 10.1037/a0014520

Pinheiro, J., Bates, D., DebRoy, S., Sarkar, D., and Team, T. R. C. (2012). *nlme: Linear and Nonlinear Mixed Effects Models.* R Packag. version 3.1.105.

Quinn, P. C., Yahr, J., Kuhn, A., Slater, A. M., and Pascalis, O. (2002). Representation of the gender of human faces by infants: a preference for female. *Perception* 31, 1109–1122. doi: 10.1068/p3331

Renzi, C., Schiavi, S., Carbon, C.-C., Vecchi, T., Silvanto, J., and Cattaneo, Z. (2013). Processing of featural and configural aspects of faces is lateralized in dorsolateral prefrontal cortex: a TMS study. *Neuroimage* 74, 45–51. doi: 10.1016/j.neuroimage.2013.02.015

Rodger, H., Vizioli, L., Ouyang, X., and Caldara, R. (2015). Mapping the development of facial expression recognition. *Dev. Sci.* doi: 10.1111/desc.12281. [Epub ahead of print].

Schneider, W., Eschman, A., and Zuccolotto, A. (2002). *E-Prime: User's Guide.* Pittsburgh, PA: Psychology Software Incorporated.

Singmann, H. (2013). *Afex: Analysis of Factorial Experiments.* R Packag. version 0.7.90.

Snijders, T. A. B., and Bosker, R. J. (1999). *Multilevel Analysis: An Introduction to Basic and Advanced Multilevel Modeling.* London: SAGE.

Stanislaw, H., and Todorov, N. (1999). Calculation of signal detection theory measures. *Behav. Res. Methods, Instrum. Comput.* 31, 137–149. doi: 10.3758/BF03207704

Tanaka, J. W., Kay, J. B., Grinnell, E., Stansfield, B., and Szechter, L. (1998). Face recognition in young children: when the whole is greater than the sum of its parts. *Vis. Cogn.* 5, 479–496. doi: 10.1080/713756795

Tiddeman, B. (2005). Towards realism in facial image transformation: results of a wavelet mrf method. *Comput. Graph. Forum* 24, 449–456. doi: 10.1111/j.1467-8659.2005.00870.x

Tiddeman, B. (2011). "Facial feature detection with 3D convex local models," in *Autom. Face Gesture Recognit* (Santa Barbara, CA), 400–405. doi: 10.1109/FG.2011.5771433

Tottenham, N., Borscheid, A., Ellertsen, K., Marcus, D., and Nelson, C. A. (2002). *The NimStim Face Set*. Available online at: http://www.macbrain.org/faces/index.htm

Tottenham, N., Tanaka, J. W., Leon, A. C., McCarry, T., Nurse, M., Hare, T. A., et al. (2009). The NimStim set of facial expressions: judgments from untrained research participants. *Psychiatry Res.* 168, 242–249. doi: 10.1016/j.psychres.2008.05.006

Valentine, T. (2001). "Face-space models of face recognition," in *Computational, Geometric, and Process Perspectives on Facial Cognition: Contexts and Challenges*, eds M. J. Wenger and J. T. Townsend (Mahwah, NJ: Psychology Press), 83–113.

Wild, H. A., Barrett, S. E., Spence, M. J., O'Toole, A. J., Cheng, Y. D., and Brooke, J. (2000). Recognition and sex categorization of adults' and children's faces: examining performance in the absence of sex-stereotyped cues. *J. Exp. Child Psychol.* 77, 269–291. doi: 10.1006/jecp.1999.2554

Willenbockel, V., Sadr, J., Fiset, D., Horne, G. O., Gosselin, F., and Tanaka, J. W. (2010). Controlling low-level image properties: the SHINE toolbox. *Behav. Res. Methods* 42, 671–684. doi: 10.3758/BRM.42.3.671

Xiao, W. S., Fu, G., Quinn, P. C., Qin, J., Tanaka, J. W., Pascalis, O., et al. (2015). Individuation training with other-race faces reduces preschoolers' implicit racial bias: a link between perceptual and social representation of faces in children. *Dev. Sci.* doi: 10.1111/desc.12241. [Epub ahead of print].

Zebrowitz, L. A., and Fellous, J. (2003). Trait impressions as overgeneralized responses to adaptively significant facial qualities: evidence from connectionist modeling. *Pers. Soc. Psychol. Rev.* 7, 194–215. doi: 10.1207/S15327957PSPR0703_01

Zebrowitz, L. A., Kikuchi, M., and Fellous, J. (2010). Facial resemblance to emotions: group differences, impression effects, and race stereotypes. *J. Pers. Soc. Psychol.* 98, 175–189. doi: 10.1037/a0017990

Zebrowitz, L. A., Kikuchi, M., and Fellous, J.-M. (2007). Are effects of emotion expression on trait impressions mediated by babyfaceness? Evidence from connectionist modeling. *Pers. Soc. Psychol. Bull.* 33, 648–662. doi: 10.1177/0146167206297399

Conflict of Interest Statement: The authors declare that the research was conducted in the absence of any commercial or financial relationships that could be construed as a potential conflict of interest.

Iconicity in the lab: a review of behavioral, developmental, and neuroimaging research into sound-symbolism

Gwilym Lockwood[1]* and Mark Dingemanse[2]

[1] Neurobiology of Language Department, Max Planck Institute for Psycholinguistics, Nijmegen, Netherlands, [2] Language and Cognition Department, Max Planck Institute for Psycholinguistics, Nijmegen, Netherlands

This review covers experimental approaches to sound-symbolism—from infants to adults, and from Sapir's foundational studies to twenty-first century product naming. It synthesizes recent behavioral, developmental, and neuroimaging work into a systematic overview of the cross-modal correspondences that underpin iconic links between form and meaning. It also identifies open questions and opportunities, showing how the future course of experimental iconicity research can benefit from an integrated interdisciplinary perspective. Combining insights from psychology and neuroscience with evidence from natural languages provides us with opportunities for the experimental investigation of the role of sound-symbolism in language learning, language processing, and communication. The review finishes by describing how hypothesis-testing and model-building will help contribute to a cumulative science of sound-symbolism in human language.

Keywords: iconicity, sound-symbolism, neuroimaging, psycholinguistics, linguistics, ideophones, synesthesia, cross-modal correspondence

Edited by:
Gabriella Vigliocco,
University College London, UK

Reviewed by:
Barbara C. Malt,
Lehigh University, USA
Chloe Marshall,
Institute of Education - University
College London, UK

*Correspondence:
Gwilym Lockwood,
Neurobiology of Language
Department, Max Planck Institute for
Psycholinguistics, Wundtlaan 1,
6525XD Nijmegen, Netherlands
gwilym.lockwood@mpi.nl

Specialty section:
This article was submitted to
Language Sciences,
a section of the journal
Frontiers in Psychology

Introduction

Despite the increasing acceptance and popularity of sound-symbolism research in recent years, many articles about sound-symbolism begin by defining it in opposition to arbitrariness. The traditional Saussurian (de Saussure, 1959) or Hockettian (Hockett, 1959) view of language is outlined, the strengths of arbitrariness as a productive and compositional system (Monaghan and Christiansen, 2006) are described, the psychological and neuroscientific models of language which are built around arbitrariness (Levelt et al., 1999; Friederici, 2002; Hickok and Poeppel, 2007; Hagoort, 2013) are enumerated. . . and with a flourish, the latest sound-symbolism research is uncovered to the reader. All is not what it seems!

This approach is certainly not without its uses; even relatively recently, the extent of sound-symbolism within any given language was dismissed as "vanishingly small" (Newmeyer, 1992), and so the prerogative of sound-symbolism researchers to point out the shortcomings and blind spots of an approach that sees language as strictly arbitrary is understandable. However, to continue to present sound-symbolism as an opponent to arbitrariness, rather than simply the opposite of arbitrariness, is unhelpful. The two systems are clearly happy enough to co-exist within language; with iconic links between sound/sign and meaning increasingly being accepted as a general property of language (Perniss et al., 2010; Perniss and Vigliocco, 2014), it is time for a more constructive perspective.

Despite the fast growing interest in iconicity in general (as witnessed for instance in studies of sign language and gesture), there is still a relative dearth of experimental research on sound-symbolism, especially when compared with the amount of psycholinguistic research based on arbitrary words. However, research into sound-symbolism has been steadfastly gaining influence in fields like linguistics, psycholinguistics and cognitive neuroscience, opening up new opportunities for theoretical and empirical progress. What is needed now is a perspective that unites these bodies of evidence and shows where they converge or diverge. This review article brings together experimental findings from a wide range of fields—from behavioral experiments to developmental work and neuroimaging studies—and shows that there is now an exciting opportunity to develop a holistic account of the communicative functions and causal mechanisms of sound-symbolism.

Definitions and History

The discussion of arbitrariness *versus* sound-symbolism is nothing new. Plato's *Cratylus* describes a debate between Cratylus and Hermogenes about the origin of names, with Cratylus arguing that names are meaningful in themselves and by nature, and Hermogenes arguing that names are merely signifiers[1]. Socrates, the umpire of the debate, acknowledges both points; he presents a Hamano-esque description of the "imitative significance of primary sounds corresponding to single letters of the alphabet" (Hamano, 1998), followed by the argument that any name, even if it is natural, cannot perfectly describe its referent and thus some degree of linguistic convention is inherent to all names (Sedley, 2003)[2].

Arbitrariness and iconicity, "the source of more trouble than any other aspect of communicative behavior" (Hockett, 1959), continued to set themselves apart throughout the Middle Ages and well into the twentieth century. It was only in the middle of the twentieth century that arbitrariness was fully enshrined as the principle cornerstone of language, basing linguistic theory upon de Saussure's (1959) posthumously translated and published work on the arbitrariness of the sign and Hockett's (1959) assertion that arbitrariness is one of seven—later updated to 13 (Hockett, 1960)—key design features of human language.

Competing Motivations for Arbitrariness and Sound-Symbolism

The strength of arbitrariness was identified as the ability to combine symbols into limitless conventional forms, giving language far more communicative power in terms of the range of concepts and relations it can express, while also explaining why different languages have different forms for the same concepts. Crucially though, Hockett (1960) also acknowledged that while the design feature arbitrariness gives limitless possibilities to

communication, it also "has the disadvantage of being arbitrary." This is a caveat with implications for learning and communication which has not always been addressed. Indeed, more recent studies have indicated that sound-symbolism and arbitrariness mutually pick up each other's slack. Non-arbitrary form-to-meaning relationships facilitate learning as they are grounded in existing perceptual and cognitive systems (Cuskley and Kirby, 2013) and enable the grouping of similar words into categories (Farmer et al., 2006). Arbitrariness facilitates the learning of specific word meanings (Monaghan et al., 2011) and prevents the confusion of concepts which are similar but critically different (such as two almost identical mushrooms; one edible, one poisonous; Corballis, 2002).

A system based solely on arbitrariness would pose immense learning difficulties, with no link between linguistic form and human experience, and would make communication less direct and vivid; a system based solely on sound-symbolism would prevent specificity of communication because it can only offer limited conceptual distinctions (Bühler, 1990). The recognition that sound-symbolism and arbitrariness coexist in language is echoed in recent theoretical syntheses of arbitrariness and iconicity (Perniss et al., 2010; Perniss and Vigliocco, 2014). They can coexist because each brings its own advantages for learning words and using them in communication. By supplying perceptual analogies for vivid communication, sound-symbolism allows for communication to be *effective*; by providing the lexicon with greater depth and distinction, arbitrariness allows for the *efficient* communication of concepts. The two systems lend themselves better to different communicative uses, which do not preclude each other, and are in fact complementary. The research is slowly leading the field toward a complementary view of language which features both sound-symbolism and arbitrariness, but there are a few obstacles in the way, not least coming up with a widely-accepted and consistently-applied understanding of exactly what sound-symbolism actually is.

Types of Sound-Symbolism

While arbitrariness is defined by the absolute lack of relation between form and meaning, defining sound-symbolism is somewhat harder; the sheer variety of depth and type of links between form and meaning, both within and across languages, means that there is no simple opposite of arbitrariness. Perniss et al. (2010) and Schmidtke et al. (2014) cover various subtypes of sound-symbolism in detail; a quick overview will be given here. The term *iconicity* is the closest cover-all term for communicative signs showing a resemblance between form and meaning, used as "a blanket term for a broad range of phenomena, including what has been referred to in the literature as sound-symbolism, mimetics, ideophones, and iconicity" (Perniss et al., 2010). Iconicity can be applied to communication in visual, spoken, and other modalities, can be manifested at all levels from phonetics to discourse, and is perhaps even present in animal communication (Hockett, 1959).

In this review paper, we use the term *sound-symbolism* to refer to iconicity in spoken language. Hinton et al. (1994, 2006) define sound-symbolism as "the direct linkage between sound and meaning," and divide it into *corporeal, imitative,*

---

[1] However, this entire debate was not conducted out of academic curiosity; rather, Cratylus had told Hermogenes that Hermogenes was not his real, natural name, assigned as it was by his parents. Thus provoked, Hermogenes became the first documented proponent of arbitrariness, arguing that any given group of people can determine their own labels for concepts and if he calls himself Hermogenes then he has the absolute right to do so since it is only a label for the person he is, thank you very much.

[2] Socrates concludes the debate by saying that it is far better to study the things themselves rather than their names, a suggestion which is somewhat less useful for models of language.

conventional, and *synesthetic* sound-symbolism. Cuskley and Kirby (2013) refine the latter two into *conventional* and *sensory* sound-symbolism. Conventional sound-symbolism is the regular correlation between specific sounds or clusters and specific meanings (such as with phonaesthemes). Conventional sound-symbolism can also cover the correlation between sounds and grammatical categories, which is broadly equivalent to what Monaghan et al. (2011, 2014) call *systematicity*. This definition of conventional sound-symbolism has a wider scope than most, as it goes further than Hinton et al. (1994, 2006) who do not consider sound-symbolism as extending to grammatical categories, while Monaghan et al. (2011, 2014) also consider systematicity to be separate from sound-symbolism, which they limit to phonaesthemes and sensory sound-symbolism. Sensory sound-symbolism is a natural connection where the word's form imitates aspects of the referent within or across modalities, and this imitation is often obvious across languages.

This classification echoes the description of sound systems outlined by Von Humboldt (1836). "Since words always correspond to concepts, it is natural for related concepts to be designated by related sounds." Von Humboldt lists three ways in which sounds designate concepts: *direct imitation*, which broadly follows imitative sound-symbolism or onomatopoeia; *symbolic designation*, whereby sounds "partly in themselves and partly by comparison with others produce for the ear an impression similar to that of the object upon the soul," and which most closely resembles sensory sound-symbolism with the acknowledgment of some degree of conventionalism; and *analogical designation*, whereby "words whose meanings lie close to one another are likewise accorded similar sounds; but … there is no regard here to the character inherent in these sounds themselves," which most closely resembles conventional sound-symbolism driven by statistical association, or systematicity. A closely related distinction is Gasser et al.'s (2010) two-way classification of iconicity as *absolute* or *relative*. *Absolute* iconicity is where there is a direct relation between form and meaning (as in onomatopoeic words for animal sounds). *Relative* iconicity is where related forms are associated with related meanings, as when a contrast between the vowels [i:a] depicts an analogous contrast in magnitude.

Many different terms and definitions have been used for sound-symbolic words, but *ideophone* is now the most widely used and accepted (Voeltz and Kilian-Hatz, 2001). Nuckolls (1999) defines ideophones as "lexicalised sound-imitative words," while Dingemanse (2012) provides a more specific definition of ideophones as "marked words which depict sensory imagery." Ideophones typically exhibit sensory sound-symbolism, although there is always some degree of conventionalization involved as well. Thus the Japanese ideophone *kirakira* "glittering" shows sensory sound-symbolism in that reduplication in the word is associated with a continuous meaning and the vowel [i] is associated with brightness, but it also has conventionalized aspects in that not all aspects of its meaning can be deduced from its sounds.

Sound-symbolism is not confined solely to ideophones; in fact, the majority of sound-symbolism research has focused on cross-modal relations between individual sounds and sensory meanings, such as vowels and object size. There are also sound-symbolic links between certain combinations of sounds and meanings. Phonaesthemes are "frequently recurring sound-meaning pairings that are not clearly contrastive morphemes" (Bergen, 2004), such as such as *tw-* in English words like *twist, tweak, twizzle, twirl*, and *twine*. They show a mix of conventional and sensory sound-symbolism (Kwon and Round, 2014), and are thought to be drivers of neologisms in language (Malkiel, 1994). Again, Von Humboldt (1836) wrote of such conventionalized forms having "undoubtedly exerted a great and perhaps exclusive dominance on primitive word-designation … and the new increment is formed by analogy with what is already present." This philosophical legacy has posed the question of how sound-symbolism constitutes and affects language; it is now the responsibility of modern experimental approaches to bring iconicity out of the wild and into the lab to resolve the argument between Cratylus and Hermogenes with evidence as well as reason.

Behavioral Experiments

There is a long history of behavioral research on sound-symbolism, most of which has investigated the mappings between consonant/vowel types and the size or shape of visual stimuli in variations on experiments performed by Sapir (1929), Newman (1933), and Köhler (1947). Half a century of Generativism saw sound-symbolism research fall out of favor somewhat, but this approach was brought back into fashion around the turn of the century (Waugh, 1994; Kita, 1997; Ramachandran and Hubbard, 2001; Klamer, 2002), and described in detail in Perniss et al. (2010). To begin with, it was enough simply to show that certain sounds have some kind of effect; this was an important rediscovery which brought sound-symbolism in from the cold and into the wider attention of the field. More recently, there have been several studies in the last few years which have attempted to tease apart the separate roles of vowels and consonants, either by testing participants with individual phonemes or with non-words. These studies have also examined the effect of specific sounds on various different modalities, including strength, light, and taste.

Forced Choice Tasks With Non-Words

The standard paradigm in behavioral sound-symbolism experiments is the *kiki-bouba* paradigm. Originally developed by Köhler (1947), participants see two shapes—one spiky and one round—and two non-words—*takete* and *maluma* [later adapted to *kiki* and *bouba* by Ramachandran and Hubbard (2001)]. Participants are then asked to say which non-word goes with which shape. Participants generally map the round shape with the "round" non-words (*maluma/bouba*) and the spiky shape with the "spiky" word (*takete/kiki*). Despite the methodologically sparse descriptions in Ramachandran and Hubbard (2001), this effect appears to be strong and consistent, and is the most well-known result showing that the relation between sound and meaning is not entirely arbitrary. This paradigm, and most variations of it, is perhaps the most obvious example of sensory sound-symbolism.

Building on the *kiki-bouba* paradigm, various experiments have found consistent effects with better-controlled stimuli. The paradigm is affected by altering both individual consonants and vowels, but not by mode of presentation, as the effect was consistent regardless of whether the stimuli were presented auditorily or visually (Nielsen and Rendall, 2011). Systematically altering the placement of consonants and vowels in novel words addressed the shortcomings of Ramachandran and Hubbard's (2001) study, where the 95% success rate was down to the obvious distinction created by the non-words and novel shapes which were deliberately designed to be as different as possible. A follow-up non-word/shape matching experiment revealed a learning bias toward sound-symbolism, albeit a weak one (Nielsen and Rendall, 2012). Two groups of participants were investigated; one which had been implicitly taught a congruent sound-symbolic pattern (plosives and spiky shapes, sonorants and curvy shapes) and one which had been implicitly taught an incongruent sound-symbolic pattern (plosives and curvy shapes, sonorants and spiky shapes). The first group performed above chance in the matching task while the second group performed at chance level, which demonstrates a learning bias toward sound-symbolism. In a novel word generation task (Nielsen and Rendall, 2013), participants were found to use both vowels and consonants to form sound-symbolic associations. Participants used sonorant consonants and rounded vowels for curvy *bouba* figures and plosive consonants and non-rounded vowels for spiky *kiki* figures. Participants also favored vowels with relatively close articulation to the co-articulated consonant (such as a frontal [i] following the strident consonants [t] and [k] and the "frontal" consonants [m], and [n]) and showed a dispreference for combining consonants and vowels which were relatively further apart. This suggested once more that consonants trump vowels when it comes to non-word sound-symbolic perception of visual contours, but that both types of sound do have a role.

The *kiki-bouba* paradigm has also been informative about language in populations different from psychology undergraduate students participating for course credit (Henrich et al., 2010). A first cross-linguistic and cross-cultural replication of Köhler's (1947) *maluma-takete* paradigm was Davis's (1961) study of English and Tanzanian children. More recently, Bremner et al. (2013) replicated the *kiki-bouba* paradigm with Himba participants in Namibia for sound-to-shape matching but not taste-to-shape matching. The Himba have no written language and very little exposure to Western culture, which is helpful in ruling out cultural or orthographic effects such as associations with brand names or associations with the shape of the letters (such as how the letter K is spikier than the letter O).

Finally, developmental disorders involving impaired cross-modal integration also affect participants' accuracy at the *kiki-bouba* paradigm. High functioning autistic participants were significantly worse than non-autistic participants at matching *kiki*-like words to spiky shapes and *bouba*-like words to curvy shapes, although they still categorized the stimuli at above-chance level; low functioning autistic participants performed at chance level (although this may be due to the nature of the task; Occelli et al., 2013). Occelli et al. (2013) theorize that this is linked to a global deficiency in multisensory integration in autistic people, suggesting that the cross-modal correspondence effect is linked to motor and sensory integrative processes in the left inferior frontal gyrus. Dyslexic Dutch speakers, meanwhile, perform above chance at *kiki-bouba* paradigms but worse than non-dyslexic Dutch speakers (Drijvers et al., 2015). This reinforces the claim that cross-modal abstraction is involved in making sound-symbolic links.

Task Effects

The robustness of the *kiki-bouba* paradigm relies in part on the nature of forced choice. When it uses four target stimuli rather than two, participants are less successful at making congruent sound-symbolic matches (Aveyard, 2012). Moreover, the use of three rounds of testing showed that participants use different strategies depending on whether the paradigm is a two- or four-alternative forced choice task. When there were only two choices, participants used a consonantal sound-symbolic strategy instantly, and general accuracy for incongruent trials improved over three rounds of testing, indicating that participants were able to use separate strategies for congruent and incongruent trials after some experience. When the number of choices was increased to four, participants were less aware of the manipulation and were slower to incorporate consonantal sound-symbolism into their decision making, although this did emerge by the third round. The main effect of linking sonorants to curviness and plosives to spikiness is in line with most behavioral research, but introduces some important variables which show how easily this sensitivity to consonantal sound-symbolism can be affected by experimental set-up.

Moving Beyond Shape

While the *kiki-bouba* paradigm has been very popular for sound-symbolism research into shape, other experimental approaches are more useful for investigating other sensory modalities. Hirata et al. (2011) found an effect of lightness on sound sensitivity. Participants were better able to identify consonants when they heard and saw congruent sound–light pairings (i.e., voiceless consonants with light visual stimuli, voiced consonants with dark visual stimuli) than incongruent sound–light pairings. However, there was no effect of consonant type when participants had to identify whether a visual stimulus was light or dark.

Links between sound and emotion have also been investigated, but these are more likely to rely on indexical interpretations of affective prosody rather than on iconicity in the sense of structural resemblance (Majid, 2012).

Most of the research presented so far has focused on the properties of consonants, but sensory sound-symbolism with vowels is well-attested too, especially for size (Sapir, 1929). Thompson and Estes (2011) and Thompson (2013) investigated sound-symbolism and object size links by addressing the forced dichotomy of two-alternative forced choice matching in a slightly different way from Aveyard (2012). They showed five different sizes of novel object set against a picture of a cow as a point of comparison, and asked participants to choose the most appropriate name from a selection of three-syllable non-words which varied the number of small-sounding (such as [i]) and large-sounding (such as [a]) vowels. Participants chose non-words with increasing numbers of large phonemes for increasingly large objects, which shows that sound-symbolism

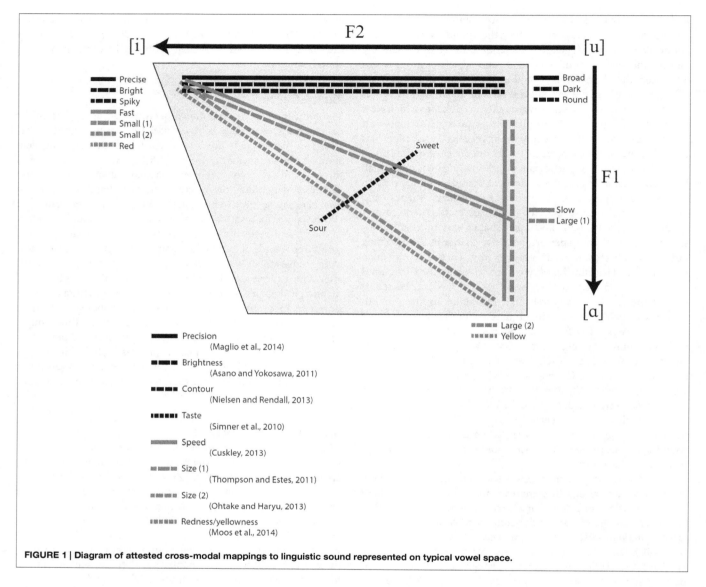

FIGURE 1 | Diagram of attested cross-modal mappings to linguistic sound represented on typical vowel space.

marks graded cross-modal mappings rather than just marking contrasts. Meanwhile, it appears that the evidence for an acoustic mechanism for sound-symbolism is stronger than that for a kinaesthetic mechanism, a perennial debate which goes back to Sapir (1929) and Newman (1933). Ohtake and Haryu (2013) performed a series of experiments which separated acoustic features of vowels and the size of the oral cavity while asking participants to categorize the size of a visual object. Participants were faster to categorize object size when hearing the vowels [a] and [i] in congruent conditions, i.e., when [a] was presenting with a large object and [i] with a small object. However, there was no effect when participants categorized object size while holding objects in their mouths to simulate the oral cavity shape made when pronouncing the vowels [a] and [i]. This suggests that the main driver of the effect is the acoustic properties of the vowels, rather than their articulatory properties.

The acoustic properties of vowels have also been found to elicit cross-modal correspondences related to taste (Simner et al., 2010).

Participants were given taste samples of four taste types—sweet, sour, bitter, and salty—and adjusted four sliders—F1, F2, voice discontinuity, and spectral balance—to create a vowel sound which best fit the taste. Participants consistently assigned lower F1 and F2 frequencies (approximating higher, more back vowels) to sweet flavors and higher F1 and F2 frequencies (approximating lower, more front vowels) to sour flavors, with salty and bitter flavors falling in between. They posit that these patterns may have influenced vocabulary construction for taste terminology. Interestingly, this spectrum does not quite fit along the same lines as most sound-symbolic vowel associations, which tend to run on a spectrum from [i] to [a] as illustrated in **Figure 1**. Given that Anglophones find it especially hard to describe and discriminate between tastes and smells according to their properties (as opposed to their sources) when compared to other senses (Majid and Burenhult, 2014), perhaps it is to be expected that Anglophone participants may not map sounds onto tastes in the same way as other senses. It is also hard to say what kind of sound-symbolic links drive this effect. It is probably sensory sound-symbolism, but there may be conventional aspects involved; the word *sour* is pronounced with a lower vowel than the word *sweet*, which mirrors the associations made by the participants.

Differences between back vowels and front vowels have been found in various studies. Cuskley (2013) investigated non-words and visual motion by asking participants to direct the motion of a ball to match a non-word. Participants made the ball travel more slowly in response to back vowels, and made the ball travel more quickly in response to front vowels and syllable reduplication with vowel alternation (the apophonic direction of vowel alternation in reduplicated syllables was not tested; forms such as *kigu* and *kugi* were treated as the same). However, whether this mapping is consistent is unclear; Thompson (2013) performed a similar study and found only a small and non-statistical trend toward assigning faster ratings to names containing front vowels.

Maglio et al. (2014) linked front vowels to conceptual precision with two studies on vision and concepts. Participants were asked to perform a geographical analysis of a fictional city. When the city's name featured more front vowels than back vowels, participants divided the city into smaller, more precise geographic regions, and *vice versa*, which Maglio et al. (2014) refer to as visual precision. Participants were also more precise when asked to describe the actions of a person when there was a front vowel association. They saw a person writing a list and were told that this person was performing a "sheeb task" or a "shoob task"; when asked to describe the person's behavior, participants replied with conceptual precision about the action in the front vowel condition (e.g., "the person is writing a list" when performing the "sheeb task"), and replied with conceptual breadth about the action in the back vowel condition (e.g., "the person is getting organized" when performing the "shoob task"). This may actually be an indirect measure of the typical vowel-size correspondences, with the participants associating back vowels with size in general and then applying the size distinction to visual or conceptual precision. Maglio et al. (2014) then performed a series of experiments on high versus low-level thought; these linked front vowels to low-level thought and back vowels to high-level thought. Back vowels in an ice-cream product name made people focus on how good it tastes rather than how easily accessible it is; back vowels in a skin lotion product name made people focus on how effective it is, rather than how attractive the packaging is; and back vowels in a back pain treatment made people focus on how long-lasting the pain relief is, rather than how arduous the procedure is. Maglio et al.'s (2014) research provides interesting evidence that specific vowel changes may elicit different mental representations. This probably examines conventional sound-symbolism rather than sensory sound-symbolism, as vowel size does not map onto literal sensory size but a more metaphorical magnitude of abstract concepts.

Some studies have linked cross-modal associations between linguistic stimuli and color to synesthesia. Moos et al. (2014) investigated vowel sound and color associations in synesthetes and control participants. They found that increased F2 (i.e., higher vowels) was associated with increased redness on the color spectrum, while increased F1 (i.e., lower vowels) was associated with increased yellowness. This was found in both synesthetes and non-synesthetes, although far more strongly in the synesthetes, which suggests that grapheme-color synesthesia is at least partially based on acoustic properties of the sounds associated to the graphemes, and provides further evidence that synesthesia may be an exaggeration of general cross-modal associations which most people have. Shin and Kim (2014) likewise investigated color associations in synesthetes by comparing the associations of Japanese, Korean, and English graphemes in trilingual synesthetes. Despite the small sample size, they found that color associations were broadly similar across participants and across languages for graphemes which expressed the same sounds, showing that grapheme-color synesthesia for individual graphemes is based on the sounds which the graphemes express. In experiments with synesthetic Japanese speakers, Asano and Yokosawa (2011) found that consonants and vowels independently influence the colors which synesthetes ascribe to the hiragana and katakana Japanese writing systems, and that this effect was not due to visual form. Their results show a tendency for front vowels and voiceless consonants to be associated with brighter colors, and for back vowels and voiced consonants to be associated with darker colors, which follows the general synesthetic patterns set out by Marks (1978). The fact that most of the participants are synesthetic in these three studies makes it hard to say which type of sound-symbolism is under investigation here, but it is likely to be sensory sound-symbolism.

Summary of Attested Cross-Modal Correspondences

Non-word behavioral experiments have been useful in establishing broadly consistent cross-modal associations between sound and other sensory modalities, and these seem to overlap with synesthetic associations. When presenting full non-words, consonants seem to have greater prominence than vowels in terms of what participants perceive and how they formulate sound-symbolic strategies; however, both consonants and vowels do influence participants' judgments. Voiced consonants and low back vowels are consistently associated with roundness, darkness in color, darkness in light intensity, and slowness (although in the case of voiced consonants, only by comparison with voiceless consonants). Voiceless consonants and high front vowels are consistently associated with spikiness, brightness in color, brightness in light intensity, and quickness. Moreover, vowel height and size is linked with physical size, with low vowels and back vowels being linked to big objects and high vowels and front vowels being linked to small objects. Taste conflates the two acoustic properties of vowels; sweetness is linked with high back vowels and saltiness is linked with low front vowels. This is illustrated in **Figures 1** and **2**.

Moving Beyond Non-Words

Despite the progress made with behavioral research on non-words, the insights it provides into language processing are limited. Non-word stimuli are carefully designed to provide maximal distinction between the sensory properties of the referent and the linguistic factors of interest, such as consonant

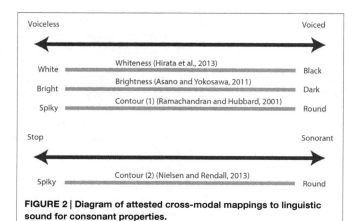

FIGURE 2 | Diagram of attested cross-modal mappings to linguistic sound for consonant properties.

voicing, vowel height and backness, and lip rounding. Not only does this introduce experimenter bias concerning which properties of language are sound-symbolic, it also means that the language stimuli used are not necessarily reflective of spoken language if such maximal distinctions do not occur naturally, and any existing findings may be an overstatement of the cross-modal associations that people make with real language. One way to address this problem is to use existing sound-symbolic words to address the question of how sound-symbolism in natural language is (or is not) associated with other sensory modalities; and among existing sound-symbolic words, ideophones are a prime source of information about sound-symbolic mappings (Dingemanse, 2012).

Most experimental work on ideophones has been conducted using Japanese, which has an extensive, commonly-used and well-documented set of ideophones (Kita, 1997; Hamano, 1998; Akita, 2009a). Most studies have found that participants with no knowledge of Japanese perform significantly above chance at guessing the meaning of ideophones. Oda (2000) performed a series of forced choice tasks with Japanese ideophones on two groups of native English speakers. The first group heard a native Japanese speaker read out the ideophones and were asked to focus on the sound before performing the tasks. The second group heard a native Japanese speaker read out the ideophones and were then asked to pronounce the words themselves before performing the tasks. The two tasks were picking the correct ideophone out of three options for one English definition, and matching two minimal pair ideophones to the two English definitions, which were accompanied by illustrations of the texture or movement. Both groups could guess the meaning of the ideophones at an above chance level of accuracy, and this accuracy was modulated by articulation; the group which pronounced the words themselves were significantly better at matching unfamiliar ideophones to English definitions. In opposition to studies such as Ohtake and Haryu (2013), Oda's (2000) result suggests that articulation does play a role in establishing the form-meaning relationship of ideophones. The question over whether sound-symbolism is driven by acoustic *or* articulatory mappings is perhaps too reductive; it seems that both mechanisms are involved depending on the nature of the task.

Iwasaki et al. (2007a) conducted similar experiments with Japanese pain vocabulary, and found that non-Japanese speakers could accurately categorize ideophones expressing pain according to the type of pain they express. However, Japanese sound-symbolism is not always entirely transparent to other speakers. In another study, Iwasaki et al. (2007b) found that English speakers with no knowledge of Japanese could make accurate semantic judgments about ideophones which referred to specific sound qualities but the same speakers made very different semantic judgments about ideophones concerning beauty and pleasantness. It is unclear whether this is due to the fact that sound-to-sound mappings do not cross modalities and are therefore more transparent, whether these particular ideophones expressing beauty were just more on the conventional side of the continuum and therefore less obviously iconic, or due to cultural differences over what constitutes beauty.

Iwasaki et al. (2007b) further found that English speakers were relatively better at categorizing ideophones describing manners of laughter (e.g., giggling and chuckling according to semantic dimensions like pitch and gracefulness) than ideophones describing manners of walking (e.g., strolling and lumbering according to semantic dimensions like pace and steadiness). Iwasaki et al. (2007b) attributed this to the same kind of vowel and consonant voicing contrasts which have been found in non-word studies, such as large vowels being linked with large strides and loud laughs. However, it also shows that ideophones are not completely intuitive to speakers of other languages and depend in some part on the specific semantic context provided by the experimental set-up. In a developmental study, Imai et al. (2008) generated some novel ideophones for manners of motion based on Hamano's (1998) phonosemantic classification of Japanese ideophones, and Japanese adult participants completely agreed with the novel ideophones' intended meanings. This supports the idea that at least some of the sound-symbolic patterns in Japanese ideophones are sufficiently systematic enough to be productive (Oda, 2000; Yoshida, 2012). When naïve English speakers were tested with these novel ideophones, the intended meanings were still categorized at above chance level, thus confirming previous behavioral research on Japanese ideophones with novel forms. All of these studies with Japanese ideophones show that there is enough sensory sound-symbolism in ideophones for speakers of other languages to be sensitive to the meanings, and that there may be additional conventional sound-symbolism in ideophones which is more informative for native speakers.

The Role of Prosody

Similar above chance categorization patterns have been found with ideophones in various languages, not just Japanese. Mitterer et al. (2012) took ideophones from five languages across five semantic domains, and presented naïve participants with four versions of the stimuli in two-alternative forced choice tasks—the original ideophone recordings, a rich resynthesis using the original recordings' phoneme durations and prosody, a phoneme-only resynthesis and a prosody-only resynthesis. Ideophones in the original recordings and in the rich resynthesis condition were both categorized at above-chance accuracy, but ideophones in the phoneme-only and prosody-only resynthesis conditions were not. This indicates that both phonemes and prosody are important for cross-linguistic effects of iconicity. This finding is corroborated by evidence that around 80% of ideophones are given special prosodic attention and emphasis in natural speech—prosodically foregrounded (Dingemanse, 2013)—and that certain prosodic profiles in non-words can have reliable semantic associations (Nygaard et al., 2009b).

Some non-ideophonic lexical words also show these effects. Kunihira (1971) conducted experiments using apparently arbitrary Japanese words in forced choice tests and found that English speakers were able to accurately categorize them, even though they were not ideophones. Responses were most accurate when the words were pronounced with "expressive voice," i.e., exaggerated prosody. This suggests sound-symbolic interpretations can be elicited even for arbitrary words—a viewpoint that reinforces the crucial role of expressive prosody. Nygaard et al. (2009a) used Kunihira's stimuli in a learning task, and found that English speakers were quicker to learn and quicker to respond to Japanese words paired with correct English translations (e.g., *hayai* and *fast*) than when paired with opposite (e.g., *slow*) or unrelated (e.g., *blunt*) English translations. Nygaard et al. (2009a) stop short of linking particular sounds or properties of the words to particular meanings, instead suggesting that reliable sound-meaning mappings—regardless of whether this sound-symbolism is sensory (i.e., presumably recognizable across languages) or conventionalized (i.e., recognizable only within a particular language)—"may constrain novel word learning and subsequent word retrieval and recognition by guiding processing to properties and meaning within a particular semantic context."

The same research group expanded the scope of this research to include antonym contrasts in 10 different languages; monolingual English speakers allocated the antonyms correctly at above chance level in two-alternative forced choice testing, although consistency varied across individual items and may indicate the inherent probabilistic variability in the degree of sound-symbolism in supposedly arbitrary words (Namy et al., submitted; Tzeng et al., submitted). These findings were partially replicated in a study comparing synesthetes and non-synesthetes, which found that both groups guessed certain meanings at above chance accuracy, and that the synesthetes did so more strongly than the non-synesthetes (Bankieris and Simner, 2015). However, there are two crucial caveats with these stimuli. Firstly, six of the 10 languages used in these studies are rich in ideophones and poor in ordinary adjectives (Indonesian, Korean, Tamil, Mandarin, Turkish, and Yoruba), which means that this study may well have indirectly studied ideophones rather than arbitrary antonyms. Secondly, the four non-ideophonic languages (Dutch, Albanian, Gujurati, and Romanian) are all Indo-European; this means that they cannot be treated as independent because of potentially shared linguistic features, and moreover their meanings may be more transparent to native English speakers if they are cognates, especially in the case of Dutch and Romanian. Unfortunately, these studies are not yet publicly available (despite their crucial role in other published work), and so we cannot do more than speculate here.

Developmental Experiments

While the extensive behavioral literature attests that sound-symbolism has persistent and varied effects on language processing and use, a frequent criticism is that these patterns of association are conditioned because of orthographic influences; people might only consider the sound [b] to be rounder than the sound [k] because the letter *b* is rounder than the letter *k*. However, studies on early language development have shown that this is not the case. Studies with pre-literate children and young infants rule out such orthographic effects. Developmental experiments with infants also provide a different window into sound-symbolism from learning experiments with adults. Experiments with infants examine existing cross-modal associations and how infants exploit these during early language development, whereas learning experiments with adults examine how sound-symbolism affects memory, and are necessarily influenced by the adults' first language.

Mixed Results for kiki-bouba Paradigms

The *kiki-bouba* paradigm, with its sensory sound-symbolism links, can be easily adapted for infants and young children, although results have been mixed. Ozturk et al. (2013) and Fort et al. (2013) tested 4-month-old infants with preferential looking procedures, using fully reduplicated non-words with no word-internal vowel contrasts (e.g., *kiki*, *bubu*). Ozturk et al. (2013) presented one shape together with one auditory non-word and measured gaze duration, while Fort et al. (2013) presented two shapes side by side together with one auditory non-word and investigated whether infants preferred looking at a particular shape. The additional complexities of Fort et al.'s (2013) experimental set-up proved to be too much for the infants, as they found no preferential looking effects; they "tentatively argue that the complexity of their design might have masked the infants' emerging sound-symbolic matching abilities." However, Ozturk et al. (2013) found that infants looked for longer durations at shapes which were presented with incongruent non-words. Moreover, they found that this only happened for non-words where both vowels and consonants were typically sound-symbolic; the infants would match *bubu* with the curvy shape and *kiki* with the spiky shape, but would not make the same distinctions when comparing *kiki* and *kuku* or *bibi* and *bubu*. The adult control group, on the other hand, only needed either a vowel contrast or a consonant contrast to make cross-modal associations. When taken together, these results suggest that there is an effect of sound-symbolism in infants, but that it needs both consonants and vowels to make the stimuli maximally distinct and that only very straightforward designs may detect the effect. This also appears to show that infants are less sensitive to sound-symbolic contrasts than adults are, which implies that increased exposure to language in fact increases sensitivity to sound-symbolic associations. This is supported by a study on pitch-size associations in 4- and 6-month-old infants, which found that 6-month-old infants make typical associations between pitch and size while 4-month-old infants do not (Fernández-Prieto et al., 2015). The apparent conflict in results between Fort et al. (2013) and Ozturk et al. (2013) shows that iconicity may be strong enough for infants to detect, but not strong enough for this effect to persist through more complicated tasks.

Maurer et al. (2006) replicated Ramachandran and Hubbard's (2001) *kiki-bouba* results with 2.5-year-old children, which ruled out orthography as a confound as these children could not yet read. Spector and Maurer (2013) developed this experiment with slightly updated stimuli, using fully reduplicated non-words with no word-internal vowel contrasts rather than the typical *kiki-bouba* words used in the previous study. The toddlers were presented with two visual shapes, and then asked by an adult to point to the non-word of interest (e.g., "can you point to the *koko*?"). As predicted, the toddlers associated curvy shapes with rounded vowels and spiky shapes with non-rounded vowels. One possible factor is the direct interaction with an adult experimenter rather than pre-recorded stimuli. Nygaard et al. (2009b) have established that adults use exaggerated and semantically-predictable prosodic profiles when pronouncing non-words in child-directed speech, and this may have provided the kind of prosodic foregrounding which helps to identify ideophones in natural language.

There have also been several developmental studies on the acquisition and use of Japanese ideophones, which show that both Japanese and non-Japanese children are highly sensitive to the sound-symbolic properties of Japanese ideophones. Iwasaki et al. (2007b) cite Ishiguro (1993), who found that children create their own idiosyncratic ideophones before fully acquiring conventional ones, and that children acquire ideophones expressing sound before acquiring ideophones expressing motion, shape, psychological states, or other sensory modalities. This ties in with Iwasaki et al.'s (2007b) and Oda's (2000) research, which showed that participants with no knowledge of Japanese were more accurate at categorizing ideophones expressing sound, and confirms the prevalence of sensory sound-symbolism in ideophones.

The Sound-Symbolic Bootstrapping Hypothesis

Imai et al. (2008) created novel Japanese ideophonic motion verbs and tested them on Japanese and English-speaking adults (as described in the behavioral section). They then tested 25-month-old Japanese children with a verb learning task, and found that the children could generalize the ideophonic verbs to new situations, but could not do the same for the non-sound-symbolic verbs. Imai et al. (2008) concluded that sound-symbolism provides a scaffold on which children can map semantic and syntactic information. Echoing Gentner and Boroditsky's (2001) arguments that actions unfold over time and are impermanent whereas objects are stable, which is why children tend to focus on objects and tend to acquire nouns first, Imai et al. (2008) propose that the sound-symbolic scaffolding provided by the ideophonic verbs helps children to isolate the action and therefore facilitates verb learning. Kantartzis et al. (2011) replicated Imai et al.'s (2008) results in experiments with English children using the same novel verbs based on Japanese sound-symbolic patterns. This provided evidence toward a cross-linguistic—or, perhaps more accurately, language-independent—early sensitivity toward sound-symbolism, and also shows that Japanese ideophones

contain sensory sound-symbolism and not just conventional sound-symbolism. Kantartzis et al. (2011) also point out that it is unclear what exactly the English children recognize as sound-symbolic; it could be the phonetics, the phonotactics, the prosody, or a combination of all three.

Yoshida (2012) developed the paradigm further and carried out more extensive tests, making several important points. Firstly, sound-symbolism aided verb acquisition in Japanese and English children equally, despite the Japanese children's greater exposure to and familiarity with the Japanese mimetic-style novel verbs. Secondly, this equal language-independent sensitivity to sound-symbolism exists despite the vast difference in general iconic input between Japanese (where parents make extensive use of ideophones to children) and English (where parents do use a lot of onomatopoeia to children, but they do so more idiosyncratically and less often than Japanese parents do). Thirdly, by including both novel verbs and novel actors in the task, she showed that the sound-symbolic scaffolding proposed by Imai et al. (2008) Imai and Kita (2014) helps children to isolate the action by excluding the identity of the actor, rather than just by focusing on the action. Yoshida (2012) proposes that infants are universally sensitive toward sound-symbolism, but this sensitivity attenuates in adulthood as their native language's conventionalized forms dictate which possible forms of sound-symbolism are acceptable; this mirrors the well-established pattern of infant sensitivity to cross-linguistic phonemic differences, which attenuates with age. The sound-symbolic bootstrapping hypothesis is also supported by ideophone usage studies, which have shown that Japanese children as young as 2 years old use ideophonic verbs frequently and productively (Akita, 2009b) and that Japanese parents are five times more likely to use ideophones to children than they were to other adults when describing the same scene (Maguire et al., 2010). The finding that ideophones are more geared toward children initially appears to sit uncomfortably with the finding of Ozturk et al. (2013), which suggested that infants were less sensitive to sound-symbolism than adults. However, perhaps a reasonable middle ground is that children are more sensitive to sound-symbolism as long as there are enough sources in the input to make associations from, while adults are less sensitive to sound-symbolism in terms of forming associations but can form associations from a more limited input.

Finally, Laing's (2014) reanalysis of a longitudinal case study (Elsen, 1991) provides another example of how sound-symbolism bootstraps language acquisition. Laing examined Elsen's detailed dataset of German infant Annalena and investigated the development and role of onomatopoeic forms. Annalena used onomatopoeic forms extensively, constituting almost 40% of her vocabulary at 11 months, but the relative proportion of onomatopoeia in Annalena's vocabulary tailed off with age. Annalena systematically replaced onomatopoeic forms with conventional words according to her phonological ability, meaning that onomatopoeic forms were retained longer when their conventional forms were phonologically more difficult. This shows how both sensory and conventional sound-symbolism in infancy works alongside the developing lexicon and can bootstrap phonological development.

Neuroimaging Experiments

Behavioral research into sound-symbolism has been instrumental in telling us that there is a robust effect of sound-symbolism on language tasks, and that this effect can be modulated by various different linguistic changes. However, neuroimaging research is needed to establish how the brain recognizes, processes, and constructs sound-symbolism. There has been far less neuroimaging research on sound-symbolism than behavioral, but the handful of existing studies make interesting suggestions about sensory embodiment, synesthesia, and multisensory integration.

ERP and fMRI Evidence

Some neuroimaging experiments on ideophones have essentially used behavioral paradigms with simultaneous EEG recording to investigate ERPs. Kovic et al. (2010) conducted a novel word learning experiment, which established that participants were quicker to identify novel objects with congruent sound-symbolic non-word names than incongruent or arbitrary non-word names. They then tested two groups of participants; one group learned congruent sound-symbolic names for pointy and round objects (i.e., *shick* for a pointy object and *dom* for a round object), the other group learned incongruent sound-symbolic names (i.e., *shick* for a round object and *dom* for a pointy object). The experiment presented a name auditorily and then an object visually, and the participants had to decide whether the object and name matched. The first group were quicker to identify correct conditions and quicker to reject incorrect conditions than the second group, which corroborates other behavioral evidence that sensory sound-symbolic congruence has an object recognition facilitation effect. Moreover, objects with congruent sound-symbolic names elicited a stronger negative wave than incongruent ones in the 140–180 ms window after the presentation of the object. This effect was observed at the occipital regions, home of the visual cortex, and Kovic et al. (2010) suggest that the early negativity represents auditory-visual integration during early sensory processing.

Arata et al. (2010) used the *kiki-bouba* paradigm on 12-month-old infants, simultaneously presenting a shape and a non-word in congruent and incongruent conditions. The infants were found to be sensitive to sound-symbolic matches and mismatches, showing differentiated wave patterns across both conditions after 200 ms post-stimulus. This may have been the P2, an ERP component which has been linked to phonological and semantic analysis. Arata et al. (2010) claim that their results support the claim that infants are synesthetic or like synesthetes (Maurer and Mondloch, 2004), potentially due to having more cortical connections than adults do, resulting in their ability to detect sound-symbolism. Asano et al. (2015) performed a similar experiment on 11-month-old infants, this time presenting the stimuli sequentially; the infants were first shown a spiky or curvy novel object, and then heard the non-word *kipi* or *moma*. This study found a later effect, with more negative ERPs in the 400–550 ms window for incongruent stimuli compared to congruent stimuli. Asano et al. (2015) argue that infants use sensory sound-symbolic congruency to anchor novel sounds onto meaning, thus enabling them to establish that linguistic sounds have real world referents.

There are fewer neuroimaging experiments specifically aimed at revealing the brain locations associated with ideophone use and understanding, probably because of the relative lack of knowledge of ideophones outside the field of linguistics. However, a few neuroimaging studies using ideophones do exist. Osaka and his group conducted a series of fMRI studies (Osaka et al., 2003, 2004; Osaka and Osaka, 2005, 2009; Osaka, 2009, 2011), which show that Japanese ideophones activate the relevant sensory cortical areas. Ideophones expressing laughter activate the "laughter module" (Osaka et al., 2003) across the visual cortex, extrastriate cortex, and the premotor cortex, and also the striatal reward area. Ideophones expressing pain (e.g., *chikuchiku* for a needle-prick kind of pain, *gangan* for a throbbing headache) activate the cingulate cortex, the part of the brain which also processes actual pain. Ideophones expressing crying (e.g., oioi for *wailing*, *mesomeso* for sniveling) activate similar areas to the laughter ideophones, suggesting that crying and laughing are processed as positive and negative equivalents, but they also activate the inferior frontal gyrus and anterior cingulate cortex in the same way as the pain ideophones, suggesting that implied crying "involves some degree of concomitant emotional pain" (Osaka, 2011). Ideophones suggestive of gaze direction and manner of walking activate the frontal eye field and extrastriate visual cortex respectively. All of these ideophones activate the visual cortex and premotor cortex, which Osaka's group argue is responsible for the vividness of the mental imagery conjured up by ideophones. However, the main limitation with these studies is that they all compared ideophones to non-words. As arbitrary words will also activate relevant sensory areas of the cortex when compared with non-words (Zwaan, 2004), this is uninformative about the special properties of sound-symbolism.

Ideophones Versus Arbitrary Words in Natural Language

Two neuroimaging studies have directly compared ideophones and arbitrary words. Lockwood and Tuomainen (2015) used EEG to investigate the difference between ideophonic adverbs and arbitrary adverbs by presenting Japanese speakers with sentences where the only difference was whether the adverb was sound-symbolic or not. Participants performed an unrelated sentence judgment task and were unaware of the nature of the experiment. The ideophones elicited a greater P2 and a late positive complex, both of which are in line with Arata et al.'s (2010) and Asano et al.'s (2013, 2015) findings. Lockwood and Tuomainen (2015) argue that the greater P2 in response to the ideophones represents the multisensory integration of sound and sensory processing. They also claim that while this effect is due to cross-modal associations rather than representative of true synesthesia, the same neural mechanisms may be involved. They speculate that it is the distinctive phonological profile of ideophones which enables, or engages, the multisensory integration process. This is also in line with the conclusions of Occelli et al.'s (2013) behavioral study on autistic participants.

Kanero et al. (2014) performed two fMRI studies where participants watched animations while simultaneously hearing ideophones or arbitrary words with related to a particular modality—motion in the first experiment and shape in the second. They observed that words which participants rated as closely matching the animations elicited greater activation across the cortex than low-match words. The right posterior superior temporal sulcus (rpSTS) was activated specifically in response to ideophone trials, and not arbitrary word trials. Kanero et al. (2014) take this to mean that the right posterior STS is a critical hub for processing Japanese ideophones, and possibly sound-symbolism in general. They argue that this goes beyond simple embodiment, as the rpSTS is not a perceptual or sensorimotor area related to the word meaning. Instead, Kanero et al. (2014) suggest that ideophones have a dual nature; part arbitrary linguistic symbol, part iconic symbol, and that the posterior STS works as a hub of multimodal integration. This is in line with a long tradition in the ideophone literature that emphasizes the combination of iconic aspects (such as vowel size contrasts) and arbitrary aspects (such as conventional word forms) in ideophones (e.g., Diffloth, 1994). However, as ideophones contain both sensory and conventional sound-symbolism, it is difficult to tease apart the separate contributions of each type with native speakers.

There has also been a study which used fMRI and fractional anisotropy (FA) to investigate sound-symbolism in apparently arbitrary words. Using the same antonym stimuli and experimental set-up as Namy et al., (submitted) and Tzeng et al., (submitted), Revill et al. (2014) found that there was increased activation in the left superior parietal cortex in response to words which participants found sound-symbolic compared to words which they did not. Furthermore, they found a correlation between functional anisotropy in the left superior longitudinal fasciculus and participants' individual sensitivity to sound-symbolism. Revill et al. (2014) argue that sound-symbolic words engage cross-modal sensory integration to a greater extent than arbitrary words, and that this cross-modal sensory integration is what facilitates word to meaning mappings (although due to the caveats mentioned above, it is not quite clear what kind of sound-symbolism is under investigation here). They also argue that these correspondences may reflect some form of iconicity or embodiment, but do not speculate whether the main driver of the sound-symbolic effect is acoustic or articulatory.

Finally, Meteyard et al. (2015) investigated the phonological and semantic basis of iconicity with aphasic patients, and used it to addressed theoretical questions rather than just demonstrating an effect. They tested left-hemisphere aphasic patients with four aphasia assessment tests which assess phonology, semantics, and the combination of phonology and semantics, and looked at the processing differences between iconic and non-iconic English words (which are mostly conventionally sound-symbolic with some sensory sound-symbolic properties). Aphasics had an especially consistent processing advantage for iconic words in auditory lexical decision and reading aloud tasks, which specifically involve the mapping between phonology and semantics rather than either phonology or semantics alone. They present two potential theoretical implications, which are not mutually exclusive. Firstly, iconic words may have additional connections from the semantic system to modality-specific features, meaning that iconic words are more robust in aphasic patients because they are represented with greater redundancy

within the language system itself. This means that the iconic word processing advantage is protected from damage in a similar way to high frequency, high imageability, and early acquired words. Alternatively, iconic words may be represented by direct connections between phonological form and modality-specific information. This is in line with both the embodiment semantics literature, which claims that iconic words have an extra route to activate experience, and the neuroimaging work of Kanero et al. (2014); under this account, the iconic word processing advantage in aphasics is because iconic words are additionally processed in cross-modal integration brain areas, including right hemisphere regions which are unaffected by left hemisphere damage. This study is probably the best account of how iconicity mediates between semantics and phonology rather than being specific to one or both.

Summary and Future Directions

The wealth of research on sound-symbolism in the last few years has consolidated three main findings. Firstly, people consistently make multiple cross-modal sensory associations to specific sounds under experimental conditions, and the direction of the cross-modal sensory association—light or dark, fast or slow, etc.,—is related to vowel height, vowel size, and consonant voicing of the sounds involved. Secondly, people can consistently guess the meanings of sound-symbolic words in foreign languages at an above chance level, and that this is related to phonemes and prosody. Thirdly, children are sensitive to sound-symbolism and that ideophones help children acquire verbs (or at least, verbal meanings in the domain of motion) regardless of which language they are learning, meaning that children's sensitivity to ideophones is likely to be driven by the sound-symbolic phonemes and prosody. There are not yet enough neuroimaging experiments on sound-symbolism to make solid conclusions, but so far it appears that sound-symbolic words activate sensory areas more strongly than arbitrary words and that the processing of sound-symbolic words appear to involve some kind of multisensory integration (or at least more multisensory integration when compared to arbitrary words).

From Observation to Explanation

The vast majority of these studies have focused on showing that there *is* an effect and have strongly made the case for sound-symbolism; the next step is to investigate how this effect *works*. Prior work has supplied several important pieces of the puzzle. There are linguistic typologies and frameworks for understanding sound-symbolism, such as those of Hinton et al. (2006), Perniss and Vigliocco (2014), Dingemanse (2012), and Cuskley and Kirby (2013). There are some cognitive accounts of structure mapping (Gentner, 1983), of the mental faculties for sound-symbolism (Marks, 1978; Ramachandran and Hubbard, 2001), and of how sound-symbolism scaffolds language acquisition (Imai and Kita, 2014). There is also a host of psychological evidence from cross-modal correspondences. However, two crucial missing pieces in the literature are specific hypotheses of how neural mechanisms may support sound-symbolism, and solid neuroimaging evidence which tests them.

Broadly speaking, psychological studies have addressed the question of which particular sounds have which particular cross-modal correspondences, while linguistic studies have addressed the question of what properties sound symbolic words have which make them sound-symbolic. The current challenge in sound-symbolism research is to pull together the different strands of research into one coherent field. Linguistic, psychological, and cognitive research programs have individually made predictions about the form, use, and function of sound-symbolism; this is now a perfect opportunity for cross-disciplinary collaboration to develop a neuroscientific model of sound-symbolism which makes predictions that can be empirically tested with neuroimaging methods.

Interdisciplinary Integration

One attempt at interdisciplinary integration is when Ramachandran and Hubbard (2001) used the *kiki-bouba* paradigm to inform their more general synesthetic bootstrapping model of language evolution. They postulate that there is a synesthetic correspondence between visual object shape represented in the inferior temporal lobe and sound represented in the auditory cortex, and that this synesthetic correspondence may either happen through direct cross-activation or may be mediated by the angular gyrus. The first possibility has been interpreted as predicting that relevant sensory areas would be more strongly activated for sound-symbolic words compared to arbitrary words; the second possibility predicts that the angular gyrus would be more strongly activated for sound-symbolic words compared to arbitrary words. Both of these hypotheses can be built on with further neuroimaging work, but of the sound-symbolism experiments that do mention it, they tend either show that there is a significant effect and move on, or they hedge their conclusions by suggesting that there may be a synesthetic or embodiment mechanism without elaborating on how it might work.

Perniss and Vigliocco (2014) also provide a relatively fleshed out model. They propose that iconicity exists to provide the link between linguistic form and human experience by establishing reference and displacement through sensorimotor embodiment of linguistic form, and that the cross-linguistic variability in iconicity shows how different languages strike a balance between two basic constraints—the need to link language to human experience and the need for an efficient communication system. This suggestion provides fertile ground for hypothesis testing, especially with language development literature which can be framed in terms of investigating the emergence of reference and displacement with respect to iconicity. The next step for this model is to hypothesize how the brain processes sound-symbolism and cross-modal correspondences. Perhaps there is a role here for Meteyard et al.'s (2015) suggestion that iconic words may be supported by additional connectivity between semantic or phonological representations and perceptuo-motor information.

Recent research on sound-symbolism has established that sound-symbolism is widespread across languages, that it has cross-modal correspondences with other senses, that this has an effect on behavior and development, and that it elicits distinct brain signals. We are now at an exciting juncture where we can start approaching this phenomenon from an integrated interdisciplinary perspective. Ideophones and sound-symbolism from natural languages provide us with opportunities for the experimental investigation of the role of sound-symbolism in meaning, interpretation, and perception. Through hypothesis-testing and model-building, these experiments will help contribute to a cumulative science of sound-symbolism in human language.

Acknowledgments

This work was funded by an IMPRS Ph.D. fellowship from the Max Planck Society to GL and an NWO Veni grant to MD.

References

Akita, K. (2009a). *A Grammar of Sound-Symbolic Words in Japanese: Theoretical Approaches to Iconic and Lexical Properties of Mimetics*. Kobe: Kobe University.

Akita, K. (2009b). "The acquisition of the constraints on mimetic verbs in Japanese and Korean," in *Japanese/Korean Linguistics*, Vol. 16, ed. Y. Takubo (Stanford, CA: CSLI Publications), 163–177.

Arata, M., Imai, M., Kita, S., Thierry, G., and Okada, H. (2010). Perception of sound symbolism in 12 month-old infants: an ERP study. *Neurosci. Res.* 68, e300. doi: 10.1016/j.neures.2010.07.1333

Asano, M., Imai, M., Kita, S., Kitajo, K., Okada, H., and Thierry, G. (2015). Sound symbolism scaffolds language development in preverbal infants. *Cortex* 63, 196–205. doi: 10.1016/j.cortex.2014.08.025

Asano, M., Kitajo, K., Thierry, G., Kita, S., Okada, H., and Imai, M. (2013). Linguistic experience alters the processing of sound symbolism: an ERP study. *Presented at the Sound-Symbolism Workshop 2013*, Tokyo.

Asano, M., and Yokosawa, K. (2011). Synesthetic colors are elicited by sound quality in Japanese synesthetes. *Conscious. Cogn.* 20, 1816–1823. doi: 10.1016/j.concog.2011.05.012

Aveyard, M. E. (2012). Some consonants sound curvy: effects of sound symbolism on object recognition. *Mem. Cogn.* 40, 83–92. doi: 10.3758/s13421-011-0139-3

Bankieris, K., and Simner, J. (2015). What is the link between synaesthesia and sound symbolism? *Cognition* 136, 186–195. doi: 10.1016/j.cognition.2014.11.013

Bergen, B. K. (2004). The psychological reality of phonaesthemes. *Language* 80, 290–311.

Bremner, A. J., Caparos, S., Davidoff, J., de Fockert, J., Linnell, K. J., and Spence, C. (2013). "Bouba" and "Kiki" in Namibia? A remote culture make similar shape-sound matches, but different shape-taste matches to Westerners. *Cognition* 126, 165–172. doi: 10.1016/j.cognition.2012.09.007

Bühler, K. (1990). *Theory of Language: The Representational Function of Language*. Amsterdam: John Benjamins Publishing.

Corballis, M. C. (2002). *From Hand to Mouth: The Origins of Language*. Princeton, NJ: Princeton University Press.

Cuskley, C. (2013). Mappings between linguistic sound and motion. *Public J. Semiotics* 5, 39–62.

Cuskley, C., and Kirby, S. (2013). "Synaesthesia, cross-modality, and language evolution," in *Oxford Handbook of Synaesthesia*, eds J. Simner and E. M. Hubbard (Oxford: Oxford University Press), 869–907.

Davis, R. (1961). The fitness of names to drawings. a cross-cultural study in Tanganyika. *Br. J. Psychol.* 52, 259–268. doi: 10.1111/j.2044-8295.1961.tb00788.x

de Saussure, F. (1959). *Course in General Linguistics*. New York: Philosophical Library.

Diffloth, G. (1994). "i: big, a: small," in *Sound Symbolism*, eds L. Hinton, J. Nichols, and J. J. Ohala (Cambridge: Cambridge University Press), 107–114.

Dingemanse, M. (2012). Advances in the cross-linguistic study of ideophones. *Lang. Linguist. Compass* 6, 654–672. doi: 10.1002/lnc3.361

Dingemanse, M. (2013). Ideophones and gesture in everyday speech. *Gesture* 13, 143–165. doi: 10.1075/gest.13.2.02din

Drijvers, L., Zaadnoordijk, L., and Dingemanse, M. (2015). "Sound-symbolism is disrupted in dyslexia: implications for the role of cross-modal abstraction processes," in *Proceedings of the 37th Annual Meeting of the Cognitive Science*

Society, eds D. Noelle, R. Dale, A. S. Warlaumont, J. Yoshimi, T. Matlock, C. D. Jennings et al. (Austin, TX: Cognitive Science Society), 602–607.

Elsen, H. (1991). *Erstspracherwerb, Der Erwerb des deutschen Lautsystems*. Wiesbaden: Deutscher Universitäts Verlag.

Farmer, T. A., Christiansen, M. H., and Monaghan, P. (2006). Phonological typicality influences on-line sentence comprehension. *Proc. Natl. Acad. Sci. U.S.A.* 103, 12203–12208. doi: 10.1073/pnas.06021 73103

Fernández-Prieto, I., Navarra, J., and Pons, F. (2015). How big is this sound? Crossmodal association between pitch and size in infants. *Infant Behav. Dev.* 38, 77–81. doi: 10.1016/j.infbeh.2014.12.008

Fort, M., Weiss, A., Martin, A., and Peperkamp, S. (2013). Looking for the bouba-kiki effect in prelexical infants. *Presented at the 12th International Conference on Auditory-Visual Speech Processing*, Annecy, 71–76.

Friederici, A. D. (2002). Towards a neural basis of auditory sentence processing. *Trends Cogn. Sci.* 6, 78–84. doi: 10.1016/S1364-6613(00)01839-8

Gasser, M., Sethuraman, N., and Hockema, S. (2010). "Iconicity in expressives: an empirical investigation," in *Experimental and Empirical Methods in the Study of Conceptual Structure, Discourse, and Language*, eds S. Rice and J. Newman (Stanford, CA: CSLI Publications), 163–180.

Gentner, D. (1983). Structure-mapping: a theoretical framework for analogy*. *Cogn. Sci.* 7, 155–170. doi: 10.1207/s15516709cog0702_3

Gentner, D., and Boroditsky, L. (2001). "Individuation, relativity, and early word learning," in *Language Acquisition and Conceptual Development*, eds M. Bowerman and S. C. Levinson (Cambridge University Press). 215–256.

Hagoort, P. (2013). MUC (Memory, Unification, Control) and beyond. *Front. Lang. Sci.* 4:416. doi: 10.3389/fpsyg.2013.00416

Hamano, S. (1998). *The Sound-Symbolic System of Japanese*. Tokyo: Center for the Study of Language and Information.

Henrich, J., Heine, S. J., and Norenzayan, A. (2010). The weirdest people in the world? *Behav. Brain Sci.* 33, 61–83. doi: 10.1017/S0140525X0999152X

Hickok, G., and Poeppel, D. (2007). The cortical organization of speech processing. *Nat. Rev. Neurosci.* 8, 393–402. doi: 10.1038/nrn2113

Hinton, L., Nichols, J., and Ohala, J. J. (1994). *Sound Symbolism*. Cambridge: Cambridge University Press.

Hinton, L., Nichols, J., and Ohala, J. J. (2006). *Sound Symbolism*. 2nd Edn. Cambridge: Cambridge University Press.

Hirata, S., Ukita, J., and Kita, S. (2011). Implicit phonetic symbolism in voicing of consonants and visual lightness using Garner's speeded classification task. *Percept. Mot. Skills* 113, 929–940. doi: 10.2466/15.21.28.PMS.113.6.929-940

Hockett, C. (1959). Animal "languages" and human language. *Hum. Biol.* 31, 32–39.

Hockett, C. (1960). The origin of speech. *Sci. Am.* 203, 89–97. doi: 10.1038/scientificamerican0960-88

Imai, M., and Kita, S. (2014). The sound symbolism bootstrapping hypothesis for language acquisition and language evolution. *Philos. Trans. R. Soc. B Biol. Sci.* 369, 20130298. doi: 10.1098/rstb.2013.0298

Imai, M., Kita, S., Nagumo, M., and Okada, H. (2008). Sound symbolism facilitates early verb learning. *Cognition* 109, 54–65. doi: 10.1016/j.cognition.2008. 07.015

Ishiguro, H. (1993). Onomatope no hassei. *Gengo* 22, 26–33.

Iwasaki, N., Vinson, D. P., and Vigliocco, G. (2007a). "How does it hurt, kiri-kiri or siku-siku? Japanese mimetic words of pain perceived by Japanese speakers and English speakers," in *Applying Theory and Research to Learning Japanese as a Foreign Language*, ed. M. Minami (Newcastle: Cambridge Scholars Publishing), 2–19.

Iwasaki, N., Vinson, D. P., and Vigliocco, G. (2007b). What do English speakers know about gera-gera and yota-yota? A cross-linguistic investigation of mimetic words for laughing and walking. *Jap. Lang. Educ. Around Globe* 17, 53–78.

Kanero, J., Imai, M., Okuda, J., Okada, H., and Matsuda, T. (2014). How sound symbolism is processed in the brain: a study on Japanese mimetic words. *PLoS ONE* 9:e97905. doi: 10.1371/journal.pone.0097905

Kantartzis, K., Imai, M., and Kita, S. (2011). Japanese sound-symbolism facilitates word learning in English-speaking children. *Cogn. Sci.* 35, 575–586. doi: 10.1111/j.1551-6709.2010.01169.x

Kita, S. (1997). Two-dimensional semantic analysis of Japanese mimetics. *Linguistics* 35, 379–415. doi: 10.1515/ling.1997.35.2.379

Klamer, M. (2002). Semantically motivated lexical patterns: a study of Dutch and Kambera expressives. *Language* 78, 258–286. doi: 10.1353/lan.2002.0101

Köhler, W. (1947). *Gestalt Psychology; an Introduction to New Concepts in Modern Psychology*, Rev. Edn. Oxford: Liveright.

Kovic, V., Plunkett, K., and Westermann, G. (2010). The shape of words in the brain. *Cognition* 114, 19–28. doi: 10.1016/j.cognition.2009.08.016

Kunihira, S. (1971). Effects of the expressive voice on phonetic symbolism. *J. Verbal Learning Verbal Behav.* 10, 427–429. doi: 10.1016/S0022-5371(71)80042-7

Kwon, N., and Round, E. R. (2014). Phonaesthemes in morphological theory. *Morphology* 25, 1–27. doi: 10.1007/s11525-014-9250-z

Laing, C. E. (2014). A phonological analysis of onomatopoeia in early word production. *First Lang.* 34, 387–405. doi: 10.1177/0142723714550110

Levelt, W. J. M., Roelofs, A., and Meyer, A. S. (1999). A theory of lexical access in speech production. *Behav. Brain Sci.* 22, 1–38. doi: 10.1017/S0140525X99001776

Lockwood, G., and Tuomainen, J. (2015). Ideophones in Japanese modulate the P2 and late positive complex responses. *Lang. Sci.* 6, 933. doi: 10.3389/fpsyg.2015.00933

Maglio, S. J., Rabaglia, C. D., Feder, M. A., Krehm, M., and Trope, Y. (2014). Vowel sounds in words affect mental construal and shift preferences for targets. *J. Exp. Psychol. Gen.* 143, 1082–1096. doi: 10.1037/a0035543

Maguire, M. J., Hirsh-Pasek, K., Golinkoff, R. M., Imai, M., Haryu, E., Vanegas, S., et al. (2010). A developmental shift from similar to language-specific strategies in verb acquisition: a comparison of English, Spanish, and Japanese. *Cognition* 114, 299–319. doi: 10.1016/j.cognition.2009.10.002

Majid, A. (2012). Current emotion research in the language sciences. *Emot. Rev.* 4, 432–443. doi: 10.1177/1754073912445827

Majid, A., and Burenhult, N. (2014). Odors are expressible in language, as long as you speak the right language. *Cognition* 130, 266–270. doi: 10.1016/j.cognition.2013.11.004

Malkiel, Y. (1994). "Regular sound development, phonosymbolic orchestration, disambiguation of homonyms," in *Sound Symbolism*, eds L. Hinton, J. Nichols, and J. J. Ohala (Cambridge: Cambridge University Press), 207–221.

Marks, L. E. (1978). *The Unity of the Senses: Interrelations Among the Modalities*. New York: London Academic Press.

Maurer, D., and Mondloch, C. J. (2004). "Neonatal synesthesia: a re-evaluation," in *Attention on Synesthesia: Cognition, Development and Neuroscience*, eds L. Robertson and N. Sagiv (Oxford: Oxford University Press), 193–213.

Maurer, D., Pathman, T., and Mondloch, C. J. (2006). The shape of boubas: sound-shape correspondences in toddlers and adults. *Dev. Sci.* 9, 316–322. doi: 10.1111/j.1467-7687.2006.00495.x

Meteyard, L., Stoppard, E., Snudden, D., Cappa, S. F., and Vigliocco, G. (2015). When semantics aids phonology: a processing advantage for iconic word forms in aphasia. *Neuropsychologia* doi: 10.1016/j.neuropsychologia.2015.01.042 [Epub ahead of print]

Monaghan, P., and Christiansen, M. H. (2006). "Why form-meaning mappings are not entirely arbitrary in language," in *Proceedings of the 28th Annual Conference of the Cognitive Science Society* (Mahwah, NJ: Lawrence Erlbaum), 1838–1843.

Monaghan, P., Christiansen, M. H., and Fitneva, S. A. (2011). The arbitrariness of the sign: learning advantages from the structure of the vocabulary. *J. Exp. Psychol. Gen.* 140, 325–347. doi: 10.1037/a0022924

Monaghan, P., Shillcock, R. C., Christiansen, M. H., and Kirby, S. (2014). How arbitrary is language? *Philos. Trans. R. Soc. B Biol. Sci.* 369, 20130299. doi: 10.1098/rstb.2013.0299

Moos, A., Smith, R., Miller, S. R., and Simmons, D. R. (2014). Cross-modal associations in synaesthesia: vowel colours in the ear of the beholder. *i-Perception* 5, 132–142. doi: 10.1068/i0626

Mitterer, H., Schuerman, W., Reinisch, E., Tufvesson, S. and Dingemanse, M. (2012). "The limited power of sound symbolism," *Proceedings of the 16th Annual Conference on Architectures and Mechanisms for Language Processing*. Riva des Garda, Italy, 27.

Newman, S. S. (1933). Further experiments in phonetic symbolism. *Am. J. Psychol.* 45, 53. doi: 10.2307/1414186

Newmeyer, F. J. (1992). Iconicity and generative grammar. *Language* 68, 756. doi: 10.2307/416852

Nielsen, A., and Rendall, D. (2011). The sound of round: evaluating the sound-symbolic role of consonants in the classic Takete-Maluma phenomenon. *Can. J. Exp. Psychol.* 65, 115–124. doi: 10.1037/a0022268

Nielsen, A., and Rendall, D. (2012). The source and magnitude of sound-symbolic biases in processing artificial word material and their implications for language learning and transmission. *Lang. Cogn.* 4, 115–125. doi: 10.1515/langcog-2012-0007

Nielsen, A., and Rendall, D. (2013). Parsing the role of consonants versus vowels in the classic Takete-Maluma phenomenon. *Can. J. Exp. Psychol.* 67, 153–163. doi: 10.1037/a0030553

Nuckolls, J. B. (1999). The case for sound symbolism. *Ann. Rev. Anthropol.* 28, 225–252. doi: 10.1146/annurev.anthro.28.1.225

Nygaard, L. C., Cook, A. E., and Namy, L. L. (2009a). Sound to meaning correspondences facilitate word learning. *Cognition* 112, 181–186. doi: 10.1016/j.cognition.2009.04.001

Nygaard, L. C., Herold, D. S., and Namy, L. L. (2009b). The semantics of prosody: acoustic and perceptual evidence of prosodic correlates to word meaning. *Cogn. Sci.* 33, 127–146. doi: 10.1111/j.1551-6709.2008.01007.x

Occelli, V., Esposito, G., Venuti, P., Arduino, G. M., and Zampini, M. (2013). The takete-maluma phenomenon in autism spectrum disorders. *Perception* 42, 233–241. doi: 10.1068/p7357

Oda, H. (2000). *An Embodied Semantic Mechanism for Mimetic Words in Japanese.* Bloomington: Indiana University.

Ohtake, Y., and Haryu, E. (2013). Investigation of the process underpinning vowel-size correspondence. *Jap. Psychol. Res.* 55, 390–399. doi: 10.1111/jpr.12029

Osaka, N. (2009). Walk-related mimic word activates the extrastriate visual cortex in the human brain: an fMRI study. *Behav. Brain Res.* 198, 186–189. doi: 10.1016/j.bbr.2008.10.042

Osaka, N. (2011). Ideomotor response and the neural representation of implied crying in the human brain: an fMRI study using onomatopoeia1. *Jap. Psychol. Res.* 53, 372–378. doi: 10.1111/j.1468-5884.2011.00489.x

Osaka, N., and Osaka, M. (2005). Striatal reward areas activated by implicit laughter induced by mimic words in humans: a functional magnetic resonance imaging study. *Neuroimage* 16, 1621–1624. doi: 10.1097/01.wnr.0000181581.18636.a7

Osaka, N., and Osaka, M. (2009). Gaze-related mimic word activates the frontal eye field and related network in the human brain: an fMRI study. *Neurosci. Lett.* 461, 65–68. doi: 10.1016/j.neulet.2009.06.023

Osaka, N., Osaka, M., Kondo, H., Morishita, M., Fukuyama, H., and Shibasaki, H. (2003). An emotion-based facial expression word activates laughter module in the human brain: a functional magnetic resonance imaging study. *Neurosci. Lett.* 340, 127–130. doi: 10.1016/S0304-3940(03)00093-4

Osaka, N., Osaka, M., Morishita, M., Kondo, H., and Fukuyama, H. (2004). A word expressing affective pain activates the anterior cingulate cortex in the human brain: an fMRI study. *Behav. Brain Res.* 153, 123–127. doi: 10.1016/j.bbr.2003.11.013

Ozturk, O., Krehm, M., and Vouloumanos, A. (2013). Sound symbolism in infancy: evidence for sound-shape cross-modal correspondences in 4-month-olds. *J. Exp. Child Psychol.* 114, 173–186. doi: 10.1016/j.jecp.2012.05.004

Perniss, P., Thompson, R. L., and Vigliocco, G. (2010). Iconicity as a general property of language: evidence from spoken and signed languages. *Front. Psychol.* 1:227. doi: 10.3389/fpsyg.2010.00227

Perniss, P., and Vigliocco, G. (2014). The bridge of iconicity: from a world of experience to the experience of language. *Philos. Trans. R. Soc. B Biol. Sci.* 369, 20130300. doi: 10.1098/rstb.2013.0300

Ramachandran, V. S., and Hubbard, E. M. (2001). Synaesthesia—a window into perception, thought and language. *J. Conscious. Stud.* 8, 3–34.

Revill, K. P., Namy, L. L., DeFife, L. C., and Nygaard, L. C. (2014). Cross-linguistic sound symbolism and crossmodal correspondence: evidence from fMRI and DTI. *Brain Lang.* 128, 18–24. doi: 10.1016/j.bandl.2013.11.002

Sapir, E. (1929). A study in phonetic symbolism. *J. Exp. Psychol.* 12, 225–239. doi: 10.1037/h0070931

Schmidtke, D. S., Conrad, M., and Jacobs, A. M. (2014). Phonological iconicity. *Lang. Sci.* 5, 80. doi: 10.3389/fpsyg.2014.00080

Sedley, D. N. (2003). *Plato's Cratylus.* Cambridge: Cambridge University Press.

Shin, E., and Kim, C.-Y. (2014). Both "나" and "조" are yellow: cross-linguistic investigation in search of the determinants of synesthetic color. *Neuropsychologia* 65, 25–36. doi: 10.1016/j.neuropsychologia.2014.09.032

Simner, J., Cuskley, C., and Kirby, S. (2010). What sound does that taste? Cross-modal mappings across gustation and audition. *Perception* 39, 553–569. doi: 10.1068/p6591

Spector, F., and Maurer, D. (2013). Early sound symbolism for vowel sounds. *i-Perception* 4, 239–241. doi: 10.1068/i0535

Thompson, P. (2013). *Phonetic Symbolism for Size, Shape, and Motion.* Ph.D. thesis, Warwick: University of Warwick.

Thompson, P., and Estes, Z. (2011). Sound symbolic naming of novel objects is a graded function. *Q. J. Exp. Psychol.* 64, 2392–2404. doi: 10.1080/17470218.2011.605898

Voeltz, F. K. E., and Kilian-Hatz, C. (2001). *Ideophones.* Amsterdam: John Benjamins Publishing.

Von Humboldt, W. (1836). *On Language: On the Diversity of Human Language Construction and Its Influence on the Mental Development of the Human Species.* ed. M. Losonsky (Cambridge: Cambridge University Press).

Waugh, L. R. (1994). Degrees of iconicity in the lexicon. *J. Pragmat.* 22, 55–70. doi: 10.1016/0378-2166(94)90056-6

Yoshida, H. (2012). A cross-linguistic study of sound symbolism in children's verb learning. *J. Cogn. Dev.* 13, 232–265. doi: 10.1080/15248372.2011.573515

Zwaan, R. (2004). The immersed experiencer: toward an embodied theory of language comprehension. *Psychol. Learn. Motiv.* 44, 35–62. doi: 10.1016/S0079-7421(03)44002-4

Conflict of Interest Statement: The authors declare that the research was conducted in the absence of any commercial or financial relationships that could be construed as a potential conflict of interest.

Drugs As Instruments: Describing and Testing a Behavioral Approach to the Study of Neuroenhancement

Ralf Brand[1]*, Wanja Wolff[2] and Matthias Ziegler[3]

[1] Sport and Exercise Psychology, University of Potsdam, Potsdam, Germany, [2] Department of Sport Science, Sport Psychology, University of Konstanz, Konstanz, Germany, [3] Department of Psychology, Psychological Diagnostics, Humboldt Universität zu Berlin, Berlin, Germany

Edited by:
Roger Lister Kneebone,
Imperial College London, UK

Reviewed by:
Con Stough,
Swinburne University of Technology,
Australia
Alexandra Cope,
University of Leeds, UK

*Correspondence:
Ralf Brand
ralf.brand@uni-potsdam.de

Specialty section:
This article was submitted to
Performance Science,
a section of the journal
Frontiers in Psychology

Neuroenhancement (NE) is the non-medical use of psychoactive substances to produce a subjective enhancement in psychological functioning and experience. So far empirical investigations of individuals' motivation for NE however have been hampered by the lack of theoretical foundation. This study aimed to apply drug instrumentalization theory to user motivation for NE. We argue that NE should be defined and analyzed from a behavioral perspective rather than in terms of the characteristics of substances used for NE. In the empirical study we explored user behavior by analyzing relationships between drug options (use over-the-counter products, prescription drugs, illicit drugs) and postulated drug instrumentalization goals (e.g., improved cognitive performance, counteracting fatigue, improved social interaction). Questionnaire data from 1438 university students were subjected to exploratory and confirmatory factor analysis to address the question of whether analysis of drug instrumentalization should be based on the assumption that users are aiming to achieve a certain goal and choose their drug accordingly or whether NE behavior is more strongly rooted in a decision to try or use a certain drug option. We used factor mixture modeling to explore whether users could be separated into qualitatively different groups defined by a shared "goal × drug option" configuration. Our results indicate, first, that individuals' decisions about NE are eventually based on personal attitude to drug options (e.g., willingness to use an over-the-counter product but not to abuse prescription drugs) rather than motivated by desire to achieve a specific goal (e.g., fighting tiredness) for which different drug options might be tried. Second, data analyses suggested two qualitatively different classes of users. Both predominantly used over-the-counter products, but "neuroenhancers" might be characterized by a higher propensity to instrumentalize over-the-counter products for virtually all investigated goals whereas "fatigue-fighters" might be inclined to use over-the-counter products exclusively to fight fatigue. We believe that psychological investigations like these are essential, especially for designing programs to prevent risky behavior.

Keywords: psychoactive drugs, non-addictive behavior, cognitive enhancement, drug instrumentalization, user types

INTRODUCTION

Use of psychoactive drugs is common in most societies. Use of caffeine, alcohol, and nicotine is particularly widespread; illicit drugs such as cocaine or marijuana are consumed less frequently (Kandel et al., 1997). There is disproportionate growth in medically unsupervised use (i.e., abuse) of prescription drugs, particularly opioids and stimulants, especially among adolescents and young adults (Johnston et al., 2010; United Nations, 2011).

Psychological research on motivations for using psychoactive drugs is often concerned with addiction and theories of drug use often focus on addiction (e.g., O'Brien et al., 1992; Koob and LeMoal, 1997; Baker et al., 2004). Given the known costs of addiction, both for the individual and for society, it is clearly an important research target. Many drug users should not be considered addicted however; for example 95% of alcohol consumers (Anderson and Baumberg, 2006), around 92% of nicotine users (Baumeister et al., 2008) and 91% of caffeine users (Meredith et al., 2013) should not be considered addicted[1]. It is likely that similar figures apply to abuse of prescription drugs (United Nations, 2011).

The starting point for our investigation was the growing number of research articles on university students' use of psychoactive pharmacological products for the purpose of enhancing cognitive performance. It has been reported that 6-8% of university students in Germany (Middendorff et al., 2015) and perhaps the same or an even higher proportion in the United States (Smith and Farah, 2011, report a rather uninformative guestimate of 2–50%) have abused drugs such as Modafinil (a wakefulness-promoting drug usually prescribed to treat shift-work sleep disorder and narcolepsy) for this purpose. Recently the presumed motivation for such drug use has prompted research on the cognitive effects of pharmaceutical drugs (e.g., benchmarking effect sizes of different dopaminergics; Fond et al., 2015) as well as several nutraceuticals (e.g., Ginseng and Bacopa benchmarked against Modafinil; Neale et al., 2013) and the ethics of usage (e.g., whether safe pharmacological enhancement could help resolve societal inequalities; Glannon, 2015). Research on students' motivation to try and perhaps subsequently persist with using such performance enhancing substances is much less elaborated. This research aimed to investigate substance users' motivated behavior systematically, i.e., from a psychological perspective.

Drug Instrumentalization Theory

Drug instrumentalization theory (DI theory; Müller and Schumann, 2011a,b) suggests that non-addictive drug use can be explained in functional terms, as a purposeful, goal-directed process. For example the wakefulness-promoting prescription drug Modafinil might be used to enhance academic performance. It is a matter of fact, however, that some students prefer to use caffeinated, non-prescription products for this purpose (Franke et al., 2011). Others might know that a strong cup of filter coffee (Walsh et al., 1990) is at least as effective a stimulant as many caffeinated over-the-counter products and perhaps more so, and prefer this option. DI theory suggests that the starting point for explaining the non-addictive use of drugs should be to consider the purpose for which they are taken; before considering the specific characteristics of the various substances that could be used for that purpose. DI theory proposes a non-exhaustive list of goals relevant to instrumental drug use; these goals are presented in **Table 1** along with examples from the domains discussed here and in the following sections.

Another claim of DI theory is that repeated, non-addictive drug use should be modeled as a two-step process: "(1) the seeking and consumption of a psychoactive drug in order to change the present mental state into a previously learned mental state, which then allows for (2) better performance of other, previously established behaviors and better goal achievement" (Müller and Schumann, 2011a, p. 295). Whilst we largely endorse the proposed first step, we think that from a psychological perspective the second step needs readjustment with regard to the qualifier "better" that implies factual improvement in performance and goal achievement.

Subjective expectations are important determinants of human behavior (e.g., Armitage and Conner, 2001). We argue that the presumed functions of a substance are an essential factor in motivation and perhaps even more important than the chosen substance's subsequent effects on performance (Wolff and Brand, 2013). This behavioral approach (Wolff and Brand, 2013; Wolff et al., 2014; Brand and Koch, 2016) differs from more substance-based approaches adopted by other authors (e.g., Franke et al., 2014; Maier and Schaub, 2015). It is our view that—in the terminology of learning theory—drug use is reinforced by the *subjective state* that this behavior, which was intended as a means to an end, produces. This reinforcement is moderated by the physiological and other observable effects of the drug which thus influence subsequent usage; a drug which proves more effective in producing the desired goal might come to be used more frequently.

This account implies, however, that objectively "better" performance and goal achievement is not a necessary consequence of instrumental drug use. We therefore suggest modifying the proposed claim about how individuals instrumentalize drugs to: (1) the seeking and consumption of a potentially psychoactive drug with the aim of reinstating a previously learned mental state that allows for (2) subjectively enhanced goal achievement.

Instrumental Use of Psychoactive Drugs to Enhance Cognitive Performance: One Aspect of Neuroenhancement

One aim of this article is to embed the active debate on what has been called pharmacological "cognitive enhancement" (e.g., Hildt and Franke, 2013) in the broader context of DI theory's (Müller

---

[1] According to ICD criteria addiction (termed dependence syndrome by the WHO) is a "cluster of physiological, behavioral, and cognitive phenomena in which the use of substances takes on a much higher priority for a given individual than other behaviors that once had greater value. A central descriptive characteristic of the dependence syndrome is the desire to take the psychoactive drugs. There may be evidence that return to substance use after a period of abstinence leads to a more rapid reappearance of other features of the syndrome than occurs with nondependent individuals" (cited from "World Health Organization, Management of substance abuse, Dependence syndrome," last modified 2016, http://www.who.int/substance_abuse/terminology/definition1/en/).

TABLE 1 | Instrumentalization goals as proposed by DI theory (Müller and Schumann, 2011a,b) with behavioral examples.

No.	Instrumentalization goal	Label[a]	Behavioral example[b]
[1]	Improved cognitive performance	Cognitive performance	Using methylphenidate to feel more concentrated and alert
[2]	Counteracting fatigue	Fatigue	Using caffeine to counteract fatigue
[3]	Improved social interaction	Social interaction	Using alcohol or other drugs at parties to be more talkative, disinhibited, and self-confident
[4]	Facilitated sexual behavior	Sexual behavior	Using drugs like alcohol or cocaine to increase the likelihood of and pleasure during sexual intercourse
[5]	Facilitated recovery from psychological stress	Stress recovery	Using cannabis to recover from a stressful day at work
[6]	Coping with psychological stress	Stress coping	Using alcohol to reduce perceived stress level before an important meeting
[7]	Euphoria and hedonia	Euphoria	Using cannabis, alcohol, or other to induce intense well-being and positive feelings
[8]	Self-medication for mental problems	Self-medication	Using antidepressants, cannabis or alcohol to reduce depressive symptoms, regain control over one's mental state, and enhance functioning in everyday life
[9]	Sensory curiosity and facilitating spiritual and religious activities	Sensory curiosity	Using hallucinogenic drugs (e.g., MDMA) to facilitate spiritual experiences

[a] Short labels for the goal detailed in the previous column.
[b] This list of examples is illustrative rather than exhaustive.

and Schumann, 2011a,b) framework theory for non-addictive psychoactive drug consumption.

Enhancements can be tried with the aim of enhancing cognitive functioning (e.g., working memory, task flexibility) and enabling increased effort (e.g., in order to stay awake and study longer; see Zelli et al., 2015), aims which might be regarded as analogous to two of the DI theory instrumentalization goals, "improved cognitive performance" and "counteracting fatigue." One might try to attain these goals by using a suitable over-the-counter product, e.g., caffeine pills, herbal substances; however some people regard over-the-counter medication as being fine for mild or occasional symptoms but less suited to treatment of severe symptoms, for which more potent drugs are necessary (United Nations, 2011). These individuals might also believe that recognized medical drugs are safer than illicit drugs, even when used unsupervised and hence although they would be unwilling to try the illegal drug "speed" (amphetamine), they might decide to try Modafinil (a prescription drug) in an attempt to enhance cognitive performance or counteract fatigue.

It is obvious from this example that diverse substances can be used in pursuit of the same goal (equifinality). It is also possible to use a single drug as an instrument for attaining several different goals (multifinality); for example cocaine users report using this illicit substance to enhance cognitive performance, as well as to facilitate social interactions and induce euphoria (Boys et al., 2001). Research focused on the use or abuse of pharmacological products to enhance cognitive performance has so far largely neglected this second aspect, multifinality, of instrumental drug use (e.g., Mazanov et al., 2013; Franke et al., 2014; Sattler et al., 2014; Wolff et al., 2014).

This point, the widely neglected aspect of multifinality in the respective studies, calls into question current usage of the terms "cognitive enhancement." It unjustifiably narrows the phenomenon under investigation. Similar criticisms have been made by researchers who note that many of the substances

used for "cognitive enhancement" are not very effective for this purpose (Zohny, 2015). We propose using the umbrella term *neuroenhancement* (*NE*) instead[2]. It is important to emphasize our suggestion that using this term in the proposed way thus refers to a *behavior* that is *explicitly connected* with a *specific goal*: We define this behavior, NE, as the non-medical use of psychoactive substances (and technology; e.g., Clark and Parasuraman, 2014) for the purpose of producing a subjective enhancement in psychological functioning and experience.

It is important to note that in pursuit of, for example, enhanced cognitive performance, individuals may instrumentalize any substance or technology which they think might help them to reach their goal. The attribution of relevant efficacy to the substance or technology is sufficient to qualify their behavior as attempted NE behavior and to investigate this behavior's motivational roots (Wolff and Brand, 2013).

This Study

Building upon the above-described argument, in the first stage of our empirical study we explored user behavior by analyzing patterns of relationships between chosen drug options ("over-the-counter products," "prescription drugs," and "illicit drugs"; e.g., Franke et al., 2014) and instrumental goals ("better cognitive performance and reduced fatigue," "better social interaction," "facilitation of sexual behavior," "enhanced recovery from and coping with psychological stress," "euphoria and hedonia," "more attractive physical appearance," "self-medication for mental problems," "sensory curiosity and facilitation of spiritual and religious activities"; Müller and Schumann, 2011a). We aimed to find and then confirm empirical patterns that would help us to address the question of whether NE behavior should be

---

[2] Although there is no evidence that (all) eligible substances actually enhance neural activity, the umbrella term's prefix "neuro-" seems to be acceptable here because of its widespread and established use in social science research.

considered a goal-directed behavior in which the choice of drug is predicated on its presumed functionality in relation to that goal or whether the choice of a drug option (e.g., an over-the-counter product but not an illicit drug) is primarily driven by other factors.

The second stage of our analysis explored whether users could be segregated into qualitatively different groups on the basis of the combination of the psychological variable "goal" and the attribute "drug option" (they were classified in these terms in the first stage). We did this because inter-individual differences are important when it comes to monitoring and preventing risky behaviors (cf. Kreuter and Wray, 2003; Rimer and Kreuter, 2006).

In summary, we hoped to make a theoretically informed contribution to the psychological literature which would help to define the boundaries of NE research and provide empirical evidence which could be used to inform programs targeting the misuse of problematic substances (e.g., Wilens et al., 2008).

METHODS

Study Sample

The focus here was on university students. A non-exhaustive manual search of the internet resources of public and private German, Swiss and Austrian universities yielded the email addresses of 853 student associations for study programs in Biology, Computer Science, Economics, Educational Sciences, English and German language and literature studies, Electrical Engineering, Health Sciences, Law, Mathematics, Medical Sciences, Physics and Psychology. These student associations were contacted and asked to distribute the link to our online questionnaire using their student mailing lists. We are unable to assess how many student associations from which universities actually complied with this request.

Participation was voluntary and no compensation was offered for participation. Participants were informed that they would be able to complete the questionnaire anonymously (i.e., without giving their name or contact address). They were also informed in advance that they could decide to stop working through the questionnaire at any time without disadvantaging themselves in any way and that their answers would not be stored unless they clicked the "send data" button at the end of the questionnaire. The study was carried out in accordance with recommendations of the ethical committee of the University of Potsdam.

In total, 2771 students began working through the questionnaire. Around 50% ($n = 1438$) completed it and sent us their answers. The mean age of this group of responders was 23.95 ± 5.43 years; 950 (66%) were women. We did not collect data on the study programs in which these participants were enrolled.

Measures

Drug instrumentalization was assessed separately for each goal. Participants were first asked if they had ever used any substance to achieve a given goal. Participants then responded to three dichotomous (yes/no) items relating to whether they had already used an over-the-counter product, a prescription drug or an illicit drug in pursuit of this goal. We decided to assess the

goal "enhancement or rebuilding of cognitive performance" with two questions (one for the "enhancement of..." and one for the "rebuilding of..." aspect) as these statements reflect distinct processes; the goal "facilitated recovery from and coping with psychological stress" was treated similarly. Participants thus indicated their pattern of behavior with respect to 27 goal × drug option combinations. In the remainder of the article we will refer to this set of items as the DI questionnaire.

Statistical Analyses

All statistical analyses were conducted using the statistical programs R (R Development Core Team, 2013) and MPlus 7 (Muthén and Muthén, 2013). The factorial structure of drug instrumentalization as assessed by the DI questionnaire (instrumentalization goals × drug option) was explored using exploratory factor analysis (EFA; psych package; Revelle, 2014) and confirmed using confirmatory factor analysis (CFA; lavaan package, Rossel, 2012). The dataset was randomly split in half to allow for independent EFA and CFA. Model tests were done according to the guidelines of Beauducel and Wittmann (2005), Hu and Bentler (1999), and Heene et al. (2011). We looked at the global model test as well as the fit indices $RMSEA$ (< 0.05), $SRMR$ (< 0.08), and CFI ($= 0.95$). A robust ML estimator was used to correct for violations of multivariate normal distribution. Missing data were dealt with using the FIML method. After this the complete dataset was subjected to factor mixture model (FMM) analysis to determine whether the latent structure was person-homogeneous, in other words to find qualitatively different groups of users. FMMs have several advantages over traditional methods of latent class identification. Specifically, FMMs allow drug instrumentalization to be modeled as an individual difference variable within a CFA model (e.g., Leite and Cooper, 2010). FMMs can be used for the analysis of data with underlying continuous constructs whilst simultaneously modeling population heterogeneity as they incorporate categorical and continuous latent variables (Lubke and Muthen, 2005, 2007). The procedure we followed in calculating and reporting our FMM analysis has been described in more detail elsewhere (Ziegler et al., 2015).

RESULTS

Descriptive Statistics

Descriptive statistics for all investigated variants of drug instrumentalization are visualized as a heat map in **Figure 1**. First, descriptive statistics indicated that all investigated goals were instrumentalized by at least some of the sample (the goal instrumentalized by the smallest proportion was "improving physical appearance": 18.6%). Second, answers indicated that in this sample all three drug options were employed in pursuit of the goals we investigated. Third, there was large variation between the frequencies with which specific "goal × drug option" configurations appeared; for example 87.2% of our participants reported that they had used over-the-counter products to fight fatigue but only 0.6% reported that they had used prescription drugs to facilitate sexual encounters.

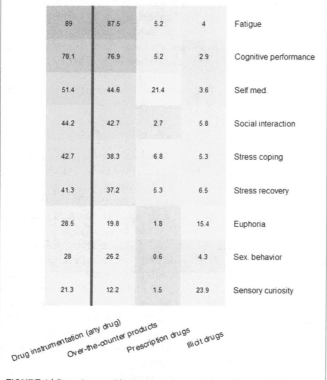

FIGURE 1 | Prevalence of instrumental use of drugs in pursuit of each goal irrespective of drug option (left column) and as a function of the three drug options (three right columns). Multiple positive responses were possible and therefore values in the colored columns do not add up to the values presented in the left column.

TABLE 2 | The exploratory three-factor model for responses to the DI questionnaire.

Drug-types × DI goals	Factor 1	Factor 2	Factor 3	h^2	u^2
ILLICIT DRUGS					
... × Fatigue	0.70	0.24	−0.06	0.54	0.46
... × Stress coping	0.57	0.03	0.08	0.33	0.67
... × Stress recovery	0.60	0.08	−0.01	0.36	0.64
... × Cognitive performance	0.61	0.24	−0.03	0.43	0.57
... × Euphoria	0.65	−0.03	0.16	0.45	0.55
... × Sex. behavior	0.47	0.17	0.04	0.25	0.75
... × Self-med	0.44	0.02	0.08	0.20	0.80
... × Social interaction	0.54	0.07	0.16	0.32	0.68
... × Sensory curiosity	0.54	0.02	0.19	0.33	0.67
PRESCRIPTION DRUGS					
... × Euphoria	0.31	0.16	0.09	0.13	0.87
... × Sensory curiosity	0.38	0.04	0.15	0.17	0.83
... × Stress coping	0.09	0.80	0.07	0.66	0.34
... × Fatigue	0.24	0.61	−0.02	0.43	0.57
... × Cognitive performance	0.28	0.60	0.00	0.44	0.56
... × Social interaction	0.13	0.53	0.00	0.30	0.70
... × Stress recovery	0.05	0.45	0.13	0.22	0.78
... × Self-med.	0.08	0.38	0.14	0.17	0.83
... × Sex. behavior	0.24	0.31	0.02	0.15	0.85
OVER-THE-COUNTER SUBSTANCES					
... × Sensory curiosity	0.34	−0.04	0.33	0.22	0.78
... × Euphoria	0.24	−0.03	0.37	0.19	0.81
... × Stress coping	0.12	0.11	0.47	0.24	0.76
... × Stress recovery	0.14	0.11	0.39	0.19	0.81
... × Social interaction	0.21	0.07	0.38	0.19	0.81
... × Self-med.	−0.03	0.08	0.37	0.14	0.86
... × Sex. behavior	0.20	0.01	0.30	0.13	0.87
... × Fatigue	0.03	−0.05	0.46	0.21	0.79
... × Cognitive performance	0.03	0.00	0.47	0.22	0.78

Factor Analyses

Parallel analysis (Horn, 1965) suggested that seven factors could be extracted. The minimum average partial test (Velicer, 1976) suggested a three factor solution. To choose a solution the two- to seven-factor solutions were extracted using principal axis factoring and geominT rotation with the R package psych (Revelle, 2014). The three-factor solution was the most plausible, reflecting patterns held together by the three drug options "over-the-counter products," "prescription drugs," and "illicit drugs." Factor loadings for this solution are given in **Table 2**. Consequently, in the subsequent CFA we tested this model, labeling the three factors "over-the-counter DI," "prescription DI," and "illicit DI." In the first step we tested the three measurement models for each factor separately, following advice by Ziegler and Hagemann (2015) according to which misfit within single measurement models might be harder to detect in the complete model otherwise. In each factor measurement model the nine items relating to whether a given drug option had been used to achieve specific goals were included in the analyses. The items and loadings for each factor measurement model are shown in **Table 3**. Analyses of model fit indicated that in all three cases measurement models described the data well (**Table 3**). We then added the same correlated residuals to all the measurement models ("fatigue" with "cognitive performance"; "euphoria" with "sensory curiosity") and ran a final analysis to assess the fit of the overall model (**Figure 2**). In order to achieve acceptable model fit three correlated error terms had to be included ("self-medication using prescription drugs" with "self-medication using over-the-counter drugs"; "sensory curiosity using illicit drugs" with both "sensory curiosity using of over-the-counter drugs" and "sensory curiosity using prescription drugs"). The fit indices for the complete model were $\chi^2 = 759.44$, $df = 312$, $p < 0.001$; $CFI = 0.90$; $RMSEA = 0.03$; $SRMR = 0.06$. This analysis indicated that the 27-item DI questionnaire was best be described by three drug option factors, each consisting of nine items with an identical format reflecting nine different aspects of drug instrumentalization and hence that drug instrumentalization behavior is primarily accounted for by the drug option rather than by specific instrumental goals.

Factor Mixture Models

Building on differentiation of our three latent factors of drug instrumentalization, the second goal was to investigate whether latent variables differentiating between types of instrumental drug users could be identified. Simply put, we were interested

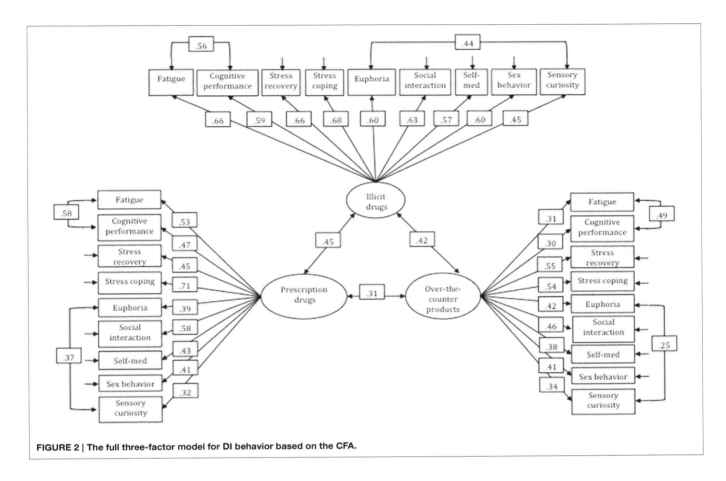

FIGURE 2 | The full three-factor model for DI behavior based on the CFA.

in whether qualitatively different classes of functional drug use could be identified with respect to each of the three drug options. Separate FMMs consisting of the nine items relating to use of each drug option (over-the-counter products; prescription drugs, illicit drugs) for DI were tested. Loadings on the latent usage variable were assumed to be equal for all classes in order to ensure that a similar latent variable was measured (factorial invariance). A robust maximum likelihood estimator was used to address the non-normality of the data. As to the acceptable model fits of the measurement models underlying these analyses (see **Table 3**) problems due to the exploitation of residual patterns are unlikely (Bauer and Curran, 2004). There was marginal evidence for the validity of a two-class solution, and only in the case of the over-the-counter DI factor (Lo-Mendel-Rubin test: $p = 0.058$; adjusted Lo-Mendel-Rubin test: $p = 0.059$)[3]. This suggests that we have two qualitatively different classes of users within the latent factor of over-the-counter products in our data. The values of the intercepts revealed that the average responses of the classes were different for almost all items. The first class (87.5% of the participants in our sample) could be described as having a higher

propensity to use over-the-counter products in pursuit of diverse goals (**Table 4**); we termed this class of users "neuroenhancers." The second class of users had a generally lower propensity to use over-the-counter products (as indicated by the much lower intercept values in **Table 4**) and used over-the-counter products almost exclusively to fight fatigue; this class of users was termed "fatigue-fighters."

DISCUSSION

The aim of this study was to develop a theoretical conception of NE behavior that would account for original empirical data on drug instrumentalization among university students. The patterns of participants' responses to the DI questionnaire suggested that NE behavior is probably based on a primary decision about usage of a class of drugs (drug option).

In other words the EFA and CFA suggested that rather than identifying a goal or motivation (e.g., "I want to fight tiredness") and then instrumentally using the different drug options that might enable them to achieve this goal (e.g., to identify the most effective one) individuals seem to instrumentally use a given drug option and then accept the constraints this places on goal attainment (e.g., "I am willing to use over-the-counter products but not to abuse prescription drugs even if this limits how effectively I can fight my tiredness").

---

[3] We compared this two-class solution with a 1-class and a 3-class solution on the basis of a sample-size adjusted BIC. The lowest value occurred for the 2-class solution (11453.57), both other solutions were close together (1-class: 13141.95; 3-class: 13223.84). The 3-class solution had p-values of 0.23 for both Lo-Mendel tests. Taken together these tests support the validity of the 2-class solution.

TABLE 3 | Factor loadings for three CFA measurement models and fit indices for these models.

	Latent factor		
	Over-the-counter substances	Prescription drugs	Illicit drugs
STANDARDIZED FACTOR LOADINGS			
Fatigue	0.31*	0.48*	0.65*
Cognitive performance	0.30*	0.45*	0.62*
Stress recovery	0.57*	0.44*	0.62*
Stress coping	0.53*	0.68*	0.68*
Euphoria	0.46*	0.46*	0.61*
Social interaction	0.51*	0.62*	0.59*
Self-med.	0.39*	0.43*	0.55*
Sex. behavior	0.41*	0.39*	0.52*
Sensory curiosity	0.36*	0.35*	0.46*
FIT INDICES			
χ^2 (df)	80.44* (25)	166.22* (25)	68.33* (25)
CFI	0.93	0.92	0.98
RMSEA	0.056	0.087	0.05
SRMR	0.041	0.047	0.028

*$p < 0.05$.

TABLE 4 | Descriptive statistics for class solutions of the factor mixture models.

	Class I		Class II	
DI-Goals	Intercept*	S.E	Intercept*	S.E
Social interaction	0.432	0.014	0.350	0.050
Sex. behavior	0.269	0.013	0.183	0.042
Cognitive performance	0.879	0.009	−0.017	0.020
Fatigue	0.854	0.010	0.981	0.022
Stress coping	0.408	0.014	0.161	0.052
Stress recovery	0.383	0.014	0.244	0.059
Self-med.	0.457	0.014	0.333	0.052
Sensory curiosity	0.123	0.009	0.092	0.026
Euphoria	0.193	0.011	0.193	0.011

*$p < 0.001$.

Results from the FMM analysis can tentatively be interpreted as supporting the notion of two qualitatively different classes of users. Both of them predominantly used over-the-counter products; they were termed "neuroenhancers" and "fatigue-fighters." "Neuroenhancers" were characterized by a higher propensity to instrumentally use over-the-counter products for virtually all the goals specified in DI theory (improving cognitive performance and overcoming fatigue were endorsed with the largest propensity; **Table 4**). In contrast "fatigue-fighters" seemed to instrumentalize over-the-counter products solely for fighting fatigue. No comparable qualitative difference in patterns of usage was found among users of prescription drugs and illicit drugs.

DI theory provided the framework for this research. We started by asking participants about their instrumental use of over-the-counter products and their abuse of prescription and illicit drugs for the goals specified in DI theory. We did not ask about any other kind of drug use. In our sample of university students we found evidence that in the group of participants all drug options were used for all the proposed goals. In our view this finding corroborates one of the central claims of DI theory, namely that individuals' instrumental use of drugs cannot be adequately explained—or investigated—without addressing the specific goal(s) which motivated this use. Although users might respond positively when asked if they have used a given drug to enhance their cognitive performance, other co-existent goals might better account for their behavior. Studies of people's motivations or reasons for using drugs that they believe have the potential to enhance cognitive performance should therefore not be limited to consideration of this particular goal. This study revealed that *multifinality*, i.e., using one instrument to pursue several goals, is an important pattern of behavior in the context of use of psychoactive substances to produce a subjective enhancement in psychological functioning and experience, i.e., neuroenhancement.

Discussion of Factor Analyses Results

Factor analyses revealed the existence of three drug option-related factors, over-the-counter product DI, prescription drug DI, and illicit drug DI, but no goal-related factors. The various instrumentalization goals appeared in each of the three drug option factors instead. This indicates that participants' primary decision related to the drug option(s) they were willing to use instrumentally. In practice this meant that if, for example, an individual resorted to using an over-the-counter product in an attempt to enhance cognitive performance then he or she was more likely to use over-the-counter products in pursuit of some other goal. An alternative pattern of results would have been that the primary decision was about which goal to pursue via use of drugs and secondarily what drug option might be the most effective tool for achieving that goal. Such a pattern would have been reflected in a set of factors representing different instrumentalization goals (or patterns of goals). A third possibility is that there might have been systematic links between drug options and specific goals, e.g., the use of over-the-counter products for facilitation of social interaction and using prescription drugs for facilitating sexual encounters. We did not observe this kind of goal-dependent switching between drug options in our sample. Our preliminary, cautious interpretation of these results, in terms of instrumental (i.e., means-end) drug use, is that individuals use drugs as instruments for pursuing a variety of goals, but that willingness to instrumentalize a drug option takes priority over attainment of a specific goal in the decision-making process. Although we found marked differences in the frequency with which specific drug options were chosen as tools for pursuing specific goals on a descriptive level, factor analyses revealed that there was more consistency in the type of instrument an individual chose, irrespective of goal. It is possible that individuals' attributions of functionality are general to a drug option and aligned with their usage behavior, for example, an individual who believes that only prescription drugs are both powerful and safe enough to allow to enable one to attain one's objectives might use methylphenidate (instead of a simple energy drink) to enhance his or her concentration and would similarly choose to use prescription antidepressants (rather than

Ginkgo biloba products) to enhance his or her subjective quality of life.

Generally speaking, one result is that the observed variance-covariance matrix was best explained by three correlated factors representing the three different drug options. The more inclined an individual is to use a given drug option for one specific goal, the more likely it is that he or she will choose the same option as an aid to attaining other goals. In contrast, a willingness to use one option as an instrument for attaining a specific goal, e.g., an over-the-counter product to facilitate sexual behavior, does not imply a similar willingness to use other options, e.g., illicit drugs, in pursuit of that goal.

Discussion of Factor Mixture Modeling Results

We found some support for the idea of two different user classes for over-the-counter products. The two classes could be described in terms of "neuroenhancers" and "fatigue-fighters." The possible existence of two qualitatively different classes of user indicates that individuals differ not only with respect to what options they are willing to use for DI—as the factor analyses showed—but also, in the case of use of over-the-counter products, with respect to what goals they pursue using drugs. The class of participants who were inclined to use drugs in pursuit of a variety of goals (the neuroenhancers) seems to see drugs as effective instruments for pursuing the rather general goal "modulation of performance." The second class seems to consist of individuals who only use drugs as instruments for "staying awake" (the fatigue-fighters) and largely abstain from other forms of instrumental drug use.

We suggest—although at this stage it is only a hypothesis—that "neuroenhancers" use drugs proactively, and truly as enhancers i.e., in pursuit of supra-normal performance, whereas "fatigue-fighters" use drugs more reactively, as a means of overcoming a deficit (sub-normal performance). In future research it will be interesting replicate the two class solution we observed and to investigate the drivers behind (these) different patterns of behavior.

Latent classes were only identified within the over-the-counter product DI factor. At present we can only speculate about why no latent classes were identified within the other DI factors. One possible reason is that instrumental use of prescription and illicit drugs is a more socially sensitive behavior than instrumental use of over-the-counter products (Dietz et al., 2013) and thus we failed to detect latent user classes within the other DI factors because participants did not report their use of these drug options truthfully. Similarly, the low rates of use of these drug options might have made it impossible to distinguish different classes of users. In our sample the reported prevalence of drug use in pursuit of the DI goals more directly related to academic performance (counteracting fatigue, enhancing cognitive performance, stress recovery) was comparable with previous reports (cf. McCabe et al., 2005; Mache et al., 2012). In our opinion there is a second plausible explanation for the failure to detect different latent classes of user in the cases of prescription and illicit drugs. Given the generally lower prevalence of DI using prescription drugs and illicit drugs, it is possible that different

classes of latent user have simply not yet emerged in society. This might be because the only legally obtainable drugs which are generally known as instruments for attaining the various goals specified in DI theory (regardless of their actual efficacy) are over-the-counter products. In other words the university students in our sample might consider themselves "experts" on DI with over-the-counter products but not with the other drug options. In future research it would be interesting to investigate whether "knowledge about drugs" and "drug availability" emerge as latent classes in analysis of DI.

Drug Instrumentalization in This Sample

Our sample was a self-selected convenience sample of university students and therefore does not permit inferences about the general population. Nevertheless, our recruitment strategy targeted students studying the most popular academic subjects in Germany, Switzerland and Austria; we were thus able to recruit a large, diverse sample of university students.

We found empirical support for instrumental use of drugs in pursuit of all the goals specified in DI theory. The reported lifetime prevalence of use of any drug in pursuit of goals varied enormously between goals. The majority of our participants had used drugs as instruments to counteract fatigue (89.0%) and enhance cognitive performance (78.1%). Drug instrumentalization with respect to certain goals seems to be the norm amongst the student population, whereas instrumental use of drugs in pursuit of others is relatively uncommon. One straightforward explanation for these differences is that some goals were of greater personal importance to our sample than others. This might also account for the recent spike in public attention (e.g., Partridge et al., 2011; Rath, 2012) and scientific attention to performance enhancement and its reported prevalence in academia (e.g., Maher, 2008). The two goals most commonly pursued via drugs in our study are very closely linked to the domain of structured learning. The relative frequency of instrumental drug use in pursuit of these goals might simply reflect the heightened importance of academic performance in society.

An alternative explanation is that the observed differences in how frequently goals are pursued via drugs reflect subjective perceptions of what drug options are most effective for which goals. The drug options most frequently used for all the goals we investigated was over-the-counter drugs. The most frequently targeted goals might represent those which folk psychopharmacology connects most closely with over-the-counter products, namely "overcoming fatigue," "improving cognitive performance," "coping with stress," "recovering from demands," and "facilitating social interaction." Prescription drugs were used most frequently for "self-medication" and illicit drugs were used most frequently for "sensory curiosity." There is intuitive appeal to this account, as it implies that individuals choose substances that are generally thought to be effective for the goals in which they are interested. If one wants to self-medicate for mental problems, prescription drugs are the most promising candidate as they are marketed (and designed) as effective treatments for mental problems. Similarly, illicit substances are commonly perceived as a good way of attaining a euphoric state.

A very important issue that needs to be resolved by further investigations however is that moral intuitions, perceptions about cultural tolerance and acceptable risk-taking, together with institutional and societal ambivalence to enhancing substances (and illicit drugs especially) might differ between countries and cultures. The phenomenology we found in our European sample might not correspond with the situation in Arab countries (e.g., Wolff et al., 2016). Cross-cultural comparisons should be conducted to shed light on this.

Limitations

This study used DI theory as the basis for research into the psychology of drug instrumentalization. We feel our results provide some important insight into the kinds of means-end (i.e., instrumental action-goal) relationship. Some limitations of the research should, however, be discussed along with questions that remain to be addressed in future research.

Goals and drug options might differ in terms of their social desirability and hence the extent to which relevant behavior is over- or under-reported. Randomized response technique (RRT, Greenberg et al., 1969) is a method of maximizing respondent anonymity in order to reduce the impact of social desirability bias on responses. This method was not suitable for our purposes as it is impossible to infer affirmation or denial of a certain behavior on the individual level from this type of data. We could not have investigated the factorial structure of drug instrumentalization or identified latent drug use classes with data collected using RRT. Use of indirect indicators is another option for dealing with social desirability bias (Greenwald et al., 2009), for example, the Implicit Association Test (Greenwald et al., 1998) has been shown to be valid predictor of athletes' doping test results (Brand et al., 2014) that is hard to distort (Wolff et al., 2015). Further studies should investigate whether indirect tests are needed or helpful in acquiring valid self-report data on NE behavior.

We did not ask for information about exactly which drugs university students had used for drug instrumentalization. We were thus not able to make assessments on specific substances. DI behavior seems to be driven largely by an individual's perception of the functions of a drug option rather than by its objective functional profile. This does not imply that future studies should refrain from assessing the use of specific drugs. Information about what drugs are perceived as effective instruments for attaining certain goals would be valuable.

It has been shown that FMM analyses can yield artificial solutions in case of non-normality or when ill fitting models are analyzed (Bauer and Curran, 2004). Even though the models analyzed here had acceptable model fit and a robust maximum likelihood estimator was used, the results should be interpreted with care. The 2-class solution fit better than a 1- or 3-class solution. Still, the direct test of significance was only marginally significant with the given sample size. Moreover, considering our questionnaire format, it cannot be ruled out that minor dependencies between items occured. Considering the explorative nature of this study as well as the high plausibility of its findings, the 2-class solution should be regarded as a feasible working hypothesis at least. Thus, future research should replicate our finding trying different questionnaire formats and more diverse samples.

Practical Implications and Conclusion

Knowing what an individual hopes to achieve by using a drug enables one to take a more informed approach to dealing with such behavior; this might involve endorsement, monitoring, preventive strategies, treatment, or prohibition. For example, use of an illicit drug for self-medication might warrant a different response from use of the same drug for hedonistic purposes. Another issue is that ethical evaluation of different DI goals might be perceived ambiguous in parts of the society. For example doping in sport (although not yet explicitly labeled as a DI behavior) is widely seen as unethical and is the target of widespread public disapproval. There is at present no definitive ethical verdict on the most prevalent form of DI, namely use of drugs in pursuit of enhanced cognitive performance (e.g., Farah, 2012; Caviola et al., 2014; Maslen et al., 2014). Our results elucidate the complex psychological processes underlying NE. It is likely that there are various forms of NE; regardless of whether one analyzes behavior according to the type of drug or drug option involved or behavior according to the goal pursued. When dealing with somebody who abuses Ritalin it is important to know whether the aim is deficit recovery or mitigation (i.e., to cope with and recover from academic demands) or enhanced performance (in this example supra-normal concentration). Unregard of the pursued purpose abusing this drug is a problem. But the arguments needed to convince a person to refrain from this abuse might be different.

In conclusion the aim of this article was to propose to, first, consequently account for the motivational roots of NE behavior in future investigations. Second, we feel that the proposed approach to the research topic, namely defining NE as the non-medical use of psychoactive substances for the purpose of producing a subjective enhancement in psychological functioning and experience, will help to overcome the conceptual limitations which have hampered research dedicated to the abuse of pharmacological products for the purpose of enhancing cognitive performance thus far (Zohny, 2015). Last but not least, we have provided empirical evidence that university students using NE might be classified according to their motivation or goal, e.g., "neuroenhancers" or "fatigue-fighters" and that this captures fundamental differences in NE behavior. We believe that such forms of differentiation between users are essential to devising techniques for deterring risky behavior among university students.

AUTHOR CONTRIBUTIONS

RB and WW developed this research question. WW conducted the empirical part of the study. RB, WW, and MZ jointly analyzed the data and cooperatively wrote this report.

ACKNOWLEDGMENTS

We thank Sandra Lindemann for her assistance in data collection.

REFERENCES

Anderson, P., and Baumberg, B. (2006). *Alcohol in Europe.* London: Institute of Alcohol Studies.

Armitage, C., and Conner, M. (2001). Efficacy of the theory of planned behaviour: a meta-analytic review. *Br. J. Soc. Psychol.* 40, 471–499. doi: 10.1348/014466601164939

Baker, T. B., Piper, M. E., McCarthy, D. E., Majeskie, M. R., and Fiore, M. C. (2004). Addiction motivation reformulated: an affective processing model of negative reinforcement. *Psychol. Rev.* 111, 33–51. doi: 10.1037/0033-295X.111.1.33

Bauer, D. J., and Curran, P. J. (2004). The integration of continuous and discrete latent variable models: potential problems and promising opportunities. *Psychol. Methods* 9, 3–29. doi: 10.1037/1082-989X.9.1.3

Baumeister, S., Kraus, L., Stonner, T., and Metz, K. (2008). Tabakkonsum, nikotinabhängigkeit und trends. Ergebnisse des epidemiologischen Suchtsurveys 2006. *Sucht* 54, 26–35. doi: 10.1024/2008.07.04

Beauducel, A., and Wittmann, W. W. (2005). Simulation study on fit indexes in CFA based on data with slightly distorted simple structure. *Struct. Equ. Modeling* 12, 41–75. doi: 10.1207/s15328007sem1201_3

Boys, A., Marsden, J., and Strang, J. (2001). Understanding reasons for drug use amongst young people: a functional perspective. *Health Educ. Res.* 16, 457–469. doi: 10.1093/her/16.4.457

Brand, R., and Koch, H. (2016). Using caffeine pills for performance enhancement. An experimental study on university students' willingness and their intention to try neuroenhancements. *Front. Psychol.* 7:101. doi: 10.3389/fpsyg.2016.00101

Brand, R., Wolff, W., and Thieme, D. (2014). Using response-time latencies to measure athletes' doping attitudes: the brief implicit attitude test identifies substance abuse in bodybuilders. *Subst. Abuse Treat. Prev. Policy* 9:36. doi: 10.1186/1747-597X-9-36

Caviola, L., Mannino, A., Savulescu, J., and Faulmuller, N. (2014). Cognitive biases can affect moral intuitions about cognitive enhancement. *Front. Syst. Neurosci.* 8:195. doi: 10.3389/fnsys.2014.00195

Clark, V. P., and Parasuraman, R. (2014). Neuroenhancement: enhancing brain and mind in health and in disease. *Neuroimage* 85, 889–894. doi: 10.1016/j.neuroimage.2013.08.071

Dietz, P., Striegel, H., Franke, A. G., Lieb, K., Simon, P., and Ulrich, R. (2013). Randomized response estimates for the 12-month prevalence of cognitive-enhancing drug use in university students. *Pharmacotherapy* 33, 44–50. doi: 10.1002/phar.1166

Farah, M. J. (2012). Neuroethics: the ethical, legal, and societal impact of neuroscience. *Ann. Rev. Psychol.* 63, 571–591. doi: 10.1146/annurev.psych.093008.100438

Fond, G., Micoulaud-Franchi, J. A., Macgregor, A., Richieri, R., Miot, S., Lopez, R., et al. (2015). Neuroenhancement in healthy adults, part I: pharmaceutical cognitive enhancement: a systematic review. *J. Clin. Res. Bioeth.* 6:213. doi: 10.4172/2155-9627.1000213

Franke, A. G., Bagusat, C., Rust, S., Engel, A., and Lieb, K. (2014). Substances used and prevalence rates of pharmacological cognitive enhancement among healthy subjects. Eur. Arch. Psychiatry Clin. Neurosci. 264, 83–90. doi: 10.1007/s00406-014-0537-1

Franke, A. G., Christmann, M., Bonertz, C., Fellgiebel, A., Huss, M., and Lieb, K. (2011). Use of coffee, caffeinated drinks and caffeine tablets for cognitive enhancement in pupils and students in Germany. *Pharmacopsychiatry* 44, 331–338. doi: 10.1055/s-0031-1286347

Glannon, W. (2015). "Reflections on neuroenhancement," in *Handbook of Neuroethics*, eds J. Clausen and N. Levy (Dordrecht: Springer), 1251–1265.

Greenberg, B. G., Abul-Ela, A. A., Simmons, W. R., and Horvitz, D. G. (1969). The unrelated question randomized response model: theoretical framework. *J. Am. Stat. Assoc.* 64, 520–539. doi: 10.1080/01621459.1969.10500991

Greenwald, A. G., McGhee, D. E., and Schwartz, J. L. K. (1998). Measuring individual differences in implicit cognition: the implicit association test. *J. Pers. Soc. Psychol.* 74, 1464–1480. doi: 10.1037/0022-3514.74.6.1464

Greenwald, A. G., Poehlman, T. A., Uhlmann, E. L., and Banaji, M. R. (2009). Understanding and using the implicit association test: III. Meta-analysis of predictive validity. *J. Pers. Soc. Psychol.* 97, 17–41. doi: 10.1037/a0015575

Heene, M., Hilbert, S., Draxler, C., Ziegler, M., and Buehner, M. (2011). Masking misfit in confirmatory factor analysis by increasing unique variances: a cautionary note on the usefulness of cutoff values of fit indices. *Psychol. Methods* 16, 319–336. doi: 10.1037/a0024917

Hildt, E., and Franke, A. G. (Eds.). (2013). *Cognitive Enhancement: An Interdisciplinary Perspective.* New York, NY: Springer.

Horn, J. L. (1965). A rationale and test for the number of factors in factor analysis. *Psychometrika* 30, 179–185. doi: 10.1007/BF02289447

Hu, L. T., and Bentler, P. M. (1999). Cutoff criteria for fit indexes in covariance structure analysis: conventional criteria versus new alternatives. *Struct. Equ. Modeling* 6, 1–55. doi: 10.1080/10705519909540118

Johnston, L. D., O'Malley, P. M., Bachman, J. G., and Schulenberg, J. E. (2010). *Monitoring the Future National Results on Adolescent Drug Use: Overview of Key Findings, 2009 (NIH Publication No. 10-7583).* Bethesda, MD: National Institute on Drug Abuse.

Kandel, D., Chen, K., Warner, L. A., Kessler, R. C., and Grant, B. (1997). Prevalence and demographic correlates of symptoms of last year dependence on alcohol, nicotine, marijuana and cocaine in the US population. *Drug Alcohol Depend.* 44, 11–29. doi: 10.1016/S0376-8716(96)01315-4

Koob, G. F., and LeMoal, M. (1997). Drug abuse: hedonic homeostatic dysregulation. *Science* 278, 52–58. doi: 10.1126/science.278.5335.52

Kreuter, M. W., and Wray, R. J. (2003). Tailored and targeted health communication: strategies for enhancing information relevance. *Am. J. Health Behav.* 27, S227–S232. doi: 10.5993/AJHB.27.1.s3.6

Leite, W. L., and Cooper, L. A. (2010). Detecting social desirability bias using factor mixture models. *Multivar. Behav. Res.* 45, 271–293. doi: 10.1080/00273171003680245

Lubke, G. H., and Muthen, B. (2005). Investigating population heterogeneity with factor mixture models. *Psychol. Methods* 10, 21–39. doi: 10.1037/1082-989X.10.1.21

Lubke, G. H., and Muthen, B. O. (2007). Performance of factor mixture models as a function of model size, covariate effects, and class-specific parameters. *Struct. Equ. Modeling* 14, 26–47. doi: 10.1080/10705510709336735

Mache, S., Eickenhorst, P., Vitzthum, K., Klapp, B. F., and Groneberg, D. A. (2012). Cognitive-enhancing substance use at German universities: frequency, reasons and gender differences. *Wien. Med. Wochenschr.* 162, 262–271. doi: 10.1007/s10354-012-0115-y

Maher, B. (2008). Poll results: look who's doping. *Nature* 452, 674–675. doi: 10.1038/452674a

Maier, L. J., and Schaub, M. P. (2015). The use of prescription drugs and drugs of abuse for neuroenhancement in Europe: not widespread but a reality. *Eur. Psychol.* 20, 155–166. doi: 10.1027/1016-9040/a000228

Maslen, H., Faulmuller, N., and Savulescu, J. (2014). Pharmacological cognitive enhancement-how neuroscientific research could advance ethical debate. *Front. Syst. Neurosci.* 8:107. doi: 10.3389/fnsys.2014.00107

Mazanov, J., Dunn, M., Connor, J., and Fielding, M. L. (2013). Substance use to enhance academic performance among Australian university students. *Perform. Enhanc. Health* 2, 110–118. doi: 10.1016/j.peh.2013.08.017

McCabe, S. E., Knight, J. R., Teter, C. J., and Wechser, H. (2005). Non-medical use of prescription stimulants among US college students: prevalence and correlates from a national survey. *Addiction* 100, 96–106. doi: 10.1111/j.1360-0443.2005.00944.x

Meredith, S. E., Juliano, L. M., Hughes, J. R., and Griffiths, R. R. (2013). Caffeine use disorder: a comprehensive review and research agenda. *J. Caffeine Res.* 3, 114–130. doi: 10.1089/jcr.2013.0016

Middendorff, E., Poskowsky, J., and Becker, K. (2015). *Formen der Stresskompensation und Leistungssteigerung bei Studierenden: Wiederholungsbefragung des HISBUS-Panels zu Verbreitung und Mustern studienbezogenen Substanzkonsums.* Hannover: DZHW.

Müller, C. P., and Schumann, G. (2011a). Drugs as instruments: a new framework for non-addictive psychoactive drug use. *Behav. Brain Sci.* 34, 293–310. doi: 10.1017/S0140525X11000057

Müller, C. P., and Schumann, G. (2011b). To use or not to use: expanding the view on non-addictive psychoactive drug consumption and its implications. *Behav. Brain Sci.* 34, 328–347. doi: 10.1017/S0140525X1100135X

Muthén and Muthén (2013). *MPLUS (Version 7).* Los Angeles, CA: Muthén & Muthén.

Neale, C., Camfield, D., Reay, J., Stough, C., and Scholey, A. (2013). Cognitive effects of two nutraceuticals Ginseng and Bacopa benchmarked against modafinil: a review and comparison of effect sizes. *Br. J. Clin. Pharmacol.* 75, 728–737. doi: 10.1111/bcp.12002

O'Brien, C. P., Childress, A. R., McLellan, A. T., and Ehrman, R. (1992). "A learning model of addiction," in *Research Publications: Association for Research in Nervous and Mental Disease*, eds C. P. O'Brien and J. H. Jaffe (New York, NY: Raven Press), 157–177.

Partridge, B. J., Bell, S. K., Lucke, J. C., Yeates, S., and Hall, W. D. (2011). Smart drugs "as common as coffee": media hype about neuroenhancement. *PLoS ONE* 6:e28416. doi: 10.1371/journal.pone.0028416

Rath, M. (2012). Energy drinks: what is all the hype? The dangers of energy drink consumption. *J. Am. Acad. Nurse Pract.* 24, 70–76. doi: 10.1111/j.1745-7599.2011.00689.x

R Development Core Team (2013). *R: A Language and Environment for Statistical Computing.* Vienna: R Foundation for statistical computing.

Revelle, W. (2014). *Psych: Procedures for Personality and Psychological Research (Version 1.4.5).* Evanston, IL: Northwestern University.

Rimer, B. K., and Kreuter, M. W. (2006). Advancing tailored health communication: a persuasion and message effects perspective. *J. Commun.* 56, 184–201. doi: 10.1111/j.1460-2466.2006.00289.x

Rossel, Y. (2012). lavaan: an r package for structural equation modeling. *J. Stat. Softw.* 48, 1–36. doi: 10.18637/jss.v048.i02

Sattler, S., Mehlkop, G., Graeff, P., and Sauer, C. (2014). Evaluating the drivers of and obstacles to the willingness to use cognitive enhancement drugs: the influence of drug characteristics, social environment, and personal characteristics. *Subst. Abuse Treat. Prev. Policy* 9:8. doi: 10.1186/1747-597X-9-8

Smith, M. E., and Farah, M. J. (2011). Are prescription stimulants "smart pills"? The epidemiology and cognitive neuroscience of prescription stimulant use by normal healthy individuals. *Psychol. Bull.* 137, 717–741. doi: 10.1037/a0023825

United Nations (2011). *The Non-Medical Use of Prescription Drugs. Policy Direction Issues.* Vienna: United Nations Office on Drug and Crimes.

Velicer, W. F. (1976). Determining number of components from matrix of partial correlations. *Psychometrika* 41, 321–327. doi: 10.1007/BF02293557

Walsh, J. K., Muehlbach, M. J., Humm, T. M., Dickins, Q. S., Sugerman, J. L., and Schweitzer, P. K. (1990). Effect of caffeine on physiological sleep tendency and ability to sustain wakefulness at night. *Psychopharmacology* 101, 271–273. doi: 10.1007/BF02244139

Wilens, T. E., Adler, L. A., Adams, J., Sgambati, S., Rotrosen, J., Sawtelle, R., et al. (2008). Misuse and diversion of stimulants prescribed for ADHD: a systematic review of the literature. *J. Am. Acad. Child Adolesc. Psychiatry* 47, 21–31. doi: 10.1097/chi.0b013e31815a56f1

Wolff, W., and Brand, R. (2013). Subjective stressors in school and their relation to neuroenhancement: a behavioral perspective on students' everyday life "doping." *Subst. Abuse Treat. Prev. Policy* 8:23. doi: 10.1186/1747-597X-8-23

Wolff, W., Brand, R., Baumgarten, F., Lösel, J., and Ziegler, M. (2014). Modeling students' instrumental (mis-)use of substances to enhance cognitive performance: Neuroenhancement in the light of job-demands-resources theory. *BioPsychoSocial Med.* 8:12. doi: 10.1186/1751-0759-8-12

Wolff, W., Sandouqa, Y., and Brand, R. (2016). Using the simple sample count to estimate the frequency of prescription drug neuroenhancement in a sample of Jordan employees. *Int. J. Drug Policy* 31, 51–55. doi: 10.1016/j.drugpo.2015.12.014

Wolff, W., Schindler, S., and Brand, R. (2015). The effect of implicitly incentivized faking on explicit and implicit measures of doping attitude: when athletes want to pretend an even more negative attitude to doping. *PLoS ONE* 10:e0118507. doi: 10.1371/journal.pone.0118507

Zelli, A., Lucidi, F., and Mallia, L. (2015). The complexity of neuroenhancement and the adoption of a social cognitive perspective. *Front. Psychol.* 6:1880. doi: 10.3389/fpsyg.2015.01880

Ziegler, M., and Hagemann, D. (2015). Testing the unidimensionality of items: pitfalls and loopholes. *Eur. J. Psychol. Assess.* 31, 231–237. doi: 10.1027/1015-5759/a000309

Ziegler, M., Maaß, U., Griffith, R., and Gammon, A. (2015). What is the nature of faking? Modeling distinct response patterns and quantitative differences in faking at the same time. *Organ. Res. Methods* 20, 1–25. doi: 10.1177/1094428115574518

Zohny, H. (2015). The myth of cognitive enhancement drugs. *Neuroethics* 8, 257–269. doi: 10.1007/s12152-015-9232-9

Conflict of Interest Statement: The authors declare that the research was conducted in the absence of any commercial or financial relationships that could be construed as a potential conflict of interest.

Introducing a Short Measure of Shared Servant Leadership Impacting Team Performance through Team Behavioral Integration

Milton Sousa[1]* and Dirk Van Dierendonck[2]

[1] *Leadership Knowledge Centre, Nova School of Business and Economics, Lisbon, Portugal,* [2] *Centre for Leadership Studies, Rotterdam School of Management, Erasmus University, Rotterdam, Netherlands*

The research reported in this paper was designed to study the influence of shared servant leadership on team performance through the mediating effect of team behavioral integration, while validating a new short measure of shared servant leadership. A round-robin approach was used to collect data in two similar studies. Study 1 included 244 undergraduate students in 61 teams following an intense HRM business simulation of 2 weeks. The following year, study 2 included 288 students in 72 teams involved in the same simulation. The most important findings were that (1) shared servant leadership was a strong determinant of team behavioral integration, (2) information exchange worked as the main mediating process between shared servant leadership and team performance, and (3) the essence of servant leadership can be captured on the key dimensions of empowerment, humility, stewardship and accountability, allowing for a new promising shortened four-dimensional measure of shared servant leadership.

Keywords: servant leadership, shared leadership, team behavioral integration, self-managed teams, measure

Edited by:
*Pablo Fernández-Berrocal,
University of Malaga, Spain*

Reviewed by:
*M. Teresa Anguera,
University of Barcelona, Spain
Elliot J. Roth,
Rehabilitation Institute of Chicago,
USA*

*Correspondence:
*Milton Sousa
milton.sousa@novasbe.pt*

Specialty section:
*This article was submitted to
Organizational Psychology,
a section of the journal
Frontiers in Psychology*

INTRODUCTION

This article explores the role of shared servant leadership in affecting team performance through the mediating role of team behavioral integration. We bring forward the idea that in a self-managed team, the collective composition of servant like leadership behaviors by individual team members can be conducive of team performance. This is based on the principle that leadership can be seen as a process emerging from the interaction between agents, as opposed to an influencing process that flows from a central leader alone. Such a collectivist view is reflected in models such as team, shared, complex, network and collective leadership (Yammarino et al., 2012). We hypothesize that, when combined, the servant leadership behaviors advanced by Van Dierendonck and Nuijten (2011), based on empowerment, stewardship, humility and accountability, will be particularly applicable in the context of shared leadership, as they naturally reflect and support a process whereby "it is only the collective that matters and single leaders *disappear* so to speak" (Yammarino et al., 2012; p. 398). We further advance that improved team behavioral integration, in its three aspects of joint decision making, information exchange and collective behavior, will be the mechanism through which shared servant leadership will have an impact on the team's performance. **Figure 1** depicts the conceptual model that guides this research.

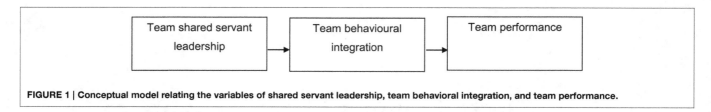

FIGURE 1 | Conceptual model relating the variables of shared servant leadership, team behavioral integration, and team performance.

In addition to this conceptual proposition, through our studies, we introduce a short measure of servant leadership, based on the original instrument by Van Dierendonck and Nuijten's (2011). Traditional team rating surveys are relatively simple (each member rates the overall team leadership) but rather inaccurate in assessing shared leadership (e.g., Pearce and Sims, 2002; Avolio et al., 2003). Round-robin approaches, whereby each team member assesses everyone else in the team individually from which a team level score is composed, provide much more accuracy but are time-consuming, especially when surveys are long. Having a shorter survey that reduces completion time while keeping the essence of the original measure would be useful and practical. This new measure will be a more practical tool for assessing shared leadership through a collective assessment of the leadership present in the team (Gockel and Werth, 2010), with the improved accuracy of a round-robin data collection method.

In order to test our conceptual model and validate the new short measure, two studies were conducted based on confirmatory factor analysis. We start by further elaborating on the concepts and corresponding constructs of shared leadership, servant leadership and team behavioral integration, as well as the underlying principles supporting the relationship between them.

CONSTRUCTS AND MODEL OPERATIONALIZATION

Shared Leadership

Shared leadership is defined as "a dynamic, interactive influence process among individuals in groups for which the objective is to lead one another to the achievement of group or organizational goals or both" (Pearce and Conger, 2003; p. 1). Shared leadership changes the focus from a vertical leadership approach where one leader influences several followers to a horizontal approach where leadership becomes a joint activity of the team members showing leadership behavior toward each other (Bligh et al., 2006). Research on shared leadership has already shown its potential use in better understanding team effectiveness in terms of ratings by managers, customers and self-ratings (e.g., Pearce and Sims, 2002; Hoch et al., 2010).

Shared leadership gains increased relevance in the context of self-managed teams, as the absence of a clear hierarchy likely provides fertile ground for shared leadership to emerge. The ideas behind self-managed teams originate from socio-technical systems theory (Stewart and Manz, 1995). It is a way of organizing that combines both the social and the technical aspects of work. Instead of working as individuals with individual targets, employees work together in teams and are jointly responsible for team targets. With the absence of a direct supervisor, these

teams have relatively more freedom to plan their own work. This can bring a strong sense of empowerment within the individual team members and opens the way for a more shared form of leadership instead of the more traditional hierarchical types. One needs to bear in mind that despite the absence of an appointed leader within a self-managed team, some kind of informal leadership will likely appear (Wolff et al., 2002). Team leaders help define team objectives, keep a team focused on team goals, and provide coordination between team members. Even in self-managed teams these roles are necessary. What distinguishes shared leadership from centralized leadership, especially in self-managed teams, is that these leadership roles are often fulfilled by different team members instead of only one, in a fluid process. As was proposed by West et al. (2003), a lack of leadership clarity can be detrimental for team performance, especially if this leads to conflict over the leadership role or the direction that a team should take. However, when one sees leadership as a process instead of a single one-to-many power relationship, this clarity can be achieved through a mutually reinforcing shared leadership process.

The Operationalization of Shared Leadership

Capturing shared leadership in teams is not easy. Previous attempts have often focused on the influence of the team as a whole or on how team members in general show leadership behavior (Gockel and Werth, 2010). For example, Pearce and Sims (2002) asked participants to rate their team members jointly on shared leadership. A similar approach was used by Avolio et al. (2003) and in a more recent study by Hoch et al. (2010). Basically, items from leadership measures are reformulated from "my leader…" into "my team members…." The main disadvantage of these measures is their lack of accuracy as one cannot know the point of reference taken by respondents when evaluating the team as a whole (Gockel and Werth, 2010). In order to overcome this problem, in the present study, shared leadership is measured through a round-robin approach whereby team members are individually assessed on their servant leadership behaviors toward each respondent, which makes it possible to consider it a relational construct (Mayo et al., 2003). The collective team average is then calculated, representing the total amount of servant leadership behavior demonstrated in the team, which should be more accurate than asking participants to rate the team as a whole. While this method has similarities with the social network analysis methods suggested by Gockel and Werth (2010) in terms of data collection, it has some distinct differences with regard to interpretation. In social network analysis, shared leadership is assessed mainly through the measures of centralization and density (Gockel and Werth, 2010). Such measures are indirect characteristics of the network topography, as they provide ratios instead of actual leadership scores. However, as we aimed to validate the short measure of servant leadership, we needed to ensure a direct measure of the amount of shared servant leadership in the team instead of using indirect ratios. We see therefore our approach as an extension and improvement of the team rating approach suggested by Gockel and Werth (2010) through the inclusion of round-robin measures of servant leadership, helping to overcome the inaccuracy of team level measures.

Servant Leadership as a Model for Shared Leadership

Robert Greenleaf (1904–1990) introduced the notion of servant leadership after reading Herman Hesse's Journey to the East (Greenleaf, 1977). This book portrays the archetype of a servant-first leader that inspired Greenleaf to extrapolate this notion to the context of modern organizations. Greenleaf's (1977) concept of servant leadership is very much focused on this initial motivation to serve as the following quote testifies: "The servant-leader is servant first…It begins with the natural feeling that one wants to serve, to serve first. Then conscious choice brings one to aspire to lead" (Greenleaf, 2002; p. 7). As such, the servant leader's major concern is the development and growth of others. Spears (1996; p. 33) highlights how "servant leadership emphasizes increased service to others; a holistic approach to work; promoting a sense of community; and the sharing of power in decision making."

The relevance of servant leadership for team functioning has been demonstrated in several recent studies that focused on servant leadership in a hierarchical setting. Walumbwa et al. (2010) showed that team level servant leadership was related to higher individual organizational commitment, self-efficacy and supervisor rated organizational citizenship behavior. Hu and Liden (2011) found that team-level servant leadership was related to team performance, team organizational citizenship behavior and team potency. The results of Schaubroeck et al. (2011) are similar in that they compared team-level transformational leadership with team-level servant leadership and showed that servant leadership was related to team performance through affect-based trust in the leader and team psychological safety. All three studies confirm the relevance for team functioning of servant leadership as shown by the direct supervisor. The present study builds on their insights by its focus on shared servant leadership in self-managed teams without a direct supervisor. We advance that aspects of servant leadership such as a servant-first attitude (Greenleaf, 1977), humility (Russell, 2001; Patterson, 2003; Van Dierendonck, 2011), and the ability to perform while focusing on the good of the whole (Van Dierendonck, 2011) will be supportive of the antecedents of shared leadership suggested by Carson et al. (2007) such as shared purpose, social support or having a voice.

Given its increasing adoption and validity in different cultural settings including the Netherlands, UK, Italy, Finland and Portugal (Hakanen and Van Dierendonck, 2011; Van Dierendonck and Nuijten, 2011; Bobbio et al., 2012; Sousa and van Dierendonck, 2014), we opted to use the measurement development study by Van Dierendonck and Nuijten (2011) providing a rather comprehensive and solid instrument, based on 8 dimensions and 30 items. These include: empowerment (7 items), accountability (3 items), standing back (3 items), humility (5 items), authenticity (4 items), courage (2 items), forgiveness (3 items), and stewardship (3 items). From this whole set, the dimensions of empowerment, stewardship, accountability and humility were suggested by Van Dierendonck and Nuijten (2011) as forming core aspects of servant leadership behavior. With this study we aim to confirm these four dimensions as the essential attributes of shared servant leadership within a self-management team context. Given the extensive amount of mutual one-to-one estimates between team members to calculate shared servant leadership in a round-robin approach, such a shortened measure will also prove far more practical. We posit that team members who show servant leadership behavior will actively empower and develop other team members, show humility toward one another, provide direction in day-to-day work by mutually holding others accountable, and emphasize the importance to act as stewards who work for the good of the team as a whole. In the next chapter we further elaborate on the specific impact of these dimensions of servant leadership, as a shared process, on team behavioral integration.

Shared Servant Leadership and Team Behavioral Integration

Team behavioral integration was suggested to be a key fundamental aspect of collective leadership (Friedrich et al., 2009; Yammarino et al., 2010, 2012). Likewise, we posit that shared servant leadership will be reflected in higher levels of team behavioral integration. As such, team behavioral integration is introduced into our theoretical model as a mediating variable to help understand the possible beneficial influence of shared leadership on team performance.

Hambrick (1994; p. 188) defined team behavioral integration as "the degree to which the group engages in mutual and collaborative interaction." Originally proposed to capture effective functioning performance in top management teams, team behavioral integration consists of three interrelated components that capture both social and task related dimensions (Hambrick, 1994; Siegel and Hambrick, 1996). The social dimension is captured on the component of collaborative behavior (Hambrick, 1994), which builds on the concept social integration. Social integration is mainly an affective construct reflected on social interaction, attraction to the group and satisfaction with other team members (O'Reilly et al., 1989). This affective and emotional bond carries however risks on the quality of decision making due to the fear of damaging relationships within the team. Consequently, for social integration to be effective it needs therefore to be combined with other task related behaviors (Schweiger and Sandberg, 1989). Hambrick (1994) encapsulated these task related behaviors in the constructs of joint decision making and information exchange.

Simsek et al. (2005) further elaborate on these three different dimensions. The authors support that collective behavior can be translated into behaviors of mutual support in managing workload, flexibility about switching responsibilities to make work easier for each other and the willingness of team members to help each other in meeting deadlines (Simsek et al., 2005). Joint decision making can be observed through the care in communicating interdependencies among team members, creating shared understanding of joint problems and each other's needs, as well as openly discussing expectations of each other (Simsek et al., 2005). Concerning information exchange, Simsek et al. (2005) consider both quantitative (e.g., number of ideas being created) and qualitative aspects (e.g., level of creativity and innovation, and the quality of proposed solutions toward problems).

The relevance of team behavioral integration for team performance was particularly emphasized by three studies that related top management team behavioral integration to company performance (Simsek et al., 2005; Lubatkin et al., 2006; Carmeli, 2008). Other studies showed its relevance for individual improvisation (Magni et al., 2009) and better quality of strategic decisions (Carmeli and Schaubroeck, 2006). On a related note, team leadership has been positioned as essential for developing shared mental models, collective information processing and team metacognition (Zaccaro et al., 2001). Also, shared leadership in teams has been related to greater collaboration, coordination, cooperation and group cohesion (Ensley et al., 2003), which are similar concepts to the three dimensions of team behavioral integration.

Given these considerations, as a people-centered mutually supporting leadership model, we suggest that the aggregate composition of servant leadership behaviors by individuals toward one another (shared servant leadership), will likely directly or indirectly enhance team behavioral integration. In the following text, we note some particularly noteworthy potential linkages based on the four dimensions of servant leadership outlined before as essential for the shared leadership context.

Empowerment refers to a motivational concept which includes empowering leadership behavior for encouraging self-directed decision making, information sharing, and coaching for innovative performance (Konczak et al., 2000). Based on this definition empowerment seems to affect both information exchange and joint decision making, as it opens up the channels of communication in support of joint coordination. Empowerment is also a base condition for shared leadership to emerge (Yammarino et al., 2012), whereby team members are able to trust each other on their ability to perform different tasks. It means that team members mutually encourage taking initiative, diligently share information, support each other in decision making and help others understanding new challenges and topics. In teams demonstrating high levels of shared leadership, one would expect members to often agree on sharing tasks such that those less knowledgeable can grow and learn, in a true mutually empowering fashion. Within team behavioral integration, this mutually supporting orientation can be captured in the social dimension of collective behavior.

Humility is about modesty reflected in a servant-leader's tendency to give priority to the interest of others, acknowledging mistakes and giving room to learn. For shared leadership to emerge in a team it is essential that the team members are able to acknowledge their limitations and the fact that other people can contribute in different ways and according to their level of development. In addition, as a collectivist form of leadership, shared leadership means that any individual team member needs to be able to move into the background when necessary (Yammarino et al., 2012). This allows others to assume leading roles as demanded by the task at hand. From a task oriented point of view, humility will support the quantity of information exchange by acknowledging the value of everyone's contribution and ideas. At the same time, humility can affect joint decision making as it will instill a culture of dialog and genuine interest in mutual understanding through humble inquiry (Schein, 2013), fostering creativity and innovative thinking. From a social integration perspective, humility can support collective behavior as it amplifies the importance of the whole above self-interest and creates a space for reaching out to other team members when in need.

Accountability is about providing direction taking into account other people's abilities, needs, and input, while holding them responsible for their achievements. In a team with shared leadership this role might be partaken among several members or eventually rotated. It also means that all members assume responsibility for each other's work and will mutually hold each other accountable for their contribution. This shared responsibility and accountability forms a cornerstone of shared leadership behavior (Pearce and Conger, 2003). In addition, accountability is mostly associated with the practical aspects of work, also present in servant leadership. Defining tasks, work processes, objectives, deadlines and control mechanisms remains critical for work to be done effectively. As such, this dimension will likely be most relevant for the task related aspects of team behavioral integration. It can support joint decision making as it emphasizes the need to mutually agree on targets, task assignments, methods and processes while ensuring execution and performance. At the same time, accountability can stimulate both the quantity and the quality of information exchange. On the quantity of information, it can prevent team members from free riding or not being sufficiently involved, increasing the number of ideas and solutions being considered. On the quality aspect, accountability will make members thoughtful of the relevance and effectiveness of their ideas and proposed solutions.

Stewardship refers to stimulating others to act in the common interest and to take a viewpoint that focuses on the good of the whole. These core aspects have been shown to contribute to followers experiencing a more challenging work setting, a sense of psychological empowerment and higher organizational commitment (Asag-gau and Van Dierendonck, 2011). This aspect of servant leadership brings an element of self-transcendence, by putting others and the mission above the self. In light of this definition, when all team members act as stewards, it becomes accepted that the team is more important than any individual, again a base condition for shared leadership to emerge (Pearce and Conger, 2003; Yammarino et al., 2012).

From an affective perspective, stewardship seems therefore to be particularly relevant for the aspect of collective behavior, as it emphasizes the importance of the whole and staying on course to achieve the team's objectives. From a task oriented point of view, stewardship will enable joint decision making as it stimulates team members to understand joint problems and each other's needs in the context of a larger picture. It can also support information exchange by increasing the quality of solutions being proposed through a higher focus on the relevant team challenges that need to be addressed (ensuring the relevance of information being exchanged).

In light of the possible links established above, it can be expected that if team members on average show more of these mutual and supportive servant leadership behaviors toward each other (empowerment, humility, accountability, and stewardship), team behavioral integration will be strengthened, which will lead to better overall team performance. Together the above reasoning can be summarized in the following hypotheses:

Hypothesis 1: Given its emphasis on mutual empowerment, accountability, stewardship and humility, shared servant leadership will be positively related to team behavioral integration.

Hypothesis 2: As a reflection of good team functioning, team behavioral integration will operate as a mediating variable between shared servant leadership and team performance.

In a nutshell, the present study aims to test the mediating effect of shared servant leadership on team performance through team behavioral integration. A round-robin approach was used to collect the data, which allows for a more accurate measure of the amount of shared servant leadership in a team. The study also aims to validate a short measure of servant leadership for the shared leadership context based on the four key dimensions of empowerment, stewardship, accountability and humility. Several control variables were included to take into account possible third variable effects, namely academic competence and team familiarity.

METHODS STUDY 1

Data Collection

In order to validate our model, it was important to have a large sample of self-managed teams (without a formal leader) going through a similar assignment and in comparable contextual circumstances, to allow for objective performance comparison. This is hard to find in an organizational context. For that reason, a simulation based assignment in a Business Administration program was used.

The simulation is based on realistic scenarios extracted from real cases pertaining to the activities of Human Resource Management (HRM) departments. The simulation lasts 2 weeks with intense teamwork in groups of four. It is important to note that during this 2 week period this assignment is their only activity for the course, reducing interference, and conflicting goals. The simulation is a major activity requiring substantial time and focus. Each team represented the HRM department

of a company where HR relevant decisions had to be made for the company. These decisions, concerning realistic recruitment, selection and retention policies, had to be taken on a daily basis for 8 days. In the morning, feedback was given on how their company was doing in comparison to the companies of the other teams. New decisions had to be taken before the end of each day. It is important to note that no leader was appointed in the teams. They were instructed to function as a self-managed team. The participants were asked to fill out a survey on their team functioning, 1 week after the simulation directly following handing in their final report, giving extra course credits. Data has been collected through an online survey in accordance with the ethical guidelines of the American Psychological Association. The ethical rules and regulations of the University were also applied. As such, (i) participation was completely voluntary, (ii) data collection through a self-report survey is exempted from an institutional ethics committee's approval, and (iii) the subjects filled out the survey for extra course credit (no money has been given). Subjects were informed about the nature of the study on the first webpage. Informed consent was given by clicking on the "Next" button.

Participants

Respondents were third year undergraduate Business Administration students participating in a HRM course. Only the results of the teams that had all four members filling out the surveys were included in the study. This provides a full database with reports of all team members on each other. The sample included 61 teams, totalling 244 students (response percentage of 71%). Of them 65 % were male and 35% female. The average age was 21.0 ($SD = 1.5$) years.

Measures
Shared Servant Leadership

All participants were asked to rate the leadership behavior they perceived from their fellow team members in a round-robin fashion (whereby every team member evaluates all other team members' behaviors). For the developmental purpose of this survey, where we also wanted to test the validity of the short measure, all 30 items from the Servant Leadership Survey (SLS; Van Dierendonck and Nuijten, 2011) were incorporated. As explained before, items were reformulated to indicate the level of servant leadership shown by each team members toward the person filling out the survey (i.e., instead of asking questions in relation to the leader, they were asked in relation to each team member individually). In addition, questions were provided in the past tense, referring to the period of the project, as opposed to a stable management relationship from the original survey. For example, one of the original empowerment items was reformulated from "My manager gives me the information I need to my work well" to "<name of team member> gave me the information I needed to do my work well." In another example, this time from the accountability dimension, the following item was rephrased from "My manager holds me responsible for the work I carry out" to "<name of team member> held me responsible for the work I carried out." Such adaptations were done for all 30 items from the original survey. Ratings were to be given on a 5-point Likert scale, ranging from *never* to *very often*. For all participants, the answers to all items were averaged to indicate the mean level of the servant leadership behavior as received from the other team members.

Based on this data, team shared servant leadership becomes the combined servant leader behavior of team members shown toward one another. This gives an indication of the average level of shared leadership in a team, which is similar to approach 1 in the Gockel and Werth (2010) paper but with the advantage of including round-robin measures for a more accurate assessment of the total average amount of shared leadership. One should note that there is no need for checking for consensus among the different team members because items refer to the servant leadership behavior shown by each team member individually and not on the overall servant leadership level of the team.

Team Behavioral Integration

Team behavioral integration was measured with the three-dimensional measure developed by Simsek et al. (2005), including collective behavior, information exchange and joint decision making. Each dimension was measured with three items. Before aggregating the data to team level, the consensus among the different team members was checked with regard to their assessment of team behavioral integration. The Rwg(j) scores (James et al., 1984) were calculated. As an additional test, the intraclass correlation (ICC1) was also calculated. This correlation gives an estimate of the related consistency among the team members. We also tested whether the operationalization of team behavioral integration acknowledged its three-dimensional conceptualization.

Team Performance

During the simulation, the teams received feedback about their performance on several company indicators, generated by the simulation software. These indicators were also transformed into an overall score which was communicated to the teams after each round. Performance in this paper is their final ranking on the simulation, which gives an indication of their overall performance throughout the eight decision rounds. Their overall end score was differentiated between 6 (for the teams whose score belonged to the lowest 10%) and 10 (for groups belonging to the highest 10%).

Control Variables

Past research has argued that team member familiarity may affect team performance (e.g., Gruenfeld et al., 1996). Therefore, we took in member familiarity as a control variable. Respondents were to judge how well they knew each team member on a scale from 1 (*not at all*) to 5 (*very well*). These scores were added together and aggregated to team level to create a team score of familiarity. Academic competence of the individual team members may also influence team performance. Respondents were asked to give an estimate of their average grade of other courses. Course grade is used as a proxy for general mental capacity, their learning style, and their motivation to put in an effort to reach high grades. These individual scores were averaged within a team for a score of a team's average academic competence. No index for within group agreement was calculated for the control variables as team members are not necessarily similar in the degree to which they know their fellow team members, nor in their average grade. In this situation the team average would still be an accurate reflection of member familiarity and intellectual capacity (cf. Gruenfeld et al., 1996).

Assessing the Validity of the New Servant Leadership Short Measure

The factorial validity of the hypothesized four-dimensional structure (humility, empowerment, stewardship, and accountability) of the new shortened version of the servant leadership survey was tested in both studies. The mean item-scores across team members were used as input for Mplus 6 (Muthén and Muthén, 2009). The nested (multi-level) structure of the dataset (i.e., participants in teams) was accounted for, thereby guaranteeing the correct error variances. In addition, in order to test the validity of the shortened version, in study 1 we compared the underlying variance of the full servant leadership scale with all 30 items with 8 dimensions to that of the reduced version with 15 items and only 4 dimensions. A model was tested where the four dimensions were allowed to load together on one second-order factor. In addition, all 30 items of the original scales were allowed to load on one underlying factor. This factor signifies the total underlying servant leadership variance of the full measure. The second order servant leadership factor (representing the underlying variance of the four dimensions theorized to be most important for shared servant leadership in self-managed teams) was allowed to correlate with the leadership factor which was determined by all 30 items.

Model Validation

Following Anderson and Gerbing (1988), we first tested the adequacy of the measurement model of the latent constructs using Mplus 6 (Muthén and Muthén, 2009) before actually testing the relations in the full model. To operationalize the latent construct of servant leadership, the four dimensions were used as manifest indicators. For the three team behavioral integration sub-dimensions, the items of each scale were used as indicators. In this way these latent constructs were determined by three or four indicators, which is the recommended practice if the goal is to study a variable at an overall level of generality and one wants to reduce the level of nuisance and bias that may come from working with the separate items directly (Bandalos, 2002). Team performance, academic competence and team familiarity were used as manifest variables. After validating the measurement model, the conceptual model was tested in both studies, with structural equation models with latent and manifest variables using Mplus 6 (Muthén and Muthén, 2009). As a final confirmation step, the indirect effects of the most significant mediating factors of team behavioral integration were tested with bootstrapping (Preacher et al., 2008).

METHODS STUDY 2

The setup of the second study is in essence a replica of the first one but this time based on students from the following year. This allowed again for a more accurate comparison between results from both studies. The aim of the second study was to confirm the findings of the first study. As such, during study 2, only the short measure of servant leadership validated in study 1 was used (15 items) with all other measures being exactly the same.

Like in the first study, participants were third year undergraduate Business Administration students participating in a HRM course that included a HRM-simulation of 2 weeks with intense teamwork in groups of four. Only the results of the teams that had all four members filling out the surveys were included in the study. This provides a full database with reports of all team members on each other. The sample included 72 teams, totalling 288 students (response percentage of 72%). Of them 62% were male and 38% female. The average age was 20.9 ($SD = 1.3$) years. The same ethical rules and regulations of for data collection from the first study were applied to this second study.

RESULTS STUDY 1

Validity of the Short Shared Servant Leadership Measure

Before testing the whole model, the validity of the short measure was evaluated. Initially, the fit of the hypothesized 4-dimensional structure corresponding to the short version of the servant leadership measure was compared to a 1-dimensional structure (all items loading on one leadership dimension). The fit indices were $X^2 = 263,887$, $df = 129$, CFI = 0.91, TLI = 0.89, RMSEA = 0.07, SRMR = 0.07, for the 4-dimensional model, and $X^2 = 648.989$, $df = 135$, CFI = 0.66, TLI = 0.61, RMSEA = 0.13, SRMR = 0.10, for the 1-dimensional model. The 4-dimensional model clearly shows the best fit, confirming the underlying multi-dimensional structure of servant leadership within this context. However, one comparative fit index (TLI) was still below 0.90, indicating some misfit in the measurement model. Items that either loaded low (i.e., a standardized factor loading lower than 0.40) on their proposed dimension or where the modification indices indicated a cross-loading on one of the other dimensions were removed. This resulted in the removal of three items from empowerment, humility and stewardship (one item from each subscale). The resulting 4-dimensional model had excellent fit indices ($X^2 = 139.185$, $df = 84$, CFI = 0.93, TLI = 0.92, RMSEA = 0.06, SRMR = 0.06). The 4-dimensional model with one underlying dimension showed a comparable fit: $X^2 = 157.561$, $df = 86$, CFI = 0.94, TLI = 0.93, RMSEA = 0.06, SRMR = 0.06. These results confirm that the short shared servant leadership measure in this paper is a 4-dimensional concept with one underlying second order factor. The internal consistencies are 0.80 for empowerment (6 items), 0.88 for accountability (3 items), 0.60 for stewardship (2 items), and 0.75 for humility (4 items). Overall, the reliability of these subscales is good. Please note that internal consistency also depends on the number of items. Stewardship has only two items, 0.60 is with only two items still respectable (as will be seen later, this value is higher in study 2).

As explained before, in order to test the validity of the shortened version, we compared the underlying variance of the full servant leadership scale with all 30 items with 8 dimensions to that of the reduced version with 15 items and only 4 dimensions. The correlation between the factor capturing the full range of the servant leadership measure and the one representing the shortened measure was 0.90. In other words, the short scale consisting of only 4 out the 8 dimensions and half the number of items (15 instead of 30), still represents 81% of the variance of the full scale.

Validity of the Team Behavioral Integration Construct

Concerning the mediating variable, team behavioral integration, it was important to assess its three-dimensional nature. Indeed, the three-dimensional model, showed a much better fit compared to the one-dimensional model ($X^2 = 42.24$, $df = 24$, CFI = 0.93, TLI = 0.90, RMSEA = 0.11, SRMR = 0.07, vs. $X^2 = 121.49$, $df = 27$, CFI = 0.64, TLI = 0.51, RMSEA = 0.24, SRMR = 0.13). The internal consistencies were 0.85 for collective behavior (3 items), 0.75 for information exchange (3 items), and 0.74 for joint decision making (3 items). In addition, as a collective assessment, we wanted to confirm the extent to which behavioral integration results could be aggregated at team level. The Rwg(j) scores were 0.86 for collective behavior, 0.92 for information exchange and 0.78 for joint decision making. Additional insight is gained through the intraclass correlation (ICC1). The ICC1 scores were 0.19 for collective behavior, 0.16 for information exchange and 0.34 for joint decision making. Overall, it can be concluded that there is enough overlap between team members to calculate average team behavioral integration scores.

Validity of the Measurement Model

The output variable for team performance and the control variables of academic competence and team familiarity were used as manifest variables. Following Anderson and Gerbing (1988), we tested the adequacy of the measurement model of the latent constructs of shared servant leadership and team behavioral integration before actually testing the relations in the full model. The relative fit indices were excellent ($X^2 = 73,569$, $df = 59$, CFI = 0.96, TLI = 0.95, RMSEA = 0.06, SRMR = 0.07), confirming our operationalization of shared servant leadership and team behavioral integration with four and three separate constructs, respectively.

Validity of the Conceptual Model

Once the measurement model was confirmed, the hypothesized model was tested, showing only a moderate fit ($X^2 = 146.286$, $df = 95$, CFI = 0.88, TLI = 0.84, RMSEA = 0.09, SRMR = 0.09). By checking the significance of the paths and the modification indices, several improvements were suggested. Interestingly, neither control variable (average team academic competence or team familiarity) were significantly related to team performance. As a result, they were removed from the model. Additionally, the paths between collective behavior and joint decision making and team performance were not significant. The adjusted model with the non-significant paths fixed at zero has an excellent fit. ($X^2 = 91.645$, $df = 71$, CFI = 0.95, TLI = 0.93, RMSEA = 0.07, SRMR = 0.08). **Table 1** shows the individual mean

TABLE 1 | Descriptives and intercorrelations of study variables at team level—study 1.

	M	SD	1	2	3	4	5	6	7	8	9
1. Academic competence	70.14	2.87									
2. Team familiarity	3.46	0.83	0.15								
3. Collective behavior	6.14	0.48	0.13	−0.15							
4. Information exchange	4.94	0.47	−0.01	−0.10	0.38*						
5. Joint decision making	5.31	0.41	−0.01	0.15	0.53*	0.43*					
6. Empowerment	3.36	0.34	0.00	0.28*	0.38*	0.39*	0.57*				
7. Accountability	3.41	0.43	0.18	0.37	−0.00	0.08	0.33*	0.40*			
8. Stewardship	3.91	0.40	0.29*	−0.02	0.20	0.08	0.32*	0.51*	0.11		
9. Humility	3.01	0.90	0.13	0.34	0.25*	0.31*	0.37*	0.73*	0.31*	0.48	
10. Team performance	7.92	1.34	−0.08	−0.12	0.10	0.56*	0.16	0.08	−0.16	−0.11	0.12

n = 61.
*$p < 0.05$.

values, standard deviations and intercorrelations of the variables of study 1.

Figure 2 shows the standardized model. As it can be seen, shared servant leadership is related to all three elements of behavioral integration. This shows that shared servant leadership behavior within self-managed teams is closely related to a stronger collective functioning. There is also an indirect relation to performance, notably through information exchange in the team.

In a final step, this indirect role of information exchange in the relation between servant leadership and team performance was tested with bootstrapping (Preacher et al., 2008). The standardized estimated indirect coefficient was 0.21 ($p = 0.01$; 95% confidence interval ranged between 0.07 and 0.34), confirming its mediating role.

Conclusion

This first study seems to confirm the first hypothesis that shared team servant leadership does have an effect on team behavioral integration. Concerning the second hypothesis, within the team behavioral integration construct, information exchange seems to play a more prominent role as a mediating variable, which confirms the prominence of this factor as suggested by Yammarino et al. (2012). The fact that academic competence and team familiarity do not seem to influence this set of relations only comes to strengthen the apparent power of shared servant leadership on bringing teams to a higher performing level.

Another important and promising development from this first study is the validity and reliability of the short measure for shared servant leadership based on 4 dimensions and 15 items, as opposed to the original consisting of 8 dimensions and 30 items. This allows capturing the essence of shared servant leadership as a model based on four key dimensions: humility, empowerment, stewardship and accountability as advanced in our third hypothesis. On a more practical level, this short measure eases research through the reduced number of items in the survey, which is quite relevant when using an extensive round-robin approach to measure team shared leadership.

In order to confirm the conclusions and findings explained before, a second similar study was developed. The findings of this second study will now be explained.

RESULTS STUDY 2

Validity of the Short Shared Servant Leadership Measure

The fit of the new developed 4-dimensional measure from was compared to a 1-dimensional structure (all items loading on one leadership dimension). The fit indices were $X^2 = 165.896$, $df = 84$, CFI = 0.95, TLI = 0.94, RMSEA = 0.06, SRMR = 0.05, for the 4-dimensional model, and $X^2 = 535.909$, $df = 90$, CFI = 0.73, TLI = 0.68, RMSEA = 0.13, SRMR = 0.09, for the 1-dimensional model. The 4-dimensional model with one underlying dimension showed a comparable fit: $X^2 = 165.149$, $df = 86$, CFI = 0.95, TLI = 0.94, RMSEA = 0.06, SRMR = 0.05. The standardized factor loading of the sub-dimensions on the second order factor were: 0.94 for empowerment, 0.51 for accountability, 0.88 for stewardship, and 0.96 for humility. The internal consistencies were 0.81 for empowerment (6 items), 0.90 for accountability (3 items), 0.69 for stewardship (2 items), and 0.77 for humility (4 items). Taken together, these results confirm the factorial validity of the shared servant leadership measure as developed in study 1, as a 4-dimensional concept with one underlying second order factor.

Validity of the Team Behavioral Integration Construct

The internal consistencies for the team behavioral integration measure were 0.89 for collective behavior (3 items), 0.86 for information exchange (3 items), and 0.90 for joint decision making (3 items). All demonstrating good results. As in study 1, we checked the overlap between team members in their estimation to confirm our use of aggregated team scores for team behavioral integration. The Rwg(j) scores (James et al., 1984) were 0.91 for collective behavior, 0.94 for information exchange and 0.89 for joint decision making. The ICC1 scores were 0.31 for collective behavior, 0.59 for information exchange and 0.41

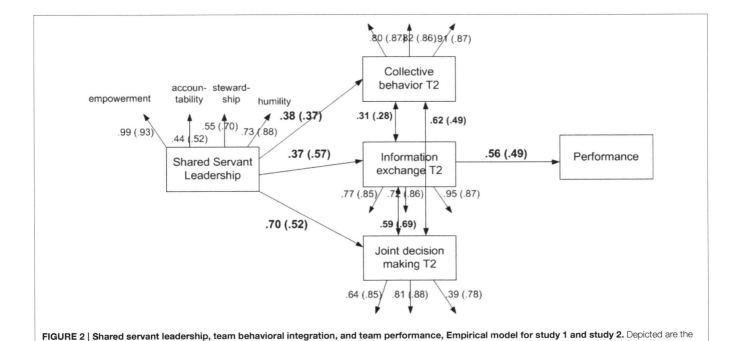

FIGURE 2 | Shared servant leadership, team behavioral integration, and team performance, Empirical model for study 1 and study 2. Depicted are the standardized values. Between brackets are the values for study 2.

for joint decision making, again allowing us to aggregate results at team level.

Validity of the Conceptual Model

Next, the model from study 1 was tested in this study to see if it could be replicated with an independent sample within a similar setting. The latent model was determined in the same way as in study 1. The fit was again good: $X^2 = 112.966$, $df = 71$, CFI = 0.94, TLI = 0.92, RMSEA = 0.09, SRMR = 0.07. There were no significant improvements suggested by the modification indices. The indirect role of information exchange in the relation between servant leadership and team performance was again tested with bootstrapping (Preacher et al., 2008). The standardized estimated indirect coefficient was 0.28 ($p < 0.001$; 95% confidence interval ranged between 0.16 and 0.40), confirming its mediating role. The standardized factor loadings of the resulting model can be found between brackets in **Figure 2**. **Table 2** shows the individual mean values, standard deviations and intercorrelations of the variables of study 2.

Conclusion

The results of the second study confirmed the findings of the first study, both in terms of the effect of shared servant leadership on team behavioral integration and the mediating role of information exchange in explaining the relationship between shared servant leadership and team performance. In addition, we were able to confirm once again the validity of the short version of the servant leadership measure. We now give a more general discussion on these findings and some indications for future research.

DISCUSSION

The research reported in this paper was designed to study the specific role of shared servant leadership in self-managed teams. The fact that we were able to replicate results in two studies separated by 1 year gives us confidence in our main findings. The most important findings were: (1) shared servant leadership has a very significant impact on team behavioral integration (confirming our first hypothesis), (2) information exchange plays a prominent role as a mediating variable between shared servant leadership and team performance (partially confirming the second hypothesis), and (3) a short measure of shared servant leadership was introduced consisting of four key dimensions (empowerment, humility, stewardship and accountability) and 15 items which appears to be valid and reliable. The results demonstrating the influence of shared servant leadership on team behavioral integration are a clear contribution to the servant leadership field. In a time when collectivist forms of leadership and self-managed teams seem to be gaining relevance in organizational work, it is interesting to notice how shared leadership processes and in particular shared servant leadership can be determinant in increasing collective behavior, information exchange and shared decision making. This confirms the perspective that leadership needs to be seen as a mutual process of taking ownership and initiative and not only as a one-to-others power relationship. There are multiple paths to creating teams that function, and centralized leadership can surely be one of them, but our results seem to demonstrate that shared leadership can also be quite effective in that process. Further research will be needed to understand the specific conditions under which shared leadership or centralized leadership become

TABLE 2 | Descriptives and intercorrelations of study variables at team level—study 2.

	M	SD	1	2	3	4	5	6	7
1. Collective behavior	6.00	0.42							
2. Information exchange	5.17	0.49	0.38*						
3. Joint decision making	5.35	0.50	0.47*	0.70*					
4. Empowerment	3.37	0.38	0.31*	0.47*	0.46*				
5. Accountability	3.32	0.46	0.30*	0.46*	0.34*	0.43*			
6. Stewardship	3.21	0.36	0.16	0.40*	0.40*	0.69*	0.37*		
7. Humility	3.16	0.37	0.25*	0.39*	0.42*	0.81*	0.54*	0.60*	
8. Team performance	7.47	1.74	0.12	0.50*	0.44*	0.16	0.16	0.11	0.18

n = 72.
*p < 0.05.

more appropriate for generating team behavioral integration. At the same time, through this study we show that servant leadership, with its focus on others, might be a model particularly suited for shared leadership in teams. Further investigating the role of each of the specific servant leadership dimensions on team behavioral integration will be important, while confirming the theoretical relationships established in this paper between these two constructs.

An essential theoretical contribution consists on a better understanding of the role of behavioral integration as a mediating variable between shared leadership and performance. Firstly, as explained before, team behavioral integration, already an important aspect in top management team performance (Simsek et al., 2005; Lubatkin et al., 2006), was shown to be influenced by the extent that team members showed servant leadership behavior toward each other. Our second finding suggests that information exchange was the most relevant dimension for the performance of self-managed teams in both our studies, which supports the importance attributed to this construct for shared leadership (Yammarino et al., 2012). We were however somewhat surprised to observe that neither collective behavior nor joint decision making acted as mediating variables, as advanced in our hypothesis. It is likely, however, that the context will affect the relative importance of the separate team behavioral integration dimensions. We suggest that the particular influence of information exchange on team performance in our studies, compared to collective behavior and joint decision making, might have to do with the knowledge-intensive nature and short time span of the simulations in both assignments. In other words, when work is mainly related to the production of knowledge in a short period of time, the ability to quickly tap into the team's existing knowledge though effective information exchange might be the main driver of performance. This would be true for both information quantity (i.e., number of ideas and solutions being offered) and quality (i.e., relevance and effectiveness of the solutions). It seems therefore that the affective social integration aspect of collective behavior, demonstrated through behaviors of mutual support and social interaction, might be less relevant when teams need to work over short periods of time under high pressure. In addition, one should also note that the operationalization of joint decision making by Simsek et al. (2005) emphasizes that the needs and perspectives

of different members are considered. The consequence being that joint decision processes are therefore by definition more time consuming. The short nature of the team assignments in this study and the need to quickly iterate between decisions and the simulation results (as opposed to highly complex decisions with multiple stakeholders over longer periods, as in the case of top management teams), might therefore help explain why joint decision making does not seem to play a relevant role for these particular cases. As such, we would expect collective behavior (as a measure of social integration and affective bond among team members) and joint decision making (as a time intensive task oriented dimension) to take an increasingly important role on performance over longer and more complex multi-stakeholder projects or when time pressure is not so high. Such contexts would be closer to the cases of top management teams, upon which most team behavioral integration literature has been developed. Further studies comparing short team assignments to longer and more complex team projects might shed some more light on this differentiated functioning of team behavioral integration.

Finally, the third finding of this paper on the short measure of shared servant leadership is rather promising from both a theoretical and practical perspective. The servant leadership survey that was the base of the current measure had to be modified to meet psychometric criteria and, at the same time, be practical for a round-robin approach of measuring shared leadership. A four-dimensional shared servant leadership scale is introduced that is in line with earlier theorizing on servant leadership (Van Dierendonck and Nuijten, 2011). The version that came out of our theoretical arguments and was confirmed in the analyses across two studies encompasses four core dimensions of servant leadership, namely: empowerment, humility, accountability and stewardship. We were able to observe that the short scale still represented 81% of the variance of the full scale. With only 15 items, instead of 30, this shortened survey can more easily be incorporated into future research on shared servant leadership and be of particular utility when using a round-robin approach with many mutual items between team members.

When considering the limitations of our study, we acknowledge that a student sample following a business simulation as the basis of the team work might not be entirely indicative of an organizational or business context. Regardless, the simulation's rather realistic scenarios, extracted from real-life cases does create a close-to-real environment when it comes to the actual decision being made. In addition our simulation based sample has multiple advantages. It guarantees the high response rate in most teams needed to test our hypothesis, which is very hard to realize in field studies. Teams had exactly the same assignment, eliminating the influence of aspects related to differing assignment complexities. The simulation took place within a limited time-span, being the main activity of the participants, reducing the influence of other work related demands in the team functioning. Also, most team studies use supervisory ratings of performance. Here it is feedback provided by the simulation program itself, which gives it a more objective and consistent character. Finally, a major strength is that we were able to replicate the findings of one study in the second study 1 year later, under the same circumstances and with the same type of assignment (something that would be very hard to realize outside an educational environment). At any rate, while there is supporting evidence to the parallels that can be established between students and other populations in their behavior in achievement settings (e.g., Locke, 1986; Brown and Lord, 1999), as our results seem to show, team behavioral integration might work differently depending on the duration, pressure and complexity of projects. Further studies in organizational

or business settings would definitely be welcome to confirm our findings and further elaborate on the workings of team behavioral integration.

In conclusion, in view of the increasing popularity of collectivistic forms of leadership and self-managed teams in particular, getting additional insights into the processes that influence their effectiveness is crucial. The findings of this study emphasize the important role of shared servant leadership on team behavioral integration and its potential effect on performance through information exchange, further supporting the idea that servant leadership might be particularly suitable for shared leadership. Moreover, we are able to confirm the specific relevance of the four dimensions of empowerment, humility, accountability and stewardship as the key fundamental aspects of shared servant leadership, as well as the validity of the corresponding short measure.

AUTHOR CONTRIBUTIONS

The article is the result of a joint effort and co-authorship is fully shared. The leading role shifted from the initial stages of field research to the final writing and editing of the document, as follows: Design and implementation of the field research (DV with the support of MS). Analysis of results (MS and DV jointly). Writing and editing of article (MS with the support of DV).

REFERENCES

Anderson, J. C., and Gerbing, D. W. (1988). Structural equation modeling in practice: a review and recommended two-step approach. *Psychol. Bull.* 103, 411–423. doi: 10.1037/0033-2909.103.3.411

Asag-gau, L., and Van Dierendonck, D. (2011). The impact of servant leadership on organizational commitment among the highly talented: the role of challenging work conditions and psychological empowerment. *Eur. J. Int. Manage.* 5, 463–483. doi: 10.1504/EJIM.2011.042174

Avolio, B. J., Sivasubramaniam, N., Murry, W. D., Jung, D., and Garger, J. W. (2003). "Development and preliminary validation of a team multifactor leadership questionnaire," in *Shared Leadership: Reframing the Hows and Whys of Leadership*, eds C. L. Pearce and J. A. Conger (Thousand Oaks, CA: Sage Publications), 143–172. doi: 10.4135/9781452229539.n7

Bandalos, D. L. (2002). The effects of item parceling on goodness-of-fit and parameter estimate bias in structural equation modelling. *Struct. Equation Model.* 9, 78–102.

Bligh, M. C., Pearce, C. L., and Kohles, J. C. (2006). The importance of self- and shared leadership in team based knowledge work. A meso-model of leadership dynamics. *J. Manage. Psychol.* 21, 296–318. doi: 10.1108/02683940610663105

Bobbio, A., Van Dierendonck, D., and Manganelli, A. M. (2012). Servant leadership in Italy and its relation to organizational variables. *Leadership* 8, 229–243. doi: 10.1177/1742715012441176

Brown, D. J., and Lord, R. G. (1999). The utility of experimental research in the study of transformational/charismatic leadership. *Leadersh. Q.* 10, 531–539. doi: 10.1016/S1048-9843(99)00029-6

Carmeli, A. (2008). Top management team behavioral integration and the performance of service organizations. *Group Organ. Manage.* 33, 712–735. doi: 10.1177/1059601108325696

Carmeli, A., and Schaubroeck, J. (2006). Top management team behavioral integration, decision quality, and organizational decline. *Leadersh. Q.* 17, 441–453. doi: 10.1016/j.leaqua.2006.06.001

Carson, J. B., Tesluk, P. E., and Marrone, J. A. (2007). Shared leadership in teams: an investigation of antecedent conditions and performance. *Acad. Manage. J.* 50, 1217–1234. doi: 10.2307/20159921

Ensley, M. D., Pearson, A., and Pearce, C. L. (2003). Top management team process, shared leadership, and a new venture performance: a theoretical model and research agenda. *Hum. Resour. Manage. Rev.* 13, 329–346. doi: 10.1016/S1053-4822(03)00020-2

Friedrich, T. L., Vessey, W. B., Schuelke, M. J., Ruark, G. A., and Mumford, M. D. (2009). A framework for understanding collective leadership: the selective utilization of leader and team expertise within networks. *Leadersh. Q.* 20, 933–958. doi: 10.1016/j.leaqua.2009.09.008

Gockel, C., and Werth, L. (2010). Measuring and modeling shared leadership. Traditional approaches and new ideas. *J. Pers. Psychol.* 9, 172–180. doi: 10.1027/1866-5888/a000023

Greenleaf, R. K. (1977). *Servant Leadership: A Journey into the Nature of Legitimate Power and Greatness.* Mahwah, NJ: Paulist Press.

Greenleaf, R. K. (2002). *Servant Leadership: A Journey into the Nature of Legitimate Power and Greatness.* Mahwah, NJ: Paulist Press.

Gruenfeld, D. H., Mannix, E. A., Williams, K. Y., and Neale, M. A. (1996). Group composition and decision making: how member familiarity and information distribution affect process and performance. *Organ. Behav. Hum. Decis. Process.* 67, 1–15. doi: 10.1006/obhd.1996.0061

Hakanen, J., and Van Dierendonck, D. (2011). Servant leadership and life satisfaction: the mediating role of justice, job control, and burnout. *Int. J. Servant-Leadersh.* 7.

Hambrick, D. C. (1994). Top management groups: a conceptual integration and reconsideration of the "team" label. *Res. Organ. Behav.* 16, 171–213.

Hoch, J. E., Pearce, C. L., and Welzel, L. (2010). Is the most effective team leadership shared? The impact of shared leadership, age diversity, and coordination on team performance. *J. Pers. Psychol.* 9, 105–116. doi: 10.1027/1866-5888/a000020

Hu, J., and Liden, R. C. (2011). Antecedents of team potency and team effectiveness: an examination of goal and process clarity and servant leadership. *J. Appl. Psychol.* 96, 851–862. doi: 10.1037/a0022465

James, L. R., Demaree, R. G., and Wolfe, G. (1984). Estimating within-group interrater reliability with and without response bias. *J. Appl. Psychol.* 69, 85–98. doi: 10.1037/0021-9010.69.1.85

Konczak, L. J., Stelly, D. J., and Trusty, M. L. (2000). Defining and measuring empowering leader behaviors: developing of an upward feedback instrument. *Educ. Psychol. Meas.* 60, 301–313. doi: 10.1177/00131640021970420

Locke, E. A. (1986). "Generalizing from laboratory to field: ecological validity or abstraction of essential elements," in *Generalizing from Laboratory to Field Settings*, ed E. A. Locke (Englewood Cliffs, NJ: Prentice Hall), 3–9.

Lubatkin, M. H., Simsek, Z., Ling, Y., and Veiga, J. F. (2006). Ambidexterity and performance in small- to medium-sized firms: the pivotal role of top management team behavioral integration. *J. Manage.* 32, 646–672. doi: 10.1177/0149206306290712

Magni, M., Proserpio, L., Hoegl, M., and Provera, B. (2009). The role of team behavioral integration and cohesion in shaping individual improvisation. *Res. Policy* 38, 1044–1053. doi: 10.1016/j.respol.2009.03.004

Mayo, M., Meindl, J. R., and Pastor, J.-C. (2003). "Shared leadership in work teams: a social network approach," in *Shared Leadership, Reframing the How's and the Why's of Leadership*, eds C. L. Pearce and J. A. Conger (Thousand Oaks, CA: Sage Publications), 193–214.

Muthén, L. K., and Muthén, B. O. (2009). *MPlus User's Guide, 6th Edn.* Los Angeles, CA: Muthén and Muthén.

O'Reilly, C. A., Caldwell, D. F., and Barnett, W. P. (1989). Work group demography, social integration, and turnover. *Adm. Sci. Q.* 34, 21–37.

Patterson, K. (2003). *Servant Leadership: A Theoretical Model.* Doctoral dissertation, Regent University. ATT 3082719.

Pearce, C. L., and Conger, J. A. (2003). "All those years ago: the historical underpinnings of shared leadership," in *Shared Leadership: Reframing the Hows and Whys of Leadership*, eds C. L. Pearce and J. A. Conger (Thousand Oaks, CA: Sage Publications), 1–20.

Pearce, C. L., and Sims, H. P. Jr. (2002). Vertical versus shared leadership as predictors of the effectiveness of change management teams: an examination of aversive, directive, transactional, transformational, and empowering leader behaviors. *Group Dyn. Theory Res. Pract.* 6, 172–197. doi: 10.1037/1089-2699.6.2.172

Preacher, K. J., Rucker, D. D., and Hayes, A. F. (2008). Addressing moderated mediation hypotheses: theory, methods, and prescriptions. *Multivariate Behav. Res.* 42, 185–227. doi: 10.1080/00273170701341316

Russell, R. F. (2001). The role of values in servant leadership. *Leadersh. Organ. Dev. J.* 22, 76–84. doi: 10.1108/01437730110382631

Schaubroeck, J., Lam, S. S. K., and Peng, A. C. (2011). Cognition-based and affect-based trust as mediators of leader behavior influences on team performance. *J. Appl. Psychol.* 96, 863–871. doi: 10.1037/a0022625

Schein, E. H. (2013). *Humble Inquiry: The Gentle Art of Asking Instead of Telling.* San Francisco, CA: Berrett-Koehler Publishers.

Schweiger, D. M., and Sandberg, W. R. (1989). The utilization of individual capabilities in group approaches to strategic decision-making. *Strateg. Manage. J.* 10, 31–43. doi: 10.1002/smj.4250100104

Siegel, P. A., and Hambrick, D. C. (1996). "Business strategy and the social psychology of top management teams," in *Advances in Strategic Management*, Vol. 13, eds J. A. C. Baum and J. E. Dutton (Greenwich, CT: JAI Press), 91–119.

Simsek, Z., Veiga, J. F., Lubatkin, M. H., and Dino, R. N. (2005). Modeling the multilevel determinants of top management team behavioural integration. *Acad. Manage. J.* 48, 69–84. doi: 10.5465/AMJ.2005.15993139

Sousa, M., and van Dierendonck, D. (2014). Servant leadership and engagement in a merge process under high uncertainty. *J. Organ. Change Manage.* 27, 877–899. doi: 10.1108/JOCM-07-2013-0133

Spears, L. (1996). Reflections on Robert K. Greenleaf and servant-leadership. *Leadersh. Organ. Dev. J.* 17, 33–35. doi: 10.1108/01437739610148367

Stewart, G. L., and Manz, C. C. (1995). Leadership for self-managing work teams: a typology and integrative model. *Hum. Relat.* 48, 747–771. doi: 10.1177/001872679504800702

Van Dierendonck, D. (2011). Servant leadership: a review and synthesis. *J. Manage.* 37, 1228–1261. doi: 10.1177/0149206310380462

Van Dierendonck, D., and Nuijten, I. (2011). The servant leadership survey: development and validation of a multidimensional measure. *J. Bus. Psychol.* 26, 249–267. doi: 10.1007/s10869-010-9194-1

Walumbwa, F. O., Hartnell, C. A., and Oke, A. (2010). Servant leadership, procedural justice climate, service climate, employee attitudes, and organizational citizenship behavior: a cross-level investigation. *J. Appl. Psychol.* 95, 517–529. doi: 10.1037/a0018867

West, M. A., Borrill, C. S., Dawson, J. F., Brodbeck, F., Shapiro, D. A., and Haward, B. (2003). Leadership clarity and team innovation in health care. *Leadersh. Q.* 14, 393–410. doi: 10.1016/S1048-9843(03)00044-4

Wolff, S. B., Pescosolido, A. T., and Urch Druskatt, V. (2002). Emotional intelligence as the basis of leadership emergence in self-managing teams. *Leadersh. Q.* 13, 505–522. doi: 10.1016/S1048-9843(02)00141-8

Yammarino, F. J., Mumford, M. D., Connelly, M. S., and Dionne, S. D. (2010). Leadership and team dynamics for dangerous military contexts. *Mil. Psychol.* 22, S15. doi: 10.1080/08995601003644221

Yammarino, F. J., Salas, E., Serban, A., Shirreffs, K., and Shuffler, M. L. (2012). Collectivistic leadership approaches: putting the "we" in leadership science and practice. *Ind. Organ. Psychol.* 5, 382–402. doi: 10.1111/j.1754-9434.2012.01467.x

Zaccaro, S. J., Rittman, A. L., and Marks, M. A. (2001). Team leadership. *Leadersh. Q.* 12, 451–483. doi: 10.1016/S1048-9843(01)00093-5

Conflict of Interest Statement: The authors declare that the research was conducted in the absence of any commercial or financial relationships that could be construed as a potential conflict of interest.

The Item versus the Object in Memory: On the Implausibility of Overwriting As a Mechanism for Forgetting in Short-Term Memory

C. Philip Beaman[1]* and Dylan M. Jones[2]

[1] Centre for Cognition Research, School of Psychology and Clinical Language Sciences, University of Reading, Reading, UK,
[2] School of Psychology, Cardiff University, Cardiff, UK

The nature of forgetting in short-term memory remains a disputed topic, with much debate focussed upon whether decay plays a fundamental role (Berman et al., 2009; Altmann and Schunn, 2012; Barrouillet et al., 2012; Neath and Brown, 2012; Oberauer and Lewandowsky, 2013; Ricker et al., 2014) but much less focus on other plausible mechanisms. One such mechanism of long-standing in auditory memory is overwriting (e.g., Crowder and Morton, 1969) in which some aspects of a representation are "overwritten" and rendered inaccessible by the subsequent presentation of a further item. Here, we review the evidence for different forms of overwriting (at the feature and item levels) and examine the plausibility of this mechanism both as a form of auditory memory and when viewed in the context of a larger hearing, speech and language understanding system.

Keywords: auditory cognition, short-term memory, memory, forgetting, auditory scene analysis

Edited by:
Jerker Rönnberg,
Linköping University, Sweden

Reviewed by:
Emily M. Elliott,
Louisiana State University, USA
Lars Nyberg,
Umeå University, Sweden

*Correspondence:
C. Philip Beaman
c.p.beaman@reading.ac.uk

Specialty section:
This article was submitted to
Auditory Cognitive Neuroscience,
a section of the journal
Frontiers in Psychology

Like many cognitive capabilities, language is grounded in memory. A failure to appreciate what has just gone drastically limits the ability to comprehend the present and any capacity to anticipate the future. Both long-term memory (for semantics and other lexical and world knowledge) and short-term memory (a record of the immediate past) are implicated in this process. In the current paper, a particular focus is placed upon the relationship between memory and language reception (e.g., hearing) rather than production (e.g., speaking). Although the latter is clearly of importance – both as an aspect of language in which memory must play its part and as a means by which (via overt or sub-vocal rehearsal) information is maintained in short- or longer-term memory (Craik and Watkins, 1973; Ward et al., 2003; Ward and Tan, 2004; Taylor et al., 2015) – a focus on the nature of the auditory-perceptual input suggests constraints on how any system accepting such input must be configured.

A key feature of the classical short-term memory (STM) research program is the importance of serial order (Lashley, 1951; Conrad, 1960; Murdock, 1968, 1983; Lewandowsky and Murdock, 1989; Henson, 1998; Brown et al., 2000; Botvinick and Plaut, 2006; Burgess and Hitch, 2006). Words, letters, or digits are presented sequentially and participants required to recall the items in the order in which they were presented. Short-term memory tasks are usually deliberately designed so that the associations to be held across multiple items (words, digits, letters) are arbitrary. Performance in such tasks is framed in terms of its proximity to verbatim recall of all the items, namely the correct item in its position at presentation. Implicitly, short-term memory theorists make the assumption that the "item" (the word, letter, or digit of interest)—rather than the relationship between items—is the most meaningful unit of analysis. Moreover, identification of the item at recall is the basis for correct scoring in the memory test. Despite known problems with identifying the "item" in anything other than a logically circular way (Miller, 1956) such an approach is defensible in cases where the items are well-known and taken from a small, circumscribed set (e.g., digits) and where recollection of an item at a time collapses into a requirement to select the most likely candidate given the degraded or incomplete information available (Nairne, 1990). This contrasts starkly with the situation in most everyday language, in which structured, non-arbitrary relationships are available between individual elements represented at multiple levels (phonotactic, syntactic, semantic, pragmatic) and the identification of a single "item" is neither necessary nor sufficient to comprehend the meaning of the sequence.

By considering veridical recall of arbitrary items rather than the relationships between them, much of interest is lost with regards to later analyses. A key component of perception is in organizing as well as registering information and of interest is whether, in registering and organizing the stimuli prior to retrieval, the perceptual system represents them in a way that harmonizes with the retrieval requirements in standard short-term memory tasks. Given the emphasis on the iterative retrieval of items across the to-be-remembered sequence, does the perceptual system, for instance, cluster items at a supra-item level in such a way as to aid or to hamper efficient retrieval? In other words, does perception result in 'items' corresponding exactly to items specified in terms of the linguistic taxonomy (such as single syllables, words, or digits) on which the sequence is nominally based? In the event of supra-item organization, how are items grouped or transformed? Is there grouping of adjacent elements (as with chunking, classically) or are non-adjacent items organized into a greater whole? Within item-focussed approaches to short-term memory—ones that assume recall is a product of an aggregation of elemental actions—forgetting may be explained by the 'overwriting' of items by subsequent events. If supra-segmental organization occurs, is overwriting still a plausible mechanism?

Here, we explore how the registration of events in memory reflects auditory input and, in particular, the organizational processes that are at play. On the basis of key phenomena in auditory perception we consider potential implications for the structure of short-term memory and, in particular, the nature of forgetting.

THE "STANDARD" MODEL OF MEMORY

The modal model of memory, informed by neuropsychological case data, has always assumed a functional and structural distinction between short-term and long-term memory, with the former fed by largely unspecified perceptual input processes, frequently depicted as a buffer storage system (Shallice and Cooper, 2010). In long-term memory, where the notion of memory as a reliable, veridical system has long since been dismissed and a reconstructive account of recall is generally accepted (Bartlett, 1932), suppression, inhibition and blocking of

the memory trace have all been discussed as possible explanations of forgetting (for example in the context of the misinformation effect in eyewitness memory). In contrast, discussions of short-term and sensory memory have been less open to the idea of memory distortion as normal and recall as a reconstructive activity. In consequence, processes that highlight deterioration of the representation such as decay and overwriting (respectively) have predominated as mechanisms for forgetting and active supra-segmental organizational processes (such as grouping into objects), which may equally hamper recall when they are inconsistent with retrieval requirements, have been largely ignored.

Much has already been written both critiquing the evidence for decay (e.g., Neath and Nairne, 1995; Nairne, 2002; Lewandowsky and Oberauer, 2008, 2009, 2015; Lewandowsky et al., 2008; Oberauer and Lewandowsky, 2008, 2013; Brown and Lewandowsky, 2010; Neath and Brown, 2012) and defending the concept (Altmann and Gray, 2002; Portrat et al., 2008; Altmann, 2009; Barrouillet et al., 2011; Altmann and Schunn, 2012) so, rather than repeating now-familiar arguments about decay versus some other (often unspecified)[1] form of interference as the source of forgetting (see Ricker et al., 2014, for a review), here we will specifically consider interference by overwriting as it appears from the perspective of auditory perception and the organization of the auditory environment.

The introduction of overwriting or displacement as a key determinant of forgetting over the short-term can be traced back to early studies of auditory sensory memory. Classically, a restricted-capacity acoustic sensory memory trace, overwritten by subsequent auditory events (Crowder and Morton, 1969), is available to supplement end-of-sequence recall otherwise only supported by "post-categorical" short-term memory systems dedicated to verbal memory but otherwise blind to sensory modality or the perceptual origins of the memoranda. This venerable account is nonetheless still extant and has been incorporated into more recent formulations of the contribution of sensory memory to immediate recall of auditory-verbal material (e.g., Page and Norris, 1998, and Burgess and Hitch, 1999, both make reference to an auditory input buffer overwritten by subsequent data). Latterly, other formulations of short-term memory have also utilized overwriting as a means of implementing interference and hence forgetting. For example, in providing a framework for short-term memory that eschews decay as a concept, Nairne (1990, 2002), Neath and Nairne (1995), Neath (2000), Oberauer and Kliegl (2006), Oberauer and Lange (2008), Lewandowsky et al. (2009), and Oberauer (2009) explicitly replace decay with overwriting as an explanatory concept. For memory of specifically auditory origin, therefore, three claims have been made:

(1) An auditory sensory store is overwritten, an item at a time, during encoding (e.g., Crowder and Morton, 1969; Page

---

[1]In fact, Lewandowsky et al. (2009, box 4) postulate at least four possible alternatives to trace decay and Ricker et al. (2014, Table 1) suggest five possibilities, all of which – as with decay itself – may be implemented in different ways (e.g., Lewandowsky and Farrell, 2011).

and Norris, 1998; Burgess and Hitch, 1999; Mercer and McKeown, 2010a).

(2) Both modality specific (sensory) and modality-independent (post-categorical, phonological) features are overwritten during encoding (e.g., Neath and Nairne, 1995; Neath, 2000).

(3) Features are overwritten via neural competition removing the availability of feature-units at a post-encoding phase (Oberauer and Kliegl, 2006; Oberauer and Lange, 2008; Oberauer, 2009).

It is interesting that the "precategorical" acoustic nature of the auditory sensory store (Crowder and Morton, 1969) arose because of prior theoretical commitments to a model of word recognition—the logogen model—which assumed a single system for recognizing both written and spoken words (Morton, 1964, 1969). Subsequent to this, changes to the logogen model (Morton, 1979) removed this theoretical constraint and introduced separate auditory and visual input logogens so that the idea that overwriting occurred at an early processing stage was retained even though the original *a priori* reasons for assuming that overwriting occurred prior to word-identification had vanished. The Crowder and Morton (1969) view is, despite its commitment to a pre-categorical (presumably continuous) representational format a classically item-based data buffer system of the first-in, first-out variety. Their approach can be contrasted with the forms of overwriting implemented in models by Nairne (1990) and Lange and Oberauer (2005).

In Nairne's (1990) feature model of immediate memory, individual items are represented as vectors of features, which may represent modality-specific or modality-independent information. The eponymous features were speculatively identified with patterns of neural firing by Beaman et al. (2008) and, although their exact nature and status has never been formally defined, it is at this level that overwriting operates within the model. Feature overwriting works by an incoming item deleting identical features already held as part of the representation of immediately preceding item. For example, if the third feature of item *n+1* of a sequence takes the same value as item *n* of the same sequence then the item-level representation of *n* is denuded of this feature, the representation becomes degraded as a consequence and *n* is henceforth less likely to be correctly recalled when cued to do so at some point in the future.

In contrast, the version of overwriting put forward by Lange and Oberauer (2005) and Oberauer and Kliegl (2006) interference is not limited to the preceding item. Like the approach of Nairne (1990), the model is once again feature-based; in this instance, however, different items are represented as patterns of activation across a subset of the features ("feature units") available system-wide and representations compete for access to their constituent feature units. Where a given representation loses this competition, the feature unit is captured by that competitor and is not available as part of the item representation of the "losing" representation. In this way a particular representation is degraded, thus impeding recall. The neural competition for features is framed in terms of synchronized firing of neurons as a mechanism of binding together the features that belong to the representation of an item (Raffone and Wolters, 2001). Feature units possessing features belonging to the same representation fire synchronously, whereas units belonging to different representations fire out of synchrony.

The principal difficulty with overwriting as the sole, or key, determinant of failure to recall in these or any other accounts is that while many studies have reported greater interference when irrelevant information (e.g., from a secondary task; Lange and Oberauer, 2005) is related to the memoranda, or when the list items are themselves similar along a specific dimension (e.g., the phonological similarity effect; Conrad, 1964; Conrad and Hull, 1964; Baddeley, 1966) other studies have shown the opposite. Overwriting in the three accounts given above assumes that interference occurs between similar items or items with similar features – acoustic items displace earlier acoustic items in a precategorical store (Crowder and Morton, 1969) or features are overwritten if they are shared between successive items (Nairne, 1990) or if they are supported by common feature units (Lange and Oberauer, 2005). These assumptions readily account for data in which interference is observed at recall between items that are similar along one or more crucial dimensions. However, Mercer and McKeown (2010a,b) found that complex tones were more accurately identified in a same-different task when followed by distractors containing *novel* frequencies – those frequencies not present in the target - when compared to a condition in which the distractors shared frequencies with the target. This pattern of results is directly contrary to that which would naturally occur if similarity-based overwriting was in operation.

Interestingly, Mercer and McKeown (2010b) also concluded in favor of an overwriting account – but in their model, directly contrary to assumptions made by other theorists about overwriting, "interference is principally caused by tones that include *novel* features since these will be most potent in "overwriting" the contents of the auditory spectral short-term memory buffer" (Mercer and McKeown, 2010b, p. 1258, emphasis added). In other words, this model assumes overwriting by items which are representationally distinct from the preceding input, rather than by items which share features with earlier items. Whether overwriting is assumed to occur amongst similar or dissimilar items/features is, of course, an *a priori* decision for any theorist attempting to construct a model (Lewandowsky and Farrell, 2011) but it is unlikely that similar items would be overwritten in some cognitive systems and dissimilar items overwritten elsewhere. To allow that closely related cognitive and perceptual subsystems work on diametrically opposed principles is, at best, un-parsimonious and contrary to Occam's Razor. If overwriting is to be accepted then a consistent set of rules should apply (Surprenant and Neath, 2009). Nor is the study by Mercer and McKeown (2010b) (which involved fairly "low-level" and non-verbal acoustic stimuli) unique in its findings. An earlier study by Nairne and Kelley (1999) showed that the phonological similarity effect observed with verbal stimuli is reversed after relatively brief periods of distraction, resulting in better performance in a serial order reconstruction test for phonologically similar lists than for phonologically dissimilar lists. If overwriting is seen as necessary to account for forgetting caused by interference effects between similar items, then reversing these similarity effects casts doubt upon the need for overwriting.

Finally, task requirements—which are unlikely to directly influence low-level processes such as overwriting/displacement of patterns of neural firing or competition for neural feature units—also play a substantial role in similarity effects for which overwriting is offered as an explanatory mechanism. Despite numerous documented similarities between immediate free and serial recall (Beaman and Jones, 1998; Bhatarah et al., 2006, 2008; Ward et al., 2010; Grenfell-Essam and Ward, 2012; Grenfell-Essam et al., 2013; Spurgeon et al., 2014) similarity effects within the to-be-recalled list —supposedly reflecting the impact of item-representations degraded by direct over-writing (Nairne, 1990) or competition for specific feature units (Oberauer and Kliegl, 2006)—depress performance on immediate serial recall tasks but enhance performance in free recall (Fournet et al., 2003). Once again it is difficult to reconcile such findings with a low-level, item-based and automatic overwriting interference process without appealing to a higher-level activity that negates, and more than negates, the negative effect of similarity-based overwriting. To account for the reversal of the phonological similarity effect, Nairne and Kelley (1999) proposed that a period of distraction allows phonological similarity to be used as a cue to select candidate items for serial reconstruction of order (e.g., any correct item must share a rime with all other items) and similar suggestions are equally applicable to free, or item, recall situations (e.g., Watkins et al., 1974; Saint-Aubin and Poirier, 1999). However, such accounts are necessarily *post hoc* and—if overwriting occurs—strategies such as these must be sufficiently ubiquitous and powerful enough to not only negate but *reverse* the similarity effects otherwise observed. Exigencies of space mean that the interesting issue of retrieval mode and streaming cannot here be addressed fully but we note that free recall is in part controlled by strategic retrieval factors so that we may expect effects such as those of similarity to be different dependent upon the mode of recall and, critically, scoring technique employed. A stream of similar-sounding items will necessarily lose order cues relative to a dissimilar stream up until the point that items become so dissimilar that stream coherence is lost (Jones et al., 1999). There are no such necessary consequences for retrieval of individual items so scoring criteria at test are crucial in the appearance and form of similarity effects.

AUDITORY SCENE ANALYSIS: SOME PRELIMINARIES

If a structural account of forgetting is set aside, what remains? Perceptual organization has profound consequences not just for the coherence of our experience of the world but also for the accessibility of information contained within it. Perception itself is directly linked to memory, as, for example, the perception of loudness is determined by a temporal integration of acoustic power; the perceived loudness of a burst of white noise depends upon its duration (Scharf, 1978) demonstrating that perception is reliant upon memory in a manner which renders the simple

idea that incoming stimuli "automatically" overwrite pre-existing representations problematic. There is a mass of evidence showing powerful effects of perceptual organization and, as with vision, it is useful to think of auditory perception in terms of objects. So, despite being intrinsically evanescent in a way that the visual world is often not, successive events are assembled into temporally extended objects in a way that allows several "streams" of information to co-exist. Note that this is immediately different from the situation assumed within most models of verbal STM, which concentrate upon memory for a single list, and require further work to allow simultaneous representation of multiple lists or streams within the same representational space. Generally, the rules of organization follow Gestalt principles that are based on the physical attributes of the stimuli: proximity, similarity, closure, symmetry, common fate, continuity, among others. So, auditory perception is an active process that partitions the auditory world into auditory objects or streams, a process known generically as *auditory scene analysis* (Bregman, 1990). It is difficult to overstate the importance that these forces of organization have on what may be retrieved from an auditory scene, even when the scene comprises a few simple stimuli.

Necessarily, stream formation involves memory. A succession of individual stimuli achieves stream quality by a process that depend on not just a single but many preceding stimuli, a process that requires storage. Streams take time to form and less compelling streams can vacillate and break down. In everyday environments, scene analysis typically results in several simultaneous streams, such as the instruments of a rock bank or orchestra, or indeed a domestic scene of refrigerator noise, radio and conversation. Also, the principles by which this is achieved are embodied in musical polyphony: the rules of composition—though in a non-acoustic language—allow a composer to generate an intelligible and coherent rendition of harmonic and melodic intent.

So, the logic adopted here is that auditory memory is intimately connected to auditory perception and that in turn the study of auditory perception suggests ways in which auditory-verbal memory is organized. Furthermore, we know that this organization is not veridical, in as much as it does not faithfully represent an item-by-item sequence, free of item clusters. As we will see later, the item-clusters produced by auditory perception are very much richer and more diverse than those considered by current models of verbal STM.

It is useful to consider specific instances, using some very simple non-verbal stimuli, of how perceptual organization of sound brings about changes to perception before returning to the case of verbal memory. The first example shows how the context in which stimuli appear works to shape what we may know of them. Take the very simple case of two short tones, A and B, the same in every respect except that they are a semi-tone apart, presented in quick succession (see **Figure 1**). When faced with the task of reporting the order as being high-low or low-high, most listeners find they can make the discrimination quite easily. However, if flankers (F_1 and F_2)—sharing almost the same pitch and tempo as A and B (see again **Figure 1**)— are inserted either side of them then we observe a dramatic reduction in the capacity to report the order of A and B. How might this come about?

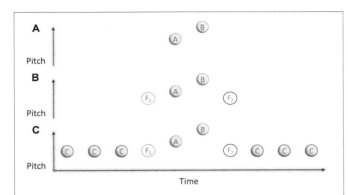

FIGURE 1 | Arrangement of stimuli in the experiment of Bregman and Rudnicky (1975). (A) Shows two stimuli—A and B—differing slightly in pitch. (B) Shows the case where two stimuli (flankers) of identical pitch—F1 and F2—flank the AB pair. (C) Shows the case in which a sequence of stimuli—the captor C stimuli—precede and follow the flanker stimuli. The flankers and captors share pitch and timing.

One way to think in terms of overwriting and to suppose that the second flanker (or indeed both flankers) somehow interfere with the representation of A and B, making their comparison less easy. Another way is frame the change in context in terms of object formation. Whilst presented as a pair, A and B formed a single object and at the same time constituted its boundaries. Adding the flankers created a new object and new boundaries, with A and B now constituting its innards, so that now the order information contained in A and B becomes more difficult to address. This is a familiar situation in STM where current recall of the items and order of the first and last few items gives rise to primacy and recency effects, with recall of items in the correct order very much worse toward the center of the list.

A simple further addition to this auditory scene shows how implausible the overwriting explanation turns out to be in the case of simple tones. If we add a further two stimuli (C_1 and C_2 in Figure 1) either side and sharing both pitch and tempo with the flankers then we witness a remarkable transformation: if we now ask a listener to judge the pitch order of A and B, close to full efficiency (that is, the level of performance when A and B are presented in isolation) is restored. Clearly, according to the overwriting view (and indeed, most interference theories of forgetting) adding more stimuli should – if anything – produce more overwriting, not less. However, the outcome of adding the C stimuli is readily understood in terms of auditory scene analysis. The C stimuli act as 'captors,' that is, by virtue of their greater similarity to the F stimuli than to the AB pair, two objects are formed; the one: $CCCF_1F_2CCC$, the other: AB. The flankers are captured, releasing AB to become a separate, and therefore an independently addressable, entity thereby restoring memory for the order of A and B.

This setting shows several remarkable qualities of auditory scene analysis with a number of important implications for the way we understand memory. The first and most profound is that the future shapes the past: perception is retroactive. What follows from this has great relevance to our current discussion about the plausibility of overwriting as an explanatory construct.

Critically, the perceptibility of AB is only decided when both F_2 and CCC are presented, but even then both F_2CCC and AB are distinguishable only with reference to F_1 and CCC. The first point that follows from this is that it is important therefore to think in terms of the emergent properties of the stimulus ensemble (the object), not merely as an aggregation of the properties of individual stimuli. The second point is that items need not be temporally adjacent in order to form into objects.

A second illustration lends weight to the first while at the same time addressing the natural skepticism that such a simple setting involving the mere 'perception' of tones A and B could have more general repercussions for more complex settings that we think as being characteristic of the study of 'memory.' Here again, the listener is asked to compare two tones but this time asked to make the judgment about whether they are the same or different in pitch (Jones et al., 1997).

Figure 2 shows the arrangement of stimuli used by Jones, Macken, and Harries (following, for example, Deutsch, 1972, 1978a,b; Semal and Demany, 1991, 1993; Starr and Pitt, 1997; Mathias and von Kriegstein, 2014). First, a standard stimulus—a tone—is followed either by a blank interval or a filled interval and then, some seconds later, by a comparison stimulus: another tone. The listener is asked to ignore stimuli that come between the standard and comparison tones in making their judgment.

The key variable of interest is the content of the interval and its effects on the accuracy of the comparison judgment. Having a sequence of tones in the interval similar in pitch and timbre to the standard and comparison (see Figure 2) has a dramatic effect of reducing the accuracy of the same-different judgment. If, instead of having tones, we have speech stimuli (say a sequence of words), comparison judgment improves considerably, to a level that is close to when there are no interpolated stimuli. This result is conventionally interpreted in an overwriting framework: memory for the standard is compromised by similar stimuli interpolated between it and the comparison (e.g., Semal and Demany, 1991, 1993; Mathias and von Kriegstein, 2014). However, another of the conditions in the study of Jones et al. (1997) makes this interpretation implausible. If the number of interpolated tones is doubled then any reasonable interpretation the overwriting account suggests that performance cannot improve and should, in fact, deteriorate. If overwriting interferes only with the immediately preceding item (as with Nairne, 1990) then the level of interference remains the same, although the increase in the number of sources competing for consideration at recall could still negatively affect overall performance. If overwriting is not restricted to immediately preceding items (as with Lange and Oberauer, 2005) then performance should deteriorate, and appreciably so given the rise in number of interfering sources. In the event, the opposite turns out to be true; performance improves significantly.

If we construe the setting in terms of auditory scene analysis, this last result is entirely intelligible. In object terms, the proximity of the standard to the interpolated tones and the similarity of their physical character (sharing tone-like qualities), along with its shared timing, increases the likelihood that it will be incorporated with them into an object, thereby reducing its identity as a separate entity. When the interpolated material is

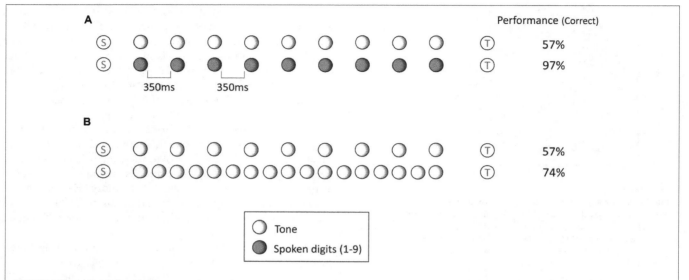

FIGURE 2 | The stimuli used by Jones et al. (1997). Both parts of the figure show an arrangement of tones both each with an initial standard tone (S) and final test tone (T), but with different interpolated sequences. Participants are asked to make a 'same' or 'different' judgment in terms of the pitch of the tones. Performance in terms of percent correct responses is shown on the right. **(A)** Shows two cases: one with interpolated tones and the other with interpolated spoken digits. **(B)** Shows the case of the standard rate of presentation and below the case where the number of stimuli is doubled.

speech, of course this tendency will be much less likely. Doubling the number of interpolated tone stimuli is likely to produce an outcome similar to that seen with interpolated speech stimuli: by virtue of shared timing (in addition to shared pitch and timbre) the interpolated stimuli will in this case form an object separate from the standard. The judgment of similarity is once again based on two stimuli distinct from the interpolated stimuli: the scene comprises three objects, a standard, a distinct interpolated stream, and the comparison.

Streaming thus produces important consequences for our judgment of the plausibility of overwriting as an explanatory mechanism and for hearing and memory. The context in which stimuli appear has powerful repercussions for what we can retrieve of stimuli. As we shall go on to consider, the fact that auditory stimuli appear in chronological order does not mean that that access to temporally adjacent stimuli is guaranteed. So, for instance, if we present a sequence in alternating male-female voices ($M_1F_2M_3F_4M_5F_6$), two streams are formed ($M_1M_3M_5$ and $F_2F_4F_6$) a situation that contrasts with a single (e.g., male) stream: $M_1M_2M_3M_4M_5M_6$. By forming two distinct streams it will become more difficult to retrieve chronologically adjacent stimuli (e.g., $M_1F_2M_3F_4$ will be harder to retrieve than $M_1M_2M_3M_4$), but easier to retrieve stream-adjacent (and chronologically non-adjacent) stimuli (e.g., $M_1M_3M_5$ will be easier to retrieve in the alternating voices case) if cued to retrieve the utterances in strict temporal order of their occurrence. Notice that—as suggested earlier—the stream can contain non-adjacent elements. This contrasts with the typical interpretations of 'chunking' (and also "grouping") that invariably refer to an aggregation of temporally adjacent elements. Auditory scene analysis shows that even quite remote elements may be assembled into an organized whole. This is why scene analysis and chunking are slightly different mechanisms and why it is important to consider remote elements

in any scene analysis (see Jones, 1993, 1999; Jones et al., 1996; for extended discussions). This relates to the question of overwriting because temporally remote and non-adjacent items can have a greater effect upon memory for any given target item than does the immediately subsequent item, a result which is inconsistent with at least two forms of overwriting (Crowder and Morton, 1969; Nairne, 1990)

Perhaps the simplest and most telling prediction from the overwriting hypothesis is that sequences with fewer shared features should be easier to retrieve than those with many shared features. This follows from such ideas as the relative distinctiveness principle, the suggestion that an item (or series of items) perceived to be discriminable on some dimension(s) from its fellows is easier to recall by virtue of psychological distinctiveness (a principle which is consistent with overwriting as an underlying mechanism, although other mechanisms may produce such an outcome; Surprenant and Neath, 2009; Neath, 2010). Evidence already reviewed indicates that this is not always the case, and further data indicate that streaming may be a useful concept in explaining outcomes that run contrary to this principle.

Very distinct non-speech sounds, when presented quickly in a sequence are easy to recognize, so that listeners can judge they are present but are less able to indicate the order in which they appeared. So, if a sequence of very different sounds—a high-pitched tone, a hiss, a low-pitched tone and a buzz—are heard in a repeating cycle, listeners are able to name each of the sounds. However, they cannot report their order correctly, even if the period of listening is extended indefinitely (Warren et al., 1969; see also Jones et al., 1999). However, if a sequence of four spoken digits—spoken in the same voice—is presented under the same conditions, the order can be readily reported. The key difference between these two settings is in the level of commonality in acoustic content: acoustically the digits form a variation on a common ground and so quickly form a stream, but for the non-voice sounds each element constitutes a separate entity and streaming is less easy to achieve.[2] Consider how such a situation would be addressed by Nairne's (1990) feature model, in which automatic overwriting forms a large part. The identity of the stimuli themselves would be represented in secondary memory, so the task would simply be to match the correct primary memory representation to the correct secondary memory identity in the correct order. The task would be made difficult by the fact that overwriting would degrade the primary memory representations such that the primary-secondary memory match would become more problematic and, potentially, confused. This confusion would clearly be more prevalent in the situation under which the most overwriting occurred – when the stimuli come from a common source (spoken digits) and share common acoustic and lexical features. These results pose grave difficulties for an overwriting account; distinct sequences should be subject to less overwriting, but the results are diametrically opposite. The explanation comes from stream formation: when the stimuli are perceived as originating from a common source they form a single stream within which order is preserved.

AUDITORY SCENE ANALYSIS: THE 'SUPRASEGMENTAL' APPROACH APPLIED TO VERBAL MEMORY

In view of the problems outlined earlier, we wish to outline an alternative framework in which retrieval (in both sensory and short-term memory) is constrained by perceptual principles. The primary line of argument we wish to pursue is that the need to maintain a coherent stream of information over time constrains the processes operating within memory and hence automatic and immediate overwriting of an item representation or the features representing an item is not a tenable explanation for forgetting. The auditory scene analysis principles outlined above, however, were introduced with reference to simple auditory stimuli (e.g., tones) and in what follows these are expanded to encompass more traditional verbal memory phenomena.

Within auditory memory, overwriting was originally proposed as an explanation for the interference associated with a post-stimulus suffix (Crowder and Morton, 1969) so we turn first to this phenomenon and possible alternative accounts.

The Failure of Overwriting: Capturing the Suffix

Classically, the existence of acoustic storage termed the "precategorical acoustic store" (PAS; Crowder and Morton, 1969) was assumed to precede "post-categorical" verbal storage (where modality of origin – spoken or written – is irrelevant, a common abstract representation is shared by all stimuli, regardless of input modality). Its existence was inferred from the auditory recency

effect, in which the final item of an auditorily presented list for serial recall is recalled at near-ceiling levels compared to the much smaller recency effect obtained with visually presented lists of the same verbal items. The reason that this has been attributed to a restricted capacity acoustic store is that elsewhere along the list performance on visually and auditorily presented lists is broadly equivalent (but see Beaman, 2002; Macken et al., 2015) and is affected in a similar manner by standard verbal manipulations such as phonological similarity, word-length, and concurrent articulation. The final piece of evidence provided in support of PAS was that the presence of a post-stimulus suffix effectively eliminates this final-item advantage, leading Crowder and Morton (1969) to conclude that the stimulus suffix effect "depends upon selective displacement of information from PAS" (Crowder and Morton, 1969, p. 369).

Crowder and Morton (1969) assumed an item-by-item displacement system rather than feature-based overwriting and one reason for disputing the feature-based interference account of the stimulus suffix effect comes from data showing that stimulus suffixes which are phonemically similar to the memoranda do not necessarily show larger suffix effects (Crowder and Cheng, 1973) and—like the other similarity-based interference effects already reviewed—may also show smaller effects (Carr and Miles, 1997). Another reason for questioning feature-based overwriting comes from studies of *streaming* the suffix. It is well established that the stimulus suffix effect depends at least in part upon the suffix being perceived as originating from the same sources, or stream, as the to-be-recalled list. So, for example, variations in the spatial location, timbre and pitch of the suffix relative to the list reduces the size of the suffix effect whereas similar manipulations varying suffix frequency, emotionality and meaning have no such effect (Morton et al., 1971). Other manipulations varying the "speech-like" qualities of the suffix similarly moderate the size of the suffix effect (Morton et al., 1981). Manipulations of the top-down interpretation of the suffix likewise show that forcing the suffix to be grouped with, or apart from, the list affects the auditory memory interference effect (Crowder, 1971; Frankish and Turner, 1984; Neath et al., 1993). So, for example, ambiguous stimuli, which can be perceived as either speech or non-speech, can be treated as a speech suffix on the basis of labeling them as such (Ayres et al., 1979; Neath et al., 1993). However, other non-speech stimuli do not show a suffix effect unless contextual effects also force them to be perceived as speech (Morton and Chambers, 1976; Ottley et al., 1982). These results show that physically identical stimuli, which bear physically identical relationships to the memoranda, can produce different memory effects depending upon context and expectation. At best, therefore, any interference effect obtained under such circumstances can only be ascribed only in part to the physical overwriting of the memory trace.

Perhaps most intriguingly, the effects of a repeated suffix have also been shown to reduce the disruption observed (Crowder, 1971, 1978; Morton, 1976). With a repeated suffix, the same suffix item is presented multiple times in quick succession and in tempo with the list sequence (as usually also happens with a single suffix). The reduced effect of the suffix when repeated in this way, even though the first presentation of the repeated

---

[2]The rate of presentation in these studies is fast and this prevents verbal labeling; when the speed of presentation is slowed performance improves but only to a relatively small degree.

suffix is physically identical to the presentation of a single suffix, is difficult to reconcile with an overwriting account based upon physical or feature similarity between successive items since the relationship between the suffix and the list items is equivalent in the two conditions. Critically, a repeated suffix only becomes a repeated suffix at the point of its re-presentation; logically, therefore, automatic overwriting occasioned by the first presentation of the suffix must already have occurred at this point. Data such as these have led to suggestions that the suffix effect might reflect the simultaneous action of overwriting, accounting for the reduced suffix effect still observed, and perceptual grouping, accounting for the difference between single and repeated suffix effects (e.g., Morton, 1976). According to these accounts, the repeated suffix forms a perceptual group apart from the to-be-remembered list whereas the single suffix is perceived as part of this list. It follows from this that the sole cause of the disruption observed in the repeated suffix condition is from overwriting. A single item suffix likewise overwrites the final item but also further depresses memory performance by increasing the functional size of the memory set (the list length) by an extra item (e.g., Nairne, 1990).

These data undermine the importance of overwriting as the source of the suffix memory disruption effect but do not rule out the possibility that overwriting occurs; perhaps it is merely contributing only part of the observed disruption. Later data reported by Nicholls and Jones (2002) are, however, less equivocal. In their experiments, Nicholls and Jones (2002) interleaved a sequence of irrelevant items between the to-be-remembered list items such that the suffix, when presented, was perceptually grouped with, or "captured" by, these irrelevant items. The sequence comprised the item 'ah,' which was also used as the suffix in a traditional suffix effect condition (see Figure 3). When no-suffix, suffix and captured suffix conditions are compared, it is clear that in the captured suffix condition performance approximates that to the no-suffix condition[3]. In the captured suffix condition the recency effect was fully restored and there was no suffix effect on the final list-item when the suffix was grouped, or streamed, with the sequence of irrelevant items. In contrast, the suffix presented alone continued to produce a suffix effect. Unlike the repeated suffix manipulation which reduced but did not eliminate the suffix effect, these data cannot easily be explained by the joint operation of overwriting and grouping since—in this case—the grouping (or streaming) manipulation removed the suffix effect entirely and hence the need to assume overwriting as the basis of the suffix effect.

Thus, the proposition that auditory-sensory memory is necessarily automatically overwritten is untenable. However, the suffix effect is only a single line of evidence. Recently, doubts about overwriting have been reinforced by findings from a paradigm using alternating voices for each list item and observing the consequences for memory of streams created in this way (Hughes et al., 2009). A suffix presented in a different voice reduces the suffix effect (Morton et al., 1971), consistent with the idea that overwriting depends on similarity between

the suffix and the final list item but also consistent with the idea that a different voice suffix is grouped apart from the list items. If overwriting is automatic and based solely upon such physical properties and relationships between successive items, then presenting the to-be-recalled list in alternating voices (e.g., male-female-male and so on), should limit the overwriting observed between successive items compared to the same items presented in a single voice because the feature similarity is reduced by the voice change. Hence, overall recall should be enhanced relative to single-voice presentation. Alternatively, if perceptual organization is important so that items presented in different voices are streamed as coming from distinct sources, then recalling the items in the correct serial order should be harder. As noted in early research on auditory attention, items are preferentially recalled according to the stream or channel from which they are perceived to originate (e.g., Broadbent, 1958; for an extensive discussion see Hughes et al., in press) such that if the two voices are perceived as two separate streams then to recall the items in correct serial order requires participants to shift alternately between streams in order to reconstruct the serial order of the list. This extra cognitive requirement imposes a behavioral cost such that a list of alternating voices is not recalled as well as the same items presented in a single voice (Hughes et al., 2009; see Figure 4). Again this talker-variability effect calls into question the predominance of overwriting, which would predict the opposite pattern of results.

Time, Space and Voice-Based Grouping Effects

The talker-variability effect, together with the different-voice suffix effect, supports the assumption that lists presented in different voices are perceptually grouped apart and that this influences the appearance of memory phenomena. Such assumptions find further support from early work on auditory attention (Broadbent, 1958) together with current theories of low-level auditory perception, within which auditory stream segregation (Bregman, 1990) plays a central role. One further line of evidence, however, serves to emphasize the relationship between perceptual organization and what seem superficially to be wholly mnemonic processes (suffix and talker-variability effects).

Work on grouping within auditory memory by Frankish and Turner (1984), Frankish (1985, 1989, 1995) directly examines the effect of perceptual grouping on subsequent recall. In a series of experiments, Frankish (1985, 1989, 1995) demonstrated that coherent groups can be formed within lists presented for immediate serial recall. These groups are defined by boundaries that exhibit the same, or similar, primacy and recency effects at recall as the longer lists of which they form a part. For example in a control (ungrouped) list, recency occurs only at the end of the list. However, in a 9-item list which is organized into three groups of three items each—for example by a delay in presentation between items 3 and 4 and between items 6 and 7—recency is seen for the final item of group 1 (at serial position 3, which must therefore be relatively immune to the suffix effects of

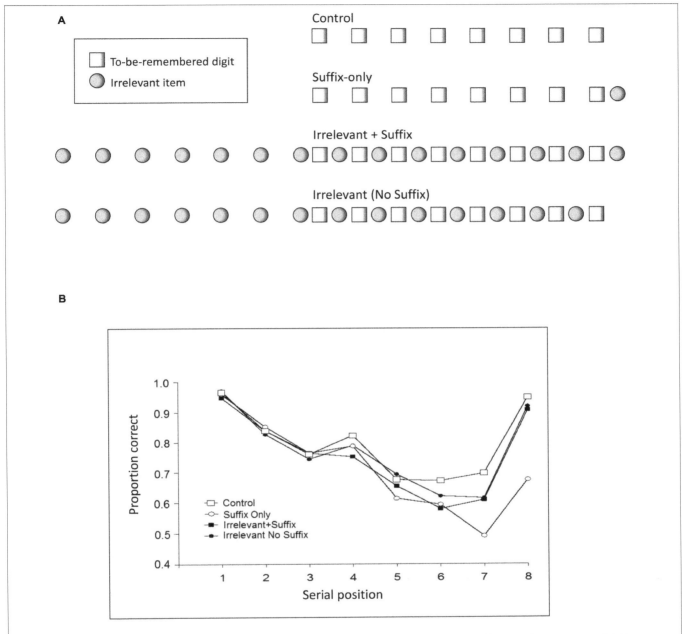

FIGURE 3 | (A) Shows schematically the arrangement of stimuli used by Nicholls and Jones (2002). The control condition comprises a sequence of eight to-be-remembered digits. The suffix-only condition has a spoken irrelevant item 'zero' at the end of the to-be-remembered sequence. The Irrelevant + Suffix condition shows a sequence of irrelevant stimuli ('zero') beginning well before the irrelevant sequence and culminating with an item after the last digit in the to-be-remembered sequence. The 'Irrelevant (No Suffix)' condition is the same as the Irrelevant + Suffix condition without a terminal suffix. **(B)** Shows the performance associated with each of those conditions as a function of the presentation position of the stimuli within the to-be-remembered sequence.

item 4). Grouping is effective when it employs exactly those principles of perceptual organization important for reducing the suffix effect. These principles include change of voice, delay in presentation, and change of spatial location, all of which have been confirmed as producing within-list recency effects associated with groups (Frankish, 1989). The principles of grouping in auditory-verbal memory, it appears, are readily inferred from the data showing a reduction of the suffix

effect. Additionally, Frankish (1985) showed that, with *visual* presentation, there is little extra grouping advantage by inserting extra pauses after the third and sixth items in the nine-item list. Frankish (1985) found no obvious difference between the serial position curves produced when participants are asked to subjectively group visual lists and those produced when the presentation of the lists was grouped by half second pauses (Experiment 1).

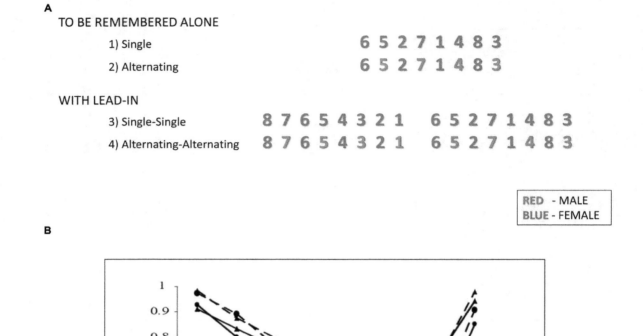

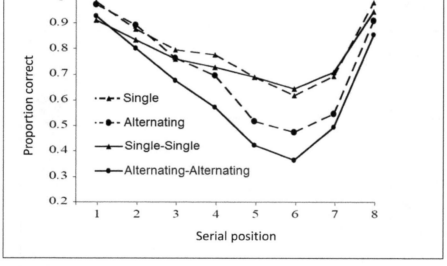

FIGURE 4 | (A) Shows a sub-set of stimuli used by Hughes et al. (2009). To-be-remembered stimuli are first shown in isolation with lists either all from the same voice (Single) and then shown with alternating male and female voices (Alternating). Participants are required to report all the list in the sequence in which it was presented. Then lists with lead-in are shown. In the first case both the lead-in and the to-be-remembered list are in the same voice (Single–Single) and then in alternating voices (Alternating-Alternating). **(B)** Shows the performance associated with each of those conditions as a function of the presentation position of the stimuli within the to-be-remembered sequence.

In a further study, Frankish (1989) showed that an extra pause of only 80 ms following the third and sixth items had as much effect as an extra half-second pause. Likewise, when the middle three digits were differentiated from the others by either voice (male vs. female) or spatial channel (left vs. right ear), the effects of these manipulations were equivalent to those of the temporal change. In addition, the study demonstrated that the voice distinction alone is as effective as voice plus pause. That is, if the middle three digits are in a different voice from the first and last three, then inserting a pause of half a second after the third and sixth digits, thereby, in addition, temporarily isolating the middle three digits, has no further effect.

These effects appear to reflect the automatic segmentation of auditory lists in a manner that is more powerful than the strategic grouping that operates on visually presented lists which produces less of an effect and is more readily disrupted (Hitch et al., 1996). Although a number of researchers (e.g., Hitch et al., 1996; Farrell, 2012) have concentrated on the role of timing—and of extended pauses—in creating groups, Frankish's results clearly show that perceptual groups can be created using cues other than elongated pauses between list items. This observation is important because it shows that factors other than consolidation and rehearsal of a recently completed group (in the pause before the next group arrives) are responsible for creating these group boundaries. It also shows that the group boundaries can be established very quickly – parsing the list into subgroups almost instantaneously as the stimuli are encountered. Thus, although providing temporal cues to grouping and allowing (or encouraging; Taylor et al., 2015) prosodic, group-based rehearsal to emerge is one means of parsing the input, it is not the only way in which within-list organization can emerge. Crucially for current purposes, the perceptual segmentation of auditory lists is one that requires the constant comparison of the current and preceding auditory input. Automatic overwriting of previous stimuli by incoming information would interfere with the allocation of the current (incoming) stimulus to the appropriate perceptual stream, which may have been established over several preceding items.

Principles of Organization: Similarity-Based Streaming

Generally, theories of short-term memory memory fail to acknowledge (or at most, pay lip-service to) the idea that events might be organized—and re-organized—according to perceptual streams. Rather, current theories view short-term memory as post-categorical, item-based encoding within a single, to-be-recalled list. The item here is defined by the experimenter *a priori* rather than inferred from the behavior of the participant. Those characteristics of the stimuli that denote common origin, that connote streams—among them similarity of pitch, timbre, location, and proximity in time—are ignored by such accounts, which also overlook the fluidity and flexibility of systems within which items are organized—and re-organized—according to their perceived belonging to one or more sources of origin. We argue that this is a profound mistake.

In the first instance, it is logical to assume that whatever form representations take in memory is constrained by the way in which information is available perceptually. The existence of natural organizational principles, known since the advent of Gestalt psychology, implies that multiple streams of information co-exist within memory in a way that is inconsistent with strict overwriting as the mechanism for forgetting. In the second instance, treating memoranda as discrete and independent items within the experimental participants' cognitive systems because they were conceived and presented as such by the experimenter is an unwarranted assumption. The assumption arises directly from the idea that representations are, almost by definition, abstract and "post-categorical," whereas in fact very few studies have examined the extent to which memory results can be accounted for by categorical vs. *continuous* storage systems (Frankish, 2008; Joseph et al., 2015). Taken to the extreme, it is clear that the recall of individual items is not independent, and whilst few models make this mistake, the amount and type of information relating the experimenter-defined items to one another and to a perceived locus of origin is impoverished in current theories. The relationship between items is formally often one merely of time or position (e.g., Page and Norris, 1998; Brown et al.,

2007). Commonality of perceptual characteristics rarely plays a role because all of the elements within the memoranda are automatically assigned to a single list-structure, something that presumably occurs at a pre-mnemonic processing stage. Where between-item similarity is considered (as for example, to model the phonological similarity effect) this may often be at a distinct stage from positional similarity. For example, the primacy model of Page and Norris (1998) in which positional errors between localist representations occur naturally along the "primacy gradient" then forward items onto an explicitly phonological distributed representation stage prior to output in order to implement item confusion errors (Beaman, 2000)[4].

Missing from all of these accounts is any measure of *stream-based similarity* such that elements within the memoranda are allocated to one stream or another based upon a common theme or thread running through the sequence and which serves to distinguish this stream from another. Stream-based similarity, according to this analysis, is necessary to account for the effects reviewed above – the reduction or elimination of suffix effects, the talker variability effect, the perceptual grouping effect and so on. The thread of similarity that acts to hold elements together is, however, precisely the source of interference that would consistently and continually degrade individual item representations under an overwriting account.

The availability of information about the stream to which the stimuli belong is precisely what is needed to account for moderation and abolition of suffix effects, between-talker variability effects, and within-list grouping effects as reviewed here. Discontinuities in time (i.e., elongated breaks between groups) have been used to account for within-list temporal grouping effects (Nairne, 1990; Hitch et al., 1996; Farrell, 2012). This mechanism follows naturally from the idea of overwriting, since a break is naturally interpreted as a pause in which information can be consolidated and/or within which retroactive interference (such as overwriting) will not occur. Such accounts do not properly address the effects of very short pauses between groups which are more parsimoniously conceived of as groupings caused by discontinuities in rhythm rather than time *per se*, nor are they able to account for grouping effects caused by intonation, timbre or spatial location. For the same reasons, speaker-variability effects and reduced suffix effects are not predicted by such accounts because the models do not maintain the correct types of information to give rise to such effects. To do so, not only must information about physical characteristics be maintained in addition to whatever post-categorical or more abstract labels that may be assumed, but also information must be held about the stream as a whole rather than individual items in isolation, and incoming information (e.g., a post-list suffix) interpreted in terms of the information held and

---

[4]This is a mirror image of how the feature model addresses the same situation: in the feature model, item-based confusions arise naturally from the distributed representation of items as vectors of feature values but positional errors only occur when an item independently "drifts" along the position dimension (Neath, 1999, 2000).

prior expectations it elicits, as shown both by contextual suffix effects and by experiments repeating and streaming the suffix. The main conclusions point to the intimacy of perception and memory, or perhaps even to their wholesale integration. Certainly, no attribution to the action of auditory memory should be entertained until a thoroughgoin analysis of how auditory streaming could explain the same phenomena has been dismissed. Only after streaming processes have yielded the super-ordinate structure of the material being remembered can other approaches – such as overwriting – be entertained as explanatory constructs.

AUTHOR CONTRIBUTIONS

This manuscript was co-written by CPB and DJ. Figures were provided by DJ.

FUNDING

The research reported in this article was supported by Economic and Social Research Council (UK) grant ES/L00710X/1 awarded to Philip Beaman and Dylan M. Jones.

REFERENCES

Altmann, E. M. (2009). Evidence for temporal decay in short-term episodic memory. *Trends Cogn. Sci.* 13, 279–279. doi: 10.1016/j.tics.2009.04.001

Altmann, E. M., and Gray, W. D. (2002). Forgetting to remember: the functional relationship of decay and interference. *Psychol. Sci.* 13, 27–33. doi: 10.1111/1467-9280.00405

Altmann, E. M., and Schunn, C. D. (2012). Decay versus Interference: a new look at an old interaction. *Psychol. Sci.* 23, 1435–1437. doi: 10.1177/0956797612446027

Ayres, T. J., Jonides, J., Reitman, J. S., Egan, J. C., and Howard, D. A. (1979). Differing suffix effects for the same physical suffix. *J. Exp. Psychol. Hum. Learn. Mem.* 5, 315–321.

Baddeley, A. D. (1966). The influence of acoustic and semantic similarity on long-term memory for word sequences. *Q. J. Exp. Psychol.* 18, 302–309. doi: 10.1080/14640746608400055

Barrouillet, P., De Pape, A., and Langerock, N. (2012). Time causes forgetting from working memory. *Psychon. Bull. Rev.* 19, 87–92. doi: 10.3758/s13423-011-0192-8

Barrouillet, P., Portrat, S., Vergauwe, E., Diependaele, K., and Camos, V. (2011). Further evidence for temporal decay in working memory. *J. Exp. Psychol. Learn. Mem. Cogn.* 337, 1302–1317.

Bartlett, F. C. (1932). *Remembering: A Study in Experimental and Social Psychology.* Cambridge: Cambridge University Press.

Beaman, C. P. (2000). Neurons amongst the symbols? *Behav. Brain Sci.* 23, 468–470. doi: 10.1017/S0140525X00233359

Beaman, C. P. (2002). Inverting the modality effect in serial recall. *Q. J. Exp. Psychol.* 55A, 371–389. doi: 10.1080/02724980143000307

Beaman, C. P., and Jones, D. M. (1998). Irrelevant sound disrupts order information in free recall as in serial recall. *Q. J. Exp. Psychol.* 51A, 615–636. doi: 10.1080/713755774

Beaman, C. P., Neath, I., and Surprenant, A. M. (2008). Modeling distributions of immediate memory effects: no strategies needed? *J. Exp. Psychol. Learn. Mem. Cogn.* 34, 219–229. doi: 10.1037/0278-7393.34.1.219

Berman, M. G., Jonides, J., and Lewis, R. L. (2009). In search of decay in verbal short-term memory. *Mem. Cogn.* 35, 317–333. doi: 10.1037/a0014873

Bhatarah, P., Ward, G., and Tan, L. (2006). Examining the relationship between free recall and immediate serial recall: the effect of concurrent task performance. *J. Exp. Psychol. Learn. Mem. Cogn.* 32, 215–229.

Bhatarah, P., Ward, G., and Tan, L. (2008). Examining the relationship between free recall and immediate serial recall: the serial nature of recall and the effect of test expectancy. *Mem. Cogn.* 36, 20–34. doi: 10.3758/MC.36.1.20

Botvinick, M., and Plaut, D. C. (2006). Short-term memory for serial order: a recurrent neural network model. *Psychol. Rev.* 113, 201–233. doi: 10.1037/0033-295X.113.2.201

Bregman, A. S. (1990). *Auditory Scene Analysis.* Cambridge, MA: MIT Press.

Bregman, A. S., and Rudnicky, A. I. (1975). Auditory segregation: stream or streams? *J. Exp. Psychol. Hum. Percept. Perform.* 1, 263–267.

Broadbent, D. E. (1958). *Perception and Communication.* London: Pergamon.

Brown, G. D., Preece, T., and Hulme, C. (2000). Oscillator-based memory for serial order. *Psychol. Rev.* 107, 127–181. doi: 10.1037/0033-295X.107.1.127

Brown, G. D. A., and Lewandowsky, S. (2010). "Forgetting in memory models: arguments against trace decay and consolidation failure," in *Forgetting*, ed. S. Della Sala (Hove: Psychology Press), 49–75.

Brown, G. D. A., Neath, I., and Chater, N. (2007). A temporal ratio model of memory. *Psychol. Rev.* 114, 539–576. doi: 10.1037/0033-295X.114.3.539

Burgess, N., and Hitch, G. J. (1999). Memory for serial order: a network model of the phonological loop and its timing. *Psychol. Rev.* 106, 551–581. doi: 10.1037/0033-295X.106.3.551

Burgess, N., and Hitch, G. J. (2006). A revised model of short-term memory and long-term learning of verbal sequences. *J. Mem. Lang.* 55, 627–652. doi: 10.1016/j.jml.2006.08.005

Carr, D., and Miles, C. (1997). Rhyme attenuates the auditory suffix effect: alliteration does not. *Q. J. Exp. Psychol.* 50A, 518–527. doi: 10.1080/027249897392008

Conrad, R. (1960). Serial order intrusions in immediate memory. *Br. J. Psychol.* 51, 45–48. doi: 10.1111/j.2044-8295.1960.tb00723.x

Conrad, R. (1964). Acoustic confusions in immediate memory. *Br. J. Psychol.* 55, 75–84. doi: 10.1111/j.2044-8295.1964.tb00899.x

Conrad, R., and Hull, A. J. (1964). Information, acoustic confusion, and memory span. *Br. J. Psychol.* 55, 429–432. doi: 10.1111/j.2044-8295.1964.tb00928.x

Craik, F. I. M., and Watkins, M. J. (1973). The role of rehearsal in short-term memory. *J. Verb. Learn. Verb. Behav.* 12, 599–607. doi: 10.1016/S0022-5371(73)80039-8

Crowder, R. G. (1971). Waiting for the stimulus suffix: decay, delay, rhythm, and readout in immediate memory. *Q. J. Exp. Psychol.* 23, 324–340. doi: 10.1080/14640746908401829

Crowder, R. G. (1978). Mechanisms of auditory backward masking in the stimulus suffix effect. *Psychol. Rev.* 85, 502–524. doi: 10.1037/0033-295X.85.6.502

Crowder, R. G., and Cheng, C.-M. (1973). Phonemic confusability, precategorical acoustic storage, and the suffix effect. *Percept. Psychophys.* 13, 145–148. doi: 10.3758/BF03207250

Crowder, R. G., and Morton, J. (1969). Precategorical acoustic storage (PAS). *Percept. Psychophys.* 5, 365–373. doi: 10.3758/BF03210660

Deutsch, D. (1972). Effect of repetition of standard and comparison tones on recognition memory for pitch. *J. Exp. Psychol.* 93, 156–162. doi: 10.1037/h0032496

Deutsch, D. (1978a). Delayed pitch comparisons and the principle of proximity. *Percept. Psychophys.* 23, 227–230. doi: 10.3758/BF03204130

Deutsch, D. (1978b). Interference in pitch memory as a function of ear of input. *Q. J. Exp. Psychol.* 30, 282–287. doi: 10.1080/14640747808400675

Farrell, S. (2012). Temporal clustering and sequencing in short-term memory and episodic memory. *Psychol. Rev.* 119, 223–271. doi: 10.1037/a0027371

Fournet, N., Juphard, A., Monnier, C., and Roulin, J.-L. (2003). Phonological similarity in free and serial recall: the effect of increasing retention intervals. *Int. J. Psychol.* 38, 384–389. doi: 10.1080/00207590344000204

Frankish, C. (1985). Modality-specific grouping effects in short-term memory. *J. Mem. Lang.* 24, 200–209. doi: 10.1016/j.cognition.2013.08.017

Frankish, C. (1989). Perceptual organization and precategorical acoustic storage. *J. Exp. Psychol. Learn. Mem. Cogn.* 15, 469–479.

Frankish, C. (1995). Intonation and auditory grouping in immediate serial recall. *Appl. Cogn. Psychol.* 9, 5–22. doi: 10.1002/acp.2350090703

Frankish, C. (2008). Precategorical acoustic storage and the perception of speech. *J. Mem. Lang.* 58, 815–836. doi: 10.1016/j.jml.2007.06.003

Frankish, C., and Turner, J. (1984). Delayed suffix effect at very short delays. *J. Exp. Psychol. Learn. Mem. Cogn.* 10, 767–777.

Grenfell-Essam, R., and Ward, G. (2012). Examining the relationship between free recall and immediate serial recall: the role of list length, strategy use, and test expectancy. *J. Mem. Lang.* 67, 106–148. doi: 10.1016/j.jml.2012.04.004

Grenfell-Essam, R., Ward, G., and Tan, L. (2013). The role of rehearsal on the output order of immediate free recall of short and long lists. *J. Exp. Psychol. Learn. Mem. Cogn.* 39, 317–347. doi: 10.1037/a0028974

Henson, R. N. A. (1998). Short-term memory for serial order: the start-end model. *Cogn. Psychol.* 36, 73–137. doi: 10.1006/cogp.1998.0685

Hitch, G. J., Burgess, N., Towse, J. N., and Culpin, V. (1996). Temporal grouping effects in immediate recall: a working memory analysis. *Q. J. Exp. Psychol.* 49A, 116–139. doi: 10.1080/027249896392829

Hughes, R. W., Chamberland, C., Tremblay, S., and Jones, D. M. (in press). Perceptual-motor determinants of auditory-verbal serial short-term memory. Journal of Memory and Language.

Hughes, R. W., Marsh, J. E., and Jones, D. M. (2009). Perceptual-gestural (mis)mapping in serial short-term memory: the impact of talker variability. *J. Exp. Psychol. Learn. Mem. Cogn.* 35, 1411–1425. doi: 10.1037/a0017008

Jones, D. M. (1993). "Objects, streams and threads of auditory attention," in *Attention: Selection, Awareness, and Control: Atribute to Donald Broadbent*, eds A. D. Baddeley and L. Weiskrantz (New York, NY: Clarendon Press), 87–104.

Jones, D. M. (1999). The cognitive psychology of auditory distraction: the 1997 BPS Broadbent Lecture. *Br. J. Psychol.* 90, 167–187. doi: 10.1348/000712699161314

Jones, D. M., Alford, D., Bridges, A., Tremblay, S., and Macken, W. J. (1999). Organizational factors in selective attention: the interplay of acoustic distinctiveness and auditory streaming in the irrelevant sound effect. *J. Exp. Psychol. Learn. Mem. Cogn.* 25, 464–473.

Jones, D. M., Beaman, C. P., and Macken, W. J. (1996). "The object-oriented episodic record model," in *Models of Short-Term Memory*, ed. S. E. Gathercole (Hove: Psychology Press), 209–238.

Jones, D. M., Macken, W. J., and Harries, C. (1997). Disruption of short-term recognition memory for tones: streaming or interference? *Q. J. Exp. Psychol. Learn. Mem. Cogn.* 50A, 337–357. doi: 10.1080/713755707

Joseph, S., Iverson, P., Manohar, S., Fox, Z., Scott, S. K., and Husain, M. (2015). Precision of working memory for speech sounds. *Q. J. Exp. Psychol. Learn. Mem. Cogn.* 68, 2022–2040. doi: 10.1080/17470218.2014.1002799

Lange, E., and Oberauer, K. (2005). Overwriting of phonemic features in serial recall. *Memory* 13, 333–339. doi: 10.1080/09658210344000378

Lashley, K. S. (1951). "The problem of serial order in behavior," in *Cerebral Mechanisms in Behavior. The Hixon Symposium*, ed. L. A. Jeffress (New York, NY: Wiley), 112–136.

Lewandowsky, S., and Farrell, S. (2011). *Computational Modelling in Cognition: Principles and Practice*. Thousand Oaks, CA: Sage.

Lewandowsky, S., Geiger, S. M., and Oberauer, K. (2008). Interference-based forgetting in verbal short-term memory. *J. Mem. Lang.* 59, 200–222. doi: 10.1016/j.tics.2008.12.003

Lewandowsky, S., and Murdock, B. B. Jr. (1989). Memory for serial order. *Psychol. Rev.* 96, 25–57. doi: 10.1037/0033-295X.96.1.25

Lewandowsky, S., and Oberauer, K. (2008). The word length effect provides no evidence for decay in short-term memory. *Psychon. Bull. Rev.* 15, 875–888. doi: 10.3758/PBR.15.5.875

Lewandowsky, S., and Oberauer, K. (2009). No evidence for temporal decay in working memory. *J. Exp. Psychol. Learn. Mem. Cogn.* 35, 1545–1551. doi: 10.1037/a0017010

Lewandowsky, S., and Oberauer, K. (2015). Rehearsal in serial recall: an unworkable solution to the non-existent problem of decay. *Psychol. Rev.* 122, 674–699. doi: 10.1037/a0039684

Lewandowsky, S., Oberauer, K., and Brown, G. D. A. (2009). No temporal decay in verbal short-term memory. *Trends Cogn. Sci.* 13, 120–126. doi: 10.1016/j.tics.2008.12.003

Macken, B., Taylor, J., and Jones, D. (2015). Limitless capacity: a dynamic object-oriented approach to short-term memory. *Front. Psychol.* 6:293. doi: 10.3389/fpsyg.2015.00293

Mathias, S. R., and von Kriegstein, K. (2014). Percepts, not acoustic properties, are the units of auditory short-term memory. *J. Exp. Psychol. Learn. Mem. Cogn.* 40, 445–450.

Mercer, T., and McKeown, D. (2010a). Interference in short-term auditory memory. *Q. J. Exp. Psychol. Learn. Mem. Cogn.* 63, 1256–1265. doi: 10.1080/17470211003802467

Mercer, T., and McKeown, D. (2010b). Updating and feature overwriting in short-term memory for timbre. *Atten. Percept. Psychophys.* 72, 2289–2303. doi: 10.3758/APP.72.8.2289

Miller, G. A. (1956). The magical number seven, plus or minus two: some limits on our capacity for processing information. *Psychol. Rev.* 101, 343–352. doi: 10.1037/0033-295X.101.2.343

Morton, J. (1964). A preliminary functional model for language behaviour. *Int. Audiol.* 3, 216–225. doi: 10.3109/05384916409074089

Morton, J. (1969). Interaction of information in word recognition. *Psychol. Rev.* 76, 165–178. doi: 10.1037/h0027366

Morton, J. (1976). Two mechanisms in the stimulus suffix effect. *Mem. Cogn.* 4, 144–149. doi: 10.3758/BF03213156

Morton, J. (1979). "Facilitation in word recognition: experiments causing change in the logogen model," in *Processing of Visible Language*, eds P. A. Kolers, M. E. Wrolstad, and H. Bouma (New York, NY: Plenum), 259–268.

Morton, J., and Chambers, S. M. (1976). Some evidence for "speech" as an acoustic feature. *Br. J. Psychol.* 67, 31–45. doi: 10.1111/j.2044-8295.1976.tb01495.x

Morton, J., Crowder, R. G., and Prussin, H. A. (1971). Experiments with the stimulus suffix effect. *J. Exp. Psychol.* 91, 169–190. doi: 10.1037/h0031844

Morton, J., Marcus, S. M., and Ottley, P. (1981). The acoustic correlates of "speechlike": a use of the suffix effect. *J. Exp. Psychol. Learn. Mem. Cogn. Gen.* 110, 568–593.

Murdock, B. B. Jr. (1968). Serial order effects in short-term memory. *J. Exp. Psychol. Learn. Mem. Cogn. Monogr. Suppl.* 76, 1–15. doi: 10.1037/h0025694

Murdock, B. B. Jr. (1983). A distributed model for serial-order information. *Psychol. Rev.* 90, 316–338. doi: 10.1037/0033-295X.90.4.316

Nairne, J. S. (1990). A feature model of immediate memory. *Mem. Cogn.* 18, 251–269. doi: 10.3758/BF03213879

Nairne, J. S. (2002). Remembering over the short-term: the case against the standard model. *Annu. Rev. Psychol.* 53, 53–81. doi: 10.1146/annurev.psych.53.100901.135131

Nairne, J. S., and Kelley, M. R. (1999). Reversing the phonological similarity effect. *Mem. Cogn.* 27, 45–53. doi: 10.3758/BF03201212

Neath, I. (1999). Modelling the disruptive effects of irrelevant speech on order information. *Int. J. Psychol.* 34, 410–418. doi: 10.1080/002075999399765

Neath, I. (2000). Modeling the effects of irrelevant speech on memory. *Psychon. Bull. Rev.* 7, 403–423. doi: 10.3758/BF03214356

Neath, I. (2010). Evidence for similar principles in episodic and semantic memory: the presidential serial position function. *Mem. Cogn.* 38, 659–666. doi: 10.3758/MC.38.5.659

Neath, I., and Brown, G. D. A. (2012). Arguments against memory trace decay: a SIMPLE account of Baddeley & Scott. *Front. Cogn.* 3:35. doi: 10.3389/fpsyg.2012.00035

Neath, I., and Nairne, J. S. (1995). Word-length effects in immediate memory: overwriting trace-decay theory. *Psychon. Bull. Rev.* 2, 429–441. doi: 10.3758/BF03210981

Neath, I., Surprenant, A. M., and Crowder, R. G. (1993). The context-dependent stimulus suffix effect. *J. Exp. Psychol. Learn. Mem. Cogn. Learn. Mem. Cogn.* 19, 698–703.

Nicholls, A. P., and Jones, D. M. (2002). Capturing the suffix: cognitive streaming in immediate serial recall. *J. Exp. Psychol. Learn. Mem. Cogn.* 28, 12–28.

Oberauer, K. (2009). Interference between storage and processing in working memory: feature overwriting, not similarity-based competition. *Mem. Cogn.* 37, 346–357. doi: 10.3758/MC.37.3.346

Oberauer, K., and Kliegl, R. (2006). A formal model of capacity limits in working memory. *J. Mem. Lang.* 55, 601–626. doi: 10.1037/a0025660

Oberauer, K., and Lange, E. B. (2008). Interference in verbal working memory: distinguishing similarity-based confusion, feature overwriting, and feature migration. *J. Mem. Lang.* 58, 730–745. doi: 10.1016/j.jml.2007.09.006

Oberauer, K., and Lewandowsky, S. (2008). Forgetting in immediate serial recall: decay, temporal distinctiveness, or interference? *Psychol. Rev.* 115, 544–576. doi: 10.1037/0033-295X.115.3.544

Oberauer, K., and Lewandowsky, S. (2013). Evidence against decay in verbal working memory. *J. Exp. Psychol. Learn. Mem. Cogn. Gen.* 142, 380–411. doi: 10.1037/a0029588

Ottley, P., Marcus, S., and Morton, J. (1982). Contextual effects in the stimulus suffix paradigm. *Br. J. Psychol.* 73, 383–387. doi: 10.1111/j.2044-8295.1982.tb01820.x

Page, M. P. A., and Norris, D. (1998). The primacy model: a new model for serial recall. *Psychol. Rev.* 105, 761–781. doi: 10.1037/0033-295X.105.4.761-781

Portrat, S., Barrouillet, P., and Camos, V. (2008). Time-related decay or interference-based forgetting in working memory? *J. Exp. Psychol. Learn. Mem. Cogn.* 34, 1561–1564.

Raffone, A., and Wolters, G. (2001). A cortical mechanism for binding in visual working memory. *J. Cogn. Neurosci.* 13, 766–785. doi: 10.1162/08989290152541430

Ricker, T. J., Vergauwe, E., and Cowan, N. (2014). Decay theory of immediate memory: from Brown (1958) to today (2014). *Q. J. Exp. Psychol.* doi: 10.1080/17470218.2014.914546 [Epub ahead of print],

Saint-Aubin, J., and Poirier, M. (1999). Semantic similarity and immediate serial recall: is there a detrimental effect on order information? *Q. J. Exp. Psychol. Learn. Mem. Cogn.* 52A, 367–394. doi: 10.1080/713755814

Scharf, B. (1978). "Loudness," in *Handbook of Perception*, Vol. 4, eds E. C. Carterette and M. P. Friedman (New York, NY: Academic Press), 187–242.

Semal, C., and Demany, L. (1991). Dissociation of pitch from timbre in auditory short-term memory. *J. Acoust. Soc. Am.* 89, 2404–2410. doi: 10.1121/1.400928

Semal, C., and Demany, L. (1993). Further evidence for an autonomous processing of pitch in auditory short-term memory. *J. Acoust. Soc. Am.* 94, 1315–1322. doi: 10.1121/1.408159

Shallice, T., and Cooper, R. (2010). *The Organisation of Mind*. Oxford: Oxford University Press.

Spurgeon, J., Ward, G., and Matthews, W. (2014). Examining the relationship between immediate serial recall and immediate free recall: common effects of Phonological Loop variables, but only limited evidence for the Phonological Loop. *J. Exp. Psychol. Learn. Mem. Cogn. Learn. Mem. Cogn.* 40, 1110–1141. doi: 10.1037/a0035784

Starr, G. E., and Pitt, M. (1997). Interference effects in short-term memory for timbre. *J. Acoust. Soc. Am.* 102, 486–494. doi: 10.1121/1.419722

Surprenant, A. M., and Neath, I. (2009). *Principles of Memory*. New York, NY: Psychology Press.

Taylor, J. C., Macken, W. J., and Jones, D. M. (2015). A matter of emphasis: linguistic stress habits modulate serial recall. *Mem. Cogn.* 43, 520–537. doi: 10.3758/s13421-014-0466-2

Ward, G., and Tan, L. (2004). The effect of the length of to-be-remembered lists and intervening lists on free recall: are-examination using overt rehearsal. *J. Exp. Psychol. Learn. Mem. Cogn. Learn. Mem. Cogn.* 30, 1196–1210.

Ward, G., Tan, L., and Grenfell-Essam, R. (2010). Examining the relationship between free recall and immediate serial recall: the effects of list length and output order. *J. Exp. Psychol. Learn. Mem. Cogn.* 36, 1207–1241. doi: 10.1037/a0020122

Ward, G., Woodward, G., Stevens, A., and Stinson, C. (2003). Using overt rehearsals to explain word frequency effects in free recall. *J. Exp. Psychol. Learn. Mem. Cogn.* 29, 186–210.

Warren, R. M., Obusek, C. J., Farmer, R. M., and Warren, R. P. (1969). Auditory sequence: confusion of patterns other than speech or music. *Science* 164, 586–587. doi: 10.1126/science.164.3879.586

Watkins, M. J., Watkins, O. C., and Crowder, R. G. (1974). The modality effect in free and serial recall as a function of phonological similarity. *J. Verb. Learn. Verb. Behav.* 13, 430–447. doi: 10.1016/S0022-5371(74)80021-6

Conflict of Interest Statement: The authors declare that the research was conducted in the absence of any commercial or financial relationships that could be construed as a potential conflict of interest.

The effect of altruistic tendency on fairness in third-party punishment

Lu Sun[1,2], Peishan Tan[1†], You Cheng[1,3†], Jingwei Chen[1] and Chen Qu[1,4]*

[1] *Center for Studies of Psychological Application, School of Psychology, South China Normal University, Guangzhou, China,* [2] *Primary School Affiliated to South China Normal University, Guangzhou, China,* [3] *Department of Psychological and Brain Sciences, Dartmouth College, Hanover, NH, USA,* [4] *School of Economics and Management and Scientific Laboratory of Economics Behaviors, South China Normal University, Guangzhou, China*

*Correspondence:
*Chen Qu,
Center for Studies of Psychological
Application, School of Psychology,
South China Normal University,
Guangzhou 510631, China
chenqu@scnu.edu.cn*

†*These authors have contributed
equally to this work.*

Specialty section:
*This article was submitted to
Personality and Social Psychology,
a section of the journal
Frontiers in Psychology*

Third-party punishment, as an altruistic behavior, was found to relate to inequity aversion in previous research. Previous researchers have found that altruistic tendencies, as an individual difference, can affect resource division. Here, using the event-related potential (ERP) technique and a third-party punishment of dictator game paradigm, we explored third-party punishments in high and low altruists and recorded their EEG data. Behavioral results showed high altruists (vs. low altruists) were more likely to punish the dictators in unfair offers. ERP results revealed that patterns of medial frontal negativity (MFN) were modulated by unfairness. For high altruists, high unfair offers (90:10) elicited a larger MFN than medium unfair offers (70:30) and fair offers (50:50). By contrast, for low altruists, fair offers elicited larger MFN while high unfair offers caused the minimal MFN. It is suggested that the altruistic tendency effect influences fairness consideration in the early stage of evaluation. Moreover, the results provide further neuroscience evidence for inequity aversion.

Keywords: altruistic tendency, third-party punishment, unfair, ERP, MFN

Introduction

Altruistic punishment refers to punishment imposed by individuals who punish free riders in the group although it is costly and yields no material benefits for the punishers. This punishment may achieve and sustain social cooperation (Fehr and Gächter, 2002). Altruistic punishment includes second-party punishment and third-party punishment. Second-party punishment refers to punishment inflicted by the person who suffered from the violation. For example, in the ultimatum game (Güth et al., 1982), the receiver can reject the unfair offer from the proposer; the rejection of the receiver is regarded as second-party punishment. Third-party punishment refers to the circumstances in which a third party who did not directly suffer from the violation is willing to pay a cost to punish the violator (Fehr and Fischbacher, 2004a,b).

The third-party punishment of dictator game is an effective tool to explore altruistic punishment and fairness distribution (Eckel and Grossman, 1996). However, the costly punishment violates the classic homo economicus theory that humans are always in pursuit of profit maximization. In the game, the dictator can decide how to distribute the money while the receiver can only accept unconditionally. After observing the distribution and level of cooperation, the otherwise disinterested third party can determine whether to pay a cost to punish the individuals who violate the cooperation social norms (Fehr and Fischbacher, 2003). Compared with second-party punishment, third-party punishment could minimize violations of social norms and maintain social equality; examples of third-party punishers are the justice system and police (Marlowe et al., 2008).

Inequality aversion theory holds that third-party punishment is the result of someone resisting inequality. More specifically, individuals abandon self-interest voluntarily to pursue a more equitable result. Several studies have found that participants exhibit aversion against inequality and impose punitive measures to reduce the pecuniary gap between people (Fehr and Schmidt, 1999; Dirk and Martin, 2006). Bolton and Ockenfels (2000) found that punishment is imposed in order to make the violator's amount of money close to the average level.

Several lines of evidence support the viewpoint of inequity aversion theory. First, Falk and Fischbacher's (2006) reciprocity theory predicts that people tend to reward kind actions and punish unkind actions. Their evidence suggests that the evaluation of a kind action is based not only on its consequences but also on its underlying intention.

Second, some researchers explain third-party punishment in terms of cognition and emotion. When people internalize a specific culture, morality that follows social norms will be formed. Internal self-punishment will be elicited if the social norms are violated (Masclet et al., 2003). Masclet et al. (2003) believes the internal pressure is a kind of sense of guilt, which is the reason why people want to punish violators even when they have not experienced directly. When observing violations committed by others, people can experience negative emotions such as the desire for revenge, the urge to fight or anger (Bosman and van Winden, 1999; Glaeser and Sacerdote, 2000; Decker et al., 2003; Abbink et al., 2004).

Neuroscience research provides further evidence for inequity-aversion theory (Pérez and Kiss, 2012). In one functional magnetic resonance imaging (fMRI) study (Singer et al., 2006), male volunteers who observed an unfair confederate receiving pain showed lower empathy-related activation, accompanied by reward-related activation that might represent the desire for revenge. A positron emission tomography (PET) study (De Quervain et al., 2004) investigating the neural mechanism of third-party punishment in a trust game found that subjects with stronger activations in the dorsal striatum, which has been implicated in the processing of rewards, were willing to incur greater costs in order to punish. Moreover, when subjects, acting as third parties, determined to pay a cost to punish the norm violators, ventral medial prefrontal cortex (vmPFC) and medial prefrontal cortex (mPFC) showed greater activation than in costless punishment. It is thought that there is a trade-off relation underling the monetary punishment behavior. Specifically, participants need to weigh the emotional satisfaction and monetary loss from the punishment at the same time, which is indicated by vmPFC and mPFC, to integrate the cognitive conflict with the decision-making processing.

Actually, a number of people do not enact third-party punishment. This is not inconsistent with inequity aversion theory, which holds that attitudes on inequity distribution should affect third-party punishment. However, aside from the research on the neural mechanisms of third-party punishment, only a few studies have explored individual differences in this behavior. Haruno and Frith (2009) explored how social value orientation, as an individual difference, affects anchoring attitudes toward resource division. Results revealed that the prosocials disliked large absolute differences in distributions (inequity aversion), whereas the individualists were unaffected by such differences. Moreover, the extent of inequity aversion in prosocials was predicted by activity in the amygdala and appeared to be impervious to cognitive load.

In the current study, altruistic tendency was introduced as an individual difference predicting altruistic punishment. In addition to behavioral results from the punishment of dictator game, event-related potential (ERP) technique was employed to assess the neural process of fairness consideration in altruistic punishments.

Medial frontal negativity (MFN) was referred to a family of negative-going ERPs peaking between 200 and 350 ms at frontocentral recording sites. MFN is associated with performance evaluation, including error-related negativity (ERN; Falkenstein et al., 1990; Gehring et al., 1990) and feedback-related negativity (FRN; Miltner et al., 1997). Some studies have found that MFN is sensitive to the violation of social expectancy or social norms (Boksem and De Cremer, 2010; Van der Veen and Sahibdin, 2011; Wu et al., 2011, 2012; Qu et al., 2013b). In an ultimatum game study, Wu et al. (2011) reported that compared with moderately unequal offers, highly unequal offers generated larger MFN indicating that the MFN can reflect a general violation of social expectancy. In present study, we predict that high altruists and low altruists would show different patterns in MFN because of different social expectancy.

We also examined another ERP component, P300, as an ERP component that has attracted interest in emotion and attention research. As shown in previous studies, P300 is sensitive to the valence and the magnitude; positive feedback generated larger P300 negative feedback (Wu and Zhou, 2009; Leng and Zhou, 2010; Qu et al., 2014). Yeung and Sanfey (2004) posited that the P300 is modulated by the individual's attention and emotional experience in result evaluations. Researchers have also found that P300 is significantly larger in reward conditions than in punishment or non-reward conditions (Hajcak et al., 2005; Bellebaum and Daum, 2008).

Therefore, the present research, employing the ERP technique, tested whether and how altruistic tendency affects third-party punishment. For behavioral results, we hypothesized that unfair offers would elicit more third-party punishments according to inequity aversion theory, and altruistic tendencies would moderate third-party punishments. Compared with low altruists, high altruists would show more third-party punishment when observing the unfair offer. As for the ERP results, MFN outcomes with larger violation of expectancy should elicit larger MFN than outcomes in line with expectancy. For high altruists, an expected outcome is the fair offer, while the unfair offer is an unexpected result. The opposite pattern should be found for low altruists. Therefore, we expected that when the high altruists observed the unfair offer, greater MFN would be elicited, whereas the low altruists would show greater MFN when a fair offer was observed. Considering the P300 is associated with the emotional arousal, we assume that the unfair offer would elicit larger P300 than the fair offer. High and low altruists will show variation in the pattern of P300, and show different punishment behavior.

Materials and Methods

Participants

Seventy right-handed undergraduate students from the South China Normal University voluntarily participated in the first stage of the research, and then a distribution task was used as a pretest through which thirty-two participants (22 females and 10 males,18–24 years of age) were selected to take part in the formal experiment. The mean age of the participants was 21.4 years. Participants reported no physical or mental illness and reported normal eyesight. Informed consent was obtained from all participants, and the research was approved by the Human Research Ethics Committee of South China Normal University.

Material

The third-party punishment dictator game was presented using the E-Prime experimental program. We applied color bars to present the allocations of the dictator. The horizontal viewing angle of each target picture was 3° and the vertical viewing angle was 1.5°.

Design and Procedure

The design was a two factor mixed design with the first factor referring to the level of fairness (Fair offer, Medium Unfair offer, High Unfair offer) and the second factor referring to the altruistic tendency (High, Low). Recent studies have shown that the dictator game is an effective paradigm to differentiate altruistic behavior (Benenson et al., 2007; Carpenter et al., 2008; Rotemberg, 2008). Thus we used the dictator game to identify participants with high and low altruistic tendencies. Participants were presented with a pair of rewards (totally 100 Yuan) for self and the other, 35 times. Three predetermined allocations including a low altruistic tendency allocation (90:10), medium altruistic tendency allocation (70:30), and high altruistic tendency allocation (50:50) were presented. We assigned participants to a certain category (high altruist, low altruist) if they made consistent decisions more than 75% of the time. Finally, 32 participants were selected for the formal experiment, 16 (3 male, 13 female) high altruists and 16 (7 males, 9 females) low altruists.

Our experiment adopted a modified paradigm of the third-party punishment of dictator game (Qu et al., 2014). In the formal task, participants were assigned a role of third party and received an initial endowment of 50 Yuan. They first witnessed a distribution of 100 Yuan between two players (the dictator and the receiver). Subsequently, the participants would have an opportunity to adjust the distribution by subtracting 15 Yuan from their endowment to turn the unfair offer into a fair offer in order to punish the dictator. The fairness factor includes three levels: Fair offer refers to both dictator and receiver owning 50 Yuan, Medium Unfair offer refers to 70 Yuan for the dictator and 30 Yuan for the receiver, and High Unfair offer refers to 90 Yuan for the dictator and 10 Yuan for the receiver. In other words, if the distribution is 90:10, the participant can spend 15 Yuan to punish the dictator, thus the distribution result will become 50:50. Before starting the dictator game, the participants were informed that the dictator results come from another group of over 300 participants who had participated previously. All participants were paid 20 Yuan as a basic payment, and were informed that an extra reward would be paid according to their decisions in the task. We randomly chose one trial's balance as his extra reward. After the experiment, we asked all the participants whether they believe that they were playing against the real human players, most of the participants considered they encountered the real person in the game. Participants were debriefed, paid, and thanked.

Participants were seated comfortably in an audio-shielded room with a fabric cap and were required to gaze at the screen center, which was 1 m away in front of their eyes. Participants were asked to read detailed task instructions. All participants had 20 trials to practice until they fully understood the task. The formal experiment process is shown in **Figure 1**. In each round of the game, every participant was required to gaze at a fixation point that appeared as "+" in the center of the screen for 800–1000 ms. Then the initial allocation scheme of the dictator was shown on the screen. A color bar was presented for 1500 ms, with a portion in red on the left side representing the score of the dictator, and a portion in blue on the right side representing the score of the recipient. Next, a selection window was given, and the participant was prompted to press the "F" or "J" key on the keyboard within 2 s to indicate whether to change the allocation of the dictator. After the decision-making, the subject would see a fixation point "+" for 800–1000 ms and then observe the final distribution and his/her score in this round. This was one trial of the task. If the participant was willing to turn the unfair offer into a fair offer, he/she would be deducted 15 Yuan; if not, the final offer would be consistent with the initial allocation, and thus the third party (participant) would retain 50 Yuan. The three fairness levels were presented in random order and each condition had 50 trials, thus there were 150 trials in the experiment. From the beginning of the formal task, EEG data and the frequency of punishment by each participant were recorded.

Record of ERP

EEGs were recorded from 32 scalp sites at 500 Hz rate. All electrodes were embedded in an elastic cap. The EEG signals were amplified with a band pass of 0.01–100 Hz by online filtering of BrainAmps (Brain Products, Munich). All electrode recordings were referenced online to the right mastoid and off-line re-referenced to the average of the left and right mastoids. The horizontal electrooculograms (HEOGs) were monitored with off-line electrodes located in both laterals of the eyes, the vertical electrooculograms (VEOGs) were placed above and below the left eye. Brain Vision Analyzer (analysis software) was performed to exclude the eye-movement signal by using independent component analysis for continuous data. Trials with EEG artifacts that exceeded ±80 μV from the mean amplitude during the recording epoch were eliminated. EEG data were measured and analyzed by no-phase-shift low-pass digital

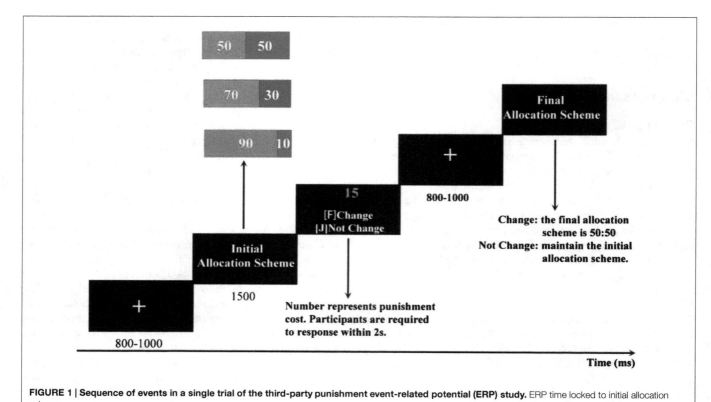

FIGURE 1 | Sequence of events in a single trial of the third-party punishment event-related potential (ERP) study. ERP time locked to initial allocation scheme.

filtering of 20 Hz. EEG epochs of 1000 ms, within a 200 ms pre-stimulus baseline, would be superimposed to analyze after the initial allocation scheme.

Based on the procedure used in previous research (Gering and Willoughby, 2002; Hajcak et al., 2005), MFN is maximal on the frontocentral electrodes, thus data from electrode sites Fz, FCz, Cz were pooled for analysis. For P300 analysis, the largest amplitude appears in the posterior sites, so a pooling of Cz, Pz electrodes was used for analysis. The mean amplitude of MFN is between 290 and 390 ms, while the mean amplitude of P300 is between 400 and 600 ms.

Results

Behavioral Results

The frequency of the third-party punishment by level of high and low altruistic tendency was presented in **Table 1**. Considering the possible gender difference, we regard the gender factor as a covariate. A 3 (fairness: Fair, Medium Unfair, High Unfair) × 2 (altruistic tendency: High, Low) repeated measures analysis of variance (rm-ANOVA) was applied to analyze the frequency of third-party punishment. Altruistic tendency was the between-subjects variable, fairness was the within-subjects variable, gender was covariate. The results show significant main effects of the fairness [$F(2,58) = 22.542, p < 0.001$] and altruistic tendency [$F(1,29) = 12.505, p = 0.001$]. The interaction between fairness and altruistic tendency was significant, [$F(2,58) = 5.352,$

$p = 0.006$]. Furthermore, the simple effect analysis suggested that for low altruists, the medium and high unfair offers generated more punitive behaviors than fair offers (both $p < 0.001$), the difference of the punishments between fair and medium unfair offers was significant, $p = 0.002$. For high altruists, they significantly showed less punishments in fair and medium unfair offers than in high unfair offers (both $p < 0.001$), but the difference between fair and medium unfair offers was not significant.

ERP Results

Two female participants were excluded because of displaying excessive artifacts in EEG recording. The remaining 30 participants included 15 high altruists (3 male and 12 female) and 15 low altruists (7 male and 8 female). **Table 2** presents the means and SD of MFN and P300 amplitudes in three different distribution schemes. **Figure 2** shows the average waveforms to different allocations for high and low altruists.

TABLE 1 | Frequency of third-party punishment by level of altruistic tendency.

Allocation scheme	High altruists	Low altruists
50: 50	0	0
70: 30	14.19 ± 20.50	5.12 ± 5.30
90: 10	44.88 ± 6.75	27.81 ± 10.76

TABLE 2 | Average amplitude and SD of medial frontal negativity (MFN) and P300 in different distribution schemes, by level of altruistic tendency.

Electrode	Fair (50: 50)				Medium unfair (70: 30)				High unfair (90: 10)			
	High altruists		Low altruists		High altruists		Low altruists		High altruists		Low altruists	
	M	SD	M	SD	M	SD	M	SD	M	SD	M	SD
MFN												
Fz	−1.15	4.79	0.93	4.14	−2.03	4.37	0.17	3.11	−3.31	3.67	3.65	4.07
FCz	−0.27	3.65	0.76	3.91	−1.25	4.18	0.27	2.89	−3.15	3.44	2.93	3.77
Cz	1.57	4.04	1.69	4.20	0.48	3.99	1.45	3.13	−1.12	2.91	3.91	3.95
P300												
Cz	3.32	4.84	1.08	4.41	4.23	2.96	1.38	3.26	4.43	3.55	5.46	5.02
Pz	4.02	3.99	2.18	3.48	5.62	3.66	2.64	3.31	6.26	4.19	7.24	4.43

For the MFN amplitude, gender as a covariate, a 2 (altruistic tendency: High, Low) × 3 (fairness: Fair, Medium Unfair, High Unfair) × 3 (electrode location: Fz, FCz, Cz) rm-ANOVA revealed a significant main effect of altruistic tendency, $F(1,27) = 5.63$, $p = 0.03$: amplitude of high altruists (−1.13 ± 0.9 μV) was markedly greater than low altruists (1.75 ± 0.86 μV). The interaction between altruism level and fairness was significant, $F(2,54) = 14.53$, $p < 0.001$. More specifically, amplitudes seen in high altruists and low altruists varied in different ways across the three allocations. For high altruists, the significant difference across allocations [$F(2,27) = 6.68$, $p = 0.004$] showed that MFN amplitude of high unfair offers (−2.52 ± 0.89 μV) was more negative-going than fair offers (0.031 ± 1.03 μV) and medium unfair offers (−0.94 ± 0.9 μV), ($p = 0.004$, $p = 0.05$), whereas the medium unfair offers (−0.94 ± 0.9μV) did not differ significantly with fair offers (0.031 ± 1.03 μV), ($p = 0.60$). Low altruists also showed significant variance in fairness consideration, $F(2,27) = 10.31$, $p < 0.001$: MFN in fair offers (1.15 ± 1.03 μV) and medium unfair offers (0.60 ± 0.91 μV) was more negative-going than in high unfair offers (3.49 ± 0.90 μV), ($p = 0.008$, $p = 0.001$); but no difference was found between medium unfair and fair offers, $p = 0.90$ (**Figure 3A**). A non-significant main effect reflected no difference across fairness levels, $F(2,54) = 1.69$, $p = 0.20$. The main effect of electrode location was not significant, $F(2,54) = 0.90$, $p = 0.37$. In addition, there were no interactions between electrode location and altruistic tendency, $F(2,54) = 3.74$, $p = 0.06$ or fairness and electrode location, $F(4,108) = 0.32$, $p = 0.80$. Likewise, no significant interaction was found between electrode location, fairness and altruistic tendency, $F(4,108) = 0.38$, $p = 0.76$.

For the amplitude of P300, we also considered gender as a covariate, a 2 (altruistic tendency: High, Low) × 3 (fairness: Fair, Medium Unfair, High Unfair) × 2 (electrode location: Pz, Cz) ANOVA yielded a significant interaction between altruistic tendency and fairness level, $F(2,54) = 5.48$, $p = 0.008$. Simple effect analysis found that P300 showed a significant difference of fairness levels for low altruists, $F(2,27) = 117.17$, $p < 0.001$ but not for high altruists, $F(2,27) = 1.50$, $p = 0.24$. For low altruists, P300 amplitude for high unfair offers (6.33 ± 1.06 μV) was more positive than fair offers (1.60 ± 1.05 μV) and

medium unfair offers (1.97 ± 0.80 μV), (both $p < 0.001$), but difference between fair offers (1.60 ± 1.05 μV) and medium unfair offers (1.97 ± 0.80 μV) was not significant, $p = 0.66$ (**Figure 3B**). No main effect of altruistic tendency was found, $F(1,27) = 1.35$, $p = 0.26$. The main effect of fairness did not reach significant, $F(2,54) = 2.71$, $p = 0.08$. No significant interaction was found between altruistic tendency and electrode location [$F(1,27) = 0.008$, $p = 0.93$] or between electrode location and fairness [$F(2,54) = 0.52$, $p = 0.59$]. The interaction among electrode location, fairness level and altruistic tendency was also not significant, $F(2,54) = 0.14$, $p = 0.86$.

To isolate variance in the ERP associated with the MFN and P300 from other overlapping ERP components, we created difference waves by subtracting each low altruist ERP from its appropriate corresponding high altruist ERP (Hajcak et al., 2005; Holroyd and Krigolson, 2007). Specifically, for each participant and channel, we created three difference waves by (1) subtracting the fairness ERP in the low altruist condition from the high altruist condition, creating a "fairness" difference wave; (2) subtracting the medium unfairness ERP in the low altruist condition from the high altruist condition, creating a "medium unfairness" difference wave; (3) subtracting the high unfairness ERP in the low altruist condition from the high altruist condition, creating a "high unfairness" difference wave. The amplitude of each difference wave was measured for each participant and electrode as the most negative deflection and the most positive deflection within the 0–800 ms following stimulus onset. Consistent with previous studies (Gering and Willoughby, 2002; Hajcak et al., 2005), MFN amplitude was evaluated at channel Fz, FCz, Cz, and P300 amplitude was evaluated at channel Cz, Pz, where they are normally maximal.

Following previous research, we adopted the algorithm of Holroyd and Krigolson (2007) to measure if MFN was affected by late positive component (especially P300). We carried out two sets of t-tests to compare results in the FCz and Pz locations, first for high altruists and second for low altruists. Results revealed that high altruistic tendency participants showed significantly larger amplitude at FCz than at Pz in all fairness conditions. For fair offers, the amplitude at FCz (−0.27 ± 3.65 μV) was significantly greater than at Pz (4.55 ± 3.00 μV), $t(14) = −6.14$, $p < 0.001$, and in medium unfair offers, amplitude in FCz

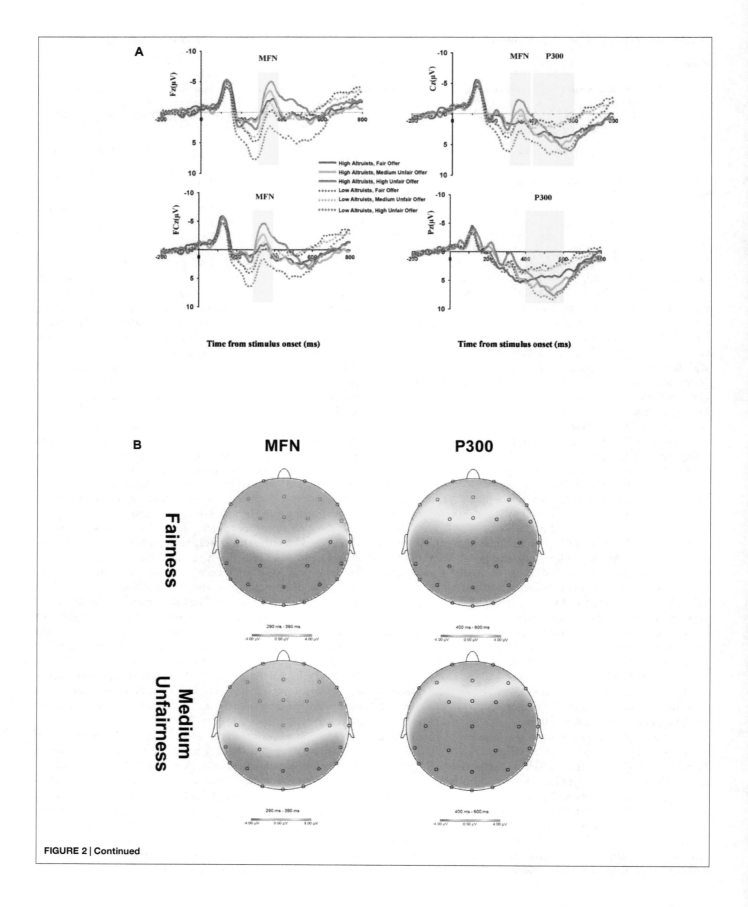

FIGURE 2 | Continued

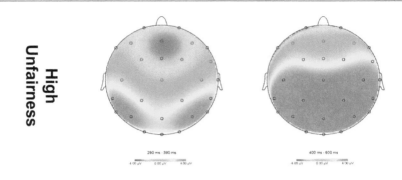

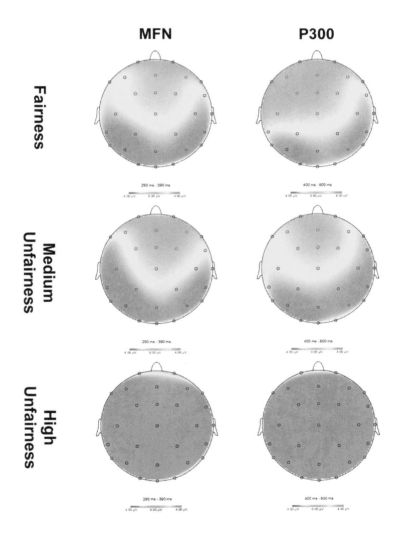

FIGURE 2 | Continued
Event-related potential data associated with high and low altruists. (A) Grand-average ERP waveforms to different allocations for high altruists and low altruists. The shaded 290–390 ms and 400–600 ms time windows were used to measure the medial frontal negativity (MFN) and P300 magnitude, respectively. **(B)** The scalp distribution of the MFN and P300 difference waves on different levels of unfairness of the high altruists. **(C)** The scalp distribution of the MFN and P300 difference waves on different levels of unfairness of the low altruists.

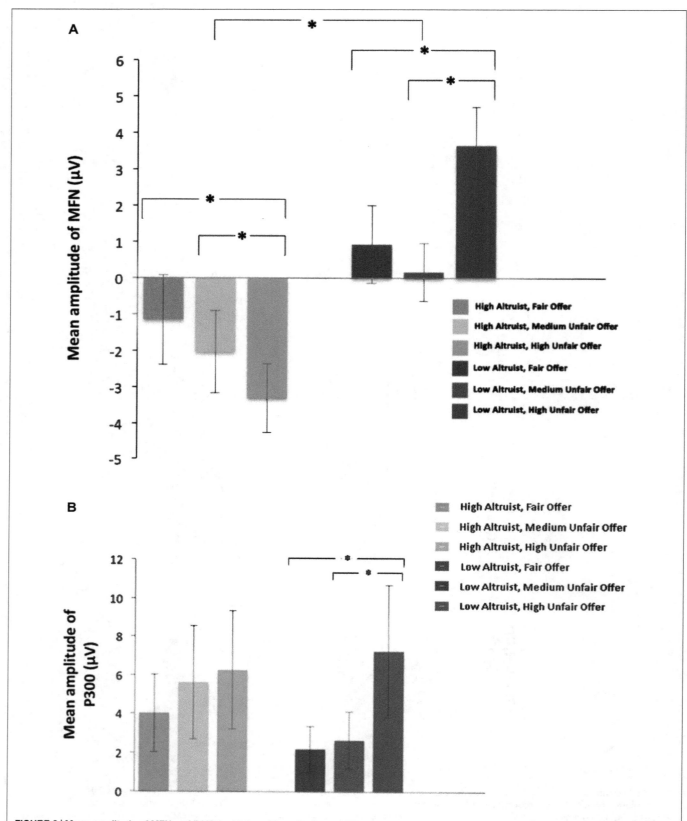

FIGURE 3 | Mean amplitude of MFN and P300 for high and low altruists at different fairness levels. (A) MFN amplitude recorded in Fz channels. **(B)** P300 amplitude recorded in Pz channels.*Significant difference refers to a $p < 0.05$. Error bars represent SE.

$(-1.25 \pm 4.18 \ \mu V)$ was also significantly greater than in Pz $(3.21 \pm 3.45 \ \mu V)$, $t(14) = -4.06$, $p < 0.01$. Moreover, in high unfair offers, amplitude in FCz $(-3.15 \pm 3.44 \ \mu V)$ was significantly more positive than in Pz $(1.59 \pm 4.81 \ \mu V)$, $t(14) = -3.32$, $p < 0.01$. t-tests in the subgroup of low altruistic tendency participants showed that FCz $(0.76 \pm 3.91 \ \mu V)$ was greater than Pz for fair offers $(2.61 \pm 3.40 \ \mu V)$,$t(14) = -2.17$, $p < 0.05$. The same pattern emerged for medium unfair offers, $(0.27 \pm 0.75 \ \mu V; 2.55 \pm 3.12 \ \mu V, t(14) = -2.64, p < 0.05)$, but the t-test result for high unfair offers found no significant difference between FCz $(2.93 \pm 3.77 \ \mu V)$ and Pz $(3.84 \pm 3.28 \ \mu V)$, $t(14) = -1.09$, $p = 0.296$. All of these results indicated that the MFN components were mainly distributed in the front of the scalp, not significantly affected by P300.

Additional evidence of the relationship between P300 and behavioral performance was obtained by testing the correlations between P300 responding to fairness levels in either high or low altruists and their behavioral performance in each group (as there is no punitive behavior confronting fair offers in either group, here we only consider medium unfair and high unfair conditions for both groups). For high altruists, behavioral performances under both medium unfair situation and high unfair situation were correlated significantly with corresponding P300s $[r(15) = 0.57, p < 0.01; r(15) = 0.84, p < 0.001]$. And the consistent behavioral patterns remained significant even when gender was controlled $[r(12) = 0.86, p < 0.001; r(12) = 0.55, p < 0.05]$. For low altruists, their behavioral performance under medium unfair and high unfair offers correlated significantly with corresponding P300 $[r(15) = 0.61, p < 0.05; r(15) = 0.52, p < 0.05]$. Also, this relationship remained significant when gender was controlled $[r(12) = 0.61, p < 0.05; r(12) = 0.59, p < 0.05]$. In other words, participants' behavioral performance was predicted by the P300 under corresponding condition, and the relationship was not diminished when the relationship between gender and these two variables were taken into account.

Discussion

This study tested whether altruistic tendency affects altruistic punishment and examined the neural process of fairness consideration. Consistent with prior research, third parties were more likely to punish unfair offers than fair offers, even at expense to themselves. However, altruistic tendency appeared to influence third-party punishment, in that high altruists imposed more of this type of punishment than low altruists. ERP results also indicated that altruistic tendency modulated the fairness consideration of the outcome. For high altruists, high unfair offers elicited larger MFN than medium unfair offers and fair offers; for low altruists, in contrast, fair offers elicited larger MFN, and high unfair offers caused the minimal MFN, which suggest that the altruistic tendency effect influence fairness consideration in the early stage of evaluation.

The behavioral results replicated third-party punishments and extend previous research finding altruistic tendency influences the punishments. In the experiment, all participants were paid 50 Yuan as initial endowment, and they were informed that

they can spend 15 Yuan to alter the unfair allocation to the fair one; the cost could not be compensated within expectation, after the pay cost, the third party (participant) would own the least payment in three. However, most participants chose irrational altruistic punishment, thus support the inequity aversion theory. The present research extends our understanding of altruistic behaviors by focusing on individual differences in third-party punishment. Third-party punishment, as a kind of irrational behavior in economic decision making, is not shown by all people. Economic societies are constituted by members with a variety of altruistic tendencies. Therefore, further research is necessary to consider these individual differences. It will be particularly important to explore the psychological and neural mechanism of fairness consideration toward population who show less altruistic punishments.

Use of the ERP technique enabled us to explore how altruistic tendency affects fairness consideration. Specifically, for high altruists, unfair offers elicited a larger MFN and for low altruists, fair offers elicited larger MFN. According to the expectancy deviation theory of MFN, unexpected outcomes cause a larger MFN (Oliveira et al., 2007); in our study, the same allocation elicited different MFN reaction patterns, which suggests that high and low altruists hold differential expectations about allocation. Hence, MFN was enhanced when high altruists saw the unfair allocation because it conflicted with their expectations, and it was enhanced when low altruists saw the fair allocation, which conflicted with their expectations.

The ERP results shed light on the relationship between the altruistic tendency and third-party punishment, in addition to providing further electrophysiological evidence in support of the inequity aversion hypothesis. Previous studies who studied the decision-making process in the dictator game showed that decisions are the result of a two-step process. In the first step, decision makers generate an automatic, intuitive proposal. The second step is a more deliberative phase in which decision makers adjust their proposals based on motivation and cognitive resources, a process that is modulated by social context, such as the perceived interpersonal closeness of the dictator with the receiver (Cappelletti et al., 2011; Grimm and Mengel, 2011; Rand et al., 2012; Cornelissen et al., 2013). In line with the social intuitionist model, the current ERP results suggest that the effect of altruistic tendency on altruistic punishment occurs in the early stage of the outcome evaluation, which provides further cognitive neuroscience evidence for the intuition dominant two-step processing theory. An important finding in this regard is that high and low altruists appeared to differ in inequity aversion. More specifically, for high altruists, the aversion to unfairness elicited greater MFN and led to paid altruistic punishment in more than 95% of the tasks; for low altruists, their concern was more about pursuit of their maximal self-interests. From the perspective of the low altruists, the dictator should pursue the maximization of self-interest, and high unfair allocation may be an expectable result. Because unfair offers do not trigger strong aversion, unfair outcomes elicited a smaller MFN and caused less punishment.

The ERP results also showed that high altruists had more negative-going MFN in response to high unfair offers, whereas there was no significant difference between medium unfair offers and fair offers. By contrast, for low altruists, MFN was significantly larger for fair offers compared with low and high unfair offers. This shows that MFN in all allocations for high and low altruists was binary, not ternary. MFN relates to a rough primary processing for allocations, which only evaluates whether the outcome was good or not (Hajcak et al., 2006; Leng and Zhou, 2010). Although many studies have found that MFN may represent more complicated information regarding outcomes, likely to be ternary or even polynary, the presentation of outcome materials in previous research was apparent and no subsequent task was introduced after the outcome appeared (Leng and Zhou, 2010; Luo et al., 2011; Qu et al., 2013a). In our experiment, after the distribution outcome was given, participants were required to decide whether to pay to punish the dictator, so participants could only make a simple dichotomous choice. For the behavioral results, we observed that the low altruists showed less frequency of the third-party punishment behaviors toward high unfair offers. For MFN, the high altruists showed larger MFN related to high unfair offers than moderate unfair offers and fair offers, but the low altruists showed the opposite patterns. We infer that because MFN occurs in the early stage of the outcome evaluation, it just reflects the awareness of fairness rather than affect the punishment behaviors of the participants. Therefore, behavioral results were inconsistent with the MFN results.

For high altruists, there was no significant difference in P300 depending on the fairness of the allocation; for low altruists, high unfair allocation induced more positive P300. Both for high altruists and for low altruists, behavioral performances under both medium unfair situation and high unfair situation were correlated significantly with corresponding amplitude of P300. More specifically, P300 might be related to altruist's punishments, larger amplitude of P300 predicts more third-party punishments.

This study only explored the influence of altruistic tendency on fairness consideration, and did not explore how altruistic tendency impacts the participants' willingness to pay to punish after becoming aware of the unfairness. In the end of the experiment, many participants reported that they had been aware of the unfairness in the tasks. However, they were not willing to pay such a high price to change the unfair allocation. Thus, further research will examine the trade-off processing in deciding the costly punishment.

Conclusion

This study is the first to examine the influence of altruistic tendency on third-party punishment and the neurophysiological process underlying fairness consideration. Behavioral results showed that compared with low altruists, high altruists delved out more third-party punishment; ERP results indicated that altruistic tendency also affected the awareness of fairness in the early stage of evaluation: for high altruists, high unfair allocation elicited more negative-going MFN amplitude, but for low altruists, fair offer triggered greater MFN. Specifically, these results demonstrate a stronger inequity aversion in high altruists than in low altruists, which may cause more punishment behavior.

Acknowledgment

This work was supported by the Program for National Natural Science Foundation of China (31470995).

References

Abbink, K., Sadrieh, A., and Zamir, S. (2004). Fairness, public good, and emotional aspects of punishment behavior. *Theory Decis.* 57, 25–57. doi: 10.1007/s11238-004-3672-8

Bellebaum, C., and Daum, I. (2008). Learning-related changes in reward expectancy are reflected in the feedback-related negativity. *Eur. J. Neurosci.* 27, 1823–1835. doi: 10.1111/j.1460-9568.2008.06138.x

Benenson, J. F., Pascoe, J., and Radmore, N. (2007). Children's altruistic behavior in the dictator game. *Evol. Hum. Behav.* 28, 168–175. doi: 10.1016/j.evolhumbehav.2006.10.003

Boksem, M. A., and De Cremer, D. (2010). Fairness concerns predict medial frontal negativity amplitude in ultimatum bargaining. *Soc. Neurosci.* 5, 118–128. doi: 10.1080/17470910903202666

Bolton, G. E., and Ockenfels, A. (2000). ERC: a theory of equity, reciprocity, and competition. *Am. Econ. Rev.* 90, 166–193. doi: 10.1007/s001820050072

Bosman, R. A. J., and van Winden, F. A. (1999). *The Behavioral Impact of Emotions in a Power to Take Game. 99-039/1.* Amsterdam: Tinberegn Institute.

Cappelletti, D., Güth, W., and Ploner, M. (2011). Being of two minds: ultimatum offers under cognitive constraints. *J. Econ. Psychol.* 32, 940–950. doi: 10.1016/j.joep.2011.08.001

Carpenter, J., Connolly, C., and Myers, C. K. (2008). Altruistic behavior in a representative dictator experiment. *Exp. Econ.* 11, 282–298. doi: 10.1007/s10683-007-9193-x

Cornelissen, G., Dewitte, S., and Warlop, L. (2013). Social value orientation as a moral intuition. *J. Int. Linguist. Assoc.* doi: 10.2139/ssrn.978469

Decker, T., Stiehler, A., and Strobel, M. (2003). A comparison of punishment rules in repeated public good games an experimental study. *J. Conflict Resolut.* 47, 751–772. doi: 10.1177/0022002703258795

De Quervain, D. J., Fischbacher, U., Treyer, V., Schellhammer, M., Schnyder, U., Buck, A., et al. (2004). The neural basis of altruistic punishment. *Science* 305, 1254–1258. doi: 10.1126/science.1100735

Dirk, E., and Martin, R. (2006). Inequality aversion, efficiency, and maximin preferences in simple distribution experiments: comment. *Am. Econ. Rev.* 96, 1912–1917. doi: 10.1257/aer.96.5.1912

Eckel, C. C., and Grossman, P. J. (1996). Altruism in anonymous dictator games. *Games Econ. Behav.* 16, 181–191. doi: 10.1006/game.1996.0081

Falk, A., and Fischbacher, U. (2006). A theory of reciprocity. *Games Econ. Behav.* 54, 293–315. doi: 10.1016/j.geb.2005.03.001

Falkenstein, M., Hohnsbein, J., Hoormann, J., and Blanke, L. (1990). "Effects of errors in choice reaction tasks on the ERP under focused and divided attention," in *Psychophysiological Brain Research*, eds C. Brunia, A. Gaillard, and A. Kok (Tilburg: Tilburg University Press), 192–195.

Fehr, E., and Fischbacher, U. (2003). The nature of human altruism. *Nature* 425, 785–791. doi: 10.1038/nature02043

Fehr, E., and Fischbacher, U. (2004a). Social norms and human cooperation. *Trends Cogn. Sci. (Regul. Ed.)* 8, 185–190. doi: 10.1016/j.tics.2004.02.007

Fehr, E., and Fischbacher, U. (2004b). Third-party punishment and social norms. *Evol. Hum. Behav.* 25, 63–87. doi: 10.1016/s1090-5138(04)00005-4

Fehr, E., and Gächter, S. (2002). Altruistic punishment in humans. *Nature* 415, 137–140. doi: 10.1038/415137a

Fehr, E., and Schmidt, K. M. (1999). A theory of fairness, competition, and cooperation. *Q. J. Econ.* 114, 817–868. doi: 10.1162/003355399556151

Gehring, W. J., Coles, M. G. H., Meyer, D. E., and Donchin, E. (1990). The error-related negativity: an event-related brain potential accompanying errors (abstract). *Psychophysiology* 27:S34.

Gering, W. J., and Willoughby, A. R. (2002). The medial frontal cortex and the rapid processing of monetary gains and losses. *Science* 295, 2279–2282. doi: 10.1126/science.1066893

Glaeser, E. L., and Sacerdote, B. (2000). The Determinants of Punishment:Deterrence, incapacitation and vengeance. *J. Legal Stud.* 32, 283–322. doi: 10.3386/w7676

Grimm, V., and Mengel, F. (2011). Let me sleep on It: delay reduces rejection rates in ultimatum games. *Econ. Lett.* 111, 113–115. doi: 10.1016/j.econlet.2011.01.025

Güth, W., Schmittberger, R., and Schwarze, B. (1982). An experimental analysis of ultimatum bargaining. *J. Econ. Behav. Organ.* 3, 367–388. doi: 10.1016/0167-2681(82)90011-7

Hajcak, G., Holroyd, C. B., Moser, J. S., and Simons, R. F. (2005). Brain potentials associated with expected and unexpected good and bad outcomes. *Psychophysiology* 42, 161–170. doi: 10.1111/j.1469-8986.2005.00278.x

Hajcak, G., Moser, J. S., Holroyd, C. B., and Simons, R. F. (2006). The feedback-related negativity reflects the binary evaluation of good versus bad outcomes. *Biol. Psychol.* 71, 148–154. doi: 10.1016/j.biopsycho.2005.04.001

Haruno, M., and Frith, C. D. (2009). Activity in the amygdala elicited by unfair divisions predicts social value orientation. *Nat. Neurosci.* 13, 160–161. doi: 10.1038/nn.2468

Holroyd, C., and Krigolson, O. (2007). Reward prediction error signals associated with a modified estimation task. *Psychophysiology* 44, 913–917. doi: 10.1111/j.1469-8986.2007.00561.x

Leng, Y., and Zhou, X. (2010). Modulation of the brain activity in outcome evaluation by interpersonal relationship: an ERP study. *Neuropsychologia* 48, 448–455. doi: 10.1016/j.neuropsychologia.2009.10.002

Luo, Q. L., Wang, Y., and Qu, C. (2011). The near-miss effect in slot-machine gambling: modulation of feedback-related negativity by subjective value. *Neuroreport* 22, 989–993. doi: 10.1097/wnr.0b013e32834da8ae

Marlowe, F. W., Berbesque, J. C., Barr, A., Barrett, C., Bolyanatz, A., Cardenas, J. C., et al. (2008). More 'altruistic' punishment in larger societies. *Proc. Biol. Sci.* 275, 587–592. doi: 10.1098/rspb.2007.1517

Masclet, D., Noussair, C., Tucker, S., and Villeval, M.-C. (2003). Monetary and nonmonetary punishment in the voluntary contributions mechanism. *Am. Econ. Rev.* 93, 366–380. doi: 10.1257/000282803321455359

Miltner, W. H., Braun, C. H., and Coles, M. G. (1997). Event-related brain potentials following incorrect feedback in a time-estimation task: evidence for a "generic" neural system for error detection. *J. Cogn. Neurosci.* 9, 788–798. doi: 10.1162/jocn.1997.9.6.788

Oliveira, F. T., McDonald, J. J., and Goodman, D. (2007). Performance monitoring in the anterior cingulate is not all error related: expectancy deviation and the representation of action-outcome associations. *J. Cogn. Neurosci.* 19, 1994–2004. doi: 10.1162/jocn.2007.19.12.1994

Pérez, R. L., and Kiss, H. J. (2012). Do People Accurately Anticipate Sanctions? *South. Econ. J.* 79, 300–321. doi: 10.4284/0038-4038-2011.033

Qu, C., Huang, Y. Y., Wang, Y., and Huang, Y. (2013a). The delay effect on outcome evaluation: results from an event-related potential study. *Front. Hum. Neurosci.* 7:748. doi: 10.3389/fnhum.2013.00748

Qu, C., Wang, Y., and Huang, Y. (2013b). Social exclusion modulates fairness consideration in the ultimatum game: an ERP study. *Front. Hum. Neurosci.* 7:505. doi: 10.3389/fnhum.2013.00505

Qu, L., Dou, W., Cheng, Y., and Qu, C. (2014). The processing course of conflicts in third-party punishment: an event-related potential study. *PsyCh J.* 3, 214–221. doi: 10.1002/pchj.59

Rand, D. G., Greene, J. D., and Nowak, M. A. (2012). Spontaneous giving and calculated greed. *Nature* 489, 427–430. doi: 10.1038/nature11467

Rotemberg, J. J. (2008). Minimally acceptable altruism and the ultimatum game. *J. Econ. Behav. Organ.* 66, 457–476. doi: 10.1016/j.jebo.2006.06.008

Singer, T., Seymour, B., O'Doherty, J. P., Stephan, K. E., Dolan, R. J., and Frith, C. D. (2006). Empathic neural responses are modulated by the perceived fairness of others. *Nature* 439, 466–469. doi: 10.1038/nature04271

Van der Veen, F. M., and Sahibdin, P. P. (2011). Dissociation between medial frontal negativity and cardiac responses in the ultimatum game: effects of offer size and fairness. *Cogn. Affect. Behav. Neurosci.* 11, 516–525. doi: 10.3758/s13415-011-0050-51

Wu, Y., Hu, J., van Dijk, E., Leliveld, M. C., and Zhou, X. (2012). Brain activity in fairness consideration during asset division: does the initial ownership playa role? *PLoS ONE* 7:e39627. doi: 10.1371/journal.pone.0039627

Wu, Y., and Zhou, X. (2009). The P300 and reward valence, magnitude, and expectancy in outcome evaluation. *Brain Res.* 1286, 114–122. doi: 10.1016/j.brainres.2009.06.032

Wu, Y., Zhou, Y., van Dijk, E., Leliveld, M. C., and Zhou, X. (2011). Social comparison affects brain responses to fairness in asset division: an ERP study with the ultimatum game. *Front. Hum. Neurosci.* 5:131. doi: 10.3389/fnhum.2011.00131

Yeung, N., and Sanfey, A. G. (2004). Independent coding of reward magnitude and valence in the human brain. *J. Neurosci.* 24, 6258–6264. doi: 10.1523/jneurosci.4537-03.2004

Conflict of Interest Statement: The authors declare that the research was conducted in the absence of any commercial or financial relationships that could be construed as a potential conflict of interest.

The cognitive-behavioral system of leadership: cognitive antecedents of active and passive leadership behaviors

Edina Dóci[1]*, Jeroen Stouten[2] and Joeri Hofmans[1]

[1] Faculty of Psychology and Educational Sciences, Vrije Universiteit Brussel, Brussel, Belgium, [2] Department of Psychology, University of Leuven, Leuven, Belgium

Edited by:
Darren Good,
Pepperdine University Graziadio
School of Business and Management,
USA

Reviewed by:
Erik L. Carlton,
The University of Memphis, USA
Anita Howard,
Case Western Reserve University,
USA

*Correspondence:
Edina Dóci,
Faculty of Psychology
and Educational Sciences, Vrije
Universiteit Brussel, Pleinlaan 2,
1050 Brussel, Belgium
edina.doci@vub.ac.be

Specialty section:
This article was submitted to
Organizational Psychology,
a section of the journal
Frontiers in Psychology

In the present paper, we propose a cognitive-behavioral understanding of active and passive leadership. Building on core evaluations theory, we offer a model that explains the emergence of leaders' active and passive behaviors, thereby predicting stable, inter-individual, as well as variable, intra-individual differences in both types of leadership behavior. We explain leaders' stable behavioral tendencies by their fundamental beliefs about themselves, others, and the world (core evaluations), while their variable, momentary behaviors are explained by the leaders' momentary appraisals of themselves, others, and the world (specific evaluations). By introducing interactions between the situation the leader enters, the leader's beliefs, appraisals, and behavior, we propose a comprehensive system of cognitive mechanisms that underlie active and passive leadership behavior.

Keywords: transformational leadership, transactional leadership, core self-evaluations, cognitive antecedents of leadership, leaders' beliefs

Introduction

The Full Range of Leadership Model portrays leadership as a pool of behaviors, ranging from highly passive to highly active (Avolio and Bass, 2001, p. 4; Avolio, 2010, p. 66; Sosik and Jung, 2011, p. 9). The model suggests that all leaders display both active and passive leadership, but that they do so with different frequency. Thus, some leaders have a stronger tendency to engage in active behaviors, while others are more likely to act passively. However, the Full Range of Leadership Model – or any other theory for that matter – falls short of explaining *why* some leaders are inclined to engage in active and others in passive behaviors, in other words, what the cognitive antecedents are that explain the differences in active and passive leadership behavior between different individuals. Furthermore, it also fails to clarify why the same leader would behave more actively in one situation than in another. Answering both questions is of particular importance for the leadership domain, both from a theoretical and a practical point of view.

Whereas researchers have in the last decades set out to examine dispositional, person-related antecedents of the full range of leadership behaviors (Barling et al., 2000; Judge and Bono, 2000; Peterson et al., 2009; Resick et al., 2009), surprisingly little attention has been paid to studying the antecedents of their within-person fluctuations (Nielsen and Cleal, 2011). Because relationships that exist at the between-person level do not necessarily apply to the within-person level (Hamaker, 2012), theorizing about and studying both between- and within-leader differences is crucial to arrive at a solid understanding of leadership behavior. Provided that intra-individual fluctuations in behaviors supplement inter-individual fluctuations (Tett and Guterman, 2000; Fleeson, 2001; Marshall and Brown, 2006; McNiel and Fleeson, 2006), there is a need for leadership theory that integrates intra-personal dynamism with stability, thereby conceptualizing them as two facets of the same phenomenon.

Furthermore, in recent decades researchers have accumulated a substantial amount of evidence showing the positive effects of active, transformational leadership behaviors on employee well-being and work outcomes (Bass, 1996, 1997; Yukl, 1999; Bass et al., 2003; Skogstad et al., 2007). Promoting active leadership behaviors among leaders is therefore highly beneficial both for individuals and organizations. However, solely knowing which dispositions go hand in hand with active leadership behaviors does not offer a sufficient theoretical basis for effective intervention. Only by incorporating intra-individual variation in leadership behavior into the scope of investigation, and by identifying the cognitive mechanisms that trigger favorable leadership behaviors, is it possible to offer relevant contributions for practitioners. We suggest this for a simple reason: it is easier for leaders to alter the way they think when it interferes with effective behaviors than to change their 'unhelpful' dispositions. Furthermore, to date most training programs merely teach new behaviors to leaders. However, if the cognitive mechanisms that trigger leadership behaviors are overlooked, interventions can hardly have long-lasting effects (Emiliani, 2003), given that leaders' impulses to think and act in a certain way are likely to override their fading memory of the learned behaviors (Day, 2001; Powell and Yalcin, 2010).

In the present paper, we embark on offering theoretical answers to two questions that are crucial to improving our understanding of leadership behavior: (1) what are the cognitive antecedents that explain inter-individual differences in leadership behavior, and (2) what are the cognitive antecedents that explain intra-individual differences in leadership behavior. To this end, we propose the Cognitive-Behavioral System of Leadership (see **Figure 1**), a model that undertakes to explain both the stability and the dynamism in leaders' behavior. To do so, we draw on one of the most influential interactionist theories, the Cognitive Affective Personality System (CAPS) theory (Mischel and Shoda, 1995). According to the CAPS theory, the same situational features are encoded differently in the minds of different individuals. For example, while an accounting task activates the encoding 'easy' for person A, it activates the encoding 'difficult' for person B. These encodings (e.g., *easy/difficult*) then activate other cognitive units, such as appraisals (e.g., *I can/cannot cope with this task*), beliefs (e.g., *I am a competent/incompetent person*), expectancies (e.g., *anticipating success/failure*), affects (e.g., *enthusiasm/anxiety*), goals (e.g., *problem solving/escaping*), and so on. Finally, a behavioral response (e.g., *proactive coping behavior/avoidance behavior*) is activated. The accessibility of certain cognitive units and the stable sequence of cognitive unit activation distinctive to a person is what accounts for the relative stability of behavior, while the different activation sequences set into motion by different situational features

explain the flexibility in a person's behavior (Mischel and Shoda, 1995; Schmitt et al., 2003). For example, in a socially (and not intellectually) challenging situation person B's belief of incompetence does not get activated, and therefore s/he will engage in active rather than avoidance behaviors. The basic tenets of the CAPS model have already received support in the context of leadership theory, with Vroom and Jago (2007) suggesting that the stable sequences of cognitive unit activation are responsible for the patterns of variability in the actions, thoughts, and feelings of leaders across different situations.

In the present article, we focus on two types of cognitive units drawn from different levels of a leader's cognitive map. First, building on the core evaluations theory (Judge et al., 1997), we look at leaders' fundamental beliefs about themselves, others, and their environment. These *core evaluations* are cognitive units that are relatively stable within one person, and affect every other unit above them. We suggest that, because they influence all appraisals, expectancies, and behavioral scripts, they shape leaders' trait-like, dispositional tendencies for leadership behavior. Second, we turn our attention to leaders' appraisals of the self, others, and the environment. These *specific evaluations* vary over time and between different circumstances for one leader, as they are triggered by a particular context. As such, they can explain the fluctuating, state-like dynamics in a leader's behavior. Together, core evaluations and specific evaluations help to explain the interplay of stability *and* variability in leadership behavior.

In the analysis below, the role of core evaluations and specific evaluations in the emergence of leadership behavior is discussed in more detail. Subsequently, discussion moves onto the dynamic interplay between the stable trait and the variable state level of our model, and the interactions between the situation, the leader's core evaluations, specific evaluations, and behavior. Besides proposing original relationships, we also aim to incorporate diverse, existing knowledge about the antecedents of leadership behavior into one coherent model. Therefore, some of the suggested relationships do not have great novelty value of themselves.

The Full Range of Leadership Model

According to the Full Range of Leadership Model (Avolio and Bass, 1991), at the passive end of the leadership spectrum lies the *lack of leadership*. *Laissez faire* is the management style characterized by the avoidance of taking leadership responsibilities, decisions, and actions, even in dire circumstances. Moving further along the passive-active continuum, the next leadership behavior is *passive management by exception*. This term refers to a management style whereby the leader does not act until problems get out of hand. Next on the scale is *active management by exception*, a management style characterized by looking out for mistakes, problems, and violations of the rules, and monitoring, controlling, and disciplining subordinates. This leadership style is active in the

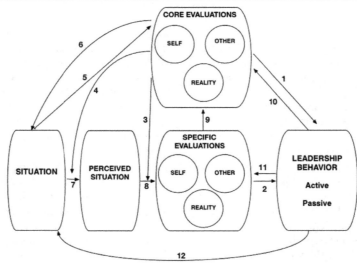

Figure 1 | The cognitive-behavioral system of leadership.

Proposition

(1) Core self-evaluations and leadership style	Arrow 1	Leader's core self-evaluations positively predict active and negatively predict passive leadership, such that the more positive a leader's core self-evaluations are, the more frequently s/he will engage in active and the less frequently in passive leadership behaviors.
(2) Specific self-evaluations and leadership behavior	Arrow 2	Leaders' specific self-evaluations positively predict active and negatively predict passive leadership behaviors, such that the more positive a leader's specific self-evaluations are in a situation, the more likely that s/he will display active and the less likely s/he will display passive leadership behaviors.
(3) Core other-evaluations and leadership style	Arrow 1	Leaders' core other-evaluations positively predict active and negatively predict passive leadership, such that the more positive a leader's core other-evaluations are, the more frequently s/he will engage in active and less frequently in passive leadership behaviors.
(4) Specific other-evaluations and leadership behavior	Arrow 2	Leaders' specific other-evaluations positively predict active and negatively predict passive leadership behaviors, such that the more positive a leader's specific other-evaluations are in a situation, the more likely that s/he will display active and the less likely s/he will display passive leadership behaviors.
(5) Core world-evaluations and leadership style	Arrow 1	Leaders' core world-evaluations positively predict active and negatively predict passive leadership, such that the more positive a leader's core world-evaluations are, the more frequently s/he will engage in active and less frequently in passive leadership behaviors.
(6) Specific world-evaluations and leadership behavior	Arrow 2	Leaders' specific world-evaluations positively predict active and negatively predict passive leadership behaviors, such that the more positive a leader's specific world-evaluations are in a situation, the more likely that s/he will display active and the less likely s/he will display passive leadership behaviors.
(7) The cognitive conditions of active leadership		Leaders' self-, other-, and world-evaluations (both on the trait and state level) will interact, such that they will amplify each other's positive effect when predicting active leadership.
(8) The emergence of specific evaluations	Arrow 3	Leaders' core evaluations will moderate the relationship between the situational features and specific evaluations.
(9) Core evaluations and objective and perceived situation	Arrow 4	Leaders' core evaluations will moderate the relationship between objective situational features and perceived situational features
(10) Situations solidify/modify core evaluations	Arrow 5	Situational features to which the leader is frequently exposed shape the leader's core evaluations over the long term, such that (1) when the two are aligned (e.g., supportive organization and positive core evaluations), frequently experienced situations reinforce core evaluations, and (2) when the two are non-aligned (e.g., hostile organization and positive core evaluations), situations may modify core evaluations.
(11) Core evaluations and situation selection	Arrow 6	The more positive a leader's core evaluations are, the more likely s/he will enter – socially or intellectually – challenging situations (while the more negative the leaders' core evaluations are, the more likely s/he will avoid such situations).
(12) Specific evaluations solidify/modify core evaluations	Arrow 9	The leader's frequently repeated specific evaluations shape the leader's core evaluations over the long term, such that (1) when the two are aligned, specific evaluations reinforce core evaluations, and (2) when the two are non-aligned, specific evaluations may modify core evaluations

(Continued)

Figure 1	Continued		
(13) Situations shape specific evaluations	Arrows 7–9	Situations shape the leader's core evaluations by (re)shaping the leader's specific evaluations.
(14) Leadership behaviors shape core evaluations	Arrow 10	The leader's recurrent behaviors shape the leader's core evaluations over the long term, such that (1) when the two are aligned with each other (positive core evaluations and active leadership behaviors, or negative core evaluations and passive behaviors), behaviors reinforce core evaluations, and (2) when the two are non-aligned, behaviors may modify core evaluations.
(15) Leadership behaviors shape situational features and specific evaluations	Arrows 5 and 12; Arrows 9 and 10	The leader's behavior shapes the leader's core evaluations through (1) modifying the situational features, and (2) modifying the leader's specific evaluations.

sense that the leader takes control of the situation instead of the situation controlling the leader. The leader actively monitors the deeds of the subordinate and intervenes when the subordinate's performance does not live up to expected standards. Even though active management by exception is clearly an active way of managing in comparison to laissez faire and passive management by exception, it is nevertheless a reactive rather than proactive way of leading. Therefore its midway position on the passivity-activity continuum. Sitting further toward the active end of the scale is *contingent reward* leadership, whereby reward are made contingent on subordinates' performance, and the necessary steps in order to be rewarded are stipulated. Contingent reward leadership implies a higher level of activeness and initiation than the previous behaviors, as the leader sets goals, identifies objectives, and structures expectations. However, a considerable amount of energy is still spent on 'reacting,' following up on objectives, rewarding, and punishing subordinates. Management by exception behaviors and contingent reward leadership fall under the umbrella term 'transactional leadership.' In all transactional leadership behaviors the leader-subordinate relationship is essentially based on the principle of mutually self-interested exchange. Transactional leaders' schema of leadership suggests that employees get their work done in exchange for financial and other reward from their leaders. Besides rewarding them, transactional leaders 'motivate' their subordinates by monitoring, controlling, and punishing them (Bass, 1991, 1999; Barling et al., 2011).

Transformational leadership, on the other hand, is based on the leader's ability to motivate subordinates by providing them with an appealing vision and stimulating challenges, and by being an inspiring role model. The four transformational behaviors, which highly intercorrelate (Avolio et al., 1999), constitute the active end of the leadership spectrum. *Individualized consideration* refers to the extent to which the leader attends to each subordinate's needs, provides them with empathy and compassion, listens to them actively, recognizes their strengths, and helps to develop their skills by acting as a mentor or coach. *Intellectual stimulation* refers to the extent to which the leader challenges the subordinates' beliefs and assumptions, takes risks, and promotes independent thinking on the part of subordinates. *Inspirational motivation* refers to the extent to which the leader articulates an inspiring vision, creates a sense of purpose and provides the subordinates with high but realistic standards. *Idealized influence* refers to the extent to which the

leader acts with integrity and as a role model for high ethical behavior, is driven by what is best for the subordinates and the organization, stands up for her/his values, addresses crises head-on, and acts charismatically (Bass, 1999; Kirkbride, 2006; Barling et al., 2011). (Because of their high intercorrelations, throughout the article we discuss the four transformational behaviors collectively, as facets of the same leadership style.) In sum, transformational leadership is characterized by highly (pro)active behaviors, such as innovating, risk-taking and challenging others, elevating expectations, shaping meaning and creating purpose.

As mentioned above, transactional leadership can also take on active forms, as the name 'active management by exception' indicates. Indeed, it requires a considerable level of alertness and action-orientation from the leader to closely monitor subordinates and maintain an early warning system should mistakes arise (Kirkbride, 2006). The Full Range of Leadership Model suggests that it is nevertheless a less active form of leading than transformational behaviors. The reason for this is that even though active management by exception entails attention, vigilance and action, it is nevertheless reactive in the sense that the leader attends mainly to deviations and corrects subordinates' behaviors when performance deteriorates from required standards (Bass, 1997; Avolio et al., 1999). Transformational leadership behaviors, instead, are approach-oriented, initiating, pro-active ways of leading, whereby the leader inspires and stimulates subordinates to reach more than they thought was possible.

Explaining Stable, Inter-Individual Differences in Leadership Behavior: Core Evaluations

We propose that, in order to understand leaders' dispositional tendencies to display active or passive leadership behavior, we must identify their core beliefs: their deepest, most enduring understandings about the self, others, and the world (Beck, 1967, 2011). The reason is that core beliefs are deep cognitive structures that guide the selection, encoding, and evaluation of all stimuli (Beck, 1967), with a major impact on subsequent behavior (Segal, 1988). In other words, beliefs influence the formation of appraisals, which in turn activate behaviors. For example, if a person believes that the world is an unfair place, s/he may perceive any criticism as hostile, and as a result act vengefully when being criticized. Identifying a leader's underlying beliefs therefore provides insight into the relative stability in his/her cognitive and behavioral patterns (McGregor, 1960; Krishnan, 2001; Emiliani, 2003; Tickle et al., 2005; Washington et al., 2006; Pastor and Mayo, 2008).

People hold beliefs about every segment of life (e.g., women are gentle, traveling is exciting, learning is difficult, etc.). However, according to *core evaluations theory* (Judge et al., 1997), there are only a small number of fundamental beliefs that underlie every subsequent appraisal. Such beliefs are referred to as *core evaluations*, that is, bottom-line, all-encompassing, and evaluative beliefs that an individual holds. Core evaluations comprise three areas, namely the self, other people, and the world (Judge et al., 1997). In this article, we argue that individual differences in the three types of core evaluations (i.e., core self-evaluations, core other-evaluations, and core world-evaluations) account for individual differences in leaders' inclinations to practice active or passive leadership behaviors (**Figure 1**, arrow 1). For example, leaders who fundamentally trust the world to be a safe place will generally be more inclined to take initiatives and risks than leaders who see the world as a dangerous place. Before elaborating on the relationship between leaders' core evaluations and behavioral tendencies, we will introduce the idea that 'specific evaluations' of the self, others, and the world explain within-person fluctuations in leadership behavior.

Explaining Intra-Individual Differences in Leadership Behavior: Specific Evaluations

Behaviors are not driven directly by the situation, but rather by the perceptions and interpretations of the situation by the subject (Lewin, 1951; Weiner, 1980; Ajzen, 1991; Mischel and Shoda, 1995; Kuppens et al., 2009). Building on this premise, we suggest that momentary leadership behavior results from the meaning that the leader attributes to any situation, that is, how s/he perceives him/herself, others, and the environment in a certain context. Such appraisals are the leader's *state core evaluations* or *specific evaluations* that – as opposed to core evaluations – fluctuate across situations (for state core self-evaluations, see Judge and Kammeyer-Mueller, 2011; Nübold et al., 2013).

Specific evaluations fluctuate because situations change. In some situations Leader A feels that s/he can cope well with the demands of the situation, while in others s/he may experience a lesser degree of confidence and control. Sometimes Leader A finds the subordinate s/he is interacting with reliable, while at other times s/he perceives the subordinate to be unreliable. Even if Leader A usually appraises the organizational environment to be safe and just, occasionally s/he may perceive it as threatening and unfair. We suggest that such different appraisals will trigger different behavioral responses within the same leader (**Figure 1**, arrow 2). For example, when a leader feels capable of coping with a task's

demands, s/he may also be capable of actively inspiring and challenging others, while in a situation where s/he does not feel in control of the situation, s/he may be inclined to remain passive.

Core Evaluations, Specific Evaluations and Leadership Behavior

Core Self-Evaluations and Leadership

Core self-evaluations are the fundamental evaluations an individual holds about him/herself and her/his capabilities, self-worth, and ability to cope (Judge et al., 1997). It is a higher-order trait indicated by four lower-order traits: locus of control, generalized self-efficacy, self-esteem, and neuroticism. Locus of control refers to a person's belief about the causes of events in his/her life. People with an internal locus of control believe that they shape the events in their lives, while people with an external locus of control attribute the causes of events to external factors such as luck or other people's actions (Rotter, 1966). Generalized self-efficacy refers to a person's beliefs about being able to cope successfully with a wide range of life-situations (Smith, 1989). Self-esteem refers to a person's self-acceptance, self-liking and self-respect (Judge et al., 1997), and neuroticism refers to one's tendency to experience long-lasting, negative emotions (Costa and McCrae, 1992).

Resick et al. (2009) have found that leaders with positive core self-evaluations are more likely to be transformational than leaders with negative core self-evaluations because they possess the necessary self-confidence required to perform transformational behaviors. People with negative core self-evaluations believe that they cannot cope successfully with challenging situations, and therefore they are inclined to engage in avoidance coping behaviors (Kammeyer-Mueller et al., 2009). We suggest that leaders who have strong inclinations to engage in passive forms of leadership – such as neglecting their responsibilities or avoiding action altogether – may do so because of their negative core self-evaluations.

Proposition 1: Leader's core self-evaluations positively predict active and negatively predict passive leadership, such that the more positive a leader's core self-evaluations are, the more frequently s/he will engage in active and the less frequently in passive leadership behaviors. (**Figure 1**, arrow 1).

Specific Self-Evaluations (State Core Self-Evaluations) and Leadership Behavior

Although core-self evaluations have predominantly been studied as a stable, person-related characteristic, there is by now widespread agreement that core self-evaluations should be seen as a trait- *and* state-based construct (Judge and Kammeyer-Mueller, 2004; Judge et al., 2012). This implies that a person's core self-evaluations fluctuate (i.e., the state part) around a fixed point (i.e., the trait part). In line with this idea, recent research has demonstrated that one's state core self-evaluations (*we use the terms state core self-evaluations and specific self-evaluations interchangeably*) indeed vary across situations (Debusscher et al., 2015; Dóci and Hofmans, 2015), just as has been shown regarding its constituent parts: self-esteem (Heatherton and Polivy, 1991), neuroticism (McNiel and Fleeson, 2006; Debusscher et al., 2014), and self-efficacy (Bandura, 2006).

As mentioned above, empirical evidence supports the notion that leaders with positive core self-evaluations are more likely to be predominantly transformational than leaders with negative core self-evaluations (Resick et al., 2009). We suggest that this relationship holds true on the state level too, that is, the more a leader feels in control, confident, and capable in a situation, the more likely s/he will challenge, inspire, stimulate, and coach others. Conversely, we also suggest that the less the leader feels in control and capable, the more likely s/he will display passive behaviors. An experimental study conducted by Dóci and Hofmans (2015) provided initial empirical evidence in support of this assumption by showing that state core-self evaluations were positively related to subordinate ratings of transformational leadership behavior.

Proposition 2: Leaders' specific self-evaluations positively predict active and negatively predict passive leadership behaviors, such that the more positive a leader's specific self-evaluations are in a situation, the more likely that s/he will display active and the less likely s/he will display passive leadership behaviors. (**Figure 1**, arrow 2).

The Criteria of Self-evaluations

From situation to situation, the criteria against which one evaluates oneself may differ. These criteria are dictated by the particular context, that is, the skills and competencies a certain situation requires. For example, while giving a presentation at a conference, one's self-evaluations primarily depend on one's appraisal of his/her scientific knowledge and presentation skills. In a dating situation, however, the same person's self-evaluation may largely be a function of that person's appraisal of her/his physical appearance. Thus, while the frame of reference for self-evaluations is 'brains' at a conference, it may be 'looks' in a dating situation.

When it comes to leadership, we suggest that there are two central domains in which one needs to feel capable, in order to arrive at positive self-evaluations (and engage in active behaviors): (1) handling people and (2) handling tasks. We expect these two dimensions of self-evaluations to be relatively independent from one another, meaning that one can evaluate oneself positively on one dimension and negatively on the other. For example, a manager at an airplane manufacturing plant with an organizational psychology background may feel confident about motivating his/her subordinates, but insecure when it comes to understanding the engineering problems at hand. Conceptualizing these two domains as distinct facets of self-evaluations is in line with research on the multi-faceted nature of self-esteem, that has shown that the sense of competence and the sense of social worth are two discrete dimensions (Tafarodi and Swann, 1995). Moreover, the two facets of self-evaluations we propose (handling tasks and handling people effectively) correspond to the two main behavioral requirements of the leadership role identified by the Ohio State Leadership Studies: *initiating structure* and *consideration*. These two criteria have been found to be independent from each other, so that the leader's position on one dimension does not predict the leader's position on the other dimension (Fleishman, 1953; Weissenberg and Kavanagh, 1972).

We suggest that for practicing highly active leadership behaviors, a leader must evaluate him/herself as capable in both domains. A leader needs to feel socially confident to coach, stimulate, and inspire subordinates, and to act charismatically. Furthermore, the leader also needs to feel confident in relation to tasks in order to challenge assumptions, demonstrate competence, and offer innovative solutions. When the leader has low confidence in one or both domains, s/he may no longer be capable of displaying highly active, transformational leadership. Thus, we suggest that feeling confident about managing people *and* tasks are necessary (but not sufficient) pre-conditions for performing active leadership behaviors.

Core Other-Evaluations and Leadership

Core evaluations of others (hereafter: core other-evaluations) refer to the implicit theory that an individual holds about other people, that is, whether others can generally be trusted (Judge et al., 1997). We propose that this fundamental belief plays a crucial role in leaders' active behavioral inclinations. To be inclined to challenge, stimulate, inspire, and coach subordinates, a leader needs to believe that people are trustworthy, implying, in the leadership context, that people can be expected to fully discharge their work duties. Leaders who do not trust others may instead be prone to closely monitor subordinates and look out for mistakes. Furthermore, we suggest that leaders who have confidence in others may be more inclined to engage in interactions with their subordinates, as trust generates sociability (Fukuyama, 1995). Leaders who are apprehensive about others may instead be inclined to be socially passive and avoid interactions with their subordinates.

It has been found those leaders' implicit followership theories, that is, their beliefs about what followers their perceptions are like in general, shape of and behaviors toward their subordinates (Goodwin et al., 2000; Sy, 2010). This line of research underscores the need for studying other-evaluations when trying to understand the differences between active and passive leadership behavior. Research that has shown that transformational and transactional leaders have distinct schemas about subordinates (Goodwin et al., 2000) points in the same direction. In particular, Pastor and Mayo (2008) found that transformational leaders were more likely to hold Y-beliefs than non-transformational leaders. Leaders with Y beliefs think that under the right circumstances, subordinates are reliable motivated to work and eager to take on responsibilities. Instead, leaders with X-beliefs see subordinates as inherently lazy and inclined to avoid tasks and responsibilities; therefore, they believe that subordinates must be closely monitored and controlled (McGregor, 1960). We suggest that Y beliefs are underpinned by a leader's predisposition to evaluate people positively.

Proposition 3: Leaders' core other-evaluations positively predict active and negatively predict passive leadership, such that the more positive a leader's core other-evaluations are, the more frequently s/he will engage in active and less frequently in passive leadership behaviors. (**Figure 1**, arrow 1).

Specific Other-Evaluations and Leadership Behavior

In the previous section we discussed how core other-evaluations may incline leaders to perceive subordinates as generally trustworthy or untrustworthy. However, despite the existence of such a general tendency, people's momentary level of trust varies as a function of who they are in interaction with (Mayer et al., 1995). Even though it has not yet been thoroughly examined in the framework of the Full Range of Leadership Model, extensive research has shown that leaders do change their behavior as a function of their perception of the subordinate (Lowin and Craig, 1968; Witkin et al., 1977; Turban and Jones, 1988). In particular, LMX theory claims that leaders change their behavior based on their evaluation of the abilities and attitudes of the different subordinates (Dansereau et al., 1975). When leaders trust their subordinates, they give them more time and attention, challenge them, and provide them with more opportunities to develop themselves than when they do not trust the subordinates (Graen and Uhl-Bien, 1995). Research has shown that when the level of trust toward a subordinate is low, leaders are more likely to emphasize their authority position and tighten control (Georgesen and Harris, 2006), intensify monitoring (Mayer and Gavin, 2005), and give subordinates less information, responsibility, and autonomy (Mayer et al., 1995).

Because trust is multidimensional and domain-specific (Lewicki et al., 1998), we suggest that the leader's trust toward one particular subordinate also fluctuates. This fluctuation may be a function of the situation's demands, and the leader's evaluation of the subordinate's capability and commitment to fulfill these demands. We predict that on occasions when the leader evaluates a particular subordinate positively, s/he will be inclined to perform active leadership behaviors characterized by pursuing contact with the subordinate, providing him/her with attention, support, stimulation, and inspiration. When the leader instead sees the same subordinate in a more negative light, s/he will be prone to emphasize her/his authority, tighten up control, intensify monitoring, or avoid the subordinate altogether. In sum, the more positively the leader evaluates a subordinate, the more inclined the leader will be to engage in active, and the less inclined to engage in passive leadership behaviors. As mentioned above, this proposition is closely aligned with the basic tenets of LMX theory. This is not a surprise given that active leadership behaviors have been shown to be closely associated with leader member exchange, as research has demonstrated that leader-member exchange acts as a mediator between transformational behaviors and positive work outcomes (Wang et al., 2005). This link implies that the same underlying cognitive mechanism may contribute to the emergence of both phenomena.

Proposition 4: Leaders' specific other-evaluations positively predict active and negatively predict passive leadership behaviors, such that the more positive a leader's specific other-evaluations are in a situation, the more likely that s/he will

display active and the less likely s/he will display passive leadership behaviors. (**Figure 1**, arrow 2).

The Criteria of Other-Evaluations

Similarly to self-evaluations, we suggest that the evaluation of others is based on different criteria in different contexts. For example, in a hospital, person A (the patient) may find person B (the surgeon) trustworthy if person B has steady hands and a low mortality record. However, if A and B get married after the operation, fidelity may become the major criterion of B's trustworthiness. Trust in another person is a belief that can be divided into several, independent components, so that the same individual can find one person (or group of people) trustworthy in one dimension, and untrustworthy in another (Mayer et al., 1995).

We suggest that for a leader to fully trust a subordinate, and therefore engage in highly active leadership behaviors; at least two criteria must be fulfilled. First, the leader must believe that the subordinate is *reliable* enough to perform his/her duties. Second, the leader must trust the subordinate to be *capable* of performing such duties, because even if the subordinate is willing to perform well, if s/he is not capable of doing so, convincing results cannot be realized. Obviously, a person can be perceived to be capable but not reliable, and vice versa.

Distinguishing between these trust domains corresponds to McAllister's (1995) assertion that cognition-based trust is a function of the evaluation of the other person's competence and reliability. We suggest that the leader needs to perceive the subordinate as both reliable *and* capable in order to perform highly active behaviors. To provide the subordinate with caring and emotional support, the leader must consider the subordinate reliable, and therefore worthy of a reciprocally positive attitude (*see Social Exchange Theory*, Emerson, 1976). Furthermore, to encourage the subordinate to think for him/herself, to stimulate and challenge him/her, and to solicit the subordinate's ideas, the leader must trust the subordinate to be capable. If the leader evaluates the subordinate to be incapable and/or unreliable, the leader may instead be inclined to give clear instructions and follow up on them closely, to be on the lookout for mistakes and deviations, to closely control the subordinate, or to ignore him/her altogether.

The above-identified criteria for other-evaluations are closely in line with the situational leadership model (Hersey and Blanchard, 1969). The situational leadership model suggests that effective leaders must adapt their leadership behavior to the maturity level of the subordinate, which is represented by the subordinate's level of competence and commitment. While the resemblance between the two models is obvious, they also differ in a core feature, namely that one of them describes the most fruitful, while the other describes the most probable leaderships behaviors in a situation. The situational leadership model is a contingency model that concerns the effectiveness of leadership behaviors in relation to subordinates with differing features, and describes the most functional and desirable managing style in particular circumstances. Our model, on the other hand, introduces the leadership behaviors that are the most likely to occur in certain circumstances. Thus, the two models firmly complement each other.

Core World-Evaluations and Leadership

Core evaluations of the world (hereafter 'core world-evaluations') are an individual's deeply held beliefs about the world around him/her (Judge et al., 1997), that is, whether the world can be trusted or not. The original core-evaluations theory distinguishes between three core world-evaluations: believing that the world is fundamentally benevolent (or malevolent); believing that the world is fundamentally just (or unjust); and believing that the world is fundamentally exciting (or dangerous) (Judge et al., 1997).

People who believe that the world is essentially benevolent trust their environment to be a safe and good place where success and happiness can be realized and values can be upheld (Judge et al., 1997, p. 164). As such, these people have the right disposition to engage in active behaviors, as research has shown that there is a higher chance for aspiration and goal-oriented action when one believes that success is likely (Jacobs et al., 1984; Wood and Bandura, 1989; Bandura and Locke, 2003). If a leader instead believes that the world is a bad place where success is an exception, values cannot be realized, and the rule is suffering and misery (Judge et al., 1997; p. 164), there is a good chance for withdrawal and passivity, based on an expectation of non-contingency between actions and probable future outcomes (see *learned helplessness theory*; Seligman, 1975; Maier and Seligman, 1976). If a leader thinks that it is not possible to achieve goals and values in this world, s/he may be less inclined to actively pursue them. In line with this idea, research has shown that not believing in the possibility for change in the organization negatively predicts transformational behavior (Bommer et al., 2004).

Furthermore, we suggest that leaders who believe that the world is an exciting place have the mindset that is needed to think innovatively, go on undiscovered paths, and challenge widely held beliefs, while leaders who think that the world is dangerous may not take the risks the aforementioned behaviors entail. Believing that the world is exciting rather than dangerous implies a generalized sense of psychological safety, and psychological safety has been shown to promote creativity in organizations (Edmondson, 2004), to relate positively to organizational innovativeness (Baer and Frese, 2003), and to promote information sharing in a way that inspires subordinates to develop their own creative ideas (Edmondson, 2004), all of which are features of active leadership. In line with this, the perception of a supportive and challenging – and therefore exciting rather than dangerous – organizational climate has been shown to promote high creativity (McLean, 2005, for a review). Moreover, believing that the world is a dangerous place implies a proclivity to fear, and fear has been shown to predict avoidance (Craske et al., 1987). Leaders who think that the world is dangerous may thus avoid taking risks in order to prevent getting harmed or punished in the event of failure, and rather withdraw into 'safe' passivity. Furthermore, leaders who believe that the world is a malicious place, instead of encouraging independent thinking may become controlling and hyper-vigilant for mistakes made under their supervision, in an attempt to pre-empt retaliation in what is perceived to be a hostile environment.

Proposition 5: Leaders' core world-evaluations positively predict active and negatively predict passive leadership, such that the more positive a leader's core world-evaluations are, the more frequently s/he will engage in active and less frequently in passive leadership behaviors. (**Figure 1**, arrow 1).

Specific World-Evaluations and Leadership Behavior

We suggest that the momentary appraisals a leader makes about the dangerousness, fairness, and benevolence of the environment in a particular situation shape the leader's behavior in that situation. When the leader evaluates the environment positively (benevolent, just, exciting) s/he may be more inclined to challenge and stimulate others, be innovative and pursue change, than in situations when s/he appraises the environment negatively (malevolent, unjust, dangerous), inclining him/her to monitor and control subordinates or withdraw altogether.

Proposition 6: Leaders' specific world-evaluations positively predict active and negatively predict passive leadership behaviors, such that the more positive a leader's specific world-evaluations are in a situation, the more likely that s/he will display active and the less likely s/he will display passive leadership behaviors (**Figure 1**, arrow 2).

The Cognitive Conditions of Active Leadership

We suggest that highly active, transformational leadership behaviors are most likely to emerge when all three cognitive conditions are met, that is, the leader evaluates him/herself, the subordinates, *and* the environment positively. For example, even if a leader has high confidence in him/herself and also appraises the organization to be fair and supportive, but thinks that the subordinate is not competent enough, s/he may not be inclined to engage in highly inspiring and challenging behaviors toward the subordinate. Similarly, even if the leader appraises the subordinate to be competent and the organization to be benevolent, but doesn't have the self-confidence for the task at hand, s/he may not be able to engage in stimulating leadership. Finally, even if the leader believes that both him/herself *and* the subordinate are able to achieve excellent outcomes, but perceives the organizational environment as threatening, s/he may not be inclined to take risks and encourage innovativeness. Therefore, having positive evaluations of all three 'actors' provides a fertile cognitive ground for the emergence of active leadership behaviors. We suggest that negative evaluations (i.e., perceiving the self to be unable to cope, people to be untrustworthy or the context to be threatening) will instead activate defensive manoeuvers (Packer, 1985), such as avoidance behaviors or attempts at controlling others and the environment.

Proposition 7: leaders' core self-, other-, and world-evaluations (both on the trait and state level) will interact, such that they will amplify each other's positive effect when predicting active leadership.

The Dynamic Interplay between the Situation, Core Evaluations, Specific Evaluations and Leadership Behavior

The Emergence of Specific Evaluations

As argued above, different situations trigger different specific evaluations (**Figure 1**, arrows 7 and 8). For example, in a situation where subordinate X arrives late to a meeting, Leader A will evaluate X negatively, while in a situation where X arrives on time, Leader A may see X in a more positive light. However, specific evaluations are not only shaped by the situation, but rather by the interaction between the situation and the leader's core evaluations (Kammeyer-Mueller et al., 2009). In the previous example, where subordinate X arrived late to a meeting (situational feature), Leader A, who holds the view that subordinates in general are unreliable (negative core other-evaluations), may think 'He's late because he couldn't care less' (negative specific other-evaluations). Leader B, however, who thinks that subordinates in general are reliable, may not attribute importance to being late, thus maintaining her/his positive image of X.

> **Proposition 8:** Leaders' core evaluations will moderate the relationship between the situational features and specific evaluations. (**Figure 1**, arrow 3).

Interaction between Core Evaluations and the Situation

We propose that a leader's core evaluations shape the leader's perception of the situation. They predispose the leader to notice and magnify some features of the situation and ignore others, thereby attributing certain meanings to the features in such a way that they become aligned with the leader's core evaluations (Kammeyer-Mueller et al., 2009). For example, leaders with negative core other evaluations may be prone to notice and magnify small deviations from the rules and perceive them as violations, while leaders with positive core other evaluations may not pay attention to such deviations. When subordinate X arrives 10 min late to the meeting, Leader A with positive core other-evaluations may think 'X is a little bit late,' while B, the leader with less confidence in others, may think 'X is very late.' In line with our reasoning, the *differential exposure hypothesis* suggests that people with positive core self-evaluations are less likely to interpret work situations as stressful as people with negative core self-evaluations (Kammeyer-Mueller et al., 2009). People with positive core self-evaluations also experience their job as more challenging because their positive predisposition makes them focus on the positive qualities of the job (Judge et al., 2000).

> **Proposition 9:** Leaders' core evaluations will moderate the relationship between objective situational features and perceived situational features. (**Figure 1**, arrow 4).

Self-Preserving Mechanisms of the System

Human systems have their self-organizing dynamics and mechanisms to preserve themselves and their coherence

(McGinn and Young, 1996). This, we suggest, holds true for the Cognitive-Behavioral System of Leadership too. In what follows, we will discuss the mechanisms through which the system remains self-preserving.

Situations Solidify Core Evaluations

Being exposed to certain working conditions over a long time period may lead to the maturation of core evaluations, as long-term working conditions have the potential to shape personality traits (Wille et al., 2013; Wille and De Fruyt, 2014). For example, the originally mildly negative core other-evaluations of Leader F may become absolute and incontestable after years of directing a school for dropouts, where students are often aggressive or absent, and teachers are cynical and negligent.

Specific Evaluations Solidify Core Evaluations

Repeated appraisals of the self, others, and the world (i.e., specific evaluations) across various situations cement the beliefs held about the self, others, and the world (i.e., core evaluations). This happens because repeated encodings increase the chronic accessibility of these cognitive units and make the neuron pathways become automatic (Mischel and Shoda, 1995). If the above-mentioned Leader F perceives students and teachers to be untrustworthy on a day-to-day basis, this will result in the solidification of her/his negative belief about people in general. Note that specific evaluations therefore mediate the link between the situation and core evaluations, a suggestion that is in line with the sociogenomic model of personality and its view of environments shaping personality traits by affecting states (Roberts and Jackson, 2008).

Leadership Behaviors Shape the Situation and Specific Evaluations and Solidify Core Evaluations

Another 'tool' for maintaining beliefs is behavior itself. Leaders preserve their beliefs by acting the way they do. The Cognitive-Behavioral System of Leadership is a self-reinforcing cycle in which the leader's behaviors set positive and negative self-fulfilling prophecies into motion, that in turn validate the preconceptions that elicited the behaviors. This may happen through modifying the features of the context, as people tend to alter their environments to achieve consistency with their personality traits (Caspi et al., 2005). The modified context then provides the leader with further opportunities to collect evidence about the accuracy of his/her beliefs. For example, a leader with a generalized negative opinion about subordinates may engage in active management by exception behavior, focusing on followers' mistakes and failures to meet standards. Consequently, subordinates may start to live up to the negative expectations (*Golem effect*; Eden, 1992), lower their efforts, and therefore confirm the leader's negative ideas about subordinates. Consider also the *laissez faire* leader, who regularly verifies his/her sense of inefficacy by avoidance behaviors that may lead to a weakened status within the organization or even demotion. As passive leadership behaviors have poorer work outcomes (Bass, 1999), the negative core self-evaluations of leaders engaging in passive behaviors can easily be reinforced. Active leadership behaviors, on the other hand, may reinforce leaders' positive evaluations. In line with social exchange theory (Emerson, 1976), positive expectations and subsequent behavioral investments lead to reciprocated loyalty and enhanced efforts on the part of subordinates. The leaders, driven by their positive expectations, display active leadership behaviors such as coaching, supporting, inspiring, stimulating the subordinates, and thereby set positive self-fulfilling prophecies into motion (*Pygmalion effect*; Eden, 1990). When working under active, transformational leadership, the subordinates perform better (Walumbwa et al., 2008), become more innovative (Reuvers et al., 2008), and motivated (Dvir et al., 2002). Consequently, the leader's positive core other-evaluations get reinforced. Moreover, the success experiences of leaders who perform active, transformational behaviors (Walumbwa et al., 2008; Tsai et al., 2009) may further enhance the leaders' positive beliefs about the self (James, 1890; Bandura, 1977).

Furthermore, behavior also shapes the leader's specific evaluations. For example, when a leader avoids a new challenge and starts procrastinating, s/he may immediately feel less in control than before the onset of the procrastination. If the procrastination becomes habitual, it may lead to consolidation of the leader's negative self-image. Through regularly activating certain specific evaluations by displaying habitual behaviors, leaders further reinforce their core evaluations. And in the self-reinforcing cognitive-behavioral cycle, the fortified beliefs trigger the regular reoccurrence of specific evaluations, behaviors, and situations that are in line with the belief.

Core Evaluations and Situation Selection

Another way the cognitive-behavioral system preserves itself can be understood by the concept of situation selection. Situation selection is an effective way of expressing and maintaining one's personality, by entering situations that are in line with one's attitudes, motives, and expectations, and avoiding others that contradict them (Emmons and Diener, 1986; Frederickx and Hofmans, 2014). For example, leaders with positive core self-evaluations may be inclined to enter situations in which they are challenged, as they believe that they can successfully cope with the challenges and are inspired by them. Leaders with negative core self-evaluations may be prone to avoid challenging situations that entail a 'potential for failure' (Judge et al., 2000, p. 238). However, by avoiding such situations they cannot collect counter-evidence for their negative beliefs. By preventing the disconfirmation of their own fears (Wells et al., 1996), they sustain the coherence of their belief system. Avoidance behaviors are often aimed at preventing the painful feeling that follows the activation of a negative belief; nevertheless, they confirm such beliefs (Young et al., 2003).

Stable but Not Static: Dynamic System

Beside its inclination to preserve its internal coherence, just like any other organic system, the leaders' cognitive-behavioral system is also capable of change and reformation. New situations, new appraisals, and new behaviors – if rehearsed repeatedly – may lead to (slow-paced) change in the deep cognitive structures. For example, even though a person's appraisals of other people's reliability are partially determined by the person's a priori expectations, new experiences have the potential of modifying such expectations, in the event that they strongly contradict them (Kramer, 1999). Such new experiences can be triggered by a major change that occurs in the individual's environment. Within the new circumstances, the features of frequently arising situations alter, the new features trigger new specific evaluations, and these specific evaluations call for novel behaviors. Such changes in the environment can be, for instance, a new position with entirely different tasks that fit the leader's talents a lot better (or worse) than the previous position; or a new, outstandingly supportive (or hostile) work environment in comparison to the previous workplace. These changes will lead to new, different day-to-day experiences that can transform a leader's core evaluations. These changes happen slowly and gradually, as described by the sociogenomic personality school in its suggestion that states which are experienced continuously over long time periods cause changes in the neuroanatomical structures of the brain and lead to the modification of traits (Roberts and Jackson, 2008). Another pathway of change in core evaluations may originate within the leader. This route is paved with the leaders' attempts to change her/his behaviors, appraisals and beliefs, possibly emerging from the recognition that the old cognitive and behavioral patterns are no longer helpful or functional. Repeated challenging and conscious amending of a person's appraisals *and* behaviors (often guided by coaching, training, or therapy) can slowly modify the deep, cognitive structures (Beck, 1964, 1972, 1991; Felmingham et al., 2007).

Stability and Dynamism

In sum, leaders' core evaluations may be maintained *or* modified (1) by being exposed frequently to certain situational features; (2) by repeated specific evaluations; or (3) by repeated leadership behavior. Whether the core evaluations are reinforced or adapted depends on whether the situational features, the specific evaluations, and the behaviors are in concordance or contradiction with the leader's core evaluations.

Proposition 10: Situational features to which the leader is frequently exposed shape the leader's core evaluations over the long term, such that (1) when the two are aligned (e.g., supportive organization and positive core evaluations), frequently experienced situations reinforce core evaluations, and (2) when the two are non-aligned (e.g., hostile organization and positive core evaluations), situations may modify core evaluations. (**Figure 1**, arrow 5).

Proposition 11: The more positive a leader's core evaluations are, the more likely s/he will enter – socially or intellectually – challenging situations (while the more negative the leaders' core evaluations are, the more likely s/he will avoid such situations; **Figure 1**, arrow 6).

Proposition 12: The leader's frequently repeated specific evaluations shape the leader's core evaluations over the long term, such that (1) when the two are aligned, specific evaluations reinforce core evaluations, and (2) when the two are non-aligned, specific evaluations may modify core evaluations (**Figure 1**, arrow 9).

Proposition 13: Situations shape the leader's core evaluations by (re)shaping the leader's specific evaluations (**Figure 1**, arrows 7–9).

Proposition 14: The leader's recurrent behaviors shape the leader's core evaluations over the long term, such that (1) when the two are aligned with each other (positive core evaluations and active leadership behaviors, or negative core evaluations and passive behaviors), behaviors reinforce core evaluations, and (2) when the two are non-aligned, behaviors may modify core evaluations (**Figure 1**, arrow 10).

Proposition 15: The leader's behavior shapes the leader's core evaluations through (1) modifying the situational features (**Figure 1**, arrows 5 and 12), and (2) modifying the leader's specific evaluations (**Figure 1**, arrows 9 and 11).

Discussion

What makes some leaders inclined to act in active ways and others in passive ways, and what makes someone an active leader in one situation and a passive one in another? In this article we build on core evaluations theory (Judge et al., 1997) and argue that in any leadership situation entered, leaders assess (1) their own capacities to cope with the task and the interpersonal demands of the situation; (2) the competence and willingness of their subordinate(s) to perform their tasks; and (3) the benevolence, fairness, and dangerousness of the context. Based on the results of their evaluations, they engage in a given leadership behavior (obviously, in most cases this process is swift, automatic, and unconscious).

We suggest that the more the leader perceives him/herself to be able to cope with challenges, others to be trustworthy and the environment to be safe and reliable, the more active behaviors s/he will pursue. If a leader feels insecure or threatened, to prevent feared events from happening s/he may avoid challenges and engage in highly passive leadership behaviors, such as dodging leadership responsibilities altogether (laissez faire) or at least until there is a crisis (passive management by exception). Another response to a low sense of confidence in the self or others may be the close monitoring of events and hyper-vigilance (active management by exception), as an attempt at taking control over the seemingly threatening, uncooperative or inept environment. A moderate level of confidence in the internal and external world is sufficient for the emergence of moderately active behaviors, such as identifying objectives and targets, combined with behaviors that nevertheless still serve the function of mildly controlling people and events, such as rewarding and following up on subordinates (contingent reward). Finally, only a strong sense of efficacy, control and confidence regarding the self, other people and the external world offer the psychological resources that are necessary for the emergence of highly active leadership behaviors, such as demonstrating competence, thinking innovatively, elevating expectations and standards, being inspirational and challenging and stimulating others (transformational behaviors).

In conclusion, we suggest that the more a leader evaluates him/herself, others, and the environment positively, the more s/he will be in possession of the basic psychological resources that are required to engage in complex, (pro)active leading behaviors (see conservation of resources theory, Hobfoll, 1989). Evaluating one or more of the three factors (self, others, environment) negatively triggers less active, 'safety' behaviors, such as avoidance or monitoring and controlling subordinates. Thus, leaders' fleeting evaluations of themselves, others, and the context (their specific evaluations) shape how they act in any given situation and therefore explain within-person fluctuations in leadership behavior. Such momentary evaluations will be partially predicted by the features of the situation at hand. Furthermore, they will be influenced by the leaders' core evaluations, that is, their inherent tendency to have a generalized high or low opinion of themselves, other people, and their environment. These core evaluations work as filters when perceiving and categorizing information, inclining the individual to make appraisals in line with the core evaluations, and to act accordingly. Thus, core evaluations explain the leaders' propensity to engage in a certain kind of leadership behavior. We suggest that leaders who have the tendency to evaluate themselves, others, and their environment positively will have a sustained inclination to be active leaders.

Implications for Leadership Research and Limitations

Because our propositions pertain to both the between- (i.e., core evaluations) and within-leader level (i.e., specific evaluations), studies that go beyond the typical cross-sectional between-subjects design are needed in order to test them. Examples of such designs are daily diary studies (Bolger et al., 2003), in which leaders can be asked about their leadership behavior, the circumstances, and their core self-, other-, and world-evaluations on a day-to-day basis. Another alternative is to conduct experience sampling studies (e.g., Nielsen and Cleal, 2011) where leaders can be asked to rate their leadership behavior, the circumstances, and their core self-, other-, and world-evaluations at random moments throughout their working life. Whereas such designs are harder to implement than the traditional, cross-sectional, between-subjects designs because they, among other things, place considerable demands on the participants, they yield valuable information about within-person changes in leadership behavior and the core evaluations; and this information is necessary to test our propositions. Moreover, such designs allow for the analysis of time-lagged effects, which allows testing the directionality of the proposed relationships.

What complicates the empirical study of our propositions is that measures for core other evaluations and core world evaluations are presently missing (a measure for core self evaluations exists; see Judge et al., 2003). Therefore, there is a need for the development of such instruments. When doing so, it may also be fruitful to identify the overlaps and correlations between the three core evaluations. We expect that negative core evaluations are interconnected (Packer, 1985; Beck, 2011), that is, the lack of trust in others (negative core other-evaluations) will positively correlate with beliefs about the world being a malevolent, unfair, and dangerous place (negative core world-evaluations). Furthermore, seeing the self as helpless, vulnerable, and unable to cope (negative core self-evaluations) will overlap with perceiving the world as a dangerous, unfair, and malevolent place and with seeing other people as untrustworthy. We expect these correlations to exist both on the trait and state level (and between the three positive core evaluations too).

Finally, our model evidently cannot fully explain the emergence of active and passive leadership behaviors. Even though positive beliefs and positive appraisals are prerequisites for active leadership, they cannot entirely predict it. For example, research has shown that affective antecedents have a strong influence on the emergence of transformational and charismatic behaviors (e.g., Walter and Bruch, 2007, 2009; Seo et al., 2008). Leaders must also be in possession of a repertoire of active leadership behavioral scripts to be able to respond to situations with such behaviors. For adaptive behavioral responses to emerge, the accurate appraisal of the situation is necessary but not sufficient, insofar as the individual does not possess a rich behavioral arsenal (Eaton et al., 2009). Furthermore, active leadership behaviors are not equally beneficial in all circumstances. For example, research has shown that transformational leadership behaviors are less beneficial in conditions of high stress (Seltzer et al., 1989), in projects that don't require the generation of new knowledge (Keller, 2006), and in relation to subordinates with an individualistic mindset (Jung and Avolio, 1999). Therefore, in certain contexts the versatile leader may favor transactional behaviors over transformational ones, based on the consideration that the aforementioned behaviors will be more efficient (in line with contingency theories, e.g., Hersey and Blanchard, 1969). Our model, therefore, aims to provide a basic framework with wide applicability, but cannot alone explain leadership tendencies, and thus intends to complement other approaches that explain the emergence of active and passive leadership.

Acknowledgments

This research was funded by the Agency for Innovation by Science and Technology (IWT) doctoral grant, dossier number: 111323.

References

Ajzen, I. (1991). The theory of planned behavior. *Organ. Behav. Hum. Decis. Process.* 50, 179–211. doi: 10.1016/0749-5978(91)90020-T

Avolio, B. J. (ed) (2010). *Full Range Leadership Development.* Thousand Oaks, CA: Sage.

Avolio, B. J., and Bass, B. M. (1991). *The Full Range of Leadership Development: Basic and Advanced Manuals.* Binghamton, NY: Bass, Avolio, & Associates.

Avolio, B. J., and Bass, B. M. (eds) (2001). *Developing Potential Across a Full Range of Leadership: Cases on Transactional and Transformational Leadership.* London: Psychology Press.

Avolio, B. J., Bass, B. M., and Jung, D. I. (1999). Re-examining the components of transformational and transactional leadership using the Multifactor Leadership Questionnaire. *J. Occup. Organ. Psychol.* 72, 441–462. doi: 10.1348/096317999166789

Baer, M., and Frese, M. (2003). Innovation is not enough: climates for initiative and psychological safety, process innovations, and firm performance. *J. Organ. Behav.* 24, 45–68. doi: 10.1002/job.179

Bandura, A. (1977). Self-efficacy: toward a unifying theory of behavioral change. *Psychol. Rev.* 84, 191–215. doi: 10.1037/0033-295X.84.2.191

Bandura, A. (2006). "Guide for constructing self-efficacy scales," in *Self-Efficacy Beliefs of Adolescents*, eds F. Pajares and T. Urdan (Greenwich, CT: Information Age Publishing), 307–337.

Bandura, A., and Locke, E. A. (2003). Negative self-efficacy and goal effects revisited. *J. Appl. Psychol.* 88, 87–99. doi: 10.1037/0021-9010.88.1.87

Barling, J., Christie, A., and Hoption, A. (2011)). "Leadership," in *APA Handbook of Industrial and Organizational Psychology: Building and Developing the Organization*, Vol. 1, ed. S. Zedeck (Washington, DC: American Psychological Association), 183–240.

Barling, J., Slater, F., and Kelloway, E. K. (2000). Transformational leadership and emotional intelligence: an exploratory study. *Leadersh. Organ. Dev. J.* 21, 157–161. doi: 10.1108/01437730010325040

Bass, B. M. (1991). From transactional to transformational leadership: learning to share the vision. *Organ. Dyn.* 18, 19–31. doi: 10.1016/0090-2616(90)90061-S

Bass, B. M. (1996). *A New Paradigm of Leadership: An Inquiry into Transformational Leadership.* Alexandria, VA: U. S. Army Research Institute for the Behavioral and Social Sciences.

Bass, B. M. (1997). Does the transactional-transformational paradigm transcend organizational and national boundaries? *Am. Psychol.* 52, 130–139. doi: 10.1037/0003-066X.52.2.130

Bass, B. M. (1999). Two decades of research and development in transformational leadership. *Eur. J. Work Organ. Psychol.* 8, 9–32. doi: 10.1080/135943299398410

Bass, B. M., Avolio, B. J., Jung, D. I., and Berson, Y. (2003). Predicting unit performance by assessing transformational and transactional leadership. *J. Appl. Psychol.* 88, 207–218. doi: 10.1037/0021-9010.88.2.207

Beck, A. T. (1964). Thinking and depression: theory and therapy. *Arch. Gen. Psychiatry* 10, 561–571. doi: 10.1001/archpsyc.1964.01720240015003

Beck, A. T. (1967). *Depression: Clinical, Experimental, and Theoretical Aspects*, Vol. 32. Philadelphia, PA: University of Pennsylvania Press.

Beck, A. T. (1972). *Depression; Causes and Treatment.* Philadelphia: University of Pennsylvania Press.

Beck, A. T. (1991). Cognitive therapy: a 30-year retrospective. *Am. Psychol.* 46, 368–375. doi: 10.1037/0003-066X.46.4.368

Beck, J. S. (2011). *Cognitive Behavior Therapy: Basics and Beyond.* New York, NY: Guilford Press.

Bolger, N., Davis, A., and Rafaeli, E. (2003). Diary methods: capturing life as it is lived. *Annu. Rev. Psychol.* 54, 579–616. doi: 10.1146/annurev.psych.54.101601.145030

Bommer, W. H., Rubin, R. S., and Baldwin, T. T. (2004). Setting the stage for effective leadership: antecedents of transformational leadership behavior. *Leadersh. Q.* 15, 195–210. doi: 10.1016/j.leaqua.2004.02.012

Caspi, A., Roberts, B. W., and Shiner, R. L. (2005). Personality development: stability and change. *Annu. Rev. Psychol.* 56, 453–484. doi: 10.1146/annurev.psych.55.090902.141913

Costa, P. T., and McCrae, R. R. (1992). *Revised NEO Personality Inventory (NEO PI-R) and NEO Five-Factor Inventory (NEO FFI): Professional Manual.* Odessa, FL: Psychological Assessment Resources.

Craske, M. G., Sanderson, W. C., and Barlow, D. H. (1987). The relationships among panic, fear, and avoidance. *J. Anxiety Disord.* 1, 153–160. doi: 10.1016/0887-6185(87)90005-3

Dansereau, F., Graen, G., and Haga, W. J. (1975). A vertical dyad linkage approach to leadership within formal organizations: a longitudinal investigation of the role making process. *Organ. Behav. Hum. Perform.* 13, 46–78. doi: 10.1016/0030-5073(75)90005-7

Day, D. (2001). Leadership development: a review in context. *Leadersh. Q.* 11, 581–613. doi: 10.1016/S1048-9843(00)00061-8

Debusscher, J., Hofmans, J., and De Fruyt, F. (2014). The curvilinear relationship between state neuroticism and momentary task performance. *PLoS ONE* 9:e106989. doi: 10.1371/journal.pone.0106989

Debusscher, J., Hofmans, J., and De Fruyt, F. (2015). The effect of state core self-evaluations on task performance, organizational citizenship behaviour, and counterproductive work behaviour. *Eur. J. Work Organ. Psychol.* 1–15. doi: 10.1080/1359432X.2015.1063486 [Epub ahead of print].

Dóci, E., and Hofmans, J. (2015). Task complexity and transformational leadership: the mediating role of leaders' state core self-evaluations. *Leadersh. Q.* 26, 436–447. doi: 10.1016/j.leaqua.2015.02.008

Dvir, T., Eden, D., Avolio, B. J., and Shamir, B. (2002). Impact of transformational leadership on follower development and performance: a field experiment. *Acad. Manag. J.* 45, 735–744. doi: 10.2307/3069307

Eaton, N. R., South, S. C., and Krueger, R. F. (2009). The Cognitive–Affective Processing System (CAPS) approach to personality and the concept of personality disorder: integrating clinical and social-cognitive research. *J. Res. Pers.* 43, 208–217. doi: 10.1016/j.jrp.2009.01.016

Eden, D. (1990). *Pygmalion in Management: Productivity as a Self-Fulfilling Prophecy.* Lexington, MA: Lexington Books/DC Heath and Com.

Eden, D. (1992). Leadership and expectations: pygmalion effects and other self-fulfilling prophecies in organizations. *Leadersh. Q.* 3, 271–305. doi: 10.1016/1048-9843(92)90018-B

Edmondson, A. C. (2004). "Psychological safety, trust, and learning in organizations: a group-level lens," in *Trust in Organizations: Dilemmas and Approaches*, eds R. Kramer and K. Cook (New York, NY: Russell Sage Foundation), 239–272.

Emerson, R. M. (1976). Social exchange theory. *Annu. Rev. Sociol.* 2, 335–362. doi: 10.1146/annurev.so.02.080176.002003

Emiliani, M. L. (2003). Linking leaders' beliefs to their behaviors and competencies. *Manag. Decis.* 41, 893–910. doi: 10.1108/00251740310497430

Emmons, R. A., and Diener, E. (1986). Situation selection as a moderator of response consistency and stability. *J. Pers. Soc. Psychol.* 51, 1013–1019. doi: 10.1037/0022-3514.51.5.1013

Felmingham, K., Kemp, A., Williams, L., Das, P., Hughes, G., Peduto, A., et al. (2007). Changes in anterior cingulate and amygdala after cognitive behavior therapy of posttraumatic stress disorder. *Psychol. Sci.* 18, 127–129. doi: 10.1111/j.1467-9280.2007.01860.x

Fleeson, W. (2001). Towards a structure- and process-integrated view of personality: traits as density distributions of states. *J. Pers. Soc. Psychol.* 80, 1011–1027. doi: 10.1037/0022-3514.80.6.1011

Fleishman, E. A. (1953). The description of supervisory behavior. *J. Appl. Psychol.* 37, 1–6. doi: 10.1037/h0056314

Frederickx, S., and Hofmans, J. (2014). The role of personality in the initiation of communication situations. *J. Individ. Differ.* 35, 30–37. doi: 10.1027/1614-0001/a000124

Fukuyama, F. (1995). *Trust: The Social Virtues and the Creation of Prosperity.* New York, NY: Free Press, 61–67.

Georgesen, J., and Harris, M. (2006). Holding onto power: effects of powerholders' positional instability and expectancies on interactions with subordinates. *Eur. J. Soc. Psychol.* 36, 451–468. doi: 10.1002/ejsp.352

Goodwin, V. L., Wofford, J. C., and Boyd, N. G. (2000). A laboratory experiment testing the antecedents of leader cognitions. *J. Organ. Behav.* 21, 769–788. doi: 10.1002/1099-1379(200011)21:7<769::AID-JOB53>3.0.CO;2-J

Graen, G. B., and Uhl-Bien, M. (1995). Relationship-based approach to leadership: development of leader-member exchange (LMX) theory of leadership over 25 years: applying a multi-level multi-domain perspective. *Leadersh. Q.* 6, 219–247. doi: 10.1016/1048-9843(95)90036-5

Hamaker, E. L. (2012). "Why researchers should think "within-person": a paradigmatic rationale," in *Handbook of Methods for Studying Daily Life*, eds M. R. Mehl and T. S. Conner (New York, NY: Guilford Publications), 43–61.

Heatherton, T. F., and Polivy, J. (1991). Development and validation of a scale for measuring state self-esteem. *J. Pers. Soc. Psychol.* 60, 895–910. doi: 10.1037/0022-3514.60.6.895

Hersey, P., and Blanchard, K. H. (1969). *Management of Organizational Behavior.* Englewood Cliffs, NJ: Prentice-Hall.

Hobfoll, S. E. (1989). Conservation of resources: a new attempt at conceptualizing stress. *Am. Psychol.* 44, 513–524. doi: 10.1037/0003-066X.44.3.513

Jacobs, B., Prentice-Dunn, S., and Rogers, R. W. (1984). Understanding persistence: an interface of control theory and self-efficacy theory. *Basic Appl. Soc. Psychol.* 5, 333–347. doi: 10.1207/s15324834basp0504_6

James, W. (1890). *The Principles of Psychology*, Vol. 1. Cambridge, MA: Harvard University Press. doi: 10.1037/11059-000

Judge, T. A., and Bono, J. E. (2000). Five-factor model of personality and transformational leadership. *J. Appl. Psychol.* 85, 751–765. doi: 10.1037/0021-9010.85.5.751

Judge, T. A., Bono, J. E., and Locke, E. A. (2000). Personality and job satisfaction: the mediating role of job characteristics. *J. Appl. Psychol.* 85, 237–249. doi: 10.1037/0021-9010.85.2.237

Judge, T. A., Erez, A., Bono, J. E., and Thoresen, C. J. (2003). The core self-evaluations scale: development of a measure. *Pers. Psychol.* 56, 303–331. doi: 10.1111/j.1744-6570.2003.tb00152.x

Judge, T. A., Hulin, C. L., and Dalal, R. S. (2012). *Job Satisfaction and Job Affect. The Oxford Handbook of Industrial and Organizational Psychology.* New York, NY: Oxford University Press (forthcoming).

Judge, T. A., and Kammeyer-Mueller, J. D. (2004). "Core self-evaluations, aspirations, success, and persistence: an attributional model," in *Attribution Theory in the Organizational Sciences: Theoretical and Empirical Contributions (HC)*, ed. M. J. Martinko (Greenwich, CT: IAP), 111–132.

Judge, T. A., and Kammeyer-Mueller, J. D. (2011). Implications of core self-evaluations for a changing organizational context. *Hum. Resource Manag. Rev.* 21, 331–341. doi: 10.1016/j.hrmr.2010.10.003

Judge, T. A., Locke, E. A., and Durham, C. C. (1997). The dispositional causes of job satisfaction: a core evaluations approach. *Res. Organ. Behav.* 19, 151–188.

Jung, D. I., and Avolio, B. J. (1999). Effects of leadership style and followers' cultural orientation on performance in group and individual task conditions. *Acad. Manag. J.* 42, 208–218. doi: 10.2307/257093

Kammeyer-Mueller, J. D., Judge, T. A., and Scott, B. A. (2009). The role of core self-evaluations in the coping process. *J. Appl. Psychol.* 94, 177–195. doi: 10.1037/a0013214

Keller, R. T. (2006). Transformational leadership, initiating structure, and substitutes for leadership: a longitudinal study of research and development project team performance. *J. Appl. Psychol.* 91, 202–210. doi: 10.1037/0021-9010.91.1.202

Kirkbride, P. (2006). Developing transformational leaders: the full range leadership model in action. *Industrial Commer. Train.* 38, 23–32. doi: 10.1108/00197850610646016

Kramer, R. M. (1999). Trust and distrust in organizations: emerging perspectives, enduring questions. *Annu. Rev. Psychol.* 50, 569–598. doi: 10.1146/annurev.psych.50.1.569

Krishnan, V. R. (2001). Value systems of transformational leaders. *Leadersh. Organ. Dev. J.* 22, 126–132. doi: 10.1108/01437730110389274

Kuppens, P., Stouten, J., and Mesquita, B. (2009). Individual differences in emotion components and dynamics: introduction to the special issue. *Cogn. Emot.* 23, 1249–1258. doi: 10.1080/02699930902985605

Lewicki, R. J., McAllister, D. J., and Bies, R. J. (1998). Trust and distrust: new relationships and realities. *Acad. Manag. Rev.* 23, 438–458. doi: 10.2307/259288

Lewin, K. (1951). *Field Theory in Social Science.* New York, NY: Harper.

Lowin, A., and Craig, J. R. (1968). The influence of level of performance on managerial style: an experimental object-lesson in the ambiguity of correlational data. *Organ. Behav. Hum. Perform.* 3, 440–458. doi: 10.1016/0030-5073(68)90020-2

Maier, S. F., and Seligman, M. E. (1976). Learned helplessness: theory and evidence. *J. Exp. Psychol. Gen.* 105, 3–46. doi: 10.1037/0096-3445.105.1.3

Marshall, M. A., and Brown, J. D. (2006). Trait aggressiveness and situational provocation: a test of the traits as situational sensitivities (TASS) model. *Pers. Soc. Psychol. Bull.* 32, 1100–1113. doi: 10.1177/0146167206288488

Mayer, R. C., Davis, J. H., and Schoorman, F. D. (1995). An integrative model of organizational trust. *Acad. Manag. Rev.* 20, 709–734. doi: 10.2307/258792

Mayer, R. C., and Gavin, M. B. (2005). Trust in management and performance: who minds the shop while the employees watch the boss? *Acad. Manag. J.* 48, 874–888. doi: 10.5465/AMJ.2005.18803928

McAllister, D. J. (1995). Affect-and cognition-based trust as foundations for interpersonal cooperation in organizations. *Acad. Manag. J.* 38, 24–59. doi: 10.2307/256727

McGinn, L. K., and Young, J. E. (1996). "Schema-focused therapy," in *Frontiers of Cognitive Therapy*, ed. P. M. Salkovskis (New York, NY: Guilford Press), 182–207.

McGregor, D. (1960). *The Human Side of the Enterprise*. New York, NY: McGraw Hill.

McLean, L. D. (2005). Organizational culture's influence on creativity and innovation: a review of the literature and implications for human resource development. *Adv. Dev. Hum. Resour.* 7, 226–246. doi: 10.1177/1523422305274528

McNiel, J. M., and Fleeson, W. (2006). The causal effects of extraversion on positive affect and neuroticism on negative affect: manipulating state extraversion and state neuroticism in an experimental approach. *J. Res. Pers.* 40, 529–550. doi: 10.1016/j.jrp.2005.05.003

Mischel, W., and Shoda, Y. (1995). A cognitive-affective system theory of personality: reconceptualizing situations, dispositions, dynamics, and invariance in personality structure. *Psychol. Rev.* 102, 246–268. doi: 10.1037/0033-295X.102.2.246

Nielsen, K., and Cleal, B. (2011). Under which conditions do middle managers exhibit transformational leadership behaviors? — An experience sampling method study on the predictors of transformational leadership behaviors. *Leadersh. Q.* 22, 344–352. doi: 10.1016/j.leaqua.2011.02.009

Nübold, A., Muck, P. M., and Maier, G. W. (2013). A new substitute for leadership? Followers' state core self-evaluations. *Leadersh. Q.* 24, 29–44. doi: 10.1016/j.leaqua.2012.07.002

Packer, E. (1985). *Understanding the Subconscious*. Laguna Hills, CA: Jefferson School of Philosophy, Economics, and Psychology/TOF Pub.

Pastor, J. C., and Mayo, M. (2008). Transformational leadership among Spanish upper echelons: the role of managerial values and goal orientation. *Leadersh. Organ. Dev. J.* 29, 340–358. doi: 10.1108/01437730810876140

Peterson, S. J., Walumbwa, F. O., Byron, K., and Myrowitz, J. (2009). CEO positive psychological traits, transformational leadership, and firm performance in high-technology start-up and established firms. *J. Manage.* 35, 348–368. doi: 10.1177/0149206307312512

Powell, K. S., and Yalcin, S. (2010). Managerial training effectiveness: a meta-analysis 1952-2002. *Pers. Rev.* 39, 227–241. doi: 10.1108/00483481011017435

Resick, C. J., Whitman, D. S., Weingarden, S. M., and Hiller, N. J. (2009). The bright-side and the dark-side of CEO personality: examining core self-evaluations, narcissism, transformational leadership, and strategic influence. *J. Appl. Psychol.* 94, 1365–1381. doi: 10.1037/a0016238

Reuvers, M., van Engen, M. L., Vinkenburg, C., and Wilson-Evered, E. (2008). Transformational leadership and innovative work behaviour: exploring the relevance of gender differences. *Creat. Innov. Manage.* 17, 227–244. doi: 10.1111/j.1467-8691.2008.00487.x

Roberts, B. W., and Jackson, J. J. (2008). Sociogenomic personality psychology. *J. Pers.* 76, 1523–1544. doi: 10.1111/j.1467-6494.2008.00530.x

Rotter, J. B. (1966). Generalized expectancies for internal versus external control of reinforcement. *Psychol. Monogr. Gen. Appl.* 80, 1–28. doi: 10.1037/h0092976

Schmitt, M., Eid, M., and Maes, J. (2003). Synergistic person x situation interaction in distributive justice behavior. *Pers. Soc. Psychol. Bull.* 29, 141–147. doi: 10.1177/0146167202238379

Segal, Z. V. (1988). Appraisal of the self-schema construct in cognitive models of depression. *Psychol. Bull.* 103, 147–162. doi: 10.1037/0033-2909.103.2.147

Seligman, M. E. P. (1975). *Helplessness: On Depression, Development, and Death*. San Francisco, CA: W. H. Freeman.

Seltzer, J., Numerof, R. E., and Bass, B. M. (1989). Transformational leadership: is it a source of more burnout and stress? *J. Health Hum. Resour. Adm.* 12, 174–185.

Seo, M., Jin, S., and Shapiro, D. L. (2008). Do happy leaders lead better? Affective and attitudinal antecedents of transformational leadership behavior. *Paper Presented at the Academy of Management Annual Conference*, Anaheim, CA.

Skogstad, A., Einarsen, S., Torsheim, T., Aasland, M. S., and Hetland, H. (2007). The destructiveness of laissez-faire leadership behavior. *J. Occup. Health Psychol.* 12, 80–92. doi: 10.1037/1076-8998.12.1.80

Smith, R. E. (1989). Effects of coping skills training on generalized self-efficacy and locus of control. *J. Pers. Soc. Psychol.* 56, 228–233. doi: 10.1037/0022-3514.56.2.228

Sosik, J. J., and Jung, D. D. (2011). *Full Range Leadership Development: Pathways for People, Profit and Planet*. New York, NY: Taylor & Francis.

Sy, T. (2010). What do you think of followers? Examining the content, structure, and consequences of implicit followership theories. *Organ. Behav. Hum. Decis. Process.* 113, 73–84. doi: 10.1016/j.obhdp.2010.06.001

Tafarodi, R. W., and Swann, W. B. Jr. (1995). Self-linking and self-competence as dimensions of global self-esteem: initial validation of a measure. *J. Pers. Assess.* 65, 322–342. doi: 10.1207/s15327752jpa6502_8

Tett, R. P., and Guterman, H. A. (2000). Situation trait relevance, trait expression, and cross-situational consistency: testing a principle of trait activation. *J. Res. Pers.* 34, 397–423. doi: 10.1006/jrpe.2000.2292

Tickle, E. L., Brownlee, J., and Nailon, D. (2005). Personal epistemological beliefs and transformational leadership behaviours. *J. Manage. Dev.* 24, 706–719. doi: 10.1108/02621710510613735

Tsai, W. C., Chen, H. W., and Cheng, J. W. (2009). Employee positive moods as a mediator linking transformational leadership and employee work outcomes. *Int. J. Hum. Resour. Manage.* 20, 206–219. doi: 10.1080/09585190802528714

Turban, D. B., and Jones, A. P. (1988). Supervisor-subordinate similarity: types, effects, and mechanisms. *J. Appl. Psychol.* 73, 228–234. doi: 10.1037/0021-9010.73.2.228

Vroom, V. H., and Jago, A. G. (2007). The role of the situation in leadership. *Am. Psychol.* 62, 17–24. doi: 10.1037/0003-066X.62.1.17

Walter, F., and Bruch, H. (2007). "Investigating the emotional basis of charismatic leadership: the role of leaders' positive mood and emotional intelligence," in *Research on Emotion in Organizations*, Vol. 3, eds C. E. J. Härtel, N. M. Ashkanasy, and W. J. Zerbe (Amsterdam: Elsevier). doi: 10.1016/s1746-9791(07)03003-9

Walter, F., and Bruch, H. (2009). An affective events model of charismatic leadership behavior: a review, theoretical integration, and research agenda. *J. Manage.* 35, 1428–1452. doi: 10.1177/0149206309342468

Walumbwa, F. O., Avolio, B. J., and Zhu, W. (2008). How transformational leadership weaves its influence on individual job performance: the role of identification and efficacy beliefs. *Pers. Psychol.* 61, 793–825. doi: 10.1111/j.1744-6570.2008.00131.x

Wang, H., Law, K. S., Hackett, R. D., Wang, D., and Chen, Z. X. (2005). Leader-member exchange as a mediator of the relationship between transformational leadership and followers' performance and organizational citizenship behavior. *Acad. Manage. J.* 48, 420–432. doi: 10.5465/AMJ.2005.17407908

Washington, R. R., Sutton, C. D., and Feild, H. S. (2006). Individual differences in servant leadership: the roles of values and personality. *Leadersh. Organ. Dev. J.* 27, 700–716. doi: 10.1108/01437730610709309

Weiner, B. (1980). *Human Motivation*. New York, NY: Holt, Rinehart & Winston.

Weissenberg, P., and Kavanagh, M. J. (1972). The independence of initiating structure and consideration: a review of the evidence. *Pers. Psychol.* 25, 119–130. doi: 10.1111/j.1744-6570.1972.tb01095.x

Wells, A., Clark, D. M., Salkovskis, P., Ludgate, J., Hackmann, A., and Gelder, M. (1996). Social phobia: the role of in-situation safety behaviors in maintaining anxiety and negative beliefs. *Behav. Ther.* 26, 153–161. doi: 10.1016/S0005-7894(05)80088-7

Wille, B., and De Fruyt, F. (2014). Vocations as a source of identity: reciprocal relations between Big Five personality traits and RIASEC characteristics. *J. Appl. Psychol.* 99, 262–281. doi: 10.1037/a0034917

Wille, B., Hofmans, J., Feys, M., and De Fruyt, F. (2013). Maturation of work attitudes: correlated change with Big Five personality traits and reciprocal effects over 15 years. *J. Organ. Behav.* 35, 507–529. doi: 10.1002/job.1905

Witkin, H. A., Moore, C. A., Goodenough, D. R., and Cox, P. W. (1977). Field-dependent and field-independent cognitive styles and their educational implications. *Rev. Educ. Res.* 47, 1–64. doi: 10.3102/00346543047001001

Wood, R., and Bandura, A. (1989). Social cognitive theory of organizational management. *Acad. Manage. Rev.* 14, 361–384. doi: 10.5465/AMR.1989.4279067

Young, P. J. E., Klosko, P. J. S., and Weishaar, M. E. (2003). *Schema Therapy: A Practitioner's Guide*. New York, NY: Guilford Press.

Yukl, G. (1999). An evaluation of conceptual weaknesses in transformational and
   charismatic leadership theories. *Leadersh. Q.* 10, 285–305. doi: 10.1016/S1048-
   9843(99)00013-2

Conflict of Interest Statement: The authors declare that the research was
conducted in the absence of any commercial or financial relationships that could
be construed as a potential conflict of interest.

Development of Visual Motion Perception for Prospective Control: Brain and Behavioral Studies in Infants

Seth B. Agyei, F. R. (Ruud) van der Weel and Audrey L. H. van der Meer *

Developmental Neuroscience Laboratory, Department of Psychology, Norwegian University of Science and Technology, Trondheim, Norway

Edited by:
Daniela Corbetta,
University of Tennessee, USA

Reviewed by:
Rick O. Gilmore,
The Pennyslvania State University,
USA
Greg D. Reynolds,
University of Tennessee, USA

*Correspondence:
Audrey L. H. van der Meer
audrey.meer@svt.ntnu.no

Specialty section:
This article was submitted to
Movement Science and Sport
Psychology,
a section of the journal
Frontiers in Psychology

During infancy, smart perceptual mechanisms develop allowing infants to judge time-space motion dynamics more efficiently with age and locomotor experience. This emerging capacity may be vital to enable preparedness for upcoming events and to be able to navigate in a changing environment. Little is known about brain changes that support the development of prospective control and about processes, such as preterm birth, that may compromise it. As a function of perception of visual motion, this paper will describe behavioral and brain studies with young infants investigating the development of visual perception for prospective control. By means of the three visual motion paradigms of occlusion, looming, and optic flow, our research shows the importance of including behavioral data when studying the neural correlates of prospective control.

Keywords: brain and behavioral development, visual motion perception, optic flow processing, perceptual information for action, prospective control

According to Gibson's ecological theory of visual perception, direct and precise specification of objects and events in the environment provides information for direct perception through the pattern of light reflected from the surrounding to an observer (Gibson, 1966, 1979). Integral to this theory is the concept of affordances, which refers to what the environment affords or offers the observer. For example, surfaces of the environment may afford the observer locomotion, collision with other objects, and other behaviors that may be beneficial or injurious. Thus, it is important for affordances to be perceived efficiently. According to the theory, information for visual perception is inherent in the ambient light when an observer looks at a visual scene. As such, information about the surface layout and layouts of different objects and places in the environment projects from the dynamic ambient optic array of light that reaches the eye, which then specifies action possibilities to the observer. With movement, the dynamic optic array (flow field) specifies information about direction of motion and the relative movement of objects and the observer. This pattern of visual information that results from an observer's own motion is referred to as optic flow (Gibson, 1979).

The visual motion perception that is achieved by changes in optic array information becomes crucial for environmental navigation. Optic flow patterns afford the adjustment of posture, perception of time-to-contact, avoidance of obstacles, and reaching a target efficiently by specifying the appropriate heading direction. Infants respond to radial flow patterns using defensive responses such as backward head movements and eye blinks (e.g., Kayed and van der Meer, 2000, 2007). Such responses suggest that young infants use perceptual information to execute adaptive motor responses (Shirai and Yamaguchi, 2010). In this paper, we discuss the development of the visuo-cognitive systems, especially visual motion perception for the control of anticipatory actions during early infancy. We provide information that contributes to the understanding of the development of visual motion perception for prospective control and the developmental impairments associated with motion perception following preterm birth. Understanding functional brain development and the possible developmental anomalies of premature birth is important to ensure early intervention and diagnosis of preterm infants at risk of developing neurological impairments.

INFORMATION FOR PROSPECTIVE CONTROL

For effective navigation to reach a destination, it is vital to perceive the visual scene and then guide forthcoming actions through the coupling together of perceptual information, cognition, and the subsequent motor execution of intended actions. This ability is referred to as prospective control (Lee, 1993, 1998; von Hofsten, 1993). Prospective control is primarily concerned with future events or future goals to be realized (see also Turvey, 1992). Without sufficient prospective control, individuals may experience problems when responding to changes in the environment. Problems may include difficulties with performing everyday tasks such as the control of walking speed and direction to reach an intended destination. Controlling speed and direction during locomotion may depend on the extent of the complexity or familiarity associated with the visual flow information. As the speed of simulated forward motion increases, latencies in response to motion activity become longer (Vilhelmsen et al., 2015a). Thus, visual scenes that are perceived as being complex and naturally infrequent or unfamiliar may affect the output of cortical responses. Constant modification of integrated inputs from the visual system concerning the nature of the visual scene is therefore necessary. This modification must be dynamic enough to incorporate the constantly changing contextual information from the environment to provide accurate prospective control information.

During visually guided actions, an observer reaches an ideal state when he acts to produce a certain pattern of visual flow. This pattern is characterized by an invariant property that is left unchanged across conditions whenever the observer is in the ideal state (Fajen, 2005). Thus, when current conditions are set constant, information about one's future trajectory is used to modify deviations from the ideal state in order to eventually reach the intended outcome or destination. Over the years, models of visually guided actions for locomotion have been proposed (see Fajen, 2005). Among these models are the bearing angle model and the affordance-based model. In the bearing angle model (e.g., Lenoir et al., 1999; Fajen and Warren, 2007), an observer is on a collision course with an object if the object's bearing remains constant. Thus, to avoid collision an observer must change his speed and/or direction if there is a fixed bearing angle between the observer and the object (see also recent studies by Bootsma et al., 2015 for an extension of this model). The bearing angle model has been used by numerous studies over the years to investigate interception and detection of collisions, and obstacle avoidance in humans and other animals (see e.g., Cutting

et al., 1995; Chardenon et al., 2004; Ghose et al., 2006). However, its numerous limitations (see review by Fajen, 2013) including failure to take locomotor capabilities and limits of observers into consideration, and to account for coordination of speed and direction during locomotion, have made its approach unsuitable to predict guided movement of observers in the presence of other moving objects (Fajen et al., 2013). The affordance-based model, which originates from Gibson's ecological theory, rectifies such limitations. It incorporates the ability to choose actions and guide locomotion by taking into account body dimensions and dynamics (Warren and Whang, 1987; van der Meer, 1997; Fajen, 2007, 2013). It also accounts for how speed and direction are coordinated (Warren and Rushton, 2007, 2009; Bastin et al., 2010). However, specific actions observers have to select to actualize the intended motor outcome, and the directions observers have to follow to reach their desired target fall outside the scope of what this model predicts. For successful performance during visually guided action, it is ultimately important for an observer to perceive the available possibilities for action and to behave in order to keep the desired prospective action within the range of possible actions (Fajen, 2007).

According to Gibson's ecological theory, it is important to identify stimulus variables that are necessary to specify perceived aspects of the environment. Specifying variables (optical invariants) are patterns of ambient-energy arrays that are left unchanged by certain transformations (Fajen, 2005). Tau (Lee, 1976) is an example of a specifying variable that estimates time-to-contact information for timing interceptive actions. Further studies show that an alternative source of optical information when estimating time-to-collisions is the use of non-specifying variables (e.g., visual angle and expansion rate) that do not relate to specific environmental factors (see Michaels et al., 2001; Smith et al., 2001; Jacobs and Michaels, 2006). Thus, in contrast to optical invariants such as tau that is unaffected by changes in environmental conditions, non-specifying variables are influenced by environmental factors such as speed and size of objects (Runeson and Vedeler, 1993; van der Meer et al., 1994; Fajen, 2005). Studies have shown that in estimating time-to-collision, observers may use tau information independently (e.g., Yilmaz and Warren, 1995) or in conjunction with the use of non-specifying variables (e.g., Jacobs et al., 2001; Smith et al., 2001). In this paper, studies are presented that show age-related differences in the use of specifying and non-specifying optical variables, as well as the developmental changes in the use of such variables for prospective control during perceptuo-motor tasks in infants.

Perception of visual information for locomotion includes being able to accurately time and efficiently guide movements. The introduction of the tau-coupling theory has helped to explain how organisms are able to guide their movements through the closure of motion gaps (van der Weel et al., 2007). Tau of a motion gap is the time to closure of the motion gap at its current rate (Lee, 1998). When two or more taus are coupled over a period of time, they remain in constant proportion over the specific time period (Lee, 2009). Their relationship is defined by the coupling constant, K, which defines the speed profile of the gap closure. When reaching with the hand to catch a moving object, motion gaps exist between the hand and the object, or between the hand and the estimated interception point of the object, or between the object and the interception point. For the hand to be at the correct place to catch the moving object, tau of the motion-gap between the hand and the interception point, and the tau of the motion gap between the object and the interception point must be coupled together. Thus, external information about the motion of the object tau-guides the hand in an extrinsic tau-coupling process (Lee et al., 2001). In an intrinsic tau-coupling, tau of the gap between the hand and the stationary object is performed when self-guided action is coupled with an intrinsic tau value generated in the nervous system (Lee, 2009). Tau information is in the form of electrical energy that flows in neuronal assemblies in the nervous system. Tau information in the nervous system serves as a template for movement control upon which proprioceptive feedback can be used for prospective control (Lee, 2009). Intrinsic tau-coupling activity can be observed, for example, during the control of sucking in infants where the sucking pressure follows a pressure curve predicted by tau-coupled movement (Craig and Lee, 1999), or during the control of balance in children and adults (Austad and van der Meer, 2007; Spencer and van der Meer, 2012).

THE NEURONAL BASIS OF VISUAL MOTION PERCEPTION

In determining how visual perception is mediated in the brain, studies in humans and other primates have investigated the cerebral networks specialized for perception of visuo-spatial information over the past years. Several studies associate the structural and functional organization of the dorsal and ventral streams in the overall processing of visual information (e.g., see review by Creem and Proffitt, 2001). Perception of spatial aspects of stimuli such as the direction and speed of motion is processed via the dorsal visual stream (Creem and Proffitt, 2001), with the ventral visual stream primarily suggested to be involved in object recognition (Milner and Goodale, 2008). Neurons within the middle temporal complex (MT/V5+) of the dorsal visual stream are generally sensitive to radial motion processing including information from looming stimuli (Greenlee, 2000). The dorsal medial superior temporal (dMST) area is specifically implicated in optic flow processing (Duffy and Wurtz, 1991; Greenlee, 2000). The MT+ complex has also been found to play an important role in the control of continuous eye movement and in catch-up saccades to a moving target during the perception of motion information (Orban de Xivry and Lefèvre, 2007).

Over the years, non-invasive electroencephalogram (EEG), with its high temporal resolution in the millisecond scale, has been used to study the neuronal basis of motion perception and the functional specializations of cortical structures. EEG records brain electrical activities primarily from pyramidal neurons. In visual perception tasks, visual evoked potential (VEP) waveforms in EEG are generally assumed to represent responses of cortical neurons to changes in afferent activity (Brecelj, 2003). VEP waveforms are dominated by a motion-sensitive negativity (N2) during visual motion processing. The N2 is assumed to originate in area MT/V5, with adult N2 latencies reported around

130–150 ms (Probst et al., 1993; Heinrich et al., 2005) and around 180–220 ms in 8-month-old infants (van der Meer et al., 2008a).

Together with VEPs, EEG analysis in the time-frequency domain is used to isolate event-related frequency changes that reflect oscillatory mechanisms underlying neuronal populations (Hoechstetter et al., 2004). Event-related time-frequency responses (TSE, time spectral evolution) represent interactions of local cortical neurons that control the frequency components of an ongoing EEG (Pfurtscheller and Lopes da Silva, 1999). Using spectral profiles within specific frequency bands, different classes of oscillations have been distinguished over the years: delta-band (1–4 Hz), theta-band (4–7 Hz), alpha-band (7–13 Hz), beta-band (13–30 Hz), and gamma-bands (30–150 Hz). These rhythms are thought to reflect neurophysiological processes that exhibit functionally different roles. These roles include signal detection and decision making with the use of delta frequency (Başar et al., 2000), the control of inhibition and cortical processing with alpha-band waves (Klimesch et al., 2007), involvement in multisensory stimulation and the shifting of neural systems to a state of attention using beta-band activity (Khader et al., 2010), and the utilization of bottom-up and top-down memory matching of information for perception using gamma frequency (Herrmann et al., 2010). Several adult studies have found evidence for the modulation of the natural frequencies by motion stimuli (e.g., see review by Saby and Marshall, 2012), with little evidence for such activity reported in infants. Low-frequency EEG rhythms are reported in infants (e.g., Orekhova et al., 2006), with event-related theta oscillations found to provide information for impending collisions in the infant brain (van der Weel and van der Meer, 2009). Some of the studies presented in this paper will show further evidence for the use of theta-alpha and other frequency oscillations during the processing of visual information for the control of prospective actions in infants.

EARLY DEVELOPMENT OF VISUAL PERCEPTION FOR PROSPECTIVE CONTROL

Since perception of information for prospective control plays an important role for everyday survival, the developmental processes that mediate visual perception throughout life are expected to be increasingly efficient after birth. One of the earliest indicators of prospective control behavior in infants is the ability to continuously pursue a moving target with head and eye movements (von Hofsten and Rosander, 1996). Smooth visual pursuit of a moving target involves fixing gaze on the target and matching eye movements with the speed of the moving target. This helps to anticipate and predict the target's trajectory. Rudimentary perception of visual flow appears within the first weeks after birth (Shirai and Yamaguchi, 2010). Infants younger than 6–8 weeks are unable to efficiently discriminate between motion directions or smoothly pursue small moving objects, but they show rapid improvements between 6 and 14 weeks of age (Gilmore et al., 2007; Rosander et al., 2007). Young infants exhibit sensitivity to information for impending collision very early in development, with infants between 3 and 6 weeks shown to perceive optical collisions by responding with defensive blinks and head movements (e.g., Náñez, 1988). Even neonates as young as 3 days old exhibit responses through backward head movements when exposed to backwards flow stimuli (Jouen et al., 2000; Shirai and Yamaguchi, 2010). Such responses in very young infants may be the result of multimodal integrative and cooperative processes in which visual, vestibular, and proprioceptive senses are involved rather than a direct consequence of motion perception (Jouen et al., 2000).

Around 2 months of age, infants are already able to show prospective control as they continuously track objects using smooth pursuit eye movements and a gain geared to the velocity of the moving target (Rosander and von Hofsten, 2002). From 3 to 5 months, infants discriminate between virtual flow displays that depict at least 22° changes in heading direction (Gilmore et al., 2004). Around 6 months of age, they further follow moving objects on a linear path using predictive head and eye movements (Jonsson and von Hofsten, 2003). At this age, infants reach for a moving target by not aiming for the current position of the object but predictively aiming for a position further ahead on the path where the hand and the object will meet (van der Meer et al., 1994; von Hofsten et al., 1998; Jonsson and von Hofsten, 2003). When moving objects that are being tracked move temporarily out of view, infants should anticipate where and when the object would reappear again. This ability seems to be developed around 6 months of age (Johnson et al., 2003).

Studies using anticipatory and compensatory postural adjustment to study prospective control have found mobile infants around the end of the first year of life to show peak postural compensation to visual flow information (e.g., Bertenthal et al., 1997; Lejeune et al., 2006). Witherington et al. (2002) studied infants between 10 and 17 months of age to investigate early development of anticipatory postural activity in support of pulling action. Infants retrieved toys by pulling open cabinet drawers while a force resisting the pulling action was applied to the drawers. Infants' anticipatory postural adjustments and the temporal specificity of anticipatory activities progressively improved with age as infants learned to stand and walk. By improving anticipatory postural responses, balance control is also enhanced (Santos et al., 2010). Thus, prospective control plays an important role in keeping balance during standing and locomotion. In evaluating whether infants who are able to walk show greater sophistication compared to non-walking infants when anticipating postural disturbances induced by a continuously moving platform, Cignetti et al. (2013) reported that the acquisition of independent walking improves sensorimotor control of posture. Other studies also show that infants with locomotor experience typically respond more to peripheral flow than pre-locomotor infants and that the developmental shift in using flow-field information for postural control may be more closely linked to locomotor experience (e.g., Higgins et al., 1996). With the development of self-generated actions including self-locomotion experience, what is perceived and the ensuing anticipatory actions considerably improve in the developing brain (van der Meer et al., 2008a; James and Swain, 2011). Thus, the functional detection of visual flow information

develops hand in hand with self-produced locomotion in normally developing infants (van der Meer et al., 2008a).

Unlike normally developing full-term infants, preterm infants show differential brain development that is particularly evident from abnormalities in tissue microstructure, cerebral morphology, and white matter damage (see review by Counsell and Boardman, 2005). Preterm infants are therefore at a higher risk of developing neurological and perceptuo-motor problems (see Taylor et al., 2009). These abnormalities underlie various cognitive and behavioral impairments, including deficits in visual perception and other neurodevelopmental disorders that are associated with preterm birth (de Jong et al., 2012). Preterm children show deficits in perception of global motion, global form, and biological motion, with impairment of the dorsal visual stream particularly implicated as a possible cause of such developmental problems (Taylor et al., 2009). Because of these impairments, identifying at-risk preterm infants is necessary to offer appropriate early intervention to those who need it.

By using brain and behavioral data mainly from occlusion, looming, and optic flow studies, we further discuss the development of visual perception for the control of prospective actions during the first year of life. Prospective control behavior in infants is shown through predictive gaze and reaching movements, and different timing strategies for obstacle avoidance. We show that the development of prospective control substantially improves with age. We illustrate how preterm infants show developmental delays in the processing of prospective control information by comparing full-term infants' responses with responses of preterm infants. The relationship between behavioral development and the development of the underlying neuronal processes is highlighted through EEG measurements of neuronal electrical activity as a function of perception of visual motion information.

INTERCEPTION TASKS WITH TEMPORARY OCCLUSION

With visual occlusion tasks, we investigated infants' prospective control and the ability to maintain object permanence—the understanding that an object exists even if it is out of sight. The development of the mediating neural structures of such processes was also studied. By combining behavioral measurements of eye, head, and hand-reaching movements together with EEG analysis of neuronal gamma oscillations, we could study infants' ability to follow, maintain attention on, and predict the arrival of a moving object as it disappears behind an occluder and reappears shortly afterwards.

When reaching for a moving object, infants must use prospective control to guide their hand-reaching movements to intercept the moving object. To study prospective control in catching, van der Meer et al. (1994) investigated the control of hand and gaze movements as infants reached for a toy moving at different speeds. The toy was occluded from view by a screen during the final part of its approach. Infants could reach to catch the toy when it was at a certain distance or time away from them. To effectively catch the toy, a strategy based on distance is less efficient as it is dependent on the approach velocity of the toy. Thus, reaching to catch the toy when it is approaching at a fast velocity leaves very limited time to extend the arm to make an interceptive movement. A strategy based on time-to-contact, however, is most efficient since it leaves the same amount of time to carry out the interceptive movement irrespective of the toy's approach velocity. Infants around 11 months of age anticipated with their gaze and hand the reappearance of the toy as it emerged from behind the occluder. Their hands started moving forward before the toy had even disappeared behind the occluder in order to catch the toy as soon as it reappeared. Prospective gaze and hand action was coupled to certain times before the toy's reappearance. Thus, information that was picked up before the disappearance of the toy behind the occluder was used to regulate gaze and hand movement. When infants between 20 and 48 weeks of age were studied longitudinally, infants' gaze anticipated the reappearance of the moving toy as soon as they were able to successfully catch the toy. Infants' anticipatory gaze movements suggest that this ability is a prerequisite for the onset of reaching for moving objects. As corroborated by various studies (e.g., Aguiar and Baillargeon, 1999), the findings indicate that object permanence is present in infants earlier than the suggested 8 months by Piaget (1954). The ability to successfully catch a fast-moving object coincides with infants' ability to use perceptual information to initiate a reaching movement. Initiation of the hand movement should begin when the toy is a certain time away from them, instead of a certain distance away, thus making available the same average time for the catching movement whether the toy is moving slowly or quickly.

How do neurologically at-risk preterm infants perform in comparison with full-term infants on tasks that rely heavily on prospective control? van der Meer et al. (1995) studied healthy full-term infants and low-birthweight preterm infants longitudinally between 20 and 48 weeks of age to investigate whether infants classified as being neurologically at-risk of brain damage have similar prospective control ability as full-term infants, and if not, whether their lowered ability could be indicative of brain damage. Infants' ability to reach for a toy moving at different speeds was studied. At the first reaching session each infant's gaze successfully anticipated the reappearance of the moving toy. However, reaching onset and prospective control of gaze and hand movements varied considerably between the full-term and preterm infants. From 24 weeks onwards, the full-term infants anticipated the moving toy with their gaze, but gaze anticipation was delayed in all the preterm infants until 40 or 48 weeks of age. As a group, the preterm infants started reaching late for the toy. Three started to reach at 28 weeks corrected age, 8 weeks later than the full-term control infants. Some preterm infants geared their actions to the distance instead of the time that the toy was from the catching point, which caused problems with faster moving toys. Almost all the preterm infants anticipated the reappearance of the moving toy with their hand at the final testing session at 48 weeks of age. They also started showing signs of using the time strategy to adapt their actions according to the length of time that the toy was from the reappearance point at this age. Two of the preterm infants still appeared to be using the less efficient distance strategy

when shifting their gaze and initiating their hand movement to reach for the toy at 48 weeks of age. The same two infants also showed the poorest anticipation of the toy's reappearance. These two preterm infants were later diagnosed with mild and moderate cerebral palsy at around 2 years of age. Hence, poor development of prospective control on the catching task could potentially serve as an indicator of possible brain damage.

Further, with normally developing full-term and preterm infants between 22 and 48 weeks of age, we longitudinally investigated the timing strategy infants use to initiate and guide the hand when catching a moving object and whether the guiding action is influenced by the use of timing strategies (Kayed and van der Meer, 2009). Little difference was found between full-term and preterm infants' use of timing strategies. Preterm infants showed about the same development as full-term infants both in timing the catch and in continuously guiding hand movement. Variation in the functionality and length of the tau-coupling between the hand and the toy was influenced by the timing strategy the infants were using to initiate the hand movement. The younger preterm and full-term infants used a distance strategy to initiate hand movement when they started to reach for the moving toy. This resulted in a high number of unsuccessful attempts at catching the toy. They performed shorter and less functional tau-coupling that was characterized by non-controlled collisions with the hand accelerating toward the toy when they used the distance strategy. However, the older infants around the end of the first year of life switched to a time strategy when reaching for the moving toy. They performed longer and more functional tau-coupling between the hand and the toy, with better controlled collisions with the hand decelerating toward the toy. They showed a marked improvement in the number of successful catches. One preterm infant failed to switch to a time strategy and showed poor prospective control with a higher number of unsuccessful catches compared to other infants. This preterm infant may later have perceptuo-motor problems.

To further investigate the use of prospective control in catching and how it could be used as a tool to detect signs of brain dysfunction, Aanondsen et al. (2007) studied adolescents between 14 and 15 years of age who were either born as preterm very-low-birthweight (VLBW), full-term small for gestational age (SGA), or full-term appropriate for gestational age (AGA) infants. They were presented with a moving target that approached from the side at three different accelerations. The experiment was conducted as a blind study without knowing beforehand the participants' neurological status such as birth status, gestational age, birthweight, and their cerebral magnetic resonance imaging (MRI) results. All participants used the time-to-contact strategy to initiate their hand movements except three adolescents (two preterm VLBW and one full-term SGA). They rather used the less advanced distance or velocity timing strategy to guide the initiation of at least one of their hands to catch the moving target. Based on their timing strategies, the three adolescents were classified as at risk for neurological problems. Their cerebral MRI confirmed this classification. It showed them to have reduced white matter tissue, dilation of the ventricular system, and/or pathology in the corpus callosum. The findings showed that the ability to use prospective information

for catching could be a reliable tool to help detect diffuse signs of motor dysfunction that may not be readily detectable using only standard neuropsychological tests.

To investigate the neural correlates underlying prospective control, Holth et al. (2013) coupled adults' gaze control during deceleration in a visual tracking task with their EEG activity. Participants followed with their gaze a horizontally moving car that was temporally occluded and pushed a button to stop the car as soon as it reappeared from behind the occluder on a large screen placed 80 cm in front of them (see **Figure 1A**). The car moved under three different constant decelerations. The button-press response was defined as either a hit or a miss depending on how much of the car was visible in the target area when it was stopped. A hit response was defined as at least half of the car being visible after pressing the button. Different events were used to time-lock the averaged event-related potential (ERP) waveforms, including stimulus onset, push-button responses, and eye jumps across the occluder. When ERP waveforms were time-locked to the prospective gaze shift over the occluder, participants were successful in discriminating between the three decelerating speeds. Thus, participants' parietal activity indicated that they were able to differentiate between the different car decelerations but only when their averaged EEG was time-locked to the eye jump event and only when they managed to stop the car successfully. No such effect was found when ERP waveforms were time-locked to any of the other events. The findings indicate that a traditional stimulus-onset time-locking procedure is likely to distort the averaged EEG signal. This distortion may consequently hide important activity differences, especially in the parietal cortex that may provide information about the prospective timing of decelerating object motion during occlusion. The observations strongly suggest active incorporation of behavioral data into EEG analysis to provide valuable information that would be lost otherwise, when studying the neural correlates of prospective control.

Further longitudinal EEG studies showed that infants' ability to smoothly track a moving object undergoing occlusion (see **Figure 1A**) and to predict its reappearance increases considerably between the ages of 4 and 12 months (Twenhöfel et al., 2013). Infants showed more instances of shifting gaze predictively over the occluder with age (**Figures 1B,C**). The older infants showed a more consistent pattern of anticipatory eye movements in response to the moving target. The results corroborate previous studies showing that anticipatory eye movements improve considerably in the course of the first year of life (see e.g., Gredebäck and von Hofsten, 2004). In order to successfully track an object over an occlusion period, object permanence must be developed. Rosander and von Hofsten (2004) suggested that smooth pursuit of moving targets and predictive occluder tracking depend on the ability to anticipate future motion based on the prediction of a continuous motion trajectory of a moving object. Because of a 100–200 ms visuo-motor delay that the smooth pursuit system has to overcome during the tracking of moving objects (see Schlag and Schlag-Rey, 2002), smooth pursuit must be adjusted predictively to compensate for this delay within which a visual target may have moved significantly.

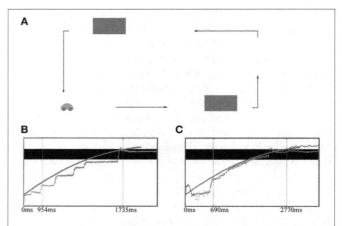

FIGURE 1 | Occlusion experimental set-up (A), and gaze data (↑ position and → time) for a typical slow deceleration in a 4-month-old infant (B) and a 12-month-old infant (C). (A) The car traveled horizontally on a rectangular path under one of three deceleration conditions, fast (10% deceleration), medium (50% deceleration), and slow (90% deceleration). The two green boxes temporarily occluded the car from its path of travel. **(B,C)** The black bar represents the occluder, and the green squares represent the car motion, while the red and blue dots represent the right and the left eye, respectively. Yellow dots are missing data. The left markers in each graph represent the catch up event (the moment at which the horizontal eye velocity equals the speed of the car for the first time), while the right markers represent the point in time at which the car starts to reappear from behind the occluder. The 4-month-old infant shows typical saccadic tracking to keep up with the target motion **(B)**, whereas the 12-month-old infant follows the car with smooth pursuit **(C)**. The 12-month-old infant shows an anticipatory saccade to the end of the occluder before car reappearance, while the 4-month-old infant shows no such prospective eye movement.

With the development of object permanence, the older infants may have used visuo-motor integration to successfully predict the object's trajectory and to continuously track its movement.

The predictive gaze shift was accompanied by a divergence and a shift in gamma band topography with age. Neuronal gamma band topography shifted from occipital areas in the dorsal stream in the younger infants to anterior temporal areas in the ventral stream in the older infants when the underlying neuronal source activities were analyzed. The divergence in gamma band topography may possibly reflect developmental changes in neuronal mechanisms serving object tracking over transient occlusion periods during the course of the first year of life. Previous studies have also implicated gamma activity in complex object processing in regions distributed along the ventral and dorsal pathways (e.g., Lachaux et al., 2005; Hoogenboom et al., 2006). The shift of gamma activity in neuronal regions may suggest different strategies of occluder tracking with age. Younger infants may be guided mainly using spatio-temporal information processed via the dorsal pathway to fill perceptual gaps over transient occlusions. The ventral pathway activation in the older infants may suggest further incorporation of object features during perceptual representations of moving objects. Thus, the gamma activation could represent top-down processing (high-speed memory comparison) of the object template that was maintained over the perceptual gap with the perceived stimulus (see Herrmann and Mecklinger, 2001). The ventral stream activation is in accordance with the suggestion that vision for perception (a typical ventral stream task) could replace vision for action (mainly a dorsal stream task) in order to successfully guide 11-month-old infants' arm reaching movements in an occlusion situation (van Wermeskerken et al., 2011). The developmental progression in regional cortical shift of oscillatory activity suggests that the development of object permanence and prospective control become more prominent around the end of the first year of life.

Unlike full-term infants, preterm infants show delayed development in the continuous eye tracking of moving objects. While full-term infants around 12 months smoothly followed the moving target in 64% of all trials, preterm infants around the same age (corrected for prematurity) showed smooth pursuit in only 35% of the presented trials. The lower proportion of predictive eye movements in the preterm infants compared to the full-term infants may be a reflection of a weak object representation (Munakata, 2001) and a delay in the influence of functional object representations on eye movements (Hollingworth et al., 2008). However, their ability to make anticipatory eye movements was relatively similar to the full-term infants. Thus, they were able to disengage attention from tracking the moving object during an occlusion period and then predictively re-orient gaze over the occluder after the object's reappearance despite showing difficulties with smooth pursuit. Disturbances in the development of the motion perception pathways and other complications associated with premature birth may impair motion processing and contribute to preterm infants' reduced ability to track moving objects. To compensate for their less functioning smooth pursuit system, it has been suggested that preterm infants may use saccadic eye movements and head movements to continuously follow a moving target, although this results in less efficient smooth pursuit than that observed in full-term infants (Grönqvist et al., 2011).

LOOMING VIRTUAL STIMULI ON A COLLISION COURSE

How does the infant brain process information about imminent collisions? By simulating a looming object on a direct collision course toward infants, it is possible to investigate brain activities in response to looming information. Looming refers to the last part of the approach of an object that is accelerating toward the infant (Kayed and van der Meer, 2007). To prevent an impending collision with the looming object, infants must use a timing strategy that ensures they have enough time to estimate when the object is about to hit them in order to perform the appropriate behavioral response. Defensive blinking is widely considered as an indicator for sensitivity to information about looming objects on a collision course. Infants must use time-to-collision information to precisely time a blinking response so that they do not blink too early and reopen their eyes before the object makes contact or blink too late when the object may have already made contact. An accurate defensive response helps to prevent

injury to the infants. For a successful defensive response to avoid collisions, development of prospective control is important. Infants must use looming visual information to correctly time anticipatory responses to avoid impending collisions.

The timing strategies that infants use to determine when to make a defensive blink to a looming virtual object on a collision course were investigated using full-term infants between 22 and 30 weeks of age in a cross-sectional behavioral study (Kayed and van der Meer, 2000). The youngest infants used a strategy based on visual angle (analogous to the distance strategy) to time defensive blinks. Thus, they blinked too late when the looming object approached at high accelerations. The oldest infants, on the other hand, used a time strategy allowing them to blink in time for all the approach conditions of the virtual object. When precise timing is required, the use of the less advantageous visual-angle strategy may lead to errors in performance compared to the use of a time strategy that allows for successful performance irrespective of object size and speed.

Further longitudinal studies of full-term and preterm infants at 22 and 30 weeks of aged showed that with age, the majority of infants switched from using a strategy based on visual angle to a strategy based on time to time their blinks (Kayed and van der Meer, 2007; Kayed et al., 2008). Some of the infants used a time strategy even already at 22 weeks, with such infants maintaining the use of this strategy on subsequent testing sessions. None of the infants switched back to using a strategy based on visual angle after using a time strategy. One preterm infant showed delayed development compared to the other infants since he was using a timing strategy based on visual angle for all loom speeds. This caused him to blink late on the majority of trials even when he was 30 weeks of age. In infants, the inability to switch from a timing strategy that is susceptible to errors to a strategy that affords successful defensive blinking might reflect an inadequate potential for flexibility. Flexibility may be required to help adjust appropriately to local environmental conditions and to successfully interact with the environment, especially since good timing is essential to avoid obstacles during navigation.

With the presentation of a looming virtual object on a direct collision course, we then investigated the developmental differences between full-term and preterm infants using high-density EEG. Infants were studied longitudinally at 4 and 12 months. The looming stimulus was programmed to loom toward the infant with different accelerations, which finally came up to the infant's face to simulate a visual collision experience (see **Figure 2A**). Looming-related peak VEP responses were analyzed using source dipoles in occipital areas. Results showed a developmental trend in the prediction of an object's time-to-collision in full-term infants. With age, average VEP duration (processing time) in full-term infants decreased, with peak VEP response closer to the loom's time-to-collision (van der Weel and van der Meer, 2009; van der Meer et al., 2012). Full-term infants around 12 months of age used the more sophisticated and efficient time strategy to time their brain responses to the virtual collision. Their looming-related brain responses were fixed at a constant time-to-collision irrespective of visual loom speed (**Figure 2B**), an indication of the development of prospective control at this age (van der Meer et al., 2015). The use of such

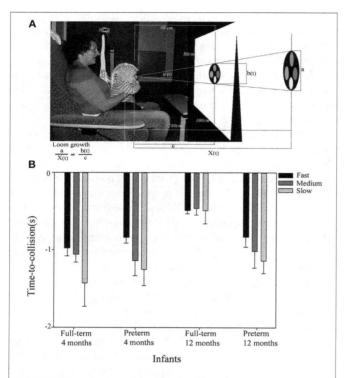

FIGURE 2 | Looming experimental setup (A), and averaged looming-related VEP peak responses (with SDs) in full-term and preterm infants (B). (A) Infants were shown a flat 2-dimensional circle filled with four smaller colored circles. The looming stimuli simulated an object approaching from a distance on a direct collision course under constant accelerations of -21.1, -9.4, $-5.3\,\text{ms}^{-2}$ for fast loom (2 s), medium loom (3 s), and slow loom (4 s), respectively. The bottom left equation describes the growth of the visual loom. The looming stimuli approached the infant as the image on the screen grew symmetrically and stopped when the image filled the entire screen. **(B)** With increasing age, the full-term infants responded significantly closer to the loom's time-to-collision compared to the pre-term infants. Only the older full-term infants responded at a fixed time-to-collision irrespective of loom speed, an indication that only the full-term infants at 12 months had switched from a visual angle strategy to the more sophisticated time strategy when timing their looming-related VEP peak responses.

a timing strategy based on a fixed time-to-collision may reflect infants' levels of neural maturity and locomotion experience. Maturity and experience are important factors needed for accurate timing of prospective actions in response to looming objects to ensure successful evasive maneuvers during navigation.

However, unlike full-term infants, preterm infants did not show such improvements with age but continued to use the less efficient timing strategy based on the loom's visual angle even at 12 months (**Figure 2B**). This suggested that preterm infants have problems with prospective control during the first year of life, showing their brain responses too early in the looming sequence and therefore not adequately taking into account the loom's different accelerations.

By localizing brain source activity for looming stimuli approaching at different speeds and using extrinsic tau-coupling analysis, the temporal dynamics of post-synaptic neuronal activity in the first year of life was further investigated (van der Weel and van der Meer, 2009). Tau-coupling analysis

calculated tau of the peak-to-peak source waveform activity and the corresponding tau of the loom speeds. Source dipoles that modeled brain activities within the visual areas of interest, O1, Oz, and O2 were fitted around peak looming VEP activity to give a direct measure of brain source activities on a trial-by-trial basis. Using full-term pre-locomotor infants at 5–7 and 8–9 months and crawling infants at 10–11 months of age, synchronized theta-band activity in response to the looming stimulus was found. This was consistent with other studies that identified oscillations in the theta range as important for registration and processing of visual perceptual information (e.g., Kahana et al., 2001). Extrinsic tau-coupling analysis on the source waveform activities showed evidence of strong and long tau-coupling in all infants. The oldest infants showed brain activity with a temporal structure that was consistent with the temporal structure present in the visual looming stimuli. Thus, in the course of development, the temporal structure of different looming stimuli may be sustained during processing in the more mature infant brain. Sustaining the temporal structure may provide increasingly accurate time-to-collision information about looming danger as infants become more mobile with age. Infants at 10–11 months differentiated well between the different loom speeds with increasing values of the tau-coupling constant, K, for the faster loom. The younger infants were not able to differentiate between the looms, with the worst performance observed in infants at 5–7 months. The findings may suggest mature neural networks for processing impending collision information in the oldest infants compared to the youngest. At 5–7 months, such neural networks may not have been developed but could rather be in the process of being established at 8–9 months of age, which coincides with the onset of crawling in infants. Thus, with better control of self-produced locomotion, the perceptual ability to recognize looming danger, and perform the necessary prospective action to avoid impending collision markedly improves.

In the developing brain, not only is visual information important for the performance of prospective actions, but also integration of information from multiple senses is necessary and fundamental to perception. To investigate whether the auditory system also plays a role in prospective control, van der Meer et al. (2008b) used an auditory-guided rotation paradigm in a behavioral study of infants at 6–9 months of age. Infants lay in a prone position with magnetic sensors fastened to their head and body to measure direction and velocity of rotation as they responded to auditory stimulation from their mothers. Infants were able to consistently choose the shortest way over the longest way to rotate to their mothers who were positioned behind them. The infants showed prospective control by rotating with a higher peak velocity as the angle to be covered between themselves and their mother's position increased. In line with affordance theory, we showed that the auditory system can function as a functional listening system. Auditory information may be used as a source of perceptual information to help guide behaviors adequately in the environment. Mobile infants may use auditory information that offers them the most efficient method for action relative to their own position in space and a desired position to reach in the environment (also see Morrongiello, 1988; Middlebrooks and Green, 1991; van der Meer and van der Weel, 2011).

However, when visual and auditory looming information are simultaneously present in an audiovisual looming stimulus, prelocomotor full-term infants show earlier looming-related brain responses to the auditory loom than to the visual loom (Agboada et al., 2015). Longitudinal studies show that peak visual and auditory looming activation responses in infants at 3–4 months occur earlier in the looming sequence compared to older infants at 9–10 months. The results indicate a developmental trend in the prediction of time-to-collision information in infancy where the recruitment of neuronal assemblies in higher cortical areas, particularly in the parietal cortex, is implicated in the processing of looming-related information as infants age. With an evolutionary bias for survival prioritizing an early auditory response over that of visual response in audiovisual looming perception, it is likely that audiovisual integration in infants could be heavily influenced by their spatial attention being captured by a visual loom. In order words, visual looming-related responses that appear relatively late in a looming sequence could be a reflection of infants' active attention shown to a visual loom over that of an auditory loom (see Corbetta et al., 1990).

OPTIC FLOW INFORMATION SIMULATING SELF-MOTION

With an optic flow paradigm, we have explored the development of visual motion perception during the first year of life by using both evoked (VEP) and induced (time-spectral evolution, TSE) brain responses to simulated self-motion. Using EEG in 8-month-old infants and adults, van der Meer et al. (2008a) studied brain electrical activity as a function of perception of structured optic flow and random visual motion. Brain activities related to the processing of motion stimuli were different in infants and adults both in VEP and induced activities of EEG. Adults and infants had shorter N2 latencies for structured optic flow than random visual motion. Infants showed longer latencies in both motion conditions compared to adults, with the longest latencies observed for random visual motion. While infants used the slower theta-band frequency during the processing of visual information, adults used the faster beta-band activity in response to the motion conditions. The findings show that infants that are not yet capable of walking may detect optic flow less efficiently compared to adults and they may be more affected by the lack of structure present in random visual motion. When the speed of structured forward optic flow information was varied in adults and infants at 4–5 and 8–10 months, Vilhelmsen et al. (2015a,b) showed that differences in N2 peak latency occurred in the adults and the older infants but not in the infants at 4–5 months. N2 latencies were found to decrease with age, with shortest N2 latency observed for the lowest speed of motion. Unlike the younger infants, the older infants may have had a more developed neurobiological system that contributed to an improved detection of visual motion, similar to the adult participants. Motion-sensitive cortical areas continue to develop through infancy to adulthood (Gilmore et al., 2007), which lead to more efficient processing of different speeds of motion with age.

In relating behavioral changes such as locomotion experience to accompanying changes in brain activities, prelocomotor infants at 3–4 months and infants at 11–12 months with self-produced locomotion experience were longitudinally studied using an optic flow paradigm (Agyei et al., 2015, 2016). Both full-term and preterm infants were studied to investigate the effect of prematurity on the processing of optic flow information. The infants were presented with three motion conditions (forwards and reversed optic flow, and random visual motion) together with a static non-flow condition. The younger infants had no crawling experience while the older infants had on average, about 2.5 months of crawling experience.

Full-term infants differentiated between the three motion conditions with shortest latency for forwards optic flow and longest latency for random visual motion, but only at 11–12 months (**Figure 3**). This improvement in visual motion perception with age was possibly due to significant neural developments such as increasing myelination of connecting fibers (Paus et al., 2001; Grieve et al., 2003; Loenneker et al., 2011) and maturation of local glucose metabolic rates (Chugani et al., 1996; Klaver et al., 2011). Thus, rapid progressive improvement in the functional processing of motion information as infants get older may account for the shorter latencies observed in infants at 11–12 months. The shortest latency for forwards optic flow could suggest faster sensitivity development to radial motion that corresponds to forward movement rather than to reversed or random directions. Further, when mothers carry infants, the infants experience passive locomotion where they are tuned to the dominant statistics of their experienced visual environment (Raudies et al., 2012; Raudies and Gilmore, 2014). Infants' passive experience of visual flow, especially during fast flow speeds, occurs as a result of their downward head direction and closer proximity to ground surfaces when being carried (Raudies et al., 2012). However, only self-generated actions may lead to a stronger link between perception and action in the developing brain (James and Swain, 2011). Thus, only the older full-term infants who had crawling experience from self-movement were better at distinguishing between the motion conditions compared to the younger infants who only had passive locomotion experience from being carried around.

The preterm infants did not differentiate between the three motion conditions at 11–12 months or improve their latencies with age. Studies show that preterm infants at corrected age of 2–3 months are delayed several weeks compared to full-term infants when differentiating between changes of direction (e.g., Braddick et al., 2005; Birtles et al., 2007). Considering that the preterm infants had similar crawling experience as the full-term infants, their inability to differentiate between the motion conditions when older could have resulted from abnormalities in white matter that may underlie impairment of the dorsal visual stream. Thus, axonal electrical impulses could be impaired, resulting in unimproved latencies with age. It is possible that preterm infants' unimproved latencies with age could also reflect a normal delay related to premature birth that could be recovered at a later age. However, at 3–4 months and irrespective of visual motion condition, preterm infants had significantly shorter latencies than full-term infants. Since the preterm infants were tested corrected

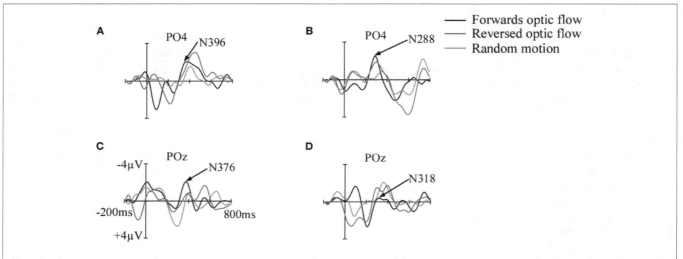

FIGURE 3 | Grand average motion VEPs in full-term infants at 3–4 months (A) and 11–12 months (B), and in preterm infants at 3–4 months (C) and 11–12 months (D). Amplitudes are on the y-axis and latencies on the x-axis. The actual N2 peak latencies for forwards optic flow are indicated at PO4 in full-term infants and POz in preterm infants. Differences in N2 peak latencies for the three motion conditions were observed only in full-term infants at 12 months where latency increased from forwards optic flow to reversed optic flow and random motion.

for prematurity, one contributing factor to this faster perceptual response could be the longer exposure to and experience of visual flow in the younger preterm infants compared to the term infants at 3–4 months.

When TSE of the motion conditions were compared with TSE of the static non-flow dot pattern, both infant groups showed desynchronized theta-band activity that was more prevalent in the younger infants (**Figure 4**). Low-frequency theta-band oscillation is a general sign of immaturity in infancy (e.g., Orekhova et al., 2006). The more prevalent theta-band desynchronization in the younger infants could suggest relatively larger neural networks and lesser specialization when processing radial motion information at this age. Further, synchronized alpha-beta band activity was seen only in the full-term infants at 11–12 months. The emergence of faster alpha-beta band frequency activity only at 11–12 months could indicate a gradual progression from less specialized, slower oscillating, and relatively immature larger oscillatory cell assemblies at 3–4 months to a more adult-like pattern of motion specialization where cell assemblies have fewer but more specialized neurons. This could explain why full-term infants at 11–12 months are better at establishing more rapid coupling between spatially separated brain regions, allowing for improved visual motion perception.

The possible impairment of the dorsal stream responsible for processing visual motion could be the reason why the preterm infants at 11–12 months showed no such progression in oscillatory patterns. Since the dorsal visual stream develops and matures relatively early (Hammarrenger et al., 2007), being born preterm may have disrupted the association fibers and synaptic development in the dorsal stream that help to fine-tune cortical growth during late fetal and early extrauterine life (Huppi et al., 1998; Mewes et al., 2006). The disruption in the development of the dorsal visual stream because of premature

birth may have impeded efficient cortical growth and contributed to the absence of higher frequency oscillatory activities when the preterm infants were older. Further, individual analysis showed abnormally high latencies in response to optic flow in three preterm infants (see also van der Meer et al., 2015). Because of the possible greater degree of impairment of the dorsal stream in these preterm infants, a follow-up study when the preterm infants reach school age is necessary to investigate whether these infants still have impaired dorsal stream-related functions, and the effect of the impairment on everyday life.

CONCLUSION

Information about how the visual system responds to visual motion through the interconnection of behavioral and neural processes has been presented to help advance our understanding of the development of visual perception for prospective control in infancy. Infants show a developmental progress with age as they use visual perceptual information to help guide the execution of anticipatory actions of eye, head, and hand movements. The processing of visual information and the development of object permanence become more efficient around the end of the first year of life. Infants show marked improvements in looming-related brain responses and the ability to switch from a distance or visual-angle strategy to the more efficient time strategy to help tau-guide their reaching movements. With age, infants recognize and differentiate between different radial motions, and show a progression from low- to high-frequency neuronal oscillations during the processing of visual information. Self-produced locomotion experience and the ongoing neural maturational processes may be factors that contribute to the efficiency of visual motion perception during development. Unlike full-terms, preterm infants may have impairments in the

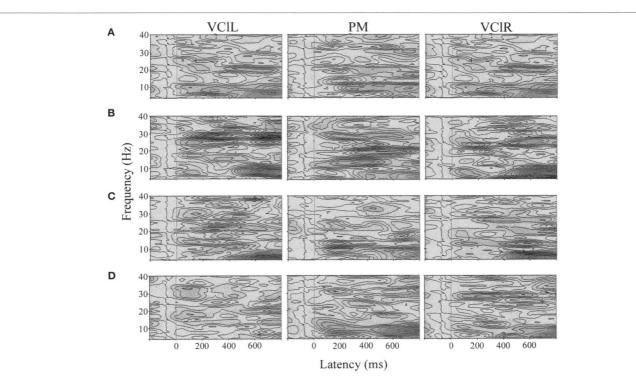

FIGURE 4 | TSE plots across brain regions of interest (VCIL, visual cortex lateral left; PM, parietal midline; VCIR, visual cortex lateral right) when the motion conditions were compared with the static non-flow condition in a typical full-term infant at 4 months (A) and 12 months (B), and in a typical preterm infant at 4 months (C) and 12 months (D). Induced synchronized and desynchronized activities appear in red and blue colored contours, respectively. Induced theta-band desynchronized activities were observed in all the visual areas of interest in the full-term and preterm infants at both ages, with induced alpha-beta band synchronized activities observed in two or more visual areas only in the full-term infants at 12 months. Stimulus onset is the vertical red line at 0 ms, with epoch from −200 to 800 ms.

functioning of the dorsal visual stream. Impaired functioning of the dorsal stream may contribute to their relatively poorer performances during the processing of visual information. Early detection and identification of preterm infants who could be at risk for developmental problems is thus necessary to help provide early intervention programmes required for their optimal development. When studying the neural correlates of prospective control in infancy, it is of the utmost importance to incorporate behavioral data into EEG analyses to get a better understanding of how the development of brain and behavior is intimately linked.

AUTHOR CONTRIBUTIONS

SA, FW, and AM have contributed equally to the conception and design of the work and are accountable for all aspects of the work. SA has drafted the work, FW and AM have contributed equally to revising it critically for intellectual content.

FUNDING

This project has partly been made possible by the Norwegian ExtraFoundation for Health and Rehabilitation.

REFERENCES

Aanondsen, C. M., van der Meer, A. L. H., Brubakk, A. M., Evensen, K. A. I., Skranes, J. S., Myhr, G. E., et al. (2007). Differentiating prospective control information for catching in at-risk and control adolescents. *Dev. Med. Child Neurol.* 49, 112–116. doi: 10.1111/j.1469-8749.2007.00112.x

Agboada, D., van der Meer, A. L. H., and van der Weel, F. R. (2015). Infants' cortical responses to audiovisual looming studied with high-density EEG. *Cogn. Behav. Psychol.* 7, 152–160. doi: 10.5176/2251-1865_cbp15.07

Aguiar, A., and Baillargeon, R. (1999). 2.5-month-old infants' reasoning about when objects should and should not be occluded. *Cogn. Psychol.* 39, 116–157. doi: 10.1006/cogp.1999.0717

Agyei, S. B., Holth, M., van der Weel, F. R., and van der Meer, A. L. H. (2015). Longitudinal study of perception of structured optic flow and random visual motion in infants using high-density EEG. *Dev. Sci.* 18, 436–451. doi: 10.1111/desc.12221

Agyei, S. B., van der Weel, F. R., and van der Meer, A. L. H. (2016). Longitudinal study of preterm and full-term infants: high-density EEG analyses of cortical activity in response to visual motion. *Neuropsychologia.* doi: 10.1016/j.neuropsychologia.2016.02.001

Austad, H., and van der Meer, A. L. H. (2007). Prospective dynamic balance control in healthy children and adults. *Exp. Brain Res.* 181, 289–295. doi: 10.1007/s00221-007-0932-1

Başar, E., Başar-Eroğlu, C., Karakaş, S., and Schürmann, M. (2000). Brain oscillations in perception and memory. *Int. J. Psychophysiol.* 35, 95–124. doi: 10.1016/S0167-8760(99)00047-1

Bastin, J., Fajen, B. R., and Montagne, G. (2010). Controlling speed and direction during interception: an affordance-based approach. *Exp. Brain Res.* 201, 763–780. doi: 10.1007/s00221-009-2092-y

Bertenthal, B. I., Rose, J. L., and Bai, D. L. (1997). Perception-action coupling in the development of visual control of posture. *J. Exp. Psychol. Hum. Percept. Perform.* 23, 1631–1643. doi: 10.1037/0096-1523.23.6.1631

Birtles, D. B., Braddick, O. J., Wattam-Bell, J., Wilkinson, A. R., and Atkinson, J. (2007). Orientation and motion-specific visual cortex responses in infants born preterm. *Neuroreport* 18, 1975–1979. doi: 10.1097/WNR.0b013e3282f228c8

Bootsma, R. J., Ledouit, S., Casanova, R., and Zaal, F. T. J. M. (2015). Fractional-order information in the visual control of lateral locomotor interception. *J. Exp. Psychol. Hum. Percept. Perform.* doi: 10.1037/xhp0000162. [Epub ahead of print].

Braddick, O., Birtles, D., Wattam-Bell, J., and Atkinson, J. (2005). Motion- and orientation-specific cortical responses in infancy. *Vision Res.* 45, 3169–3179. doi: 10.1016/j.visres.2005.07.021

Brecelj, J. (2003). From immature to mature pattern ERG and VEP. *Doc. Ophthalmol.* 107, 215–224. doi: 10.1023/B:DOOP.0000005330.62543.9c

Chardenon, A., Montagne, G., Laurent, M., and Bootsma, R. J. (2004). The perceptual control of goal- directed locomotion: a common control architecture for interception and navigation? *Exp. Brain Res.* 158, 100–108. doi: 10.1007/s00221-004-1880-7

Chugani, H. T., Muller, R. A., and Chugani, D. C. (1996). Functional brain reorganization in children. *Brain Dev.* 18, 347–356. doi: 10.1016/0387-7604(96)00032-0

Cignetti, F., Zedka, M., Vaugoyeau, M., and Assaiante, C. (2013). Independent walking as a major skill for the development of anticipatory postural control: evidence from adjustments to predictable perturbations. *PLoS ONE* 8:e56313. doi: 10.1371/journal.pone.0056313

Corbetta, M., Miezin, F. M., Dobmeyer, S., Shulman, G. L., and Petersen, S. E. (1990). Attentional modulation of neural processing of shape, color, and velocity in humans. *Science* 248, 1556–1559. doi: 10.1126/science.2360050

Counsell, S. J., and Boardman, J. P. (2005). Differential brain growth in the infant born preterm: current knowledge and future developments from brain imaging. *Semin. Fetal Neonatal Med.* 10, 403–410. doi: 10.1016/j.siny.2005.05.003

Craig, C. M., and Lee, D. N. (1999). Neonatal control of nutritive sucking pressure: evidence for an intrinsic tau-guide. *Exp. Brain Res.* 124, 371–382. doi: 10.1007/s002210050634

Creem, S. H., and Proffitt, D. R. (2001). Defining the cortical visual systems: "what", "where", and "how." *Acta Psychol.* 107, 43–68. doi: 10.1016/S0001-6918(01)00021-X

Cutting, J. E., Vishton, P. M., and Braren, P. A. (1995). How we avoid collisions with stationary and moving objects. *Psychol. Rev.* 102, 627–651. doi: 10.1037/0033-295X.102.4.627

de Jong, M., Verhoeven, M., and van Baar, A. L. (2012). School outcome, cognitive functioning, and behaviour problems in moderate and late preterm children and adults: a review. *Semin. Fetal Neonatal Med.* 17, 163–169. doi: 10.1016/j.siny.2012.02.003

Duffy, C. J., and Wurtz, R. H. (1991). Sensitivity of MST neurons to optic flow stimuli. II. Mechanisms of response selectivity revealed by small-field stimuli. *J. Neurophysiol.* 65, 1346–1359.

Fajen, B. R. (2005). Perceiving possibilities for action: on the necessity of calibration and perceptual learning for the visual guidance of action. *Perception* 34, 717–740. doi: 10.1068/p5405

Fajen, B. R. (2007). Affordance-based control of visually guided action. *Ecol. Psychol.* 19, 383–410. doi: 10.1080/10407410701557877

Fajen, B. R. (2013). Guiding locomotion in complex, dynamic environments. *Front. Behav. Neurosci.* 7:85. doi: 10.3389/fnbeh.2013.00085

Fajen, B. R., Parade, M. S., and Matthis, J. S. (2013). Humans perceive object motion in world coordinates during obstacle avoidance. *J. Vis.* 13, 1–13. doi: 10.1167/13.8.25

Fajen, B. R., and Warren, W. H. (2007). Behavioral dynamics of intercepting a moving target. *Exp. Brain Res.* 180, 303–319. doi: 10.1007/s00221-007-0859-6

Ghose, K., Horiuchi, T. K., Krishnaprasad, P. S., and Moss, C. F. (2006). Echolocating bats use a nearly time-optimal strategy to intercept prey. *PLoS Biol.* 4:e108. doi: 10.1371/journal.pbio.0040108

Gibson, J. J. (1966). *The Senses Considered as Perceptual Systems.* Boston, MA: Houghton-Mifflin.

Gibson, J. J. (1979). *The Ecological Approach to Visual Perception.* Hillsdale, NJ: Lawrence Erlbaum Associates.

Gilmore, R. O., Baker, T. J., and Grobman, K. H. (2004). Stability in young infants' discrimination of optic flow. *Dev. Psychol.* 40, 259–270. doi: 10.1037/0012-1649.40.2.259

Gilmore, R. O., Hou, C., Pettet, M. W., and Norcia, A. M. (2007). Development of cortical responses to optic flow. *Vis. Neurosci.* 24, 845–856. doi: 10.1017/s0952523807070769

Gredebäck, G., and von Hofsten, C. (2004). Infants' evolving representations of object motion during occlusion: a longitudinal study of 6- to 12-month-old infants. *Infancy* 6, 165–184. doi: 10.1207/s15327078in0602_2

Greenlee, M. W. (2000). Human cortical areas underlying the perception of optic flow: brain imaging studies. *Int. Rev. Neurobiol.* 44, 269–292. doi: 10.1016/S0074-7742(08)60746-1

Grieve, P. G., Emerson, R. G., Fifer, W. P., Isler, J. R., and Stark, R. I. (2003). Spatial correlation of the infant and adult electroencephalogram. *Clin. Neurophysiol.* 114, 1594–1608. doi: 10.1016/S1388-2457(03)00122-6

Grönqvist, H., Brodd, K. S., and Rosander, K. (2011). Development of smooth pursuit eye movements in very prematurely born infants: the low-risk subgroup. *Acta Paediatr.* 100, 5–11. doi: 10.1111/j.1651-2227.2011.02247.x

Hammarrenger, B., Roy, M.-S., Ellemberg, D., Labrosse, M., Orquin, J., Lippe, S., et al. (2007). Developmental delay and magnocellular visual pathway function in very-low-birthweight preterm infants. *Dev. Med. Child Neurol.* 49, 28–33. doi: 10.1017/s0012162207000084.x

Heinrich, S. P., Renkl, A. E., and Bach, M. (2005). Pattern specificity of human visual motion processing. *Vision Res.* 45, 2137–2143. doi: 10.1016/j.visres.2005.02.008

Herrmann, C. S., Fründ, I., and Lenz, D. (2010). Human gamma-band activity: a review on cognitive and behavioral correlates and network models. *Neurosci. Biobehav. Rev.* 34, 981–992. doi: 10.1016/j.neubiorev.2009.09.001

Herrmann, C. S., and Mecklinger, A. (2001). Gamma activity in human EEG is related to highspeed memory comparisons during object selective attention. *Vis. cogn.* 8, 593–608. doi: 10.1080/13506280143000142

Higgins, C. I., Campos, J. J., and Kermoian, R. (1996). Effect of self-produced locomotion on infant postural compensation to optic flow. *Dev. Psychol.* 32, 836–841. doi: 10.1037/0012-1649.32.5.836

Hoechstetter, K., Bornfleth, H., Weckesser, D., Ille, N., Berg, P., and Scherg, M. (2004). BESA source coherence: a new method to study cortical oscillatory coupling. *Brain Topogr.* 16, 233–238. doi: 10.1023/B:BRAT.0000032857.55223.5d

Hollingworth, A., Richard, A. M., and Luck, S. J. (2008). Understanding the function of visual short-term memory: transsaccadic memory, object correspondence, and gaze correction. *J. Exp. Psychol.* 137, 163–181. doi: 10.1037/0096-3445.137.1.163

Holth, M., van der Weel, F. R., and van der Meer, A. L. H. (2013). Combining findings from gaze and electroencephalography recordings to study timing in a visual tracking task. *Neuroreport* 24, 968–972. doi: 10.1097/WNR.0000000000000020

Hoogenboom, N., Schoffelen, J. M., Oostenveld, R., Parkes, L. M., and Fries, P. (2006). Localizing human visual gamma-band activity in frequency, time and space. *Neuroimage* 29, 764–773. doi: 10.1016/j.neuroimage.2005.08.043

Huppi, P. S., Maier, S. E., Peled, S., Zientara, G. P., Barnes, P. D., Jolesz, F. A., et al. (1998). Microstructural development of human newborn cerebral white matter assessed *in vivo* by diffusion tensor magnetic resonance imaging. *Pediatr. Res.* 44, 584–590. doi: 10.1203/00006450-199810000-00019

Jacobs, D. M., and Michaels, C. F. (2006). Lateral interception I: operative optical variables, attunement, and calibration. *J. Exp. Psychol. Hum. Percept. Perform.* 32, 443–458. doi: 10.1037/0096-1523.32.2.443

Jacobs, D. M., Runeson, S., and Michaels, C. F. (2001). Learning to visually perceive the relative mass of colliding balls in globally and locally constrained task ecologies. *J. Exp. Psychol. Hum. Percept. Perform.* 27, 1019–1038. doi: 10.1037/0096-1523.27.5.1019

James, K. H., and Swain, S. N. (2011). Only self-generated actions create sensori-motor systems in the developing brain. *Dev. Sci.* 14, 673–678. doi: 10.1111/j.1467-7687.2010.01011.x

Johnson, S. P., Amso, D., and Slemmer, J. A. (2003). Development of object concepts in infancy: evidence for early learning in an eye-tracking paradigm. *Proc. Natl. Acad. Sci. U.S.A.* 100, 10568–10573. doi: 10.1073/pnas.1630655100

Jonsson, B., and von Hofsten, C. (2003). Infants' ability to track and reach for temporarily occluded objects. *Dev. Sci.* 6, 86–99. doi: 10.1111/1467-7687.00258

Jouen, F., Lepecq, J.-C., Gapenne, O., and Bertenthal, B. I. (2000). Optic flow sensitivity in neonates. *Infant Behav. Dev.* 23, 271–284. doi: 10.1016/S0163-6383(01)00044-3

Kahana, M. J., Seelig, D., and Madsen, J. R. (2001). Theta returns. *Curr. Opin. Neurobiol.* 11, 739–744. doi: 10.1016/S0959-4388(01)00278-1

Kayed, N. S., Farstad, H., and van der Meer, A. L. H. (2008). Preterm infants' timing strategies to optical collisions. *Early Hum. Dev.* 84, 381–388. doi: 10.1016/j.earlhumdev.2007.10.006

Kayed, N. S., and van der Meer, A. (2000). Timing strategies used in defensive blinking to optical collisions in 5- to 7-month-old infants. *Infant Behav. Dev.* 23, 253–270. doi: 10.1016/S0163-6383(01)00043-1

Kayed, N. S., and van der Meer, A. (2007). Infants' timing strategies to optical collisions: a longitudinal study. *Infant Behav. Dev.* 30, 50–59. doi: 10.1016/j.infbeh.2006.11.001

Kayed, N. S., and van der Meer, A. L. H. (2009). A longitudinal study of prospective control in catching by full- term and preterm infants. *Exp. Brain Res.* 194, 245–258. doi: 10.1007/s00221-008-1692-2

Khader, P. H., Jost, K., Ranganath, C., and Rosler, F. (2010). Theta and alpha oscillations during working-memory maintenance predict successful long-term memory encoding. *Neurosci. Lett.* 468, 339–343. doi: 10.1016/j.neulet.2009.11.028

Klaver, P., Marcar, V., and Martin, E. (2011). Neurodevelopment of the visual system in typically developing children. *Prog. Brain Res.* 189, 113–136. doi: 10.1016/B978-0-444-53884-0.00021-X

Klimesch, W., Sauseng, P., and Hanslmayr, S. (2007). EEG alpha oscillations: the inhibition – timing hypothesis. *Brain Res. Rev.* 3, 63–88. doi: 10.1016/j.brainresrev.2006.06.003

Lachaux, J., George, N., Tallon-Baudry, C., Martinerie, J., Hugueville, L., Minotti, L., et al. (2005). The many faces of the gamma band response to complex visual stimuli. *Neuroimage* 25, 491–501. doi: 10.1016/j.neuroimage.2004.11.052

Lee, D. N. (1976). A theory of visual control of braking based on information about time-to-collision. *Perception* 5, 437–459. doi: 10.1068/p050437

Lee, D. N. (1993). "Body-environment coupling," in *The Perceived Self: Ecological and Interpersonal Sources of Self-Knowledge*, ed U. Neisser (Cambridge: Cambridge University Press), 43–67.

Lee, D. N. (1998). Guiding movement by coupling taus. *Ecol. Psychol.* 10, 221–250. doi: 10.1080/10407413.1998.9652683

Lee, D. N. (2009). General tau theory: evolution to date. *Perception* 38, 837–850. doi: 10.1068/pmklee

Lee, D. N., Georgopoulos, A. P., Clark, M. J. O., Craig, C., and Port, N. L. (2001). Guiding contact by coupling the taus of gaps. *Exp. Brain Res.* 139, 151–159. doi: 10.1007/s002210100725

Lejeune, L., Anderson, D. I., Campos, J. J., Witherington, D. C., Uchiyama, I., and Barbu-Roth, M. (2006). Responsiveness to terrestrial optic flow in infancy: does locomotor experience play a role? *Hum. Mov. Sci.* 25, 4–17. doi: 10.1016/j.humov.2005.10.004

Lenoir, M., Musch, E., Janssens, M., Thiery, E., and Uyttenhove, J. (1999). Intercepting moving objects during self-motion. *J. Mot. Behav.* 31, 55–67. doi: 10.1080/00222899909601891

Loenneker, T., Klaver, P., Bucher, K., Lichtensteiger, J., Imfeld, A., and Martin, E. (2011). Microstructural development: organizational differences of the fiber architecture between children and adults in dorsal and ventral visual streams. *Hum. Brain Mapp.* 32, 935–946. doi: 10.1002/hbm.21080

Mewes, A. U. J., Hüppi, P. S., Als, H., Rybicki, F. J., Inder, T. E., McAnulty, G. B., et al. (2006). Regional brain development in serial magnetic resonance imaging of low-risk preterm infants. *Pediatrics* 118, 23–33. doi: 10.1542/peds.2005-2675

Michaels, C. F., Zeinstra, E. B., and Oudejans, R. R. D. (2001). Information and action in punching a falling ball. *Q. J. Exp. Psychol. A* 54, 69–93. doi: 10.1080/02724980042000039

Middlebrooks, J. C., and Green, D. M. (1991). Sound localization by human listeners. *Annu. Rev. Psychol.* 42, 135–159. doi: 10.1146/annurev.ps.42.020191.001031

Milner, A. D., and Goodale, M. A. (2008). Two visual systems re-viewed. *Neuropsychologia* 46, 774–785. doi: 10.1016/j.neuropsychologia.2007.10.005

Morrongiello, B. A. (1988). Infants' localization of sounds along two spatial dimensions: horizontal and vertical axes. *Infant Behav. Dev.* 11, 127–143. doi: 10.1016/S0163-6383(88)80001-8

Munakata, Y. (2001). Graded representations in behavioral dissociations. *Trends Cogn. Sci.* 5, 309–315. doi: 10.1016/S1364-6613(00)01682-X

Náñez, J. (1988). Perception of impending collision in 3- to 6-week-old human infants. *Infant Behav. Dev.* 11, 447–463.

Orban de Xivry, J.-J., and Lefèvre, P. (2007). Saccades and pursuit: two outcomes of a single sensorimotor process. *J. Physiol.* 584, 11–23. doi: 10.1113/jphysiol.2007.139881

Orekhova, E. V., Stroganova, T. A., Posikera, I. N., and Elam, M. (2006). EEG theta rhythm in infants and preschool children. *Clin. Neurophysiol.* 117, 1047–1062. doi: 10.1016/j.clinph.2005.12.027

Paus, T., Collins, D. L., Evans, A. C., Leonard, G., Pike, B., and Zijdenbos, A. (2001). Maturation of white matter in the human brain: a review of magnetic resonance studies. *Brain Res. Bull.* 54, 255–266. doi: 10.1016/S0361-9230(00)00434-2

Pfurtscheller, G., and Lopes da Silva, F. H. (1999). Event-related EEG/MEG synchronization and desynchronization: basic principles. *Clin. Neurophysiol.* 110, 1842–1857. doi: 10.1016/S1388-2457(99)00141-8

Piaget, J. (1954). *The Construction of Reality in the Child*. New York, NY: Basic Books.

Probst, T., Plendl, H., Paulus, W., Wist, E. R., and Scherg, M. (1993). Identification of the visual motion area (area V5) in the human brain by dipole source analysis. *Exp. Brain Res.* 93, 345–351. doi: 10.1007/bf00228404

Raudies, F., and Gilmore, R. O. (2014). Visual motion priors differ for infants and mothers. *Neural Comput.* 26, 2652–2668. doi: 10.1162/NECO_a_00645

Raudies, F., Gilmore, R. O., Kretch, K. S., Franchak, J. M., and Adolph, K. E. (2012). "Understanding the development of motion processing by characterizing optic flow experienced by infants and their mothers," in *IEEE International Conference on Development and Learning and Epigenetic Robotics* (San Diego, CA).

Rosander, K., Nystrom, P., Gredeback, G., and von Hofsten, C. (2007). Cortical processing of visual motion in young infants. *Vision Res.* 47, 1614–1623. doi: 10.1016/j.visres.2007.03.004

Rosander, K., and von Hofsten, C. (2002). Development of gaze tracking of small and large objects. *Exp. Brain Res.* 146, 257–264. doi: 10.1007/s00221-002-1161-2

Rosander, K., and von Hofsten, C. (2004). Infants' emerging ability to represent occluded object motion. *Cognition* 91, 1–22. doi: 10.1016/S0010-0277(03)00166-5

Runeson, S., and Vedeler, D. (1993). The indispensability of precollision kinematics in the visual perception of relative mass. *Percept. Psychophys.* 53, 617–632. doi: 10.3758/BF03211738

Saby, J. N., and Marshall, P. J. (2012). The utility of EEG band power analysis in the study of infancy and early childhood. *Dev. Neuropsychol.* 37, 253–273. doi: 10.1080/87565641.2011.614663

Santos, M. J., Kanekar, N., and Aruin, A. S. (2010). The role of anticipatory postural adjustments in compensatory control of posture: electromyographic analysis. *J. Electromyogr. Kinesiol.* 20, 388–397. doi: 10.1016/j.jelekin.2009.06.006

Schlag, J., and Schlag-Rey, M. (2002). Through the eye, slowly: delays and localization errors in the visual system. *Nat. Rev. Neurosci.* 3, 191–215. doi: 10.1038/nrn750

Shirai, N., and Yamaguchi, M. K. (2010). How do infants utilize radial optic flow for their motor actions?: a review of behavioral and neural studies. *Jpn. Psychol. Res.* 52, 78–90. doi: 10.1111/j.1468-5884.2010.00426.x

Smith, M. R. H., Flach, J. M., Dittman, S. M., and Stanard, T. (2001). Monocular optical constraints on collision control. *J. Exp. Psychol. Hum. Percept. Perform.* 27, 395–410. doi: 10.1037/0096-1523.27.2.395

Spencer, L. M., and van der Meer, A. L. H. (2012). TauG-guidance of dynamic balance control during gait initiation across adulthood. *Gait Posture* 36, 523–526. doi: 10.1016/j.gaitpost.2012.05.017

Taylor, N. M., Jakobson, L. S., Maurer, D., and Lewis, T. L. (2009). Differential vulnerability of global motion, global form, and biological motion processing in full-term and preterm children. *Neuropsychologia* 47, 2766–2778. doi: 10.1016/j.neuropsychologia.2009.06.001

Turvey, M. T. (1992). Affordances and prospective control: an outline of the ontology. *Ecol. Psychol.* 4, 173–187. doi: 10.1207/s15326969eco0403_3

Twenhöfel, A., Holth, M., van der Weel, F. R., and van der Meer, A. L. H. (2013). "Changing behaviour/changing brain activity: gaze control and brain development in 4- to 12-month-old infants," in *Studies in Perception and Action XII*, eds T. J. Davis, P. Passos, M. Dicks, and J. A. Weast-Knapp (New York, NY: Psychology Press), 84–87.

van der Meer, A. L. H. (1997). Visual guidance of passing under a barrier. *Early Dev. Parent.* 6, 149–157.

van der Meer, A. L. H., Agyei, S. B., Vilhelmsen, K., Zotcheva, E., Slinning, R., and van der Weel, F. R. (2015). "The development of visual motion perception in infancy with high-density EEG," in *Poster Presented at the 21st Annual Meeting of the Organization for Human Brain Mapping* (Honolulu, HI). Available online at: https://ww4.aievolution.com/hbm1501/index.cfm?do=abs.viewAbs&abs=1405

van der Meer, A. L. H., Fallet, G., and van der Weel, F. R. (2008a). Perception of structured optic flow and random visual motion in infants and adults: a high-density EEG study. *Exp. Brain Res.* 186, 493–502. doi: 10.1007/s00221-007-1251-2

van der Meer, A. L. H., Ramstad, M., and van der Weel, F. R. (2008b). Choosing the shortest way to mum: auditory guided rotation in 6- to 9-month-old infants. *Infant Behav. Dev.* 31, 207–216. doi: 10.1016/j.infbeh.2007.10.007

van der Meer, A. L. H., Svantesson, M., and van der Weel, F. R. (2012). Longitudinal study of looming in infants with high-density EEG. *Dev. Neurosci.* 34, 488–501. doi: 10.1159/000345154

van der Meer, A. L. H., and van der Weel, F. R. (2011). "Auditory guided arm and whole body movements in young infants," in *Advances in Sound Localization*, ed P. Strumillo (Vienna: InTech), 297–314.

van der Meer, A. L. H., van der Weel, F. R., and Lee, D. N. (1994). Prospective control in catching by infants. *Perception* 23, 287–302. doi: 10.1068/p230287

van der Meer, A. L. H., van der Weel, F. R., Lee, D. N., Laing, I. A., and Lin, J. P. (1995). Development of prospective control of catching moving objects in preterm at-risk infants. *Dev. Med. Child Neurol.* 37, 145–158. doi: 10.1111/j.1469-8749.1995.tb11984.x

van der Weel, F. R., Craig, C., and van der Meer, A. L. H. (2007). "The rate of change of tau," in *Closing the Gap: The Scientific Writings of David N. Lee*, eds G. J. Pepping, and M. A. Grealy (London: Lawrence Erlbaum Associates), 305–365.

van der Weel, F. R., and van der Meer, A. L. H. (2009). Seeing it coming: infants' brain responses to looming danger. *Naturwissenschaften* 96, 1385–1391. doi: 10.1007/s00114-009-0585-y

van Wermeskerken, M., van der Kamp, J., Te Velde, A. F., Valero-Garcia, A. V., Hoozemans, M. J. M., and Savelsbergh, G. J. P. (2011). Anticipatory reaching of seven- to eleven-month-old infants in occlusion situations. *Infant Behav. Dev.* 34, 45–54. doi: 10.1016/j.infbeh.2010.09.005

Vilhelmsen, K., van der Weel, F. R., and van der Meer, A. L. H. (2015a). A high-density EEG study of differences between three high speeds of simulated forward motion from optic flow in adult participants. *Front. Syst. Neurosci.* 9:146. doi: 10.3389/fnsys.2015.00146

Vilhelmsen, K., van der Weel, F. R., and van der Meer, A. L. H. (2015b). "Development of optic flow perception in infants: a high-density EEG study of speed and direction," in *Studies in Perception and Action XIII*, eds J. A. Weast-Knapp, M. L. Malone, and D. H. Abney (New York, NY: Psychology Press), 157–160.

von Hofsten, C. (1993). Prospective control: a basic aspect of action development. *Hum. Dev.* 36, 253–270. doi: 10.1159/000278212

von Hofsten, C., and Rosander, K. (1996). The development of gaze control and predictive tracking in young infants. *Vision Res.* 36, 81–96. doi: 10.1016/0042-6989(95)00054-4

von Hofsten, C., Vishton, P., Spelke, E. S., Feng, Q., and Rosander, K. (1998). Predictive action in infancy: tracking and reaching for moving objects. *Cognition* 67, 255–285. doi: 10.1016/S0010-0277(98)00029-8

Warren, P. A., and Rushton, S. K. (2007). Perception of object trajectory: parsing retinal motion into self and object movement components. *J. Vis.* 7, 2.1–11. doi: 10.1167/7.11.2

Warren, P. A., and Rushton, S. K. (2009). Optic flow processing for the assessment of object movement during ego movement. *Curr. Biol.* 19, 1555–1560. doi: 10.1016/j.cub.2009.07.057

Warren, W. H., and Whang, S. (1987). Visual guidance of walking through apertures: body-scaled information for affordances. *J. Exp. Psychol. Hum. Percept. Perform.* 13, 371–383. doi: 10.1037/0096-1523.13.3.371

Witherington, D. C., Hofsten, C., Rosander, K., Robinette, A., Woollacott, M. H., and Bertenthal, B. I. (2002). The development of anticipatory postural adjustments in infancy. *Infancy* 3, 495–517. doi: 10.1207/S15327078IN0304_05

Yilmaz, E. H., and Warren, W. H. (1995). Visual control of braking: a test of the?tau hypothesis. *J. Exp. Psychol. Hum. Percept. Perform.* 21, 996–1014. doi: 10.1037/0096-1523.21.5.996

Conflict of Interest Statement: The authors declare that the research was conducted in the absence of any commercial or financial relationships that could be construed as a potential conflict of interest.

The reviewer GR and handling Editor DC declared their shared affiliation, and the handling Editor states that the process nevertheless met the standards of a fair and objective review.

Measuring Individual Differences in Decision Biases: Methodological Considerations

Balazs Aczel[1]*, Bence Bago[2], Aba Szollosi[1], Andrei Foldes[1] and Bence Lukacs[3]

[1] Institute of Psychology, Eotvos Lorand University, Budapest, Hungary, [2] Paris Descartes University, Paris, France, [3] Corvinus University of Budapest, Budapest, Hungary

Individual differences in people's susceptibility to heuristics and biases (HB) are often measured by multiple-bias questionnaires consisting of one or a few items for each bias. This research approach relies on the assumptions that (1) different versions of a decision bias task measure are interchangeable as they measure the same cognitive failure; and (2) that some combination of these tasks measures the same underlying construct. Based on these assumptions, in Study 1 we developed two versions of a new decision bias survey for which we modified 13 HB tasks to increase their comparability, construct validity, and the participants' motivation. The analysis of the responses ($N = 1279$) showed weak internal consistency within the surveys and a great level of discrepancy between the extracted patterns of the underlying factors. To explore these inconsistencies, in Study 2 we used three original examples of HB tasks for each of seven biases. We created three decision bias surveys by allocating one version of each HB task to each survey. The participants' responses ($N = 527$) showed a similar pattern as in Study 1, questioning the assumption that the different examples of the HB tasks are interchangeable and that they measure the same underlying construct. These results emphasize the need to understand the domain-specificity of cognitive biases as well as the effect of the wording of the cover story and the response mode on bias susceptibility before employing them in multiple-bias questionnaires.

Keywords: decision making, heuristics and biases, individual differences, decision biases, multiple-bias questionnaires

Edited by:
Richard Rende,
Brown University, USA

Reviewed by:
Jennifer Joy-Gaba,
Virginia Commonwealth University,
USA
Sabina Kleitman,
The University of Sydney, Australia

*Correspondence:
Balazs Aczel
aczel.balazs@ppk.elte.hu

Specialty section:
This article was submitted to
Personality and Social Psychology,
a section of the journal
Frontiers in Psychology

INTRODUCTION

The heuristics and biases (HB) literature has produced a wide collection of tasks to demonstrate the systematic deviation of people's thinking from rational thought. These bias-assessment tasks are frequently employed in the field of judgment and decision making to study differences between and within groups and individuals. Measuring individual differences in the susceptibility to decision biases has become a targeted research question since it was suggested that there is an unexplored variance in rational thinking independent of cognitive abilities and intelligence (Stanovich and West, 1998, 2001; Stanovich, 1999). This notion bears relevance to the question of whether intelligence tests encompass all important aspects of rational thinking (Stanovich, 2012), or rather rationality deserves an additional assessment tool (Stanovich et al., 2011). A methodology that allows for the exploration of individual differences in cognitive biases can also help us understand how susceptible people are to the individual decision biases; whether there are independent factors behind these biases; and how effective certain debiasing methods are. Experimental settings devised for studying these questions often attempt to include a wide range of these tasks to test them in a within-subject design. The format and structure of the HB tasks, however, vary greatly, as they have been developed independently, and judgment and decision-making researchers tend to select tasks for habitual rather than empirical reasons. Nevertheless, when analyzed together, several methodological issues should be taken into consideration. In this paper, we highlight a list of methodological challenges that should be faced when measuring several HB tasks together with the aim of assessing the degree of susceptibility on an individual level, or when using performance measures of these tasks as an indicator of their shared underlying factors.

Individualized Scores

The assumption that the HB tasks share some underlying cognitive properties prompts researchers to create a composite score from the performance measures of the individual tasks (e.g., Bruine de Bruin et al., 2007; Toplak et al., 2007). Similarly, when studying the association of performance on HB tasks with other psychological factors, within-subject design is required where the performance of the participants is evaluated individually. Unfortunately, when evaluating the traditional HB tasks it is not always straightforward whether the given person violated a normative rule or not in his or her decision. Sometimes the bias can be assessed only in comparison to another decision or on a group level. From this aspect, we find that the HB tasks that measure individual biases fall into three categories.

Type-A: In this type of task, a single question is diagnostic to the person's susceptibility to violating the given normative rule. For example, in the standard tasks of the Conjunction fallacy (Tversky and Kahneman, 1983), or the Base-rate neglect (Bar-Hillel, 1980) certain answers always indicate suboptimal reasoning. For measurement purposes, sometimes the bias is calculated from an amalgamation of several versions of the question (e.g., overconfidence, Lichtenstein and Fischhoff, 1977).

Type-B: For these tasks, the answer to the given question can be regarded as indicating the person's decision bias only in relation to another decision of the individual. Therefore, the task is made of two questions in a within-subjects design. For example, the Framing effect is sometimes measured on the level of the individual by comparing the answers given to two differently framed versions of the same question within the same questionnaire (e.g., Resistance to framing in Toplak et al., 2014).

Type-C: This type of task also assesses the presence of bias by two questions, but on a group level in between-subjects design. For example, the Status Quo bias is typically studied in a way that two groups would receive the same question, but one group would also know that one of the options is the current state of affairs (e.g., Samuelson and Zeckhauser, 1988).

A main challenge for measuring individual differences with HB questions is to reconstruct Type-C tasks into Type-A or Type-B designs. For example, the Hindsight bias is often measured in two groups. In a typical hindsight bias experiment, both groups receive descriptions of a number of events, each with a few possible outcomes and the participants are asked to indicate

the likelihood of the given outcomes. For one group, however, the outcomes that actually occurred are indicated. The estimate of this group (the hindsight probability estimate) is compared to the estimate of the foresight group, which was not told about the actual outcomes. Typically, the mean estimate of the hindsight group is higher than the foresight group (Christensen-Szalanski and Willham, 1991), indicating an effect of outcome knowledge in the participants' judgments. Although this experimental design provides a sensible arrangement for the demonstration of the hindsight bias, it is unable to offer a measure for the purpose of individual difference analyses. A noteworthy attempt to provide an individualized score for Hindsight bias can be found in a study conducted by Stanovich and West (1998). In Experiment 4, they asked the participants to read two forms of 35 general knowledge questions. For the first form of questions, the correct answers were not indicated and they were asked to indicate their confidence in their responses. For the second set of questions, the correct answers were indicated and they were asked to indicate the probability that they would have answered the questions correctly. The forms were counter-balanced and the scores on the two forms were standardized based on their distributions. From these measures, the authors created an individualized hindsight score by subtracting for each individual the percentage of their correct responses on the knowledge calibration test from their percentage estimate on the hindsight test. This is a notable attempt to create a Type-B from a Type-C HB task, yet taking a closer look it might not satisfy expectations. The degree of noise on one of the forms does not necessarily correspond with the degree of noise on the other form, as an individual might actually know the answers on the hindsight form and be less confident about the answers on the foresight form. Therefore, this attempt to solve the Type-C problem does not provide the score necessary for individual difference analyses. Indices of group performance are not adequate to serve as reference points for evaluating rationality at the level of the individual.

A more promising technique to solve the Type-C problem is asking the two versions of the question from the same people, instead of testing them in two groups. This solution can be applied to the Hindsight bias by asking the participants to indicate a range of possible values for a question (Hardt and Pohl, 2003) or to give a confidence rating for their answer (Teovanović et al., 2015). Then, in a later phase, they have to recall these estimates immediately after receiving feedback for the initial question. The Framing effect has also been shown to be observable in a within-subject design (Frisch, 1993). Here, researchers prefer to place the two versions of the questions in distant parts of the questionnaire (e.g., Parker and Fischhoff, 2005), or insert a longer delay between them (e.g., 1 week in Levin et al., 2002) to decrease the effect of the memory of the first question on the second one. With higher resemblance between the two versions of the questions, it becomes more difficult to camouflage the link between the two items. In fact, the framing effect is consistently less prevalent in within-subjects comparisons than in between-subjects design (Gambara and Piñon, 2005).

Another difficulty in adapting Type-C tasks to Type-B formats occurs in cases where the effect of the current state of affairs is measured. For example, one typical way to demonstrate the status quo bias is to inform only one of two groups about the current state of affairs regarding the same decision situation. In consecutive presentation of the two questions in a within-subject arrangement, either the neutral or the status quo description must come first, and thus the results can become biased. When the neutral question precedes, the decision on this question can become the status quo; when the status quo question comes first, it can affect the interpretation of the neutral description coming later. Roca et al. (2006) described a different approach to test within-subject status quo effect. They asked the participants to choose between different ambiguous gambles where the proportion of the number of balls of two colors in the urn was unknown and they won if they drew the ball of their chosen color. Before playing the gamble, they were offered an opportunity to exchange those gambles for their non-ambiguous counterparts. This decision was contrasted with a consecutive neutral context where the participants had to choose between ambiguous and unambiguous gambles to play. Within-subject status quo bias was defined by the behavior of retaining the ambiguous gamble in the first context, but choosing the unambiguous gamble in the neutral condition. Along with demonstrating the effect of status quo bias, a strong tendency of the participants was observed to choose consistently between the contexts (65–92% of the decisions), probably due to the consecutive presentation of the two situations.

In summary, the adaption of Type-C questions to Type-B tasks is a persistent challenge for measuring individual differences in HB tasks. An added difficulty is that even when this adaption is successful people are more immune to violating the principle of invariance (Tversky and Kahneman, 1986) and tend to choose consistently (LeBoeuf and Shafir, 2003). In fact, empirical analyses show that the within-subject effect is much weaker than the between-subject effect when the expectation of decision consistency may override their default answer (Gambara and Piñon, 2005; Roca et al., 2006).

Construct Validity

Another requirement for establishing the degree to which individuals are biased in their decisions is that the incorrect answers should be due to the given cognitive bias that the question was devised to measure. In the related literature, we found surprisingly numerous cases where not all of the incorrect questions are good examples of the studied bias.

For example, West et al. (2008) describe their Gambler's Fallacy task and its scoring such as follows (pp. 932–933):

> When playing slot machines, people win something about 1 in every 10 times. Lori, however, has just won on her first three plays. What are her chances of winning the next time she plays? Choose the best answer.

The problem was followed by the choices: (a) She has better than 1 chance in 10 of winning on her next play, (b) She has <1 chance in 10 of winning on her next play, (c) She has a 1 chance in 10 that she will win on her next play. The correct response of c was scored as 1, while any other response incorrect and scored as 0.

In this example, response (b) would indicate that the participant followed the pattern predicted by the Gambler's Fallacy: if winning happened more frequently than normal then we should expect less than normal frequency to follow. However, response (a), while being incorrect, is more similar to what the hot-hand illusion (Gilovich et al., 1985) would predict, since a sequence of success is followed by increased likelihood of success. Consequently, 0 score on this question is not a valid indicator of the studied effect. Methodological problems remain present when researchers define which concrete, incorrect response would indicate the presence of the given bias. For example, Toplak et al. (2011) measured the Sunk Cost effect in two parts (p. 1289.):

> "In the first part, participants are told to imagine that they are staying in a hotel room, and they have just paid $6.95 to see a movie on pay TV. Then they are told that they are bored 5 min into the movie and that the movie seems pretty bad. They are then asked whether they would continue to watch the movie or switch to another channel. In the second part, the scenario is analogous, except that they have not had to pay for the movie. They are asked again whether they would continue to watch the movie or switch to another channel. Responses were scored as correct if the participant chose consistently across the two situations (either continuing to watch the movie in both cases, or switching to another channel in both cases), and as incorrect if the participant displayed a sunk cost (that is, continuing to watch the movie if it had been paid for but not if it was free)."

In this example, out of the four possible choices of the participant, two were scored as correct, but only one of the two remaining possible choices was scored as incorrect, the one that indicates the effect of Sunk Cost. Nevertheless, the possible case when the participant would continue to watch the movie if it hasn't been paid for, but would not watch it if it has been paid for was not scored as either correct or incorrect. It is unstated how these items were analyzed, but when the aim is to create a composite score from the HB tasks then this kind of scoring becomes problematic. Scoring these responses as 0 or disregarding the item from the composite score would both bias its validity. Discarding the participant's data from the analysis if he or she selects this combination of choices would be impractical for the aim of creating comparable within-subjects measures.

Comparability

Variation in susceptibility to different biases is a recurring question of the decision-making research program (Blais and Weber, 2001; Toplak et al., 2011). To compare the degree of susceptibility in the different biases, we have to be able to assume that the response mode of the tasks does not bias the sensitivity of the task to detect the corresponding bias, so that the chance of giving correct (and incorrect) responses for the different tasks is the same. This criterion is mostly never satisfied in studies testing HB tasks together. The chance of correct choice can be as high as 50% where the participants can choose from only between two options (e.g., the Base-rate neglect problem in Toplak et al., 2011), but in the case of open questions, this chance can be also infinitely low (e.g., the Gambler's fallacy problem in Toplak et al.,

2011). Higher chance for correct choice decreases the sensitivity of the question to measure the given bias and creates a confound when studying the variance in susceptibility among the biases. In addition, a composite score created from tasks with unadjusted sensitivity levels can underestimate the effect of less sensitive HB tasks.

Motivation

One of the criticisms that the HB research program received over the course of years is that the suboptimal performance on the cognitive bias tasks might be partly due to participants being under-motivated to allocate the necessary cognitive effort to solving the questions (Klein, 1999). In fact, one assumption behind reasoning models is that humans are "cognitive misers" (Simon, 1955; Evans and Stanovich, 2013): they are reluctant to assign effort to a task, unless it is important to them. Financial incentives were found to achieve only limited improvement in performance (Camerer and Hogarth, 1999), while rather the ecological validity of the questions increased interest in the issue. From an ecological validity perspective, HB tasks are different from real life decisions since they are made in laboratories about often artificial questions or hypothetical situations (Gigerenzer et al., 1999; Klein, 1999). While it is hard to link performance to real-life consequences (other than payment) when using questionnaires, the descriptions of the questions rarely indicate that the outcome of the decision would have, even fictional, critical consequences for or relevance to the participant's personal aims.

Aim of the Study

This study represents an attempt to increase the validity and reduce the inconsistency of multiple-bias questionnaires. We aimed to test whether different versions of the same bias task are interchangeable. Within-subject arrangements cannot exclude that one task or the answer to that would not make people answer similarly on other analogous questions, so we tested this assumption in a between-subject design. We created two versions of the same survey and tested each with a random group of people. Next, we analyzed the psychometric properties of the surveys, and we compared the correspondence between the measured susceptibility to the individual biases with their performance on the Cognitive Reflection Test (CRT; Frederick, 2005), as it is a potent predictor of performance on HB tasks (Toplak et al., 2011). By these correlations and by a Factor Analysis we aimed to assess the coherence within and the consistency between the bias surveys.

STUDY 1

Methods

Participants

One thousand two hundred and seventy nine participants (697 female) were recruited, comprising mostly university students, native speakers of Hungarian with a mean age of 22.96 years ($SD = 8.14$). Leaders of Hungarian student organizations were asked to circulate a recruiting e-mail on their respective mailing-lists. The e-mail contained a link to the online questionnaire.

TABLE 1 | An example of the adapted changes on the Gambler's Fallacy task.

Original task	Modified task
When playing slot machines, people win something 1 out of every 10 times. Julie, however, just won her first three plays. What are her chances of winning the next time she plays? ___ out of ___	You are responsible for the financial planning of a real estate broking firm Based on past data, your entrusted broker company makes profitable deals in 60% of the cases in the long term They were unsuccessful with their last nine cases. What are the chances that the 10th case will be successful?
[An answer of 1 out of 10 is the normative response and was scored as 1, while any other response was scored as 0.]	(A) 60%; (B) 70%; (C) 80%; (D) 90%
(Toplak et al., 2007, p. 111)	[Correct answer: (A)]

The participants were motivated to take part in the survey by a 50.000 HUF prize (approx. 180 USD) drawn from among those who completed the survey. Participants, who wanted to take part in the lottery, were identified by their e-mail address, which they could provide voluntarily. The research was approved by the institutional ethics committee of Eotvos Lorand University, Hungary.

One hundred two participants' results were excluded from the analysis as their answers clearly indicated that they did not understand the questions or were not motivated to answer sensibly[1]. Missing data were omitted in a pairwise manner.

Materials

Two versions of an HB task battery were administered. Both questionnaires contained the same popularly tested bias-tasks (Anchoring effect, Base-rate neglect, Conjunction fallacy, Covariation detection, Framing effect, Gambler's fallacy, Insensitivity to sample size, Monty Hall problem, Outcome bias, Probability match, Regression to the mean, Relativity bias, Sunk cost fallacy[2]), the only difference between the two versions being the wording of the questions. All testing materials were presented in Hungarian. A pilot test was conducted with volunteers to improve sensitivity and comprehensibility in which they were able to report any issues in the tasks that prevented them from fully understanding the situations. The tasks are available in the Supplementary Materials (Study 1, Extended Methods section and **Table 1**) for both tests.

As the tasks were adapted from the literature, we found it important to put notable emphasis on the issues outlined above, namely comparability, construct validity and motivation. Thus, firstly, the probability of randomly giving the correct answer was fixed at 25% for each question. Secondly, the answer options were constructed so that they measure only

---

[1] The participant's results were excluded from the analysis if their CRT answers clearly indicated that the participant was not motivated to answer sensibly. Practically, for the Bat and Ball problem of the CRT task, we excluded those participants who provided nonsensical answers (such as 55,555, 12,345, or 10,000,000) and retained those who gave the correct, intuitive incorrect answers or anything that an imaginable miscalculation could yield.

[2] Additionally, an Overconfidence bias and a Planning fallacy task were administered, but as they did not satisfy the methodological criteria of having a 25% chance-level of giving a correct answer, they were not included in the analyses.

TABLE 2 | Reliability measures of the HB composite score.

	Split-half	Cronbach's alpha
Test 1	0.38	0.37
Test 2	0.21	0.23

the bias they are supposed to measure. Finally, to increase the participants' motivation to find a good solution to the presented problems, we reframed the traditional HB tasks so that the participants should envisage themselves in the situation of a concrete decision maker where the outcome of the decision would be critical for them. We also decided to place all of the questions in one domain. Among the decision-making domains with probably the most critical outcomes are military, medical, aviation and managerial domains. We speculated that out of these, the situations described in the managerial domain are the most understandable for the widest range of participants. **Table 1** shows an example of the adapted changes on the HB tasks, such as the managerial theme, unified level of chance, and the description of critical situations in order to increase motivation.

Procedure

Participants were assigned one of the two tests via arbitrary sampling. After obtaining informed consent, they were asked to provide basic demographic data. Next, they completed the survey consisting of the HB tasks in a fixed order and the three items of the original CRT (Frederick, 2005). For each HB question, a limit constrained the participant's time to provide a response so that all participants would spend approximately the same amount of time answering the questions without being able to seek external help. To make sure that participants could properly understand the situation, they were first presented with the description with no time-pressure. After they indicated that they understood the situation and were ready continue, the answer options were revealed along with an indication of how much time they have left until they needed to give an answer. The limit ranged between 30 and 70 s based on the results of pilot testing. At the end of the experiment, participants received personal feedback of their results alongside a brief description of each task.

Scoring

For each HB task participants scored either 1 for the correct or 0 for the incorrect answer. Composite score was calculated as the sum of the scores of the HB tasks. CRT tasks were also scored 1 for correct and 0 for incorrect answers. Composite scores for the CRT tasks were calculated the same way as for the HB tasks.

Results
Reliability

Reliability measures showed very low internal consistency for the composite scores on both of the tests (**Table 2**). Both Cronbach's alpha and Split-half reliability measures were below the acceptable level. This low internal consistency questions whether items measure a single unidimensional latent construct.

Factor Analysis

A polynomial Factor Analysis with an oblique (Promax) rotation method, and with a Diagonal Weighted Least Square estimation procedure was conducted on the data, using the psych R package (Revelle, 2014). The two tests were analyzed separately; on the first test the best fitting factor structure was assessed, then an analysis with the same number of factors was conducted on the second test.

As a first step, it was tested whether the data are adequate for Factor Analysis. With regard to Test 1, the Kaiser-Meyer-Olkin factor (KMO; computed on the polychoric correlation matrix) reached an acceptable value, KMO = 0.66, and the Bartlett's test also indicated that the correlation matrix is not an identity matrix, $\chi^2_{(78)} = 620.32$, $p < 0.001$. In Test 2, similar results were observed, with regard to the KMO = 0.62, and to the Bartlett's test, $\chi^2_{(78)} = 746.34$, $p < 0.001$. These results suggested that the data are suitable for Factor Analysis.

In the first analysis, based on the Very Simple Structure criterion the analysis suggested a one-factor model, while a Parallel Analysis suggested a seven-factor model and an eigenvalue analysis suggested a six-factor model. Factor structures, beginning with one factor were examined based on the explained cumulative variances. The five-factor model proved best, as the cumulative variance for the six-factor model was 0.42 compared to 0.41 in the five-factor model. Next, items with lower than 0.3 factor loadings on any of the factors were discarded. As a Heywood case was detected with the five-factor model, the number of factors was decreased to four. For this four-factor structure (**Table 3**), model-fit indices were relatively low, but closer to the acceptable level than the other factor structures, $\chi^2_{(2)} = 8.48$, $p < 0.05$, TLI = 0.82, RMSEA = 0.07 (95% CI [0.00, 0.13]).

In the Factor Analysis of the second test, we observed similar fitting indices, $\chi^2_{(2)} = 6.58$, $p < 0.05$, TLI = 0.81, RMSEA = 0.05 (95% CI [0.00, 0.11]), however, no consistency was found between the factors of the two tests. As **Table 3** indicates, the factor structures of the two tests varied greatly. These results suggest that the wording of the different reasoning problems affects how people interpret and answer the questions. Original item-item correlations and factor correlations can be found in the Supplementary Materials.

Correlation with the CRT

To further investigate the differences between the measured biases, for both tests the correlations between the CRT composite score and each HB task were assessed separately (**Table 4**). The average CRT performance was similar in the groups ($M_{Test1} = 1.37$; $M_{Test2} = 1.27$). The Fisher-exact test[3] showed significantly different correlations in the two tests for Probability match, Base-rate neglect, Insensitivity to sample size, Monty Hall problem, and the Relativity bias.

---

[3]Correlation coefficients were compared using a Fisher r-to-z transformation (http://vassarstats.net/rdiff.html).

TABLE 3 | Results of the exploratory factor analysis for the two tests.

		Factor 1	Factor 2	Factor 3	Factor 4	Communalities
Test 1	Gambler's fallacy	0.00	−0.07	**0.53**	−0.06	0.27
	Sunk cost fallacy	0.15	−0.09	**0.37**	0.17	0.27
	Base-rate neglect	**0.98**	0.09	0.03	−0.01	0.99
	Monty Hall problem	−0.02	0.02	−0.03	**0.86**	0.73
	Insensitivity to sample size	**0.32**	−0.18	−0.06	−0.07	0.12
	Relativity bias	−0.06	0.09	**0.57**	−0.14	0.28
	Outcome bias	0.01	0.00	**0.47**	0.10	0.26
	Anchoring effect	0.09	**0.99**	0.00	0.01	0.99
Test 2	Gambler's fallacy	**0.90**	0.05	0.03	0.00	0.82
	Sunk cost fallacy	0.15	−0.10	0.16	0.24	0.15
	Base-rate neglect	0.10	−0.04	**0.51**	−0.08	0.26
	Monty Hall problem	0.05	**0.99**	−0.01	0.03	0.99
	Insensitivity to sample size	−0.10	−0.12	−0.01	0.17	0.05
	Relativity bias	−0.18	0.20	**0.40**	0.05	0.24
	Outcome bias	−0.01	0.04	−0.08	**0.68**	0.44
	Anchoring effect	−0.01	−0.11	**0.38**	−0.06	0.15

Factor loadings of 0.3 and above are in bold font. Factors with one item loading are presented only for demonstrative purposes.

TABLE 4 | Differences between the two tests in correlation with the CRT for each task.

Tasks	Correlation with the CRT composite		Fisher-exact test
	r (Test 1)	*r* (Test 2)	Z-scores
Anchoring effect	0.13**	0.004	1.85
Base-rate neglect	0.23***	−0.003	3.46***
Conjunction fallacy	−0.03	−0.10*	1.03
Covariation detection	0.05	−0.03	1.17
Framing effect	0.14*	0.05	1.32
Gambler's fallacy	0.11*	0.01	1.46
Insensitivity to sample size	0.11*	−0.04	2.19*
Monty Hall problem	0.19***	0.02	2.51*
Outcome bias	0.23***	0.16**	1.06
Probability match	0.11*	0.24***	−1.96*
Regression to the mean	−0.01	−0.04	0.44
Relativity bias	0.06	−0.09	2.19*
Sunk cost fallacy	0.08	0.14**	−0.89

*p < 0.05; **p < 0.01; ***p < 0.001.

TABLE 5 | Differences in accuracy between the two tests.

	Test 1 (%)	Test 2 (%)	$\chi^2_{(1)}$
Anchoring effect	49.27	76.41	65.61***
Base-rate neglect	41.26	35.90	2.41
Conjunction fallacy	31.99	8.21	76.02***
Covariation detection	23.90	16.98	6.49**
Framing effect	50.10	39.80	8.83**
Gambler's fallacy	34.92	30.98	1.89
Insensitivity to sample size	14.73	13.99	0.04
Monty Hall problem	23.97	22.08	0.33
Outcome bias	34.10	30.61	1.04
Probability match	22.10	43.56	50.85***
Regression to the mean	27.56	16.00	16.51***
Relativity bias	44.89	19.90	59.18***
Sunk cost fallacy	25.66	35.82	10.94***

Accuracy reflects mean percentages of correct responses for each task.
**p < 0.01; ***p < 0.001.

Differences in Accuracy between the HB Tasks

To assess the degree to which the different wording of the tasks affected the participants' susceptibility on the biases, chi-square tests were conducted on performance scores. The results revealed significant differences in terms of accuracy for Anchoring effect, Conjunction fallacy, Covariation detection, Framing effect, Probability match, Regression to the mean, Relativity bias, Sunk cost fallacy and for the overall HB composite score (**Table 5**).

Discussion

The aim of this study was to explore the psychometric properties of two versions of a newly constructed HB questionnaire. The questionnaire contained modified versions of 13 frequently used HB tasks. Through these modifications we aimed to ascertain that all questions satisfy the criteria of comparability, construct validity, and motivation. To be able to assume that the tasks are equally sensitive for detecting the given biases, we unified them by providing only one correct option and three biased options for the participants to choose from. Choosing any of the three incorrect options should indicate failure to resist the susceptibility of the same bias or fallacy. To motivate them to care about their answers they had to envisage themselves in situations of a concrete decision maker making critical decisions. Although the effect of these modifications was not directly tested in this study, they serve as methodological recommendations for the development of multiple-bias questionnaires.

To study our main research question of whether different biases reflect the same individual differences factor, we analyzed the psychometric properties of the surveys. The reliability assessment of the composite scores on both of the two tests showed very low internal consistency. The indices would not allow the questionnaire to be used for measuring the same concept. Therefore, to explore the underlying factorial structure, we employed a polynomial Factor Analysis for both tests. For Test 1 a four-factor model fitted the data best, cumulatively explaining 49% of the variance. The same structure explained 39% of cumulative variance for Test 2. In both tests some HB tasks did not reach the expected level of loading. Most surprisingly, the explorations showed very different factor structure for the two tests. For example, the Anchoring Effect constituted a separate factor in Test 1, but it was grouped with Relativity bias and Base-rate neglect in Test 2, while these latter two were in separate factors in Test 1. In Test 1 five, and in Test 2 an additional three HB tasks did not reach the necessary loading for any of the factors.

Another way to assess the shared properties of these HB tasks is to correlate their scores with the CRT composite. The CRT was argued to be the most representative test of the assumed latent rationality factor (Toplak et al., 2011). The individual correlation coefficients of the tasks were within the range of -0.09 and 0.24 reaching the level of significance only occasionally. Importantly, in five cases these correlation coefficients were significantly different for the two tests, changing valence in three tasks.

These apparent differences between the two versions of the tasks call for explanation. One possibility is that while incorrect responses on the different versions constitute the violation of the same normative rule, different wordings of the tasks may evoke different strategies and may have a greater effect on performance than previously expected. We found support for the latter in the comparison of the accuracy measures of the tasks in the two tests. By altering the wording of the tasks, the Framing effect, Anchoring effect, Relativity bias, Probability match, Outcome bias, Covariation detection, Sunk cost fallacy, Conjunction fallacy, and Regression to the mean all showed significantly different levels of difficulty.

The other possible explanation for this pattern of results is that when we modified the original HB tasks, we unintentionally decreased the validity of the questions. Although in devising these new tasks, we always aimed to keep the structure of the original tasks while changing the number of answer options and some superficial features of the tasks, some modifications might have decreased the ability of the test to measure the cognitive processes that underlie the original tasks. A limitation of this study is that we did not administer the original questions, and therefore, this assumption could not be tested directly. Study 2 was designed to explore this second possible explanation of our present results.

STUDY 2

In this study, for each of seven frequently tested cognitive biases we collected three different tasks. The different versions of the tasks have been used interchangeably in the literature to measure the given cognitive bias. We assumed that if different test questions of a bias measure the same underlying factor, then the test questions are interchangeable. We created three questionnaires for the seven biases by randomly selecting one version of each task for each questionnaire. If the different wording of the task does not alter the cognitive strategy that the participant employs when solving the task then we would expect the same pattern of factors emerging from the Factor Analysis. Also, if the different versions of the task represent the same underlying factor, then we would expect that they would correlate similarly with the CRT.

Methods
Participants
Five hundred and twenty seven native English-speaking participants (277 female, $M = 37.98$ years, $SD = 12.18$) were recruited through an online crowd-sourcing platform, CrowdFlower. In exchange for their participation, they were paid 0.30 USD for finishing the questionnaire. The research was approved by the institutional ethics committee of Eotvos Lorand University, Hungary.

Materials
Three new HB questionnaires were constructed, each consisting of seven tasks (Base-rate neglect, Conjunction fallacy, Covariation detection, Framing effect, Gambler's fallacy, Insensitivity to sample size, Sunk cost fallacy). Three versions of each task were collected from the literature and were randomly assigned to the tests (Supplementary Material, Study 2). All testing materials were presented in English. For each task, the aim was to employ questions with the same number of answer options. Where this was not possible, the number of answer options was modified to render them more similar to the other tasks. Similarly to Study 1, the CRT tasks were administered at the end of the survey.

Procedure
Participants were randomly assigned to one of the three tests. After giving informed consent, participants were asked to solve the seven HB tasks and the three CRT questions (Frederick, 2005). The first part of the framing question was administered at the beginning of the test, followed by the six other HB questions in randomized order. The second part of the risky-choice framing question was administered after the other HB questions and before the CRT tasks. No time-pressure was employed in this study.

Results
Reliability
Reliability measures showed weaker results for the composite scores than in Study 1. Both Split-half and Cronbach's alpha values were below the acceptable level (**Table 6**).

TABLE 6 | Reliability measures for the composite score of the three HB tests.

	Split-half	Cronbach's alpha
Test 1	0.35	0.08
Test 2	0.37	0.16
Test 3	0.22	−0.004

Factor Analysis

An explorative Factor Analysis, similar to Study 1, was conducted on the three tests. Prior to the Factor Analysis, data adequacy was tested identically to Study 1. With regard to Test 1, the KMO reached an acceptable level, KMO = 0.59, and the Bartlett's test was significant again, $\chi^2_{(21)} = 159.54$, $p < 0.001$. For Test 2 similar results were obtained: KMO = 0.65, Bartlett's test, $\chi^2_{(21)} = 152.92$, $p < 0.0001$. In Test 3, the KMO was smaller, KMO = 0.33, but Bartlett's test was significant, $\chi^2_{(21)} = 250.69$, $p < 0.001$. Contrary to the small KMO value in Test 3, the mean absolute correlation was relatively high, $r = 0.3$. These results suggested that a Factor Analysis can be conducted on the data.

In the first analysis, based on the Very Simple Structure criterion the analysis suggested a three-factor model, while a Parallel Analysis suggested a two-factor model and an eigenvalue analysis suggested a three-factor model. Based on explained cumulative variance, the three-factor structure fitted the data best for all of the three tests. Model-fit indices were acceptable for Test 1, $\chi^2_{(3)} = 2.04$, $p = 0.56$, TLI = 1.00, RMSEA = 0.00 (95% CI [0.00, 0.11]), and Test 2, $\chi^2_{(3)} = 3.1$, $p = 0.38$, TLI = 1.00, RMSEA = 0.02 (95% CI [0.00, 0.14]), but they were not acceptable for Test 3[4], $\chi^2_{(3)} = 22.57$, $p < 0.05$, TLI = 0.33, RMSEA = 0.21 (95% CI [0.12, 0.29]). Similarly to Study 1, different tasks belonged to different factors in each test, for example, Base-rate neglect was classified in one factor with Insensitivity to sample size, Gambler's fallacy and Sunk cost fallacy in Test 1, with Conjunction fallacy in Test 2, and with Sunk cost fallacy in Test 3 (Table 7). Original item-item correlations and factor correlations can be found in the Supplementary Materials.

Correlations with the CRT Composite Score

Similarly to Study 1, the correlation between the HB tasks and the CRT composite scores were examined; the results are presented in Tables 8, 9. No significant correlation between the Framing effect and the CRT composite scores were found (Table 8). The Fisher-exact test revealed differing levels of correlation for the Conjunction fallacy, for the Insensitivity to sample size and for the Sunk cost fallacy (Table 9). Average CRT performance was similar in each group ($M_{Test1} = 1.31$; $M_{Test2} = 1.27$; $M_{Test3} = 1.40$).

---

[4]Note that the factor structure in **Table 7** of Test 3 is only presented for demonstrational purposes. These results are not meaningful due to the low fitting indices, which suggest that the performance scores on Test 3 are not suitable to extract latent factors from.

Differences in Accuracy between the HB Tasks

As in Study 1, chi-square tests were conducted on performance scores to examine the differences between the different tests. The analyses revealed significant differences in terms of accuracy across the three versions of the HB task, except for Gambler's fallacy (**Table 10**).

Discussion

The aim of this study was to assess the properties of three versions of an HB task questionnaire. We assumed that if different test questions of a bias measure the same underlying factor, then the test questions are interchangeable. We thereby expected the same pattern of factors emerging from the Factor Analysis and similar correlation between the tasks and the CRT.

The reliability measures of the three tests were very poor, arguing against a general factor behind the HB tasks. The Factor Analysis showed a no more coherent picture of the tasks here than in Study 1. For example, in Test 1, Base-rate neglect was grouped in one factor with Sunk Cost and Gambler's fallacy, with negative loading of Insensitivity to sample size. In Test 2 Base-rate neglect was in the same factor with Conjunction fallacy, while in Test 3 Base-rate neglect was paired with the Sunk cost fallacy. Only the Insensitivity to sample size and the Gambler's fallacy tasks belong to the same factor in all three questionnaires. The three versions of the tasks showed significantly different correlations with the CRT for the Conjunction fallacy, the Insensitivity to sample size and the Sunk cost tasks. Scores of the Framing effect task did not show significant correlation with the CRT in any of the tests. The susceptibility of the tasks also greatly varies among the tests, showing similarly good performance only for the Gambler's fallacy task, for the other tests the accuracy measure significantly differed. These results shed light on a general problem with the HB tasks that might explain the unexpected findings of our Study 1.

GENERAL DISCUSSION

The objective of this paper is to highlight certain methodological questions in individual differences research of cognitive biases. In Study 1, we emphasized that the within-subjects design, which is required for measuring individual differences, brings about new challenges when multiple-bias surveys are created. The problem of turning between-subjects tasks into within-subjects tasks is especially problematic for tests of coherence rationality (the expectation that the person should decide indifferently in logically equivalent situations; Kahneman and Fredrick, 2005) such as the framing effect, as the expected behavior can become transparent to the participants. We also stressed the importance of other criteria of this design, such as comparability, construct validity, and motivation. We implemented the necessary modifications on the traditionally used HB tasks to satisfy these criteria. Participants have been found to be susceptible to the questions of the two new surveys. Nevertheless, the results of Factor Analysis indicated major inconsistencies between the two tests of the same biases. In Study 2, where we returned to using the traditional versions of the HB tasks, this inconsistency remained apparent among the

TABLE 7 | Results of the exploratory factor analysis for the three tests.

		Factor 1	Factor 2	Factor 3	Communalities
Test 1	Conjunction fallacy	0.03	0.03	**−0.49**	0.24
	Base-rate neglect	**0.48**	−0.08	0.19	0.3
	Covariation detection	0.07	0.03	**0.69**	0.5
	Insensitivity to sample size	**−0.48**	0.07	0.16	0.22
	Gambler's fallacy	**0.94**	0.06	0.05	0.93
	Framing effect	0.08	**0.99**	0.02	0.99
	Sunk cost fallacy	**0.30**	0.04	−0.06	0.09
Test 2	Conjunction fallacy	−0.24	0.06	**0.5**	0.18
	Base-rate neglect	−0.04	−0.03	**0.54**	0.26
	Covariation detection	**0.59**	−0.23	0.08	0.45
	Insensitivity to sample size	**−0.42**	−0.1	−0.13	0.27
	Gambler's fallacy	**0.85**	0.12	−0.17	0.6
	Framing effect	0.04	**0.99**	0.02	0.99
	Sunk cost fallacy	0.3	0.03	0.35	0.33
Test 3	Conjunction fallacy	0.46	−0.19	0.48	0.57
	Base-rate neglect	−0.46	0.16	**0.98**	0.99
	Covariation detection	−0.02	0.09	0.15	0.03
	Insensitivity to sample size	**0.84**	−0.02	0.13	0.69
	Gambler's fallacy	**0.55**	−0.28	0.13	0.39
	Framing effect	−0.06	**1.00**	0.11	0.99
	Sunk cost fallacy	0.05	0.07	**−0.39**	0.18

Factor loadings of 0.3 and above are marked with bold. Factors with one item loading are presented only for demonstrative purposes.

TABLE 8 | Correlations of each HB tasks with the CRT composite scores.

	Test 1	Test 2	Test 3
Base-rate neglect	0.22*	0.26***	0.28***
Conjunction fallacy	−0.16*	0.08	0.19*
Covariation detection	0.32***	0.34***	0.15*
Framing effect	0.08	0.06	−0.08
Gamblers fallacy	0.26***	0.21*	0.18*
Insensitivity to sample size	0.05	−0.34***	0.04
Sunk cost fallacy	0.09	0.23*	−0.18*

***p < 0.001; *p < 0.05.

TABLE 9 | Differences in correlation between the tests for each HB Task.

	Test 1–Test 2	Test 1–Test 3	Test 2–Test 3
Base-rate neglect	−0.40	−0.60	−0.20
Conjunction fallacy	−2.25*	−3.30***	−1.04
Covariation detection	−0.21	1.69	1.89
Framing	0.19	1.50	1.31
Gamblers fallacy	0.49	0.79	0.29
Insensitivity to sample size	3.77***	−0.38	−4.14***
Sunk cost	−1.34	2.54*	3.88***

Presented values represent Z-scores.
*p < 0.05; ***p < 0.001.

three questionnaires. It appeared that using different versions of the HB tasks resulted in remarkably different factor structures, altering correlational relations with the CRT and varying bias-susceptibility. These results raise several important questions for the research of individual differences in cognitive biases.

What does the HB Composite Score Represent?

With a few exceptions (e.g., Bruine de Bruin et al., 2007; Klaczynski, 2014), most multiple-bias questionnaires consist of one or two task items from each measured bias (e.g., Slugoski et al., 1993; Stanovich and West, 1998; Klaczynski, 2001; Toplak et al., 2007, 2011; West et al., 2008, 2012). Performance scores

on these items are regularly aggregated to create a composite score for further analyses. It is not clear, however, what we expect this composite score to represent. The view that there is a general underlying factor behind HB is rarely held. Earlier proposals for one single factor behind the diverse set of decision errors have been empirically discouraged. For example, Wyer and Srull (1989) claimed that the variety of decision and judgment biases is the result of people's general tendency to treat conditional relationships as if they were biconditional (the disposition to infer "Y is X" given "X is Y"). Assuming individual difference variation in performance, we would expect the HB to show high intercorrelation and to load highly on one factor. Factor Analysis did not support Wyer and Srull's proposal

TABLE 10 | Accuracy for each task and composite score across the three HB tests.

Tasks	Test 1 (%)	Test 2 (%)	Test 3 (%)	$\chi^2_{(2, 528)}$
Base-rate neglect	39.33	46.02	58.76	13.85***
Conjunction fallacy	34.27	9.66	24.86	30.82***
Covariation detection	38.20	56.82	31.64	24.68***
Framing effect	73.60	76.70	53.11	26.63***
Gambler's fallacy	85.96	89.20	92.66	4.16
Insensitivity to sample size	27.53	17.05	81.92	175.87***
Sunk cost fallacy	61.80	75.00	29.94	76.78***

Accuracy reflects mean percentages of correct responses for each task.
***p < 0.001.

(Slugoski et al., 1993). Studies of decision making competence found more promising rates of explained variance by one-factor models (30% for Bruine de Bruin et al., 2007; 25% for Parker and Fischhoff, 2005). However, the components of their test batteries (Resistance to Framing, Recognizing Social Norms, Under/overconfidence, Applying Decision Rules, Consistency in Risk Perception, Path Independence, and Resistance to Sunk Costs) only partially represent the traditional HB tasks. Intercorrelations on different sets of tasks were repeatedly found to be weak (0.16 for Bruine de Bruin et al., 2007; 0.12 for Parker and Fischhoff, 2005), occasionally being very weak (e.g., 0.066 for West et al., 2008; 0.03 for Slugoski et al., 1993). While the unidimensional factor bears no theoretical or empirical support, research literature shows several attempts to classify decision biases into sets of similar problems. When the researchers choose their test questions they often assume that some combination of these tasks measure probabilistic reasoning abilities (Toplak et al., 2007), the conceptual measure of rational thought (Stanovich et al., 2011), or decision competence (Bruine de Bruin et al., 2007). The most elaborated bias taxonomy was provided by Stanovich (2009, 2012). There, it is suggested that rational thinking problems can be classified according to three main categories of cognitive difficulties: the cognitive miser problem such as focal bias, override failure; mindware gaps, such as probability knowledge or alternative thinking; and the contaminated mindware such as self and egocentric processing. Stanovich suggests that errors on most of the HB tasks can be linked to one of these categories, while some biases are determined by multiple cognitive problems. It is proposed that these dimensions of rationality can be measured by specific traditional testing paradigms. From a testing perspective, Stanovich relies on the psychometric separability of these tasks to allow for a "Rationality Quotient," a comprehensive assessment of rational thought (2011). This proposal strongly depends on the assumptions that the traditionally used HB tasks can be grouped by their underlying factors, and that different versions of the same task represent the same thinking error. Some evidence for the separability of biases come from the study of Toplak et al. (2007) where in a communality analysis of Gambling fallacy, Regression to the mean, Covariation detection, Probability matching, Bayesian reasoning, Statistical reasoning, Outcome bias, and Probability reasoning tasks they

found that three categories of these tasks explained unique variance in problem gambling. Although Factor Analysis has been applied to decision bias collections, their direct aim was not exploration of such classifications (Klaczynski, 2001; Parker and Fischhoff, 2005; Bruine de Bruin et al., 2007). The recent work of Teovanović et al. (2015) has been dedicated to the examination of factorial structure on HB tasks. Performance on the Anchoring effect, Belief bias, Overconfidence bias, Hindsight bias, Base-rate neglect, Outcome bias and Sunk cost effect has been analyzed in an Exploratory Factor Analysis. They argued that their results showed low explained variance, indicating weak replicability. When they analyzed these tasks together with cognitive ability tests and thinking disposition measures in another Factor Analysis, the previously observed factors were not replicated. These findings, in accord with our own present results, indicate that contrary to previous theoretical expectations, decision biases do not form robust categories, or at least they cannot be extracted by the traditionally used HB tasks. These results question the empirical grounding that HB composite scores provide a meaningful measure for the exploration of individual differences in decision competence.

What do the Different Versions of an HB Task Measure?

Besides the surprisingly low communality of the HB tasks, the present work points to an additional concern: the observation that the different versions of the HB tasks appear to show an unexpected level of heterogeneity. In fact, in most previous studies when several tasks of the same bias have been assessed together, people's susceptibility to the different versions of the task greatly varied (e.g., West et al., 2008) and internal consistency of these tasks rarely reached acceptable levels (0.61 for Resistance to Sunk Cost in Bruine de Bruin et al., 2007; yet the same bias is 0.03 in Parker and Fischhoff, 2005). Measuring the different items of the same task in within-subjects arrangement can increase intercorrelation only by sequential effects or as a result of the participants' desire to appear to be consistent with their answers to recognizably similar questions (coherence rationality, Kahneman and Fredrick, 2005). When we found inconsistencies between the different versions of the tasks, we used between-subjects comparisons. This form of analysis is necessary in order to understand the idiosyncratic properties of the tasks, since a participant's answer on one cannot influence their answer on the other task. Although the degree of intercorrelation is not a direct indicator of whether the items measure a unidimensional latent construct (Green et al., 1977), the result that different items of a task fall into different factors strongly suggests that they either do not measure the same latent construct, or that individual items have very poor measurement properties.

Possible Causes for the Inconsistencies

At this point, it is only within the realm of speculation to suggest an explanation for this inconsistency among HB task versions. One possibility is that people interpret the questions differently than how the questions were intended by the researchers. Similarly to the studies of the framing effect, a vast body of research in survey studies (e.g., Bradburn, 1982; Schwarz, 1999) suggests that seemingly irrelevant wording of the questions and response options can have a significant effect on people's tendency to interpret and answer the questions. For example, when researchers use presumed antonyms (e.g., "forbidding" and "allowing"), participants may not treat these terms as exact opposites (Rugg, 1941). Synonymous terms (e.g., "inflation" and "prices in general"), may be interpreted differently (Ranyard et al., 2008) due to the difference between lexical and pragmatic meanings (Schwarz, 1999). Varying cover stories and the employed situational factors can easily lead to a mismatch between how the researcher and the participant interpret the question.

From a contextualist perspective, problems framed in different domains might evoke different cognitive strategies (Cosmides and Tooby, 1989; Gigerenzer and Hug, 1992). It is reasonable to assume that people show idiosyncrasy in their approach to a problem under the influence of prior knowledge or domain familiarity. For example, it has been found that people perform generally better on versions of the Wason Selection Task when presented in the context of social relations (Cosmides, 1989). Similarly, studies of risk-perception and decision making competence showed differences between domains of financial decisions, health/safety, recreational, ethical, and social decisions (Weber et al., 2002; Weller et al., 2015). It has been suggested that task content can elicit different decision mode usage (analytic, rule-based, automatic) and these modes can lead to different degrees of bias susceptibility (Blais and Weber, 2001), and also that changes in content can change decision outcome by affecting strategies and mental representations (Rettinger and Hastie, 2001). Jackson et al. (2015, submitted) have demonstrated that context is important for adjusting individuals' control thresholds, which in turn affect their recklessness and hesitancy. Therefore, the domain-specificity framework would predict inconsistencies in the different versions of tasks if they are framed in different domains as they can require different cognitive strategies and abilities.

The format of response options can also inadvertently bias the measurement of the task items. In HB literature, response options are presented in very different formats, such as open-ended questions (e.g., Toplak et al., 2011), simple choice (e.g., Klaczynski, 2001), multiple choice (e.g., Kahneman et al., 1982), or rating scales (e.g., Bruine de Bruin et al., 2007). Response mode can greatly affect people's performance (de Bruin and Fischhoff, 2000; Roediger and Marsh, 2005), confidence (Pallier et al., 2002; Jackson, submitted), and the cognitive strategies elicited (Hertwig and Chase, 1998).

The greatest difficulty in this matter is that we know very little about the underlying cognitive processes of the different HB. On the one hand, it has been shown at least for the anchoring heuristic (Epley and Gilovich, 2005) and the framing effect (Levin et al., 1998, 2002) that these are labels representing a variety of different cognitive mechanisms dependent on question content and task characteristics. On the other hand, a repeated critique of the heuristics-and-biases approach is that its labels are either so vaguely defined that they do not allow falsifiable process models (Gigerenzer and Goldstein, 1996) or the attempts to explore the

underlying processes in judgment and reasoning are unsatisfying (Fiedler, 2015; Fiedler and von Sydow, 2015).

Another possible source of inconsistency between the different versions of the tasks is that they tap into different normative models. Many critics have insisted that on certain tasks the responses judged to be wrong by the researcher are in fact correct due to the mismatch between the problem and the linked normative model (Margolis, 1987; Messer and Griggs, 2013). It has been argued that taking different linguistic or conceptual interpretations of the problems may to lead to different normative answers for tasks such as the taxicab base-rate problem (Birnbaum, 1983), the overconfidence effect (Gigerenzer, 1991), or the conjunction fallacy task (Fiedler, 1988). Therefore, it is possible that different cover stories or different wording of the tasks inadvertently change the corresponding normative models, which might require different competence from the participant.

Even if we suppose that errors on task versions of the same cognitive bias are caused by the same cognitive failure, different levels of task fluency can alter the heuristic nature of the task. On certain tasks, for example, where higher level of fluency triggers a stronger heuristic answer (Thompson et al., 2011), good performance might indicate higher reflectivity, while tasks with a lower level of fluency do not require the inhibition of the immediate answer and rather reflect people's cognitive capacity. This notion is confirmed by the significantly different correlation coefficients among the tasks of a given bias and the CRT composite scores. Arguably, the CRT measures inhibition or reflectivity (Campitelli and Labollita, 2010), and thus differences among correlation coefficients could be caused by the different level of reflectivity needed to solve the tasks. Our results, with the support of the empirical studies outlined here, may therefore suggest that the diverse collection of questions traditionally used for measuring the individual decision biases cannot be taken unconditionally as interchangeable measures of the same latent factor or cognitive mechanism. Rather, more effort is needed to explore how content, language and question format can alter or influence the assessment of a decision bias.

CONCLUSIONS

In summary, this paper represents two attempts to explore the methodological requirements for individual differences research using HB tasks. The first study highlighted the need to construct HB test items that satisfy the criteria of comparability, construct validity, and motivation. However, the results of a modified HB test battery suggested and the analysis of the second study confirmed a great level of inconsistency when these biases are measured by individual items. An overview of decision competence literature suggests that the weakness of these tests cannot be derived from the general practice of measuring biases by single (or very few) items for two reasons. Firstly, multiple-bias questionnaires show poor or unacceptable internal consistency. Secondly, the empirical results do not support the theoretical assumption that the different versions of the HB tasks measure the same underlying cognitive construct. While in the field of judgment and decision making there is a growing interest in going beyond aggregate level results by examining individual differences, the success will depend on how clearly we can understand the cognitive mechanisms behind the traditional list of HB.

ACKNOWLEDGMENTS

We would like to thank Melissa Wood, Simon Jackson, Zita Zoltay-Paprika, and Maria Dunavolgyi for their comments on an earlier draft of this manuscript as well as Gyorgy Racz for his assistance in data collection. This research was supported by the European Union and the State of Hungary, co-financed by the European Social Fund in the framework of TÁMOP 4.2.4. A/1-11-1-2012-0001 "National Excellence Program" and by the Hungarian Scientific Research Fund – OTKA, 105421. Bence Bago was supported by a doctoral fellowship from Ecole des Neurosciences de Paris Ile-de-France.

REFERENCES

Bar-Hillel, M. (1980). The base-rate fallacy in probability judgments. *Acta Psychol. (Amst).* 44, 211–233. doi: 10.1016/0001-6918(80)90046-3

Birnbaum, M. H. (1983). Base rates in bayesian inference: signal detection analysis of the cab problem. *Am. J. Psychol.* 96, 85–94. doi: 10.2307/1422211

Blais, A.-R., and Weber, E. U. (2001). Domain-specificity and gender differences in decision making. *Risk Decis. Policy* 6, 47–69. doi: 10.1017/S1357530901000254

Bradburn, N. (1982). "Question-wording effects in surveys," in *Question Framing and Response Consistency*, ed R. M. Hogarth (San Francisco, CA: Jossey-Bass), 65–76.

Bruine de Bruin, W., Parker, A. M., and Fischhoff, B. (2007). Individual differences in adult decision-making competence. *J. Pers. Soc. Psychol.* 92, 938–956. doi: 10.1037/0022-3514.92.5.938

Camerer, C. F., and Hogarth, R. M. (1999). The effects of financial incentives in experiments: a review and capital-labor-production framework. *J. Risk Uncertain.* 19, 7–42. doi: 10.1023/A:1007850605129

Campitelli, G., and Labollita, M. (2010). Correlations of cognitive reflection with judgments and choices. *Judgm. Decis. Mak.* 5, 182–191.

Christensen-Szalanski, J. J., and Willham, C. F. (1991). The hindsight bias: a meta-analysis. *Organ. Behav. Hum. Decis. Process.* 48, 147–168. doi: 10.1016/0749-5978(91)90010-Q

Cosmides, L. (1989). The logic of social exchange: has natural selection shaped how humans reason? Studies with the Wason selection task. *Cognition* 31, 187–276. doi: 10.1016/0010-0277(89)90023-1

Cosmides, L., and Tooby, J. (1989). Evolutionary psychology and the generation of culture, part II: case study: a computational theory of social exchange. *Ethol. Sociobiol.* 10, 51–97. doi: 10.1016/0162-3095(89)90013-7

de Bruin, W. B., and Fischhoff, B. (2000). The effect of question format on measured HIV/AIDS knowledge: detention center teens, high school students, and adults. *AIDS Educ. Prev.* 12, 187–198.

Epley, N., and Gilovich, T. (2005). When effortful thinking influences judgmental anchoring: differential effects of forewarning and incentives on self–generated and externally provided anchors. *J. Behav. Decis. Mak.* 18, 199–212. doi: 10.1002/bdm.495

Evans, J. S. B., and Stanovich, K. E. (2013). Dual-process theories of higher cognition advancing the debate. *Perspect. Psychol. Sci.* 8, 223–241. doi: 10.1177/1745691612460685

Fiedler, K. (1988). The dependence of the conjunction fallacy on subtle linguistic factors. *Psychol. Res.* 50, 123–129. doi: 10.1007/BF00309212

Fiedler, K. (2015). Functional research and cognitive-process research in behavioural science: an unequal but firmly connected pair. *Int. J. Psychol.* doi: 10.1002/ijop.12163. [Epub ahead of print].

Fiedler, K., and von Sydow, M. (2015). "Heuristics and biases: beyond Tversky and Kahneman's (1974) judgment under uncertainty," in *Cognitive Psychology: Revisiting the Classical Studies*, eds M. W. Eysenck and D. Groome (Los Angeles, US: Sage), 146–161.

Frederick, S. (2005). Cognitive reflection and decision making. *J. Econ. Perspect.* 19, 25–42. doi: 10.1257/089533005775196732

Frisch, D. (1993). Reasons for framing effects. *Organ. Behav. Hum. Decis. Process.* 54, 399–429. doi: 10.1006/obhd.1993.1017

Gambara, H., and Piñon, A. (2005). A meta-analytic review of framing effect: risky, attribute and goal framing. *Psicothema* 17, 325–331.

Gigerenzer, G. (1991). How to make cognitive illusions disappear: beyond "Heuristics and Biases." *Eur. Rev. Soc. Psychol.* 2, 83–115. doi: 10.1080/14792779143000033

Gigerenzer, G., and Goldstein, D. G. (1996). Reasoning the fast and frugal way: models of bounded rationality. *Psychol. Rev.* 103, 650–669. doi: 10.1037/0033-295X.103.4.650

Gigerenzer, G., and Hug, K. (1992). Domain-specific reasoning: social contracts, cheating, and perspective change. *Cognition* 43, 127–171. doi: 10.1016/0010-0277(92)90060-U

Gigerenzer, G., Todd, P. M., and Group, A. R. (1999). *Simple Heuristics that Make us Smart*. New York, NY: Oxford University Press.

Gilovich, T., Vallone, R., and Tversky, A. (1985). The hot hand in basketball: on the misperception of random sequences. *Cogn. Psychol.* 17, 295–314. doi: 10.1016/0010-0285(85)90010-6

Green, S. B., Lissitz, R. W., and Mulaik, S. A. (1977). Limitations of coefficient alpha as an index of test unidimensionality1. *Educ. Psychol. Meas.* 37, 827–838. doi: 10.1177/001316447703700403

Hardt, O., and Pohl, R. F. (2003). Hindsight bias as a function of anchor distance and anchor plausibility. *Memory* 11, 379–394. doi: 10.1080/09658210244000504

Hertwig, R., and Chase, V. (1998). Many reasons or just one: how response mode affects reasoning in the conjunction problem. *Think. Reason.* 4, 319–352. doi: 10.1080/135467898394102

Jackson, S. A., Kleitman, S., Stankov, L., and Howie, P. (2015). Decision pattern analysis as a general framework for studying individual differences in decision making. *J. Behav. Decis. Mak.* doi: 10.1002/bdm.1887. [Epub ahead of print].

Kahneman, D., and Fredrick, S. (2005). "A model of heuristic judgment," in *The Cambridge Handbook of Thinking and Reasoning*, eds K. J. Holyoak and R. G. Morrison (New York, NY: Cambridge University Press), 267–293.

Kahneman, D., Slovic, P., and Tversky, A. (1982). *Judgment Under Uncertainty: Heuristics and Biases*. Cambridge, UK: Cambridge University Press. doi: 10.1017/CBO9780511809477

Klaczynski, P. A. (2001). Analytic and heuristic processing influences on adolescent reasoning and decision–making. *Child Dev.* 72, 844–861. doi: 10.1111/1467-8624.00319

Klaczynski, P. A. (2014). Heuristics and biases: interactions among numeracy, ability, and reflectiveness predict normative responding. *Front. Psychol.* 5:665. doi: 10.3389/fpsyg.2014.00665

Klein, G. A. (1999). *Sources of Power: How People Make Decisions*. Cambridge, MA: MIT press.

LeBoeuf, R. A., and Shafir, E. (2003). Deep thoughts and shallow frames: on the susceptibility to framing effects. *J. Behav. Decis. Mak.* 16, 77–92. doi: 10.1002/bdm.433

Levin, I. P., Gaeth, G. J., Schreiber, J., and Lauriola, M. (2002). A new look at framing effects: distribution of effect sizes, individual differences, and independence of types of effects. *Organ. Behav. Hum. Decis. Process.* 88, 411–429. doi: 10.1006/obhd.2001.2983

Levin, I. P., Schneider, S. L., and Gaeth, G. J. (1998). All frames are not created equal: a typology and critical analysis of framing effects. *Organ. Behav. Hum. Decis. Process.* 76, 149–188. doi: 10.1006/obhd.1998.2804

Lichtenstein, S., and Fischhoff, B. (1977). Do those who know more also know more about how much they know? *Organ. Behav. Hum. Perform.* 20, 159–183. doi: 10.1016/0030-5073(77)90001-0

Margolis, H. (1987). *Patterns, Thinking, and Cognition: A Theory of Judgment.* Chicago, IL: University of Chicago Press.

Messer, W. S., and Griggs, R. A. (2013). Another look at Linda. *Bull. Psychon. Soc.* 31, 193–196. doi: 10.3758/BF03337322

Pallier, G., Wilkinson, R., Danthiir, V., Kleitman, S., Knezevic, G., Stankov, L., et al. (2002). The role of individual differences in the accuracy of confidence judgments. *J. Gen. Psychol.* 129, 257–299. doi: 10.1080/00221300209602099

Parker, A. M., and Fischhoff, B. (2005). Decision−making competence: external validation through an individual−differences approach. *J. Behav. Decis. Mak.* 18, 1–27. doi: 10.1002/bdm.481

Ranyard, R., Missier, F. D., Bonini, N., Duxbury, D., and Summers, B. (2008). Perceptions and expectations of price changes and inflation: a review and conceptual framework. *J. Econ. Psychol.* 29, 378–400. doi: 10.1016/j.joep.2008.07.002

Rettinger, D. A., and Hastie, R. (2001). Content effects on decision making. *Organ. Behav. Hum. Decis. Process.* 85, 336–359. doi: 10.1006/obhd.2000.2948

Revelle, W. (2014). *psych: Procedures for Personality and Psychological Research.* R package version, 1.5.4. Evanston: Northwestern University.

Roca, M., Hogarth, R. M., and Maule, A. J. (2006). Ambiguity seeking as a result of the status quo bias. *J. Risk Uncertain.* 32, 175–194. doi: 10.1007/s11166-006-9518-8

Roediger, H. L. III, and Marsh, E. J. (2005). The positive and negative consequences of multiple-choice testing. *J. Exp. Psychol. Learn. Mem. Cogn.* 31, 1155–1159. doi: 10.1037/0278-7393.31.5.1155

Rugg, D. (1941). Experiments in wording questions: II. *Public Opin. Q.* 5, 91. doi: 10.1086/265467

Samuelson, W., and Zeckhauser, R. (1988). Status quo bias in decision making. *J. Risk Uncertain.* 1, 7–59. doi: 10.1007/BF00055564

Schwarz, N. (1999). Self-reports: how the questions shape the answers. *Am. Psychol.* 54, 93–105. doi: 10.1037/0003-066X.54.2.93

Simon, H. A. (1955). A behavioral model of rational choice. *Q. J. Econ.* 69, 99–118. doi: 10.2307/1884852

Slugoski, B. R., Shields, H. A., and Dawson, K. A. (1993). Relation of conditional reasoning to heuristic processing. *Pers. Soc. Psychol. Bull.* 19, 158–166. doi: 10.1177/0146167293192004

Stanovich, K. E. (1999). *Who is Rational? Studies of Individual Differences in Reasoning.* Hillsdale, NJ: Lawrence Erlbaum.

Stanovich, K. E. (2009). *What Intelligence Tests Miss: The Psychology of Rational Thought.* New Haven, CT: Yale University Press.

Stanovich, K. E. (2012). "On the distinction between rationality and intelligence: implications for understanding individual differences in reasoning," in *The Oxford Handbook of Thinking and Reasoning,* eds K. J. Holyoak and R. G. Morrison (New York, NY: Oxford University Press), 343–365. doi: 10.1093/oxfordhb/9780199734689.013.0022

Stanovich, K. E., and West, R. F. (1998). Individual differences in rational thought. *J. Exp. Psychol. Gen.* 127, 161–188. doi: 10.1037/0096-3445.127.2.161

Stanovich, K. E., and West, R. F. (2001). Individual differences in reasoning: implications for the rationality debate? *Behav. Brain Sci.* 23, 645–665. doi: 10.1017/S0140525X00003435

Stanovich, K. E., West, R. F., and Toplak, M. E. (2011). "Intelligence and rationality," in *The Cambridge Handbook of Intelligence,* eds R. J. Sternberg and S. B. Kaufman (Cambridge, UK: Cambridge University Press), 784–826. doi: 10.1017/CBO9780511977244.040

Teovanović, P., Knežević, G., and Stankov, L. (2015). Individual differences in cognitive biases: evidence against one-factor theory of rationality. *Intelligence* 50, 75–86. doi: 10.1016/j.intell.2015.02.008

Thompson, V. A., Prowse Turner, J. A., and Pennycook, G. (2011). Intuition, reason, and metacognition. *Cogn. Psychol.* 63, 107–140. doi: 10.1016/j.cogpsych.2011.06.001

Toplak, M. E., Liu, E., MacPherson, R., Toneatto, T., and Stanovich, K. E. (2007). The reasoning skills and thinking dispositions of problem gamblers: a dual−process taxonomy. *J. Behav. Decis. Mak.* 20, 103–124. doi: 10.1002/bdm.544

Toplak, M. E., West, R. F., and Stanovich, K. E. (2011). The Cognitive Reflection Test as a predictor of performance on heuristics-and-biases tasks. *Mem. Cognit.* 39, 1275–1289. doi: 10.3758/s13421-011-0104-1

Toplak, M. E., West, R. F., and Stanovich, K. E. (2014). Rational thinking and cognitive sophistication: development, cognitive abilities, and thinking dispositions. *Dev. Psychol.* 50, 1037–1048. doi: 10.1037/a0034910

Tversky, A., and Kahneman, D. (1983). Extensional versus intuitive reasoning: the conjunction fallacy in probability judgment. *Psychol. Rev.* 90, 293–315. doi: 10.1037/0033-295X.90.4.293

Tversky, A., and Kahneman, D. (1986). Rational choice and the framing of decisions. *J. Bus.* 59, 251–278. doi: 10.1086/296365

Weber, E. U., Blais, A. R., and Betz, N. E. (2002). A domain-specific risk-attitude scale: measuring risk perceptions and risk behaviors. *J. Behav. Decis. Mak.* 15, 263–290. doi: 10.1002/bdm.414

Weller, J. A., Ceschi, A., and Randolph, C. (2015). Decision-making competence predicts domain-specific risk attitudes. *Front. Psychol.* 6:540. doi: 10.3389/fpsyg.2015.00540

West, R. F., Meserve, R. J., and Stanovich, K. E. (2012). Cognitive sophistication does not attenuate the bias blind spot. *J. Pers. Soc. Psychol.* 103, 506–519. doi: 10.1037/a0028857

West, R. F., Toplak, M. E., and Stanovich, K. E. (2008). Heuristics and biases as measures of critical thinking: associations with cognitive ability and thinking dispositions. *J. Educ. Psychol.* 100, 930–941. doi: 10.1037/a0012842

Wyer, R. S. Jr., and Srull, T. K. (1989). *Memory and Cognition in its Social Context.* Hillsdale, NJ: Lawrence Erlbaum.

Conflict of Interest Statement: The authors declare that the research was conducted in the absence of any commercial or financial relationships that could be construed as a potential conflict of interest.

Cognitive Load Does Not Affect the Behavioral and Cognitive Foundations of Social Cooperation

Laura Mieth*, Raoul Bell and Axel Buchner

Department of Experimental Psychology, Heinrich Heine University Düsseldorf, Düsseldorf, Germany

Edited by:
Anna Thorwart,
University of Marburg, Germany

Reviewed by:
Diane Swick,
VA Northern California Health Care
System, USA
Brittany S. Cassidy,
Indiana University Bloomington, USA
Danielle M. Shore,
University of Oxford, UK

*Correspondence:
Laura Mieth
Laura.Mieth@hhu.de
Raoul Bell
Raoul.Bell@hhu.de

Specialty section:
This article was submitted to
Cognition,
a section of the journal
Frontiers in Psychology

The present study serves to test whether the cognitive mechanisms underlying social cooperation are affected by cognitive load. Participants interacted with trustworthy-looking and untrustworthy-looking partners in a sequential Prisoner's Dilemma Game. Facial trustworthiness was manipulated to stimulate expectations about the future behavior of the partners which were either violated or confirmed by the partners' cheating or cooperation during the game. In a source memory test, participants were required to recognize the partners and to classify them as cheaters or cooperators. A multinomial model was used to disentangle item memory, source memory and guessing processes. We found an expectancy-congruent bias toward guessing that trustworthy-looking partners were more likely to be associated with cooperation than untrustworthy-looking partners. Source memory was enhanced for cheating that violated the participants' positive expectations about trustworthy-looking partners. We were interested in whether or not this expectancy-violation effect—that helps to revise unjustified expectations about trustworthy-looking partners—depends on cognitive load induced via a secondary continuous reaction time task. Although this secondary task interfered with working memory processes in a validation study, both the expectancy-congruent guessing bias as well as the expectancy-violation effect were obtained with and without cognitive load. These findings support the hypothesis that the expectancy-violation effect is due to a simple mechanism that does not rely on demanding elaborative processes. We conclude that most cognitive mechanisms underlying social cooperation presumably operate automatically so that they remain unaffected by cognitive load.

Keywords: dual task, working memory load, trust, social cooperation, source memory

INTRODUCTION

There is increasing interest in whether (and how) social cooperation is affected by cognitive load. Although it has been proposed that cooperation is generally decreased (Piovesan and Wengström, 2009) or enhanced (Rand et al., 2012) by cognitive load, no consensus about this issue has been reached, and there are a number of null findings and failed replications (Tinghög et al., 2013; Kessler and Meier, 2014; Verkoeijen and Bouwmeester, 2014). Focusing on how cognitive load affects specific cognitive mechanisms that are important for cooperation could be a more promising approach than looking at the global outcome of presumably many different kinds of processes involved in cooperation. Therefore, the present study examines how memory for cheating or cooperation—a necessary prerequisite for reciprocal cooperation (Trivers, 1971)—is affected by cognitive load. We were particularly interested in whether or not social expectations affect the participants' memory for the cheating or cooperation of interaction partners under cognitive load.

Examining the influence of social expectations seems particularly important because social cooperation depends fundamentally on expectations about other people's behaviors. This can be illustrated with the Prisoner's Dilemma Game (Clark and Sefton, 2001), which serves as a model for understanding human cooperation. In this game, two players independently decide whether or not to cooperate with each other. Mutual cooperation leads to reward while mutual defection leads to punishment, which reflects that more can be achieved through cooperation. However, unilateral defection leads to the highest payoff (the temptation payoff) while unilateral cooperation leads to the worst payoff (the sucker's payoff). The dilemma lies in the fact that each player can maximize his or her payoff by defecting, but mutual defection leads to a worse payoff for both players than mutual cooperation. Humans are often able to resist the selfish temptation to defect, and high levels of cooperation are often achieved even in one-shot games (Delton et al., 2011). However, given that nobody wants to be suckered, cooperation depends on people's expectations about whether or not the other player will choose to cooperate.

These expectations are strongly influenced by facial appearance (Chang et al., 2010; Olivola and Todorov, 2010). Appearance-based impressions are formed quickly (Willis and Todorov, 2006; Todorov et al., 2009) and automatically (Engell et al., 2007), but are quite stable over time. There is also a high degree of inter-individual agreement about who looks trustworthy and who does not (Todorov, 2008). These appearance-based impressions determine people's behaviors in social-dilemma games: People often cooperate with trustworthy-looking partners, and defect against untrustworthy-looking partners (van 't Wout and Sanfey, 2008; Rezlescu et al., 2012).

However, appearance-based expectations may often turn out to be false. People are somewhat better than chance when using facial appearance to predict whether partners will cooperate or cheat in social-dilemma games (Bonnefon et al., 2013), but facial appearance is a comparatively invalid source of information about a person's character, and people rely on it more than they should (Olivola and Todorov, 2010). Therefore, remembering expectancy-incongruent information is especially important to correct invalid appearance-based impressions about other persons. To correct a false impression, it is insufficient to simply recognize the face as familiar, it is also necessary to have good source memory for the association between the face and the behavior of the person (Buchner et al., 2009). For example, remembering that a trustworthy-looking person is unreliable is important to avoid being misled by the person's trustworthy appearance in the

future. This functional analysis leads to the prediction that people should have better source memory for expectancy-incongruent information than for expectancy-congruent information.

The same prediction can be derived from schema theories of memory. The schema-copy-plus-tag model (Graesser and Nakamura, 1982) implies that expectancy-congruent behaviors are represented in memory by pointers to general schemas. Expectancy-violating behaviors are tagged as schema violations. In memory tests, participants often produce a high amount of schema-congruent information due to guessing, but memory accuracy is often poor for this type of information because it is produced regardless of whether it was present at encoding or not. The discrimination between actually experienced and new information is often better for schema-atypical information. For instance, participants will guess that a trustworthy-looking face belongs to a trustworthy person, regardless of whether the behavior of the person was trustworthy or not. Learning that a trustworthy-looking person is a cheater represents a more distinct and therefore more memorable information. Indeed, several studies confirmed the idea that people remember appearance-incongruent behaviors better than appearance-congruent behaviors (Suzuki and Suga, 2010; Volstorf et al., 2011; Bell et al., 2012b).

The present study serves to test whether or not the memory advantage for expectancy-incongruent behavior depends on cognitive load. Two opposing hypotheses are tested. Source memory for cheating and cooperation may be *impaired* by cognitive load because source memory is often believed to be more fragile and more dependent on cognitive resources than familiarity-based item memory (Nieznański, 2013). Therefore, the encoding of the association between a face and cheating or cooperation may be decreased under cognitive load. Memory for expectancy-incongruent information in particular may be negatively affected because this information cannot be easily integrated into existing schemas. Expectancy-incongruent information may trigger more effortful elaborative encoding than expectancy-congruent information, which will lead to enhanced memory for this information under normal circumstances. However, these elaborative processes may depend on the mobilization of additional cognitive resources. Therefore, a reduction in available cognitive resources may eliminate the expectancy-violation effect. Consistent with this hypothesis, the source memory advantage for expectancy-incongruent information was absent in older adults (Bell et al., 2013) who may have fewer cognitive resources available than younger adults. If the memory advantage for expectancy-incongruent information is abolished under cognitive load, our ability to successfully engage in social cooperation would be impaired because this type of memory is essential for correcting maladaptive behavior tendencies.

However, it is also possible that cognitive load has *no effect* on memory for expectancy-incongruent behaviors. Remembering expectancy-incongruent information seems to be too important to vanish quickly under conditions of high cognitive load. Cooperation is particularly important in stressful situations. The human cognitive system would be badly designed if it would let go of the most important information under distracting and stressful conditions first. Therefore, the cognitive machinery specialized in categorizing other people are often assumed to be automatic (Klein et al., 2002). The same hypothesis can be based on non-functional, schema-based accounts of memory. According to the schema-copy-plus-tag model, schema-atypical information is encoded and retained in the form of unelaborated tags. This encoding strategy is assumed to be frugal in terms of processing resources, and should remain unaffected by cognitive load (Graesser and Nakamura, 1982). Accordingly, source memory for the face of a cheater is often not due to an enhanced recollection of the specific details of the cheating episode, but instead due to the rough classification of the person as a "cheater" in form of emotional tagging (Bell et al., 2012a). Arguably, these unelaborated emotional tags can be automatically encoded even under conditions of high cognitive load. Consistent with this idea, a demanding secondary task at encoding does not always lead to decreased memory for schema-atypical information, but may even result in a more pronounced schema-atypicality effect in source memory (Ehrenberg and Klauer, 2005). The automatic tagging of expectancy-violating behaviors would allow people to successfully engage in social cooperation even under stressful and distracting conditions.

The present series of experiments was designed to discriminate between these two conflicting hypotheses. The first experiment served to replicate the finding that source memory for the cheating or cooperation of others is enhanced for appearance-incongruent behaviors. To anticipate, an asymmetrical source memory advantage for appearance-incongruent cheating was found. In two further experiments, we examined whether this incongruity advantage would vanish under conditions of increased cognitive load. A fourth study was designed to validate the cognitive-load task by showing that this task does indeed interfere with (general) working-memory resources.

EXPERIMENT 1

Experiment 1 served as a replication of the effects reported by Bell et al. (2012b) with the only difference that female instead of male faces were used as stimuli. We expected to replicate the finding that people guess that trustworthy-looking faces would be associated with cooperation and untrustworthy-looking faces with cheating. Furthermore, we expected that participants would remember appearance-incongruent behaviors better than appearance-congruent behaviors. In most experiments (Suzuki and Suga, 2010; Bell et al., 2012b), this memory advantage was asymmetric in that participants remembered cheating better than cooperation when the partners looked trustworthy, but there was only a non-significant tendency toward remembering cooperation better than cheating when the partners looked untrustworthy. This asymmetry should be particularly pronounced for female faces because they elicit more positive social expectations than male faces, which means that the violation of these positive expectations is particularly salient when female faces are used (Kroneisen and Bell, 2013).

Method
Participants
One hundred and twelve students (73 of whom were female) with a mean age of 23 ($SD = 5$) participated in Experiment 1 (**Table 1**). All participants gave written informed consent in accordance with the Declaration of Helsinki. The present experiments are part of a series of experiments that has been approved by the ethics committee of the Department of Experimental Psychology at Heinrich Heine University Düsseldorf.

Materials, Procedure, and Design
The same sequential Prisoner's Dilemma Game was used as in previous studies (Bell et al., 2012b, 2013). In this game, participants were required to invest money into a joint business with partners whose faces were shown on the screen. Participants played with 20 trustworthy-looking partners and with 20 untrustworthy-looking partners. The faces were randomly drawn from a set of 40 trustworthy-looking and 40 untrustworthy-looking frontal facial photographs of women[1] with a neutral expression (250 × 375 pixel) from the FERET database (Phillips et al., 1998). In a norming study, the untrustworthy-looking faces had received low trustworthiness ratings ($M = 2.75$, $SD = 0.24$) and the trustworthy-looking faces had received high trustworthiness ratings ($M = 4.28$, $SD = 0.23$) on a scale ranging from 1 to 6. Half of the partners in each condition cooperated and the other half cheated.

Participants could familiarize themselves with the game in two practice trials. At the start of the game, they were informed that they played for real money. In each trial, participants first saw a silhouette at the left side of the screen (representing the participant), and the partner's face at the right side of the screen (**Figure 1**). Participants were required to decide whether to invest 15 cents or 30 cents (by pressing a left or right button of the response box, respectively). The decision was displayed on screen for 1 s. The investment was presented in an arrow for 500 ms before it moved to the center of the screen within 500 ms. Similarly, the partner's decision was shown in an arrow

[1] As in our previous studies (e.g., Bell et al., 2015) we only used faces from one gender because it is well known that female faces are more trustworthy than male faces (Kroneisen and Bell, 2013), and we did not want facial gender to dilute the facial trustworthiness manipulation.

TABLE 1 | Comparison of age, gender, and justice sensitivity (Schmitt et al., 2005) of Experiment 1 and 2 and Experiment 1 and 3, respectively.

	Age	Gender	Justice Sensitivity
Experiment 1	$M = 23$; $SD = 5$	female = 73 male = 39	$M = 2.93$; $SD = 0.60$
Experiment 2	$M = 24$; $SD = 5$	female = 67 male = 42	$M = 2.80$; $SD = 0.70$
Experiment 3	$M = 22$; $SD = 5$	female = 69 male = 34	—
Comparison of Experiment 1 and 2	$t(219) = 1.78$, $p = 0.08$	$\chi^2 (1) = 0.33$, $p = 0.57$	$t(219) = 1.42$, $p = 0.16$
Comparison of Experiment 1 and 3	$t(213) = 1.09$, $p = 0.28$	$\chi^2 (1) = 0.08$, $p = 0.78$	—

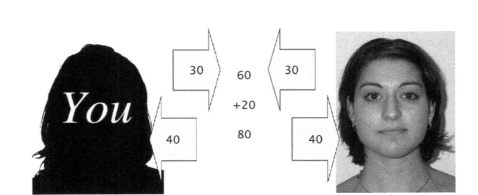

Account Balance: 100 Cents

Gain: +10 Cents

Gain: +10 Cents

Account Balance: 110 Cents

Your interactant cooperated. He invested as much as you did. You both benefit from the interaction.
With the help of your interactant you made a 10 Cent gain.

FIGURE 1 | A screenshot of the sequential prisoner's dilemma game. In this example, both the participant and the partner cooperated and invested 30 cents, resulting in a 10 cents gain for each of them. The partner's photograph shown in this example was taken from the Center for Vital Longevity (CVL) face database (Minear and Park, 2004).

for 500 ms, before it moved to the center of the screen within 500 ms. The sum of investments was then shown in the middle of the screen. After 500 ms a bonus of 1/3 of the sum of investments was added. After 500 ms, the total sum was shown. After a further 500 ms, this total sum was split up between the partners. Both the participant and the partner received half of the total sum, regardless of what they had invested. The partner's share was shown in an arrow moving toward the partner's face (500 ms). After 500 ms, the participant's share was shown in an arrow moving to the participant's silhouette (500 ms). After 1 s, the partner's gain or loss was presented, followed by the participant's gain or loss (after 500 ms). After a further 500 ms, the updated account balance of the participant was presented, and (again after 500 ms) a summary of the interaction was displayed. The next trial was initiated by the participant pressing the continue button.

A cooperating partner always reciprocated the participant's investment (either 15 or 30 cents), which resulted in a gain for both players. A cheating partner invested nothing (0 cents), which resulted in a gain for the partner at the expense of the participant, who lost money.

The payoff (gain or loss) of each player can be determined by the formula:

$$P_a = \frac{I_a + I_b + \frac{1}{3} \cdot (I_a + I_b)}{2} - I_a$$

where P_a is the payoff of Player A, I_a is the investment of Player A, and I_b is the investment of Player B. Applying this formula, it is

obvious that interacting with a cooperating partner led to a gain, and interacting with a cheating partner led to a loss of the same magnitude for the participant.

After the game, participants received the instructions for the surprise source memory test. Eighty faces were presented. Half of the faces were old (presented during the sequential Prisoner's Dilemma Game), and the other half were new. Participants were first required to rate the likability of the faces on a scale ranging from 1 (not likable at all) to 6 (very likable). After pressing the continue button, participants were asked whether or not they had seen the face during the game. If participants indicated that they had seen the face before, they were required to decide whether the face belonged to a cheater or to a cooperator. After pressing the continue button, the next face was shown. Before leaving, participants filled out a paper–pencil version of the justice sensitivity questionnaire (Schmitt et al., 2005), and were paid.

The design was a 2 × 2 repeated measures design with facial trustworthiness (trustworthy vs. untrustworthy) and behavior (cheating vs. cooperation) as independent variables. Dependent variables were game investments, likability ratings, and memory performance. A multinomial model was used to distinguish among old–new recognition, source memory, and guessing processes. Given $\alpha = 0.05$, a sample size of $N = 112$, and 80 responses in the source memory test, it was possible to detect an effect of size $w = 0.04$ (comparable to the effect sizes observed by Buchner et al., 2009; Küppers and Bayen, 2014; Bell et al., 2015; Kroneisen et al., 2015) for the comparison between source memory for cheaters and cooperators with a statistical power $(1 - \beta)$ of 0.97. The power calculation was performed using G*Power (Faul et al., 2007).

Measuring Source Memory

When examining source memory, it is important to use a measure that does not confound item recognition, source memory, and guessing (Bröder and Meiser, 2007). Therefore, we applied the widely used (Erdfelder et al., 2009) source monitoring model of Bayen et al. (1996) to measure source memory and source guessing separately.

To illustrate, the first model tree in **Figure 2** represents the cognitive states that are assumed to underlie the classification of a cheater face. With probability D_{Cheat}, participants know that the face is old (remember that they have seen the face during the game). With probability d_{Cheat}, they also have source memory for the face (remember that the person is a cheater). The source memory parameter is expressed as a conditional probability that varies between 0 and 1. A probability of 0 represents the absence of source memory while a probability of 1 represents perfect source memory. If participants fail to remember the source,

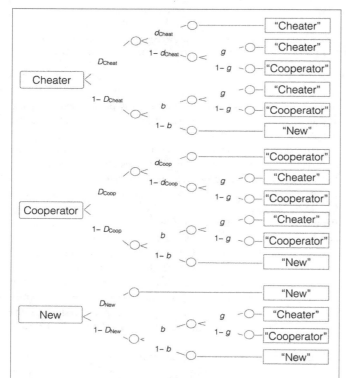

FIGURE 2 | The multinomial source memory model adapted from Bayen et al. (1996). Rounded rectangles on the left represent the items presented in the source memory test (cheater, cooperator, or new faces). The letters along the branches represent the probabilities with which certain memory states occur (D: probability to correctly recognize a face as old or new; d: conditional probability to correctly remember that the person was a cheater or a cooperator; g: conditional probability to guess that the person was a cheater; b: conditional probability to guess that a face was old). Rectangles on the right represent the participants' responses in the memory test.

which occurs with the complementary probability $1 - d_{Cheat}$, they may guess, with probability g, that the person was a cheater or, with probability $1 - g$, that the person was a cooperator. If they fail to recognize the face as old, which occurs with probability $1 - D_{Cheat}$, they may guess, with probability b, that the face is old, and may then guess that the person was a cheater with probability g, or that the person was a cooperator with probability $1 - g$. With probability $1 - b$, participants may guess that the face is new (has not been encountered during the game). The goodness-of-fit tests are based on the log-likelihood ratio statistic G^2 which is asymptotically chi-square distributed (Riefer and Batchelder, 1988; Stahl and Klauer, 2007; Singmann and Kellen, 2013). Parameter estimations and goodness-of-fit tests were calculated using multiTree (Moshagen, 2010). The observed response frequencies for Experiments 1–3 are reported in the Online Supplementary Material (Data Sheets 1–3).

Results
Game Investments
Game investments were analyzed with a repeated measures MANOVA with facial trustworthiness (trustworthy-looking vs. untrustworthy-looking) as independent variable. Participants only interacted once with each partner and thus had no chance to anticipate the behavior of the partners before they decided whether to invest or not. Therefore, only the partners' facial trustworthiness, but not their behavior could influence the investments. As expected, participants invested more money when playing with trustworthy-looking partners than when playing with untrustworthy-looking partners, $F(1,111) = 136.83$, $p < 0.001$, $\eta_p^2 = 0.55$ (see left panel of **Figure 3**).

Likability Ratings
Likability ratings were analyzed with a 2 × 2 MANOVA with facial trustworthiness (trustworthy-looking vs. untrustworthy-looking) and partner behavior (cheating vs. cooperation) as independent variables. Trustworthy-looking faces were more likable than untrustworthy-looking faces, $F(1,111) = 410.29$, $p < 0.001$, $\eta_p^2 = 0.79$. Cooperators received higher likability ratings than cheaters, $F(1,111) = 12.94$, $p < 0.001$, $\eta_p^2 = 0.10$. There was no interaction between facial trustworthiness and behavior, $F(1,111) = 1.75$, $p = 0.189$, $\eta_p^2 = 0.01$ (see left panel of **Figure 4**).

Old–New Recognition
Old–new recognition in terms of P_r (the sensitivity measure of the two-high-threshold model of old–new recognition, often referred to as corrected hit rate and given by hit rate minus false alarm rate; Snodgrass and Corwin, 1988) is shown in the left panel of **Figure 5**. A 2 × 2 MANOVA was performed with facial trustworthiness (trustworthy-looking vs. untrustworthy-looking) and partner behavior (cheating vs. cooperation) as independent variables. There was no main effect of facial trustworthiness on face recognition, $F(1,111) = 0.52$, $p = 0.472$, $\eta_p^2 < 0.01$, no main effect of partner behavior, $F(1,111) = 1.11$, $p = 0.294$, $\eta_p^2 = 0.01$, and no interaction between facial trustworthiness and behavior, $F(1,111) = 0.90$, $p = 0.346$, $\eta_p^2 < 0.01$.

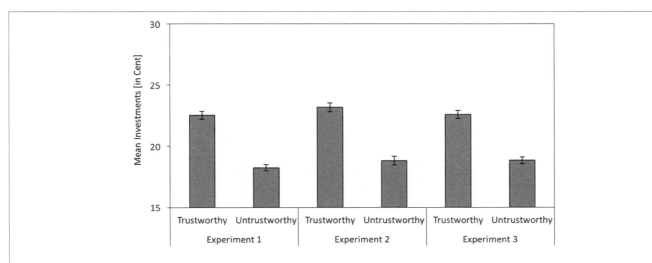

FIGURE 3 | Participants' mean investments in the social interaction game as a function of facial trustworthiness (trustworthy vs. untrustworthy) in Experiment 1 (without cognitive load) and in Experiments 2 and 3 (with cognitive load). The error bars represent the standard errors.

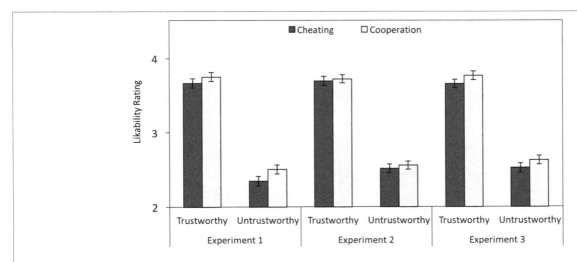

FIGURE 4 | Mean test-phase likability ratings (on a scale ranging from 1 to 6) as a function of facial trustworthiness (trustworthy vs. untrustworthy) and behavior (cheating vs. cooperation) in Experiment 1 (without cognitive load) and in Experiments 2 and 3 (with cognitive load). The error bars represent the standard errors.

Source Guessing and Source Memory

To disentangle source guessing and memory, the multinomial source monitoring model mentioned above (Bayen et al., 1996) was used. For the present study, we needed two sets of the trees displayed in **Figure 2**, one for trustworthy faces and one for untrustworthy faces. To obtain an identifiable base model, we assumed that old–new recognition does not differ as a function of partner behavior (as evidenced by the analysis of old–new recognition reported above), and does not differ between old and new faces ($D_{\text{Cheat}} = D_{\text{Coop}} = D_{\text{New}}$), which is commonly assumed when using the two high threshold model (Snodgrass and Corwin, 1988; Bayen et al., 1996). This base model fit the data well, $G^2(2) = 1.84, p = 0.398$.

First, we analyzed whether participants would show an expectancy-congruent guessing bias. When the behavior of

a recognized person is not remembered, participants have to guess whether the face was associated with cheating or cooperation. In previous studies (Bell et al., 2012b), participants guessed that trustworthy-looking persons were cooperators and that untrustworthy-looking persons were cheaters. That pattern was replicated here. If source memory was not available at test, participants showed a strong bias toward guessing that trustworthy-looking faces were previously associated with cooperation and that untrustworthy-looking faces were previously associated with cheating, $\Delta G^2(1) = 43.01$, $p < 0.001$, $w = 0.07$ (see left panel of **Figure 6**).

The left panel of **Figure 7** displays the estimates for source memory parameter d representing the conditional probability of remembering the behaviors of cheaters and cooperators given that their faces were recognized as old. Source memory was

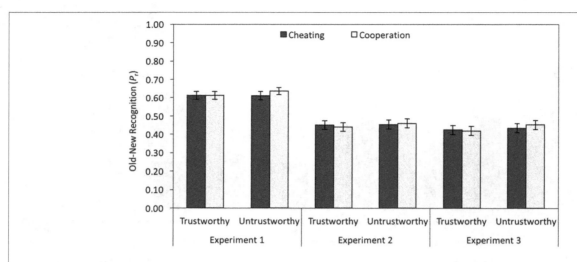

FIGURE 5 | Old–new recognition in terms of P_r (corrected hit rates) as a function of facial trustworthiness (trustworthy vs. untrustworthy) and partner behavior (cheating vs. cooperation) in Experiment 1 (without cognitive load) and in Experiments 2 and 3 (with cognitive load). The error bars represent the standard errors.

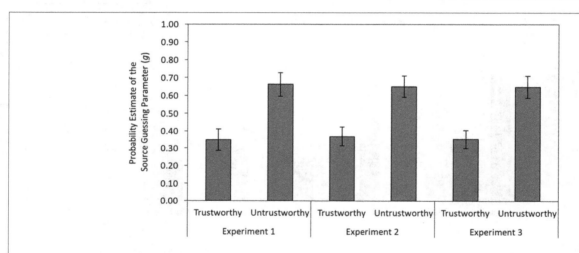

FIGURE 6 | Estimates of the guessing parameter g representing the probability to guess that a person was a cheater rather than a cooperator as a function of facial trustworthiness (trustworthy vs. untrustworthy) in Experiment 1 (without cognitive load) and in Experiments 2 and 3 (with cognitive load). The error bars represent the 95% confidence intervals.

better for cheaters than for cooperators when the faces looked trustworthy, $\Delta G^2(1) = 4.82, p = 0.028, w = 0.02$, but there was no corresponding memory advantage for cooperators over cheaters when the faces looked untrustworthy, $\Delta G^2(1) = 0.14, p = 0.704$, $w < 0.01$. Thus, we replicated the finding of an asymmetrical expectancy-violation effect (Suzuki and Suga, 2010; Bell et al., 2012b).

Discussion

In Experiment 1, as in previous studies (van 't Wout and Sanfey, 2008; Bell et al., 2012b, 2013), participants invested more money into the sequential Prisoner's Dilemma Game (trusted their partners more) when the partners looked trustworthy than when they looked untrustworthy. In the memory test, old–new recognition was not affected by facial trustworthiness and

partner behavior, consistent with a large number of previous studies showing that a person's behavior has no effect on old–new face recognition (e.g., Barclay and Lalumière, 2006; Mehl and Buchner, 2008; Buchner et al., 2009; Kroneisen and Bell, 2013). There are some reports suggesting that old–new recognition is better for untrustworthy-looking than for trustworthy-looking persons (Rule et al., 2012; Bell et al., 2013; Mattarozzi et al., 2015), but this finding was not reliably obtained across experiments (Bell et al., 2012b), and was not replicated here. Consistent with several other studies (Nash et al., 2010; Bell et al., 2012b; Cassidy et al., 2012), participants demonstrated a bias toward guessing that trustworthy-looking persons were cooperators and untrustworthy-looking persons were cheaters. Moreover, and in line with previous studies (Suzuki and Suga, 2010; Bell et al., 2012b), an asymmetric source memory advantage

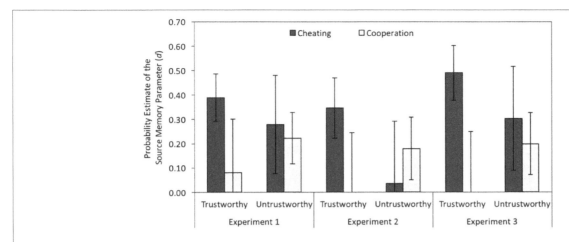

FIGURE 7 | Estimates of the source memory parameter _d_ as a function of the partners' facial trustworthiness (trustworthy vs. untrustworthy) and the partners' behavior (cheating vs. cooperation) in Experiment 1 (without cognitive load) and in Experiments 2 and 3 (with cognitive load). The error bars represent the 95% confidence intervals.

for appearance-incongruent negative information was found: Participants had better source memory for trustworthy-looking cheaters than for trustworthy-looking cooperators.

EXPERIMENT 2

Experiment 2 served to test whether a different pattern of results would be obtained under cognitive load. To impose cognitive load, a continuous choice reaction time (CRT) task with auditory stimuli was used as secondary task. This is a well established method to impose cognitive load (Naveh-Benjamin et al., 2003; Kroneisen et al., 2014), and has the advantage that it involves non-verbal stimuli and responses that do not directly interfere with the sequential Prisoner's Dilemma Game. Participants had to classify three randomly varying tones by pressing three buttons on a response box. The tones were continuously presented to guarantee a steady burden on cognitive resources. The main question was whether the expectancy-violation effect on source memory would disappear under conditions of reduced cognitive resources.

Method
Participants
One hundred and nine students (67 of whom were female) with a mean age of 24 ($SD = 5$) participated in Experiment 2. Participants in Experiment 2 did not differ from those in Experiment 1 in terms of age, gender, and justice sensitivity (**Table 1**). All participants gave written informed consent.

Materials, Procedure, and Design
Experiment 2 was identical to Experiment 1 except that participants were required to perform a secondary CRT task during the sequential Prisoner's Dilemma Game. The task was to continuously classify three piano tones (C1, F3, and B6) by pressing a black left, gray middle, or white right button on a response box, respectively. Each tone was repeated once every

second until participants made a CRT response by pressing a CRT button. Participants received no reminder of the CRT task and no explicit warning when they failed to respond to the CRT stimuli (but the repeated presentation of the same tone can be seen as an implicit warning). Before the start of the sequential Prisoner's Dilemma Game, participants received a training of the CRT task. During this training, participants received immediate feedback about their responses ("correct" in green font color or "false" or "miss" in red font color). This training continued until participants had 20 correct responses in a row.

Given that participants were not pressured to perform the secondary CRT task, it was necessary to exclude participants who did not respond to the CRT stimuli properly. As an inclusion criterion, we required a minimum of one response per trial in the Prisoner's Dilemma Game on average. Based on this criterion, datasets of 13 participants were excluded from analyses because of too few CRT responses. With the remaining sample consisting of 96 participants, it was possible to detect an effect of size $w = 0.04$ for the comparison of source memory between cheaters and cooperators with a statistical power $(1 - \beta)$ of 0.94.

Results
Game Investments
As in Experiment 1, participants invested more when playing with trustworthy-looking partners than when playing with untrustworthy-looking partners, $F(1,95) = 160.64$, $p < 0.001$, $\eta_p^2 = 0.63$ (see middle panel of **Figure 3**).

Likability Ratings
There was a main effect of facial trustworthiness on likability, $F(1,95) = 433.80$, $p < 0.001$, $\eta_p^2 = 0.82$. The effect of partner behavior was not significant, $F(1,95) = 1.13$, $p = 0.290$, $\eta_p^2 = 0.01$. There was no interaction between facial trustworthiness and behavior, $F(1,95) = 0.07$, $p = 0.794$, $\eta_p^2 < 0.01$ (see middle panel of **Figure 4**).

Old–New Recognition

Old–new recognition was lower than in Experiment 1, but the same pattern of results was obtained (see middle panel of **Figure 5**). There was neither a main effect of facial trustworthiness, $F(1,95) = 0.34$, $p = 0.563$, $\eta_p^2 < 0.01$, nor a main effect of partner behavior, $F(1,95) = 0.02$, $p = 0.897$, $\eta_p^2 < 0.01$. The two-way interaction was not significant, $F(1,95) = 0.34$, $p = 0.562$, $\eta_p^2 < 0.01$.

Source Guessing and Source Memory

The base model fit the data well, $G^2(2) = 0.32$, $p = 0.852$. As in Experiment 1, participants were more likely to guess that untrustworthy-looking faces were associated with cheating than that trustworthy-looking faces were associated with cheating, $\Delta G^2(1) = 48.32$, $p < 0.001$, $w = 0.08$ (see middle panel of **Figure 6**).

Again, source memory was better for cheating than for cooperation when the faces looked trustworthy, $\Delta G^2(1) = 5.22$, $p = 0.022$, $w = 0.03$, and source memory did not differ between cheating and cooperation when the faces looked untrustworthy, $\Delta G^2(1) = 0.67$, $p = 0.414$, $w < 0.01$ (see middle panel of **Figure 7**).

Performance in the Continuous Reaction Time Task

The description of the results is incomplete without an analysis of the performance in the CRT task because it is important to test whether or not the enhanced memory for appearance-incongruent cheating is due to a performance trade-off between the encoding of the faces and the CRT task. Therefore, we performed two 2 × 2 MANOVAs with the partner trustworthiness (trustworthy-looking vs. untrustworthy-looking) and partner behavior (cheating vs. cooperation) as independent variables and the proportion of correct responses and the response times (including only correct responses that occurred after > 100 ms) in the CRT task as dependent variables (**Table 2**). Proportion correct did not differ as a function of facial trustworthiness, $F(1,95) = 2.43$, $p = 0.122$, $\eta_p^2 = 0.02$. However, CRT performance was less accurate in the cheater condition in comparison to the cooperator condition, $F(1,95) = 5.76$, $p = 0.018$, $\eta_p^2 = 0.06$. There was no interaction between facial trustworthiness and partner behavior, $F(1,95) = 0.14$, $p = 0.704$, $\eta_p^2 < 0.01$. Response times showed a similar pattern. Response time did not differ as a function of facial trustworthiness, $F(1,95) = 0.31$, $p = 0.578$, $\eta_p^2 < 0.01$. Responses were slower in the cheater condition in comparison to the cooperator condition, $F(1,95) = 5.09$, $p = 0.026$, $\eta_p^2 = 0.05$. However, there was no interaction between facial trustworthiness and partner behavior, $F(1,95) = 0.15$, $p = 0.697$, $\eta_p^2 < 0.01$. Given that this attentional disruption did not translate into better memory for cheaters (as shown by the analyses above), this result does not seem to reflect a reallocation of cognitive resources to the cheater faces and, therefore, does not seem to reflect a performance trade-off between the memory task and the CRT task. It seems possible to speculate that experiencing cheating may result in a negative emotional response that may distract from the secondary task, but does not seem to cause a direct memory enhancement.

TABLE 2 | Mean proportion correct and response times in milliseconds in the CRT task as a function of the partners' facial trustworthiness (trustworthy vs. untrustworthy) and the partners' behavior (cheating vs. cooperation) in Experiments 2 and 3.

	Cheating		Cooperation	
	M	SE	M	SE
Experiment 2				
Proportion correct				
Trustworthy Faces	0.90	0.01	0.92	0.01
Untrustworthy Faces	0.91	0.01	0.92	0.01
Response time				
Trustworthy Faces	2,252	79	2,186	86
Untrustworthy Faces	2,240	99	2,149	86
Experiment 3				
Proportion correct				
Trustworthy Faces	0.88	0.01	0.90	0.01
Untrustworthy Faces	0.89	0.01	0.90	0.01
Response time				
Trustworthy Faces	788	13	762	13
Untrustworthy Faces	787	12	760	13

Discussion

Even though participants had to perform a secondary CRT task, the results were almost identical to those of Experiment 1. Most importantly, participants showed evidence of an appearance-congruent guessing bias and of an asymmetrical expectancy-violation effect on source memory. We conclude from these findings that the enhanced memory for expectancy-incongruent information is obtained even under conditions of cognitive load, which suggests that the encoding of this information occurs automatically and does not rely on demanding elaborative processes.

It seemed important to address the possible concern that the CRT task may simply not have been demanding enough to interfere with the primary task. In Experiment 2, participants were required to perform the secondary CRT task concurrently to the Prisoner's Dilemma Game, but no time pressure was imposed. Therefore, it may have been possible to attend to both the CRT task and the Prisoner's Dilemma Game by delaying responses in the CRT task. In Experiment 3, we therefore required participants to respond to each tone within a time interval of 2 s (which is a typical time interval in CRT studies, see Kroneisen et al., 2014).

EXPERIMENT 3

Experiment 3 was identical to Experiment 2 with the exception that the CRT task was modified to increase the continuous demands on cognitive resources.

Method

Participants

One hundred three students (69 of whom were female) with a mean age of 22 ($SD = 5$) participated in Experiment 3. The sample was similar to those in Experiments 1 and 2 (**Table 1**). All participants gave written informed consent.

Materials, Procedure, and Design

Experiment 3 was identical to Experiment 2 with the exception that the CRT task required participants to respond to each tone within 2 s, after which the next tone was presented. If participants failed to respond to a tone during a trial of the sequential Prisoner's Dilemma Game, they received a warning after the trial that reminded them of the CRT task. In contrast to Experiment 2—in which the sequential Prisoner's Dilemma Game was self-paced—the next round of the game was automatically initiated 10 s after the summary of the interaction had been displayed. Justice sensitivity was not assessed.

The data of two outliers were excluded from the analyses because these participants produced >20% CRT misses on average. The remaining sample responded to 98% of the CRT stimuli on average. With a remaining sample of 101 participants, it was possible to detect an effect of size $w = 0.04$ for the comparison between source memory for cheaters and cooperators with a statistical power $(1 - \beta)$ of 0.95.

Results

Game Investments

As in Experiments 1 and 2, participants invested more when playing with trustworthy-looking partners than when playing with untrustworthy-looking partners, $F(1,100) = 157.95$, $p < 0.001$, $\eta_p^2 = 0.61$ (see right panel of **Figure 3**).

Likability Ratings

There was a main effect of facial trustworthiness on likability with higher likability ratings for trustworthy-looking compared to untrustworthy-looking partners, $F(1,100) = 504.95, p < 0.001$, $\eta_p^2 = 0.83$. Cheaters were judged to be less likable than cooperators, $F(1,100) = 15.08$, $p < 0.001$, $\eta_p^2 = 0.13$. The interaction between facial trustworthiness and behavior was not significant, $F(1,100) = 0.05, p = 0.822, \eta_p^2 < 0.01$ (see right panel of **Figure 4**).

Old–New Recognition

There was neither a main effect of facial trustworthiness on old–new recognition, $F(1,100) = 1.49$, $p = 0.225$, $\eta_p^2 = 0.01$, nor a main effect of partner behavior, $F(1,100) = 0.21$, $p = 0.651$, $\eta_p^2 < 0.01$. The two-way interaction was also not significant, $F(1,100) = 0.57, p = 0.452, \eta_p^2 < 0.01$ (see right panel of **Figure 5**).

Source Guessing and Source Memory

The base model fit the data well, $G^2(2) = 0.87$, $p = 0.647$. As in Experiments 1 and 2, participants were significantly more likely to guess that untrustworthy-looking faces were associated with cheating than that trustworthy-looking faces were associated with cheating, $\Delta G^2(1) = 55.78, p < 0.001, w = 0.08$ (see right panel of **Figure 6**).

As in the previous experiments, there was a source memory advantage for cheaters over cooperators when the faces looked trustworthy, $\Delta G^2(1) = 12.60, p < 0.001, w = 0.04$, but source memory did not differ between cheaters and cooperators when the faces looked untrustworthy, $\Delta G^2(1) = 0.42, p = 0.519$, $w < 0.01$ (see right panel of **Figure 7**).

Performance in the Continuous Reaction Time Task

As in Experiment 2 we performed analyses of the proportion of correct responses and response times (including only correct responses that occurred after >100 ms) in the CRT task. CRT responses were faster than they were in Experiment 2, but the same pattern of results was observed (**Table 2**). Proportion correct did not differ as a function of facial trustworthiness, $F(1,100) = 0.42, p = 0.520, \eta_p^2 < 0.01$. CRT performance was less accurate in the cheater condition in comparison to the cooperator condition, $F(1,100) = 21.82, p < 0.001, \eta_p^2 = 0.18$. There was no interaction between facial trustworthiness and partner behavior, $F(1,100) = 0.55, p = 0.460, \eta_p^2 < 0.01$. Response times showed a similar pattern. Response time did not differ as a function of facial trustworthiness, $F(1,100) = 0.09, p = 0.764, \eta_p^2 < 0.01$. However, responses were slower in the cheater condition in comparison to the cooperator condition, $F(1,100) = 33.29, p < 0.001, \eta_p^2 = 0.25$. There was no interaction between facial trustworthiness and partner behavior, $F(1,100) = 0.04, p = 0.845, \eta_p^2 < 0.01$. Again, the previous analyses suggest that this attentional disruption is not associated with enhanced encoding of the cheater faces.

Discussion

Even though participants were pressured to make faster responses in the CRT task, the same pattern of results was obtained as in Experiments 1 and 2. Most importantly, we obtained evidence in favor of an expectancy-congruent guessing bias and of an asymmetric expectancy-violation effect. Therefore, it seems possible to conclude that the encoding of expectancy-incongruent information works well even under conditions of high cognitive load, presumably because it occurs automatically. At a descriptive level, the results of all three experiments are strikingly similar with the only exception that old–new recognition seems to be somewhat decreased in Experiments 2 and 3 in comparison to Experiment 1.

Given that the CRT task did not seem to have any substantial effect on source memory (or any other variable except face recognition), it may be tempting to conclude from these findings that the CRT task was simply not demanding enough. However, concluding from a non-significant finding that the cognitive load manipulation was not strong enough is problematic because this type of circular reasoning renders the prediction that cognitive load affects cooperation and memory unfalsifiable. To escape this problem, we performed a validation study to test whether the secondary task does indeed disrupt cognitively demanding working-memory processes (as intended).

EXPERIMENT 4

Experiment 4 served to validate the CRT task by testing whether it does indeed have the capacity to disrupt cognitively demanding processes. We used both a verbal memory task and a spatial memory task to test whether the CRT task interferes generally with cognitive processing and does not only selectively affect the processing of a specific type of information (Lange, 2005; Vachon et al., in press).

Method
Participants
Forty students (27 of whom were female) with a mean age of 24 ($SD = 4$) participated in Experiment 4. Participants were consecutively assigned to either the cognitive load group or the control group (i.e., Participant 1 was assigned to the cognitive load condition, Participant 2 was assigned to the control condition, and so on). All participants gave written informed consent.

Materials, Procedure, and Design
Participants performed a verbal working memory task and a spatial working memory task. Task order was counterbalanced between groups (cognitive load vs. control).

In the verbal working memory task, participants were required to remember sequences with varying sequence lengths of four to nine items. The items were randomly drawn from the set {1, 2, ... 9}. Each trial started with a visual warning that participants were required to remember the digits. The digits were presented one after another in 24 pt Arial font at the center of a computer screen for 800 ms with a 200 ms inter-stimulus interval. After a retention interval of 2 s, a number pad with the previously presented digits was shown, and participants were required to select the numbers in the correct (forward) order, using the computer mouse. Selected digits were grayed out, and could not be selected again. After all digits were selected, the number pad disappeared, and a continue button was shown. Upon clicking this button, the next trial started. The task started with a sequence length of four digits. Digit length gradually increased during the task. Participants completed three trials of each sequence length.

The spatial working memory task was identical to the verbal working memory task except that participants were required to remember the spatial locations of four to nine black dots instead of four to nine digits. The locations of the dots were not aligned (but instead randomly distributed across the screen) to make a verbal coding strategy extremely difficult. In each trial, the spatial positions were randomly drawn from a set of nine different spatial positions. The dots appeared one after another at their designated positions (800 ms on, 200 ms off). After a retention interval of 2 s, the previously presented dots were presented again at their corresponding spatial locations. The participants' task was to select the spatial locations of the dots in the order of their appearance. Selected locations were grayed out, and could not be selected again.

The working memory tasks were either completed alongside the secondary CRT task (in the cognitive load condition) or without the secondary CRT task (in the control condition). The CRT task was identical to the one used in Experiment 3. Participants were reminded of the tone classification task before each trial. Tones were presented only during visual item presentation and the retention interval of the working memory task, but not during recall. If participants did not give a response to all CRT tones, they received a warning when the recall of the items was completed.

The design was a mixed 2 × 2 design with working memory task (verbal vs. spatial) as a within-subject variable and cognitive load (cognitive load vs. control) as a between-subjects variable. The dependent variable was working memory performance according to a strict scoring criterion (only items remembered in their correct serial position were scored as correct). Given $\alpha = 0.05$, a total sample size of $N = 40$ participants, and an assumed correlation between the levels of the within-subject variable of $\rho = 0.50$, an effect of size $f = 0.50$ could be detected for the cognitive load variable with a statistical power $(1 - \beta)$ of 0.95.

Results
A 2 × 2 MANOVA with cognitive load (cognitive load vs. control) and working memory task (verbal vs. spatial) as independent variables yielded a main effect of cognitive load, $F(1,38) = 20.60$, $p < 0.001$, $\eta_p^2 = 0.35$, and of task, $F(1,38) = 70.34$, $p < 0.001$, $\eta_p^2 = 0.65$, but no interaction between cognitive load and task, $F(1,38) = 1.75$, $p = 0.193$, $\eta_p^2 = 0.04$. Cognitive load significantly decreased memory performance both in the verbal, $t(38) = 3.68$, $p = 0.001$, $\eta_p^2 = 0.26$, and in the spatial task, $t(38) = 4.05$, $p < 0.001$, $\eta_p^2 = 0.30$ (**Figure 8**). Raw data are reported in the Online Supplementary Material (Data Sheet 4).

Discussion
Experiment 4 serves as a validation study to confirm that the CRT task interferes with cognitively demanding processes. In line with our expectations, the CRT task disrupted performance in a verbal working memory task as well as in a spatial working memory task, suggesting that it does not only interfere with a specific type of information processing, but instead leads to a general decrease of cognitive resources. This rules out the possibility that the CRT

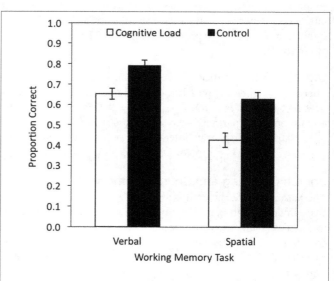

FIGURE 8 | Mean working memory performance in proportion correct as a function of working memory task (verbal vs. spatial) and cognitive load (cognitive load vs. control). The error bars represent the standard errors.

task was not demanding enough to disrupt cognitive processing, which facilitates the interpretation of the findings obtained in Experiments 1–3.

GENERAL DISCUSSION

Previous research suggests that expectations about other people's trustworthiness are formed quickly and automatically on the basis of physical appearance (Todorov et al., 2009, 2015). Trustworthiness judgments in particular are strongly affected by facial cues (Todorov, 2008). The assumption that facial cues have a strong effect on trust and social expectations (van 't Wout and Sanfey, 2008) is further confirmed by the present results. Specifically, participants invested more into the sequential Prisoner's Dilemma Game when the partners looked trustworthy than when the partners looked untrustworthy. Given that investing into the game only payed off when the partner reciprocated, this result suggests that trustworthy-looking partners were expected to cooperate more than untrustworthy-looking partners. Noticeably, this pattern of results was obtained without and with cognitive load, which confirms previous findings suggesting that the perception of facial trustworthiness is an automatic process that does not depend on the availability of cognitive resources (Bonnefon et al., 2013).

Given that appearance-based judgments about a person are often invalid (Todorov et al., 2015), it is important to update facial trustworthiness judgments with behavioral information (Rezlescu et al., 2012). It may be especially important to remember expectancy-incongruent behaviors to be able to correct a false first impression about another person. Consistent with previous studies (Suzuki and Suga, 2010; Volstorf et al., 2011; Bell et al., 2012b), source memory was better for the appearance-incongruent cheating of a trustworthy-looking person in comparison to the appearance-congruent cooperation of a trustworthy-looking person. Noticeably, memory for appearance-congruent cooperation was poor. This confirms the predictions of the schema-copy-plus-tag model (Graesser and Nakamura, 1982), which states that discriminability of schema-consistent information is poor because it will be produced at test regardless of whether it was presented at encoding or not. Schema-atypical information is more distinct, and, therefore, associated with better memory discriminability.

Memory was selectively enhanced for cheating that violated a positive expectation about a trustworthy-looking partner, but there was no similar memory advantage for cooperators over cheaters when the faces looked untrustworthy. This asymmetry was also found in previous memory experiments (Suzuki and Suga, 2010; Bell and Buchner, 2012), and it fits with a study on investments in repeated game interactions showing that participants tend to adjust their own behavior more strongly in response to a partner's defection than in response to a partner's cooperation (Chang et al., 2010). This asymmetric memory advantage for appearance-incongruent cheating over appearance-incongruent cooperation may be

particularly pronounced in the present study because only female stimulus faces were used. It is known that female faces tend to elicit positive social expectations (Kroneisen and Bell, 2013), which means that norm-violating behaviors of female partners may represent particularly strong expectancy violations (Bell et al., 2015).

Two explanations for the memory advantage for appearance-incongruent cheating were tested. According to the first account, information that does not fit into existing schemas receives more elaborative processing, which depends on the mobilization and availability of additional cognitive resources. This enhanced elaboration results in a more vivid and detailed recollection of the expectancy-incongruent information. According to the second account, schema-atypical information is retained in form of unelaborated tags. This resource-efficient encoding strategy has the advantage that unexpected information can be encoded and retained in memory even under conditions of high cognitive load. The present results support the latter view. The source memory advantage for appearance-incongruent cheating was not affected by the presence or absence of cognitive load at encoding. A similar memory advantage for appearance-incongruent cheating was obtained in all three experiments, regardless of whether participants had to perform a demanding secondary task at encoding or not. The experiments were reported separately because they were run at different times. However, when the source memory data of all experiments were combined in a single supplementary cross-experimental analysis, the conclusion that source memory was not affected by cognitive load was supported. The base model still fit the data well, $G^2(6) = 3.02$, $p = 0.807$. Source memory did not differ among experiments, $\Delta G^2(8) = 11.95, p = 0.154, w = 0.02$, which suggests that the pattern of results was not affected by the secondary task in Experiments 2 and 3.

This pattern of findings confirms the predictions of the schema-copy-plus-tag model (Graesser and Nakamura, 1982), according to which schema-violating information is retained in the form of simple tags that require only minimal elaboration, and can therefore be encoded and retained even under conditions of high cognitive load. Consistent with this interpretation, it has been previously shown that the source memory advantage for faces of cheaters is not due to a vivid recollection of the cheating episode, but rather due to emotional tagging in the sense of a rough classification of the partner as a "cheater" (Bell et al., 2012a). The encoding and retrieval of simple emotional tags may be less cognitively demanding and, therefore, less affected by a reduction in cognitive resources than other types of context memory (Rahhal et al., 2002).

This interpretation fits well with Todorov and Uleman's (2003) assumption that reading about or observing the behavior of another person leads people to draw inferences about the other person's traits (e.g., dishonest or honest) that then become linked to the other person's face. Importantly, these trait representations are assumed to include only a summary judgment about the other person's behavior, and to be comparatively unelaborated and robust (Carlston and Skowronski, 1994; Todorov and Uleman, 2002). In the study of Todorov and Uleman (2003), participants saw faces with behavior descriptions that implied character traits.

The binding between faces and traits was revealed by an enhanced false recognition of the trait labels in an implicit memory test. The most interesting finding in the present context is that the implicit memory for the association between a face and a trait was not affected by a secondary task at encoding (rehearsing 6-digit numbers), which suggests that the process of binding traits to faces is an automatic process. The present study shows parallel findings in a different paradigm where traits are directly inferred from experiences in a social-dilemma game, and memory is tested in an explicit source memory test.

Remembering appearance-congruent cooperation and cheating enables participants to update their impressions about other people, which could have beneficial effects on future social decision making. For instance, when we encounter a trustworthy-looking person, but learn subsequently that this person is not to be trusted, memory for the appearance-incongruent cheating may help to avoid being fooled by the trustworthy appearance of this person again. Obviously, this discussion implies that the memory for the partners' previous behaviors is used to inform social decision making. Previous results using repeated social-dilemma games suggest that people continue to rely on facial trustworthiness over the course of the game (in line with the persistent effect of facial trustworthiness on source guessing in the present experiment), but also succeed in adjusting their own decisions to the individual partners' previous trustworthy or untrustworthy behaviors (Chang et al., 2010; Rezlescu et al., 2012). Murty et al. (2016) directly examined the relationship between memory and economic decision making, and found that source memory (in contrast to item memory) had a beneficial effect on the participants' choices in social and non-social decision making tasks. Therefore, it seems plausible to assume that source memory for appearance-incongruent behaviors can have direct beneficial effects on social decision making.

CONCLUSION

In sum, source memory for cheaters and cooperators was highly similar across experiments, regardless of whether cognitive load was induced at encoding (Experiments 2 and 3) or not (Experiment 1). These results are compatible with the general idea that cognitive mechanisms underlying social cooperation operate highly automatically so that they remain unaffected by cognitive load. Specifically, it seems possible to encode and retain information about a person's expectancy-incongruent behavior even under conditions of high cognitive load. Remembering this type of behavior seems particularly important for the decision making process because it helps to correct maladaptive behavior tendencies. For example, it seems particularly important to remember that a trustworthy-looking person is in fact not to be trusted to avoid being fooled by the trustworthy appearance of this person in the future. Being able to remember appearance-incongruent behaviors even under conditions of cognitive load may be beneficial in that it allows people to sustain successful reciprocal cooperation even under the distracting and stressful conditions that are characteristic of everyday life.

AUTHOR CONTRIBUTIONS

LM, RB, and AB conceived and designed the experiments, supervised data collection, analyzed the data, and wrote the paper.

REFERENCES

Barclay, P., and Lalumière, M. (2006). Do people differentially remember cheaters? Hum. Nat. 17, 98–113. doi: 10.1007/s12110-006-1022-y

Bayen, U. J., Murnane, K., and Erdfelder, E. (1996). Source discrimination, item detection, and multinomial models of source monitoring. J. Exp. Psychol. Learn. Mem. Cogn. 22, 197–215.

Bell, R., and Buchner, A. (2012). How adaptive is memory for cheaters? Curr. Dir. Psychol. Sci. 21, 403–408. doi: 10.1177/0963721412458525

Bell, R., Buchner, A., Erdfelder, E., Giang, T., Schain, C., and Riether, N. (2012a). How specific is source memory for faces of cheaters? Evidence for categorical emotional tagging. J. Exp. Psychol. Learn. Mem. Cogn. 38, 457–472. doi: 10.1037/a0026017

Bell, R., Buchner, A., Kroneisen, M., and Giang, T. (2012b). On the flexibility of social source memory: a test of the emotional incongruity hypothesis. J. Exp. Psychol. Learn. Mem. Cogn. 38, 1512–1529. doi: 10.1037/a0028219

Bell, R., Giang, T., Mund, I., and Buchner, A. (2013). Memory for reputational trait information: is social–emotional information processing less flexible in old age? Psychol. Aging 28, 984–995. doi: 10.1037/a0034266

Bell, R., Mieth, L., and Buchner, A. (2015). Appearance-based first impressions and person memory. J. Exp. Psychol. Learn. Mem. Cogn. 41, 456–472. doi: 10.1037/xlm0000034

Bonnefon, J.-F., Hopfensitz, A., and De Neys, W. (2013). The modular nature of trustworthiness detection. J. Exp. Psychol. Gen. 142, 143–150. doi: 10.1037/a0028930

Bröder, A., and Meiser, T. (2007). Measuring source memory. Z. Psychol. J. Psychol. 215, 52–60.

Buchner, A., Bell, R., Mehl, B., and Musch, J. (2009). No enhanced recognition memory, but better source memory for faces of cheaters. Evol. Hum. Behav. 30, 212–224. doi: 10.1016/j.evolhumbehav.2009.01.004

Carlston, D., and Skowronski, J. (1994). Savings in the relearning of trait information as evidence for spontaneous inference generation. J. Pers. Soc. Psychol. 66, 840–856. doi: 10.1037/0022-3514.66.5.840

Cassidy, B. S., Zebrowitz, L. A., and Gutchess, A. H. (2012). Appearance-based inferences bias source memory. Mem. Cogn. 40, 1214–1224. doi: 10.3758/s13421-012-0233-1

Chang, L. J., Doll, B., van 't Wout, M., Frank, M., and Sanfey, A. G. (2010). Seeing is believing: Trustworthiness as a dynamic belief. Cogn. Psychol. 61, 87–105. doi: 10.1016/j.cogpsych.2010.03.001

Clark, K., and Sefton, M. (2001). The sequential prisoner's dilemma: evidence on reciprocation. Econ. J. 111, 51–68. doi: 10.1111/1468-0297.00588

Delton, A., Krasnow, M., Cosmides, L., and Tooby, J. (2011). Evolution of direct reciprocity under uncertainty can explain human generosity in one-shot encounters. Proc. Natl. Acad. Sci. U.S.A. 108, 13335–13340. doi: 10.1073/pnas.1102131108

Ehrenberg, K., and Klauer, K. C. (2005). Flexible use of source information: processing components of the inconsistency effect in person memory. *J. Exp. Soc. Psychol.* 41, 369–387. doi: 10.1016/j.jesp.2004.08.001

Engell, A. D., Haxby, J. V., and Todorov, A. (2007). Implicit trustworthiness decisions: automatic coding of face properties in the human amygdala. *J. Cogn. Neurosci.* 19, 1508–1519. doi: 10.1162/jocn.2007.19.9.1508

Erdfelder, E., Auer, T.-S., Hilbig, B. E., Aßfalg, A., Moshagen, M., and Nadarevic, L. (2009). Multinomial processing tree models. *Z. Psychol. J. Psychol.* 217, 108–124.

Faul, F., Erdfelder, E., Lang, A.-G., and Buchner, A. (2007). G*Power 3: a flexible statistical power analysis for the social, behavioral, and biomedical sciences. *Behav. Res. Methods* 39, 175–191. doi: 10.3758/BF03193146

Graesser, A. C., and Nakamura, G. V. (1982). "The impact of a schema on comprehension and memory," in *The Psychology of Learning and Motivation*, ed. G. H. Bower (London: Academic Press), 59–109.

Kessler, J., and Meier, S. (2014). Learning from (failed) replications: cognitive load manipulations and charitable giving. *J. Econ. Behav. Organ.* 102, 10–13. doi: 10.1016/j.jebo.2014.02.005

Klein, S., Cosmides, L., Tooby, J., and Chance, S. (2002). Decisions and the evolution of memory: multiple systems, multiple functions. *Psychol. Rev.* 109, 306–329. doi: 10.1037/0033-295X.109.2.306

Kroneisen, M., and Bell, R. (2013). Sex, cheating, and disgust: enhanced source memory for trait information that violates gender stereotypes. *Memory* 21, 167–181. doi: 10.1080/09658211.2012.713971

Kroneisen, M., Rummel, J., and Erdfelder, E. (2014). Working memory load eliminates the survival processing effect. *Memory* 22, 92–102. doi: 10.1080/09658211.2013.815217

Kroneisen, M., Woehe, L., and Rausch, L. S. (2015). Expectancy effects in source memory: how moving to a bad neighborhood can change your memory. *Psychon. Bull. Rev.* 22, 179–189. doi: 10.3758/s13423-014-0655-9

Küppers, V., and Bayen, U. J. (2014). Inconsistency effects in source memory and compensatory schema-consistent guessing. *Q. J. Exp. Psychol.* 67, 2042–2059. doi: 10.1080/17470218.2014.904914

Lange, E. B. (2005). Disruption of attention by irrelevant stimuli in serial recall. *J. Mem. Lang.* 53, 513–531. doi: 10.1016/j.jml.2005.07.002

Mattarozzi, K., Todorov, A., and Codispoti, M. (2015). Memory for faces: the effect of facial appearance and the context in which the face is encountered. *Psychol. Res.* 79, 308–317. doi: 10.1007/s00426-014-0554-8

Mehl, B., and Buchner, A. (2008). No enhanced memory for faces of cheaters. *Evol. Hum. Behav.* 29, 35–41. doi: 10.1016/j.evolhumbehav.2007.08.001

Minear, M., and Park, D. (2004). A lifespan database of adult facial stimuli. *Behav. Res. Methods Instrum. Comput.* 36, 630–633. doi: 10.3758/BF03206543

Moshagen, M. (2010). multiTree: a computer program for the analysis of multinomial processing tree models. *Behav. Res. Methods* 42, 42–54. doi: 10.3758/BRM.42.1.42

Murty, V., FeldmanHall, O., Hunter, L., Phelps, E., and Davachi, L. (2016). Episodic memories predict adaptive value-based decision-making. *J. Exp. Psychol. Gen.* 145, 548–558. doi: 10.1037/xge0000158

Nash, R. A., Bryer, O. M., and Schlaghecken, F. (2010). Look who's talking! Facial appearance can bias source monitoring. *Memory* 18, 451–457. doi: 10.1080/09658211003742706

Naveh-Benjamin, M., Guez, J., and Marom, M. (2003). The effects of divided attention at encoding on item and associative memory. *Mem. Cogn.* 31, 1021–1035. doi: 10.3758/BF03196123

Nieznański, M. (2013). Effects of resource demanding processing on context memory for context-related versus context-unrelated items. *J. Cogn. Psychol.* 25, 745–758. doi: 10.1080/20445911.2013.819002

Olivola, C. Y., and Todorov, A. (2010). Elected in 100 milliseconds: appearance-based trait inferences and voting. *J. Nonverbal Behav.* 34, 83–110. doi: 10.1007/s10919-009-0082-1

Phillips, P. J., Wechsler, H., Huang, J., and Rauss, P. J. (1998). The FERET database and evaluation procedure for face-recognition algorithms. *Image Vis. Comput.* 16, 295–306. doi: 10.1016/S0262-8856(97)00070-X

Piovesan, M., and Wengström, E. (2009). Fast or fair? A study of response times. *Econ. Lett.* 105, 193–196.

Rahhal, T., May, C., and Hasher, L. (2002). Truth and character: sources that older adults can remember. *Psychol. Sci.* 13, 101–105. doi: 10.1111/1467-9280.00419

Rand, D. G., Greene, J. D., and Nowak, M. A. (2012). Spontaneous giving and calculated greed. *Nature* 489, 427–430. doi: 10.1038/nature11467

Rezlescu, C., Duchaine, B., Olivola, C., Chater, N., and Rustichini, A. (2012). Unfakeable facial configurations affect strategic choices in trust games with or without information about past behavior. *PLoS ONE* 7:e34293. doi: 10.1371/journal.pone.0034293

Riefer, D. M., and Batchelder, W. H. (1988). Multinomial modeling and the measurement of cognitive processes. *Psychol. Rev.* 95, 318–339. doi: 10.1007/s00406-010-0151-9

Rule, N., Slepian, M., and Ambady, N. (2012). A memory advantage for untrustworthy faces. *Cognition* 125, 207–218. doi: 10.1016/j.cognition.2012.06.017

Schmitt, M., Gollwitzer, M., Maes, J., and Arbach, D. (2005). Justice sensitivity: assessment and location in the personality space. *Eur. J. Psychol. Assess.* 21, 202–211. doi: 10.1027/1015-5759.21.3.202

Singmann, H., and Kellen, D. (2013). MPTinR: analysis of multinomial processing tree models in R. *Behav. Res. Methods* 45, 560–575. doi: 10.3758/s13428-012-0259-0

Snodgrass, J. G., and Corwin, J. (1988). Pragmatics of measuring recognition memory: applications to dementia and amnesia. *J. Exp. Psychol. Gen.* 117, 34–50. doi: 10.1037/0096-3445.117.1.34

Stahl, C., and Klauer, K. (2007). HMMTree: a computer program for latent-class hierarchical multinomial processing tree models. *Behav. Res. Methods* 39, 267–273. doi: 10.3758/BF03193157

Suzuki, A., and Suga, S. (2010). Enhanced memory for the wolf in sheep's clothing: facial trustworthiness modulates face-trait associative memory. *Cognition* 117, 224–229. doi: 10.1016/j.cognition.2010.08.004

Tinghög, G., Andersson, A., Bonn, C., Böttiger, H., Josephson, C., Lundgren, G., et al. (2013). Intuition and cooperation reconsidered. *Nature* 489, 427–430.

Todorov, A. (2008). Evaluating faces on trustworthiness. *Ann. N. Y. Acad. Sci.* 1124, 208–224. doi: 10.1196/annals.1440.012

Todorov, A., Olivola, C., Dotsch, R., and Mende-Siedlecki, P. (2015). Social attributions from faces: determinants, consequences, accuracy, and functional significance. *Annu. Rev. Psychol.* 66, 519–545. doi: 10.1146/annurev-psych-113011-143831

Todorov, A., Pakrashi, M., and Oosterhof, N. N. (2009). Evaluating faces on trustworthiness after minimal time exposure. *Soc. Cogn.* 77, 813–833. doi: 10.1521/soco.2009.27.6.813

Todorov, A., and Uleman, J. (2002). Spontaneous trait inferences are bound to actors' faces: evidence from a false recognition paradigm. *J. Pers. Soc. Psychol.* 83, 1051–1065. doi: 10.1037/0022-3514.83.5.1051

Todorov, A., and Uleman, J. (2003). The efficiency of binding spontaneous trait inferences to actors' faces. *J. Exp. Soc. Psychol.* 39, 549–562. doi: 10.1016/S0022-1031(03)00059-3

Trivers, R. L. (1971). The evolution of reciprocal altruism. *Q. Rev. Biol.* 46, 35–57. doi: 10.1086/406755

Vachon, F., Labonté, K., and Marsh, J. E. (in press). Attentional capture by deviant sounds: a non-contingent form of auditory distraction? *J. Exp. Psychol. Learn. Mem. Cogn.*

van 't Wout, M., and Sanfey, A. G. (2008). Friend or foe: the effect of implicit trustworthiness judgments in social decision-making. *Cognition* 108, 796–803. doi: 10.1016/j.cognition.2008.07.002

Verkoeijen, P. P. J. L., and Bouwmeester, S. (2014). Does Intuition Cause Cooperation? *PLoS ONE* 9:e96654. doi: 10.1371/journal.pone.0096654

Volstorf, J., Rieskamp, J., and Stevens, D. R. (2011). The good, the bad, and the rare: memory for partners in social interactions. *PLoS ONE* 6:e18945. doi: 10.1371/journal.pone.0018945

Willis, J., and Todorov, A. (2006). First impressions: making up your mind after a 100-ms exposure to a face. *Psychol. Sci.* 17, 592–598. doi: 10.1111/j.1467-9280.2006.01750.x

Conflict of Interest Statement: The authors declare that the research was conducted in the absence of any commercial or financial relationships that could be construed as a potential conflict of interest.

Assessing anger regulation in middle childhood: development and validation of a behavioral observation measure

Helena L. Rohlf* and Barbara Krahé

Department of Psychology, University of Potsdam, Potsdam, Germany

An observational measure of anger regulation in middle childhood was developed that facilitated the *in situ* assessment of five maladaptive regulation strategies in response to an anger-eliciting task. 599 children aged 6–10 years ($M = 8.12$, $SD = 0.92$) participated in the study. Construct validity of the measure was examined through correlations with parent- and self-reports of anger regulation and anger reactivity. Criterion validity was established through links with teacher-rated aggression and social rejection measured by parent-, teacher-, and self-reports. The observational measure correlated significantly with parent- and self-reports of anger reactivity, whereas it was unrelated to parent- and self-reports of anger regulation. It also made a unique contribution to predicting aggression and social rejection.

Keywords: anger regulation, middle childhood, behavioral observation, aggression, social rejection

Edited by:
Yusuke Moriguchi,
Joetsu University of Education, Japan

Reviewed by:
Yoshifumi Ikeda,
Joetsu University of Education, Japan
Peter Zimmermann,
Universität Wuppertal, Germany
Annette M. Klein,
University of Leipzig, Germany

*Correspondence:
Helena L. Rohlf,
Department of Psychology, University
of Potsdam, Karl-Liebknecht-Str.
24-25, 14476 Potsdam, Germany
helena.rohlf@uni-potsdam.de

Specialty section:
This article was submitted to
Developmental Psychology,
a section of the journal
Frontiers in Psychology

Introduction

Anger is a common emotion in childhood. School-aged children have reported feeling angry once a day on average and more often described their anger intensity as strong than as moderate or low (von Salisch, 2000). Anger may be defined as "the appraisal that a goal of personal significance has been blocked and readiness to act with increased effort to overcome obstacles and achieve the goal" (Cole, 2014, p. 204). A large body of research has shown that deficits in anger regulation are related to various problematic outcomes in childhood, including aggression and peer rejection (see Lemerise and Harper, 2010; Röll et al., 2012, for reviews). Given this great importance of anger regulation skills for children's social functioning (Fabes and Eisenberg, 1992), it is essential to have valid methods for the assessment of anger regulation strategies in childhood. The present study was conducted to develop and validate an observational method for assessing anger regulation in middle childhood in response to an anger-eliciting task.

According to Gross (1998), emotion regulation is defined as "the processes by which individuals influence which emotions they have, when they have them, and how they experience and express these emotions" (p. 275). Emotion regulation includes attentional, cognitive, and behavioral attempts to manage the internal experience or the external expression of emotion (Eisenberg and Spinrad, 2004). The development of emotion regulation skills makes major progress throughout childhood (Lemerise and Harper, 2010). By the time they start school, most children have developed a set of strategies that enable them to regulate their emotions, and they have also understood that the external expression of emotions does not have to match the internal emotional experience (Saarni and von Salisch, 1993). They show an increasing use of strategies for regulating the anger expression (e.g., by substituting or neutralizing the anger expression) in order to comply with cultural display rules for the expression of emotions (Zeman and Garber, 1996). However, there is evidence that children find the regulation of anger more difficult than the regulation of other negative emotions. In a study by Zeman and Shipman (1997) children reported a lower self-efficacy regarding the regulation of the expression of anger compared to the regulation of the expression of sadness. Similarly, Waters and Thompson (2014) found that children perceived the regulation of anger as more difficult than the regulation of sadness. In addition, their study revealed that children perceive different strategies to be more effective in regulating anger compared to sadness. Notably, children rated *problem-solving behavior* to be more effective in managing the experience of anger, whereas the strategies *seeking social support* and *venting the emotion* were seen as more effective in regulating sadness. These results are in line with the theoretical conceptualization of anger as a response to the blockage of a goal: As a strategy that is directed at removing the obstacle to goal attainment, problem-solving is more likely to effectively reduce anger than strategies that focus on the emotion experience.

Although the majority of the studies on anger regulation in middle childhood have relied on parent- and self-reports of anger regulation, there are several concerns about the use of such measures. With regard to self-reports, thinking and talking about complex processes such as emotion regulation requires an appropriate level of cognitive and linguistic skills that might not have developed sufficiently at this age. Furthermore, even if a child is able to generate strategies for regulating emotional states, it remains questionable whether children's self-reports on how they might behave correspond to their behavior in a real emotion-evoking situation (Underwood, 1997b). Regarding anger in particular, children's reports may be distorted as anger is related to an impulse to act and has been shown to narrow attention, bias judgments, and influence information processing (Litvak et al., 2010). These characteristics make it difficult to behave in a reflected way in the state of anger. Thus, children who theoretically know about adaptive regulation strategies may have difficulties acting according to this knowledge when they are angry. A study by Parker et al. (2001) showed that 2nd grade children's reports about how they would express their anger in a hypothetical scenario differed substantially from their behavior in a live situation. In the live context, children reported feeling less anger, expressed less anger, and dissembled their anger more. Furthermore, the children generated fewer strategies for hiding their anger in the live context in comparison to the hypothetical context. Based on these results, the authors warned that children's self-reports in response to hypothetical vignettes should not be considered representative of their actual behavior in live situations.

Parents' ratings may provide more valid information about their children's anger regulation skills, as they have the opportunity to observe their children in anger-arousing situations. Parents, however, can only give information about their children's behavior in the family context. The emotion-related behavior children show in their family cannot easily be generalized to behavior in other contexts, such as the school. Children have reported controlling their expression of emotion significantly more in the presence of peers compared to parents (Zeman and Garber, 1996). This discrepancy might be particularly large with respect to anger as children anticipate greater negative social consequences from peers in response to displaying anger compared to other emotions (Underwood, 1997a).

These findings suggest that an observation of the children's behavior in an anger-eliciting situation might provide a better assessment of anger regulation strategies than parent- or self-reports. By recording anger regulation skills *in situ,* behavioral observations may yield more ecologically valid conclusions about anger regulation skills than self- and parent-reports. To date, observational measures of anger regulation have been primarily used in studies with children of pre-school age. For example, Tan et al. (2013) developed a paradigm in which children aged between 24 and 48 months were made to wait for a desired gift while playing with a boring toy. Two adaptive anger regulation strategies, distraction and calm bids, were identified and were found to be negatively linked to difficulties in child temperament (negative affectivity and low effortful control). The use of behavioral observation measures in studies with preschoolers is often based on the argument that the use of self-reports is not possible due to the limited cognitive abilities of children at this age (e.g., Helmsen and Petermann, 2010). The results of the study of Parker et al. (2001) described above indicate that the same reasoning can be applied to school age children. However, when conducting behavioral observations in middle childhood, it is crucial to know how valid the obtained data of anger regulation actually is and whether observational measures can add additional information beyond parent- or self-reports. In our study we addressed this question by assessing anger regulation through behavioral observation as well as parent- and self-reports and by examining the associations of these different methods with aggression and social rejection. This enabled us to examine if the observational measure can explain unique variance of these two outcomes. To our knowledge, there are no studies to date that have directly addressed this issue.

Emotion regulation is not limited to successful, adaptive regulation strategies but also includes maladaptive strategies (Eisenberg and Spinrad, 2004). However, regulation strategies are not generally good or bad, as their adaptivity can vary across different contexts (Gross, 1998). Thus, strategies can have different consequences depending on the situation in which they are used and depending on characteristics of the person who uses them, such as age and gender. Therefore, in the present study we defined the adaptivity of the anger regulation strategies specifically in terms of their consequences on aggression and social rejection. Accordingly, our classification into adaptive and maladaptive strategies was based on studies that investigated the associations of anger regulation strategies with aggression and social rejection. With regard to aggression, it has been found that in frustrating situations aggressive children more often focus on the frustrating stimuli, show more external regulation (e.g., swearing or handling the task material roughly), and show a higher tendency to resign from the situational demands than do non-aggressive children (Melnick and Hinshaw, 2000; Gilliom et al., 2002; Crockenberg et al., 2008; Helmsen and Petermann, 2010). In contrast to these maladaptive forms of anger regulation, the ability to distract oneself from the source of frustration and the use of problem-oriented behavior has been found to be used more often by non-aggressive children (Orobio de Castro et al., 2005). With regard to the application of display rules about the socially acceptable expression of anger, there is evidence that non-aggressive children use display rule strategies for regulating the expression of anger more often compared to aggressive children (Underwood et al., 1992; Cole et al., 1994).

Similar findings have been obtained with regard to the link between anger regulation strategies and social rejection. Focusing on negative aspects of a frustrating task, showing less use of active distraction from a frustrating stimulus, and showing less use of display rule strategies could be identified as predictors of low social preference and social rejection (McDowell et al., 2000; Melnick and Hinshaw, 2000; Trentacosta and Shaw, 2009), respectively. Furthermore, socially rejected children have been found to express their anger more compared to their socially accepted peers (Dearing et al., 2002). Based on these results, we distinguished seven observable strategies of anger regulation: The strategies *visual focus*, *verbal focus*, *venting the anger*, and *resignation* were conceptualized as maladaptive, whereas *distraction*, *solution-orientation*, and *the use of display rule strategies* were defined as adaptive in terms of aggression and social rejection. With regard to the strategy *venting the anger*, it is important to note that this behavior is not consistently conceptualized as a regulation strategy but sometimes seen as the simple expression of the anger experience that has no regulatory function. Different authors have conceptualized anger expression and anger regulation as distinct constructs and have considered anger expression as the outcome of the regulation process or as an indicator of anger reactivity (Melnick and Hinshaw, 2000; Dearing et al., 2002). However, as we assume that such behavior includes the attempt to reduce the anger intensity, in line with other authors (Grob and Smolenski, 2005; Helmsen and Petermann, 2010), we consider external anger-related behavior, such as venting the anger, as part of anger regulation.

A further important emotion regulation strategy in childhood is *seeking social support*. Whether this strategy is adaptive or maladaptive depends on the likelihood that social support may be obtained. Research has shown that help-seeking behavior is a mediator between insecure attachment style and maladjustment (Larose and Bernier, 2001) and that seeking social support during frustrating situations effectively reduces anger in children and adolescents (Spangler and Zimmermann, 2014). However, these links have been studied in situations where supportive others were available, for example in the form of emotional support provided by mothers. In our paradigm, children encountered the anger-eliciting task in the presence of a stranger who was instructed not to respond to requests for help. If children looked at the experimenters, they did not respond, if they directly asked for help, they were told they had to manage the task on their own. In this context, repeated attempts at securing social support, despite having noticed that no help can be expected, is not considered an adaptive strategy. Consistent with this reasoning, studies that observed children in a frustrating situation in which social support was not available or only to a limited degree, did not find associations between the strategy *seeking support* and

aggression (Gilliom et al., 2002; Helmsen and Petermann, 2010). Thus, in line with the classification of regulation strategies by other authors (Grob and Smolenski, 2005), we considered this strategy to be neither adaptive nor maladaptive in our behavioral observation measure, although it may well be adaptive in other contexts in which support is actually available. To highlight this point, we refer to this category as *ineffective help-seeking* in the context of our methodological approach.

The aim of the present study was to develop and validate a method for assessing anger regulation in children through behavioral observation in an anger-eliciting situation. The measure was designed to meet two objectives: (a) to identify anger regulation strategies defined as maladaptive with regard to social rejection and aggression that are open to observation, and (b) to categorize any additional strategies in response to the anger-eliciting task to provide a comprehensive description of the children's behavioral strategies of dealing with their anger. Anger was induced through a frustration, defined as the blocking of a goal-directed activity, by presenting the children with an unsolvable task, as described in the Methods section below. A coding system of children's behavior during completion of the task facilitated the identification of the adaptive and maladaptive regulation strategies as well as additional strategies that were part of the children's behavioral repertoire in dealing with their anger during the task. The coding system was based on several studies which have used a similar approach for categorizing emotion regulation strategies (Fabes and Eisenberg, 1992; Melnick and Hinshaw, 2000; Gilliom et al., 2002; Helmsen and Petermann, 2010), and on other work addressing emotion regulation in children (Grob and Smolenski, 2005; Petermann and Wiedebusch, 2008).

Construct validity was assessed by correlating the behavioral measure with parent- and self-reports of anger regulation and anger reactivity as well as the self-reported situational anger level. Anger reactivity is theoretically distinct from anger regulation as emotional reactivity reflects individual differences in emotional responsiveness, whereas emotion regulation reflects the ability to modulate the emotional reaction (Mullin and Hinshaw, 2007). However, as the two constructs influence one another and have often found to be related (e.g., Kim-Spoon et al., 2013), anger reactivity served as a validation construct in the present study. Criterion validity was assessed by relating maladaptive anger regulation, assessed via behavioral observation, to measures of aggression and social rejection.

Two hypotheses were examined in our study:

Hypothesis 1 predicted that the observational measure of maladaptive anger regulation would show significant correlations with the parent- and self-reports of anger regulation and the conceptually related construct of anger reactivity. Given the features and limitations of parent- and self-reports of anger regulation outlined above, we expected the correlations between these two measures and the behavioral measure of anger regulation to be moderate in size. The correlations between the observational measure and the measures of anger reactivity and anger level were also expected to be moderate, as the latter measures reflect the construct of anger *reactivity*, which is conceptually distinct from anger *regulation*.

Hypothesis 2 postulated that the observational measure of maladaptive anger regulation would be positively associated with aggression and social rejection and make a unique contribution to the prediction of both outcomes beyond the effects of parent- and self-reports of anger regulation and anger reactivity.

Materials and Methods

Participants

A total of 677 children aged 6–10 years were included in this study. Data from a subsample of 78 children (42 girls and 36 boys; age: $M = 7.91$, $SD = 1.09$) was used to develop and evaluate the coding system for the behavioral observation. This subsample was selected randomly from the first 250 participants. The remaining sample of 599 children (304 girls, 295 boys) provided the data for testing the validity of the observational measure. The mean age of this sample was $M = 8.12$ ($SD = 0.92$). With regard to socio-economic status, defined by the parents' educational status, 1.6% of the mothers and 1.4% of the fathers had no or a low level school qualification, 41.6% of the mothers and 48.9% of the fathers had a medium level qualification, 22.9% of the mothers and 13.6% of the fathers had university entrance qualification, and 33.9% of the mothers and 36.1% of the fathers held a university degree.

Participants were part of a larger sample of 1658 children from 33 public elementary schools who took part in a longitudinal study on intrapersonal developmental risk factors in childhood and adolescence based at the University of Potsdam in Germany. Parental consent for videotaping the children during the behavioral observation was obtained in addition to obtaining general consent to participate in the study. Only children whose parents gave permission for their child to be videotaped completed the behavioral observation task ($n = 1183$). These children did not differ significantly from those children without consent for videotaping on any of the variables included in the present study. Due to limited resources for data coding, it was not possible to analyze all videos. After excluding videos that could not be coded due to technical issues or poor light conditions (about 15%), the 677 children whose videos were included in the coding were selected randomly.

Materials
Anger-Eliciting Task

A frustrating task designed to elicit anger was developed to assess anger regulation strategies through behavioral observation. Frustration was induced by telling the children that they could win an attractive prize if they managed to complete a task that was, in fact, almost impossible to achieve. The children were asked to build a tower out of 10 wooden toy blocks. A picture of a block tower was put in front of them, and they were instructed to build a tower that looked exactly like the tower on the picture. Three small toys and a 2:40-min hourglass were put next to the toy blocks. The experimenter sat diagonally behind the child. The children were told that they could choose one of the toys if they managed to build the tower before the hourglass had finished. The task was rigged such that two of the blocks were slightly rounded on one side. This made it almost impossible to

complete the task because the tower collapsed again and again. A demonstration video showing the task is available as Supplementary Information (parental permission for including the video as Supplementary Information to this paper was obtained for the children who feature in the video). Afterwards the children were carefully debriefed by explaining to them that the task was very difficult and that hardly anyone had ever succeeded in it. All children were rewarded with a toy of their choice regardless of their performance on the task. The task was developed and pretested in a subsample of 18 children. This subsample also served to test the desirability of the presents that were offered to the children for successful performance.

Reports of Anger Regulation, Anger Reactivity, and Anger Level

As this study was embedded within a larger study, some of the questionnaires could not be used in their full length due to time constraints. The short forms used in the present study were constructed after careful theoretical considerations, as explained below. Furthermore, some of the response formats were adapted in order to keep them homogeneous across all questionnaires used in the larger study. The number of participants for whom reports were available varied from 536 to 597 between the measures (see **Table 3**).

Parent-reported anger reactivity

The subscale Anger/Frustration of the Temperament in Middle Childhood Questionnaire (TMCQ; Simonds, 2006) was used as a parent-report measure of anger reactivity. The TMCQ assesses temperament in children aged 7–10 years. The subscale Anger/Frustration assesses the amount of negative affect shown by the child in response to the interruption of ongoing tasks or goal-blocking (e.g., "my child gets angry when she or he has trouble with a task," or "my child gets angry when she or he makes a mistake"). The scale consists of seven items, and the response scale ranges from 1 (*almost always untrue*) to 5 (*almost always true*). A total score was obtained by averaging the item scores. The internal consistency was $\alpha = 0.79$. A bilingual speaker of English and German translated the items into German, and the accuracy was checked through back-translation.

Parent-reported anger regulation

Parents rated the frequency of their child's use of three anger regulation strategies: *distraction* (one item: "when my child gets angry he or she does something that he or she enjoys"), *perseveration* (one item: "when my child gets angry, what caused his or her anger won't get out of his or her mind"), and *venting the anger* (two items: "when my child gets angry he or she shows his or her anger overtly" and "when my child gets angry he or she expresses his or her anger"). These strategies were chosen because they have been found to be either negatively (*distraction*) or positively (*perseveration*, *venting*) related to aggression and social rejection in previous studies (e.g., Helmsen and Petermann, 2010; see Introduction). The items were derived from the Questionnaire on Emotion Regulation in Children and Adolescents (FEEL-KJ; Grob and Smolenski, 2005) and rephrased for use as parent-report items. Parents rated the frequency with which their children use these strategies when they feel angry on a 5-point scale, ranging from 0 (*never*) to 4 (*always*). A total score for the strategy *venting* was obtained by averaging across the two item scores. The internal consistency was α = 0.86. Based on the results of previous studies (see introduction), the strategy *distraction* was classified as adaptive and the strategies *perseveration* and *venting* as maladaptive. In the original classification by Grob and Smolenski (2005), the strategy *venting* was grouped into the category *other strategies* and not classified as a maladaptive strategy. However, as we defined the adaptivity of the strategies in terms of their consequences on aggression and social rejection, we treated the strategy *venting* as maladaptive. The internal consistency across all four items was α = 0.59 after recoding the scores of the items for *perseveration* and *venting the anger* The latent factor based on these items showed a good fit, as shown in **Table 4**.

Self-reported level of anger and sadness during the behavioral observation

Following the behavioral observation, children were asked how angry they had felt when the tower collapsed to check if the task had been successful in eliciting anger. In addition to its function as a manipulation check, the question about the anger level served as a measure for the validation of the behavioral observation as it was assumed that the anger level would be correlated positively with the use of maladaptive strategies. As the task might have elicited sadness, children were also asked about their feelings of sadness. A three-point response scale was used for both questions: 1 (*not at all*), 2 (*somewhat*), and 3 (*a lot*).

Self-reported anger regulation

The subscale Emotion Regulation of the Intelligence and Development Scales (IDS; Grob et al., 2009) was used to assess the children's self-report of anger regulation. Children were asked with an open-ended question what they typically do if they feel angry to get rid of their anger. If they mentioned a strategy, they were asked what else they could do. The classification of the strategies was based on the system by Grob and Smolenski (2005), with three superordinate categories: (a) adaptive strategies (e.g., *distraction, solution orientation*), (b) maladaptive strategies (e.g., *resignation, perseveration*), and (c) other strategies (e.g., *social support*). As explained above, we classified the strategy *venting the anger* as maladaptive instead of grouping it into the category *other strategies*. The children's answers were written down by the interviewer and subsequently analyzed by two trained raters, who assigned 0 points for mentioning a maladaptive strategy or no strategy at all, 1 point for mentioning a strategy of the category *other strategies*, and 2 points for mentioning an adaptive strategy, in line with Grob and Smolenski (2005). Thus, the minimum score on this measure was 0 (naming no or only maladaptive strategies), and the maximum score was 4 (naming two adaptive strategies), with higher scores reflecting more adaptive anger regulation. The answers of 134 randomly selected children were double-coded to compute the inter-rater reliability. Krippendorff's alpha was 0.80.

Self-reported anger reactivity

One item from the subscale Stress Management of the brief form of the BarOn Emotional Quotient Inventory: Youth Version (BarOn EQ-i:YV Brief Form; Bar-On and Parker, 2000) was used to assess children's self-report of anger reactivity ("I get angry easily"). The BarOn EQ-I assesses the emotional and social functioning of children and adolescents aged 7–18 years. The original five-point answer format was modified into a four point-scale ranging from 1 (*never*) to 4 (*often*). A bilingual speaker of English and German translated the item into German, and the accuracy was checked through back-translation.

Aggressive Behavior

Aggressive behavior was assessed through teacher-reports of physical aggression (three items, e.g., "this child hits, shoves, or pushes peers") and relational aggression (three items, e.g., "this child spreads rumors or gossips about some peers"). The response scale ranged from 0 (*never*) to 5 (*daily*). The items were based on the items of the Children's Social Behavior Scale—Teacher Form (CSBS-T; Crick, 1996). A total score of aggressive behavior was obtained by computing the mean score of all items. The internal consistency was α = 0.91. A bilingual speaker of English and German translated the items into German, and the accuracy was checked through back-translation.

Social Rejection

Social rejection was assessed using teacher-, parent-, and self-report scales. The total score for each scale was obtained by summing up the item scores (after recoding items that were positively worded, so that higher scores indicate greater social rejection).

Teacher-reported social rejection

Teachers completed two items of the subscale Peer Relationship Problems of the teacher measure of the German version of the Strength and Difficulties Questionnaire (SDQ; Goodman, 1997; "is picked on or bullied by other children" and "is generally liked by other children") and one self-constructed item ("is often excluded when classmates play together at break time"). The response scale ranged from 0 (*not true*) to 2 (*certainly true*). Calculating the internal consistency yielded a relatively low score of α = 0.58. However, the SDQ represents frequency counts of indicators for social rejection and is therefore not required to form an internally consistent scale.

Parent-reported social rejection

Three items from the subscale Peer Relationship Problems from the parent version of the SDQ were used as a parent-report measure of the children's social rejection ("is generally liked by other children," "is picked on or bullied by other children," and "has at least one good friend"). The response scale ranged from 0 (*not true*) to 2 (*certainly true*). The internal consistency was α = 0.67.

Self-reported social rejection

Five items of the subscale Social Integration of the Questionnaire on Social and Emotional Experiences at School of Elementary School Children (FEESS; Rauer and Schuck, 2003, 2004) and three items of the subscale Peer Acceptance of the German version of the Harter-Scales (Asendorpf and van Aken, 1993) were used to measure children's self-reported social rejection (e.g., "I am liked by other children," "The other children often laugh at me"). Children indicated on a 2-point-scale whether the statements were true or not true of them ($1 = yes$, $2 = no$). The internal consistency was $\alpha = 0.62$.

Analysis of the Videotapes

The videotapes were coded using the software Eudico Linguistic Annotator (ELAN; Wittenburg et al., 2006). A coding system for the identification of regulation strategies was developed and pre-tested in an iterative process by conducting three consecutive trial codings on a subset of 20 videotapes each. Problems that occurred during the coding were successively reduced by modifying the system after each trial until a final version was reached that allowed the clear assignment of all relevant behaviors to one category. During this process, it became apparent that the strategy *distraction* had to be excluded as it turned out that the anger-eliciting situation did not offer enough opportunities for the use of this strategy. This left four maladaptive strategies (1–4), two adaptive strategies (5–6), and two further strategies (7–8) that were shown by the children but not classified as adaptive or maladaptive, as displayed in **Table 1**. Examples of behaviors representing the maladaptive and adaptive categories are provided in the demonstration video available as Supplementary Information.

The eight superordinate strategies were further differentiated into one to four sub-categories that represented observable behaviors and served as indicators for the regulation strategies. In addition to the sub-categories listed in **Table 1**, it was coded if the children's eyes were not clearly visible (e.g., because a child held one hand near to his or her eyes while building the tower) and if the children built the tower in a different order than prescribed. This enabled us to exclude these children from the analyses of the strategy *visual focus* (as it was not possible to determine what the child looked at; $n = 92$) or the strategy *solution orientation* (as due to the wrong order of the toy blocks the behavior *balancing*, which is a sub-category of the strategy *solution orientation*, could not be used; $n = 24$).

The videos were coded by two trained coders who were unaware of the children's aggression and peer rejection status. A subsample of 121 videos (about 20%) were double-coded to analyze the reliability of the coding system. Krippendorff's alphas, presented in **Table 1**, showed that three categories had an alpha below 0.80 (*visual focus on the frustrating stimuli*: $\alpha = 0.71$, *venting the anger*: $\alpha = 0.73$, and *solution orientation*: $\alpha = 0.79$). All other categories had alphas higher than 0.80, with

TABLE 1 | Coding system of the behavioral observation.

Strategy	Sub-categories	Krippendorff's α
1. Visual focus on the frustrating stimuli	1.1 Looking at the hourglass 1.2 Looking at the presents	0.71
2. Verbal focus on the frustrating stimuli	2.1 Talking negatively about the time (e.g., "time is almost up") 2.2 Talking negatively about the rewards (e.g., "but I want a present") 2.3 Talking negatively about the tower (e.g., "it's so wobbly," "it keeps falling") 2.4 Negative self-evaluation (e.g., "I can't do it")	0.92
3. Venting the anger	3.1 Verbal expression of anger (swearing, e.g., "I hate this task" or "stupid tower," grumbling) 3.2 Anger expression (contracting the eyebrows) 3.3 Handling the material roughly (e.g., smashing the toy blocks on the table)	0.73
4. Resignation	4.1 Giving up (refusing to continue for at least 3 sec)	0.99
5. Solution orientation	5.1 Testing a new strategy 5.2 Duration of balancing 5.3 Working in a focused/determined way	0.79
6. Substituting the anger expression	6.1 Smiling/laughing	0.83
7. Verbalized cognitive strategies	7.1 Positive thinking (e.g., "I can do it," "there is still enough time") 7.2 External attribution: a) Attribution on insolvability of the task ("It's not my fault, it's not possible to build this tower") b) Attribution on difficulty of the task ("It's not my fault, it's too difficult for children") 7.3 Reappraisal and information seeking (e.g., "I don't care, I have enough toys at home anyway," "Have the other kids managed to build the tower")	0.86
8. Ineffective help-seeking	8.1 Looking at the experimenter 8.2 Asking for help	0.83

the highest reliability in the category *resignation* ($\alpha = 0.99$). Overall, these coefficients indicate acceptable to good inter-rater reliability (Wirtz, 2006).

The sub-categories were event-coded, which means that every occurrence during the 2:40 min observation period was counted (Greve and Wentura, 1997). The scores for the strategies were calculated by summing the frequencies of the corresponding sub-categories. For two of the sub-categories of the strategy *solution orientation*, the event-sampling approach could not be used, as these categories did not reflect specific, countable behaviors. Instead, the duration of the attempt to balance the toy blocks on critical parts of the tower was measured in seconds, and the goal-orientation of the children's task performance was rated on a 4-point scale ranging from 0 (*very little engagement with the task*) to 3 (*extremely concentrated and dedicated performance*). The rating complemented the other two sub-categories, as solution-oriented behavior is a complex behavior that could not be fully captured by event-based behavioral indicators. Specific instructions regarding the coding of individual strategies are available as Supplementary Material.

Procedure

The instruments and procedure were approved by the Ethics Committee of the authors' university as well as the Ministry of Education, Youth, and Sport of the Federal State of Brandenburg. All self-report measures and the behavioral observation task were administered in individual sessions at the school. The parent questionnaire that assessed the child's emotion regulation, emotional reactivity, and social rejection was sent home to the parents. All children received a cinema voucher and small presents for their participation. Teachers received 5 Euros for the class kitty for each completed questionnaire. After the end of the data collection period, all participating schools received a written report about the results.

Plan of Analysis

The statistical analyses were carried out with SPSS 22 and Mplus version 7.11 (Muthén and Muthén, 2012). In order to avoid reduction of the sample size, missing values were handled by the Full Information Maximum Likelihood estimation option in Mplus. To account for the non-normal distribution of the data, the robust mlr-estimator was used. All measures used in this study were analyzed as latent variables via confirmatory factor analysis except for the single-item measures (self-reported anger regulation, self-reported anger reactivity, as well as the degree of anger and sadness elicited by the task). The measurement models of the parent-reports of anger regulation and anger reactivity were specified using the corresponding items as factor indicators. The three measures of social rejection (parent-, teacher-, and self-reports) were used as indicators of a multi-informant latent factor of social rejection. The six items of aggression served as indicators of a latent factor for aggression that comprised both forms of aggression (physical and relational). To account for the shared variance of the items of the two different forms of aggression, a method factor for physical aggression was specified.

The hypotheses were tested using correlation analyses (Hypothesis 1) and structural equation modeling (Hypothesis 2). Good model fit is indicated by a comparative fit index (CFI) above 0.95, a root-mean-square error of approximation (RMSEA) below 0.06, and a standardized root-mean-square residual below 0.08 (SRMR; Hu and Bentler, 1998). A measurement model of maladaptive anger regulation, assessed through behavioral observation, was specified using the six maladaptive strategies as factor indicators: *visual focus, verbal focus, venting, resignation, (low) solution orientation,* and *(low) substitution of the anger expression.* The strategy *substituting the anger expression,* as a display rule strategy (Zeman et al., 2006), differs from the other strategies in referring to the regulation of the external expression of anger rather than the regulation of the internal experience of anger. Different authors have emphasized the importance of the conceptual and empirical distinction between these two aspects of emotion regulation (Dearing et al., 2002; Spinrad et al., 2007). However, as the use of display rules has been shown to be adaptive regarding the development of aggression and social rejection in previous studies, we still included this strategy in the measurement model in order to examine if all strategies considered to be relevant with respect to these two outcomes served as indicators for a factor reflecting maladaptive anger regulation.

As outlined in the introduction, the strategy *ineffective help-seeking* was assumed to be neither adaptive nor maladaptive in the context of the present measure. Therefore, it was not considered in the hypotheses-testing analyses. The category *verbalized cognitive strategies* contains strategies which are generally assumed to be adaptive, as they have been found to be negatively related to measures of psychopathology (e.g., Garnefski et al., 2007). However, when measured through behavioral observation, cognitive strategies can only be identified when they are verbalized. Classifying these verbalized cognitive strategies as adaptive could result in a biased assessment of the children's anger regulation skills because children who used cognitive strategies but did not verbalize them could not be identified. These children, however, might be more mature with regard to emotion regulation skills, as they have already managed to internalize their cognitive strategies (Helmsen and Petermann, 2010). Therefore, we chose not to consider these strategies in our hypotheses-testing analyses.

Results

Behavioral Observation: Descriptive Statistics and Bivariate Correlations

The means and standard deviations of the anger regulation strategies assessed through behavioral observation are displayed in **Table 2**. The most frequently used strategies were *venting, visual focus,* and *substituting the anger expression. Resignation* had the lowest frequency. To examine gender differences, *t*-tests for independent samples were conducted rather than a MANOVA to avoid a reduction in sample size. Alpha-level adjustment for multiple testing was conducted through Bonferroni correction yielding a significance level of $p = 0.006$, and Cohen's *d* was computed

TABLE 2 | Means and correlations between the observed anger regulation strategies.

	Range	M (SD)	1.	2.	3.	4.	5.	6.	7.	8.	9.
1. Visual focus	0–39	3.96 (3.60)	1	0.33***	0.10*	0.11*	−0.36***	0.01	0.18***	0.24***	−0.19***
2. Verbal focus	0–27	2.75 (3.54)	0.30***	1	0.43***	0.17***	−0.43***	0.22***	0.58***	0.49***	−0.21***
3. Venting the anger	0–22	4.33 (3.87)	0.10*	0.42***	1	0.14**	−0.27***	0.17***	0.37***	0.16***	−0.13**
4. Resignation	0–2	0.03 (0.19)	0.13**	0.18**	0.11*	1	−0.31***	−0.07	0.05	0.15***	−0.06
5. Solution orientation[a]	–	0.02 (1.60)	−0.34***	−0.38***	−0.23***	−0.30***	1	−0.14**	−0.35***	−0.40***	0.33***
6. Substituting the anger expression	0–14	4.62 (2.94)	0.04	0.21***	0.19***	−0.10*	−0.14**	1	0.20***	0.18***	−0.02
7. Verbalized cognitive strategies	0–8	1.26 (1.35)	0.20***	0.54***	0.36***	0.05	−0.33***	0.20***	1	0.38***	−0.08
8. Ineffective help-seeking	0–25	1.67 (2.35)	0.21***	0.50***	0.16**	0.10*	−0.35***	0.18***	0.35***	1	−0.14**
9. Age	6–10	8.12 (0.92)	–	–	–	–	–	–	–	–	1

Zero-order correlations are presented above the diagonal, partial correlations controlled for age and gender are presented below the diagonal. N = 599; Exceptions: Visual focus: N = 507 (250 girls, 257 boys); solution orientation: N = 576 (293 girls, 283 boys); partial correlations: N = 486.
[a] The scores of the sub-categories of the strategy solution orientation were z-transformed prior to aggregation because of differences in response scale formats.
*p < 0.05, **p < 0.01, ***p < 0.001.

as a measure of effect size. The only significant gender difference was found on the strategy *substituting the anger expression*, $t_{(597)} = 3.99$, $p < 0.000$, $d = 0.33$, which was more often used by girls ($M = 5.07$, $SD = 2.87$) than by boys ($M = 4.16$, $SD = 2.94$).

Pearson correlation coefficients were computed to assess the bivariate associations among the strategies as well as their links with age. In addition, partial correlations, controlled for age and gender were computed. The results are displayed in **Table 2** (partial correlations are presented below the diagonal). Zero-order correlations among the strategies were low to moderate, ranging from $r = 0.01$ (*visual focus* and *substituting the anger expression*) to $r = 0.58$ (*verbal focus* and *verbalized cognitive strategies*). For the majority of the categories, significant positive correlations were found. Negative correlations were found between *solution orientation* and all other strategies. The correlations with age revealed that the frequencies of *visual focus, verbal focus, venting the anger,* and *ineffective help-seeking* decreased whereas *solution orientation* increased with age. The partial correlations, controlled for age and gender, were very similar to the zero-order correlations.

A measurement model with the six strategies did not fit the data well [$\chi^2(9, N = 599) = 103.06, p < 0.00$, RMSEA = 0.13, SRMR = 0.06, CFI = 0.79]. The factor loadings indicated that the strategy *substituting the anger expression* did not load significantly on the latent factor ($\beta = -0.07, p = 0.15$). This result confirmed the proposed difference between the five strategies of anger regulation and the one strategy referring to the regulation of the external expression of anger. Therefore, in a next step, we specified a measurement model excluding this strategy. This measurement model, displayed in **Figure 1**, showed a good fit with the data after freeing residual covariances between the indicators *solution orientation* and *visual focus* and *solution orientation* and *resignation* [$\chi^2(3, N = 599) = 8.33, p = 0.04$, RMSEA = 0.05, SRMR = 0.02, CFI = 0.99]. The factor-loading pattern reflected the assumed classification of the strategies: The loadings of the four strategies considered as maladaptive were positive, whereas the loading of the strategy *solution orientation*, the adaptive strategy, was negative. All factor loadings were

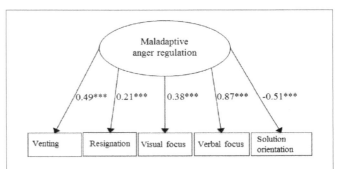

FIGURE 1 | Latent factor of maladaptive anger regulation (standardized path coefficients). ***p < 0.001; N = 599; Model fit: $\chi^2(3) = 8.33, p = 0.04$, RMSEA = 0.05, SRMR = 0.02, CFI = 0.99.

significant at $p < 0.001$. Accordingly, this model was adopted for the further analyses.

Validation Constructs: Descriptive Statistics and Correlations with Behavioral Observation

The means and standard deviations of the validation constructs, as well as their correlations with age, are displayed in **Table 3**. The majority of the children reported that they had experienced moderate (49.5%) or strong (40.8%) anger during the tower-building task. A minority of children (9.7%) reported they had not felt angry at all. A paired-sample t-test revealed that the task elicited significantly more anger than sadness, $t_{(587)} = 16.08, p < 0.001$, $d = 0.66$.

T-tests for independent samples were conducted to examine gender difference, with the significance level set at $p = 0.004$ to correct for multiple testing. There were no gender differences in the level of anger and sadness elicited by the task. The only significant difference was found on the teacher-report of aggression, $t_{(555.35)} = -5.15, p < 0.00, d = 0.44$, with boys receiving higher scores than girls (boys: $M = 1.67, SD = 0.74$; girls: $M = 1.38, SD = 0.59$). Age showed significant positive correlations with the self-report measure of anger regulation, indicating that older children reported more adaptive regulation strategies. The correlation with self-reported anger reactivity was also positive, indicating that older children more often reported to get angry easily. Furthermore, a significant positive correlation with age was found for the teacher ratings of social rejection, indicating that social rejection increased with age.

The measurement models of the validation constructs all showed a very good fit with the data (all RMSEAs < 0.05,

SRMRs < 0.02, CFIs > 0.99). All fit indices as well as the factor loadings are displayed in **Table 4**. When modeling the parent-report factors of anger regulation and anger reactivity, the residual covariance between items that were highly similar in meaning was freed. This concerned the two items that assessed the strategy *venting* in the anger regulation questionnaire as well as items of the anger reactivity scale, which overlap in content (e.g., "Gets mad when provoked by other children and" and

TABLE 3 | Means and SDs of the validation constructs and correlations with age.

Variable	N items	Range	N	M (SD)	Correlation with age
Level of anger — self-report	1	1–3	588	2.32 (0.64)	0.03
Level of sadness — self-report	1	1–3	588	1.84 (0.72)	−0.03
Maladaptive anger regulation — parent-report					
Venting	2	1–5	561	4.14 (0.91)	−0.04
Perseveration	1	1–5	554	2.97 (1.07)	0.08
Distraction	1	1–5	552	1.91 (1.05)	0.03
Anger reactivity — parent-report	7	1–5	561	2.66 (0.73)	−0.03
Anger reactivity — self-report	1	1–4	596	2.18 (1.05)	0.08*
Anger regulation — self-report	1	0–4	585	1.93 (1.17)	0.11**
Aggression — teacher-report	6	1–5	591	1.55 (0.73)	−0.01
Social rejection — teacher-report	3	3–9	536	3.67 (1.02)	0.13**
Social rejection — parent-report	3	3–9	563	3.60 (0.97)	0.02
Social rejection — self-report	5	8–16	597	9.42 (1.55)	0.06

*p < 0.05, **p < 0.01.

TABLE 4 | Model fits and factor loadings of the measurement models of the validation constructs.

Factor	Indicators	Factor loadings	N	χ^2(df)	CFI	RMSEA	SRMR
Maladaptive anger regulation—parent-report	Venting_1	0.62***	562	1.61 (1), n.s.	1.00	0.03	0.01
	Venting_2	0.55***					
	Perseveration	0.37***					
	Distraction	−0.29***					
Anger reactivity—parent-report	Reac_1	0.43***	561	22.92 (2)*	0.99	0.05	0.02
	Reac_2	0.61***					
	Reac_3	0.58***					
	Reac_4	0.52***					
	Reac_5	0.48***					
	Reac_6	0.65***					
	Reac_7	0.51***					
Aggression—teacher-report	Physical_1	0.58***	591	25.12 (6)**	0.99	0.07	0.01
	Physical_2	0.60***					
	Physical_3	0.55***					
	Relational_1	0.87***					
	Relational_2	0.88***					
	Relational_3	0.90***					
Social rejection	Teacher report	0.57***	599	0.98 (1), n.s.	1.00	0.00	0.02
	Parent-report	0.61***					
	Self-report	0.47***					

*p < 0.05; **p < 0.01; ***p < 0.001, n.s., not significant.

TABLE 5 | Correlations between the observational measure of maladaptive anger regulation and the validation constructs.

	1.	2.	3.	4.	5.	6.
1. Maladaptive anger regulation—behavioral observation[a]	1	0.11	0.12*	−0.06	0.14**	0.35***
2. Maladaptive anger regulation—parent- report[a]		1	0.73***	−0.15*	0.06	−0.05
3. Anger reactivity—parent-report[a]			1	−0.07	0.18**	0.10+
4. Anger regulation—self-report[b]				1	0.05	0.05
5. Anger reactivity—self-report[b]					1	0.13**
6. Situational anger level—self-report[b]						1

[+]$p < 0.10$; *$p < 0.05$; **$p < 0.01$; ***$p < 0.001$.
[a]Latent variable; [b]manifest variable.

"Gets very angry when another child takes his/her toy away"). All indicators loaded significantly on the respective factors with $p < 0.001$. On the parent-report factor of anger regulation, the loadings of the items for *perseveration* and *venting* were positive; the loading of the *distraction* item was negative. Thus, high scores on this factor reflected maladaptive regulation. Accordingly, this factor was labeled *maladaptive anger regulation—parent-report*.

Hypothesis 1 was examined by computing partial correlations between the observational measure of maladaptive anger regulation and the validation constructs (parent- and self-reports of anger reactivity and anger regulation and self-reported anger level), controlling for age and gender. The correlations between the observational measure of maladaptive anger regulation and the validation constructs are presented in **Table 5**. As expected, significant, positive correlations of low to medium size were found between the observational measure and the parent- and self-reports of anger reactivity as well as the self-reported anger level during the tower-building task. However, the correlations with the parent- and self-reports of anger regulation were not significant. Thus, Hypothesis 1 was partially confirmed by the data.

Associations with Aggression and Social Rejection

Structural equation modeling was used to examine the links between the observational measure of maladaptive anger regulation and aggression as well as social rejection, proposed in Hypothesis 2. The parent- and self-reports of anger regulation and anger reactivity were included as predictors to investigate whether the observational measure made an independent contribution to the prediction of the two outcome measures. Age and gender were included as covariates. In addition, the self-reported level of anger and sadness elicited by the task were included as covariates of maladaptive anger regulation as the use of regulation strategies may have been influenced by the intensity of these two emotions. As the two parent- report measures were highly correlated (see **Table 5**), we did not include both variables in the same model to avoid imprecise estimations caused by multicollinearity. Instead, two separate models were computed for each outcome. The two models for aggression are presented in **Figure 2A** (with parent-reported anger-reactivity) and **Figure 2B** (with parent-reported anger regulation), the two models for social rejection are presented in **Figure 3A** (with parent-reported

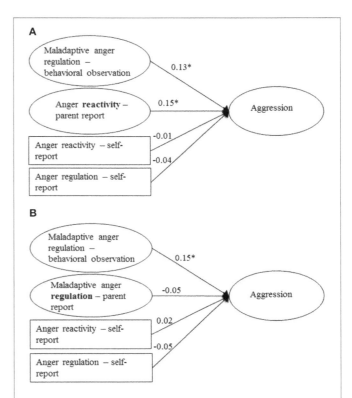

FIGURE 2 | Links between aggression and measures of anger regulation and anger reactivity (standardized path coefficients), controlled for age, gender, and anger level. The two models differ regarding the inclusion of the parent-report measures of anger reactivity **(A)** and anger regulation **(B)**, *$p < 0.05$, $N = 599$. **(A)** *Model fit:* $\chi^2(217) = 369.08$, $p < 0.00$, RMSEA $= 0.04$, SRMR $= 0.04$, CFI $= 0.97$; $R^2 = 0.04$; **(B)** *Model fit:* $\chi^2(157) = 275.45$, $p < 0.00$, RMSEA $= 0.03$, SRMR $= 0.03$, CFI $= 0.97$; $R^2 = 0.03$.

anger-reactivity) and **Figure 3B** (with parent-reported anger regulation). The fit for all models was acceptable or good (RMSEAs < 0.05, SRMRs < 0.05, CFIs > 0.94; see figure captions for full model fit information).

In line with Hypothesis 2, the observational measure of anger regulation made a unique contribution to the prediction of both aggression and social rejection beyond the parent- and self-report measures. The parent-reports of anger reactivity were also positively associated with both outcomes. The self-report measure of

Behavioral Psychology: Understanding Human Behavior

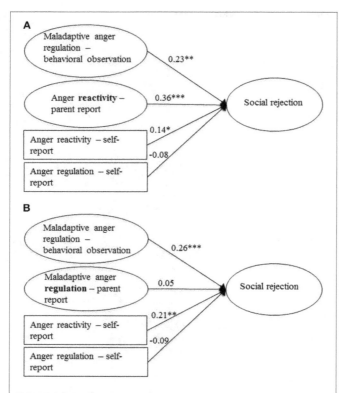

FIGURE 3 | Links between social rejection and measures of anger regulation and anger reactivity (standardized path coefficients), controlled for age, gender, and anger level. The two models differ regarding the inclusion of the parent-report measures of anger reactivity **(A)** and anger regulation **(B)**, *p < 0.05, **p < 0.01, ***p < 0.001; N = 599. **(A)** Model fit: $\chi^2(162) = 297.24$, $p < 0.00$, RMSEA = 0.04, SRMR = 0.05, CFI = 0.93. $R^2 = 0.27$. **(B)** Model fit: $\chi^2(111) = 204.28$, $p < 0.00$, RMSEA = 0.04, SRMR = 0.04, CFI = 0.93. $R^2 = 0.17$.

anger reactivity was linked to social rejection but not to aggression. Neither the parent- nor the self-reports of anger regulation were related to the two outcome measures.

Discussion

The present study was designed to develop and validate an observational measure of anger regulation strategies in an anger-eliciting situation in middle childhood. Construct validity was assessed by relating the observational measure to parent- and self-report measures of anger regulation and the conceptually related construct anger reactivity. Criterion validity was examined by linking it to aggression and social rejection.

The tower-building task was successful in inducing anger in the present sample of elementary school children. Furthermore, the task elicited significantly more anger than sadness. The task takes only a few minutes to complete and does not require any special skills, which makes it suitable for administration to a large sample of children, for instance in a school setting. The coding system, developed to analyze the children's behavior during the completion of the task, allowed the comprehensive analysis of the

children's anger regulation responses. Five strategies of emotional regulation were classified as maladaptive with regard to the development of aggression and social rejection (*visual focus, verbal focus, venting the anger, resignation*, and *low solution orientation*). A further strategy, *substituting the anger expression*, was initially included as a strategy referring to the regulation of the expression of anger, but was then excluded due to its failure to load on the latent factor of anger regulation.

The correlations with age revealed that older children less often focused on the frustrating stimuli (verbally and visually), vented their anger, and sought social support from the experimenter, while scoring higher on the strategy of solution orientation. Few gender differences were found, but girls more often substituted their anger expression with the expression of joy than did boys. These results are in line with previous evidence on age and gender differences in emotion regulation (Band and Weisz, 1988; Underwood et al., 1999; Zeman et al., 2006) and provide evidence for the construct validity of the observational measure.

Construct Validity

We assessed the construct validity of the latent factor of maladaptive anger regulation based on the behavioral observation by examining its correlations with three pertinent constructs: (a) anger regulation (parent- and self-reports), (b) anger reactivity (parent- and self-reports), and (c) self-reported anger level during the task (assuming that the more anger the task elicited, the more likely it would be that children engaged in maladaptive regulation strategies). The use of maladaptive strategies in response to the anger-eliciting task was significantly correlated with higher parent-rated and self-reported anger reactivity, and with greater self-reported anger during the behavioral observation. As expected, the correlations were moderate in size, which supports the conceptualization of emotional reactivity and emotion regulation as interrelated, but conceptually distinct constructs (Rothbart and Sheese, 2007). No significant correlations were found with parent- and self-reported anger regulation.

One possible explanation for the non-significant correlation of parents' assessment of anger regulation with the observational measure is that parents' ratings are largely limited to their children's behavior within the family context. The behavioral observation task may have evoked less anger display due to the presence of an unfamiliar experimenter and the awareness of being videotaped. The behavior during the tower-building task may more closely reflect the children's behavior within the school setting than their behavior in the family context as in the school-setting children are likely to be more concerned about the consequences of venting their anger openly. Another explanation may lie in the high correlation between the parent-ratings of anger reactivity and anger regulation found in the present study. Theoretically, a child with high anger reactivity can be skilled in anger regulation and vice versa. The high correlation indicates that the parents found it difficult to differentiate between the two constructs, which suggests that parents may not be a good source of information on anger regulation unconfounded by anger reactivity.

In conclusion, the proposed links of observed anger regulation with parent- and self-reports predicted in Hypothesis 1 were partly confirmed by the data. The lack of significant associations of observed maladaptive anger regulation strategies with parent-rated maladaptive regulation and self-reported anger regulation skills may to some extent reflect the limitations of parent- and self-reports of anger regulation, outlined in the introduction. Children in the present age group may be too young to give valid self-reports of anger regulation, and—as suggested by previous research—their self-reports of anger regulation may not correspond to their actual behavior in a real situation. Parents may be unable to differentiate between anger reactivity and anger regulation. In combination, these problems call for alternative methods for assessing anger regulation, such as behavioral observation. However, our results do not undermine the importance of parent and self- reports *per se*. Parent-reports can provide important data about the children's anger regulation at home, particularly about the external anger-related behavior. Self-reports provide valuable insights about the children's theoretical knowledge about regulations strategies. In addition, the self-report measure offers the opportunity to report internal cognitive strategies, which, as they are not observable, cannot be assessed through either behavioral observation or parent ratings. The differential suitability of the methods for assessing different anger regulation strategies highlights the importance of a multi-method approach to capture a broad range of the children's use of regulation strategies.

Criterion Validity

In line with Hypothesis 2, we found that the observational measure of maladaptive anger regulation was significantly linked to aggression measured by teacher-reports, and social rejection assessed by self-, parent-, and teacher-reports. These findings support the criterion validity of the observational measure as they are consistent with a large number of studies that also have found that children with deficits in anger regulation are rated as more aggressive and are more socially rejected than children with more adaptive regulation skills (see Lemerise and Harper, 2010, for a review). With regard to aggression, this link can be explained by the action tendency associated with anger, as this action tendency is assumed to activate aggression-related motor impulses (Berkowitz and Harmon-Jones, 2004). Accordingly, the likelihood of aggression is increased for children who use maladaptive anger regulation strategies, as these strategies do not effectively reduce the intensity and frequency of angry feelings. With regard to social rejection, our results support the notion that maladaptive forms of anger regulation may irritate peers and disturb ongoing peer interactions, leading to social rejection. In addition, low use of solution-oriented behavior may be associated with the inability to constructively solve conflicts with peers (Maszk et al., 1999).

Our results suggest that the observational measure may be more valid compared to the parent- and self-report measures of anger regulation in the present age group, as neither the parent-report nor the self-report measure were linked to aggression or social rejection.

Further evidence for the validity of the observational measure was provided by the fact that maladaptive regulation, assessed through observation, was uniquely linked to both aggression and social rejection. The significant association of observed maladaptive anger regulation with social rejection held when controlling for both self-reported and parent-reported anger reactivity, and the association with aggression held over and above a significant link with parent-reported anger reactivity. This result is in line with previous studies that have found that anger reactivity and anger regulation predict unique variance in outcome measures such as externalizing behavior problems and social functioning (Eisenberg et al., 1995, 2005).

Strengths and Limitations

We believe our study has several strengths. We employed a realistic anger-eliciting task and developed a reliable coding system for identifying maladaptive strategies of anger regulation. The task is suitable for administration in short school-based testing sessions and can therefore be used economically in large samples of children. The observational measure was compared to information obtained from the children and their parents on habitual anger regulation and anger reactivity to establish its construct validity. Moreover, we demonstrated the criterion validity of the observational method through relating it to measures of aggression and social rejection, also using data from multiple informants.

At the same time, some limitations of our study have to be mentioned. The stability of the children's anger regulation strategies in a similar task needs to be tested in future research. The generalizability of the behavior shown during the behavioral observation also remains to be tested, as the children were observed in an arranged situation that, to some extent, constrained their opportunities to act. For example, children had very limited opportunities to distract themselves from the anger-eliciting task. Therefore, as noted above, the strategy *distraction* could not be assessed through the observational measure, although it is likely that some children might have used this strategy in a natural situation. This limitation may also serve to explain why the behavioral observation measure did not correlate with the parent- and self- reports of anger regulation, as parents and children may have thought of different situations than the one assessed with the observational measure. Similarly, the presence of an unresponsive experimenter who did not provide support meant that *seeking social support*, considered adaptive in other situations, was classified as neither adaptive nor maladaptive in the present measure.

In addition, as we assessed only one adaptive strategy, namely *solution orientation*, we were not able to examine the link between the number of strategies a child uses and aggression and social rejection. Using one regulation strategy at a high level may be less adaptive than using moderate levels of several strategies, as suggested by previous findings that children who use various adaptive strategies are less aggressive than children who use just one (Gilliom et al., 2002; see also Lougheed and Hollenstein, 2012, for a similar finding with regard to internalizing problems).

Finally, the results regarding the parent-ratings of anger regulation may have been affected by the fact that we were unable to include the selected scales in full and had to adapt the items slightly for use as a parent-report measure.

Despite these limitations, our study contributed to the existing literature on the assessment of anger regulation in children by providing an easily applicable observational method for the assessment of anger regulation strategies in middle childhood. It further showed that maladaptive regulation, assessed with this new measure, contributed independently to the prediction of aggression and social rejection beyond the effect of parent- and self-reports of anger regulation and anger reactivity. Thus, our observational measure is recommended as part of a multi-method approach to studying anger regulation in childhood in which the strengths of different methods complement each other. For example, our results indicate that compared to self-reports, observational measures are better able to assess the behavior in a real anger-eliciting situation. Self-reports, on the other hand, may be more suitable for assessing the children's theoretical knowledge about emotion regulation. The results of our study provided insights about the advantages and limitations of parent-reports, self-reports, and observational measures that may be helpful for future research on anger regulation in middle childhood.

Author Contributions

Both authors have contributed substantially to the conception and design of the work as well as to the analysis of the data. HR has primarily collected, analyzed, and interpreted the data, BK has provided input and supervision to the analyses and writing up of the study. Both authors agreed to be accountable for all aspects of the work.

Acknowledgments

This research was funded by the German Research Foundation as part of the Graduate College "Intrapersonal developmental risk factors in childhood and adolescence: A longitudinal perspective" (GRK 1668). The authors would like to thank Eva Bausch for her support in coding the video data.

References

Asendorpf, J. B., and van Aken, M. A. G. (1993). Deutsche Versionen der Selbstkonzeptskalen von Harter [German version of the Harter's self-concept scales]. *Z. Entwicklungspsychol. Pädagog. Psychol.* 25, 64–86.

Band, E. B., and Weisz, J. R. (1988). How to feel better when it feels bad: children's perspectives on coping with everyday stress. *Dev. Psychol.* 24, 247–253. doi: 10.1037/0012-1649.24.2.247

Bar-On, R., and Parker, J. D. A. (2000). *The Handbook of Emotional Intelligence: Theory, Development, Assessment, and Application at Home, School, and in the Workplace.* San Franciso, CA: Jossey-Bass.

Berkowitz, L., and Harmon-Jones, E. (2004). Toward an understanding of the determinants of anger. *Emotion* 4, 107–130. doi: 10.1037/1528-3542.4.2.107

Cole, P. M. (2014). Moving ahead in the study of the development of emotion regulation. *Int. J. Behav. Dev.* 38, 203–207. doi: 10.1177/0165025414522170

Cole, P. M., Zahn-Waxler, C., and Smith, K. D. (1994). Expressive control during a disappointment: variations related to preschoolers' behavior problems. *Dev. Psychol.* 30, 835–846. doi: 10.1037/0012-1649.30.6.835

Crick, N. R. (1996). The role of overt aggression, relational aggression, and prosocial behavior in the prediction of children's future social adjustment. *Child Dev.* 67, 2317–2327. doi: 10.2307/1131625

Crockenberg, S. C., Leerkes, E. M., and Bárrig Jó, P. S. (2008). Predicting aggressive behavior in the third year from infant reactivity and regulation as moderated by maternal behavior. *Dev. Psychopathol.* 20, 37–54. doi: 10.1017/S0954579408000023

Dearing, K. F., Hubbard, J. A., Ramsden, S. R., Parker, E. H., Relyea, N., Smithmyer, C. M., et al. (2002). Children's self reports about anger regulation: direct and indirect links to social preference and aggression. *Merrill. Palmer. Q.* 48, 308–336. doi: 10.1353/mpq.2002.0011

Eisenberg, N., Fabes, R. A., Murphy, B., Maszk, P., Smith, M., and Karbon, M. (1995). The role of emotionality and regulation in children's social functioning: a longitudinal study. *Child Dev.* 66, 1360. doi: 10.2307/1131652

Eisenberg, N., Sadovsky, A., Spinrad, T. L., Fabes, R. A., Losoya, S. H., Valiente, C., et al. (2005). The relations of problem behavior status to children's negative emotionality, effortful control, and impulsivity: concurrent relations and prediction of change. *Dev. Psychol.* 41, 193–211. doi: 10.1037/0012-1649. 41.1.193

Eisenberg, N., and Spinrad, T. L. (2004). Emotion-related regulation: sharpening the definition. *Child Dev.* 75, 334–339. doi: 10.1111/j.1467-8624.2004.00674.x

Fabes, R. A., and Eisenberg, N. (1992). Young children's coping with interpersonal anger. *Child Dev.* 63, 116–128. doi: 10.2307/1130906

Garnefski, N., Rieffe, C., Jellesma, F., Terwogt, M. M., and Kraaij, V. (2007). Cognitive emotion regulation strategies and emotional problems in 9 - 11-year-old children: the development of an instrument. *Eur. Child Adolesc. Psychiatry* 16, 1–9. doi: 10.1007/s00787-006-0562-3

Gilliom, M., Shaw, D. S., Beck, J. E., Schonberg, M. A., and Lukon, J. L. (2002). Anger regulation in disadvantaged preschool boys: strategies, antecedents, and the development of self-control. *Dev. Psychol.* 38, 222–235. doi: 10.1037/0012-1649.38.2.222

Goodman, R. (1997). The Strengths and Difficulties Questionnaire: a research note. *J. Child Psychol. Psychiatry* 38, 581–586. doi: 10.1111/j.1469-7610.1997.tb01545.x

Greve, W., and Wentura, D. (1997). *Wissenschaftliche Beobachtung. Eine Einführung [Systematic Observation: An Introduction].* Weinheim: Beltz/Psychologie Verlags Union.

Grob, A., Meyer, C. S., and Arx, P. H. (2009). *Intelligence and Development Scales (IDS). Intelligenz- und Entwicklungsskalen für Kinder von 5-10 Jahren.* Bern: Huber.

Grob, A., and Smolenski, C. (2005). *Fragebogen zur Erhebung der Emotions-regulationsstratgien bei Kindern und Jugendlichen [FEEL-KJ; Questionnaire on Emotion Regulation in Children and Adolescents].* Bern: Huber.

Gross, J. J. (1998). The emerging field of emotion regulation: an integrative review. *Rev. Gen. Psychol.* 2, 271–299. doi: 10.1037/1089-2680.2.3.271

Helmsen, J., and Petermann, F. (2010). Emotionsregulationsstrategien und aggressives Verhalten im Kindergartenalter [Emotion regulation strategies and aggressive behavior of preschool children]. *Prax. Kinderpsychol. Kinderpsychiatr.* 59, 775–791. doi: 10.13109/prkk.2010.59.10.775

Hu, L., and Bentler, P. M. (1998). Fit indices in covariance structure modeling: sensitivity to underparameterized model misspecification. *Psychol. Methods* 3, 424–453. doi: 10.1037/1082-989X.3.4.424

Kim-Spoon, J., Cicchetti, D., and Rogosch, F. A. (2013). A longitudinal study of emotion regulation, emotion lability-negativity, and internalizing symptomatology in maltreated and nonmaltreated children. *Child Dev.* 84, 512–527. doi: 10.1111/j.1467-8624.2012.01857.x

Larose, S., and Bernier, A. (2001). Social support processes: mediators of attachment state of mind and adjustment in late adolescence. *Attachm. & Hum. Dev.* 3, 96–120. doi: 10.1080/14616730010024762

Lemerise, E. A., and Harper, B. D. (2010). "The development of anger from preschool to middle childhood: expressing, understanding, and regulating anger," in *International Handbook of Anger. Constituent and Concomitant Biological, Psychological, and Social Processes*, eds M. Potegal, G. Stemmler, and C. Spielberger (New York, NY: Springer), 219–229.

Litvak, P. M., Lerner, J. S., Tiedens, L. Z., and Katherine, S. (2010). "Fuel in the fire: how anger impacts judgment and decision-making," in *International Handbook of Anger. Constituent and concomitant Biological, Psychological, and Social Processes*, eds M. Potegal, G. Stemmler, and C. Spielberger (New York, NY: Springer), 287–310.

Lougheed, J. P., and Hollenstein, T. (2012). A limited repertoire of emotion regulation strategies is associated with internalizing problems in adolescence. *Soc. Dev.* 21, 704–721. doi: 10.1111/j.1467-9507.2012.00663.x

Maszk, P., Eisenberg, N., and Guthrie, I. K. (1999). Relations of children's social status to their emotionality and regulation: a short-term longitudinal study. *Merrill. Palmer. Q.* 45, 468–492.

McDowell, D. J., O'Neil, R., and Parke, R. D. (2000). Display rule application in a disappointing situation and children's emotional reactivity: relations with social competence. *Merrill. Palmer. Q.* 46, 306–324.

Melnick, S. M., and Hinshaw, S. P. (2000). Emotion regulation and parenting in AD/HD and comparison boys: linkages with social behaviors and peer preference. *J. Abnorm. Child Psychol.* 28, 73–86. doi: 10.1023/A:1005174102794

Mullin, B. C., and Hinshaw, S. P. (2007). "Emotion regulation and externalizing disorders in children and adolescents," in *Handbook of Emotion Regulation*, ed J. J. Gross (New York, NY: Guilford Press), 523–541.

Muthén, L. K., and Muthén, B. O. (2012). *Mplus User's Guide. Statistical Analysis with Latent Variables*, 7th Edn. Los Angeles, CA: Muthén and Muthén.

Orobio de Castro, B., Merk, W., Koops, W., Veerman, J. W., and Bosch, J. D. (2005). Emotions in social information processing and their relations with reactive and proactive aggression in referred aggressive boys. *J. Clin. Child Adolesc. Psychol.* 34, 105–116. doi: 10.1207/s15374424jccp3401_10

Parker, E. H., Hubbard, J. A., Ramsden, S. R., Relyea, N., Dearing, K. F., Smithmyer, C. M., et al. (2001). Children's use and knowledge of display rules for anger following hypothetical vignettes versus following live peer interaction. *Soc. Dev.* 10, 528–557. doi: 10.1111/1467-9507.00179

Petermann, F., and Wiedebusch, S. (2008). *Emotionale Kompetenz bei Kindern [Emotional Competence in Children]*, 2nd Edn. Göttingen: Hogrefe.

Rauer, W., and Schuck, K. D. (2003). *Fragebogen zur Erfassung emotionaler und sozialer Schulerfahrung von Grundschulkindern dritter und vierter Klassen [FEESS 3-4; Questionnaire on Social and Emotional Experiences at School of Elementary School Children in Third and Fourth Grade]*. Göttingen: Beltz Deutsche Schultests.

Rauer, W., and Schuck, K. D. (2004). *Fragebogen zur Erfassung emotionaler und sozialer Schulerfahrung von Grundschulkindern erster und zweiter Klassen [FEESS 1-2; Questionnaire on Social and Emotional Experiences at School of Elementary School Children in the First and Second Grade]*. Göttingen: Beltz Deutsche Schultests.

Röll, J., Koglin, U., and Petermann, F. (2012). Emotion regulation and childhood aggression: longitudinal associations. *Child Psychiatry Hum. Dev.* 43, 909–923. doi: 10.1007/s10578-012-0303-4

Rothbart, M. K., and Sheese, B. E. (2007). "Temperament and emotion regulation," in *Handbook of Emotion Regulation*, ed J. J. Gross (New York, NY: Guilford Press), 331–350.

Saarni, C., and von Salisch, M. (1993). "The socialization of emotional dissemblance," in *Lying and Deception in Everyday Life*, eds M. Lewis and C. Saarni (New York, NY: The Guilford Press), 106–125.

Simonds, J. (2006). *The Role of Reward Sensitivity and Response: Execution in Childhood Extraversion*. Unpublished doctoral dissertation. University of Oregon. Available online at: http://www.bowdoin.edu/~sputnam/rothbart-temperament-questionnaires/pdf/Simonds_Dissertation_2006.pdf [Accessed April 4, 2015]

Spangler, G., and Zimmermann, P. (2014). Emotional and adrenocortical regulation in early adolescence: prediction by attachment security and disorganization in infancy. *Int. J. Beh. Dev.* 38, 142–154. doi: 10.1177/0165025414520808

Spinrad, T. L., Eisenberg, N., and Gaertner, B. M. (2007). Measures of effortful regulation for young children. *Infant Ment. Health J.* 28, 606–626. doi: 10.1002/imhj.20156

Tan, P. Z., Armstrong, L. M., and Cole, P. M. (2013). Relations between temperament and anger eegulation over early childhood. *Soc. Dev.* 22, 755–773. doi: 10.1111/j.1467-9507.2012.00674.x

Trentacosta, C. J., and Shaw, D. S. (2009). Emotional self-regulation, peer rejection, and antisocial behavior: developmental associations from early childhood to early adolescence. *J. Appl. Dev. Psychol.* 30, 356–365. doi: 10.1016/j.appdev.2008.12.016

Underwood, M. K. (1997a). Peer social status and children's understanding of the expression and control of positive and negative emotions. *Merrill. Palmer. Q.* 43, 610–634.

Underwood, M. K. (1997b). Top ten pressing questions about the development of emotion regulation. *Motiv. Emot.* 21, 127–146. doi: 10.1023/A:1024482516226

Underwood, M. K., Coie, J. D., and Herbsman, C. R. (1992). Display rules for anger and aggression in school-age children. *Child Dev.* 63, 366–380. doi: 10.2307/1131485

Underwood, M. K., Hurley, J. C., Johanson, C. A., and Mosley, J. E. (1999). An experimental, observational investigation of children's responses to peer provocation: developmental and gender differences in middle childhood. *Child Dev.* 70, 1428–1446. doi: 10.1111/1467-8624.00104

von Salisch, M. (2000). *Wenn Kinder sich ärgern. Emotionsregulation in der Entwicklung [When Children Get Angry. Emotional Regulation in the Course of Development]*. Göttingen: Hogrefe.

Waters, S. F., and Thompson, R. A. (2014). Children's perceptions of the effectiveness of strategies for regulating anger and sadness. *Int. J. Behav. Dev.* 38, 174–181. doi: 10.1177/0165025413515410

Wirtz, M. (2006). "Methoden zur Bestimmung der Beurteilerübereinstimmung [Methods for assessing inter-rater agreement]," in *Handbuch der Psychologischen Diagnostik*, eds F. Petermann and M. Eid (Göttingen: Hogrefe), 369–380.

Wittenburg, P., Brugman, H., Russel, A., Klassmann, A., and Sloetjes, H. (2006). "ELAN: a professional framework for multimodality research," in *Proceedings of LREC 2006, Fifth International Conference on Language Resources and Evaluation*. Available online at: http://tla.mpi.nl/tools/tla-tools/elan/ [Accessed May 14, 2012]

Zeman, J., Cassano, M., Perry-Parrish, C., and Stegall, S. (2006). Emotion regulation in children and adolescents. *J. Dev. Behav. Pediatr.* 27, 155–168. doi: 10.1097/00004703-200604000-00014

Zeman, J., and Garber, J. (1996). Display rules for anger, sadness, and pain: it depends on who is watching. *Child Dev.* 67, 957–973. doi: 10.2307/1131873

Zeman, J., and Shipman, K. (1997). Social-contextual influences on expectancies for managing anger and sadness: the transition from middle childhood to adolescence. *Dev. Psychol.* 33, 917–924. doi: 10.1037/0012-1649.33.6.917

Conflict of Interest Statement: The authors declare that the research was conducted in the absence of any commercial or financial relationships that could be construed as a potential conflict of interest.

Behavioral and Neurophysiological Signatures of Benzodiazepine-Related Driving Impairments

Bradly T. Stone[1]*, Kelly A. Correa[1], Timothy L. Brown[2], Andrew L. Spurgin[2,3], Maja Stikic[1], Robin R. Johnson[1] and Chris Berka[1]

[1] Advanced Brain Monitoring, Inc., Carlsbad, CA, USA, [2] National Advanced Driving Simulator, Center for Computer Aided Design, The University of Iowa, Iowa City, IA, USA, [3] College of Pharmacy, The University of Iowa, Iowa City, IA, USA

Edited by:
Joshua Poore,
Charles Stark Draper Laboratory, USA

Reviewed by:
Joshua Fredrick Wiley,
Mary MacKillop Institute for Health
Research at Australian Catholic
University, Australia
Dick De Waard,
University of Groningen, Netherlands

*Correspondence:
Bradly T. Stone
bradlytstone@gmail.com

Specialty section:
This article was submitted to
Quantitative Psychology
and Measurement,
a section of the journal
Frontiers in Psychology

Impaired driving due to drug use is a growing problem worldwide; estimates show that 18–23.5% of fatal accidents, and up to 34% of injury accidents may be caused by drivers under the influence of drugs (Drummer et al., 2003; Walsh et al., 2004; NHTSA, 2010). Furthermore, at any given time, up to 16% of drivers may be using drugs that can impair one's driving abilities (NHTSA, 2009). Currently, drug recognition experts (DREs; law enforcement officers with specialized training to identify drugged driving), have the most difficult time with identifying drivers potentially impaired on central nervous system (CNS) depressants (Smith et al., 2002). The fact that the use of benzodiazepines, a type of CNS depressant, is also associated with the greatest likelihood of causing accidents (Dassanayake et al., 2011), further emphasizes the need to improve research tools in this area which can facilitate the refinement of, or additions to, current assessments of impaired driving. Our laboratories collaborated to evaluate both the behavioral and neurophysiological effects of a benzodiazepine, alprazolam, in a driving simulation (miniSim™). This drive was combined with a neurocognitive assessment utilizing time synched neurophysiology (electroencephalography, ECG). While the behavioral effects of benzodiazepines are well characterized (Rapoport et al., 2009), we hypothesized that, with the addition of real-time neurophysiology and the utilization of simulation and neurocognitive assessment, we could find objective assessments of drug impairment that could improve the detection capabilities of DREs. Our analyses revealed that (1) specific driving conditions were significantly more difficult for benzodiazepine impaired drivers and (2) the neurocognitive tasks' metrics were able to classify "impaired" vs. "unimpaired" with up to 80% accuracy based on lane position deviation and lane departures. While this work requires replication in larger studies, our results not only identified criteria that could potentially improve the identification of benzodiazepine intoxication by DREs, but also demonstrated the promise for future studies using this approach to improve upon current, real-world assessments of impaired driving.

Keywords: simulation, benzodiazepines, impairment, driving, EEG, neurophysiology, cognitive assessment

INTRODUCTION

Driving while impaired is illegal in most countries worldwide due to the public health and safety risks associated with this behavior. Such impairment is often illegal regardless of whether it is due to alcohol, illegal/recreational drugs, or prescription drugs. Despite its illegality, the 2013 National Survey on Drug Use and Health found that 3.8% of those aged 12 or older, an estimated 9.9 million people, self-reported driving under the influence of illicit drugs within the past year (SAMHSA, 2014). In addition to legal penalties, drugged driving comes with severe health risks as well. While the rate of fatal crashes due to drunk driving has generally been declining over the years (NHTSA, 2013), nonalcoholic-drugged driving-related fatalities have increased from 16.6% in 1999 to 28.3% in 2010 (Brady and Li, 2014). Rates of accidents, in general, have shown similar trends as well. In one study of 322 vehicular accident victims admitted to a trauma center in Maryland, urinalysis and plasma results showed that 15.8% of these victims tested positive for alcohol only, 9.9% tested positive for both alcohol and drugs, while an alarming 33.5% tested positive for drugs only (Walsh et al., 2004).

Although the risk of being involved in a fatal car accident is greatly increased by drug use (Li et al., 2013), the level of risk and prevalence is not the same across all drug types. Central nervous system (CNS) depressants, as compared to stimulants, narcotics, and cannabis, are associated with the greatest risk (Li et al., 2013). A 2007 National Highway Traffic Safety Administration study randomly selected drivers at traffic stops across the US during several time points throughout the day and found that benzodiazepines were one of the most commonly encountered drugs being used in day-time drivers (Lacey et al., 2009). These data are consistent with multiple studies and one meta-analysis showing that benzodiazepines are associated with 60–80% increased risk for vehicular accidents (Dassanayake et al., 2011). Furthermore, drivers who are at fault in an accident are 40% more likely to have been under the influence of benzodiazepines than those who are not at fault (Dassanayake et al., 2011).

Due to the public health risks associated with driving under the influence of benzodiazepines, objective assessments of the cognitive, behavioral, and physiological correlates of such impairments are needed. While alcohol related impairments are predictable, and correlated to breath alcohol content (BrAC), a recent review of the relationship between plasma concentrations of benzodiazepines and driving performance did not find a clear dose–response relationship (Verster and Roth, 2013). Therefore, detection of impairment due to other substances has relied on alternative assessments performed by Drug Recognition Experts (DREs). A DRE evaluation includes observations of many factors, including (but not limited to): physical appearance, driving behaviors, vital signs, psychomotor functioning, etc (Talpins and Hayes, 2004). These evaluations have proven to be highly successful in detecting driving impairments due to drug intoxication in general, yet, out of all drug classifications, with the exclusion of alcohol, CNS depressants are the least likely (41.7%) to be accurately recognized by DREs (Smith et al., 2002). Further research on correlates of benzodiazepine impairments is needed to validate the existing criteria and provide additional signs for DREs to rely on to increase their accuracy in drug specificity. Alternative research methods and tools may be necessary to facilitate such investigations. In particular, the utilization of a cognitive and physiological assessment with time-synced neurocognitive tasks and electroencephalography (EEG) may prove to be a successful approach toward meeting this goal.

Research has shown promise for the utilization of cognitive and behavioral performance for such an assessment. In regards to cognitive task performance, benzodiazepines decrease alertness (Verster et al., 2002; Barker et al., 2004), increase reaction times (Fernández-Guardiola et al., 1984; Suzuki et al., 1995; Münte et al., 1996; Verster et al., 2002; Barker et al., 2004; Snyder et al., 2005; Leufkens et al., 2007), impair vigilance (Koženà et al., 1995), and impair various memory functions such as verbal and working memory (Linnoila et al., 1990; Rush and Griffiths, 1997; Verster et al., 2002; Barker et al., 2004; Snyder et al., 2005; Leufkens et al., 2007). These effects are dose-dependent. For example, a 0.5 mg dose of the benzodiazepine, alprazolam, significantly slowed reaction times on simple attention tasks (Snyder et al., 2005). A 1.0 mg dose also slowed reaction times on simple attention tasks and additionally decreased accuracy on tasks assessing executive functions and learning, and increased reaction times on executive and psychomotor tasks (Snyder et al., 2005). In addition to impairing cognitive function, benzodiazepines can have adverse effects on motor control (Verster et al., 2002; Barker et al., 2004) and psychomotor functioning (Linnoila et al., 1990; Rush and Griffiths, 1997; Riba et al., 2001; Barker et al., 2004; Snyder et al., 2005). Taken together, these data suggests that this class of drug may impair various driving-related skills as driving requires the coordination of both cognitive and motor skills. In fact, studies have confirmed that benzodiazepine use is directly associated with driving impairments related to control of lateral position within the lane or completely crossing into adjacent lanes or shoulders (O'Hanlon et al., 1982; Van Laar et al., 1992, 2001; Bocca et al., 1999; Verster et al., 2002; Leufkens et al., 2007), speed control (Van Laar et al., 1992; Verster et al., 2002; Staner et al., 2005), and steering (Smiley and Moskowitz, 1986). Use of this drug has also been shown to negatively impact one's abilities to assess the surrounding environment (Verster et al., 2002; Leufkens et al., 2007; Dassanayake et al., 2011) and to slow reaction times related to driving performance (Kuitunen, 1994; Bocca et al., 1999; Vanakoski et al., 2000; Leufkens et al., 2007; Dassanayake et al., 2011).

EEG has also been utilized to measure the neurocognitive effects of benzodiazepines and driving. Benzodiazepines can affect several EEG power spectral density bandwidths linked to attention and internal processing (Buchsbaum et al., 1985; Harmony et al., 1996; Eoh et al., 2005). Research has shown benzodiazepines to be related to increases in Delta (1–3 Hz) in the bilateral frontal–temporal and temporal–occipital regions (Staner et al., 2005). Such increases in Delta, as well as Theta (3–7 Hz), have been positively correlated with fatigue while driving (Lal and Craig, 2002; Campagne et al., 2004), and could possibly serve as an indicator of benzodiazepine-related driving impairment. Benzodiazepines also decrease Alpha (8–13 Hz) band activity in the frontal, temporal, and occipital regions (Buchsbaum et al., 1985; Bond et al., 1992; Staner et al., 2005). Suppression of Alpha activity can be indicative of task-related increases in cognitive demand (Klimesch, 1999; Eoh et al., 2005) and has even been specifically linked to driving; easier simulator courses produce higher levels of Alpha than more difficult simulator courses in healthy drivers (Eoh et al., 2005). The suppression of Alpha associated with benzodiazepine use may be indicative of cognitive compensatory mechanisms being activated, leaving fewer resources for coping with higher driving demands when needed. Since increases in cognitive demand are correlated with greater likelihoods of committing errors (Fairclough et al., 2005), it is possible that the reduction in Alpha due to benzodiazepine use may also serve as an indicator for increased risk of driving errors. EEG Beta activity (13–30 Hz) is of particular interest in relation to driving abilities; as benzodiazepine use is associated with increased activity in the parietal and central regions (i.e., motor cortex) as well as in the bilateral frontal–temporal and temporal–occipital regions (Hendler et al., 1980; Buchsbaum et al., 1985; Bond et al., 1992; Staner et al., 2005). Because increased Beta activity across the motor cortex is associated with a reduction in motor movements (Baker, 2007), this could potentially be an indicator of a reduction in driving-related psychomotor functioning.

In addition to EEG metrics, ECG metrics may also be informative in assessing impairments associated with benzodiazepine use. For example, research has shown that the administration of a benzodiazepine elevates heart rate (HR; Muzet et al., 1981; DiMicco, 1987; Ueda et al., 2013). This finding could possibly be related to, and predictive of, the impairments associated with this class of drug. HR variability (HRV) may also be predictive of such impairments as its quadratic relationship with the activation of the parasympathetic nervous system (Goldberger et al., 2001) provides detail on the autonomic nervous system's functioning through the low frequency/high frequency ratio (Camm et al., 1996; Sztajzel, 2004). In fact, research has shown promise for using this metric to detect driving errors. For example, decreased HRV is related to drowsiness while driving (Murata and Hiramatsu, 2008), as well as increases in drowsiness related driving errors (Michail et al., 2008). This class of drugs has been shown to reduce HRV (Adinoff et al., 1992; Agelink et al., 2002), which, in addition to drowsiness, may also indicate impaired cognitive functioning. To this end, research has shown that those with lower HRV show decreased accuracy, and increased reaction times, on working memory and vigilance tasks (Hansen et al., 2003). For these reasons, ECG was also time-synced to the neurocognitive tasks. In summary, these findings provide a foundation establishing that the neurocognitive, physiological, and behavioral effects of benzodiazepines can both be measured and used to detect levels of driving related impairment.

While there has been extensive research on the cognitive, behavioral, and neurophysiological effects of benzodiazepines, research is needed on whether these impairments can be utilized to predict and differentiate between who is safe to drive and who is impaired due to benzodiazepine use. The variability inherently associated with real-world, on-the-road assessments, in addition to the risk for accidents, complicates the orchestration of safe and controlled research studies of benzodiazepine-related driving impairments. Innovations in virtual environments have made driving simulators a highly valid alternative to on-the-road assessments. Furthermore, driving simulator performance has been shown to be related to, and predictive of, on-the-road driving performance (Lee, 2003; Lew et al., 2005; De Winter et al., 2009; Bédard et al., 2010). Therefore, a driving simulator is the most effective platform for conducting safe, controlled, and reproducible studies on the effects of CNS active drugs, such as benzodiazepines, on driving performance.

The current study utilized such a platform to assess the use of neurocognitive, physiological, and behavioral indicators for predicting benzodiazepine-related impairment. Although performance on laboratory-based cognitive tasks have previously been shown to be related to Standard Deviation of Lateral Position (SDLP; Verster et al., 2002), an indicator of driving performance, these tasks, alone, have not been able to predict much of the variability in SDLP (Verster and Roth, 2012). By adding real-time neurophysiology to cognitive tasks, we hypothesized that we would be able to predict variability in simulated driving performance. Since simulated driving performance predicts real-world driving, such findings would not only demonstrate the promise for this alternative approach for future research on this topic, but could also lead to further validation of, and improvement upon, assessments for drugged driving related impairments.

MATERIALS AND METHODS

Participants

A total of $N = 24$ participants were recruited and enrolled following a two level screening process. Participants were recruited through a database registry ($n = 7000+$) whereby emails and phone calls were sent out to a randomized set of individuals who met the pre-screening criteria. Additionally, participants were recruited through emails sent to all 30000+ students/faculty associated with the University of Iowa. Prior to any participant screening visits, an initial phone screen was completed to increase the rate of participants passing the screening visit. The phone screening involved a variety of yes or no questions to determine preliminary eligibility.

If initially eligible, participants were required to come to the National Advanced Driving Simulator facility (NADS) at the University of Iowa's Research Park (Coralville, IA, USA), for an in-person screening visit, and to complete the informed consent protocol prior to a more rigorous screening process. Once enrolled, participants were then asked to complete the following additional screening procedures: an initial urinalysis drug screen to ensure they tested negative for all drugs, a pregnancy screen (if female), a brief physical examination of vital signs (including HR and blood pressure), and a psychiatric exam using the Columbia-Suicide Severity Rating Scale (C-SSRS). After successful completion of the physical and psychiatric screening, an in-depth survey was administered that included detailed demographics and questions about the presence and extent of any preexisting abnormalities and/or mental health issues that may put the participant at a greater risk for health complications, adverse drug reactions, or interfere with the study procedures and results. All potential enrollees were then asked to complete a brief (5–8 min) drive in the simulator to assess for the propensity of simulator sickness and to familiarize them with the operation of the simulator. Following the drive, a wellness questionnaire was administered to determine their individual risk of simulator sickness; those scoring at high risk were removed from further participation.

A total of $n = 19$ participants were selected for the analysis for this study out of the originally qualified $N = 24$. The exclusions were due to: (a) having poor EEG and/or ECG data quality ($<80\%$ good data) ($n = 1$); (b) Simulator Sickness Questionnaire indicating increased proneness to simulator sickness ($n = 1$); (c) testing positive for non-approved drug within their system on orientation visit ($n = 2$); and (d) failure to comply with study protocol ($n = 1$). The final dataset ($n = 19$) was comprised of 31.6% females with 94.7% of the participants identifying as Caucasian. This dataset had a mean age of 25.3 yr (range: 18–38 year), a mean weight of 81.19 kg (SD: 12.85 kg), and a mean height of 176.64 cm (SD: 15.85 cm).

All participants received monetary compensation for taking part in the current study. Participants were paid at the end of their last visit. Payment schedules went as follows: $25 for Orientation, $115 for first experimental session, and $135 for the second experimental session. If a participant was unable to complete the experiment, they were paid for any past visits and additional $20/h for the time they completed in their last session. All procedures were reviewed by the University of Iowa IRB, and approved prior to study implementation.

Equipment/Materials
Self-report Tools
Three self-report tools were used after final screening to (1) screen out those at higher risk of simulation sickness (Simulator Sickness Questionnaire; Kennedy et al., 1993); (2) confirm compliance with sleep and caffeine intake requirements (Intake Survey; Brown et al., 2014); and (3) to assess general sleepiness prior to drug administration (Stanford Sleepiness Scale; Johnson et al., 1990). As the class of benzodiazepine drugs are associated with increased fatigue, and the effects on driving are thought to stem, in part, to the fatigue related effects, sleepiness assessment is essential to ensure that the effects of the drug are being measured, rather than some unrelated fatigue issues.

Psychophysiology
EEG and ECG were acquired using the B-Alert® X10 wireless sensor headset (Advanced Brain Monitoring, Inc, Carlsbad, CA, USA). This system had nine referential EEG channels located according to the International 10–20 system at Fz, F3, F4, Cz, C3, C4, POz, P3, and P4 and an auxiliary channel for ECG. Linked reference electrodes were located behind each ear on the mastoid bone. ECG electrodes were placed on the right clavicle and the lower left rib. Data were sampled at 256 Hz with a high band pass at 0.1 Hz and a low band pass, fifth order filter, at 100 Hz obtained digitally with Sigma-Delta

A/D converters. Data was broadcasted to an iOS-Compatible Bluetooth transmitter using a wired configuration, which then transmitted the data wirelessly via Bluetooth to a host iOS device, where acquisition software then stored the psychophysiological data. The proprietary acquisition software also included artifact decontamination algorithms for eye blink, muscle movement, and environmental/electrical interference such as spikes and saturations. After obtaining head measurements, the B-Alert® X10 wireless sensor headset was placed on the subject's head, with accompanying leads, and the impedance was tested until optimal connectivity was achieved (<40.0 kΩs) prior to each of the three data collection sessions.

Drive Simulator
The NADS miniSim™ Research Driving Simulator is a PC-based research driving simulator with powerful scenario editing and data acquisition capabilities that is based on over a decade of research and driving simulation experience at the University of Iowa's National Advanced Driving Simulator (NADS). The miniSim™ can be configured a variety of ways, including single and multi-screen displays and desktop, 1/4-cab and 1/2 cab configurations.

miniSim™ Data Collection Mode
The miniSim™ data acquisition system (DAQ) runs every time a scenario is ran. The DAQ collects well over 100 variables for post-processing; the Runtime Measures Evaluation functionality offers the researcher the option of obtaining measures from the simulator immediately when the drive ends. Among these variables are: Mean Lane Position, Standard Deviation of Lane Position, Lane Departure, Standard Deviation of Steering Wheel Angle, Steering Entropy, Steering Bandwidth, Lateral Acceleration, Speed, Standard Deviation of Speed, Longitudinal Acceleration, and other event specific measures. The measures are reported for the entire drive. The user has total control in defining the start and end points of each event through the scenario. For the analyses presented herein, there is a focus on assessing Standard Deviation of Lane Position and Lane Departures, as these metrics have shown promise in assessing benzodiazepine-related impairments in previous studies. The Standard Deviation of Lane Position is a combination of averaging the variability in lane position across events and road conditions, as well as the variability of speed across these events (25–70 mph), and variability and driving conditions, while Lane Departure refers to any time a wheel crossed over a lane line.

A total of three scenarios were programmed with consistent events, and comparable difficulty, that included three Road type segments: Rural, Urban, and Highway; with 6–10 events in each segment. These scenarios were used equally, counterbalanced across participants so that each received two (1 per drive). The events are shown in **Table 1**.

Doses, Administration, and Design
Drugs
The study was conducted according to a double blind, placebo-controlled, within subject, cross-over design. Two dosing conditions existed: (1) administration of the benzodiazepine and

(2) administration of a matched placebo. In order to provide an identical dose, both conditions delivered an encapsulated, identical in size (size 0) and similar in weight and appearance (non-labeled, colored-blue and opaque), pill. The benzodiazepine [1 mg instant release (IR) alprazolam] was manufactured by Mylan® and obtained through the University of Iowa Hospitals and Clinics, under the DEA license of the Principal Investigator (PI). A low dose of 1mg IR alprazolam was chosen because several studies have found that this dose significantly impairs cognitive function and driving performance (Leufkens et al., 2007; Dassanayake et al., 2011). The placebo (lactose) was supplied as lactose monohydrate NF (National Formulary), manufactured by Professional Compounding Centers of America (PCCA). The placebo and the benzodiazepine were encapsulated at the University of Iowa College of Pharmacy by blinded outer capsules, made by Gallipot Inc., to ensure that administration of the drug/placebo remained blind.

Neurocognitive Assessment Tasks (M-AMP)

Participants were required to complete the Mobile Alertness Memory Profile (M-AMP) as part of the study protocol at three time points (orientation and as part of each of the two experimental sessions), with synchronized psychophysiology

TABLE 1 | Road type segments and events.

Road type segment	Event	Description
Rural	TurnOffRamp	Transition from off-ramp to rural road
Rural	Lighted	Straight section of lighted rural road
Rural	TransToDark	Partially lighted rural road
Rural	Dark	Mixture of curves and tangents without environmental lighting
Rural	TransToGravel	Transition from dark rural to gravel
Rural	Gravel	Rural gravel road with curves
Rural	Driveway	Gravel curve past a house and driveway
Rural	GravelExtension	Rural gravel road with curves
Rural	GravelTransToRural	Transition to paved rural road from gravel
Rural	RuralStraight	Ten minute rural tangent
Highway	OnRamp	Transition from urban to interstate via ramp
Highway	MergeOn	Transition from ramp to interstate
Highway	Interstate	Divided highway with traffic in same direction
Highway	MergingTraffic	Interchange with traffic that merges and forces driver to change lanes
Highway	InterstateCurves	Divided highway with curves
Highway	ExitRamp	Transition from interstate via ramp
Urban	Pullout	Entering driving lane from parking spot
Urban	Urban General	Urban environment with curves and tangents
Urban	Green Light	Intersection with green light
Urban	Yellow	Intersection with light that turns yellow as driver approaches
Urban	Left	Intersection with left turn across traffic
Urban	UrbanCurves	Less dense urban environment with curves
Urban	UrbanEarly	Urban environment with curves and tangents

from the B-Alert X10. Using an Apple iPad® (fourth generation), the tasks that were completed included:

3-Choice Active Vigilance Task (3CVT)

The three choice active vigilance task (3CVT) is a 20 min long task that requires participants to discriminate one target (70% occurrence) from two non-target (30% occurrence) geometric shapes. Each stimulus was presented for a duration of 200 ms. The inter-stimulus interval was variable and changed for each quartile of the task: 1–3 s for the 1st quartile, 1–6 s for the second and third quartiles, and 1–10 s for the last quartile. Participants were instructed to respond as quickly as possible to each stimulus by selecting the left arrow for target stimuli and the right arrow for non-target stimuli. A training period was provided prior to the beginning of the task in order to minimize practice effects.

Visual Psycho-Vigilance Task (VPVT) and Auditory Psycho-Vigilance Task (APVT)

The Visual Psycho-Vigilance Task (VPVT) and Auditory Psycho-Vigilance Task (APVT) were passive vigilance tasks that lasted 5 min each. The VPVT repeatedly presented a 10 cm circular target image for a duration of 200 ms. The target image was presented every 2 s in the center of the computer monitor, requiring the participant to respond to image onset by pressing the spacebar. The APVT consisted of an auditory tone that was played every 2 s, requiring the participant to respond to auditory onset by pressing the spacebar.

Standard Image Recognition (SIR)

The Standard Image Recognition (SIR) task was used to evaluate attention and short-term memory and takes 6 minutes to complete. The IR task included both training and testing periods. During the training period, participants were asked to memorize a series of 20 target images that were presented twice per image. To ensure the participant was attending to the target images, they were required to respond to each image by pressing the left arrow key. In the testing period, the participants were then asked to identify the target images (selecting the left arrow key for targets or right arrow key for non-target, as with the 3CVT) in a field of 100 total images (20 targets/80 non-target). This task is capable of employing several different categories of images (animals, food, sports, and travel); the animals category is always used unless the participant must restart the task, in which case images from a different category are displayed. These images were used in a counterbalanced order across participants to ensure that there were no carryover effects over time for each participants.

Protocol

Eligible participants completed a total of three visits: orientation and two experimental sessions that were identical in procedure, differing only in dosing condition.

Orientation

After completion of the screener and determination of final eligibility, participants were asked to complete an initial M-AMP with synchronized psychophysiology. The 45-min session consisted of the 3CVT (20 min), VPVT (5 min), APVT (5 min), and SIR (6 min), as well as practice and transition periods. These tasks began prior to 11:00 AM in order to ensure that diurnal variation in the EEG signal did not confound results throughout the study. If participants were unable to begin these tasks prior to 11:00 AM, a second orientation visit was scheduled. The first experimental sessions were scheduled upon completion of the M-AMP.

Experimental Sessions

The two experimental study visits were scheduled at a minimum of 5 days apart in order to allow for an adequate drug wash-out period between study visits. Experimental sessions lasted approximately 5–6 h and started at either 7:00 AM or 8:00 AM. Upon arrival for a study visit the subject was required to provide a urine specimen for drug screening and, if female, a pregnancy test. In the case of a positive drug screen, the subject was taken home and the visit was rescheduled for a later date, taking into account the time it takes for the drug to clear the participant's system. After urinalysis, the capsule (drug or placebo) was administered to participants accompanied with a full glass of water. Upon swallowing the capsule, a two-hour waiting period began. During this two hour waiting period, to allow for peak activity of the study drug, participants remained seated and relaxed in the subject prep room. Subjects were allowed to listen to music, read, and/or browse the internet, however continuous monitoring ensured that they did not fall asleep. Immediately following this waiting period, the M-AMP was administered to assess neurocognitive functioning. All M-AMP sessions began by 11:00 AM to ensure limited diurnal variation in the EEG signal. Once participants completed this test battery, they were moved into the miniSim™ room and began their drive.

The study drive consisted of four simulated nighttime segments. Each segment lasted approximately 10 minutes and included urban, freeway, and rural roadways that included a mixture of road geometries and speeds. It should be noted that this drive was designed to provide a cross section of driving environments to assess how performance varies as driving context varies and differs (Lee et al., 2010) substantially from traditional simulated road tests utilizing only straight roads at a constant speed. Therefore, as the SDLP values are considered, it is important to note some differences relative to other published data. Most published data uses a common driving environment including straight roads at a constant speed, but the research presented herein involves a diverse environment containing a variety of driving situations. The result of this is that many of our SDLP values are not directly comparable to other methodologies. Lastly, participants completed the Simulator Sickness Questionnaire in response to their experience during the study drive.

The second experimental session was scheduled at the end of the first session. After each visit, participants were taken home by a taxi service to ensure they were not driving under any potential influence due to the study procedures.

Statistics

One way ANOVAs (drug condition) were conducted for the drive metrics of SDLP and Lane Departures (LnDPs), both for the overall drive and for each event of the drive (i.e., Urban Yellow Light, Rural gravel Extension); Bonferroni adjustments were made for multiple comparisons. Our goal is not to identify drug use, but rather the impairments associated with drug use. For this reason, we stratified participants/sessions into "impaired" vs. "unimpaired" based on performance on SDLP and LnDPs. From this stratification we found that $n = 1$ placebo session was impaired, and $n = 6$ drug use sessions were unimpaired. We removed the placebo confounded session from further analysis, and included the "drug-unimpaired" in the unimpaired category after an initial assessment showed no significant differences between these sessions and the placebo-unimpaired group.

We then conducted one-way ANOVAs on the M-AMP data for performance and neurophysiologic metrics: EEG bandwidths, EEG wavelets, HR, and HR Variability, based on impairment. Tukey's range test for pairwise comparisons were used for *post hoc* tests.

In order to begin to determine the predictive value of the M-AMP on driving impairment, we regressed the M-AMP data onto the SDLP and LnDP, by M-AMP task (i.e., we regressed the 3CVT metrics separate from the VPVT, APVT, and SIR metrics). We performed several forward step-wise regressions to identify the predictive power of performance and neurophysiological metrics for each of the aforementioned tasks. During the step-wise regression, in each step, a set of *F*-tests were performed as the selection criteria to determine the explanatory power of variables and to select which variables to include in the model. The metrics identified by the regressions were then used in a cross-validated 2-Class discriminate function analysis by "impairment" status (based on SDLP and LnDP as noted) to identify the potential predictive power of the neurocognitive assessment in predicting driving impairment.

To further evaluate classification accuracy, we applied a machine learning approach (boosting) to the dataset. The boosting algorithm, AdaBoost (Freund and Schapire, 1997; Viola and Jones, 2001) combines multiple weak learners into a single strong classifier. Each weak learner is a simple decision stump that depends only on a single variable from the input training vectors. The final prediction rule is a weighted majority vote of weak learners in which the weight of each weak learner is a function of its accuracy. The error of the boosted classifier drops exponentially when the weak learners' accuracy is slightly better than random guessing. AdaBoost maintains a set of weights over the training samples to focus the training process on samples that are misclassified. This is done by increasing the weights of the training samples that are misclassified and decreasing the weights of the training samples that are correctly classified in each boosting round.

RESULTS

One Way ANOVAs
Drive

A one-way ANOVA was conducted in order to investigate the effects of the drug on SDLP throughout the driving session which revealed that those who were given the benzodiazepine ($M = 41.76$ cm, $SD = 6.10$) had significantly greater SDLP

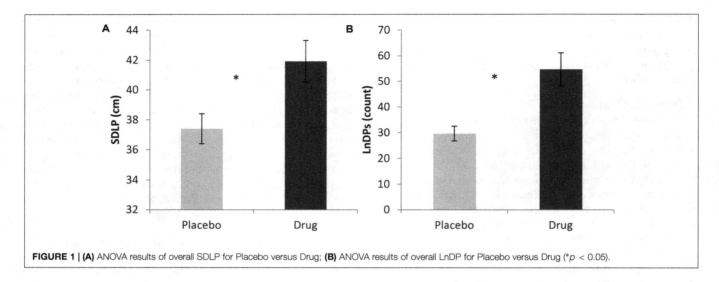

FIGURE 1 | (A) ANOVA results of overall SDLP for Placebo versus Drug; **(B)** ANOVA results of overall LnDP for Placebo versus Drug (*$p < 0.05$).

than those who were given the placebo ($M = 37.49$ cm, $SD = 4.27$), $F(1,33) = 6.12$, $p < 0.05$. For comparison, the relatively straight portion of the urban drive, when considered alone, showed the same pattern of effects with those who were given the benzodiazepine ($M = 25.73$ cm, $SD = 9.16$) having a significantly greater SDLP than those who were given the placebo ($M = 19.19$ cm, $SD = 8.49$), $F(1,18) = 6.02$, $p < 0.05$. Since the inability to maintain lane position is one of the cues officers use to predict impairment due to intoxication (NHTSA, 1997), we investigated LnDP as well. The one-way ANOVA on the sum of LnDPs for the overall drive revealed a significant difference between drug conditions, $F(1,33) = 10.11$, $p < 0.01$, with the benzodiazepine condition ($M = 54.68$, $SD = 28.72$) having significantly more LnDPs than placebo ($M = 29.6$, $SD = 11.46$). These findings are shown in **Figure 1**.

In addition to overall drive effects, ANOVAs were used to examine the events within the drive, as some are more sensitive to impaired driving than others, by design. For SDLP, we found significant differences between conditions for the following events: Urban General $F(1,33) = 4.27$, $p < 0.05$; Urban Green Light $F(1,33) = 4.66$, $p < 0.05$; Highway Interstate $F(1,33) = 10.24$, $p < 0.01$; Rural Transition to Dark, $F(1,33) = 8.18$, $p < 0.01$; and Rural Straight, $F(1,33) = 12.81$, $p < 0.001$. These data are reported in **Table 2** and shown in **Figure 2**. For LnDPs, the following events revealed significant differences between the two conditions: Highway Interstate $F(1,33) = 6.36$, $p < 0.05$; Rural Dark $F(1,33) = 5.52$, $p < 0.05$; and Rural Straight $F(1,33) = 14.24$, $p < 0.001$ (see **Table 2**; **Figure 2**).

M-AMP Impairment

One way ANOVAs were conducted to detect significant differences in performance and neurophysiology between the drug-impaired and unimpaired groups for all M-AMP tasks. The two groups significantly differed on the following physiologic metrics during the 3CVT: P3 Gamma (25–40 Hz), $F(1,33) = 4.22$, $p < 0.05$; and Midline Alpha Slow (Fz, Cz, Pz, and POz from 8 to 10 Hz), $F(1,33) = 4.22$, $p < 0.05$. For performance, we found reaction time and reaction variability to be significantly different,

TABLE 2 | One way ANOVA – drive metrics.

Metric	Road type segment-event	Condition	Mean (cm)	Standard deviation (cm)
SDLP	Urban-general*	Placebo	22.45	7.08
		Drug	28.03	8.34
	Urban-green light*	Placebo	18.77	7.95
		Drug	25.03	8.74
	Highway-interstate**	Placebo	45.5	6.4
		Drug	56.27	11.71
	Rural-transition to dark**	Placebo	26.29	6.89
		Drug	37.98	14.56
	Rural-straight***	Placebo	34.21	7.06
		Drug	50.65	17.15
LnDP	Highway-interstate*	Placebo	9	4.5
		Drug	13.84	6.26
	Rural-dark*	Placebo	4.07	2.94
		Drug	7.58	5.16
	Rural-straight***	Placebo	4.81	4.68
		Drug	16.79	11.92

*$p < 0.05$; **$p < 0.01$; ***$p < 0.001$

including: overall correct response variability, $F(1,33) = 5.07$, $p < 0.05$; variability in correct response to interference stimuli during the first quartile, $F(1,33) = 4.45$, $p < 0.05$; reaction times for correct responses across all stimuli types during the fourth quartile $F(1,32) = 4.59$, $p < 0.05$; and variability in correct response reaction times across all stimuli types during the 4th quartile, $F(1,32)$ 4.67, $p < 0.05$. The mean and SD for these findings are shown in **Table 3**.

Significant differences based on impairment were found for the other three tasks as well. For the VPVT, performance differences were found between the two groups, with the drug-impaired group having significantly more missed responses ($M = 3.92$, $SD = 4.03$) than the unimpaired group ($M = 1.24$, $SD = 2.17$), $F(1,28) = 5.52$, $p < 0.05$ (no physiologic differences were revealed). Similar to the performance differences observed

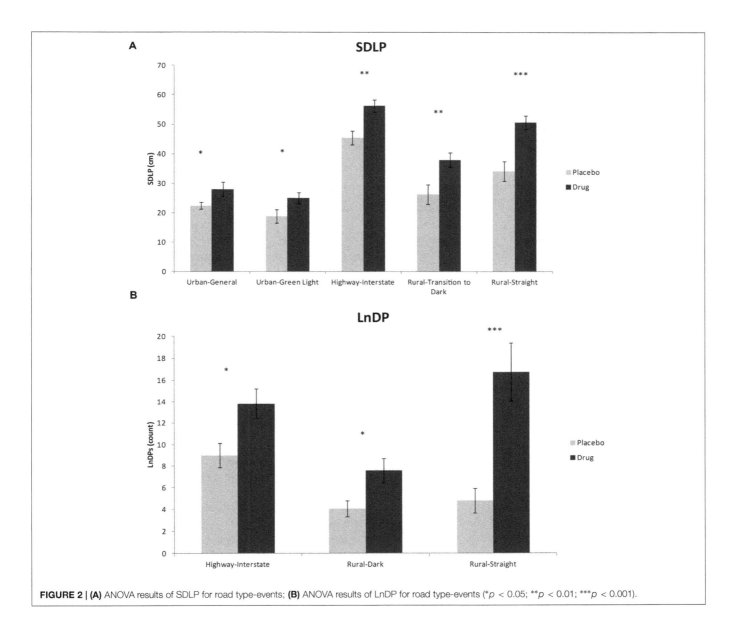

FIGURE 2 | (A) ANOVA results of SDLP for road type-events; (B) ANOVA results of LnDP for road type-events (*$p < 0.05$; **$p < 0.01$; ***$p < 0.001$).

TABLE 3 | One way ANOVA – 3CVT data.

Metric	Impairment group	Mean	Standard deviation
P3 Gamma (25–40 Hz)	Unimpaired	2.44	0.40
	Drug-impaired	2.20	0.19
Midline Alpha Slow (8–10 Hz)	Unimpaired	2.95	0.26
	Drug-impaired	3.19	0.41
Overall standard deviation of reaction time for correct-targets	Unimpaired	0.15	0.06
	Drug-impaired	0.20	0.06
Standard deviation of reaction times to interference stimuli (Q1)	Unimpaired	0.10	0.04
	Drug-impaired	0.13	0.05
Mean reaction time for correct-targets, quartile 4	Unimpaired	0.73	0.13
	Drug-impaired	0.84	0.17
Standard deviation of reaction time for correct-targets, quartile 4	Unimpaired	0.16	0.06
	Drug-impaired	0.25	0.19

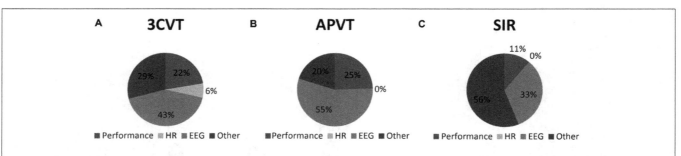

FIGURE 3 | Standard Deviation of Lateral Position (SDLP) variance explained by HR, EEG, and Performance metrics within the (A) 3CVT; (B) APVT; and (C) SIR task.

TABLE 4 | Standard Deviation of Lateral Position (SDLP) regression models.

	Standard deviation in lane departures (SDLP)		
	Metric	F	Adj. R^2
3CVT	Parietal hemispheric difference, Alpha (8–13 Hz)	6.19*	0.18
	F4 Gamma (25–40 Hz)	4.06*	0.08
	Standard deviation of reaction times to non-targets	4.6*	0.07
	Heart rate (HR)	4.53*	0.06
	Frontal hemispheric difference, Delta (1–3 Hz)	5.91*	0.07
	POz Slow Theta (3–5 Hz)	6.04*	0.06
	Reaction time to non-targets, quartile 4	6.09*	0.05
	Incorrect non-target rate, quartile 1	3.3	0.02
	Incorrect non-target rate, quartile 4	8.26**	0.04
	Accuracy overall, quartile 4	3.84*	0.02
	Overall Gamma (25–40 Hz)	5.77*	0.02
	Overall hemispheric differences, Beta (13–30 Hz)	7.5*	0.02
	Incorrect interference rate, quartile 4	5.57*	0.01
	Accuracy non-target Rate, quartile 1	7.62*	0.01
APVT	Lapses, 6 s or longer	7.03*	0.18
	Central hemispheric differences, Gamma (25–40 Hz)	3.3*	0.07
	Central hemispheric differences, Delta (1–3 Hz)	3.07*	0.06
	Frontal hemispheric difference, Fast Alpha (10–13 Hz)	2.75	0.05
	Lapses, 3 s or longer	4.5*	0.07
	C4 Theta (3–7 Hz)	3.74	0.05
	Cz Fast Alpha (10–13 Hz)	6.95*	0.08
	Fz Delta (1–3 Hz)	4.2	0.04
	C4 Sigma (12–15 Hz)	3.4	0.03
	POz Gamma (25–40)	3.39	0.03
	Central hemispheric differences, Alpha (8–13 Hz)	4.37*	0.03
	Overall hemispheric differences, Delta (1–3 Hz)	3.91*	0.02
	Parietal hemispheric difference, Sigma (12–15 Hz)	4.73*	0.03
	C4 Delta (1–3 Hz)	7.15*	0.03
	F3 Gamma (25–40 Hz)	11.24**	0.03
SIR	Frontal hemispheric difference, Slow Alpha (8–10 Hz)	7.42*	0.19
	Incorrect target rate	4.94*	0.11
	Frontal hemispheric difference, Beta (13–30 Hz)	2.37	0.05
	Central hemispheric differences, Beta (13–30 Hz)	4.92*	0.09

*$p < 0.05$; **$p < 0.01$; Adj. R^2 = adjusted R^2 value of the model when the variable was entered into the model.

for the VPVT, the APVT showed significant differences on missed responses between groups with the drug-impaired group missing more responses ($M = 8.43$, $SD = 7.94$) than the unimpaired group ($M = 1.32$, $SD = 2.87$), $F(1,34) = 14.82$, $p < 0.001$. In addition, during the APVT, the drug-impaired group had significantly more lapses (failure to respond for 3 s or longer, $M = 5.5$, $SD = 5.17$) than the unimpaired group ($M = 0.5$, $SD = 1.19$), $F(1,34) = 19.29$, $p < 0.001$. Neurophysiological differences for the APVT revealed that overall Central Theta (C3, Cz, C4; 3–7 Hz) was higher in the drug-impaired group ($M = 3.43$, $SD = 0.46$) in comparison to the unimpaired group ($M = 3.19$, $SD = 0.23$), $F(1,34) = 4.25$, $p < 0.05$. During the SIR task, the drug-impaired group also showed greater variability in reaction times ($M = 0.18$, $SD = 0.05$) compared to the unimpaired group ($M = 0.13$, $SD = 0.05$), $F(1,33) = 11.23$, $p < 0.01$, but no significant differences in accuracy or neurophysiology were found.

Forward Step Wise Regression

As individual M-AMP neurophysiologic and performance metrics were not substantially informative in identifying impairment, we explored whether the combination of multiple metrics could best predict impaired driving performance. To this end, we applied a forward step-wise regression of the M-AMP metrics within each M-AMP task onto SDLP and LnDP. For SDLP, 3CVT metrics explained 70.9% of variance, $F(14,18) = 7.62$, $p < 0.05$, primarily by hemispheric differences in parietal Alpha (8–13 Hz) (17.5%) and frontal (F4) Gamma (25–40 Hz, 8.0%). Overall, 70.9% of variance was explained by: EEG metrics (42.3%), elevated HR (6.3%), and performance (22.2%). In contrast, the VPVT metrics were not statistically significant in explaining SDLP variability. However, the APVT metrics explained 79.9%, with lapses explaining the most variability at 17.5%, and with EEG metrics making up the remainder (55.4%), $F(15,19) = 11.24$, $p < 0.01$. Finally, SIR metrics explained only 43.9% of SDLP variance, primarily with hemispheric differences (32.8%) at the frontal (F3 and F4) and central (C3 and C4) sites within Slow Alpha (8–10 Hz) and Beta (13–30 Hz). Performance metrics made up the remainder (11.1%), $F(4,29) = 4.92$, $p < 0.05$. These data are presented in **Table 4** and visualized in **Figure 3**.

For the LnDPs, the 3CVT metrics were the most explanatory, at 92.3%, $F(13,19) = 10.66$, $p < 0.01$, that relied on hemispheric parietal (P3 and P4) differences in Gamma (25–40 Hz) (19.5%) and HRV during the third quartile of the 3CVT (11.3%), with other EEG metrics making up the majority (68.5%) of the variance explained, and performance contributing 12.4%. Once again, the VPVT had a statistically insignificant model and thus was not valid in explaining variability in LnDPs. The APVT metrics, again, had high explanatory value $F(14,19) = 5.18$, $p < 0.05$, with EEG making up the majority of the metrics (58.5%) at various locations and bandwidths. Similar to SDLP, performance metrics within the APVT had a significant explanatory role (19.0%), relying primarily on lapses. HRV metrics within the APVT, though small (2.31%), also contributed to explaining lane departures, such that decreases in HRV were associated with increases in the variance in lane departures. Finally, the SIR metrics explained 63.3%; $F(5,27) = 6.7, p < 0.05$; relying on hemispheric differences (48.5%) across Alpha, Sigma, Beta, and Gamma bandwidths, as well as performance (14.8%). These data are presented in **Table 5** and visualized in **Figure 4**.

Discriminant Function Analysis (DFA)

In order to further determine if the variables found in the regression analyses could identify impairment risk, we entered these variables into a 2-class (drug-impaired/unimpaired) linear discriminate function analyses. While highly preliminary, the results are promising from the leave one out cross validation (LOOCV) method. The function was identified using the LOOCV method to examine the generalizability of the model. LOOCV uses one observation from the N = 30–32 as the validation data in order to use it as testing data for the validation model, while the rest of the data is used as training data. This process is then repeated for each observation in the dataset so that each sample is used once as the validation data. This, in turn, creates the function prediction from the regression variables. By using the significant variables from the 3CVT, APVT, and SIR regressions on SDLP, this analysis resulted in models that were 63.1, 87.0, and 76.8% accurate, respectively. For the 3CVT and SIR, only the first four variables from the regression were used because it was found that adding more variables actually reduced accuracy of the model. However, for the APVT, 13 variables were needed to obtain the aforementioned level of accuracy. Using variables identified in the Lane departure regressions, we also found promising predictive results of impairment. Again, the VPVT could not predict impairment due to an insignificant regression model. However, the 3CVT, APVT, and SIR offered promising predictive models that were 72.7, 73.4, and 77.0% accurate, respectively, with 9, 17, and 6 variables.

Machine Learning Approach – Boosting

Recognizing that the series of regressions that provided the variables to be used within the DFA has the propensity of introducing a biased estimate of the population variance accounted for, it is likely that the aforementioned models could overfit the predictor variables due to the small sample size. To account for this, an adaptive boosting approach, AdaBoost ($n = 20$ boosting rounds) was also applied to the dataset in a leave-one-out cross-validation manner. This approach aims to identify the strong boosted classifier that predicts impairment

TABLE 5 | LnDP regression models.

	Lane departures (LnDPs)		
	Metric	**F**	**Adj. R^2**
3CVT	Parietal hemispheric difference, Gamma (25–40 Hz)	6.81*	0.2
	HRV, quartile 3	4.46*	0.11
	F4 Delta (1–3 Hz)	4.24*	0.1
	F4 Slow Theta (3–5 Hz)	13.52**	0.21
	Standard deviation of reaction times to Targets, quartile 3	5.72*	0.07
	Frontal hemispheric difference, Fast Theta (5–7 Hz)	10.31**	0.08
	Midline (Fz, Cz, POz) Delta (1–3 Hz)	10.21**	0.05
	P3 Fast ThetaF (5–7 Hz)	6.17*	0.03
	Reaction time to non-targets, quartile 4	3.31	0.01
	Reaction time to non-targets, quartile 2	7.52*	0.02
	Parietal hemispheric difference, Alpha (8–13 Hz)	10.1**	0.02
	Frontal (Fz, F3, F4) Fast Theta (5–7 Hz)	7.87*	0.01
	Reaction time to interference stimuli, quartile 3	7.73*	0.01
APVT	Lapses, 6 s or longer	7.53**	0.19
	F3 Gamma (25–40 Hz)	7.54**	0.16
	Central hemispheric differences, Sigma (12–15 Hz)	7.45*	0.13
	Frontal hemispheric difference, Fast Alpha (10–13 Hz)	2.51	0.04
	F3 Delta (1–3 Hz)	4.38*	0.06
	Cz Fast Theta (5–7 Hz)	2.9	0.03
	C4 Delta (1–3 Hz)	3.18	0.03
	Central hemispheric differences, Alpha (8–13 Hz)	5.91*	0.05
	Central hemispheric differences, Beta (13–30 Hz)	5.1*	0.04
	P3 Gamma (25–40 Hz)	3.1	0.02
	Parietal hemispheric difference, Sigma (12–15 Hz)	2.25	0.01
	Parietal (Pz, P3, P4) Fast Alpha (10–13 Hz)	3.15	0.02
	C4 Gamma (25–40 Hz)	2.63	0.01
	HRV	5.18*	0.02
SIR	Frontal hemispheric difference, Slow Alpha (8–10 Hz)	6.95*	0.18
	Incorrect target rate	6.66*	0.15
	Overall hemispheric differences, Beta (13–30 Hz)	5.69*	0.11
	POz Gamma (25–40 Hz)	6.41*	0.1
	Overall hemispheric differences, Sigma (12–15 Hz)	6.7*	0.09

*$p < 0.05$; **$p < 0.01$; Adj. R^2 = adjusted R^2 value of the model when the variable was entered into the model.

risk (drug-impaired/unimpaired). Because the VPVT did not have statistically significant variables from the regressions, this task was not incorporated into the boosting analysis. However, the leave-one-out cross-validation of the remaining three tasks' metrics were able to classify "impaired" vs. "unimpaired" based on lane maintenance. Respectively, the 3CVT, APVT, and SIR were found to have 58.06, 80.56, and 71.43% accuracy in distinguishing such classifications.

DISCUSSION

Driving under the influence of drugs, especially benzodiazepines, is not only hazardous for the driver, but everyone on the road (Walsh et al., 2004; NHTSA, 2010; Dassanayake et al., 2011;

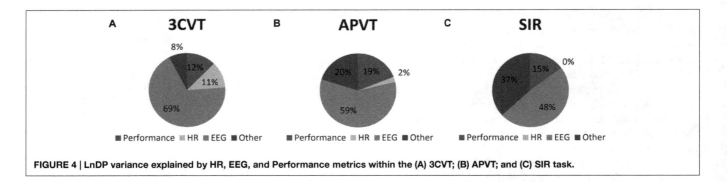

FIGURE 4 | LnDP variance explained by HR, EEG, and Performance metrics within the (A) 3CVT; (B) APVT; and (C) SIR task.

Li et al., 2013; Brady and Li, 2014). DREs are least likely to accurately recognize driving impairments due to nonalcoholic, CNS depressants (including benzodiazepines), as compared to impairment associated with other classes of drugs (Smith et al., 2002). Validation of the existing criteria for determining impaired driving, as well as the addition of new criteria, are needed to assist DREs in conducting such assessments. Studies have shown promise for utilizing cognitive, behavioral, and neurophysiological signatures associated with benzodiazepine use and impairment to aid in such investigations (Hendler et al., 1980; O'Hanlon et al., 1982; Fernández-Guardiola et al., 1984; Buchsbaum et al., 1985; Smiley and Moskowitz, 1986; Linnoila et al., 1990; Bond et al., 1992; Van Laar et al., 1992; Kuitunen, 1994; Kožena et al., 1995; Suzuki et al., 1995; Münte et al., 1996; Rush and Griffiths, 1997; Bocca et al., 1999; Vanakoski et al., 2000; Riba et al., 2001; Van Laar et al., 2001; Verster et al., 2002; Barker et al., 2004; Eoh et al., 2005; Snyder et al., 2005; Staner et al., 2005; Leufkens et al., 2007). Research has even shown laboratory tasks to be directly related to SDLP, a widely used measure of driving performance (Verster et al., 2002). However, these tasks alone cannot predict much of the variability in driving performance (Verster and Roth, 2012). It is possible that the addition of neurophysiology can help explain more of this variance. Therefore, the current study sought to determine whether all three classes of correlates could be leveraged as a new approach for validating and suggesting improvements to the current DRE evaluations.

The current findings, in agreement with previous work, indicate that SDLP and LnDP are good indicators of impairment and that the observation of poor lane position maintenance provides justification for conducting a DRE evaluation (O'Hanlon et al., 1982; NHTSA, 1997; Bocca et al., 1999; Van Laar et al., 2001; Verster et al., 2002; Leufkens et al., 2007). Our analyses were able to pinpoint specific driving conditions that make lane position maintenance especially difficult for those under the influence of benzodiazepines. These conditions include open stretches of the interstate or highway, as well as rural roadways. Thus, lane position difficulties under these driving conditions may serve as particularly useful criteria for officers to detect driving impairments associated with benzodiazepines.

Though the results presented herein are in agreeance with past literature, as previously mentioned, this dynamic environment did introduce the likelihood for higher SDLP values. This

is important to note because three of the five statistically significant segments revealed from the ANOVAs were designed to introduce more challenging maneuvers than observed in previously published work. This is particularly true for the interstate highway event. Although straight, this segment of the driving course contains slower moving traffic, which causes the drivers to circumnavigate the slower traffic by performing two lane changes. These lane changes produce higher levels of SDLP relative to the other events within the simulator. Similarly, the rural events that yielded significant differences in the ANOVA's also have elevated SDLP values. This is experienced in the Rural-Transition to Dark segment due to the curvy nature of the roadway and the short duration of time from dusk to dark while on this roadway. The Rural-Straight portion of the drive also introduces variances in SDLP values that are unlike those of past studies. Even though this segment is straight, SDLP is elevated due to the changes in participant's alertness/wakefulness as this is one of the last segments of the drive. Prior work has yielded similar results; Brown et al. (2014) used this same scenario and showed that even during daytime drives, sleepiness increased, as measured by the Stanford Sleepiness Scale, over the course of the drive and SDLP was elevated relative to earlier in the drive. These three events have been specifically included in this evaluation due to the fact that they represent more challenging environments. Therefore, they are more likely to highlight, and be sensitive to, drug effects despite not conforming to the typical environments in which they have been historically reported. On the other hand, the other two statistically significant segments revealed within the SDLP ANOVAs have values similar to previously suggested guidelines (Brookhuis et al., 2003). While the urban general section does contain a portion where the roadway is slightly curved, the urban green light segment is similar to more commonly used driving simulator environments and may best serve as a direct comparison to past literature. The fact that the urban green light segment is both environmentally similar to past literature and yields similar SDLP values suggests that the performance of participants in both conditions are comparable to that of those reported in previous studies.

The current study expanded on the findings that benzodiazepines impair lane maintenance behaviors by exploring the use of a neurocognitive assessment for explaining the lane maintenance errors of drivers under the influence of benzodiazepines. ANOVA results revealed behavioral findings consistent with this field of literature, such as increased reaction times during the 3CVT (Fernández-Guardiola et al., 1984; Suzuki et al., 1995; Münte et al., 1996; Verster et al., 2002; Barker et al., 2004; Snyder et al., 2005; Leufkens et al., 2007) and impaired vigilance on the APVT and VPVT as indicated by the missed responses and lapses (Kožena et al., 1995). However, we did not find any indications of memory impairment during the SIR. The EEG ANOVA results indicated a reduction in parietal Gamma (25–40 Hz), an elevation in Midline Alpha (8–10 Hz) during the 3CVT, and Central Theta elevation during the APVT. The central elevation in theta is consistent with findings that increases in both Delta (1–3 Hz) and Theta (3–7 Hz) are positively correlated with fatigue while driving and that benzodiazepines are associated with increased fatigue (Lal and Craig, 2002; Campagne et al., 2004). In contrast, the elevated Midline Alpha is inconsistent with most studies that find benzodiazepines decrease Alpha (8–13 Hz) in the frontal, temporal, and occipital regions (Buchsbaum et al., 1985; Bond et al., 1992; Staner et al., 2005). However, suppression of Alpha can also be an adaptive response to increasing simulation difficulty, indicating that a failure to suppress Alpha may be a sign of failure to adapt by those under the influence of a benzodiazepine (Eoh et al., 2005).

The regression and discriminate function analyses are more consistent with prior work indicating that Beta (Hendler et al., 1980; Buchsbaum et al., 1985; Bond et al., 1992; Staner et al., 2005), Frontal Delta (Buchsbaum et al., 1985; Staner et al., 2005), and Alpha over multiple regions (Buchsbaum et al., 1985; Bond et al., 1992; Staner et al., 2005) are associated with benzodiazepine use. These findings also support the combination of neurophysiology and performance in objectively assessing and predicting impairment due to benzodiazepines, as past studies failed to explain variability in SDLP using performance metrics alone (Verster and Roth, 2012). To this end, the current data indicate that combining performance metrics with neurophysiology can explain up to 79.9% of the variance in SDLP using APVT metrics alone. However, the combination of metrics within the regression analyses indicated that HR measures were only significant in explaining SDLP impairment within the 3CVT, and not in any of the other tasks. Herein, results were in agreeance with past literature, as HR during this task did increase as a result of the benzodiazepine (Muzet et al., 1981; DiMicco, 1987; Ueda et al., 2013) and was a significant predictor of SDLP. This approach yielded promising results for lane departures as well. In comparison to the SDLP results, we were able to explain more of the variance in lane departures with 3CVT metrics, explaining 92% of the variance in this measure. Similar to the results seen for SDLP, HRV was shown to have a significant explanatory power within the 3CVT task for assessment of lane departures. HRV measures showed significant explanatory power within the APVT task as well, which supports the results from previous studies showing that benzodiazepines decrease HRV (Adinoff et al., 1992; Agelink et al., 2002), decreases in HRV are related to increases in drowsiness related driving errors (Michail et al., 2008), and that decreased HRV is associated with cognitive and behavioral impairments (Hansen et al., 2003). The discriminate function classification and boosting results were even more promising, respectively, showing up to 87 and 80% accuracy in identifying impairment likelihood based on neurophysiology and

performance within cognitive tasks. While preliminary, and in need of replication in larger confirmatory studies, these results indicate the promise of this approach as a way for researchers to gain further insight into the correlates of drug impaired driving and consequently aid in the optimization of assessments of benzodiazepine impaired driving.

While promising, this study does have limitations that should be taken into account when interpreting our results. The simulated environment utilized herein contains more diverse driving scenarios than that of previous studies in order to more closely resemble real-world driving. While results from this design may have greater external validity, they do not easily lend to comparisons with past findings. Future studies utilizing the current approach could employ both types of driving environments in order to enable such comparisons. In regards to demographics, the majority of participants were young males, just as most drugged drivers are also young males (Lacey et al., 2009). This approach requires validation across genders and age groups to determine whether the models will generalize across a larger population. Additionally, we utilized a within subject design (to reduce individual differences across conditions), but with the small sample size, this may lead to an even greater likelihood of overfitting the regression and discriminant function analyses. Future research is needed to verify whether these findings can be replicated with a larger sample size. Replication and expansion of our design is also necessary in terms of dosing levels. Since participants were only dosed with 1 mg of alprazolam in the current study, our findings may only represent deficits associated with moderate to low doses of this benzodiazepine. A dose-response study should be conducted to verify whether these same correlates can predict, and classify, driving impairment due to a range of dosing levels and to reveal whether other correlates may better explain variances in performance due to a wide range of doses. Other benzodiazepines, as well as an array of CNS depressants outside of the benzodiazepine class, should also be examined to determine if the effects found within this study are limited to alprazolam, or are true for all benzodiazepines and CNS depressants. Furthermore, conditions that are known to interact with CNS depressant use, such as sleep deprivation and alcohol use, should be examined to see how their interactions affect driving impairment. Future studies should expand on these findings to include broader demographic diversity, greater sample size, dose response, administration of different benzodiazepines, and the use of other types of CNS depressants. Taking these suggested limitations and improvements into consideration, future studies should target a means of taking the research beyond the scope of a simulated environment in order to better provide the much needed support for law enforcement in ensuring public health and safety for all drivers.

FUNDING

The work presented herein was supported by the Department of Health and Human Services, National Institute for Drug Abuse (NIDA) (contract number: HHSN271201200019C).

REFERENCES

Adinoff, B., Mefford, I., Waxman, R., and Linnoila, M. (1992). Vagal tone decreases following intravenous diazepam. *Psychiatry Res.* 41, 89–97. doi: 10.1016/0165-1781(92)90101-8

Agelink, M. W., Majewski, T. B., Andrich, J., and Mueck-Weymann, M. (2002). Short-term effects of intravenous benzodiazepines on autonomic neurocardiac regulation in humans: a comparison between midazolam, diazepam, and lorazepam. *Crit. Care Med.* 30, 997–1006. doi: 10.1097/00003246-200205000-00008

Baker, S. N. (2007). Oscillatory interactions between sensorimotor cortex and the periphery. *Curr. Opin. Neurobiol.* 17, 649–655. doi: 10.1016/j.conb.2008.01.007

Barker, M. J., Greenwood, K. M., Jackson, M., and Crowe, S. F. (2004). Cognitive effects of long-term benzodiazepine use. *CNS Drugs* 18, 37–48. doi: 10.2165/00023210-200418010-00004

Bédard, M., Parkkari, M., Weaver, B., Riendeau, J., and Dahlquist, M. (2010). Assessment of driving performance using a simulator protocol: validity and reproducibility. *Am. J. Occup. Ther.* 64, 336–340. doi: 10.5014/ajot.64.2.336

Bocca, M., Le Doze, F., Etard, O., Pottier, M., L'Hoste, J., and Denise, P. (1999). Residual effects of zolpidem 10 mg and zopiclone 7.5 mg versus flunitrazepam 1 mg and placebo on driving performance and ocular saccades. *Psychopharmacology* 143, 373–379. doi: 10.1007/s002130050961

Bond, A., Silveira, J., and Lader, M. (1992). The effects of alprazolam alone and combined with alcohol on central integrative activity. *Eur. J. Clin. Pharmacol.* 42, 495–498. doi: 10.1007/BF00314857

Brady, J. E., and Li, G. (2014). Trends in alcohol and other drugs detected in fatally injured drivers in the united states, 1999–2010. *Am. J. Epidemiol.* 179, 692–699. doi: 10.1093/aje/kwt327

Brookhuis, K. A., Waard, D. D., and Fairclough, S. H. (2003). Criteria for driver impairment. *Ergonomics* 46, 433–445. doi: 10.1080/001401302/1000039556

Brown, T., Lee, J., Schwarz, C., Fiorentino, D., and McDonald, A. (2014). *Assessing the Feasibility of Vehiclebased Sensors to Detect Drowsy Driving.* Final Report No. DOT HS 811 886. Washington, DC: NHTSA.

Buchsbaum, M. S., Hazlett, E., Sicotte, N., Stein, M., Wu, J., and Zetin, M. (1985). Topographic EEG changes with benzodiazepine administration in generalized anxiety disorder. *Biol. Psychiatry* 20, 832–842. doi: 10.1016/0006-3223(85)90208-2

Camm, A., Malik, M., Bigger, J., Breithardt, G., Cerutti, S., Cohen, R., et al. (1996). Heart rate variability: standards of measurement, physiological interpretation and clinical use. Task force of the european society of cardiology and the north american society of pacing and electrophysiology. *Circulation* 93, 1043–1065. doi: 10.1161/01.CIR.93.5.1043

Campagne, A., Pebayle, T., and Muzet, A. (2004). Correlation between driving errors and vigilance level: influence of the driver's age. *Physiol. Behav.* 80, 515–524. doi: 10.1016/j.physbeh.2003.10.004

Dassanayake, T., Michie, P., Carter, G., and Jones, A. (2011). Effects of benzodiazepines, antidepressants and opioids on driving. *Drug Safe.* 34, 125–156. doi: 10.2165/11539050-000000000-00000

De Winter, J. C. F., De Groot, S., Mulder, M., Wieringa, P. A., Dankelman, J., and Mulder, J. A. (2009). Relationships between driving simulator performance and driving test results. *Ergonomics* 52, 137–153. doi: 10.1080/00140130802277521

DiMicco, J. A. (1987). Evidence for control of cardiac vagal tone by benzodiazepine receptors. *Neuropharmacology* 26, 553–559. doi: 10.1016/0028-3908(87)90147-X

Drummer, O. H., Gerostamoulos, J., Batziris, H., Chu, M., Caplehorn, J. R., Robertson, M. D., et al. (2003). The incidence of drugs in drivers killed in Australian road traffic crashes. *Forensic Sci. Int.* 134, 154–162. doi: 10.1016/S0379-0738(03)00134-8

Eoh, H. J., Chung, M. K., and Kim, S.-H. (2005). Electroencephalographic study of drowsiness in simulated driving with sleep deprivation. *Int. J. Ind. Ergon.* 35, 307–320. doi: 10.1109/EMBC.2014.6945054

Fairclough, S. H., Venables, L., and Tattersall, A. (2005). The influence of task demand and learning on the psychophysiological response. *Int. J. Psychophysiol.* 56, 171–184. doi: 10.1016/j.ijpsycho.2004.11.003

Fernández-Guardiola, A., Jurado, J. L., and Aguilar-Jimenez, E. (1984). Evaluation of the attention and sleepiness states by means of a psychophysiological test of reaction time and time estimate in man: effects of psychotropic drugs. *Curr. Ther. Res.* 35, 1000–1009.

Freund, Y., and Schapire, R. E. (1997). A decision-theoretic generalization of on-line learning and an application to boosting. *J. Comput. Syst. Sci.* 55, 119–137. doi: 10.1006/jcss.1997.1504

Goldberger, J. J., Challapalli, S., Tung, R., Parker, M. A., and Kadish, A. H. (2001). Relationship of heart rate variability to parasympathetic effect. *Circulation* 103, 1977–1983. doi: 10.1161/01.CIR.103.15.1977

Hansen, A. L., Johnsen, B. H., and Thayer, J. F. (2003). Vagal influence on working memory and attention. *Int. J. Psychophysiol.* 48, 263–274. doi: 10.1016/S0167-8760(03)00073-4

Harmony, T., Fernández, T., Silva, J., Bernal, J., Díaz-Comas, L., Reyes, A., et al. (1996). EEG Delta activity: an indicator of attention to internal processing during performance of mental tasks. *Int. J. Psychophysiol.* 24, 161–171. doi: 10.1016/S0167-8760(96)00053-0

Hendler, B. N., Cimini, C., Ma, T., and Donlin Long, M. D. (1980). A comparison of cognitive impairment due to benzodiazepines and to narcotics. *Am. J. Psychiatry* 137, 828–830. doi: 10.1176/ajp.137.7.828

Johnson, L. C., Spinweber, C., Gomez, S., and Matteson, L. (1990). Daytime sleepiness, performance, mood, nocturnal sleep: the effect of benzodiazepine and caffeine on their relationship. *Sleep* 13, 121–135.

Kennedy, R. S., Lane, N. E., Berbaum, K. S., and Lilienthal, M. G. (1993). Simulator sickness questionnaire: an enhanced method for quantifying simulator sickness. *Int. J. Aviat. Psychol.* 3, 203–220. doi: 10.1207/s15327108ijap0303_3

Klimesch, W. (1999). EEG Alpha and theta oscillations reflect cognitive and memory performance: a review and analysis. *Brain Res. Rev.* 29, 169–195. doi: 10.1016/S0165-0173(98)00056-3

Koẑena, L., Frantik, E., and Horvath, M. (1995). Vigilance impairment after a single dose of benzodiazepines. *Psychopharmacology* 119, 39–45. doi: 10.1007/BF02246052

Kuitunen, T. (1994). Drug and ethanol effects on the clinical test for drunkenness: single doses of ethanol, hypnotic drugs and antidepressant drugs. *Pharmacol. Toxicol.* 75, 91–98. doi: 10.1111/j.1600-0773.1994.tb00329.x

Lacey, J. H., Kelley-Baker, T., Furr-Holden, D., Voas, R. B., Romano, E., Ramirez, A., et al. (2009). *2007 National Roadside Survey of Alcohol and Drug use by Drivers: Drug Results National Highway Traffic Safety Administration (NHTSA, Trans.)*. Report No. HS-811 249. Washington, DC.

Lal, S. K., and Craig, A. (2002). Driver fatigue: electroencephalography and psychological assessment. *Psychophysiology* 39, 313–321. doi: 10.1017/S0048577201393095

Lee, H. C. (2003). The validity of driving simulator to measure on-road driving performance of older drivers. *Trans. Eng. Aust.* 8:89. doi: 10.3389/fnhum.2014.00772

Lee, J., Fiorentino, D., Reyes, M., Brown, T., Ahmad, O., Fell, J., et al. (2010). *Assessing the Feasibility of Vehicle-Based Sensors to Detect Alcohol Impairment (No. DOT HS 811 358)*. Washington, DC: National Highway Traffic Safety Administration.

Leufkens, T. R., Vermeeren, A., Smink, B. E., Van Ruitenbeek, P., and Ramaekers, J. G. (2007). Cognitive, psychomotor and actual driving performance in healthy volunteers after immediate and extended release formulations of alprazolam 1 mg. *Psychopharmacology* 191, 951–959. doi: 10.1007/s00213-006-0669-8

Lew, H. L., Poole, J. H., Lee, E. H., Jaffe, D. L., Huang, H. C., and Brodd, E. (2005). Predictive validity of driving-simulator assessments following traumatic brain injury: a preliminary study. *Brain Inj.* 19, 177–188. doi: 10.1080/02699050400017171

Li, G., Bradya, J. E., and Chen, Q. (2013). Drug use and fatal motor vehicle crashes: a case-control study. *Accident Anal. Prevent.* 60, 205–210. doi: 10.1016/j.aap.2013.09.001

Linnoila, M., Stapleton, J. M., Lister, R., Moss, H., Lane, E., Granger, A., et al. (1990). Effects of single doses of alprazolam and diazepam, alone and in combination with ethanol, on psychomotor and cognitive performance and on autonomic nervous system reactivity in healthy volunteers. *Eur. J. Clin. Pharmacol.* 39, 21–28. doi: 10.1007/BF02657051

Michail, E., Kokonozi, A., Chouvarda, I., and Maglaveras, N. (2008). "EEG and HRV markers of sleepiness and loss of control during car driving," in *Proceedings of the EMBS 2008. 30th Annual International Conference of the IEEE, Engineering in Medicine and Biology Society*, New Jersey, NJ: IEEE, 2566–2569.

Münte, T. F., Gehde, E., Johannes, S., Seewald, M., and Heinze, H. J. (1996). Effects of alprazolam and bromazepam on visual search and verbal recognition memory in humans: a study with event-related brain potentials. *Neuropsychobiology* 34, 49–56. doi: 10.1159/000119291

Murata, A., and Hiramatsu, Y. (2008). "Evaluation of drowsiness by HRV measures-basic study for drowsy driver detection," in *Proceedings of 4th International Workshop on Computational Intelligence & Applications* (Hiroshima: Hiroshima University), 99–102.

Muzet, A., Johnson, L. C., and Spinweber, C. L. (1981). Benzodiazepine hypnotics increase heart rate during sleep. *Sleep* 5, 256–261.

NHTSA (1997). *The Visual Detection of DWI Motorists. National Highway Traffic Safety Administration, US Department of Transportation*, Report No. DOT HS 808 677, Washington DC.

NHTSA (2009). *2007 National Roadside Survey Methodology* (Trans. DOT/NHTSA). Washington, DC: NHTSA.

NHTSA (2010). *Drug Involvement of Fatally Injured Drivers* (Trans. DOT/NHTSA). Washington, DC: NHTSA.

NHTSA (2013). *2012 Motor Vehicle Crashes: Overview* (Trans. DOT/NHTSA). Washington, DC: NHTSA.

O'Hanlon, J. F., Haak, T. W., Blaauw, G. J., and Riemersma, J. B. (1982). Diazepam impairs lateral position control in highway driving. *Science* 217, 79–81. doi: 10.1126/science.7089544

Rapoport, M. J., Lanctôt, K. L., Streiner, D. L., Bedard, M., Vingilis, E., Murray, B., et al. (2009). Benzodiazepine use and driving: a meta-analysis. *J. Clin. Psychiatry* 70, 663–673. doi: 10.4088/JCP.08m04325

Riba, J., Rodríguez-Fornells, A., Urbano, G., Morte, A., Antonijoan, R., and Barbanoj, M. J. (2001). Differential effects of alprazolam on the baseline and fear-potentiated startle reflex in humans: a dose-response study. *Psychopharmacology* 157, 358–367. doi: 10.1007/s002130100816

Rush, C. R., and Griffiths, R. R. (1997). Acute participant-rated and behavioral effects of alprazolam and buspirone, alone and in combination with ethanol, in normal volunteers. *Exp. Clin. Psychopharmacol.* 5, 28–38. doi: 10.1037/1064-1297.5.1.28

SAMHSA. (2014). Results from the 2013 National Survey on Drug Use and Health: Summary of National Findings (HHS, Trans.) NSDUH Series H-48. Rockville, MD.

Smiley, A., and Moskowitz, H. (1986). Effects of long-term administration of buspirone and diazepam on driver steering control. *Am. J. Med.* 80, 22–29. doi: 10.1016/0002-9343(86)90328-1

Smith, J. A., Hayes, C. E., Yolton, R. L., Rutledge, D. A., and Citek, K. (2002). Drug recognition expert evaluations made using limited data. *Forensic Sci. Int.* 130, 167–173. doi: 10.1016/S0379-0738(02)00384-5

Snyder, P. J., Werth, J., Giordani, B., Caveney, A. F., Feltner, D., and Maruff, P. (2005). A method for determining the magnitude of change across different cognitive functions in clinical trials: the effects of acute administration of two different doses alprazolam. *Hum. Psychopharmacol. Clin. Exp.* 20, 263–273. doi: 10.1002/hup.692

Staner, L., Ertlé, S., Boeijinga, P., Rinaudo, G., Arnal, M. A., Muzet, A., et al. (2005). Next-day residual effects of hypnotics in DSM-IV primary insomnia: a driving simulator study with simultaneous electroencephalogram monitoring. *Psychopharmacology* 181, 790–798. doi: 10.1007/s00213-005-0082-8

Suzuki, M., Uchiumi, M., and Murasaki, M. (1995). A comparative study of the psychological effects of DN-2327, a partial benzodiazepine agonist, and alprazolam. *Psychopharmacology* 121, 442–450. doi: 10.1007/BF02246492

Sztajzel, J. (2004). Heart rate variability: a noninvasive electrocardiographic method to measure the autonomic nervous system. *Swiss Med. Wkly* 134, 514–522.

Talpins, S. K., and Hayes, C. (2004). *Drug Evaluation and Classification (DEC) Program: Targeting Hardcore Impaired Drivers*. Alexandria, VA: American Prosecutors Research Institute.

Ueda, K., Ogawa, Y., Aoki, K., Hirose, N., Gokan, D., Kato, J., et al. (2013). Antagonistic effect of flumazenil after midazolam sedation on arterial-cardiac baroreflex. *Acta Anaesthesiol. Scand.* 57, 488–494. doi: 10.1111/aas.1 2035

Van Laar, M., Volkerts, E., and Verbaten, M. (2001). Subchronic effects of the GABA-agonist lorazepam and the 5-HT2A/2C antagonist ritanserin on driving performance, slow wave sleep and daytime sleepiness in healthy volunteers. *Psychopharmacology* 154, 189–197. doi: 10.1007/s002130000633

Van Laar, M. W., Volkerts, E. R., and Van Willigenburg, A. P. P. (1992). Therapeutic effects and effects on actual driving performance of chronically administered buspirone and diazepam in anxious outpatients. *J. Clin. Psychopharmacol.* 12, 86–95.

Vanakoski, J., Mattila, M. J., and Seppälä, T. (2000). Driving under light and dark conditions: effects of alcohol and diazepam in young and older subjects. *Eur. J. Clin. Pharmacol.* 56, 453–458. doi: 10.1007/s002280000167

Verster, J. C., and Roth, T. (2012). Predicting psychopharmacological drug effects on actual driving performance (SDLP) from psychometric tests measuring driving-related skills. *Psychopharmacology* 220, 293–301. doi: 10.1007/s00213-011-2484-0

Verster, J. C., and Roth, T. (2013). Blood drug concentrations of benzodiazepines correlate poorly with actual driving impairment. *Sleep Med. Rev.* 17, 153–159. doi: 10.1016/j.smrv.2012.05.004

Verster, J. C., Volkerts, E. R., and Verbaten, M. N. (2002). Effects of alprazolam on driving ability, memory functioning and psychomotor performance: a randomized, placebo-controlled study. *Neuropsychopharmacology* 27, 260–269. doi: 10.1016/S0893-133X(02)00310-X

Viola, P., and Jones, M. (2001). Rapid object detection using a boosted cascade of simple features. *Comput. Vis. Pattern Recogn.* 1, 511–518.

Walsh, J. M., Flegel, R., Cangianelli, L. A., Atkins, R., Soderstrom, C. A., and Kerns, T. J. (2004). Epidemiology of alcohol and other drug use among motor vehicle crash victims admitted to a trauma center. *Traffic Inj. Prev.* 5, 254–260. doi: 10.1080/15389580490465319

Conflict of Interest Statement: Authors Robin R. Johnson and Chris Berka are share holders in Advanced Brain Monitoring, which may benefit financially from the publication of these data. The other authors declare that the research was conducted in the absence of any commercial or financial relationships that could be construed as a potential conflict of interest.

Angels and Demons: Using Behavioral Types in a Real-Effort Moral Dilemma to Identify Expert Traits

Hernán D. Bejarano [1,2]*, Ellen P. Green [3] and Stephen J. Rassenti [2]

[1] Department of Economics, Center of Economic Research and Teaching, Aguascalientes, Mexico, [2] Economic Science Institute, Chapman University, Orange, CA, USA, [3] School for the Science of Health Care Delivery, Arizona State University, Phoenix, AZ, USA

In this article, we explore how independently reported measures of subjects' cognitive capabilities, preferences, and sociodemographic characteristics relate to their behavior in a real-effort moral dilemma experiment. To do this, we use a unique dataset, the Chapman Preferences and Characteristics Instrument Set (CPCIS), which contains over 30 standardized measures of preferences and characteristics. We find that simple correlation analysis provides an incomplete picture of how individual measures relate to behavior. In contrast, clustering subjects into groups based on observed behavior in the real-effort task reveals important systematic differences in individual characteristics across groups. However, while we find more differences, these differences are not systematic and difficult to interpret. These results indicate a need for more comprehensive theory explaining how combinations of different individual characteristics impact behavior is needed.

Keywords: cognitive capabilities, personality, preferences, real effort, abstract effort, moral dilemma, experiment, survey

Edited by:
Nikolaos Georgantzis,
University of Reading, UK

Reviewed by:
Brice Corgnet,
Chapman University, USA
Jana Peliova,
University of Economics in Bratislava,
Slovakia

*Correspondence:
Hernán D. Bejarano
bejarano@chapman.edu

Specialty section:
This article was submitted to
Personality and Social Psychology,
a section of the journal
Frontiers in Psychology

INTRODUCTION

Mainstream economic theory routinely assumes that individuals have stable, consistent preferences that at least partly determine their behavior and revealed preferences (Samuelson, 1948; Stigler and Becker, 1977). Behavioral and experimental economists have explored the validity of that assumption, and phenomena like preference reversals, endowment effects, framing, and the Ellsberg paradox imply that individuals lack stable, consistent preferences.

Most lab experiments attempt to induce consistent preferences using conditional rewards based on Smith's (1976) Induced Value Theory. In these experiments, failure to observe the behavior implied by the induced preferences leads researchers to question the narrow self-interest hypothesis and search for alternative theories. This process has contributed to a deeper understanding of preferences by examining how experimental designs and subject characteristics affect behavior (Frank and Glass, 1991; Becker, 2013). For example, experimental results imply that subjects are partially motivated by fairness (Rabin, 1993), equality (Bolton and Ockenfels, 2006), ambiguity aversion (Fox and Tversky, 1995), and identity (Akerlof and Kranton, 2000).

We argue that even with substantial improvements over the past decades in our understanding of how individual characteristics correlate with individual actions, several key questions remain: Are there systematic differences among individuals? For example, do variations in individual characteristics matter? If so, which characteristics influence behavior? Do actions reveal more than psychological indicators of behavioral types? Furthermore, little is known about how the answer to these questions depends on the elicitation method.

There are two prevalent approaches used to try to answer these questions: (1) surveying with primary experiments; and (2) adding secondary experimental tasks. In the first approach, researchers use questionnaires either before or after the primary experimental task. For example, several authors have explored how psychological characteristics influence economic behavior using this method—e.g., personality traits (Almlund et al., 2011; Ferguson et al., 2011); emotions (Pixley, 2002); and sentiments (Smith and Wilson, 2013). Corgnet et al. (2015) found that reflective individuals, as measured by the Cognitive Reflection Test (CRT), exhibited more consistently mildly altruistic actions in a lab experiment. Frederick (2005) and Burks et al. (2009) found that cognitive capabilities related to time and risk preferences. Other researchers investigated the interaction between personality traits and risk and time preferences (Rustichini et al., 2012). Researchers have also linked experimental behavior to the results of testing such for IQ (Oechssler et al., 2009; Brañas-Garza et al., 2012, 2015), social intelligence (Takagishi et al., 2010), and personality (Almlund et al., 2011; Rustichini et al., 2012). However, the findings are not consistent with one another (Ben-Ner et al., 2007; Eckel and Grossman, 2008; Borghans et al., 2009; Hirsh and Peterson, 2009; Oechssler et al., 2009; DeAngelo et al., 2015).

The alternative approach is to add secondary experiments that are designed to measure preferences or characteristics. Researchers use these measures to determine the relationship between a subject's actions in the primary experiment and their individual preferences or characteristics. Examples of this practice are the use of the Dictator Game, the Trust Game and Risk and Time Preference experiments as complements to primary experiments. Unfortunately, correlations between behavior in the primary and secondary experiments have not been consistent. For example, while characteristics such as risk preferences have accompanied behavior in games such as repeated prisoner's dilemmas and beauty-contest games (Boone et al., 1999; Sabater-Grande and Georgantzis, 2002; Goeree et al., 2003; Brocklebank et al., 2011; Lönnqvist et al., 2011; Kagel and McGee, 2014), the same characteristics sometimes failed to correlate (Aycinena et al., 2014). Another approach has found that in prisoner dilemma games, there are interesting evolutionary explanations for the existence of different types (Congleton and Vanberg, 2001).

In this article, we alter these approaches to address the inconsistencies described above. First, we utilize individual-level subject data collected on different occasions. That is, our measures of individual characteristics and preferences were collected in different experimental sessions from our primary experiment. We argue that, while difficult, using data collected from different experimental sessions implies that subjects are less likely to be influenced by portfolio and wealth effects across tasks. Secondly, we leverage a large dataset with over 30 measures of individual characteristics and preferences, the Chapman Preferences and Characteristics Instrument Set (CPCIS). These

include measures of several types such as: personality traits, preferences, strategic behavior in simple games and the socio demographics of our experimental subjects. Furthermore, the CPCIS was not designed or implemented by us, so it reduces the potential presence of any experimental demand effect. More specifically, the CPCIS not only measures characteristics that we hypothesize to influence the behavior in our primary experimental task, but also a large set of variables which a priori should not influence actions in it.

Our primary experiment, based on Green (2014), presents experimental subjects with a novel real-effort experiment with a distinct moral dilemma. Subjects in this experiment representing experts are asked to provide proofreading services to another group of subjects (customers). The quality of the expert's edits affects the customer, positively if the edits are done properly and negatively if they are done incorrectly. However, the quality of edits has no impact on the expert's personal earnings. Therefore, the experts face a moral dilemma between maximizing personal earnings and providing benefits to their customer.

Behavior in moral dilemmas is hypothesized to be influenced not only by subjects' induced payoff function and preferences for monetary rewards, but also in other-regarding preferences, subject's cognitive capabilities, values and personality traits (Bowles, 1998; Fehr and Fischbacher, 2003). Therefore, we combine observed behavior from our primary experiment, a real-effort moral dilemma task, with the individuals' measures of the CPCIS to see how individual characteristics relate to an individual's actions.

Our results provide several new insights concerning experiments with a moral dilemma. Initially, we find that simple correlational analysis provides an incomplete explanation of how individual measures relate to behavior. Both measures of preferences and other individual characteristics fail to consistently correlate with actions in our main experimental task. For example, measures of individual preferences (i.e., risk aversion, loss aversion, and time preferences) are not correlated with observed actions in the primary experiment. In contrast, some measures of strategic preferences, intelligence, and personality are significantly correlated with behavior. However, in spite of the inconsistency in correlation across individual preferences and behavior, that fact that some measures do correlate is of note. When a subject's preferences are characterized by a combination of factors such as personality, cognitive capabilities, and intelligence, as in our primary experiment, predictions of behavior become uncertain. For instance, subjects with high measures of intelligence should produce higher outcomes for their customers, whereas those same individuals may have varying levels of altruism also influencing their behavior and, thereby, theoretical predictions.

This leads us to explore individuals by behavioral groups, also known as *clusters*. Clusters are identified using the action variables "total edits" and "total incorrect edits." Cluster analysis based on these two variables allows us to distinguish between subjects who edited a lot with a high percentage of incorrect edits (the Demons) and subjects who edited sparsely with a high percentage of incorrect edits, as well as those who edited few with a high percentage of correct edits (Angels).

Behavioral group members exhibited systematic differences in their individual characteristics. We found significant differences among behavioral groups that could not be detected using simple correlation analysis, suggesting that the effect of psychological, cognitive, and demographic differences on behavior in trials with our moral dilemma experiment is nonlinear. These results indicate a need for more comprehensive theory explaining how different individual characteristics work together.

EXPERIMENTAL DESIGN AND INDIVIDUAL DATA

Experimental Design

The primary experimental design was introduced by Green (2014). The experimental design and data analyzed here are from Bejarano et al. (2016). Green's original experiment was designed to explore behavior between an expert and customer where the expert is presented with a moral dilemma. Experts are asked to provide proofreading services for a panel of customers. The quality of the expert's proofreading services affects the customer's wellbeing (in the form of monetary payment); however, the customer's wellbeing has no impact on the expert's personal earnings. Therefore, the experts are faced with a tradeoff between maximizing personal earnings and providing benefits for their customer.

The interaction between the expert and the customer took place in two phases with one group of subjects playing the role of the customer (Phase I) and another group playing the role of the expert (Phase II). In Phase I, customers were given 50 min to proofread 10 essays. Each essay had 10 typographical or spelling errors (e.g., misuse of "their" for "there" or "write" for "right"). Customers were initially endowed with $25; however, for each error they were unable to find, they lost $0.25. Phase I was designed to create customer demand for the proofreading services provided in Phase II of the experiment.

In Phase II, experts were presented with a panel of 40 customer-edited essays collected in phase I. These essays contained a total of 125 errors. To create the expert subjects, errors were highlighted when presented to the "experts." In addition to the 125 errors that were highlighted, another 250 sections of text were highlighted to create a potential for over-editing.

There were three possible payment schemes for the expert: *fee-for-service*, *capitation*, or *salary*. Under *fee-for-service*, experts were paid $0.20 per individual field of text edited. Under *salary*, experts were paid a flat rate of $25 to participate in the experiment. Under *capitation*, experts were paid $0.625 for each essay in which they edited at least one highlighted section of the text. The expert's edits directly impacted the payoff of their customer. For each incorrect edit, the experts made to the text, customers lost $0.15 and for each correct edit, customers are reimbursed $0.05.

Each payment scheme presented a different moral dilemma; that is, strategies to maximize personal earnings or minimize effort varied across payment schemes. Under *fee-for-service*, experts faced a tradeoff between maximizing the number of edits

and the quality of each edit for their customers. Under *salary*, experts faced a tradeoff between leaving the experiments early (minimizing effort) and providing services for their customers.[1] Experts paid under *capitation* faced a tradeoff between the number of customers and the quality of edits for each customer.

In addition to varying the payment scheme, we also varied the expert's ability to select among the payment schemes. Our experiment included two treatments. Under the first, *self-selection*, experts could choose among the three payment schemes. Under the second, random assignment, experts were randomly assigned to one of the three payment systems: *fee-for-service, capitation,* or *salary*.

In Green (2014), subjects were randomly assigned to these payment schemes. Consistent with experts randomly assigned in the present analysis, experts in the *fee-for-service* treatment provided significantly more services than those in either the *capitation* or *salary* treatments. This difference was caused by a significant increase in the number of unnecessary edits to the essays provided by the experts, resulting in a much lower quality of service under the *fee-for-service* option compared to the *salary* or *capitation* payment schemes.

The Chapman Preferences and Characteristics Instrument Set (CPCIS)

Starting in September 2015, the ESI required all subjects to complete the CPCIS prior to participating in ESI experiments. This instrument set required about 90 min of a subject's time and was run independently of any other experiment, at a time convenient to the subject. The data collected by this instrument set consisted of standardized measures of preferences and individual characteristics gleaned from a series of classic simple experiments and questionnaires.

Measures are calculated for and sorted into five characteristic categories: individual preferences, strategic preferences, intelligence, personality tasks, and demographic characteristics. Individual preferences measured in the CPCIS include time preferences, loss aversion, and risk aversion. Strategic preferences include *trust* (adapted from Berg et al., 1995), *fairness* (adapted from Güth et al., 1982), and *altruism* (adapted from Kahneman et al., 1986).

Intelligence is measured using classic psychology measures from Raven, the CRT, and Wonderlic. Additionally, subjects are asked to complete a simple adding task, once with incentives for correctness and once with none. Social intelligence is measured using The Reading the Mind in The Eyes task. Finally, subjects provided self-reported measures of intelligence via their SAT and ACT scores, as well as their GPA. Personality was measured using the Big Five personality test. Demographic variables included age, gender, volunteer hours per week, work hours per week, number of siblings, number of older siblings, and finally, religiosity.

Although, the tests used are somewhat arbitrary and controversial, the results predict behavior in traditional experimental games and are consistent with several behavioral

---

[1] Subjects who completed their task before the time was up were asked to raise their hand and were then given a short survey to complete silently. Once finished with the survey, subjects quietly exited the room and were paid outside of the laboratory. We found no session effects.

and experimental-economics studies that attempt to elicit relevant preferences. The goal of the CPCIS is to provide a panel dataset that includes the personality indicators most used by experimental economists, with indicators used by psychologists, sociologists, anthropologists, and other social scientists.

In order to integrate several traditional tasks within the same instrument set, tasks within CPCIS such as Raven, The Reading the Mind in The Eyes task and Wonderlic (Test, 1992) were truncated. Specifically, the CPCIS contained the odd-numbered questions from the last three series of matrices within the Raven test (Jaeggi et al., 2010), one that has also been used by Corgnet et al. (2015). Our Big Five questionnaire is based on the 44 items described by John et al. (2008). Conversely, we used an extended version of the CRT (Frederick, 2005). While the original task from Frederick (2005) has three questions, our task has seven questions (Toplak et al., 2011).

In addition to traditional games that elicit several types of other-regarding preferences, the CPCIS includes an instrument that elicits social preferences a la Bartling et al. (2009), hereafter referred to as the *BFMS task*. This task has been used to study preferences of subjects who self-select into competitive tasks (Bartling et al., 2009), as well as the relationship between cognitive capabilities and other-regarding preferences (Corgnet et al., 2015). In our experiment, we combine features of these two applications. Selection into a payment scheme is not based on competitiveness but tradeoffs between the desire to reimburse others and to maximize personal earnings. Therefore, we argue that selection into the different treatments could be related to social preferences elicited by the BFMS. In the following paragraphs, we briefly describe the BFMS that the students in the CPCIS faced[2].

The BFMS instrument is a series of binary choices with different allocations for the decision maker and a randomly matched partner (**Table 1**). Each choice presents an egalitarian alternative and a non-egalitarian alternative. In our modified BFMS instrument, subjects have to make six choices. Of these six choices, three present subjects with a choice between an egalitarian alternative and another non-egalitarian division earnings, which is at least as good or favorable for herself but detrimental for the matched partner (choices BFMS1, BFMS2, and BFMS5). In contrast, two of the other three binary choices presented to the subject ask her to choose between the egalitarian alternative and a division that is as least as favorable for the matched partner but less than or equal for the decision maker (BFMS3, BFMS6). Finally, BFMS4 is welfare-improving or increases overall earnings but by a greater amount for the matched partner.

In the CPCIS, after all of the subjects made their decisions, two of the individuals were randomly selected to have their choices determine the earnings for this task. Models describing behavior observed in the BFMS task vary across publications. Fehr and Schmidt (1999) presented a two-parameter α, β model,

where α represents aversion to disadvantageous inequality, Behindness Aversion, and β aversion to advantageous inequality, Aheadness Aversion. Fehr and Schmidt (1999) assumed that $\alpha > \beta > 0$. In contrast, Corgnet et al. (2015) related these parameters to envy and compassion and did not impose any assumption on them. The authors summarized five motivations that could make subjects select one alternative over the other. These include self-interest, altruism, egalitarianism, spitefulness, and inequality-seeking. The authors also said that individuals could have a combination of these motives while choosing among alternatives. In order to organize BFMS choices in a way useful for our analysis, we further simplified the choices within three types of preferences. Decision makers who chose alternative A more often across all six choices demonstrated egalitarian preferences. Decision makers who chose to allocate larger earnings to their matched partner than to themselves (alternative A in BFMS3, BFMS4, and BFMS5) at no cost or a small cost to their own earnings, were considered altruistic or averse to being ahead of their partner. Finally, decision makers who were more likely to choose option A in BFMS1, BFMS2, and BFMS5 were considered Spiteful. These individuals could also be considered as having demonstrated aversion to being behind their partner.

Based on these notions, we constructed three variables based on the BFMS choices for each individual. Each individual could choose between zero and six egalitarian alternatives (Egalitarianism). Also, they could choose between zero and three beneficial alternatives (Selfishness) or detrimental alternatives (Altruism). These three variables elaborate on the theory of other-regarding preferences and improve our understanding of how a subject's choices under this instrument relate to their actions in our moral dilemma experiment.

We do not claim that the measures obtained by these truncated tasks mirror those obtained by the original tests, but for the purpose of our analysis, we determine the extent to which these measures are correlated with the experimental actions.

THEORETICAL RELATIONSHIP AMONG CPCIS VARIABLES

In this section, we analyze the theoretical implications of expert preferences and characteristics. Two experimental-design features are important for our analysis. First, an expert in the self-selection treatment likely reveals something about her personal preferences in her selection of payment systems. Experts who are randomly assigned to their payment scheme will be the average of the general student population, rather than the conditional averages for the subject types that prefer a particular payment scheme. We will distinguish between these two groups in our predictions.

Second, the quality of the expert's proofreading directly impacted the customer's payment. But it had no impact on the expert's personal earnings. In the choice of a payment scheme, all experts in the self-selection treatment faced the same tradeoff, or moral dilemma, between choosing the payment scheme that

---

[2]It is not within the scope of this article to describe each task in the CPCIS in detail. Most of the tasks included in the CPCIS have been used in several experiments. In this case, we make an exception for the BFMS, assuming that it is not as well-known as the other tasks. Still, we encourage the reader to read Bartling et al. (2009) and Corgnet et al. (2015) for more detailed descriptions of this type of instrument.

TABLE 1 | Bartling binary choice task.

Binary choice variable name	Egalitarian alternative A	Non-egalitarian alternative B
BFMS1	Both subjects earn $10	Decision-Maker earns $10, Matched Partner $6
BFMS2	Both subjects earn $10	Decision-Maker earns $16, Matched Partner $4
BFMS3	Both subjects earn $10	Decision-Maker earns $10, Matched Partner $18
BFMS4	Both subjects earn $10	Decision-Maker earns, $11 Matched Partner $19
BFMS5	Both subjects earn $10	Decision-Maker earns, $12 Matched Partner $4
BFMS6	Both subjects earn $10	Decision-Maker earns $8, Matched Partner $16

would maximize personal earnings or one that would limit their maximum earnings. Therefore, selecting a payment scheme may reveal something about subjects' characteristics.

The following *ceteris paribus* predictions highlight the expected relationship between each individual characteristics and behavior in the primary experiment. However, we note that individuals do not differ from each other in *ceteris paribus* ways; therefore theoretical implications are unlikely to describe the expected differences in behavior among any two given subjects.

Predicted Behavior with Homo Economicus Preferences

The predicted behavior varies with assumptions about expert preferences that are not induced. However, there are simple predictions for the outcomes of these experiments if we assume subjects prefer to be purely self-interested (*homo economicus*). If careful editing requires bearing a real-effort or cognitive cost, a *homo economicus* expert assigned to the *salary* scheme will exert no effort and conduct no edits. A *homo economicus* expert randomly assigned to the *capitation* scheme should exert the minimum effort and only conduct one edit per essay. A *homo economicus* expert assigned to *fee-for-service* should maximize the number of edits with minimum effort and make both necessary and unnecessary edits. Furthermore, in the *selection* treatment, *homo economicus* would select *fee-for-service* 100% of the time, because under that scheme, experts can earn three times more than the maximum earnings possible under *salary* or *capitation*.

However, the experimental evidence presented in Green (2014) and Bejarano et al. (2016) demonstrates that subjects deviated from income-maximizing strategies. These results suggest that subject preferences were more complex than those of *homo economicus*. This leads us to investigate what role additional preferences might be in play in order to modify our assumptions regarding the effects of the payoff schemes on actions.

Predicted Behavior with Other Preferences and Choice-Relevant Characteristics

The experimental design has some implications concerning the relevance of other personal characteristics as well. For example, risk aversion, loss aversion, and time preferences should not affect behavior. Subjects earnings do not depend on the correctness of their editing but only on their payment system and their decision to edit or not. Payments are deterministic. Therefore, subjects do not face risks of the usual kind. Similarly, the effect of choice on

earnings is almost immediate; hence, time preferences should not influence choices.

On the other hand, a subject's actions in Phase II have an impact on the earnings of subjects who participated on Phase I. Therefore, we expect that measures of what might be regarded as social preferences should affect behavior. For example, differences in the extent of altruism is likely to affect behavior, as has been found in Dictator, Trust, Ultimatum Game, and Prisoner's Dilemma experiments. We expect measures of altruism to be positively correlated with efforts to help subjects in Phase I. Error rates should fall under *fee-for-service*, and more time (and care) should be spent editing under salary and capitation.

The three variables described above (Egalitarianism, Selfishness, Altruism) have an intrinsic relationship with what we expect to uncover with the selection and related actions in our experiment. We expect that those demonstrating Selfishness through these measures will prioritize their earnings over their customers'. Hence, these subjects will likely select *fee-for-service* and perform a larger number of edits rather than maximize their incomes, even at the expense of their customer. In contrast, those individuals that prioritize the earnings of their matched partners will likely choose *salary* and only attempt to conduct beneficial edits for the customers, even at a cognitive and time cost to themselves.

In contrast to the preference measures, predictions regarding Intelligence and demographic variables are not clear. Little is known regarding how actions in our experiment will be influenced by a subject's demographic characteristics. We also have variables that reflect Numeracy, Academic, and IQ Intelligence. To the best of our knowledge, this is the first time that researchers aimed to explore how these measures correlate with performance on incentivized linguistic tasks that affect third parties.

Cognitive Capabilities and Personality

In this section, we clarify the implications that cognitive capabilities and personality traits could have on the behavior observed in our primary experiment given their indirect relationship with strategic preferences. In a novel study, Corgnet et al. (2015) found that Chapman students with a more reflective nature were less likely than intuitive individuals to be associated with egalitarian *and* spiteful motives. The authors named the behavior of those with scores above median CRT as mildly altruistic. Given that we have access to the same subject database with the same measures of cognitive capability (CRT) and preferences for egalitarianism or spitefulness (Bartling et al., 2009), we might expect also that subjects with higher CRTs would show some type of characteristic behavior. However, it is not clear what exactly would comprise mildly altruistic behavior in our experiment. The moral dilemma at hand implies that for each treatment, experts face a different tradeoff between self-interest and customer welfare. We expect subjects with higher CRT scores to be more likely to balance this tradeoff differently in the various treatments examined because they are more likely to reflect on the cost of the tradeoff at stake.

In an attempt to relate personality traits to preferences measures, Rustichini et al. (2012) used a dataset with 1000 truck drivers. They measured the truck drivers' Big Five traits, time preference, risk aversion, truck accidents, job persistence, credit score, and body mass index (BMI). The authors found that personality traits had stronger predictive power than time preferences or risk aversion for truck accidents, job persistence, credit score, and BMI. However, the authors argue that both economic and psychological theories are needed to understand truck-driver behavior.

Big Five personality traits are also likely to help explain differences in the behavior of experts among treatments and payment systems. Unfortunately, the Big Five factors are not orthogonal. Although, qualitative predictions can often be made for individual factors, a person's particular vector of factors often includes factors with the opposite effects on the behavior of interest. For example, *openness* is associated with curiosity and a higher willingness to explore. Therefore, relatively open individuals might be more likely to conduct a larger number of edits and to spend more time on them.

Conscientiousness is associated with being dependable and disciplined. In our experiment, experts have a mission. In their mission, they know that they could affect the earnings of their customers. Higher conscientiousness is likely to be correlated positively with measures of correct edits. Agreeableness is associated with higher cooperation against the exploitation of others (Andersen et al., 2006). We expect that subjects with higher agreeableness should conduct more correct edits to increase the earnings of customers. These three dispositions, therefore, tend to induce better outcomes for the customers.

Higher extroversion is associated with higher sensitivity to rewards. In this case, the perceived nature of the reward matters. Subjects with a higher extroversion measure (maintaining the degree of preferences for others' welfare) may be driven by monetary rewards. In that case, they will be more likely to choose *fee-for-service* and to conduct unnecessary edits. However, if they perceive their reward to be correlated with the benefits of their customers, extroverts will take greater account of such effects than introverts.

Finally, neuroticism appears to be the factor that is not likely to influence the behavior of subjects in a clearly predictive way. Because the experimental environment is set up to isolate subjects from situations where moods, anxiety, and depression play a significant role, we do not expect to find any significant correlation between neuroticism and behavior.

EXPERIMENT, DATA, AND ANALYSIS

The experiments were conducted in the ESI laboratory and conference rooms at Chapman University between May 2014 and May 2016. Experimental subjects were recruited from the ESI database of more than 2000 students. Phase I was conducted either in the ESI laboratory or the ESI conference room. Phase II was conducted in the ESI's computer laboratories. Printed instructions were provided for the students to read on their own for 10 min. At the end of the 10 min, the experimental coordinator read the instructions out loud. Subjects were not able to start the experiment until they satisfactorily completed a quiz.

Many of these subjects were also recruited to participate in the CPCIS by a different recruitment email on a previous date convenient to the subject's schedule. The CPCIS sessions were implemented in the same laboratory but had no formal connection to any other experiments being conducted at ESI. The local Institutional Review Board (IRB) approved both studies. In both studies, participants received a show-up fee of 7 USD plus additional incentive payments earned by their behavior in the session.

In the primary experiment, there was a total of 20 undergraduates (customers) recruited in Phase I and 228 undergraduates (experts) recruited in Phase II. In Phase II, which was dedicated to experts performing editing services, 105 subjects were randomly assigned to their payment scheme, and 125 selected their payment scheme. Of the subjects in Phase II, 161 had completed the CPCIS; 115 of those were in the *self-selection* treatment and the other 46 were randomly assigned to one of the three payment schemes. We focus our analysis below on the behavior of those 161 subjects who participated in the primary experiment and had undertaken the CPCIS. The primary experiment lasted an average of 1 h and 15 min, and completion of the CPCIC instrument required an average of 1 h and 35 min.

In the primary experiment, expert subjects could edit correctly or incorrectly. We will focus our analysis on six experimental actions: total edits, total incorrect edits, percentage wrong, net impact on the customer earnings, expert earnings, and total editing time taken. Total edits (total incorrect) is the sum of all (incorrect) edits made by the expert over four rounds of editing. Percentage wrong was calculated by dividing total incorrect by total edited. Cumulative impact on the customer earnings, or impact, was calculated as the customer payoff generated by the expert's behavior over all four rounds. As subjects were given the opportunity to leave the experiment early, total time taken is the amount of time the experts spent editing the essays across all four rounds.

Table 2 provides a summary of the actions taken in the different treatments. As discussed in Bejarano et al. (2016), experts preferred either *fee-for-service* or *salary* over *capitation*. Those subjects who self-selected *fee-for-service* provided significantly more edits than those randomly assigned, resulting in more earnings for themselves and less help for their customers. The observed behavior between the randomly assigned *salary* treatment and those who self-selected *salary* did not significantly differ.

We begin with a correlational analysis of the relationship between subjects' actions and CPCIS measures. The correlation analysis only captures the way in which actions correlated with specific individual's characteristics. In the second part of this section, we report the results of a cluster analysis that groups subjects acting in similar ways. These clusters were most salient when subjects could self-select into one of the payment schemes. We analyze whether particular subjects' behavior or action-strategy types are revealed by actions in the experiment, and whether we observe differences across types in the *self-selected* treatment. Finally, we analyze how the observed relationships between experimental actions and CPCIS measures relate to our theoretical hypotheses.

Correlation Analysis

We start this section by exploring the individual characteristics across the six experimental subject types: self-selected and three randomly assigned into either *fee-for-service, capitation,* or *salary* types. When comparing across experimental subject types, we do not expect to see much difference between individual characteristics of those subjects that were randomly assigned individuals to the different payment schemes, because they were randomly selected from the general subject population. In contrast, we would expect to see differences in the individual characteristics of those that self-selected different payment schemes.

We proceed as follows: First, we study the correlation between experimental actions and individual characteristics for all those subjects for whom we have the CPCIS data (A summary of each of the CPCIS data measure can be found in the Appendix). This analysis, which includes the pooled set of randomly assigned and self-selected individuals, should reveal if *ceteris paribus* measures within a characteristic category are strongly correlated with actions in a particular way. Second, we use the fact that self-selecting into different payment schemes might reveal something about a subject's type to better understand behavior. Here, we analyze the correlation between each one of the payment schemes disaggregated by self-selection and randomly assigned with each of the individual characteristic measures in the CPCIS data. In both cases, we estimated the Spearman correlation coefficient[3] and test significance correcting for the multiple hypothesis effects via the Bonferroni adjustment.

In the analysis of the pooled set of subjects, there are two main findings: First and not surprisingly, variables within a characteristic category are typically highly correlated with one another. Second, we did not find any significant correlation between any of the preference measures and subject actions in the experimental treatments. The lack of correlation is consistent with our predictions of individual preferences but surprising for

those measures of strategic preferences, which were hypothesized to play a role in behavior in our primary experiment.

One exception is the correlation between all BFMS variables, measures of strategic preference, and action variables in our primary experiments. Particularly, we observed that when evaluating the correlation between the pooled data, i.e., all subjects in all treatments, selfishness correlates positively with total edited ($rs = 0.185$, $p < 0.10$). Furthermore, in all three cases, the three variables, egalitarianism, altruism and selfishness, have significant positive correlation with the amount experts earned with $rs = 0.158$, $rs = 0.221$, and $rs = 0.179$, and $p < 0.10$, respectively,. In contrast, altruism is not correlated with the number of wrong edits or its percentage. Furthermore, both egalitarianism and selfishness have a positive correlation with the number of wrong edits (and its percentage) with these respective statistics, $rs = 90.1779$, $rs = 0.214$, and $p < 0.05$ in both cases. Accounting for self-selection in general or self-selection into a particular payment scheme, all these correlations hold their significance except the correlation between the number of total edits, which now is not statistically significantly related to egalitarianism.

We found CRT measures correlated with total earnings in two dimensions: The number of correct CRT answers is positively correlated with total earnings ($r_s = 0.2348$, $r_s = 0.3030$, $p < 0.05$), and CRT impulsiveness is negatively correlated with total earnings ($r_s = -0.2270$, $p < 0.10$). This result is consistent with the findings of Corgnet et al. (2015) given that CRT relates to how compulsive/deliberative subjects are. However, these results should not be generalized since these traits could affect both the self-selection and the actions taken by subjects after this choice. Therefore, the outcome could be either driven by the self-selected portion of the subjects or not.

The lack of significant correlation between most of our measures of individual characteristics and subject actions conflicts with the theoretical hypotheses that we discussed in the previous section. *None* of the preference measures were correlated with any of the experimental action variables. Several explanations for this result are feasible. One possible explanation for the lack of correlations is that the CPCIS instrument and the primary experiment were conducted at different times by different researchers. This might imply that subjects are less likely to act in a manner consistent with the behavior characterized by their responses to the CPCIS tasks while performing in the primary experiment. Differences in the timing and circumstances of the CPCIS tasks and the primary experiments imply that their behavior in the primary experiment is less likely to reflect any implicit experimenter demand effect.

We continue our analysis by examining only correlations among those who self-selected the same treatment. This is an important step in our analysis, as the act of choosing a treatment might reveal differences in individual characteristics. To analyze this possibility, we break down the correlation analysis into two steps. First, we conduct the same correlation analysis as above but only for those subjects in the *self-selection* treatment.

Not surprisingly, there is no correlation between experimental actions and the individual characteristic measures of the CPCIS

---

[3]The Spearman's rho is a nonparametric measure of rank correlation. The assumption of monotonicity in Spearman's rho test is satisfied.

TABLE 2 | Actions summary by treatment.

Variable	Randomly assigned			Selection		
	Fee-for-service	Salary	Capitation	Fee-for-service	Salary	Capitation
Total edited	175.8	81.7	89.2	250.3	85.8	73.8
Total wrong	98.1	7.6	17.6	180.6	13.8	7.0
Total correct	77.8	74.1	71.5	69.7	72.0	66.8
Percentage correct	62%	90%	83%	40%	85%	89%
Cumulative impact	6.8	10.8	9.8	1.1	10.4	9.7
Total earnings	$35	$25	$21	$51	$25	$23
Number of subjects	39	41	25	49	70	4

for the subjects that self-selected the two most popular payment schemes[4]. The next step in our analysis is to break down the correlation analysis, controlling for self-selection into a particular payment scheme, *salary* or *fee-for-service*.

The analysis of correlation between subjects that self-selected a similar moral dilemma presents two main findings. First, almost all the finding of the analysis of the pooled set of a subject's data persists. This means that those characteristics that were not found significantly correlated persisted and presented a lack of relationship with actions and were still not correlated when disaggregating by payment scheme. In contrast, we found that the selection choice may work as a screening device of subjects with different values for those that were found significant for all the self-selected subjects. This is reflected by the fact that accounting for the particular payment schemes eliminates the significance for those relationships that were significant for the pooled set of subjects into both payment schemes. This result holds for all the correlations between actions and individual characteristics reflected by variables such as egalitarianism, altruism and selfishness, as well as CRT correct and CRT. This result could be explained if values for these variables and actions are similar among those that self-selected salary but very different for those that self-selected fee for service.

Cluster Analysis

The results of the previous section lead us to believe that there may be different types of experimental subjects. More specifically, we argue that the inconsistencies in correlations between measures of individual characteristics and observed actions are due to the fact that in our primary experiment multiple characteristics, i.e., cognitive capabilities, individual preferences, social preferences and personality traits, might affect behavior. That is, given the moral dilemma and real effort features of our primary experiment, we expect that certain individual characteristics will pull the subject's behavior in opposite directions. For example, experts with high measures of intelligence would be more likely to provide better outcomes for their customers, whereas low levels of altruism imply worse outcomes for their customers. Therefore, a subject's the combination of the individual characteristics each subject

possesses may have uncertain implications for theoretical predictions.

For this reason, we next explore if expert actions reveal behavioral types and whether behavioral groups correspond to differences in preference, cognitive, and demographic characteristics. To do this, we use cluster analysis to build behavioral groups from the actions of subjects in the selection treatment of our primary experiment.

Clusters (behavioral groups) are based on a subject's actions. Specifically, behavioral groups are created using the action variables "total edits" and "total incorrect edits." Cluster analysis based on these two variables allows us to distinguish between subjects who edited a lot with a high percentage of incorrect edits (the Demons) and subjects who edited sparsely with a high percentage of incorrect edits, as well as those who edited few with a high percentage of correct edits (the Angels).

Behavioral groups were created using the k-mean algorithm with Euclidian distances. We clustered on values of k from 2 to 6 and maximized the Calinski and Harabasz (CH) pseudo f-statistics to find the optimal clustering (Caliński and Harabasz, 1974). In order to control for the robustness of the k-mean algorithm, we ran it in a loop with 50 repetitions for each value of k. From these repetitions, we selected the cluster with the highest CH pseudo F-statistic for each value of k. Then, comparing across the k values, we selected the clustering with the highest CH pseudo f-statistic.

Behavioral Groups

Figure 1 and **Table 3** provide summaries of the cluster groupings. **Table 3** summarizes the experimental actions taken by the typical member of the five behavioral groups created by our cluster analysis. The results displayed in **Table 3** reveal three things. First, they reveal that various subjects in our primary experiment behaved in very different ways. Second, the significant differences on actions across behavioral groups imply that our cluster methodology identified different types of subjects. Lastly, a large part of subject behavior is captured by the subjects' choices of payment scheme. The payment scheme selection action completely and consistently separates the five groups into two subsets, {A, B, D} and {C, E}. No significant differences exist between any pair of groups from within either subset, but significant differences do exist between any pair of groups across subsets.

---
[4]Total time taken showed a positive correlation with self-reported GPA ($r_s = 0.1981, p < 0.10$).

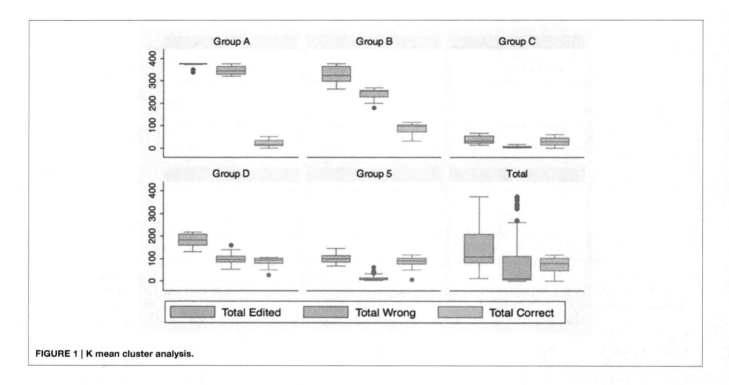

FIGURE 1 | K mean cluster analysis.

TABLE 3 | Actions summary by group.

Variable	Group A	Group B	Group C	Group D	Group E
Total edited	370	328	37	182	101
Total wrong	347	241	6	99	13
Total correct	23	87	31	83	88
Percentage correct	6%	26%	80%	46%	87%
Cumulative impact	−14	2	5	7	12
Total earnings	$74	$63	$24	$36	$25
Percentage *fee-for-service*	100%	93%	5%	90%	21%
Number of subjects	13	14	19	10	63

TABLE 4 | Summary of FPRANK comparisons across groups and individual preferences.

	Group A	Group B	Group C	Group D	Group E
Group A	–	6	5	4	3
Group B	6	–	7	5	7
Group C	5	7	–	6	4
Group D	4	5	6	–	2
Group E	3	7	4	2	–
Totals	18	25	22	17	16
% of Total	13%	18%	16%	13%	12%

However, payment choice does not capture all the dimensions of subject behavior. **Figure 1** reveals that even for those groups with a large percentage of subjects choosing the *fee-for-service* payment scheme (Groups A, B, and D), behavior varied significantly. And although a much smaller percentage of subjects chose the *fee-for-service* payment scheme, Groups C and E also displayed dissimilar behavior in other dimensions. For example, although Group E has a large number of subjects choosing *salary* rather than the *fee -for-service*, the *fee -for-service* subjects of Group E (the Angels) behaved very different than *fee-for-service* subjects in Groups A, B and D and, in particular, most different from those in Group A (the Demons).

The experimental actions from our primary experiment show strong support for the existence of behavioral types as revealed in **Table 3** and **Figure 1**. In the spirit of the ongoing claims in various fields of behavioral science, we seek to determine whether the differences in primary experimental behavior relate to individual characteristics that may be captured independently

by the CPCIS database. Understanding this question is of great importance to experimental research.

In order to test the hypotheses that there are no differences in the individual characteristics of students who have been clustered into different groups, we perform a binary comparison of the aggregate experimental actions taken by subjects in each pair of groups for each CPCIS characteristic. The complete results for the Two Sample Fligner–Policello Rank Test are displayed in **Table 5**. **Table 4** provides a summary of these results by reporting the count of the number of CPCIS characteristics in which each pair of behavioral groups differed significantly.

Although, all the groups were formed by Chapman students, each group displayed at least 2 and up to 9 significant differences in the characteristics of its membership. There were 26 characteristic differences that reinforced the basic subdivision ({A, B, D}, {C, E}) that was revealed by payment selection, but there were 23 characteristic differences between groups within

TABLE 5 | Summary statistics of action and individual characteristics.

Variable	Group A Mean	Group A Ranking		Group B Mean	Group B Ranking		Group C Mean	Group C Ranking		Group D Mean	Group D Ranking		Group E Mean	Group E Ranking	
INDIVIDUAL PREFERENCES																
Risk aversion	4.00	3	–	4.15	2	>3	4.00	3	<2	3.90	4	–	4.18	1	–
Loss aversion	3.38	3	–	3.15	5	<1	3.28	4	–	3.90	1	>5	3.46	2	–
Time preference	6.00	2	–	6.23	1	–	4.94	5	–	5.30	4	–	5.74	3	–
STRATEGIC PREFERENCES																
Trust																
Trust sent	7.69	2	–	8.46	1	–	6.11	3	–	6.00	4	–	7.37	3	–
Trust return	13.08	1	>4, 3	10.38	4	<1	13.06	2	>3	9.00	3	<1, 2	12.46	3	–
Ultimatum																
Offer	4.85	5	–	5.69	2	–	5.11	4	–	5.70	1	–	5.44	3	–
First accepted offer	3.92	1	–	3.62	4	–	3.67	3	–	3.80	2	–	3.49	5	–
Advantageous offers	0.00	4	–	0.31	2	–	0.50	1	–	0.50	1	–	0.05	3	–
Dictator																
Sent	4.31	4	<2	5.62	1	–	5.44	2	>1, 3	4.30	5	–	4.70	3	<1
Prisoners' dilemma																
Cooperative action	1.54	1	>4	1.23	4	<1	1.50	2		1.50	2	–	1.39	3	–
Bartling																
Egalitarianism	3.54	1	>5	3.07	4	–	3.21	2	>5	2.70	5	<1, 2	3.11	3	–
Altruism	0.92	5	–	1.50	1	–	1.26	3	–	1.40	2	–	1.17	4	–
Selfishness	1.54	2	>5	1.00	5	<2, 1	1.21	3	<1	1.90	1	>5, 3, 4	1.14	4	<1
INTELLIGENCE																
Psychology																
Raven	13.69	1	–	13.15	3	–	12.17	4	–	12.60	5	–	13.16	2	–
CRT	3.23	2	–	4.08	1	>5	2.67	5	<1	3.10	4	–	3.18	3	–
Wonderlic	19.77	3	–	20.23	1	>5	18.94	5	<1, 2	20.20	2	>5	19.54	4	–
Numeracy																
Adding task (Incentivized)	15.38	4	–	17.54	1	>5	14.78	5	<1	16.60	2	–	16.05	3	–
Adding task (Not Incentivized)	13.85	4	<1	17.08	1	>4, 5	12.83	5	<1, 2, 3	16.80	2	>5	15.21	3	>5
Academic																
SAT	5.15	4	–	5.38	2	>5	5.29	3	–	5.40	1	–	4.96	5	<2
ACT	6.42	1	–	6.23	2	–	5.82	5	–	5.89	4	–	6.00	3	–
GPA	3.61	2	>5	3.72	1	>5, 3	3.41	5	<2, 1, 3	3.45	4	–	3.56	3	<1, >5
Social																
Theory of mind	27.69	1	–	27.30	2	–	26.41	5	–	26.50	4	–	27.02	3	–
PERSONALITY-BIG 5																
Openness	36.54	4	–	39.08	1	–	36.94	3	–	36.40	5	–	37.28	2	–
Conscientiousness	30.77	5	–	32.23	2	–	32.06	3	–	31.10	4	–	32.51	1	–
Extroversion	28.08	1	>4	26.85	3	–	27.28	2	–	26.60	4	<1	25.86	5	–
Agreeableness	31.77	4	<3, 2, 1	31.54	5	<1, 2	33.72	3	>4	35.20	1	>4, 5	34.49	2	>4, 5
Neuroticism	25.85	1	>4, 5	24.08	2	–	21.50	4	<1	20.00	5	<1, 3	23.61	3	>5
DEMOGRAPHICS																
Age	18.85	4	–	18.62	5	<1	18.89	3	–	18.90	2	–	19.23	1	>5
Gender	1.54	2	–	1.43	5	–	1.53	3	–	1.60	1	–	1.44	4	
Volunteer hours	1.15	5	<1	1.67	1	>3, 4, 5	1.47	3	<1	1.22	4	<1	1.49	2	
Work hours	1.46	5	<1	2.25	1	>3, 4, 5	1.76	3	<1	1.89	2	–	1.60	4	<1
Number of siblings	1.23	4	<1	1.15	5	–	1.56	2	–	1.50	3	<1	1.91	1	>3, 4
Older siblings	0.77	4	–	0.46	5	<3	0.83	3	>5, <1	1.10	1	**>3**	0.88	2	–
Religiosity	1.67	3	–	1.54	4	<1	1.41	5	<2	1.90	2	>5	2.04	1	>4

Subjects who chose the capitation payment were not able to be clustered into a group. Their data is not summarized here.
Significance in ranking reported by < or > signs next to ranking.

the same subset; this allows us to differentiate between groups that have a similar predilection for payment scheme.

Table 5 displays the differences among those individual characteristics for each group. For each variable in the CPCIS, we provide the information of the mean at the group level and the number of subjects in the group. We also rank them from the highest (1) to the lowest (5) value and the sign for those differences that were statistically significant according to the results of the binary Two Sample Fligner–Policello Rank Test. We next describe how the results in **Table 5** relate to the theoretical implications discussed in Section Theoretical Relationship among CPCIS Variables.

Individual Preferences

In contrast to the correlation analysis where no measures of individual preferences were significantly different, risk aversion, and loss aversion were each significantly different between two groups (Groups B > C and Group D > Group B, respectively). This is surprising as experts' risk aversion and loss aversion profiles should not affect their behavior as the subjects are in control of their actions and thereby, their earnings. However, these results cannot be rationalized by either a non-egocentric egocentric view of preferences over other's risk and loss (Hsee and Weber, 1997). If we consider each action as a choice between an uncertain outcome (i.e., edit is potentially right or wrong) and a certain outcome (i.e., no edit means no risk) for their counterpart, the number of edits conducted would reflect one's risk aversion. However, Group C behaved more conservatively in editing than Group B, whereas Group C is less risk averse than Group B. In contrast, Group B had lower levels of loss aversion than Group D and conducted significantly more edits than Group D. This demonstrates Group B's willingness to act carelessly in decisions that negatively impact others more so than the behavior of Group D. These results provide a first indication of how difficult it is to relate measures of individual preference to behavior in a real-effort moral dilemma.

Strategic Preference

In contrast to the correlation analysis, more measures of strategic preferences were found to be significantly different. First, we predicted that subjects with higher levels of reciprocity would act more benevolently than others in our primary task; that is, these subjects would provide a higher cumulative impact (income) for their customers. However, we found that when comparing the actions in the Trust Game (reciprocity), groups with high levels of reciprocity were less benevolent to their customers. For example, groups that provided a large number of incorrect edits, such as Group A (the Demons), or relatively few edits, such as Group C, had higher rankings of reciprocity, i.e., returned more money on the trust game. However, it is important to note that in the Trust Game, reciprocity from the recipient is conditional whereas, in our experiment, expert actions toward customers are not. In our primary experiment, the benefits experts confer to their customers do not affect their own earnings. This key distinction may explain the unexpected behavior.

BFMS measures of egalitarianism, selfishness or altruism also partly contradict our theoretical predictions. Groups A and C had significantly larger measures of egalitarianism in the BFMS relative to the other groups; however, in our experiment Group A's actions reflect those of *homo economicus* and Group C's reflected those of an egalitarian. Group C has the lowest overall personal earnings and the 3rd highest cumulative impact for their customer. A similar relationship appears with measures of selfishness reported by the BFMS. Groups A and C are among those with higher levels of selfishness. The inconsistency in behavior and similarity of BFMS measures in these two Groups leads us to question the usual interpretation of the BFMS measure.

Intelligence

We found that 6 of our 9 measures of intelligence differed across groups. In contrast to the simple correlation analysis, the different behavioral groups were not drawn from the same population with respect to the CRT and Wonderlic test results. For the CRT we found that Group B, the group with the highest CRT values, also behaved in a way that could be described as mildly altruistic and selfish. Group B mostly opted for *fee-for-service* and conducted a large number of edits, thereby increasing their earnings. However, relative to Group A, who also provided a large number of edits, Group B provided more accurate edits. This behavior we characterize as mildly altruistic and selfish, and it is consistent with our theoretical predictions. Similar results were observed by Corgnet et al. (2015). Corgnet et al. observed in their experiments that individuals with high CRT scores behave in a more altruistic way.

Our final measure of intelligence that had significant differences across groups is by numeracy both in an incentivized task and not incentivized. In our theoretical predictions, we argue that there is no relationship between numeracy and the task in our primary experiment. However, upon reflection, statistically significant differences on the not incentivized Adding Task would not contradict our predictions. Notice, that this CPCIS task measures more than numeracy skills, as subjects are not presented with any monetary incentive to add correctly. Therefore, the correct additions performed in this task is also a measure of intrinsic motivation. Hence, finding that those who groups with the highest number of correct edits (Groups B, D, and E) also have the highest scores on the not incentivized Adding Task is as one would expect.

Personality

Table 5 reveals that the behavioral groups differ with regard to at least three personality measures (Extroversion, Agreeableness, and Neuroticism). Two measures, however, Openness and Conscientiousness, are not statistically different among groups. The finding that Conscientiousness does not differ amongst groups regardless of choice of payment contradicts our theoretical discussion. However, we do find two supporting results. First, Group A (the Demons) has higher levels of extroversion. This group is only composed of subjects that chose *fee-for-service*; it conducted the most edits on average and had the lowest percentage of correct edits, all of which are consistent with an extrovert's attitude toward rewards. Second, Groups D and E showed the highest values of Agreeableness. These two groups also had higher cumulative impact (the return of dollars to customers as a result of their actions). This result is consistent with the compassionated attitude associated with this trait. Finally, we also found that Neuroticism differs significantly among groups. Particularly, Groups A, B, and D, the three groups with the largest numbers of edits, presented higher values of Neuroticism than the Groups with lower numbers of edits, Groups C and E.

Demographics

Several demographic characteristics presented significant differences amongst groups. Of particular interest to our analysis are self-reported numbers of volunteer and work hours. Again, Group B ranked the highest for these two variables. We have already described the behavior of Group B as mildly altruistic and selfish, so it is encouraging that the results are consistent with our previous finding.

DISCUSSION

In general, understanding how individual characteristics influence behavior is a fundamental task of the economist, psychologist, and scientist. While crucial, scientists rarely have independent datasets that combine both an individual subject's characteristics and behavior (Caplan, 2003). In this article, we leverage a uniquely large dataset containing the individual characteristics of a subset of our experimental subjects to shed light on the relationship between subject's individual characteristics and their behavior in a real-effort moral dilemma with self-selection by payment scheme. Due to the unique nature of our primary experiment, we use two statistical approaches, correlation analysis and cluster analysis, to better understand these dynamics. Different scholars collected our two datasets at different times for different reasons. This allowed us to avoid issues associated with a sequence of primary and secondary experiments conducted by the same experimental team and setting. The following points summarize our results.

First, there is no clear majority of individual characteristics that correlate with behavior in our primary experiment. A set of a few, but interesting, significant correlation relationships were found across experimental actions. We found that no measure of individual preference, i.e., time discounting, risk and loss aversion, was significant. Furthermore, our measures of strategic preferences, which include variables such as Trust, Trustworthiness, and Altruism captured from implementation of canonical Trust and Ultimatum Games also failed to show any significant correlation with actions in a real-effort moral dilemma. These results highlight the importance of conducting reliability tests for simple statistical analyses exploring these social preferences (Charness and Rabin, 2002). Other measures of social preferences, such as those derived from Bartling et al. (2009), were significantly correlated with actions, but the results of these correlations were contradictory to our theoretical predictions.

Measures of intelligence and personality traits also often failed to correlate with observed behavior in our primary experiment. This result is consistent with previous findings (Becker et al.,

2012) and presents an additional call to a better development in the study of the relationship between personality traits and economic behavior (Almlund et al., 2011; Rustichini et al., 2012). Hence, there is a need for replication of this investigation to develop better theoretical models (Benjamin et al., 2013).

There are several arguments that may justify these inconsistencies. First, ordering of tasks has been shown to impact outcomes in experiments. For instance, Healy et al. (2016) demonstrates that by going from a single shot of a game to a repeated game, subjects' payment functions change and thereby, so do behaviors. Similarly, implementing a sequence of tasks, primary and secondary, or a battery of tasks and surveys, as with the CPCIS, could induce different behavior through wealth and portfolio effects. Here, we analyze the correlation between a single task (our primary experiment) and a battery of instruments (the CPCIS), collected on separate occasions. Therefore, behavior in our primary experiment should be less affected by the behavior of the CPCIS than if both datasets had been collected in the same session, producing less consistent correlations than otherwise.

Secondly, it is possible that the joint implementation of tasks in the CPCIS dataset generate spurious correlations. These spurious correlations could be generated from the bundling of experimental tasks, experimenter demand effects (Zizzo, 2010), or idiosyncratic effects of experimenter teams or their lab set up. For instance, researchers often only conduct secondary experiments that they believe will reveal something about their subjects. This potentially introduces an experimenter demand effect instead of the desired elicitation of additional characteristics, resulting in spurious correlations. We argue that the difficulty of finding significant correlations in our analysis, when both of the datasets were collected by separate research teams, is a call for attention to the interpretation of correlations found between primary experiments and secondary measures that are jointly collected. Furthermore, these findings open several research questions regarding how to implement and analyze the results of several experimental tasks, which *a priori* are correlated.

Following the correlation analysis, we found that actions in a primary experiment could be used to categorize subjects into groups based on their observed actions using cluster analysis (i.e., behavioral groups). Furthermore, because of the availability of the CPCIS data we could proceed one step further than several experiments, which have already utilized cluster analysis with the investigation of individual characteristics (Houser et al., 2004; Rong and Houser, 2015).

The cluster analysis reveals that individual characteristics are a distinguishing factor across behavioral groups. Individual measures of preferences (Risk and Loss aversion), strategic preferences (Trust Game, Dictator Game, Prisoners' Dilemman, and Bartling) and Intelligence (CRT, Wonderlic, and numeracy) all varied across behavioral groups. However, like the correlation analysis, the results often contradicted our theoretical predictions. Regardless, it is important to note that these behavioral groups revealed systematic differences in behavior regardless of inconsistencies with theoretical predictions. That is, due to the tension between some of our theoretical analyses of the influence of personal characteristics on behavior in our moral dilemma and the observed behavior, either our theory or our measures are still far from perfect.

Our results suggest that the effects of psychological, cognitive, and demographic differences on behavior in experiments are more complex than those implied by *ceteris paribus* hypothesis. Subjects are endowed with mixtures of individual characteristics that could present contradictory theoretical interpretations. Despite this difficulty, characteristics of subjects that chose and act similarly (i.e., belong to the same behavioral group) are more likely to be similar between each other and different from those that chose and act differently in individual characteristics. This finding could not be detected using a simple correlation analysis.

We believe that the results of our analysis shed light on the strength of the links between individual characteristics, behavior in simple strategic games, behavior in real-effort moral dilemmas.

AUTHOR CONTRIBUTIONS

Each author contributed to the design, implementation, analysis, and writing of the document.

ACKNOWLEDGMENTS

We would especially like to thank Roger Congleton for his helpful comments and suggestions.

REFERENCES

Akerlof, G. A., and Kranton, R. E. (2000). Economics and identity. *Q. J. Econ.* 115, 715–753. doi: 10.1162/003355300554881

Almlund, M., Duckworth, A. L., Heckman, J. J., and Kautz, T. D. (2011). *Personality Psychology and Economics.* No. w16822. National Bureau of Economic Research. Available online at: http://www.nber.org/papers/w16822 (Accessed July 4, 2016).

Andersen, S., Harrison, G. W., Lau, M. I., and Rutström, E. E. (2006). Elicitation using multiple price list formats. *Exp. Econ.* 9, 383–405. doi: 10.1007/s10683-006-7055-6

Aycinena, D., Bejarano, H., and Rentschler, L. (2014). *Informed Entry in Auction.* Working Paper. Available online at: http://fce.ufm.edu/wp-content/uploads/2014/12/AEP2_2015.01_WP.pdf

Bartling, B., Fehr, E., André Maréchal, M., and Schunk, D. (2009). Egalitarianism and competitiveness. *Am. Econ. Rev.* 99, 93–98. doi: 10.1257/aer.99.2.93

Becker, A., Deckers, T., Dohmen, T., Falk, A., and Kosse, F. (2012). *The Relationship between Economic Preferences and Psychological Personality Measures.* Institute for the Study of Labor (IZA), Discussion Paper No. 6470. Available online at: http://ftp.iza.org/dp6470.pdf (accessed July 4, 2016).

Becker, G. S. (2013). *The Economic Approach to Human Behavior.* University of Chicago Press.

Bejarano, H., Green, E. P., and Rassenti, S. (2016). *Payment Scheme Self-Selection in the Credence Goods Market: An Experimental Study.* No. 16-04. Economic Science Institute Working Paper No. 16-04. Available online at: http://www.chapman.edu/research-and-institutions/economic-science-institute/_files/WorkingPapers/Payment-Scheme-Self-Selection-in-the-Credence-Goods-Market1.pdf (Accessed July 4, 2016).

Benjamin, D. J., Brown, S. A., and Shapiro, J. M. (2013). Who is 'behavioral'? Cognitive ability and anomalous preferences. *J. Eur. Econ. Assoc.* 11, 1231–1255. doi: 10.1111/jeea.12055

Ben-Ner, A., Putterman, L., and Ren, T. (2007). *Lavish Returns on Cheap Talk: Non-Binding Communication in a Trust Experiment.* Available online at SSRN: http://ssrn.com/abstract=1013582

Berg, J., Dickhaut, J., and McCabe, K. (1995). Trust, reciprocity, and social history. *Games Econ. Behav.* 10, 122–142. doi: 10.1006/game.1995.1027

Bolton, G. E., and Ockenfels, A. (2006). Inequality aversion, efficiency, and maximin preferences in simple distribution experiments: comment. *Am. Econ. Rev.* 96, 1906–1911. doi: 10.1257/aer.96.5.1906

Boone, C., De Bert, B., and Van Witteloostuijn, A. (1999). The impact of personality on behavior in five Prisoner's Dilemma games. *J. Econ. Psychol.* 20, 343–377. doi: 10.1016/S0167-4870(99)00012-4

Borghans, L., Heckman, J. J., Golsteyn, B. H., and Meijers, H. (2009). Gender differences in risk aversion and ambiguity aversion. *J. Eur. Econ. Assoc.* 7, 649–658. doi: 10.1162/JEEA.2009.7.2-3.649

Bowles, S. (1998). Endogenous preferences: the cultural consequences of markets and other economic institutions. *J. Econ. Lit.* 36, 75–111.

Brañas-Garza, P., Garcia-Muñoz, T., and González, R. H. (2012). Cognitive effort in the beauty contest game. *J. Econ. Behav. Organ.* 83, 254–260. doi: 10.1016/j.jebo.2012.05.018

Brañas-Garza, P., Kujal, P., and Lenkei, B. (2015). *Cognitive Reflection Test: Whom, How, When.* Working Paper. Available online at: https://www.chapman.edu/research-and-institutions/economic-science-institute/_files/WorkingPapers/cognitive-reflection-test-whom-how-when-2015.pdf

Brocklebank, S., Lewis, G. J., and Bates, T. C. (2011). Personality accounts for stable preferences and expectations across a range of simple games. *Pers. Individ. Dif.* 51, 881–886. doi: 10.1016/j.paid.2011.07.007

Burks, S. V., Carpenter, J. P., Goette, L., and Rustichini, A. (2009). Cognitive skills affect economic preferences, strategic behavior, and job attachment. *Proc. Natl. Acad. Sci. U.S.A.* 106, 7745–7750. doi: 10.1073/pnas.0812360106

Caliński, T., and Harabasz, J. (1974). A dendrite method for cluster analysis. *Commun. Stat. Theor. Methods* 3, 1–27.

Caplan, B. (2003). Stigler–Becker versus Myers–Briggs: why preference-based explanations are scientifically meaningful and empirically important. *J. Econ. Behav. Organ.* 50, 391–405. doi: 10.1016/S0167-2681(02)00031-8

Charness, G., and Rabin, M. (2002). Understanding social preferences with simple tests. *Q. J. Econ.* 117, 817–869. doi: 10.1162/003355302760193904

Congleton, R. D., and Vanberg, V. J. (2001). Help, harm or avoid? On the personal advantage of dispositions to cooperate and punish in multilateral PD games with exit. *J. Econ. Behav. Organ.* 44, 145–167. doi: 10.1016/S0167-2681(00)00159-1

Corgnet, B., Espín, A. M., and Hernán-González, R. (2015). The cognitive basis of social behavior: cognitive reflection overrides antisocial but not always prosocial motives. *Front. Behav. Neurosci.* 9:257. doi: 10.3389/fnbeh.2015.00287

DeAngelo, G., Lang, H., and McCannon, B. (2015). *Do Psychological Traits Explain Differences in Free Riding? Experimental Evidence.* West Virginia University, Working Paper. Available online at: http://www.be.wvu.edu/phd_economics/pdf/16-08.pdf

Eckel, C. C., and Grossman, P. J. (2008). "Men, women and risk aversion: experimental evidence," in *Handbook of Experimental Economic Results*, Vol. 1, eds C. Plott and V. Smith (New York, NY: Elsevier), 1061–1073.

Fehr, E., and Fischbacher, U. (2003). Why social preferences matter–the impact of non-selfish motives on competition, cooperation and incentives. *Econ. J.* 112, 478.

Fehr, E., and Schmidt, K. M. (1999). A theory of fairness, competition, and cooperation. *Q. J. Econ.* 114, 817–868. doi: 10.1162/003355399556151

Ferguson, E., Heckman, J. J., and Corr, P. (2011). Personality and economics: overview and proposed framework. *Pers. Individ. Dif.* 51, 201–209. doi: 10.1016/j.paid.2011.03.030

Fox, C. R., and Tversky, A. (1995). Ambiguity aversion and comparative ignorance. *Q. J. Econ.* 110, 585–603. doi: 10.2307/2946693

Frank, R. H., and Glass, A. J. (1991). *Microeconomics and Behavior.* New York, NY: McGraw-Hill.

Frederick, S. (2005). Cognitive reflection and decision making. *J. Econ. Perspect.* 19, 25–42. doi: 10.1257/089533005775196732

Goeree, J. K., Holt, C. A., and Palfrey, T. R. (2003). Risk averse behavior in generalized matching pennies games. *Games Econ. Behav.* 45, 97–113. doi: 10.1016/S0899-8256(03)00052-6

Green, E. P. (2014). Payment systems in the healthcare industry: an experimental study of physician incentives. *J. Econ. Behav. Organ.* 106, 367–378. doi: 10.1016/j.jebo.2014.05.009

Güth, W., Schmittberger, R., and Schwarze, B. (1982). An experimental analysis of ultimatum bargaining. *J. Econ. Behav. Organ.* 3, 367–388. doi: 10.1016/0167-2681(82)90011-7

Healy, P. J., Azrieli, Y., and Chambers, C. P. (2016). *Incentives in Experiments: A Theoretical Analysis.* Economics Department Working paper, Ohio State University.

Hirsh, J. B., and Peterson J. B. (2009). Extraversion, neuroticism, and the prisoner's dilemma. *Person. Indiv. Diff.* 46, 254–256. doi: 10.1016/j.paid.2008.10.006

Houser, D., Keane, M., and McCabe, K. (2004). Behavior in a dynamic decision problem: an analysis of experimental evidence using a Bayesian type classification algorithm. *Econometrica* 72, 781–822. doi: 10.1111/j.1468-0262.2004.00512.x

Hsee, C. K., and Weber, E. U. (1997). A fundamental prediction error: Self-others discrepancies in risk preference. *J. Exp. Psychol.* 126, 45–53. doi: 10.1037/0096-3445.126.1.45

Jaeggi, S. M., Buschkuehl, M., Perrig, W. J., and Meier, B. (2010). The concurrent validity of the N-back task as a working memory measure. *Memory* 18, 394–412. doi: 10.1080/09658211003702171

John, O. P., Naumann, L. P., and Soto, C. J. (2008). "Paradigm shift to the integrative Big Five trait taxonomy: History, measurement, and conceptual issues," in *Handbook of Personality: Theory and Research,* Vol. 3, eds O. P. John, R. W. Robins, and L. A. Pervin (New York, NY: Guilford Press), 114–158.

Kagel, J., and McGee, P. (2014). Personality and cooperation in finitely repeated prisoner's dilemma games. *Econ. Lett.* 124, 274–277.

Kahneman, D., Knetsch, J. L., and Thaler, R. (1986). Fairness as a constraint on profit seeking: entitlements in the market. *Am. Econ. Rev.* 76, 728–741.

Lönnqvist, J.-E., Verkasalo, M., and Walkowitz, G. (2011). It pays to pay–Big Five personality influences on co-operative behaviour in an incentivized and hypothetical prisoner's dilemma game. *Pers. Individ. Dif.* 50, 300–304. doi: 10.1016/j.paid.2010.10.009

Oechssler, J., Andreas, R., and Schmitz, P. W. (2009). Cognitive abilities and behavioral biases. *J. Econ. Behav. Organ.* 72, 147–152. doi: 10.1016/j.jebo.2009.04.018

Pixley, J. (2002). Emotions and economics. *Sociol. Rev.* 50, 69–89. doi: 10.1111/j.1467-954x.2002.tb03592.x

Rabin, M. (1993). Incorporating fairness into game theory and economics. *Am. Econ. Rev.* 83, 1281–1302.

Rong, R., and Houser, D. (2015). Growing stars: a laboratory analysis of network formation. *J. Econ. Behav. Organ.* 117, 380–394.

Rustichini, A., DeYoung, C. G. D., Anderson, J. A., and Burks, S. V. (2012). *Toward the Integration of Personality and Decision Theory in the Explanation of Economic and Health Behavior.* Institute for the Study of Labor (IZA), Discussion Paper No. 6750 (IZA, 6570). Available online at: http://ftp.iza.org/dp6750dp6570.pdf (Accessed July 4, 2016).

Sabater-Grande, G., and Georgantzis, N. (2002). Accounting for risk aversion in repeated prisoners' dilemma games: an experimental test. *J. Econ. Behav. Organ.* 48, 37–50. doi: 10.1016/S0167-2681(01)00223-2

Samuelson, P. A. (1948). Consumption theory in terms of revealed preference. *Economica* 15, 243–253. doi: 10.2307/2549561

Smith, V. L. (1976). Experimental economics: induced value theory. *Am. Econ. Rev.* 66, 274–279.

Smith, V. L., and Wilson, B. J. (2013). Sentiments, Conduct, and Trust in the Laboratory. Economic Science Institute Working Paper, Chapman University.

Stigler, G. J., and Becker, G. S. (1977). De gustibus non est disputandum. *Am. Econ. Rev.* 67, 76–90.

Takagishi, H., Kameshima, S., Schug, J., Koizumi, M., and Yamagishi, T. (2010). Theory of mind enhances preference for fairness. *J. Exp. Child Psychol.* 105, 130–137. doi: 10.1016/j.jecp.2009.09.005

Test, W. P. (1992). *Wonderlic Personnel Test and Scholastic Level Exam User's Manual.* Libertyville, IL: Wonderlic Personnel Test, Incorporated.

Toplak, M. E., West, R. F., and Stanovich, K. E. (2011). The Cognitive Reflection Test as a predictor of performance on heuristics-and-biases tasks. *Mem. Cogn.* 39, 1275–1289. doi: 10.3758/s13421-011-0104-1

Zizzo, D. J. (2010). Experimenter demand effects in economic experiments. *Exp. Econ.* 13, 75–98. doi: 10.1007/s10683-009-9230-z

Conflict of Interest Statement: The authors declare that the research was conducted in the absence of any commercial or financial relationships that could be construed as a potential conflict of interest.

APPENDIX

TABLE A1 | CPCIS Taxonomy.

Measure	Method–Test (Reference)	Related elicited characteristic
INDIVIDUAL PREFERENCES		
		Preferences over:
Risk aversion	Multiple listing method (Andersen et al., 2006)	Risk over lotteries
Loss aversion	Multiple listing method (Andersen et al., 2006)	Lotteries with losses
Time	Multiple listing method (Andersen et al., 2006)	Temporarily based payments
STRATEGIC PREFERENCES		
Trust	Trust Game (Berg et al., 1995)	
Trust sent	Trustor can sent only 0 or 10	Trust
Trust SM return	Trustee respond to each possibility (Strategy Method SM)	Reciprocity
Ultimatum	Ultimatum (Güth et al., 1982)	
Offer	Strategy method, first player can send any even number between (0–20, 11 choices)	Altruism
First accepted offer	When playing as a second player, player can reject any proposal	Fairness
Number of advantageous offers rejected		Fairness
Dictator game	Dictator game (Kahneman et al., 1986)	
	Strategy method, player can send any even number between (0–20, 11 choices)	
Egalitarianism, Altruism, and Selfishness	Bartling, Fehr, Marechal, and Schunk (BFMS) Task from Bartling et al. (2009)	
Egalitarianism	Zero to six choices of an equitative alternative over non-equitative	Preferences for equitatives distribution
Altruism	Zero to three choices of a detrimental alternative over equitative alternative	Preferences for distribution that benefit others
Selfishness	Zero to three choices of a beneficial alternative over equitative alternative	Preferences for distribution that benefit herself
INTELLIGENCE		
Pyschology		
Raven	Reduced version of the Raven Test in this case subjects have to choose only 18 questions	Fluid intelligence
Cognitive reflection test (CRT)	Extended version of the CRT described by Toplak et al. (2011)	Reflection and impulsiveness
Wonderlic	Reduced version of the Wonderlic Personnel Test, 24 questions with a maximum of 6 min	
Numeracy		
Adding task correct (incentivized)	Individual has to add 10 sequences of summations and its pay for each correct addition	Numeracy capabilities with extrinsic motivation
Adding task (no incentivized)	Similar to the incentivized task but individuals are not paid by correctness	
Academic		
SAT	Self-reported	
ACT	Self-reported	
GPA	Self-reported	
Other		
The reading the mind in the eyes test	A sample test in which individuals were requested to guess the most likely emotion of 36 pictures of eyes	Theory of mind
PERSONALITY—BIG FIVE		
Openness	Big five questionnaire with 44 items, John et al., 2008	Include traits of appreciation for unusual ideas, curiosity, and variety of experience
Conscientiousness	Big five questionnaire with 44 items, John et al., 2008	Tendency to be organized, disciplined, dependable, and to prefer planned behavior
Extraversion	Big five questionnaire with 44 items, John et al., 2008	Tendency to seek stimulation by the company of others, to be talkative, energetic, and assertive

(Continued)

TABLE A1 | Continued

Measure	Method–Test (Reference)	Related elicited characteristic
Agreeableness	Big five questionnaire with 44 items, John et al., 2008	Tendency to be sympathetic, compassionate and cooperative, kind, and affectionated
Neuroticism	Big five questionnaire with 44 items, John et al., 2008	Tendency to be moody, and to experience easily emotions such as anger, anxiety, and depression
DEMOGRAPHICS		
Age	Self-reported	Numeric
Gender	Self-reported	Male or female
Volunteer hours	Self-reported	Range of number of hours allocated to voluntary work or N/A
Work hours	Self-reported	Range of hours allocated to remunerated work
Number of sibling	Self-reported	Range of number of hours allocated to remunerated work or NA
Older sibling	Self-reported	Number of siblings older than the subject
Religiosity	Self-reported	Range of the frequency of service attendance

Reminders of behavioral disinhibition increase public conformity in the Asch paradigm and behavioral affiliation with ingroup members

Kees van den Bos [1,2]*, E. A. Lind [3], Jeroen Bommelé [1†] and Sebastian D. J. VandeVondele [1]

[1] Department of Social and Organizational Psychology, Utrecht University, Utrecht, Netherlands, [2] School of Law, Utrecht University, Utrecht, Netherlands, [3] Fuqua School of Business, Duke University, Durham, NC, USA

Edited by:
Eva Jonas,
University of Salzburg, Austria

Reviewed by:
Joseph Hayes,
York University, Canada
Immo Fritsche,
University of Leipzig, Germany

***Correspondence:**
Kees van den Bos,
Department of Social
and Organizational Psychology,
Utrecht University, Heidelberglaan 1,
3584 CS Utrecht, Netherlands
k.vandenbos@uu.nl

†**Present address:**
Jeroen Bommelé,
IVO Addiction Research Institute,
Rotterdam, Netherlands

Specialty section:
This article was submitted to
Cognitive Science,
a section of the journal
Frontiers in Psychology

This paper argues that being in the Asch situation, where there is a felt need to conform to others' faulty behaviors, poses a social threat to people. Furthermore, participating in a psychology experiment in which you will have to interact with other participants might trigger sense-making processes. The paper proposes that these assumed threats or sense-making processes are likely to activate the behavioral inhibition system, making people respond in more inhibited ways than they normally would be inclined to do. As a result, people's tendency to affiliate behaviorally with persons who are similar to them can be inhibited. The implication is that lowering behavioral inhibition (by experimentally reminding people about having acted without behavioral inhibitions) should lead to more public conformity in the Asch situation and stronger behavioral affiliation with ingroup members than not being reminded about behavioral disinhibition. Findings of four experiments support this line of reasoning. These findings are discussed in terms of behavioral inhibition and behavioral affiliation. Alternative accounts of the data that focus on social belongingness threats and optimal distinctiveness are also considered.

Keywords: threats, social interaction, behavioral disinhibition, affiliation, conformity, behavior, sense-making

Introduction

In the present paper we examine the dynamics of how people respond to potentially threatening social interactions. In particular, we focus on reactions in the Asch (1951, 1955, 1956) situation, in which there is pressure to conform to the faulty answers given by other research participants. We also examine responses in psychology experiments in which people expect to interact with other participants. We argue that these kinds of social interaction situations may contain threatening or sense-making aspects for research participants and that the social interaction threats or sense-making processes may activate the behavioral inhibition system (BIS: Carver and White, 1994). We test behavioral implications of this line of reasoning by assessing how lowering behavioral inhibition by means of experimental manipulation may affect public conformity and behavioral affiliation with the other participants in the experiments. We ground our predictions by building on work on behavioral affiliation and associated literatures and aim to integrate these insights with our recently developed perspective on behavioral inhibition and disinhibition (Van den Bos and Lind, 2013).

Behavioral Affiliation

Humans are social animals, creatures that are highly interactive with, and responsive to, other members of their species (Aronson, 1972). One of the core needs of humans is the need for affiliation. "Affiliation is the act of associating or interacting with one or more other people" (Leary, 2010, p. 865). Thus, people who want to affiliate seek to be in the company of others and want to interact with these other persons.

Theorists have suggested that being with or interacting with other people is a fundamental social behavior (e.g., Murray, 1938), especially when this involves individuals who are similar to us (Schachter, 1959). Therefore, peers or others who are similar to us serve a special function in fulfilling the need for affiliation and, more generally, people's pursuit of interpersonal connection (Sherif and Sherif, 1964; Schwarz, 1973; Wolf, 2008; Sundar et al., 2009; see also Erikson, 1968).

Peers are those individuals who share a similar or equal status, are usually of roughly the same age, and often have similar interests and backgrounds, bonded by the premise of sameness (Wolf, 2008). These individuals have a significant influence on the behaviors of people, especially when people are high in need for affiliation (Leary, 2010). For example, members inside peer groups learn to develop relationships with others in a social system. Furthermore, peers, and in particular ingroup peers, constitute important social referents for conveying customs and social norms (Clausen, 1968). Moreover, research suggests that peers exert stronger influence on what people do than do other important figures such as authorities. For example, a correlational study by Schwarz (1973) suggested that peers have stronger effects on inmates' behaviors than do prison authorities. An experiment on consumer attitudes by Sundar et al. (2009) showed that peer cues are generally more persuasive than are cues received from authorities or experts with high source credibility. Similarly, Harris (1995) concluded in her review article that peers may be more important for the socialization of children than are parents and other authorities.

With the phrase "The Social Animal," Aronson (1972) highlighted that we humans have a social nature and that we have a strong tendency to affiliate with others around us, including (and probably especially) with those who are similar to us (Schachter, 1959; see also Murray, 1938; Sherif and Sherif, 1964; Clausen, 1968; Erikson, 1968; McClelland, 1987; Baumeister and Leary, 1995; Wolf, 2008). As a result of this social quality of humans, people's behaviors tend to be influenced heavily by their social surroundings. In other words, a great many human behaviors are, at their core, socially oriented behaviors.

This does not mean, though, that socially oriented behaviors are always good or benign. In fact, the notion that our susceptibility to social influence can yield both positive and negative effects on what we do forms a central part of classic and modern social psychology. The potentially deleterious effect of peer pressure is well-known and includes instances where an individual feels directly or indirectly pressured into conforming with the group to make their behavior match that of their peers, even when conformity has a less than positive impact (Erikson, 1968; Sherif and Sherif, 1968). And in his APA-medal winning book Aronson (1972) clearly pointed out that social behaviors include not only prosocial behaviors (such as helping in bystander situations or fighting injustice), but also less benevolent behaviors (such as behaviors pertaining to prejudice, aggression, and conformity with wrong answers given in the Asch paradigm). The current paper aims to address both aspects of social influence.

A key feature of the argument we present here is that humans have a natural tendency to want to affiliate with people similar to them and that when confronted with threats people often want even more to affiliate with similar others. However, to fully understand people's responses to threats, we also need to consider those threats that result from those situations in which we have the feeling we do not belong in the group or in which our feelings of optimal distinctiveness (e.g., Brewer, 1991) are threatened. There is a truly substantial amount of research on these kinds of threats in social psychology. For example, people feel threatened if they are socially excluded (e.g., Eisenberger et al., 2003) and react with all sorts of defenses to social exclusion (see, e.g., Baumeister and Tice, 1990; Twenge et al., 2001; Abrams, 2005; DeWall and Baumeister, 2006; Bernstein et al., 2008; Lakin et al., 2008; Molden et al., 2009; Aydin et al., 2010; Gunther Moor et al., 2011; Riva et al., 2012; Schaafsma and Williams, 2012). Furthermore, Simon et al. (1997) have shown that a mortality salience threat can lead people to want to be similar or dissimilar to others depending on whether their optimal distinctiveness to others had been threatened (i.e., whether their uniqueness or their similarity to others had been threatened). Thus, many issues need to be considered to provide a complete picture of the need for affiliation and people's responses to threat.

Obviously, the current paper cannot address all aspects of responses to social threats. Therefore, based on notions such as peer group affiliation (Sherif and Sherif, 1964), affiliation motivation (McClelland, 1987), and the social animal (Aronson, 1972), the present paper notes that a core issue in classic and contemporary social psychology is trying to understand when people want to be involved with their fellow companions in their surroundings, and what different forms of behaviors people may engage in when they want to be involved with these peers. The current paper focuses on these issues by examining the effects of reminders of behavioral disinhibition on conforming and affiliating with peers.

Responding to Threats in Social Interactions

One reason why people affiliate with others is to obtain relief from stressful or fearful situations (Hill, 1987). Thus, behavioral affiliation is a response often seen when people are responding to social threats. Furthermore, Schachter (1959) proposed that people who are uncertain about the nature of a situation and how they should react desire to affiliate with other people to find out (see also Leary, 2010). Therefore, following the literature on behavioral affiliation, we focus in the present paper on how people respond to threatening situations and situations in which they are at least somewhat uncertain as to how they should behave exactly.

We examine these issues by relying on recent insights that suggest that in many situations people can be surprised by what is happening and do not know how to respond to the situation at hand (see, e.g., Van den Bos et al., 2011b; Van den Bos, 2013; Van den Bos and Lind, 2013). We argue here that in these confusing situations the BIS will be activated such that people will inhibit behavioral action because they are seeking first to find out what is going on and what behavior is appropriate in the situation at hand. After people have made sense of the situation the inhibition system is deactivated and the behavioral activation system is turned on so that people can perform the behavior that they think is appropriate in the current situation (Van den Bos, 2013). We ask what implications this line of reasoning can have for our understanding of how people affiliate with and conform to peers or fellow research participants.

Asch (1951, 1955, 1956) showed that participants in his classic conformity experiments were trying to sort out what was going on in the experiments and why their fellow research participants suddenly gave wrong answers to objectively simple questions. Given that people devalue, dislike, and reject those who do not conform to their judgments, decisions, and behaviors (Schachter, 1951), people understandably conform to others' views (Cialdini et al., 1991; Leary, 2010). Furthermore, consider the situation of a participant entering the psychology laboratory in which they are told that they will have to interact with other participants. It is a well-known fact that people who do this are trying to sort out what is going on in the experiment in which they are participating and to make sense of the situation in which they now find themselves, in particular when they will have to interact with an experimenter and other participants in the experiment. As a result of these sense-making processes, research participants are susceptible to how they are evaluated by important persons present in the lab setting. These important others may include the experimenter (Cottrell et al., 1968; Cottrell, 1972) but may also include the participants' peers (Innes and Young, 1975).

We assume that the social threats encountered in the Asch situation as well as the more general sense-making processes triggered in psychology experiments in which you will have to participate with other participants inhibits your reactions. Our assumption is based in part on the insight that evaluation apprehension involves anxiety (Christensen, 1982) and fear of negative evaluation (Rosenberg, 1980), which are concepts that are related to the activation of the BIS (Gray, 1987; Gray and McNaughton, 2000). Asch (1951, 1955, 1956) showed that participants in his conformity experiments were trying to sort out what was going on in the experiments and why their fellow research participants suddenly gave wrong answers to objectively simple questions. Thus, in addition to anxiety and fear of negative evaluation, more general processes of sense-making play a role in how research participants act in (at least some) psychology experiments, particularly those experiments in which participants interact with others.

Here we acknowledge that there are different perspectives on the functioning of the BIS in the research literature (see, e.g., Latané and Nida, 1981; Gray, 1987; Monteith, 1993; Carver and White, 1994; Gable et al., 2000; Gray and McNaughton, 2000; Nigg, 2000; Sawyer and Behnke, 2002; Carver, 2005; Knyazev et al., 2006; Amodio et al., 2008). This noted, there is good evidence that the BIS is activated when people are faced with anxiety-triggering stimuli (e.g., Carver and White, 1994; Gray

and McNaughton, 2000) or, more generally, with social situations that instigate processes of sense-making (e.g., Gable et al., 2000; Van den Bos, 2013). For example, Carver and White (1994) argue that the BIS regulates people's responses to anxiety-related cues and inhibits behavior that can lead to negative or painful consequences. Furthermore, the BIS has also been used to explain self-regulation and inhibition of prejudiced responses (Monteith, 1993). Moreover, the BIS has also been linked to more general sense-making processes in social contexts, such as how people deal with novelty in their environments (Gable et al., 2000) or how they interpret and react to puzzling situations (Van den Bos et al., 2011b; Van den Bos, 2013).

Importantly, as explained in detail in Van den Bos and Lind (2013), our ideas about inhibition and disinhibition focus on behavioral (dis)inhibition in public contexts. We note that an important notion in social psychology is the idea that in public settings the presence of others can constrain people from following their personal inclinations. Thus, we argue that issues of *public* and *behavioral* inhibition are important elements in the psychology of inhibition and sense-making. *Public* because the inhibition of primary importance is often instigated by thoughts of what others will think of our actions in non-private and fundamentally social contexts, and *behavioral* because the main consequence of interest in our line of work will be the effects of inhibition on the behaviors that people subsequently show. In the current research we examine how this analysis may contribute to insights about when people affiliate with and conform to their fellow research participants.

The Current Research

In the present paper we aim to combine the insights on conformity (Asch, 1951, 1955), behavioral affiliation (Schachter, 1959; Leary, 2010), and associated literatures (Murray, 1938; Sherif and Sherif, 1964; Clausen, 1968; Erikson, 1968; Aronson, 1972; McClelland, 1987; Wolf, 2008) with the idea that people try to make sense of their surroundings, including psychology experiments in which they are taking part with other participants (Cottrell et al., 1968; Rosenberg, 1980; Christensen, 1982; Geen, 1983, 1985; Van den Bos, 2013). Specifically, we attempt to integrate these insights with recent work that suggests that people in many social situations are inhibited from showing important social behaviors (Van den Bos, 2013). That is, we argue that if participants in psychology experiments in which they are expecting to interact with others indeed are inhibited from showing their social behaviors, as has been suggested in recent papers (Van den Bos et al., 2009, 2011b; Van den Bos, 2013), and if young people such as university students are indeed oriented toward their peers, as important scholars have argued (Schwarz, 1973; Harris, 1995; Sundar et al., 2009), then it should be the case that lowering behavioral inhibition will lead people to show increased affiliation with peers or others who are close or similar to them. Our previous research shows that behavioral inhibition can be lowered by reminding people of times in the past when they acted without inhibitions (Van den Bos et al., 2009, 2011b). Thus, reminding people of past disinhibited behaviors should lead them to affiliate more (not less) with their peers.

In four studies we examine the implications of this hypothesis on the actual behavior of research participants. To connect our research directly to the influence of social threats we focus in Studies 1 and 2 on people's behavior in the Asch (1951, 1955, 1956) paradigm. That is, in Studies 1 and 2 we argue that if reminders of behavioral disinhibition indeed lead people to affiliate more with their peers, they should be willing to conform more with what their peers do. Indeed, we reveal in Studies 1 and 2 that reminding people of having acted without inhibitions leads them to conform more (not less) with the wrong answers given by fellow research participants in the Asch paradigm.

We then use Studies 3 and 4 to generalize the effects of disinhibition to other measures of peer affiliation. In particular, in Studies 3 and 4 we note that increased affiliation with peers should be shown in university students wanting to sit closer to a fellow student from their university (cf. Macrae et al., 1994; Van den Bos et al., 2007). Indeed, in Study 3 we reveal that reminding university students of having acted without inhibitions leads them to sit closer to a fellow research participant, and not closer to the experimenter. Furthermore, in Study 4 we show that reminders of behavioral disinhibition lead students to sit closer to a student from their own university, and not closer to a student from a rival other university. Thus, taken together, our four studies reveal that reminders of behavioral disinhibition increase public conformity in the Asch paradigm and behavioral affiliation with ingroup members.

In all four studies we use a behavioral disinhibition manipulation that we developed and validated in earlier research (see Van den Bos et al., 2009, 2011b). Our manipulation asks participants in the disinhibition condition to answer three simple open-ended questions that remind them about their thoughts and feelings about having behaved without inhibitions. In the control condition participants answer similar questions that do not remind participants about disinhibited behaviors.

Van den Bos et al. (2009) showed that this way of reminding (vs. not reminding) participants of having acted without behavioral inhibitions successfully lowers behavioral inhibition as assessed by a state version of the popular and well-validated measure of BIS sensitivity by Carver and White (1994). Specifically, after completing the three disinhibition questions or the three control questions, participants completed the following seven state BIS items. Following Carver and White (1994) these items asked participants to indicate to what extent they agreed or disagreed with the following statements: "At this moment, I worry about making mistakes"; "At this moment, criticism or scolding would hurt me quite a bit"; "At this moment, I would feel pretty worried or upset when I think or know somebody is angry at me"; "At this moment, I do not experience fear or nervousness, even when something bad is about to happen to me" (reverse coded); "At this moment, I would get pretty worked up when I would know that something unpleasant is going to happen"; "At this moment, I would feel worried when I would think I have done poorly at something"; "At this moment, I have very few fears compared to my friends" (reverse coded). All items were answered on 7-point scales (1 = *strongly disagree*, 7 = *strongly agree*). Reliability of the resulting state scale BIS scale was good (Cronbach's alpha = 0.76). Results reported in Van

den Bos et al. (2009) showed that the disinhibition manipulation successfully lowered behavioral inhibition such that participants in the disinhibition condition experienced significantly lower levels of state behavioral inhibition than participants in the no-disinhibition condition.

Furthermore, the disinhibition manipulation yields effects comparable to differences on Carver and White's (1994) measure of trait BIS (see Van den Bos et al., 2011a,b). In addition, the manipulation does not trigger behavioral activation [no effects were found on state versions of Carver and White, 1994, behavioral activation scales (BAS)] nor does it influence positive or negative affective states [no effects were found on the positive and negative subsets of the Positive and Negative Affect Schedule (PANAS) by Watson et al., 1988; see Van den Bos et al., 2009, 2011b]. Moreover, the manipulation does not affect self-monitoring nor experienced accountability or self-awareness (Van den Bos et al., 2011b). Participants in studies using this manipulation typically indicate no suspicion of the procedures employed during the disinhibition manipulation nor do they suspect a direct relationship between the manipulation and their subsequent reactions in other parts of the experiments (Van den Bos et al., 2009, 2011b). Furthermore, the effects of the disinhibition manipulation can be found both among students in the psychology laboratory and in non-student samples outside the psychology laboratory (Van den Bos et al., 2009, 2011b). And in all the studies that have used this manipulation, gender did not interact with the effects of the disinhibition manipulation. Gender also does not affect the findings we will report here.

Thus, the reminders of behavioral disinhibition that we use in our studies have been pretested extensively. These earlier tests show that this is a manipulation that is conceptually related to the BIS as defined by Carver and White (1994; see also Van den Bos, 2013), significantly lowers state behavioral inhibition (Van den Bos et al., 2009), yields comparable effects as associated individual difference variables (Van den Bos et al., 2011a,b), and does so without affecting alternative concepts such as behavioral activation, affective states, self-monitoring, or accountability (Van den Bos et al., 2009, 2011b). What effects do these reminders of behavioral disinhibition have on conformity and affiliation with peers?

Study 1

In Studies 1 and 2 we examine whether reminding people of having acted without inhibitions lead them to conform more in public with the wrong answers given by other participants in the Asch (1951, 1955, 1956) paradigm. In Study 1, participants completed reminders of disinhibition or no disinhibition, after which they were asked to participate in a human perception task. In this task, participants were asked to indicate publicly which of three lines was equal in length to stimulus lines. In the condition in which confederates were present, four other supposed participants gave wrong answers in 10 critical trials. We assessed how many wrong answers the actual participants gave during the critical trials. In Study 1, we compared these responses with answers given in a condition where no confederates were present.

Method
Participants and Design

Eighty-six students (31 men and 55 women) at Utrecht University participated in the study and were randomly assigned to one of the cells of the 2 (confederates: present vs. absent) × 2 (behavioral disinhibition: disinhibition vs. no disinhibition) factorial design.[1,2] Participants received 3 Euros for their participation in the study.

Procedure

The experiment was presented to the participants as consisting of two unrelated parts. In the first part, the disinhibition manipulation took place. This manipulation used the same procedures developed and extensively pretested in earlier research (for details, see Van den Bos et al., 2009, 2011a,b). Specifically, participants were asked to complete a short questionnaire of three open-ended questions. Participants in the disinhibition condition were instructed as follows:

The purpose of this questionnaire is to assess how people react to being disinhibited, that is, how people behave when they do not care about what others think of their reactions and what feelings they then experience. To this end, please complete the following three questions: Please briefly describe a situation out of your own life in which you acted without inhibitions. Please briefly describe how you behaved in the situation in which you acted without inhibitions. Please briefly describe the emotions that you experienced when you acted without inhibitions.

In the no-disinhibition condition participants completed a short questionnaire of three open-ended questions pertaining to public transportation. Specifically, participants in the no-disinhibition condition received the following instruction:

The purpose of this questionnaire is to assess how people react to using public transportation, that is, how people behave when they use public transportation and what feelings they then experience. To this end, please complete the following three questions: Please briefly describe a situation out of your own life in which you used public transportation. Please briefly describe how you behaved in the situation in which you used public transportation. Please briefly describe the emotions that you experienced when you used public transportation.

After the disinhibition manipulation, participants were informed that the first part of the study had ended and that the second part now would begin. In this part, participants were asked to participate in a study on human perception. Based on the meta-review by Bond (2005), which shows that when three or more confederates are present the tendency to conform tends to be stable, participants in the condition in which confederates were present took part in this study together with four other participants (in reality confederates who were blind to conditions). In the condition in which confederates were absent there were no other participants.

Participants were presented a total of 17 sets of vertical lines, projected on a big white screen. Each set consisted of one stimulus line and three other lines (A, B, and C). To make our stimulus materials a bit different from the original Asch materials (which consisted of horizontal lines) we used vertical lines.[3] The stimulus line was presented at the top of the screen and the three other lines beneath the stimulus line. After the presentation of each set of lines, participants were asked to indicate out loud which of the three other lines was equal in length to the stimulus line.

In the condition in which confederates were present, three confederates first gave their answers, after which the actual participant gave his or her answer, followed by the answer of the last confederate. As in the original Asch experiment, the confederates started by answering a few questions correctly but eventually began providing incorrect responses. That is, during 7 of the 17 trials (Trials 1, 2, 5, 8, 11, 14, and 17) the confederates gave the correct answers. During the 10 other trials the confederates gave a uniformly wrong answer. Our dependent variable assessed how many wrong answers (0–10) the actual participants gave during the 10 critical trials.

At the end of the experiment, participants were thoroughly debriefed. During debriefing, participants indicated no suspicion of the procedures employed nor did they suspect a direct relationship between the disinhibition manipulation and their reactions in the perception study.

Results

A 2 (confederates) × 2 (disinhibition) analysis of variance on our conformity measure (the number of wrong answers given by the participants during the critical trials) revealed a main effect of confederates being present or absent, $F(1,82) = 62.39, p < 0.001$, $\eta_p^2 = 0.43$, a main effect of disinhibition, $F(1,82) = 10.11$, $p < 0.01$, $\eta_p^2 = 0.11$, and a significant interaction between the confederates and disinhibition manipulations, $F(1,82) = 8.28$, $p < 0.01$, $\eta_p^2 = 0.09$. **Figure 1** shows the effects together with the respective standard errors. In the condition in which confederates were present, participants gave more wrong answers when they had been reminded about disinhibited behavior ($M = 4.75$, $SD = 3.19$) than when they had not been reminded about disinhibited behavior ($M = 2.35$, $SD = 2.16$), $F(1,84) = 6.34$, $p < 0.02$, $\eta_p^2 = 0.07$. In the condition in which confederates were absent, there was no significant effect of the disinhibition manipulation, $F(1,84) = 0.03$, $p = 0.86$, $\eta_p^2 = 0.00$. Participants in this condition did not gave many wrong answers following

---

[1] In all studies of this paper, gender was proportionally distributed among conditions. Furthermore, gender did not interact with the hypotheses under consideration and hence was dropped from the analyses.

[2] We report all manipulations, all data exclusions, and all measures in our studies (Simmons et al., 2012), so we note that in Study 1, 14 extra participants took part in the experiment and were removed from the analyses reported: Three participants knew about the Asch experiments, one participant indicated suspicion about the experimental procedure used, eight participants had to omitted because faults in the experimental procedures were made when running these participants, and two participants from the no-disinhibition control condition were removed from the analyses because inspecting Cook's (1977) distance measure in our main analysis (Cohen et al., 2003) revealed that they showed a distance score of more than 3.50 SDs above the mean. We further note that after assessing conformity in Studies 1 and 2, and measuring distance in Studies 3 and 4, participants completed some questionnaires. The results of these questionnaire findings are not discussed here and are available on request.

[3] Debriefing indicated that participants of Studies 1 and 2 did not see a relationship between our studies and the original Asch (1951, 1955, 1956) experiments, with the exception of the participants mentioned in Footnotes 2 and 5 who were omitted from the analyses presented.

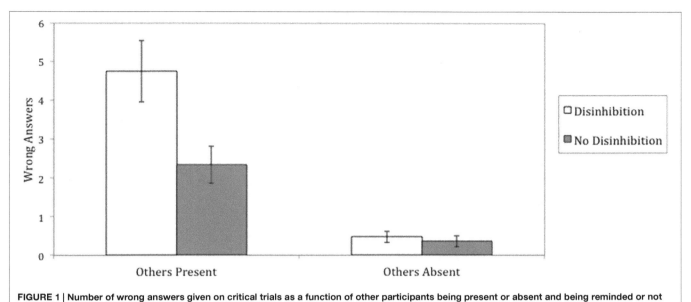

FIGURE 1 | Number of wrong answers given on critical trials as a function of other participants being present or absent and being reminded or not about disinhibited behavior (Study 1). Error bars represent standard errors of the mean.

the presence of reminders of behavioral disinhibition ($M = 0.48$, $SD = 0.77$) or following the absence of these reminders ($M = 0.36$, $SD = 0.70$).[4]

In addition, please note that when participants had not been reminded about disinhibited behavior, they gave more wrong answers following the presence as opposed to absence of confederates, $F(1,84) = 8.81$, $p < 0.01$, $\eta_p^2 = 0.09$. This replicated the original Asch finding. Furthermore, supporting our predictions, in the condition in which participants had been reminded about disinhibited behavior, the effect of confederates being present or absent was three times as large, $F(1,84) = 37.37$, $p < 0.001$, $\eta_p^2 = 0.31$, than when participants had not been reminded about disinhibited behavior.

Study 2

Study 1 reveals that reminding people of having acted without inhibitions lead them to conform more in public with the wrong answers given by other participants in the Asch (1951, 1955, 1956) paradigm. Reminders of disinhibition do not affect participants' line size perceptions when no other participants are present, suggesting that the effect of disinhibition reminders is not a perceptual phenomenon, but instigates increased conformity with peers.

Study 2 attempted to replicate the effect of reminders of behavioral disinhibition on conformity reactions. We did this

[4]Controlling for heterogeneity using the Welch–Satterthwaite approach (Satterthwaite, 1946; Welch, 1947) yielded the same results: a significant interaction between the confederates and disinhibition manipulations, $F(1,27.85) = 5.69$, $p < 0.03$, indicating a significant effect of the disinhibition manipulation when confederates were present, $F(1,25.30) = 6.62$, $p < 0.02$, and a non-significant effect when confederates were absent, $F(1,47.57) = 0.33$, $p > 0.56$. Thus, heterogeneity does not affect the conclusions regarding Study 1. Furthermore, heterogeneity of variance was not an issue in the other experiments reported in this paper.

in an experiment in which there were always three confederate participants present. After all, Study 1 showed that the effect of the disinhibition reminders was only there in the condition in which four confederates were present, and in Study 2 we wanted to see whether we could replicate the effects of the disinhibition reminders in the presence of only three confederates.

Study 2 also sought to refine our understanding of what it is in our disinhibition manipulation that causes the effect. Note that the disinhibition manipulation used in the first study reminds people of how they "react to being disinhibited, that is, how people behave when they do not care about what others think of their reactions." This is a rather general manipulation of public behavioral disinhibition (Van den Bos et al., 2009, 2011a,b). Of course, evidence for our line of reasoning would be stronger if we could specify what this manipulation entails in somewhat more detailed terms.

In a pilot study we determined that most of our participants (Utrecht University students), when asked to indicate what they did when they acted without concerns for others present in their situation, pointed out that they voiced their own opinions in the presence of others. Voicing of opinions is an important issue to people (e.g., Hirschman, 1970; Folger, 1977; Van den Bos, 1999). In Study 2, therefore, before participants took part in the Asch paradigm we exposed them to reminders of general behavioral disinhibition, no disinhibition, or reminders of voicing their own opinions without much concerns for others present. If our reminders of general behavioral disinhibition are predominantly about disinhibition pertaining to voicing one's own opinions, as our pilot study suggested, then the general disinhibition condition should yield about the same level of conformity as the condition in which people were reminded about disinhibited behaviors regarding voicing of their own opinions.

Building on Study 1, we again expected that the lowest levels of conformity would be shown in the absence of reminders of disinhibition. To make conforming a more attractive and easier to choose option we made the stimulus lines and the other lines more comparable to each other. Compared to Study 1 this should lead to more conformity in the no-disinhibition condition, hence providing a tougher test of our prediction that there should be more conformity in the disinhibition conditions (either general or voice disinhibition) than in the no-disinhibition condition.

Method
Participants and Design
Sixty-two students (15 men and 47 women) at Utrecht University participated in the study and were randomly assigned to one of the conditions of the behavioral disinhibition manipulation (general disinhibition, voice disinhibition, no disinhibition).[5] Participants were paid 3 Euros for their participation.

Procedure
As in Study 1, the disinhibition manipulation took place in the first part of the study. The no-disinhibition condition was the same as in Study 1. The instructions in the "general disinhibition" condition were the same as those used in the disinhibition conditions of Study 1. In the condition in which participants were reminded about "disinhibition regarding voice," participants were instructed as follows:

The purpose of this questionnaire is to assess how people react to being disinhibited, that is, how people voice their own opinions in the presence of others such that they do not care about what others think of their reactions and what feelings they then experience. To this end, please complete the following three questions: Please briefly describe a situation out of your own life in which you felt no inhibitions to voice your own opinions. Please briefly describe how you behaved in the situation in which you voiced your own opinions without inhibitions. Please briefly describe the emotions that you experienced when you voiced your own opinions without inhibitions.

The second part of Study 2 was the same as in Study 1, with this time three confederate participants present in all conditions and (as in the original Asch experiment) the actual participant always being the last to answer which line resembled the stimulus line.

Participants were thoroughly debriefed at the end of the experiment. Again, participants indicated no suspicion of the procedures employed and did not suspect a direct relationship between the disinhibition manipulation and their reactions in the perception study.

Results
An analysis of variance showed a significant effect of the disinhibition manipulation on our conformity measure (the number of wrong answers given by the participants during the critical trials), $F(2,59) = 3.31$, $p < 0.05$, $\eta_p^2 = 0.10$. **Figure 2** shows the effect together with the respective standard errors. When participants had been reminded about general disinhibited behavior they conformed more with the wrong answers given by the confederate participants ($M = 4.80$, SD $= 2.48$) than when they had not been reminded about disinhibited behavior ($M = 3.24$, SD $= 1.58$), $F(1,60) = 4.72$, $p < 0.04$, $\eta_p^2 = 0.07$. Furthermore, when participants had been reminded about disinhibition regarding voice they also conformed more ($M = 4.86$, SD $= 2.71$) than when they had not been reminded about disinhibited behavior, $F(1,60) = 5.14$, $p < 0.03$, $\eta_p^2 = 0.08$. Conformity did not differ between the general disinhibition and voice disinhibition conditions, $F(1,60) = 0.00, p > 0.91, \eta_p^2 = 0.00$.

Study 3

Studies 1 and 2 focused on the dynamics of how people respond to threats in social interactions, in particular Asch experiments in which there is pressure to publicly conform with faulty answers of fellow participants. Study 1 demonstrated that reminding people about having acted without inhibitions lead them to conform more with the faulty answers their fellow research participants give. Study 2 replicated this effect and in addition demonstrates that similar levels of enhanced conformity are found following reminders of general behavioral disinhibition and following reminders of having voiced one's own opinions without inhibitions.

Our line of reasoning suggested that in social threatening situations people want to behaviorally affiliate with those who are similar to them (such as their fellow research participants) but can be inhibited in showing their behavioral affiliation tendencies. After all, both behavioral affiliation (e.g., Hill, 1987) and behavioral inhibition (e.g., Gray, 1987; Gray and McNaughton, 2000) are responses that people frequently show when responding to social threats. Studies 3 and 4 aim to generalize the effects of disinhibition reminders to direct measures of peer affiliation. In particular, the student participants in Studies 3 and 4 are told that they will take part in psychology experiments with other students and we assess behavioral affiliation with peers by measuring how close our participants will sit to fellow students (Macrae et al., 1994; Van den Bos et al., 2007).

Studies 3 and 4 also extend Studies 1 and 2 by focusing on participant reactions to taking part in psychology experiments in which they merely expect to interact with other people. After all, there are many instances in which people seek to interact with others that do not involve stressful or distressing circumstances (Leary, 2010) and that involve more general sense-making processes (Van den Bos, 2013). The kind of psychology experiments on which we focus in Studies 3 and 4 may well resemble those situations that Schachter (1959) explored when noting that people who are uncertain about the nature of a situation will be motivated to affiliate with similar others to find out what to expect and how to behave in the new situation at hand.

In Study 3 we reminded our participants about times they had acted without inhibitions (disinhibition conditions) or how they act on normal days (no-disinhibition conditions). We did

---

[5]In Study 2, 14 extra participants took part and were removed from the analyses presented: Five participants knew about the Asch experiments, three participants had to omitted because faults in the experimental procedures were made when running these participants, five participants had difficulty understanding the questions asked to them, and one participant from the no-disinhibition control condition was removed from the analyses because inspecting Cook's distance measure in our main analysis indicated that this participant showed a distance score of more than 2.75 SDs above the mean.

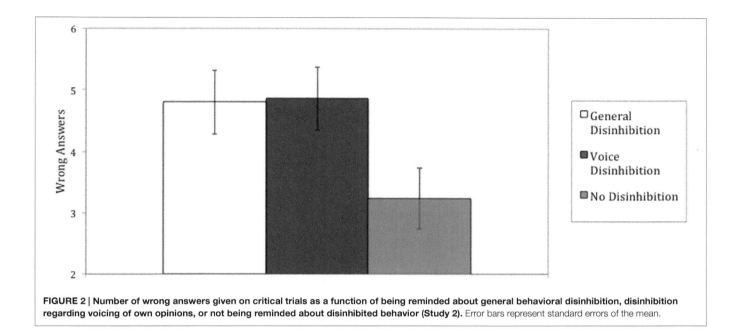

FIGURE 2 | Number of wrong answers given on critical trials as a function of being reminded about general behavioral disinhibition, disinhibition regarding voicing of own opinions, or not being reminded about disinhibited behavior (Study 2). Error bars represent standard errors of the mean.

this using the method of earlier studies that extensively pretested this manipulation of behavioral disinhibition (Van den Bos et al., 2009, 2011a,b). After this, in a separate part of the experiment, participants were brought to a big room where they saw a small desk and a row of seven chairs. Building on and extending the method used by Macrae et al. (1994; see also Van den Bos et al., 2007), the desk at the left was where the experimenter would sit and the chair on the right was where another participant would sit. The chair in which participants sat down was our dependent variable, providing an indication of how much participants wanted to be closer to the other participant or to the experimenter.

Thus, the dependent variable was the distance, in number of chairs, between the chair with the belongings on it and the chair that the participant chose to sit on. This task measures interpersonal social distance (see Holland et al., 2004). Indeed, physical and social distances have been shown to be conceptually related (Bar-Anan et al., 2007). If our hypothesis was true that behavioral disinhibition would lead participants to want to affiliate with their peers, then we should see that reminding our student participants of disinhibited behaviors would lead them to sit closer to the other participant. In other words, we should see that reminders of behavioral disinhibition should lead to behavioral affiliation with a peer, not with an authority such as an experimenter.

Another advantage of this experimental set-up was that it allowed us to assess *behavioral* affiliation. Social psychology has always been aware that it is important to show effects of its concepts on people's behavioral reactions (instead of only showing effects on cognitive responses, perceptions, affective reactions, or intentions), yet frequently our research does not provide behavioral data (Greenberg, 1987; Jones, 1998; Baumeister et al., 2007). Furthermore, from an applied point of view it is interesting to see whether just asking people to complete three questions

that remind them of their disinhibited behaviors has behavioral consequences on where they sit down in a room.

Method
Participants and Design
Sixty students (17 men and 43 women) at Utrecht University were randomly assigned to either the disinhibition or no-disinhibition conditions. Participants received 3 Euros for their participation.

Procedure
The experiment was presented to the participants as two separate studies. In the first study, the disinhibition manipulation was induced. The instructions in the disinhibition condition were the same as in Studies 1 and 2. Following earlier studies (Van den Bos et al., 2009, 2011a,b), participants in the no-disinhibition condition completed a short questionnaire of three open-ended questions pertaining to how they experience a normal day. Specifically, instructions were as follows:

The purpose of this questionnaire is to assess how people experience a normal day in their lives, that is, how people usually behave on a regular day and what feelings they then experience. To this end, please complete the following three questions: Please briefly describe a situation out of your own life in which you acted in a normal way like you do on a regular day. Please briefly describe how you behave when you act in a normal way like you do on a regular day. Please briefly describe the emotions that you experience when you act in a normal way on a regular day.

After the disinhibition manipulation the experimenter told participants that the first study had ended and that the second study now would begin. This second study would take place in another room across the hall. The experimenter, carrying some papers, escorted one participant at a time to this room. Upon entering the room, the participant saw a small desk and a row of seven chairs. The desk was placed at the left of the room. The experimenter put down his papers on the desk and pointed out that the desk was the place where he would sit during the second part of the study. On the right-hand chair hang a coat and below the chair there was a bag. The experimenter said: "You will participate in this study together with another student. You see the student is already there [pointing at the right-hand chair]. This student is now in the bathroom and will be back in a moment. Please seat yourself at one of the chairs and wait till the other student gets back. I will check how the other student is doing. After this, we will start the study." The experimenter then ostensibly started walking out of the room but did not actually leave the room until the participant had sat down on one of the chairs. In this way, the experimenter could assess in which chair the participant sat (1 = *immediately next to the other participant's chair*, 6 = *immediately next to the experimenter's desk*) and this constituted our dependent variable.

After participants sat down, they were thoroughly debriefed. Participants indicated no suspicion of the procedures employed. Furthermore, they did not suspect a direct relationship between the disinhibition manipulation in the first study and the chair in which they sat in the second study in which they participated.

Results

An analysis of variance revealed a significant effect of the disinhibition manipulation on our distance measure (sitting close to or distant from the other participant), $F(1,58) = 5.97$, $p < 0.02$, $\eta_p^2 = 0.09$. When participants had been reminded about disinhibited behavior they sat closer to the other participant ($M = 2.07$, SD $= 0.83$) than when they had not been reminded about disinhibited behavior ($M = 2.87$, SD $= 1.59$).

Study 4

In accordance with our line of reasoning Study 3 reveals that reminding people of having acted without inhibitions lead them to sit closer to a fellow research participant. The reminders of behavioral disinhibition did not lead our student participants to sit closer to the experimenter. These findings suggest that disinhibition leads to behavioral affiliation with peers, not with authorities.

The aim of Study 4 was to replicate the finding that reminding people of having acted without inhibitions lead them to affiliate behaviorally with those who are close or similar to them, and not with those who are less similar to them. To this end, participants (students at Utrecht University) again first completed the reminders of disinhibition or no disinhibition, and then were asked to take a seat in a row of seven chairs. To rule out possible alternative explanations, there was no experimenter desk in Study 4 and we varied whose belongings were on the right-hand chair in the room: These belongings were said to be from another student at Utrecht University or were from a student from a rival university. If our hypothesis was true that behavioral disinhibition would lead to behavioral affiliation especially with similar people, then we should find that reminders of behavioral disinhibition will lead our participants to sit closer to the student from their own university, but not closer to the student from the rival university.

Method
Participants and Design

Eighty students (25 men and 55 women) at Utrecht University were randomly assigned to one of the cells of the 2 (university affiliation of other student: same university vs. other university) × 2 (behavioral disinhibition: disinhibition vs. no disinhibition) factorial design. They received 3 Euros for their participation.

Procedure

The experiment was presented as two separate studies. In the first study, the disinhibition manipulation was induced in the same way as in Study 3. After this, the first study ended and the second study began. Walking to the room in which the second study would take place, the experimenter informed participants that they would participate in the second study together with another participant. The university affiliation manipulation varied whether the experimenter told our Utrecht University participants that the other participant was from Utrecht University (ingroup affiliation condition) or was from Leiden University (outgroup affiliation condition). When entering the room, participants saw a row of seven chairs. On the right-hand chair hang a coat and below the chair there was a bag. The experimenter said: "As I told you, you will participate in this study together with the other student. This student will be back in a moment. Please seat yourself at one of the chairs and wait till the other student gets back." The chair in which participants sat down (1 = *immediately next to the other participant's chair*, 6 = *furthest away from the other participant's chair*) served as the dependent variable of Study 4.

After participants sat down, they were thoroughly debriefed. Participants indicated no suspicion of the procedures employed and did not suspect a direct relationship between the disinhibition manipulation and the chair on which they sat down.

Results

A 2 (university affiliation of other student) × 2 (disinhibition) analysis of variance on the distance measure showed only a significant interaction effect between the university affiliation and disinhibition manipulations, $F(1,76) = 5.39$, $p < 0.03$, $\eta_p^2 = 0.07$. **Figure 3** illustrates the effect together with the respective standard errors. When interacting with the student from their own university, participants sat closer to the other participant when they had been reminded about disinhibited behavior ($M = 2.55$, SD $= 0.89$) than when they had not been reminded about disinhibited behavior ($M = 3.35$, SD $= 1.31$), $F(1,76) = 4.41$, $p < 0.04$, $\eta_p^2 = 0.05$. When interacting with the student from the other university, being reminded about disinhibited behavior ($M = 3.55$, SD $= 1.32$) or not being reminded about disinhibited behavior ($M = 3.10$, SD $= 1.25$) did not significantly affect where participants sat down, $F(1,76) = 1.40$, $p > 0.24$, $\eta_p^2 = 0.02$.

In addition, it is worth mentioning that in the disinhibition condition participants sat closer to the student from the same university than from the other university, $F(1,76) = 6.89$, $p < 0.02$, $\eta_p^2 = 0.08$. The effect of university affiliation was not statistically

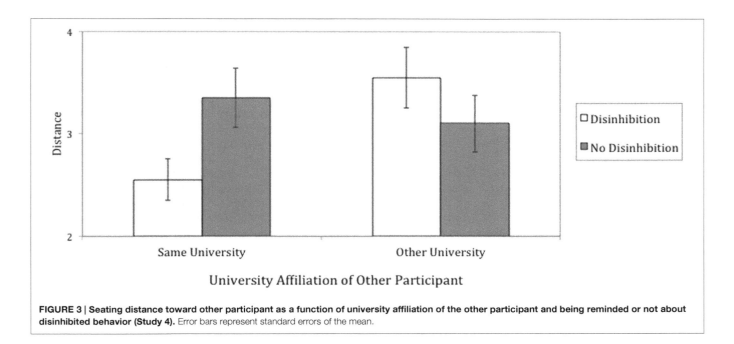

FIGURE 3 | Seating distance toward other participant as a function of university affiliation of the other participant and being reminded or not about disinhibited behavior (Study 4). Error bars represent standard errors of the mean.

significant in the no-disinhibition condition, $F(1,76) = 0.43$, $p > 0.51$, $\eta_p^2 = 0.01$.

General Discussion

Four experiments focused on the dynamics of how people respond to threats in social interactions. We examined this issue by means of Asch experiments in which there was pressure to publicly conform with faulty answers of fellow participants (Studies 1 and 2). We also studied behavioral affiliation by means of seating distance measures in psychology experiments in which people were expecting to interact with other participants (Studies 3 and 4). All studies demonstrate that reminding people of having acted without inhibitions leads them to show behaviors that are more oriented toward their peers, in these studies peers being fellow research participants who are similar or close to them.

In particular, Study 4 reveals that reminding people about having acted without inhibitions leads them to sit closer to fellow research participants from their own university, and not closer to those who are from a rival other university. This suggests that reminders of disinhibited behaviors lead people to affiliate behaviorally with people who are similar to them. This effect is in line with Study 3 in which we found that participants who had been reminded about behavioral disinhibition sat closer to a fellow research participant and not closer to the experimenter. Thus, Studies 3 and 4 suggest that disinhibited individuals want to affiliate with their peers, that is, that they want to be with those who are similar to them and not with those who have authority over them (Study 3) and not with those who are members from an outgroup (Study 4). Taken together, the current experiments reveal a pioneering finding that the disinhibited individual wants to affiliate behaviorally and conform his or her behaviors with those who are similar to them.

Possible Implications

A noteworthy aspect of all our four experiments is that we obtained our effects on the actual behavior of our participants. In this way the four studies that we report contribute to pleas that social psychology should provide behavioral data (not just cognitive responses, perceptions, affective reactions, or intentions; see, e.g., Greenberg, 1987; Jones, 1998; Vohs et al., 2006; Baumeister et al., 2007). In addition, the behavioral effects we obtained on participants' behavior are especially remarkable, we think, because we obtained them using a manipulation that consisted only of completing three questions. The findings we report here reveal that this somewhat modest manipulation yields reliable and consistent effects on participants' actual behavior.

The findings in our first Asch experiment were obtained by contrasting reactions given in the presence of confederates who gave wrong answers with reactions given in the absence of those confederates. Importantly, the effects of our disinhibition manipulation were only found in the presence of confederates and hence only when pressure to conform to fellow research participants was high and not when this pressure was absent. Pressure to conform constitutes an important threat in social interactions and is an important reason why people affiliate with others (Hill, 1987), so this is one way in which we studied the dynamics of social threats in the current paper.

Following Schachter (1959) and others (e.g., Leary, 2010) we also examined the effects of reminders of behavioral disinhibition in situations in which we assumed that participants would be at least somewhat uncertain as to how they should behave exactly. We studied this issue in psychology experiments in which participants were expecting to interact with other participants. We note explicitly that we did not have conditions in those studies (nor in Study 2) in which the assumed social threats or uncertainties about how to behave were contrasted with conditions in which threats and/or uncertainties clearly were absent. Furthermore, the assumed threatening or uncertainty-provoking aspects of these situations were not measured in our studies. One reason for this is because it may be very difficult to reliably measure perceived threat or uncertainties (see, e.g., Van den Bos, 2009; Van den Bos and Lind, 2009). This noted, we would applaud it when future research would include more control conditions as well as sensitive measures of threat or uncertainty that would show robust evidence for the line of reasoning proposed here, for example by means of moderation or mediation analyses.

When we inspected what participants wrote down when answering the questions that asked them about their disinhibited behaviors we found that they were describing situations in which they did not feel strong public constraints on their behaviors, such as when they were attending big dance parties or other events in which they felt they could do whatever they wanted to do without others constraining their behaviors (see also Van den Bos et al., 2009, 2011a,b).

Importantly, our disinhibition manipulation does not ask participants to think about situation in which they did not follow group norms, rather it is a more general manipulation that ask them to think back about situations in which they did not care about what others were thinking of their reactions. Thus, the manipulation is not a group-related manipulation *per se*. Furthermore, when we inspected what participants wrote down when answering the disinhibition questions we did not find strong evidence that participants thought about groups and their not following group norms. Thus, we do not think the disinhibition manipulation is strongly or directly related to group behavior or group norms. We think it is better viewed of as a manipulation of interpersonal disinhibited behavior, thus behavior against other people (not necessarily groups or group members).

Previous findings have shown that our disinhibition manipulation is conceptually related to the BIS (Carver and White, 1994; Van den Bos, 2013), significantly lowers state behavioral inhibition (Van den Bos et al., 2009), yields comparable effects to those of individual differences in trait behavioral inhibition (Van den Bos et al., 2011a), and does so without engendering experimenter demands or affecting alternative concepts such as behavioral activation, affective states, self-monitoring, or accountability (Van den Bos et al., 2009, 2011a,b). Study 2 extends these findings by showing that one important component of the effect of disinhibition manipulations may have to do with people feeling free to voice their own opinions in public. The findings we present here, together with earlier research (Van den Bos et al., 2009, 2011a,b), suggest that reminders of behavioral disinhibition have conceptually meaningful and statistically significant effects on what people actually do.

In developing our ideas about behavioral disinhibition, we built our theorizing not only on work on the BIS as developed by Gray (1987; Gray and McNaughton, 2000) and Carver and White (1994), but also on the work on public inhibition as defined by Latané and Nida (1981). Latané and Nida (1981) note that in public settings the presence of others can restrain people from showing their personal inclinations. For example, in a bystander dilemma a person may want to engage in helping behavior but may be restrained from doing so because of the presence of

others (bystanders) who are not helping. Similarly, we think that important elements in the psychology of inhibition and sense-making involve the issues of *public* and *behavioral* inhibition. *Public* because the inhibition of primary importance seems often to be instigated by thoughts of what others will think of our actions, and *behavioral* because the main consequence of interest in our line of work are the effects on the behaviors that people subsequently show. The studies we presented here are in line with this public and behavioral perspective on disinhibition. For example, our Studies 1 and 2 reveal that reminders of behavioral disinhibition lead to more public behavioral conformity. These findings extend insights derived from Asch's classic experiments on public conformity and contradict common sense by revealing that it is the disinhibited participant who shows more conformity.

Earlier research has highlighted the pernicious effects of behavioral disinhibition (e.g., Newman et al., 2005) and depicted behavioral disinhibition as antisocial (Lilienfeld, 1992), psychopathological (Nigg, 2000), and a source of unwanted acts (Peters et al., 2006). Along the same lines, an important theme in moral and political philosophy has been that humans should refrain from disinhibited behavior and that it would be better for the greater good if people acted with more inhibition than they normally do (e.g., Kant, 1959). In contrast, our research program thus far has highlighted more benign effects of behavioral disinhibition. For example, we showed that following reminders of behavioral disinhibition people do not suffer from the usual bystander effects that limit helping (Van den Bos et al., 2009) and are more likely to resist advantageous but unfair outcomes (Van den Bos et al., 2011b).

Going beyond these insights, the current studies provide a more nuanced perspective on behavioral disinhibition. Yes, reminders of behavioral disinhibition can lead people to conform with faulty answers given by fellow research participants (Studies 1 and 2), but our work suggests that is it is not just the case that disinhibition provokes conformity. Rather, the link between disinhibition and conformity should be understood in light of the fact that following disinhibition reminders people want to affiliate with those who are close or similar to them (Studies 3 and 4). Thus, behavioral disinhibition is best not viewed as unequivocally bad (e.g., Kant, 1959) or antisocial (Lilienfeld, 1992), but rather should be viewed of as triggering peer-oriented responses. This can lead to benign effects, such as helping of peers in need (Van den Bos et al., 2009) or rejection of outcomes that are unfairly better than outcomes of peers (Van den Bos et al., 2011b), but also to conformity with faulty behaviors of those peers (Studies 1 and 2). Behavioral disinhibition as a trigger of increased peer affiliation yields a new, more precise, and more nuanced understanding of behavioral disinhibition than seen previously in the research literature (e.g., Lilienfeld, 1992; Nigg, 2000; Suler, 2004; Peters et al., 2006; Van den Bos et al., 2009, 2011b).

An Alternative Account of the Data: Belongingness Threat and Optimal Distinctiveness

The empirical observation that reminders of behavioral disinhibition are related to more conformity and more group affiliation is an intriguing effect. In fact, we think that the counterintuitive quality may be part of what makes this effect so interesting. This noted, the exact psychological processes instigated by our reminders of behavioral disinhibition should be examined in more detail in future research. Although earlier evidence revealed that the disinhibition manipulation attenuates a state version of the Carver and White (1994) behavioral inhibition scale, and does not influence state versions of the Carver and White BAS and also does not have reliable effects on positive and negative affective states, self-monitoring, accountability, or self-awareness (Van den Bos et al., 2009, 2011b), more insights into these issues is needed. After all, there are different conceptualizations and associated measures of behavioral inhibition and activation out there and these conceptualizations and measures may well yield better insight into the exact psychological processes triggered by our disinhibition manipulation.

An important possibility that needs to be examined carefully in future research is whether being reminded of one's own socially deviant behavior can constitute a threat to social belonging and optimal distinctiveness. After all, it could be argued that being reminded about not having cared about what others think of your reactions might lead participants to realize that there have been instances in which they acted too individualistically and did not pay enough attention to important social connections. Arguably, this might threaten the balance between people wanting to belong to important social groups and form meaningful social connections and their desire to be unique individuals who stand out a bit (but not too much) from other persons, other groups, and other social connections.

Optimal distinctiveness theory (e.g., Brewer, 1991) suggests that reminders of being individuated should increase affiliative needs and thus the enhance motivation to belong to social groups. There is certainly evidence for this effect, beginning with the work presented in Brewer's (1991) initial article on that prominent model. Thus, our reminders of behavioral disinhibition might in fact have disturbed the balance of optimal distinctiveness and might have instigated belonging threats to at least some of the participants. Viewed in this way the effects reported in the present article would conceptually replicate studies demonstrating that after reminders of possible social exclusion people show affiliative tendencies, such as mimicry or norm conformity (see, e.g., Leary, 2010).

Thus, optimal distinctiveness and social belongingness threats may provide important alternative accounts of the findings we presented here. After all, an intriguing aspect of the current findings is that if the disinhibition manipulation induced people to feel free to voice their own opinions in public why they did not stick to the correct answer in the Asch paradigm? On the contrary, the manipulation seemed to have caused people to behave in such a way as to show a great deal of concern about social evaluation and a great deal of caring about what others think of their reactions. In short, optimal distinctiveness and social belonging may constitute important alternative accounts for explaining the effects of our manipulation.

We assumed that people are naturally inclined to affiliate with others but their natural inclination to affiliate with others can be inhibited. We further argued that the disinhibition manipulation allows participants to break free of this inhibited state and follow their natural inclination to affiliate with others. Importantly, our disinhibition manipulation (which involves having people think of a time in which they did not care about what others were thinking of their reactions) might cause an important affiliation threat to participants, which may partly help to explain our results.

Exploring the psychology of peer relations as well as group psychology may also be important in this regard. These concepts may share important similarities but may also differ in important ways from each other and understanding the similarities and differences between these concepts and related issues such as affiliation and belonging (Leary, 2010) may help to better understand the effects presented in the present paper.

To conclude this section, we strongly advocate for future research that would show whether and how our disinhibition manipulation is related to processes of social belonging and optimal distinctiveness. Obtaining these kinds of findings would elucidate the psychological processes underlying the behavioral effects reported here and elsewhere (see, e.g., Van den Bos et al., 2009, 2011a,b; Van den Bos and Lind, 2013). In earlier research we observed that our disinhibition manipulation successfully lowers a state version of the Carver and White (1994) BIS scale, so we also suggest that our manipulation is conceptually and empirically related to behavioral inhibition in social contexts as we defined it here and elsewhere (see, e.g., Van den Bos and Lind, 2013). More fine-grained insight into the psychological processes discussed here would add a significant contribution to theory building and would help to identify a fascinating field of research.

Other Possible Limitations

The concept of approach motivation may also help to interpret the findings reported here. For example, Harmon-Jones et al. (2013) conceptualize approach motivation as the urge to move toward something. Perhaps this suggests that our results suggest that people who overcome inhibition show approach-related behavior such that in Studies 1 and 2 people approach the opinion of their peers and that in Studies 3 and 4 people approach peers, in particular ingroup members. Thus, future research may want to focus on how approach-related behavior might be involved in the results presented here. Different operationalizations of approach motivation (see, e.g., Coan and Allen, 2003; Harmon-Jones et al., 2013) may be relevant here.

Another issue that should be examined is whether behavioral inhibition and activation are independent of each other. Many social psychologists have good reasons to consider the BIS and BAS as constituting independent systems (e.g., Carver and White, 1994; Gable et al., 2000; Gray and McNaughton, 2000), but current cognitive psychologists also tend to focus on the interaction between the BIS and BAS (e.g., Knyazev et al., 2006).

Of course, the findings of Studies 1 and 2 are limited to public conformity, which is not the same as private conformity (see Asch, 1951, 1955, 1956). This noted, Studies 1 and 2 suggest that following reminders of behavioral disinhibition people actively affiliate more with those who are similar to them, and it is certainly possible that this desire for greater affiliation will affect private, as well as public, conformity. Future research is needed to examine the effects of behavioral disinhibition on private conformity as well as its effects on additional other-oriented reactions, including relevant cognitions, feelings, and other internalized responses.

Although we believe that the effects of reminders of behavioral disinhibition are better studied using a chain of experiments (Spencer et al., 2005), rather than by attempting to tap intervening variables that may disturb the effects of the reminders, we do want to note explicitly that future research is needed to examine relevant moderators and mediators of the processes suggested by our findings. For example, in earlier research we found that differences in social value orientations moderate the effects of reminders of behavioral disinhibition on reactions to being overpaid (Van den Bos et al., 2011b). In contrast, though, social value orientations do not moderate the influence of behavioral disinhibition on reactions to bystander situations (Van den Bos et al., 2009), moral dilemmas (Van den Bos et al., 2011a), or the findings we presented in this paper. It appears that some processes, such as responses to bystander situations, moral dilemmas, behavioral affiliation settings, and conformity are so robust that they are not moderated by social value orientations, while other reactions, such as responses to being overpaid or to experiencing other mixed-motive situations, are susceptible to the moderating influence of social value orientations.

Do the findings we presented here imply that disinhibited people will seldom or never be influenced by authorities, but rather only by peers? Of course not. Research clearly shows that authorities can have strong influence on what people do (see, e.g., Cottrell et al., 1968; Milgram, 1974; Tyler and Lind, 1992). But our findings do suggest that the disinhibited individual is more likely to affiliate with their peers than with authorities

(see, e.g., Study 3). Future research should examine under what conditions affiliation with authorities becomes more likely. Future research should also explore other antecedents of behavioral affiliation and conformity, such as physical similarity (Mackinnon et al., 2011) or being mimicked by others (Van Baaren et al., 2003).

Conclusion

Building on and extending earlier work on behavioral inhibition (e.g., Latané and Nida, 1981; Carver and White, 1994; Gray and McNaughton, 2000) and behavioral disinhibition (e.g., Suler, 2004; Van den Bos et al., 2009, 2011a,b) the aim of this paper was to examine the dynamics of how people make sense of and respond behaviorally to threats in social interaction experiments. To this end, we delineated some important and unexplored effects of reminders of disinhibited behavior. In particular, we reasoned that reminders of behavioral disinhibition would want to affiliate with their peers more. Supporting this line of reasoning we found that reminders of disinhibition lead people to show more conformity with faulty answers given by their peers in the Asch paradigm (Studies 1 and 2). Our findings also revealed increased behavioral affiliation following reminders of behavioral disinhibition (Studies 3 and 4). These effects were obtained on actual behavior in both modern and classic experimental paradigms oriented toward the understanding of human behavior pertaining to public conformity (Asch, 1951, 1955, 1956) and behavioral affiliation (Macrae et al., 1994). Taken together, our studies portray the disinhibited individual as someone who in potentially threatening social interactions affiliates and conforms with his or her peers.

References

Abrams, D. (ed.). (2005). *The Social Psychology of Inclusion and Exclusion*. Oxford: Blackwell.

Amodio, D. M., Master, S. L., Yee, C. M., and Taylor, S. E. (2008). Neurocognitive components of the behavioral inhibition and activation systems: implications for theories of self-regulation. *Psychophysiology* 44, 11–19. doi: 10.1111/j.1469-8986.2007.00609.x

Aronson, E. (1972). *The Social Animal*. New York, NY: The Viking Press.

Asch, S. E. (1951). "Effects of group pressure upon the modification and distortion of judgments," in *Groups, Leadership, and Men*, ed. H. Guetzkow (Pittsburgh, PA: Carnegie Press), 177–190.

Asch, S. E. (1955). Opinions and social pressure. *Sci. Am.* 193, 31–35. doi: 10.1038/scientificamerican1155-31

Asch, S. E. (1956). Studies of independence and conformity: a minority of one against a unanimous majority. *Psychol. Monogr.* 70, 1–70.

Aydin, N., Fischer, P., and Frey, D. (2010). Turning to God in the face of ostracism: effects of social exclusion on religiousness. *Pers. Soc. Psychol. Bull.* 36, 742–753. doi: 10.1177/0146167210367491

Bar-Anan, Y., Liberman, N., Trope, Y., and Algom, D. (2007). Automatic processing of psychological distance: evidence from a Stroop task. *J. Exp. Psychol. Gen.* 136, 610–622. doi: 10.1037/0096-3445.136.4.610

Baumeister, R. F., and Leary, M. R. (1995). The need to belong: desire for interpersonal attachments as a fundamental human motivation. *Psychol. Bull.* 117, 497–529. doi: 10.1037/0033-2909.117.3.497

Baumeister, R. F., and Tice, D. M. (1990). Anxiety and social exclusion. *J. Soc. Clin. Psychol.* 9, 165–195. doi: 10.1521/jscp.1990.9.2.165

Baumeister, R. F., Vohs, K. D., and Funder, D. C. (2007). Psychology as the science of self-reports and finger movements: whatever happened to actual

behavior? *Curr. Dir. Psychol. Sci.* 16, 396–403. doi: 10.1111/j.1745-6916.2007.00051.x

Bernstein, M. J., Young, S. G., Brown, C. M., Sacco, D. F., and Claypool, H. M. (2008). Adaptive responses to social exclusion: social rejection improves detection of real and fake smiles. *Psychol. Sci.* 19, 981–983. doi: 10.1111/j.1467-9280.2008.02187.x

Bond, R. (2005). Group size and conformity. *Group Process. Intergroup Relat.* 8, 331–354. doi: 10.1177/1368430205056464

Brewer, M. B. (1991). The social self: on being the same and different at the same time. *Pers. Soc. Psychol. Bull.* 17, 475–482. doi: 10.1177/0146167291175001

Carver, C. S. (2005). Impulse and constraint: perspectives from personality psychology, convergence with theory in other areas, and potential for integration. *Pers. Soc. Psychol. Rev.* 9, 312–333. doi: 10.1207/s15327957pspr0904_2

Carver, C. S., and White, T. L. (1994). Behavioral inhibition, behavioral activation, and affective responses to impending reward and punishment: the BIS/BAS scales. *J. Pers. Soc. Psychol.* 67, 319–333. doi: 10.1037/0022-3514.67.2.319

Christensen, L. (1982). Assessment of the existence of the anxiety component in evaluation apprehension. *Soc. Behav. Pers.* 10, 117–123. doi: 10.2224/sbp.1982.10.2.117

Cialdini, R. B., Kallgren, C. A., and Reno, R. R. (1991). "A focus theory of normative conduct: a theoretical refinement and reevaluation of the role of norms in human behavior," in *Advances in Experimental Social Psychology*, Vol. 24, ed. M. P. Zanna (San Diego, CA: Academic Press), 201–234.

Clausen, J. A. (ed.). (1968). *Socialization and Society*. Boston, MA: Little Brown and Company.

Coan, J. A., and Allen, J. J. B. (2003). Frontal EEG asymmetry and the behavioral activation and inhibition systems. *Psychophysiology* 40, 106–114. doi: 10.1111/1469-8986.00011

Cohen, J., Cohen, P., West, S. G., and Aiken, L. S. (2003). *Applied Multiple Regression/Correlation Analysis for the Behavioral Sciences*, 3rd Edn. Hillsdale, NJ: Erlbaum.

Cook, R. D. (1977). Detection of influential observations in linear regression. *Technometrics* 19, 15–18. doi: 10.2307/1268249

Cottrell, N. B. (1972). "Social facilitation," in *Experimental Social Psychology*, ed. C. McClintock (New York, NY: Holt, Rinehart, & Winston), 185–236.

Cottrell, N. B., Wack, D. L., Sekerak, G. J., and Rittle, R. H. (1968). Social facilitation of dominant responses by presence of others. *J. Pers. Soc. Psychol.* 9, 245–250. doi: 10.1037/h0025902

DeWall, C. N., and Baumeister, R. F. (2006). Alone but feeling no pain: effects of social exclusion on physical pain tolerance and pain threshold, affective forecasting, and interpersonal empathy. *J. Pers. Soc. Psychol.* 91, 1–15. doi: 10.1037/0022-3514.91.1.1

Eisenberger, N. I., Lieberman, M. D., and Williams, K. D. (2003). Does rejection hurt? An fMRI study of social exclusion. *Science* 302, 290–292. doi: 10.1126/science.1089134

Erikson, E. H. (1968). *Identity: Youth and Crisis*. New York, NY: Norton.

Folger, R. (1977). Distributive and procedural justice: combined impact of "voice" and improvement of experienced inequity. *J. Pers. Soc. Psychol.* 35, 108–119. doi: 10.1037/0022-3514.35.2.108

Gable, S. L., Reis, H. T., and Elliot, A. J. (2000). Behavioral activation and inhibition in everyday life. *J. Pers. Soc. Psychol.* 78, 1135–1149. doi: 10.1037/0022-3514.78.6.1135

Geen, R. G. (1983). Evaluation apprehension and the social facilitation/inhibition of learning. *Motiv. Emot.* 7, 203–212. doi: 10.1007/BF00992903

Geen, R. G. (1985). Evaluation apprehension and response withholding in solution of anagrams. *Pers. Indivd. Dif.* 6, 293–298. doi: 10.1016/0191-8869(85)90052-2

Gray, J. A. (1987). *The Psychology of Fear and Stress*. Cambridge: Cambridge University Press.

Gray, J. A., and McNaughton, N. (2000). *The Neuropsychology of Anxiety: An Enquiry into the Functions of the Septo-hippocampal System*. Oxford: Oxford University Press.

Greenberg, J. (1987). A taxonomy of organizational justice theories. *Acad. Manag. Rev.* 12, 9–22.

Gunther Moor, B., Guroglu, B., Op de Macks, Z. A., Rombouts, S. A., Van der Molen, M. W., and Crone, E. A. (2011). Social exclusion and punishment of excluders: neural correlates and developmental trajectories. *Neuroimage* 59, 708–717. doi: 10.1016/j.neuroimage.2011.07.028

Harmon-Jones, E., Harmon-Jones, C., and Price, T. F. (2013). What is approach motivation? *Emot. Rev.* 5, 291–295. doi: 10.1177/1754073913477509

Harris, J. R. (1995). Where is the child's environment? A group socialization theory of development. *Psychol. Rev.* 102, 458–489. doi: 10.1037/0033-295X.102.3.458

Hill, C. A. (1987). Affiliation motivation: people who need people. . . but in different ways. *J. Pers. Soc. Psychol.* 52, 1008–1018. doi: 10.1037/0022-3514.52.5.1008

Hirschman, A. O. (1970). *Exit, Voice and Loyalty: Responses to Declines in Firms, Organizations, and States*. Cambridge, MA: Harvard University Press.

Holland, R. W., Roeder, U., van Baaren, R. B., Brandt, A., and Hannover, B. (2004). Don't stand so close to me: self-construal and interpersonal closeness. *Psychol. Sci.* 15, 237–242. doi: 10.1111/j.0956-7976.2004.00658.x

Innes, J. M., and Young, R. F. (1975). The effect of presence of an audience, evaluation apprehension and objective self-awareness on learning. *J. Exp. Soc. Psychol.* 11, 35–42. doi: 10.1016/S0022-1031(75)80007-2

Jones, E. E. (1998). "Major developments in five decades of social psychology," in *The Handbook of Social Psychology*, 4th Edn, Vol. 1, eds D. T. Gilbert, S. T. Fiske, and G. Lindzey (Boston, MA: McGraw-Hill), 3–57.

Kant, I. (1959). *Foundation of the Metaphysics of Morals*. Indianapolis, IN: Bobbs-Merrill. (Original work published in 1785.)

Knyazev, G. G., Schutter, D. J., and Van Honk, J. (2006). Anxious apprehension increases coupling of delta and beta oscillations. *Int. J. Psychophysiol.* 61, 283–287. doi: 10.1016/j.ijpsycho.2005.12.003

Lakin, J. L., Chartrand, T. L., and Arkin, R. M. (2008). I am too just like you: nonconscious mimicry as an automatic behavioral response to social exclusion. *Psychol. Sci.* 19, 816–822. doi: 10.1111/j.1467-9280.2008.02162.x

Latané, B., and Nida, S. (1981). Ten years of research on group size and helping. *Psychol. Bull.* 89, 308–324. doi: 10.1037/0033-2909.89.2.308

Leary, M. R. (2010). "Affiliation, acceptance, and belonging: the pursuit of interpersonal connection," in *Handbook of Social Psychology*, 5th Edn, Vol. 2,

eds S. T. Fiske, D. T. Gilbert, and G. Lindzey (Hoboken, NJ: Wiley), 864–897.

Lilienfeld, S. O. (1992). The association between antisocial personality and somatization disorders: a review and integration of theoretical models. *Clin. Psychol. Rev.* 12, 641–662. doi: 10.1016/0272-7358(92)90136-V

Mackinnon, S., Jordan, C., and Wilson, A. (2011). Birds of a feather sit together: physical similarity predicts seating choice. *Pers. Soc. Psychol. Bull.* 37, 879–892. doi: 10.1177/0146167211402094

Macrae, C. N., Bodenhausen, G. V., Milne, A. B., and Jetten, J. (1994). Out of mind but back in sight: stereotypes on the rebound. *J. Pers. Soc. Psychol.* 67, 808–817. doi: 10.1037/0022-3514.67.5.808

McClelland, D. C. (1987). *Human Motivation*. Cambridge: Cambridge University Press.

Milgram, S. (1974). *Obedience to Authority: An Experimental View*. New York, NY: Harper & Row.

Molden, D. C., Lucas, G. M., Gardner, W. L., Dean, K., and Knowles, M. L. (2009). Motivations for prevention or promotion following social exclusion: being rejected versus ignored. *J. Pers. Soc. Psychol.* 96, 415–431. doi: 10.1037/a0012958

Monteith, M. J. (1993). Self-regulation of prejudiced responses: implications for progress in prejudice-reduction efforts. *J. Pers. Soc. Psychol.* 65, 469–485. doi: 10.1037/0022-3514.65.3.469

Murray, A. H. (1938). *Explorations in Personality*. New York, NY: Oxford University press, 531–545.

Newman, J. P., MacCoon, D. G., Vaughn, L. J., and Sadeh, N. (2005). Validating a distinction between primary and secondary psychopathy with measures of Gray's BIS and BAS constructs. *J. Abnorm. Psychol.* 114, 319–323. doi: 10.1037/0021-843X.114.2.319

Nigg, J. T. (2000). On inhibition/disinhibition in developmental psychopathology: views from cognitive and personality psychology and a working inhibition taxonomy. *Psychol. Bull.* 126, 220–246. doi: 10.1037/0033-2909.126.2.220

Peters, F., Perani, D., Herholz, K., Holthoff, V., Beuthien-Baumann, B., Sorbi, S., et al. (2006). Orbitofrontal dysfunction related to both apathy and disinhibition in frontotemporal dementia. *Dement. Geriatr. Cogn. Disord.* 21, 373–379. doi: 10.1159/000091898

Riva, P., Romero Lauro, L. J., DeWall, C. N., and Bushman, B. J. (2012). Buffer the pain away: stimulating the right ventrolateral prefrontal cortex reduces pain following social exclusion. *Psychol. Sci.* 23, 1473–1475. doi: 10.1177/0956797612450894

Rosenberg, M. J. (1980). Experimenter expectancy, evaluation apprehension, and the diffusion of methodological angst. *Behav. Brain Sci.* 3, 472–474. doi: 10.1017/S0140525X00006208

Satterthwaite, F. E. (1946). An approximate distribution of estimates of variance components. *Biometrics* 2, 110–114. doi: 10.2307/3002019

Sawyer, C. R., and Behnke, R. R. (2002). Behavioral inhibition and the communication of public speaking state anxiety. *West. J. Commun.* 66, 412–422. doi: 10.1080/10570310209374747

Schaafsma, J., and Williams, K. D. (2012). Exclusion, intergroup hostility, and religious fundamentalism. *J. Exp. Soc. Psychol.* 48, 829–837. doi: 10.1016/j.jesp.2012.02.015

Schachter, S. (1951). Deviance, rejection, and communication. *J. Abnorm. Soc. Psychol.* 46, 190–207. doi: 10.1037/h0062326

Schachter, S. (1959). *The Psychology of Affiliation*. Stanford, CA: Stanford University Press.

Schwarz, B. (1973). Peer versus authority effects in a correctional community. *Criminology* 11, 233–257. doi: 10.1111/j.1745-9125.1973.tb00597.x

Sherif, M., and Sherif, C. (1964). *Reference Groups*. Chicago, IL: Regnery.

Simmons, J. P., Nelson, L. D., and Simonsohn, U. (2012). A 21-word solution. *Dialogue* 26, 4–7. doi: 10.2139/ssrn.2160588

Simon, L., Greenberg, J., Arndt, J., Pyszczynski, T., Clement, R., and Solomon, S. (1997). Perceived consensus, uniqueness, and terror management: compensatory responses to threats to inclusion and distinctiveness following mortality salience. *Pers. Soc. Psychol. Bull.* 23, 1055–1065. doi: 10.1177/01461672972310006

Spencer, S. J., Zanna, M. P., and Fong, G. T. (2005). Establishing a causal chain: why experiments are often more effective than mediational analyses in examining psychological processes. *J. Pers. Soc. Psychol.* 89, 845–851. doi: 10.1037/0022-3514.89.6.845

Suler, J. (2004). The online disinhibition effect. *Cyberpsychol. Behav.* 7, 321–326. doi: 10.1089/1094931041291295

Sundar, S. S., Xu, Q., and Oeldorf-Hirsch, A. (2009). Authority vs. peer: how interface cues influence users. *Paper Presented at the 27th International Conference on Human Factors in Computing Systems*, Boston.

Twenge, J. M., Baumeister, R. F., Tice, D. M., and Stucke, T. S. (2001). If you can't join them, beat them: effects of social exclusion on aggressive behavior. *J. Pers. Soc. Psychol.* 81, 1058–1069. doi: 10.1037/0022-3514.81.6.1058

Tyler, T. R., and Lind, E. A. (1992). "A relational model of authority in groups," in *Advances in Experimental Social Psychology*, Vol. 25, ed. M. P. Zanna (San Diego, CA: Academic Press), 115–191.

Van Baaren, R. B., Holland, R. W., Steenaert, B., and Van Knippenberg, A. (2003). Mimicry for money: behavioral consequences of imitation. *J. Exp. Soc. Psychol.* 39, 393–398. doi: 10.1016/S0022-1031(03)00014-3

Van den Bos, K. (1999). What are we talking about when we talk about no-voice procedures? On the psychology of the fair outcome effect. *J. Exp. Soc. Psychol.* 35, 560–577. doi: 10.1006/jesp.1999.1393

Van den Bos, K. (2009). Making sense of life: the existential self trying to deal with personal uncertainty. *Psychol. Inq.* 20, 197–217. doi: 10.1080/10478 400903333411

Van den Bos, K. (2013). "Meaning making following activation of the behavioral inhibition system: how caring less about what others think may help to make sense of what is going on," in *The Psychology of Meaning*, eds K. D. Markman, T. Proulx, and M. J. Lindberg (Washington, DC: American Psychological Association), 359–380.

Van den Bos, K., Euwema, M. C., Poortvliet, P. M., and Maas, M. (2007). Uncertainty management and social issues: uncertainty as important determinant of reactions to socially deviating people. *J. Appl. Soc. Psychol.* 37, 1726–1756. doi: 10.1111/j.1559-1816.2007.00235.x

Van den Bos, K., and Lind, E. A. (2009). "The social psychology of fairness and the regulation of personal uncertainty," in *Handbook of the Uncertain Self*, eds R. M. Arkin, K. C. Oleson, and P. J. Carroll (New York, NY: Psychology Press), 122–141.

Van den Bos, K., Müller, P. A., and Van Bussel, A. A. L. (2009). Helping to overcome intervention inertia in bystander's dilemmas: behavioral disinhibition can improve the greater good. *J. Exp. Soc. Psychol.* 45, 873–878. doi: 10.1016/j.jesp.2009.03.014

Van den Bos, K., and Lind, E. A. (2013). "On sense-making reactions and public inhibition of benign social motives: an appraisal model of prosocial behavior," in *Advances in Experimental Social Psychology*, Vol. 48, eds J. M. Olson and M. P. Zanna (San Diego, CA: Academic Press), 1–58.

Van den Bos, K., Müller, P. A., and Damen, T. (2011a). A behavioral disinhibition hypothesis of interventions in moral dilemmas. *Emot. Rev.* 3, 281–283. doi: 10.1177/1754073911402369

Van den Bos, K., Van Lange, P. A. M., Lind, E. A., Venhoeven, L. A., Beudeker, D. A., Cramwinckel, F. M., et al. (2011b). On the benign qualities of behavioral disinhibition: because of the prosocial nature of people, behavioral disinhibition can weaken pleasure with getting more than you deserve. *J. Pers. Soc. Psychol.* 101, 791–811. doi: 10.1037/a0023556

Vohs, K. D., Mead, N. L., and Goode, M. R. (2006). The psychological consequences of money. *Science* 314, 1154–1156. doi: 10.1126/science.1132491

Watson, D., Clark, L. A., and Tellegen, A. (1988). Development and validation of brief measures of positive and negative affect: the PANAS scales. *J. Pers. Soc. Psychol.* 54, 1063–1070. doi: 10.1037/0022-3514.54.6.1063

Welch, B. L. (1947). The generalization of "Student's" problem when several different population variances are involved. *Biometrika* 34, 28–35. doi: 10.2307/2332510

Wolf, S. (2008). *Peer Groups: Expanding Our Study of Small Group Communication*. Thousand oaks, CA: Sage.

Conflict of Interest Statement: The authors declare that the research was conducted in the absence of any commercial or financial relationships that could be construed as a potential conflict of interest.

15

Deployment of Attention on Handshakes

Mowei Shen, Jun Yin, Xiaowei Ding, Rende Shui and Jifan Zhou*

Department of Psychology and Behavioral Sciences, Zhejiang University, Hangzhou, China

Understanding the social structures between objects, organizing, and selecting them accordingly, is fundamental to social cognition. We report an example that demonstrates the object association learned from social interactions could impact visual attention. Particularly, when two hands approach each other to perform a handshake, they tend to be attended to as a unit because of the cooperative relationship exhibited in the action: even a cue presented on a non-target hand may facilitate a response to the targets that appear on the non-cued hand (Experiment 1), indicating that attentional shift between two hands was facilitated; furthermore, the response to a target on one hand is significantly impaired by a distractor on the other hand (Experiment 2), implying that it is difficult to selectively confine attention to a single hand. These effects were dependent on the existence of the hands when cue and target appeared (Experiment 3); neither perceptual familiarity, or physical fit can explain all the attention effects (Experiment 4). These results have bearings on the perceptual root of social cognition.

Keywords: visual organization, attention, social relationship, attentional unit, social cognition

Edited by:
Narayanan Srinivasan,
University of Allahabad, India

Reviewed by:
Sumitava Mukherjee,
Indian Institute
of Management-Ahmedabad, India
Mark Fenske,
University of Guelph, Canada
Eric Taylor,
University of Toronto, Canada

*Correspondence:
Jifan Zhou
jifanzhou@zju.edu.cn

Specialty section:
This article was submitted to
Cognitive Science,
a section of the journal
Frontiers in Psychology

INTRODUCTION

Social relation between objects (or agency) has significant meanings for mankind. People's interactions assign social properties to the structure of agents; for example, people who help each other have cooperative relationships. Understanding social structure and organizing agents accordingly is important in daily life, because we frequently need to pool individuals who cooperate with each other into groups and distinguish allies from opponents. Since social relationship defines the social units we process during social cognition, the mental system should organize and select information according to social relationship at some early stage of processing, before high-level social cognition. The human visual system is equipped with remarkably efficient computation modules to extract social properties from low-level visual features, including the impression of animacy, others' goals and intentions (Heider and Simmel, 1944; Dittrich and Lea, 1994; Scholl and Tremoulet, 2000; Schlottmann et al., 2006; Gao et al., 2009, 2010). And those perceived social information is able to affect lower-level perceptual processing. For example, our previous research demonstrated that social cues affect the causal perception of physical events (Zhou et al., 2012), and social relationship shapes the visual organization of objects that dynamically interact with each other (Yin et al., 2013). Thus, noting that social structure is important for humans to organize the observed word, we speculated that social information may modulate attention in enabling the social-based deployment of processing resource.

Despite the importance of social structures, the traditional research about attention majorly focused on physical structures, which are defined by physical relationships between objects, such as proximity, symmetry, and continuity. According to those structures, the visual system group the visual elements into processing units at different levels, such as figure-ground segregation, object forming, and perceptual grouping (Wertheimer, 1923; Marr, 1982; Treisman, 1986; Scholl, 2001; Palmer, 2003), based on some fundamental perceptual principles, such as Gestalt laws (Sternberg, 2003). It enables us to see a well-structured visual world rather than discrete visual elements. Attention deployment is guided by such physical structures; a great example is the well-studied "same-object advantage" effect (Duncan and Duncan, 1984; Kahneman et al., 1992; Egly et al., 1994; Moore et al., 1998; Flombaum and Scholl, 2006), which shows that attention automatically spreads within an object defined by real or illusory contours. In addition to objects, a similar effect was suggested to occur for perceptual groups (Driver et al., 2001; Scholl, 2001). That is, attention automatically spreads within a group, and it is difficult to attend to a single object in a group without also selecting the other objects.

Indeed, recent studies revealed that social information also has a profound impact on attention deployment. Joint attention (Frischen et al., 2007) is probably the best example of that: participants' performance on an object detection task was facilitated when a preceding face cue gazed toward the location of the target. This gaze cueing effect occurs rapidly with very brief presentation of gaze cues (Friesen and Kingstone, 1998), and occurs such that the gaze cue does not necessarily predict the direction of, or even predicts the direction opposite to, the target location (Driver et al., 1999; Friesen et al., 2004). Moreover, the gaze-following attention shift may occur without the awareness of the presentation of gaze cues (Sato et al., 2007). These findings suggest that the visual system automatically aligns attention with that of others based on the received social information—other's gaze direction, which signals their locus of attention.

The gaze cueing effect demonstrates that attention deployment is modulated by the social relationship defined by the interaction between other people and objects. In addition to gaze, other body parts that are involved in social interaction, such as hands, also affect attention. For instance, attention prioritizes stimuli in near-hand space (Reed et al., 2006), and the attentional system treat the surface of one's own hands differently from other surface, therefore shifting attention from hands to other surface (including other hands) is costly (Taylor and Witt, 2014; Taylor et al., 2015). These hand-based effects on attention, together with the visuomotor priming caused by hands (e.g., Bruzzo et al., 2008; Liuzza et al., 2012), facilitate manual action and help people understand the relationships in social interactions. Our previous research also showed that social interaction between objects (or agents) affects attention deployment (Yin et al., 2013). In this study, a chasing motion including two predators and one prey was presented to participants. In the condition that predators cooperated to chase the prey, the predators were perceived as a group, such that the exogenous attentional cue appearing on one of the two predators could facilitate the response to the target presented on the other (uncued) predator. This automatic attention spreading did not occur when the predators acted in a competitive manner to chase the prey suggesting that the social relationship (cooperative/competitive relationship in this case) obtained from the dynamic motion display can guide our attention deployment.

Based on those findings, the current study aimed to generalize the social-based attention effect to socially related objects acquired from social learning. Baron-Cohen (1995) suggested that the behavior of joint attention is performed by an innate module attuned to the visual appearance of the eyes. Furthermore, the ability to perceive causality and animacy (the foundation of detecting cooperative/competitive chasing) from motion display is considered to be innate (see Scholl and Tremoulet, 2000 for a review). Thus, social-based attention effects may occur on only stimuli that are processed by innate domain-specific modules that developed through evolution to adapt to social life. However, neither this hypothesis nor its alternative hypotheses have been directly examined; thus, it is still unclear exactly what type of social information is able to modulate attention deployment. Here, we tested whether such effects occur on learned socially related objects, in order to add a new type of social-based attention deployment to the known body of knowledge of attention.

The current study used a handshake scene, in which two hands approach each other to perform a handshake, to examine the attention effect induced by socially related objects (i.e., the two hands). The handshake scene was selected because of the following considerations: (1) the handshake is a greeting gesture learned in social interaction, not an innate behavior; not even a universal behavior. (2) Handshakes symbolize friendship, agreement, congratulatory sentiments, and hence provide social information about cooperative relationship between individuals. Thus, the hands involved in the handshake scenes may be treated as a social unit, leading to modulation on attention deployment. (3) Handshakes are so common in daily social interactions that people have learned the association of the two hands going to perform a handshake; thus, the social meaning is easily understood and more likely to instantly impact attention deployment. Compared to physical cues, information about the social relationship of objects are not usually obvious or instantly available; thus, if the social structure of scenes impact attention, it would most likely occur in visual scenes in which the social relationship of objects has been well learned in our daily life. (4) The motion involved in handshakes is relatively simple; thus, handshakes can be manipulated and controlled in laboratory settings.

If the socially related objects (i.e., the two hands) were treated as a unit during attentional processes, similar to perceptual units defined by physical cues, then we could hypothesize that (1) when attention is cued to one hand, the response to a target presented on the other hand would be quicker because the attentional shift from the cued hand to the other is facilitated; and (2) a distractor presented on one hand would significantly interfere with a target presented on the other hand because it would be difficult to selectively confine attention to just one hand. These two hypotheses were tested in the following experiments.

EXPERIMENT 1

Experiment 1 explored whether two hands that are approaching to perform a handshake would facilitate attentional shift between two hands. This social-based attention effect was examined using a cueing task similar to that used by Moore et al. (1998). In this task, participants are presented with a display where two hands (one showing its palm and the other showing its back) are approaching each other, creating the impression that they will perform a handshake. Subsequently, the hands return to their initial positions, and a target randomly appears on one hand. Before the target appears, one of the hands is cued by the onset of a white square. In most trials, the cue appears on the same hand as that where the target will be presented (*valid* trials); in the remaining trials, the cue appears on the other hand (*invalid* trials). Typically, the response to the target is faster when the cue is valid than when it is invalid. However, if the two hands are treated as an attentional unit bound by their social relationship, then attentional shift between the cued hand to the non-cued hand, decreasing the RT difference between the valid and invalid trials. Consequently, the cueing effect should be weakened when the hands are approaching to perform a handshake. Three control conditions were designed as follows: the *both-back* condition, in which the backs of both of the hands were shown; the *both-palm* condition, in which the palms of both hands were shown; and the *reversed-hand* condition, in which a palm and the back of a hand were presented, as in the *handshake* condition, except that one of the hands was shown upside-down. In all three of the control conditions, it was impossible to create the impression of a handshake.

Methods
Participants
Students from Zhejiang University aged between 18 and 26 years (~21 on average) were recruited to participate in this and following experiments. All were right-handed, had normal or corrected-to-normal vision and were naïve about the purpose of the experiments. The participants received financial rewards after completing the experiment. The experimental protocol was approved by the Institutional Review Board at the Department of Psychology and Behavioral Sciences, Zhejiang University; participants gave written informed consent prior to their participation.

Twenty naïve students (11 men and 9 women) participated in Experiment 1. To ensure adequate power, the sample size was determined by a power analysis based on predicted effect size using G*power 3 (Faul et al., 2007, 2009). Based on the results of our pilot studies, we predicted a medium effect size ($f^2 = 0.15$, according to Cohen, 1988) for our experimental design. With the alpha level set at 0.01, the suggested sample size was approximately 20 individuals. The sample sizes of the following experiments were determined by the same rule.

Design and Procedure
The participants were tested individually in a darkened room while seated approximately 60 cm from the screen. All displays were presented on a gray background on a Samsung 19″ CRT monitor, which subtended approximately 28.3° in visual angle.

Each trial began with a separate presentation of two hands; these presentations were separated by a white fixation cross (0.5° × 0.5°). The fixation was presented at the center of the screen; the visual angle between the fixation and each fingertip was 2°. The appearance of the two hands was in accordance with one of the four hand-approaching display types shown in **Figure 1A**. After being stationary for 100 ms, the hands began to approach each other until the images overlapped by 0.7°. Following this display, the overlapped hands vanished and immediately reappeared at their initial locations. After an interval of 400 ms, a cue (a 1.2° × 1.2° white square) was presented at the center of one hand for 100 ms. Following a variable interstimulus interval (ISI; 150–250 ms), a target and a distractor appeared on the two hands. The target was a *T* or an *L*, whereas the distractor was one of three *T–L* hybrid characters, which were identical to those used by Moore et al. (1998). These characters subtended 0.73° × 0.73° each and were randomly oriented at one of four orientations (0, 90, 180, or 270°). The participants were asked to report whether the target was a *T* or an *L* as quickly as possible by pressing the right or left buttons on a standard keyboard. They were explicitly informed that the displays of hand movement were irrelevant to the task and could, therefore, be ignored. The target and distractor remained visible until a response was made. The next trial began after a 1.5–2.5-s intertrial interval. If no response was made within 2 s, the next trial began immediately.

Each participant completed 360 trials (90 trials in each of the 4 hand-approaching display conditions). In two-thirds of the trials (i.e., 60 trials in each condition), the cue and target appeared on the same hand; these trials were valid trials. In the remaining one-third of the trials, the cue and target appeared on different hands; these trials were invalid trials. All of the trials were presented in random order.

Results and Discussion
The mean RTs for correct responses in the four conditions are shown in **Figure 2A**. The RT data were submitted to a 2 (validity) × 4 (hand-approaching display) repeated-measures ANOVA. The main effect of validity was significant, $F(1,19) = 95.80$, $p < 0.001$, $\eta_p^2 = 0.83$, but that of hand-approaching display was not significant, $F(3,57) = 1.84, p > 0.05$, $\eta_p^2 = 0.09$. The interaction between validity and approach display was significant, $F(3,57) = 3.86$, $p < 0.05$, $\eta_p^2 = 0.17$, indicating that the cueing effect varied across the hand-approaching display conditions. **Figure 2B** shows the mean RT differences between the valid and invalid trials, which reflect the facilitation induced by the attention cue. A *post hoc* LSD test revealed that the mean RT difference in the handshake condition was significantly smaller than that in the control conditions (*handshake* vs. *both-back*, $p < 0.01$; *handshake* vs. *both-palm*, $p < 0.05$; *handshake* vs. *reversed-hand*, $p < 0.001$). Thus, the cueing effect was weakened in the handshake condition, compared to each of the three different control conditions. As shown in **Figure 2**, this weakened cueing effect stemmed from both the faster responses in the invalid trials (*handshake* vs. *both-back*, $p < 0.05$; *handshake* vs.

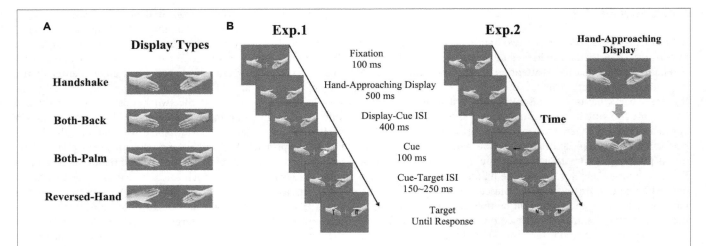

FIGURE 1 | Depiction of the four hand-approaching display conditions (A) and the procedure of Experiments 1 and 2 (B). The four hand-approaching display conditions were as follows: (1) the palm of one hand and the back of the other were displayed such that they were prepared for a handshake (the *handshake* condition); (2) the backs of both hands were displayed (the *both-back* condition); (3) the palms of both hands were displayed (the *both-palm* condition); and (4) the palm of one hand and the back of the other were displayed, but one of the hands was upside-down (the *reversed-hand* condition). The beginning and the end of the hand-approaching display were showed at the right. In Experiment 1, the task was to report whether a *T* or an *L* was presented on one of the hands; the cue was valid or invalid (here, the invalid condition is shown). In Experiment 2, the task was to report whether an *N* or an *X* appeared on the hand indicated by the arrow; the character presented on the other hand was compatible or incompatible with the target (here, the compatible condition is shown).

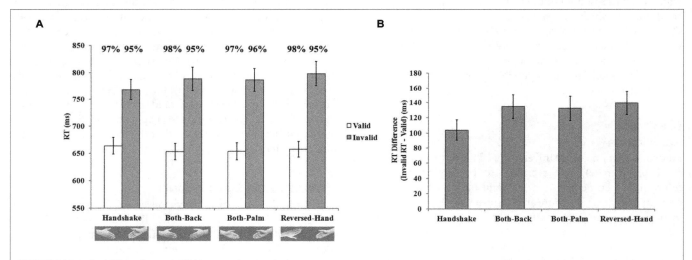

FIGURE 2 | Results of Experiment 1. (A) Mean reaction time (RT) varied as a function of hand-approach display and cue validity. Mean accuracy rates for every condition was shown above the corresponding bars. **(B)** The mean RT difference between invalid and valid trials varied according to the hand-approach display. Error bars indicate standard errors.

both-palm, $p < 0.05$; *handshake* vs. *reversed-hand*, $p < 0.01$) and the slower responses in the valid trials (relatively weak, but there was a trend toward significance, *handshake* vs. *both-back*, $p = 0.06$; *handshake* vs. *both-palm*, $p = 0.06$; *handshake* vs. *reversed-hand*, $p = 0.10$) compared to the control conditions.

The same ANOVA was conducted for the accuracy data, revealing significant main effect of validity, $F(1,19) = 20.31$, $p < 0.001$, $\eta_p^2 = 0.52$. It suggested that the responses were more accurate on valid than invalid trials (97% vs. 95%). No other effect reached statistical significance, $Fs < 2.25$, $p > 0.12$. Thus there was no speed-accuracy tradeoff.

The faster responses in the invalid trials indicated that attentional shift from the cued hand to the other hand was facilitated. Therefore, the processing of targets that appeared on the uncued hand was speeded. Meanwhile, the attentional resources allocated to the cued hand were diluted, leading to the slower processing of targets that appeared on the cued hand. The hypothesis that two hands approaching to perform a handshake would be treated as an attentional unit—and, hence, that the cueing effect would be weakened—was supported by the results of Experiment 1.

EXPERIMENT 2

Experiment 2 employed an interference task to investigate whether the handshake display would increase the interference between the two hands. In this task, an arrow is presented in the center of the screen to indicate the hand on which the target will be presented (here, the rate of cue validity was 100%). Then, a target appeared on the cued hand and a distractor concurrently appears on the other hand. The distractor may be the same character as the target (*compatible* trials) or a different character (*incompatible* trials). Typically, participants' responses to the target are more rapid in compatible than in incompatible trials; this RT difference reflects the interference effect. Much like in Experiment 1, we manipulated the hand-approaching display conditions. We posited that if the two hands were treated as an attentional unit when they seemed poised to perform a handshake, then participants would be unable to selectively confine their attention to a single hand without attending to the other. We thus expected the incompatible distractor to produce greater interference compared to the control conditions, in which the hands were not socially related.

Methods

Twenty naïve Zhejiang University students (9 men and 11 women) participated and received financial rewards. None of them had participated in Experiment 1.

The hand-approaching displays were identical to those in Experiment 1 (see **Figure 1**). Following the display, an arrow that pointed to the right or left was presented above the fixation. With an ISI of 150–250 ms, a target appeared on the hand where the arrow was pointing, and a distractor was presented on the other hand. The target and the distractor were either an *N* or an *X*. In half of the trials, the target and distractor were compatible (i.e., both *N* or both *X*); in the remaining half of the trials, the target and distractor were incompatible. The participants' task was to report whether the target was an *N* or an *X* as quickly as possible by pressing the left or right buttons, respectively. The target and distractor remained on the screen until a response was made. A 2 (compatibility: compatible, incompatible) × 4 (hand-approaching display) within-subjects design was used. Each participant completed 560 total trials, with 70 trials in each condition. The trials were presented at random.

Results and Discussion

A 2 (compatibility) × 4 (hand-approaching display) repeated-measures ANOVA indicated a significant main effect of compatibility, $F(1,19) = 21.43$, $p < 0.001$, $\eta_p^2 = 0.53$, but no main effect of hand-approaching display, $F(3,57) = 1.15$, $p > 0.05$, $\eta_p^2 = 0.06$. The interaction between these two variables was significant, $F(3,57) = 6.94$, $p < 0.01$, $\eta_p^2 = 0.27$, indicating that the interference effect varied across hand-approaching display conditions. To compare the interference effect across the four hand-approaching displays, we submitted the mean RT difference between the compatible and incompatible trials to a single factor (hand-approaching display) repeated-measures ANOVA with *post hoc* LSD test. The results revealed a significant main effect,

$F(3,57) = 6.89$, $p < 0.01$, $\eta_p^2 = 0.27$, and the interference effect was significantly larger in the handshake condition than in the control conditions, $ps < 0.05$. As shown in **Figure 3**, faster RT in the compatible trials [*handshake* vs. *both-back*, $p < 0.05$; *handshake* vs. *both-palm*, $p = 0.18$ (not significant between these two conditions); *handshake* vs. *reversed-hand*, $p < 0.01$] jointly contributed with slower RT in the incompatible trials (for all paired comparisons, $p < 0.05$) to the largest interference effect in the handshake condition.

The same ANOVA was conducted for the accuracy data. No effect was significant, $Fs < 2.59$, $p > 0.12$, suggesting no speed-accuracy tradeoff.

This result implied that the distractor shared attentional resources with the target, leading to a facilitation of responses with a compatible distractor and a delayed response with an incompatible distractor.

EXPERIMENT 3

Experiment 3 was conducted to examine what would happen when hands were not presented after the hand-approaching display. Our hypothesis to be tested was that social information modulates the attention deployment on the related objects, if it was true, then the effect should be specific to the two hands – nothing would happen if the hands disappeared, because the objects to be attend to went away in this case. Otherwise, if the hand-approaching display induced a general attention effect, such as increasing the breadth of attention or facilitating the attentional shift between all objects, and the effect lasted for a certain time to affect the subsequent task, it would still occur when hands were removed after the approaching action. Because the displays in the previous experiments all contained two hands, it was difficult to distinguish whether the observed results occurred due to a general effect affecting all objects. In Experiment 3, both the hands were removed *after* the hand-approaching display, and the targets and distractors were presented directly onto the background, to test whether the effects found in Experiments 1 and 2 were dependent on the image of the hands.

Methods

This experiment involved two sub-experiments. One sub-experiment used the cueing task that served as the control situation in Experiment 1; the other used the interference task that served as the control of Experiment 2. Each of the sub-experiments included 20 participants (10 men and 10 women in each sub-experiment).

The sub-experiment with the cueing task was similar to Experiment 1; however, we added a condition in which the hands disappeared prior to target onset. While the procedure was identical to Experiment 1 in the hands-present condition, the hands disappeared following the cue offset in the hands-disappear condition. Because adding the hands-disappear condition doubled the length of the experiment, we removed the both-back condition and the both-palm condition, which were not significantly different from the reversed-hand condition in

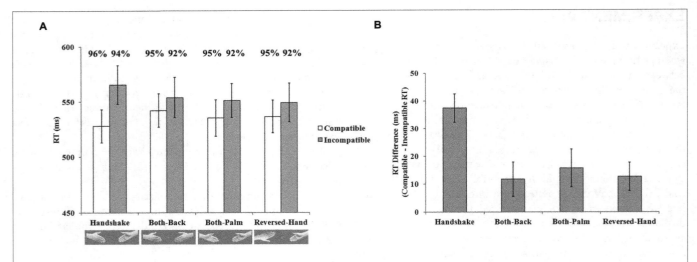

FIGURE 3 | Results of Experiment 2. (A) Mean RT varied as a function of hand-approaching display and compatibility. Mean accuracy rates for every condition was shown above the corresponding bars. **(B)** The mean RT difference between compatible and incompatible trials according to the hand-approaching display is shown. Error bars indicate standard errors.

the previous experiments. Such changes allowed us to maintain an appropriate experimental duration. This sub-experiment employed a 2 (hands status: hands-present, hands-disappear) × 2 (hand-approaching display: handshake, reversed-hand) × 2 (validity: valid, invalid) within-subjects design. The total number of trials, presented in a random order, was 360.

Similarly, the sub-experiment with the interference task had an additional hands-disappear condition, in which the hands disappeared after the cue offset. Again, we removed the both-back condition and the both-palm condition. Thus, this sub-experiment used a 2 (hands status: hands-present, hands-disappear) × 2 (hand-approaching display: handshake, reversed-hand) × 2 (compatibility: compatible, incompatible) within-subjects design. Each participant completed 240 trials (30 in each condition).

Results and Discussion
Cueing Task
Figure 4A shows the mean RTs for correct trials in the four conditions of the cueing task. To examine the social-information-induced attention effect in different hands status (hands-present/hands-disappear), we ran a 2 (hands status) × 2 (hand-approaching display) × 2 (validity) repeated-measures ANOVA for the mean RTs in correct trials. The result showed significant main effects of hand-approaching display, $F(1,19) = 9.14, p < 0.01, \eta_p^2 = 0.33$, and validity, $F(1,19) = 42.81, p < 0.001, \eta_p^2 = 0.69$. The interaction between hands status and validity was significant, $F(1,19) = 8.03, p < 0.05, \eta_p^2 = 0.30$. And the interaction between hand-approaching display and validity was significant, $F(1,19) = 5.28, p < 0.05, \eta_p^2 = 0.22$. Other effects were failed to reach significance, $Fs < 1.33, ps > 0.26$, including the 3-way interaction, although when hands were present the mean RT difference between valid and invalid trials was smaller in the handshake condition than in the reversed-hand condition (see **Figure 4B**), $t(19) = 3.37, p < 0.01$, which

replicating the result of Experiment 1; while this difference was not significant when hands were removed, $t(19) = 0.86, p = 0.40$. The insignificant 3-way interaction was probably because that the differential RTs were in the same direction for the hands-present and hands-disappear conditions: the handshake display led to smaller cueing effect than the reversed-hand display, in both the hands-present and hands-disappear conditions, although the difference of the cueing effect between handshake and reversed-hand conditions was numerically larger when hands were present (19 ms vs. 8 ms).

The accuracy data were submitted to the same ANOVA. The only significant effect was validity, $F(1,19) = 10.34, p < 0.01, \eta_p^2 = 0.35$, indicating that the accuracy was higher when cue was valid than invalid (97% vs. 94%). The interaction between hands status and validity was marginally significant, $F(1,19) = 3.53, p = 0.08, \eta_p^2 = 0.16$. Other effects were not significant, $Fs < 2.76, ps > 0.11$.

Based on the insignificant 3-way interaction of the RT data, it was not able to make a conclusive answer to the question whether the attention effects induced by handshake display dependent on the image of the hands. One possible explanation for that is the handshake display might produce a general effect that facilitating the attention shifts between all objects (probably very weak), which contributed to the effects found in Experiments 1 and 2; but it cannot completely explain the results, since the effect in the hands-disappear conditions is smaller than that in the hands-present condition. Thus, the whole picture would be clearer in combination of the interference effect.

Interference Task
Figure 4C shows the mean RTs for correct trials in the four conditions of the interference task. For the interference task, the 2 (hands status) × 2 (hand-approaching display) × 2 (compatibility) repeated-measures ANOVA revealed significant main effect of compatibility, $F(1,19) = 7.57, p < 0.05, \eta_p^2 = 0.29$.

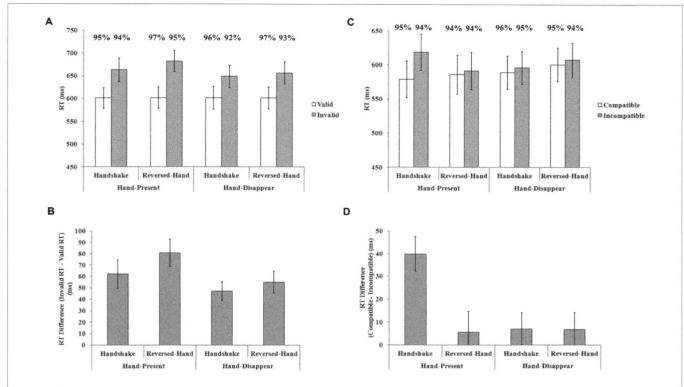

FIGURE 4 | Results of Experiment 3. (A) and (B) respectively, depict the mean RT and RT difference between the invalid and valid trials for the cueing task.
(C) and (D) respectively, depict the mean RT and RT difference between the compatible and incompatible trials for the interference task. Error bars indicate standard errors. Mean accuracy rates for every condition was shown above the corresponding bars.

The other two main effects were not significant, $Fs < 0.37$, $ps > 0.55$. All the 2-way interactions were significant: hands status × hand-approaching display, $F(1,19) = 7.44$, $p < 0.05$, $\eta_p^2 = 0.28$; hands status × compatibility, $F(1,19) = 4.90$, $p < 0.05$, $\eta_p^2 = 0.21$; hand-approaching display × compatibility, $F(1,19) = 10.55$, $p < 9.01$, $\eta_p^2 = 0.36$. The 3-way interaction was significant, $F(1,19) = 6.17$, $p < 0.05$, $\eta_p^2 = 0.25$, indicating that hands status and hand-approaching display interact together to impact the interference effect. As shown in **Figure 4D**, when the hands were present, the interference effect in the handshake condition was significantly larger than that in the reversed-hand condition, $t(19) = 4.11$, $p < 0.001$; while this difference is not significant when hands were removed, $t(19) = 0.03, p = 0.97$. The ANOVA for accuracy data found no significant effect, $Fs < 2.24$, $ps > 0.15$. These results suggested that the handshake display increased the interference effect only when the hands were present.

Thus, the result of this sub-experiment clearly showed that the interference effect induced by the handshake display vanished when hands were removed. The result of the cueing task was consistent, as the weakened cueing effect induced by the handshake display did fade away in the hands-disappear condition, although the interaction failed to reach statistical significance. Combining the results from both sub-experiments, this experiment showed that the effect is transient and dependent on the existence of the two hands,

providing further evidence to support our hypothesis that the handshake display modulated the attention deployment on the hands.

EXPERIMENT 4

Before conclusions can be drawn, other alternative accounts must be excluded. In addition to its social meaning, the handshake display used in Experiments 1 and 2 is significantly different from the control conditions in two aspects. The first difference is related to perceptual familiarity. People frequently view handshakes but rarely view the scenes depicted in the control conditions; because two hands approaching each other are typically perceived as a grouped entity in an everyday handshake, the display of two approaching hands may activate the representation of two hands holding together. If this account is accurate, then it is probable that social information is not the key factor in determining the attention effect; rather, it is prior experience (i.e., the learned association between objects, also including learned social relationships) that leads to attending to both of the displayed hands, thus not only socially related objects but all kinds of objects that have learned object associations would produce similar attention effects. The second difference is physical fit. That is, the hands in the handshake condition could lock on to each other but the hands in the both-back and both-palm conditions could not. Although the hands in the reversed-hand condition are capable of grasping each other, this act is not as easy to see as in the handshake condition. Thus, the attention effect might be attributed to the physical fit between the two hands rather than social implications.

To test whether mere perceptual familiarity or physical fit result in the attention effects, we introduced a *hand-cup* condition and a *plug-socket* condition in addition to the handshake and reversed-hand conditions. In the hand-cup condition, one of the two hands in the handshake condition was replaced by a cup, which appeared as if it was going to be caught by the hand. In the plug-socket condition, the hands were replaced by a plug and a matching socket, creating the impression that the plug will be plugged into the socket. Both scenes are generally familiar to participants, and the object associations in these scenes are well learned. For the student participants in the present study, the two new scenes may have been even more familiar than the handshake scene. Participants drank from cups several times each day, and plugged in laptops or cell phones frequently. By contrast, these young students were less likely to view handshake scenes on a daily basis. Moreover, the objects (hand and cup, plug and socket) that appeared in each scene were a clear fit with each other.

Hence, according to the perceptual familiarity and physical fit account, we should observe similar attention effects in these two conditions, because the objects are familiar and fit together well. However, compared to the handshake scene that exhibits a clear social relationship between two men, the hand-cup scene is a much less social situation because it shows an active behavior toward a passive object; and the plug-socket scene shows a non-social relationship, which is determined by their shapes that are physically fit with each other. Thus, if social relationship is the key factor to modulate the deployment of attention, the handshake condition should lead to different results from the other two conditions.

Method

Again, Experiment 4 involved two sub-experiments with separate cueing and interference tasks. Twenty naïve Zhejiang University students (9 men and 11 women) participated in the cueing version and another 20 students (11 men and 9 women) participated in the interference version.

The procedure of the cueing and interference task was similar to that of Experiments 1 and 2, respectively, except that the both-back and both-palm conditions were replaced by the hand-cup and plug-socket condition. The cup, plug, and socket had the same width as the hand, and their approaching display adopted the same moving pattern: the hand and cup (or, the plug and socket) moved to approach each other until the images overlapped by $0.7°$. In the cueing task, a cue was presented at one of the objects (which could be a hand, cup, plug, or socket, depending on the condition), followed by a target and a distractor appeared on the two objects. Again, participants performed a "T-or-L" task as quickly as possible. All the parameters (color, shape, size, and duration, etc.) of the cue and target were identical to those of Experiment 1. In the interference task, a central cue (the same arrow as Experiment 2) was presented after the approaching display. Following the cue, a target appeared on the cued object, and a distractor appeared on the uncued object. The same "N-or-X" task was performed. All other experimental details of the interference task were identical to those of Experiments 2.

The cueing task sub-experiment employed a 2 (validity) × 4 (hand-approaching display: *handshake, hand-cup, plug-socket,* and *reversed hand*) within-subjects design, with 90 trials (in which 60 trials were cue-valid, and 30 trials were cue-invalid) in each of the 4 hand-approaching display conditions, resulting in 360 trials in total. The interference task sub-experiment employed a 2 (compatibility) × 4 (hand-approaching display) within-subjects design, with 70 trials in each combined condition, resulting in 560 total trials in total. All of the trials were presented in random order.

Results and Discussion
Cueing Task

Figure 5 (left) shows the mean RTs for correct responses in the cueing task. A 2 (validity) × 4 (hand-approaching display) repeated-measures ANOVA revealed significant main effects of validity, $F(3,57) = 105.39$, $p < 0.001$, $\eta_p^2 = 0.85$, and hand-approaching display, $F(3,57) = 3.99$, $p < 0.05$, $\eta_p^2 = 0.17$, indicating that RT varied with cue validity and display type. However, the interactive effect failed to reach statistical significance, $F(3,57) = 2.49$, $p = 0.09$, $\eta_p^2 = 0.12$, suggesting that the cueing effect did not vary much across the hand-approaching display conditions. The cueing effect, namely the mean RT difference between valid and invalid trials, for the handshake condition (115 ms) was smaller but not significantly so compared to the reverse-hand condition (139 ms), $t(19) = 1.63$, $p = 0.12$. It was also not significantly different from that of the hand-cup (121 ms) and plug-socket (108 ms) display.

The same ANOVA was conducted for the accuracy data, revealing significant main effect of validity, $F(1,19) = 15.06$, $p < 0.001$, $\eta_p^2 = 0.44$. It suggested that the responses were more accurate on valid than invalid trials (97% vs. 94%). No other effect reached statistical significance, $Fs < 1.54, p > 0.22$.

Thus, compared to the control conditions, the handshake condition showed nothing special in modulating the cueing effect, because the cueing effect failed to be significantly smaller than the control conditions. That was not the expected result, so we returned to the result of Experiment 1. After comparing the data from the two Experiments, we found that the cueing effect for the reverse-hand condition remained unchanged (140 ms in Experiment 1 and 139 ms in Experiment 4), although the overall RT decreased; on the other hand, the cueing effect for the handshake condition increased slightly (from 104 ms in Experiment 1 to 115 ms in Experiment 4). As for the hand-cup and plug-socket condition, the cueing effect was low. Thus, we speculated that the familiar non-socially paired objects are also able to facilitate attentional shift between the related objects, and that this facilitative effect is not exclusively for socially related objects. Moreover, since the cueing effect is sensitive to variable factors, such as cue validity, perceptual load, and the subjective organization of stimuli (Chen, 1998; He et al., 2004; Ho and

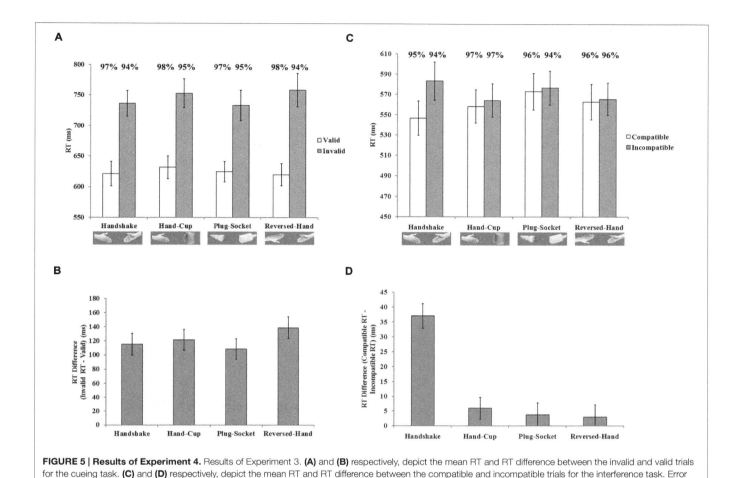

FIGURE 5 | Results of Experiment 4. Results of Experiment 3. **(A)** and **(B)** respectively, depict the mean RT and RT difference between the invalid and valid trials for the cueing task. **(C)** and **(D)** respectively, depict the mean RT and RT difference between the compatible and incompatible trials for the interference task. Error bars indicate standard errors. Mean accuracy rates for every condition was shown above the corresponding bars.

Atchley, 2009), the facilitated attentional shift is likely to be attenuated when other frequently paired objects are presented at the same time. Specifically, when there were three different kinds of paired objects in the same experiment, making most of the trials included related objects, the attentional system might switch to an "easy-shift" mode in those trials while treat the only different condition – the reversed-hand condition in a special way. In this case, the handshake condition is treated equally with the hand-cup and plug-socket conditions, therefore diluting the effect induced by the handshake scene, compared to Experiment 1. That is a possible explanation for this experiment failing to obtain a significant smaller cueing effect in the handshake condition than in the reversed-hand condition.

Interference Task

Figure 5 (right) shows the mean RTs for correct responses in the interference task. A 2 (compatibility) × 4 (hand-approaching display) repeated-measures ANOVA revealed a significant main effect of compatibility, $F(1,19) = 29.60$, $p < 0.001$, $\eta_p^2 = 0.61$. The main effect of hand-approaching display was also significant, $F(3,57) = 5.75$, $p < 0.01$, $\eta_p^2 = 0.23$, suggesting that RTs varied with the "background" of the target (i.e., responses were slowest with the plug-socket background). The interaction was

significant, $F(3,57) = 18.44$, $p < 0.001$, $\eta_p^2 = 0.49$, indicating that the interference effect varied across hand-approaching display conditions. The mean RT difference between the compatible and incompatible trials was significant in only the handshake condition, $t(19) = 8.95$, $p < 0.001$. In all control conditions, the mean RTs were not significantly different between the compatible and incompatible trials, $ps > 0.12$.

The same ANOVA was conducted for the accuracy data, revealing significant main effect of hand-approaching display, $F(3,17) = 4.00$, $p < 0.05$, $\eta_p^2 = 0.41$. It suggested that the accuracy varied with the background of the target and distractor. No other effect reached statistical significance, $Fs < 1.03$, $p > 0.32$.

Thus, the handshake display showed its specificity in the interference task because of the significant interference effect. The possible reasons for the divergent results of the cueing and interference task are discussed in the General Discussion. Our results indicate that not all learned object associations lead to the attention effects induced by the handshake display; therefore, there must be something inherent in the handshake scene such that the attentional system treats the two hands as an inseparable unit. The key factor, we speculated, is likely to be the social information contained in it.

GENERAL DISCUSSION

This study demonstrates that, when two hands approach each other, seemingly to perform a handshake, the response to the target presented on one hand facilitated the attentional cue presented on the non-target hand (Experiment 1), and responses to a target on one hand was significantly impaired by a distractor on the other hand (Experiment 2). We confirmed that these effects were dependent on the existence of the hands, thus were due to modulating of the deployment of attention on the hands (Experiment 3). The findings were also not explained merely by perceptual familiarity or physical fit, because other paired objects that are common in daily life did not show the same effects (Experiment 4).

The Social Nature of Attention Deployment

The handshake display contains several visual features and pieces of semantic information; hence, one might argue that the observed attention effects may not be the result of social factors. We posit, however, that the attention effects observed in the current experiments is associated with social factors for three reasons. First, similarity is not the cause of the attention effects. In the both-hand and both-palm conditions, the two hands displayed more similarities than those displayed in the handshake condition; yet, there was no such effect in the former two conditions. Second, the attention effects cannot be attributed to the impending action implied by the display, because all of the control conditions involved approach actions. Third, merely watching other peoples' hands that are not socially related cannot lead to the attention effects. Taylor et al. (2015) showed that the attention shift across others' hands is nothing special, but just like any other surface. Thus, in the current study, the social information brought by the handshake action should be the key factor to cause the attention effects. Fourth, mere perceptual familiarity and physical fit do not lead to exactly the same effects. Experiment 4 demonstrated that other familiar paired objects (such as hand and cup or plug and socket, which lock onto each other in a similar manner to hands) did not show the same pattern in modulating attention deployment—that is, the learned object associations facilitated the attentional shift from the cued object to the other, but the interference effect occurred only between the hands approaching to perform handshake. Thus, these results could not be solely explained by learned object associations; rather, the social information conveyed by the handshake action is likely to play an important role.

Based on the above reasons, we argue that the social relationship exhibited by the handshake scene leads to the attention effects observed in both the cueing and interference tasks, although we do not exclude the possibility that such pre-learned associations is needed for social information to induce such effects. Further studies are thus required to examine whether

a novel social relationship between objects would lead to the same results.

Humans can make high-level cognitive inferences about the relationships between objects, intentionally regard them as a unit, and redeploy attention accordingly. Does the attention effect in mutual approaching hands, therefore, result from high-level cognitive inferences? We argue that it in fact occurs at a perceptual level. First, if the experimental manipulation were transparent to participants, then they might have intentionally employed strategies to modulate their responses. However, the hand-approaching display manipulation, and the task in the current experiments—to report the identity of the target—were ostensibly unrelated to the purpose of our experiments, which was to investigate how socially related objects modulate attention deployment. Thus, it was unlikely that the participants intended to respond according to experimenter expectations. Second, post-experiment interviews confirmed that participants failed to discern the actual purpose of the study. Indeed, the majority of participants believed that the hand-approaching display was employed to distract them and attempted to ignore it as a result. Thus, the effect occurred involuntarily, providing evidence that socially related objects do not affect attention deployment via higher-level cognitive processes.

The Interaction between Social Processing and Attention Deployment

Converging with research in the gaze cueing effect (Frischen et al., 2007) and the attentional consequences induced by social interaction (Yin et al., 2013), the current findings provide further evidence that our visual system deploy attention according to social information. Such social-based attention deployment is probably achieved through the interaction between social and perceptual processes. Previous studies (Beck and Palmer, 2002; Kimchi and Hadad, 2002) have demonstrated that perceptual organization interacts with higher-level processes rather than working in a purely stimulus-driven, bottom-up fashion (Neisser, 1967; Beck, 1975; Marr, 1982; Treisman, 1986). In addition, Palmer et al. (2003) suggested that visual organization occurs at each level of representation rather than at a single level, and that the organization relies on features extracted from different levels. Thus, the interactive processes between the social and perceptual system enables organization according to various sources of visual information, including the social structure of a visual scene, such that attention could be deployed based on the perceptual units defined by the social relationship among objects.

Indeed, a growing body of research has indicated that vision is more social than expected. On the one hand, the visual system can recover social properties from the physical properties of objects and events. For example, although simple mechanical interactions between objects convey little information, the visual system can infer their social properties, producing strong impressions of animacy (Heider and Simmel, 1944; Scholl and Tremoulet, 2000;

Schlottmann et al., 2006) and recovering social structures, such as causality, goals and intentions, from their interactions (Michotte, 1954/1963; Dasser et al., 1989; Dittrich and Lea, 1994; Gao et al., 2009, 2010). On the other hand, social information offers effective cues for lower-level perceptual processing. For example, a gaze cue guides our attention (Langton et al., 2000; Frischen et al., 2007), and changes in facial expressions influence the causal perceptions of physical events (Zhou et al., 2012). Furthermore, the present study revealed that even a lower-level perceptual process, such as attentional selection, is affected by social factors. Such effect is not unique to the handshake scene. Rather, it is more likely a common phenomenon that occurs in different social situations. Yin et al. (2013) demonstrated that a cooperative relationship, which was reflected in the dynamic chases, led to attentional consequence induced by the perceptual grouping of cooperative objects. In those cases, social information provides additional cues for the process through which people form effective inferences about the external world structure. More importantly, it reveals that social properties are assigned to visual representations early at the perceptual stages, suggesting that social processing begins to interact with visual perception at fundamental visual processes. The perceptual foundation of subsequent processing is thereby established to understand social structures and interact with other people. For example, if we observe two people talking to each other, we are likely to choose a path around them (rather than between them) when passing by. If these people are treated as a unit from the start at the perceptual stage and attention is deployed accordingly, then the cognitive system will plan a path around them without explicitly considering the social consequences of each possible path. Further studies should be conducted to examine the social-based attention effects in such real-life situations, applying the cognitive ethology approach (Kingstone et al., 2008; Kingstone, 2009), in order to generalize the experimental phenomena obtained from controlled lab situation to more stimulus-rich situations.

In addition, further studies are needed to investigate how social information modulate attention. Take the facilitated attentional shift in the handshake condition for an example, there are at least three possible mechanisms[1] of this effect: First, the hands are perceptually grouped due to their social relationship, thus attention automatically spread within the perceptual group, leading to speeded attentional shift between two hands. Second, the handshake display speeds the disengagement of attention from one hand, therefore attention is easier to orient to the other hand. Third, the handshake display may "reset" the attention allocation to direct the focus to the middle of the display, resulting in faster responses in the invalid trials and slower responses in the valid trials, thus the cueing effect is weakened. Those possible accounts need to be tested to reveal the mechanisms of social-based attention modulation in follow-up research.

---

[1] Thanks for a reviewer for pointing out the latter two possibilities.

Differences and Similarities between Social and Non-social Paired Objects

Experiment 4 revealed that the handshake display was similar to other non-social paired objects in facilitating attentional shift between objects—the response to the target present on one object was quicker when the other object was cued. However, they were different in the interference task, that is, the between-object interference occurred in only the handshake condition. This divergence is noteworthy, as it seems that the specificity of the social information included in the handshake display greatly reflects the interference effect.

It has been reported that the familiarity of the stimulus leads to the grouping of objects and consequently affects attention. For example, familiar words (Kumada and Humphreys, 2001) and action relationships (Humphreys and Riddoch, 2007) affect attentional selection, such that one attends to the related objects as a single unit. Our finding extends this line of research, suggesting that the learned social relationship between objects leads to a similar effect. The different behavior in the interference task suggests that it is more difficult to regard the socially related objects as two parts, leading to more difficulty in inhibiting the distractor on one of the objects, compared to the case of non-socially related objects. At least under the current experimental settings, the interference task may be more sensitive in detecting the specific attentional effect induced by socially related objects. Further study is needed to clarify what and how socially related objects differ from other familiar pairs in modulating attention.

CONCLUSION

In summary, we demonstrated one example, the handshake-induced attention effects, as the evidence for the assumption that attention deployment can be modulated by the learned social relationships between objects. Generalization of such effects is required to further test this assumption, and to get more evidence to fully understand the role of social information in attention processes.

AUTHOR CONTRIBUTIONS

JZ, JY, and MS conceived and designed the experiments. JY and XD performed the experiments and collected the data. JY, JZ, and MS performed the data analyses. All authors contributed to the result interpretation and manuscript writing. All authors approved the final version of the manuscript for submission.

ACKNOWLEDGMENTS

This research is supported by the National Natural Science Foundation of China (No. 31571119, No. 31170975), and the Fundamental Research Funds for the Central Universities (No. 2015QNA3021).

REFERENCES

Baron-Cohen, S. (1995). "The eye direction detector (EDD) and the shared attention mechanism (SAM): two cases for evolutionary psychology," in *Joint Attention Its Origins and Role in Development*, eds C. Moore and P. J. Dunham (Hillsdale, NJ: Lawrence Erlbaum Associates, Publishers), 41–59.

Beck, D. M., and Palmer, S. E. (2002). Top-down influences on perceptual grouping. *J. Exp. Psychol. Hum. Percept. Perform.* 28, 1071–1084.

Beck, J. (1975). Relation between similarity grouping and perceptual constancy. *Am. J. Psychol.* 88, 397–409. doi: 10.2307/1421770

Bruzzo, A., Borghi, A. M., and Ghirlanda, S. (2008). Hand–object interaction in perspective. *Neurosci. Lett.* 441, 61–65. doi: 10.1016/j.neulet.2008.06.020

Chen, Z. (1998). Switching attention within and between objects: the role of subjective organization. *Can. J. Exp. Psychol.* 52, 7–17. doi: 10.1037/h0087274

Cohen, J. (1988). *Statistical Power Analysis for the Behavioral Sciences*, 2nd Edn. Hillsdale, NJ: Lawrence Earlbaum Associates.

Dasser, V., Ulbaek, I., and Premack, D. (1989). The perception of intention. *Science* 243, 365–367. doi: 10.1126/science.2911746

Dittrich, W. H., and Lea, S. E. (1994). Visual perception of intentional motion. *Perception* 23, 253–268. doi: 10.1068/p230253

Driver, J., Davis, G., Ricciardelli, P., Kidd, P., Maxwell, E., and Baron-Cohen, S. (1999). Gaze perception triggers reflexive visuospatial orienting. *Vis. Cogn.* 6, 509–540. doi: 10.1080/135062899394920

Driver, J., Davis, G., Russell, C., Turatto, M., and Freeman, E. (2001). Segmentation, attention and phenomenal visual objects. *Cognition* 80, 61–95. doi: 10.1016/S0010-0277(00)00151-7

Duncan, J., and Duncan, J. (1984). Selective attention and the organization of visual information. *J. Exp. Psychol. Gen.* 113, 501–517. doi: 10.1037/0096-3445.113.4.501

Egly, R., Driver, J., and Rafal, R. D. (1994). Shifting visual attention between objects and locations: evidence from normal and parietal lesion subjects. *J. Exp. Psychol. Gen.* 123, 161–177. doi: 10.1037/0096-3445.123.2.161

Faul, F., Erdfelder, E., Buchner, A., and Lang, A.-G. (2009). Statistical power analyses using G*Power 3.1: tests for correlation and regression analyses. *Behav. Res. Methods* 41, 1149–1160. doi: 10.3758/BRM.41.4.1149

Faul, F., Erdfelder, E., Lang, A.-G., and Buchner, A. (2007). G*Power 3: a flexible statistical power analysis program for the social, behavioral, and biomedical sciences. *Behav. Res. Methods* 39, 175–191. doi: 10.3758/BF03193146

Flombaum, J. I., and Scholl, B. J. (2006). A temporal same-object advantage in the tunnel effect: facilitated change detection for persisting objects. *J. Exp. Psychol. Hum. Percept. Perform.* 32, 840–853.

Friesen, C. K., and Kingstone, A. (1998). The eyes have it! Reflexive orienting is triggered by nonpredictive gaze. *Psychon. Bull. Rev.* 5, 490–493. doi: 10.3758/BF03208827

Friesen, C. K., Ristic, J., and Kingstone, A. (2004). Attentional effects of counterpredictive gaze and arrow cues. *J. Exp. Psychol. Hum. Percept. Perform.* 30, 319–329.

Frischen, A., Bayliss, A. P., and Tipper, S. P. (2007). Gaze cueing of attention: visual attention, social cognition, and individual differences. *Psychol. Bull.* 133, 694–724. doi: 10.1037/0033-2909.133.4.694

Gao, T., McCarthy, G., and Scholl, B. J. (2010). The wolfpack effect: perception of animacy irresistibly influences interactive behavior. *Psychol. Sci.* 21, 1845–1853. doi: 10.1177/0956797610388814

Gao, T., Newman, G. E., and Scholl, B. J. (2009). The psychophysics of chasing: a case study in the perception of animacy. *Cogn. Psychol.* 59, 154–179. doi: 10.1016/j.cogpsych.2009.03.001

He, X., Fan, S., Zhou, K., and Chen, L. (2004). Cue validity and object-based attention. *J. Cogn. Neurosci.* 16, 1085–1097. doi: 10.1162/0898929041502689

Heider, F., and Simmel, M. (1944). An experimental study of apparent behavior. *Am. J. Psychol.* 57, 243–259. doi: 10.2307/1416950

Ho, M. C., and Atchley, P. (2009). Perceptual load modulates object-based attention. *J. Exp. Psychol. Hum. Percept. Perform.* 35, 166–11. doi: 10.1037/a0016893

Humphreys, G. W., and Riddoch, M. J. (2007). How to define an object: evidence from the effects of action on perception and attention. *Mind Lang.* 22, 534–547. doi: 10.1111/j.1468-0017.2007.00319.x

Kahneman, D., Treisman, A., and Gibbs, B. J. (1992). The reviewing of object files: object-specific integration of information. *Cogn. Psychol.* 24, 175–219. doi: 10.1016/0010-0285(92)90007-O

Kimchi, R., and Hadad, B. S. (2002). Influence of past experience on perceptual grouping. *Psychol. Sci.* 13, 41–47. doi: 10.1111/1467-9280.00407

Kingstone, A. (2009). Taking a real look at social attention. *Curr. Opin. Neurobiol.* 19, 52–56. doi: 10.1016/j.conb.2009.05.004

Kingstone, A., Smilek, D., and Eastwood, J. D. (2008). Cognitive ethology: a new approach for studying human cognition. *Br. J. Psychol.* 99, 317–340. doi: 10.1348/000712607X251243

Kumada, T., and Humphreys, G. W. (2001). Lexical recovery on extinction: interactions between visual form and stored knowledge modulate visual selection. *Cogn. Neuropsychol.* 18, 465–478. doi: 10.1080/02643290042000224

Langton, S. R. H., Watt, R. J., and Bruce, V. (2000). Do the eyes have it? Cues to the direction of social attention. *Trends Cogn. Sci.* 4, 50–59. doi: 10.1016/S1364-6613(99)01436-9

Liuzza, M. T., Setti, A., and Borghi, A. M. (2012). Kids observing other kids' hands: visuomotor priming in children. *Conscious. Cogn.* 21, 383–392. doi: 10.1016/j.concog.2011.09.015

Marr, D. (1982). *Vision*. San Francisco, CA: Freeman.

Michotte, A. (1954/1963). *The Perception of Causality* (trans. T. R. Miles and E. Miles). London: Methuen.

Moore, C. M., Yantis, S., and Vaughan, B. (1998). Object-based visual selection: evidence from perceptual completion. *Psychol. Sci.* 9, 104–110. doi: 10.1111/1467-9280.00019

Neisser, U. (1967). *Cognitive Psychology*. New York, NY: Appleton-Century-Crofts.

Palmer, S. E. (2003). "Perceptual organization and grouping," in *Perceptual Organization in Vision: Behavioral and Neural Perspectives*, eds R. Kimchi, M. Behrmann, and C. R. Olson (Mahwah, NJ: Lawrence Erlbaum Associates), 3–43.

Palmer, S. E., Brooks, J. L., and Nelson, R. (2003). When does grouping happen? *Acta Psychol.* 114, 311–330. doi: 10.1016/j.actpsy.2003.06.003

Reed, C. L., Grubb, J. D., and Steele, C. (2006). Hands up: attentional prioritization of space near the hand. *J. Exp. Psychol. Hum. Percept. Perform.* 32, 166–177.

Sato, W., Okada, T., and Toichi, M. (2007). Attentional shift by gaze is triggered without awareness. *Exp. Brain Res.* 183, 87–94. doi: 10.1007/s00221-007-1025-x

Schlottmann, A., Ray, E. D., Mitchell, A., and Demetriou, N. (2006). Perceived physical and social causality in animated motions: spontaneous reports and ratings. *Acta Psychol.* 123, 112–143. doi: 10.1016/j.actpsy.2006.05.006

Scholl, B. J. (2001). Objects and attention: the state of the art. *Cognition* 80, 1–46. doi: 10.1016/S0010-0277(00)00152-9

Scholl, B. J., and Tremoulet, P. D. (2000). Perceptual causality and animacy. *Trends Cogn. Sci.* 4, 299–309. doi: 10.1016/S1364-6613(00)01506-0

Sternberg, R. J. (2003). *Cognitive Psychology*, 3rd Edn. Belmont, CA: Thomson Wadsworth.

Taylor, J. E. T., Pratt, J., and Witt, J. K. (2015). Joint attention for stimuli on the hands: ownership matters. *Front. Psychol.* 6:543. doi: 10.3389/fpsyg.2015.00543

Taylor, J. E. T., and Witt, J. K. (2014). Altered attention for stimuli on the hands. *Cognition* 133, 211–225. doi: 10.1016/j.cognition.2014.06.019

Treisman, A. (1986). "Properties, parts, and objects," in *Handbook of Perception and Human Performance*, Vol. 2, eds K. R. Boff, L. Kaufman, and J. P. Thomas (New York, NY: Wiley), 1–70.

Wertheimer, M. (1923). Untersuchungen zur Lehre von der Gestalt. II. *Psychol. Res.* 4, 301–350. doi: 10.1007/BF00410640

Yin, J., Ding, X., Zhou, J., Shui, R., Li, X., and Shen, M. (2013). Social grouping: perceptual grouping of objects by cooperative but not competitive relationships in dynamic chase. *Cognition* 129, 194–204. doi: 10.1016/j.cognition.2013.06.013

Zhou, J., Huang, X., Jin, X., Liang, J., Shui, R., and Shen, M. (2012). Perceived causalities of physical events are influenced by social cues. *J. Exp. Psychol. Hum. Percept. Perform.* 38, 1465–1475. doi: 10.1037/a0027976

Conflict of Interest Statement: The authors declare that the research was conducted in the absence of any commercial or financial relationships that could be construed as a potential conflict of interest.

Compulsive Buying Behavior: Clinical Comparison with Other Behavioral Addictions

Roser Granero [1,2], Fernando Fernández-Aranda [1,3,4], Gemma Mestre-Bach [3], Trevor Steward [1,3], Marta Baño [1,3], Amparo del Pino-Gutiérrez [5], Laura Moragas [3], Núria Mallorquí-Bagué [1,3], Neus Aymamí [3], Mónica Gómez-Peña [3], Salomé Tárrega [2], José M. Menchón [3,4,6] and Susana Jiménez-Murcia [1,3,4*]

[1] Ciber Fisiopatología Obesidad y Nutrición (CIBERObn), Instituto de Salud Carlos III, Barcelona, Spain, [2] Departament de Psicobiologia i Metodologia de les Ciències de la Salut, Universitat Autònoma de Barcelona, Barcelona, Spain, [3] Pathological Gambling Unit, Department of Psychiatry, Bellvitge University Hospital-IDIBELL, Barcelona, Spain, [4] Department of Clinical Sciences, Faculty of Medicine, University of Barcelona, Barcelona, Spain, [5] Nursing Department of Mental Health, Public Health, Maternal and Child Health, Nursing School, University of Barcelona, Barcelona, Spain, [6] Ciber de Salud Mental (CIBERSAM), Instituto de Salud Carlos III, Barcelona, Spain

Edited by:
Matthias Brand,
University Duisburg-Essen, Germany

Reviewed by:
Daria Joanna Kuss,
Nottingham Trent University, UK
Astrid Müller,
Hannover Medical School, Germany

*Correspondence:
Susana Jiménez-Murcia
sjimenez@bellvitgehospital.cat

Specialty section:
This article was submitted to
Psychopathology,
a section of the journal
Frontiers in Psychology

Compulsive buying behavior (CBB) has been recognized as a prevalent mental health disorder, yet its categorization into classification systems remains unsettled. The objective of this study was to assess the sociodemographic and clinic variables related to the CBB phenotype compared to other behavioral addictions. Three thousand three hundred and twenty four treatment-seeking patients were classified in five groups: CBB, sexual addiction, Internet gaming disorder, Internet addiction, and gambling disorder. CBB was characterized by a higher proportion of women, higher levels of psychopathology, and higher levels in the personality traits of novelty seeking, harm avoidance, reward dependence, persistence, and cooperativeness compared to other behavioral addictions. Results outline the heterogeneity in the clinical profiles of patients diagnosed with different behavioral addiction subtypes and shed new light on the primary mechanisms of CBB.

Keywords: behavioral addictions, compulsive buying behavior, gambling disorder, internet gaming disorder, internet addiction, sex addiction

INTRODUCTION

Compulsive buying behavior (CBB), otherwise known as shopping addiction, pathological buying or compulsive buying disorder, is a mental health condition characterized by the persistent, excessive, impulsive, and uncontrollable purchase of products in spite of severe psychological, social, occupational, financial consequences (Müller et al., 2015b). Whereas, ordinary non-addicted consumers state value and usefulness as their primary motives for shopping, compulsive buyers make purchases in order to improve their mood, cope with stress, gain social approval/recognition, and improve their self-image (Lejoyeux and Weinstein, 2010; Karim and Chaudhri, 2012; McQueen et al., 2014; Roberts et al., 2014). Although the aftermath of protracted CBB includes feelings of regret/remorse over purchases, shame, guilt, legal and financial problems, and interpersonal difficulties, people with CBB fail in their attempts to stop compulsive buying (Konkolÿ Thege et al., 2015).

The frequency of CBB has increased worldwide during the two last decades. A recent meta-analysis estimated a pooled prevalence of 4.9% for CBB in adult representative samples, with higher ratios for university students, those of non-community origin and shopping-specific participants (Maraz et al., 2015). However, prevalence estimations in epidemiological research vary and can range from 1 to 30% depending on the type of sample studied (Basu et al., 2011).

One major difficulty in estimating CBB prevalence is that the categorization of this psychopathological condition in international classification systems continues to be debated and consensus on diagnosis criteria has yet to be reached. As a matter of fact, the concept of "addiction" itself was a contentious subject matter in the preparation of the Diagnostic and Statistical Manual of Mental Disorders fifth edition (DSM-5; American Psychiatric Association, 2013; Piquet-Pessôa et al., 2014). Currently the available operational definitions for CBB have relied on similarities with disorders in the impulsive control spectrum (Potenza, 2014; Robbins and Clark, 2015), mainly linked to substance use disorders (Grant et al., 2013), obsessive-compulsive disorder (Weinstein et al., 2015), eating disorders (Fernández-Aranda et al., 2006, 2008; Jiménez-Murcia et al., 2015) and other behavioral addictions such as gambling disorder (Black et al., 2010), Internet gaming disorder (IGD) and Internet addiction (Suissa, 2015; Trotzke et al., 2015), and sexual addiction (Derbyshire and Grant, 2015; Farré et al., 2015).

The specific etiology of CBB is still unknown. Diverse factors have been proposed as likely contributors and the few CBB studies conducted to date have largely been centered on neurobiological factors, with research on genetic factors and CBB being nonexistent. As in substance use disorders, brain imaging studies in people with CBB and other behavioral addictions have consistently found abnormalities in frontoparietal regions, reward processing, and limbic systems (Raab et al., 2011; Baik, 2013; Leeman and Potenza, 2013; Probst and van Eimeren, 2013; Vanderah and Sandweiss, 2015). However, the presently available neurological evidence does not fully explain how concrete neural mechanisms and cognitive processes can cause normal-shopping behavior to become addictive in the absence of exogenous drug stimulation (Clark, 2014; Engel and Caceda, 2015). Unlike in other addictive conditions, it has been stated that the development of CBB depends on the presence of particular cultural mechanisms, such as a market-based economy, a wide variety of available goods, disposable income, and materialistic values (Unger et al., 2014).

Regarding the CBB phenotype, research studies highlight shared common features with other behavioral addictions (El-Guebaly et al., 2012; Choi et al., 2014; Grant and Chamberlain, 2014; Di Nicola et al., 2015). Gray's Reinforcement Sensitivity Theory, which has been applied to other behavioral addictive disorders, argues that high levels of behavioral approach system (BAS) predispose individuals to engage in impulsive behaviors (Franken et al., 2006). It has also been used to explain the addictive processes underlying CBB: both reinforcement-punishment systems seem to participate in the onset and development of this disorder (Davenport et al., 2012). Although

in clinical samples, a greater association has been found between this disorder and higher levels of behavioral activation (Claes et al., 2010; Müller et al., 2014). Furthermore, dysfunctional emotion regulation also seems to be implied in the phenotype of behavioral addictions, particularly in aspects such as managing cravings and withdrawal symptoms(Kellett et al., 2009; Williams and Grisham, 2012).

The early onset of problematic behavior is also considered a common feature of these addictive activities, and epidemiological research has found that addictive behaviors tend to become problematic in late adolescence (Balogh et al., 2013; Maraz et al., 2015). It is during this stage of development when impulsivity and risky behaviors may be most socially tolerated or even promoted by peers, which could constitute a potential risk factor for developing an addiction (Dayan et al., 2010; Hartston, 2012). It must be highlighted however that some representative surveys in Europe in the recent years have demonstrated increases in the estimated prevalence of behavioral addictions in older adult populations (Mueller et al., 2010).

The study of the CBB phenotype and related personality traits has also generated consistent results with other behavioral addictions. Research has shown that compulsive buying is characterized by high impulsivity scores, novelty seeking and compulsivity (Black et al., 2012; Di Nicola et al., 2015; Munno et al., 2015), along with high levels in both positive and negative urgency traits (Rose and Segrist, 2014), coinciding with the findings obtained in gambling disorder (Janiri et al., 2007; Tárrega et al., 2015), IGD or in sexual addictions (Jiménez-Murcia et al., 2014b; Farré et al., 2015).

Finally, CBB is associated with significant comorbidity, particularly with psychiatric conditions that are also highly prevalent in other behavioral addictions (Mueller et al., 2010; Aboujaoude, 2014), such as mood disorders, anxiety disorders, substance use, other impulse control disorders, and eating disorders (Fernández-Aranda et al., 2006, 2008).

Heterogeneous features in both clinical and personality aspects have also been reported when comparing CBB with other behavioral addictions. Firstly, epidemiological studies point to strong sex differences (Fattore et al., 2014): whereas CBB is more prevalent in women (Otero-López and Villardefrancos, 2014), gambling disorder (Ashley and Boehlke, 2012), and sexual addiction (Farré et al., 2015) are more prevalent in men.

Regarding CBB patients' psychopathological state, to our knowledge few studies with clinical samples have assessed the specific differences between CBB and other behavioral additions. As such, the objectives of this study are: (a) to ascertain the most relevant socio-demographic and clinical characteristics associated to CBB in a large clinical sample of patients with behavioral addictions; and (b) to compare the CBB profile with other behavioral addictions (sexual addiction, IGD, Internet addiction, and gambling disorder).

MATERIALS AND METHODS

Sample

All the patients who arrived at the Pathological Gambling Unit in the Psychiatry Department at Bellvitge University Hospital in Barcelona (Spain), from January 2005 to August 2015, were potential participants in this study. Exclusion criteria for the study were the presence of an organic mental disorder, intellectual disability, or active psychotic disorder. Bellvitge University Hospital is a public hospital certified as a tertiary care center for the treatment of behavioral addictions and oversees the treatment of highly complex cases. The catchment area of the hospital includes over two million people in the Barcelona metropolitan area.

All participants were diagnosed according to DSM-IV criteria (SCID-I; First et al., 1996) and using specific questionnaires for each disorder. Interviews were conducted by psychologists and psychiatrists with more than 15 years of experience in the field.

The study sample included $n = 3324$ patients, who were classified into five groups according to their diagnostic subtype: CBB ($n = 110$), sexual addiction ($n = 28$), IGD ($n = 51$), Internet addiction ($n = 41$), and gambling disorder ($n = 3094$). Mutual exclusivity criterion was required to include the patients in the groups, that is, the addictions considered in this study did not occur at the same time to allow for the estimation and comparison of the specific clinical state of each behavioral addiction type (39 patients were excluded from our analyses for meeting the criteria of having more than one behavioral addiction).

Measures
Evaluation of Current and Lifetime Substance use Disorders and Impulsive Related Behaviors
Patients were assessed using a structured clinical face-to-face interview modeled after the Structured Clinical Interview for DSM-IV (SCID-I; First et al., 1996), covering the lifetime presence of impulsive behaviors, namely alcohol and drug abuse, comorbid impulse control disorders (such as CBB, sexual addiction, and IGD and Internet addiction).

Diagnostic Questionnaire for Pathological Gambling According to DSM Criteria (Stinchfield, 2003)
This 19-item questionnaire allows for the assessment of DSM-IV (American Psychiatric Association, 1994) diagnostic criteria for pathological gambling (in the present study called GD). Convergent validity with the SOGS scores in the original version was very good [$r = 0.77$ for representative samples and $r = 0.75$ for gambling treatment groups (Stinchfield, 2003)]. Internal consistency in the Spanish adaptation used in this study was $\alpha = 0.81$ for the general population and $\alpha = 0.77$ for gambling treatment samples (Jiménez-Murcia et al., 2009). In this study, the total number of DSM-5 criteria for GD was analyzed. Cronbach's alpha in the sample was very good ($\alpha = 0.81$).

South Oaks Gambling Screen (SOGS) (Lesieur and Blume, 1987)
This self-report, 20-item, screening questionnaire discriminates between probable pathological, problem, and non-problem gamblers. The Spanish validated version used in this study has shown excellent internal consistency ($\alpha = 0.94$) and test-retest reliability ($r = 0.98$; Echeburúa et al., 1994). Consistency in the sample of this work was adequate ($\alpha = 0.76$).

Diagnostic Criteria for Compulsive Buying According to McElroy et al. (1994)
These criteria have received wide acceptance in the research community, although their reliability and validity have not yet been determined (Tavares et al., 2008). It's worth noting that no formal diagnostic criteria for CBB have been accepted for the DSM or the ICD−10. At present, it is recommended that CBB diagnosis be determined via detailed face−to−face interviews which explore "buying attitudes, associated feelings, underlying thoughts, and the extent of preoccupation with buying and shopping" (Müller et al., 2015b).

Diagnostic Criteria for IGD According to Griffiths and Hunt (1995, 1998)
To assess IGD diagnosis and to establish the level of dependence on video games, clinical experts conducted a clinical face-to-face interview considering the scale designed by Griffiths and Hunt (1995, 1998). This interview evaluated aspects such as the frequency of the problematic behavior, the interference generated in daily functioning because of maladaptive use of video games or the presence of tolerance and difficulties in abstinence management.

Diagnostic Criteria for Sexual Addiction According to DSM-IV-TR (American Psychiatric Association, 2000)
To assess sexual addiction, a battery of items was administered, which were based on the proposed definition in the DSM-IV-TR (American Psychiatric Association, 2000) in the Sexual Disorders Not Otherwise Specified section (302.9). In making our assessment, the following clinical description was given special weight: "distress about a pattern of repeated sexual relationship involving a succession of lovers who are experienced by the individual only as things to be used."

Diagnostic Criteria for Internet Addiction According to Echeburúa (1999)
To assess Internet addiction, a clinical interview that adapts the nine criteria from Echeburúa (1999) in yes/no responses was used. Four to six scores indicate a risk of dependency and 7–9 an already established problem. Internet addiction categorization is focused on excessive and continuous use of the Internet (social networking, watching videos, television series, and movies online, etc.). These items also explore the urge to carry out this behavior or the failed attempts to reduce its frequency.

Temperament and Character Inventory-Revised (TCI-R) (Cloninger, 1999)
The TCI-R is a reliable and valid 240-item questionnaire which measures seven personality dimensions: four temperament (novelty seeking, harm avoidance, reward dependence, and persistence) and three character dimensions (self-directedness, cooperativeness, and self-transcendence). All items are measured on a 5-point Likert-type scale. The scales in the Spanish revised version showed adequate internal consistency (Cronbach's alpha α mean value of 0.87; Gutiérrez-Zotes et al., 2004). Cronbach's alpha (α) in the sample used in this study is in the good to excellent range (index for each scale is included in **Table 2**).

Symptom Checklist-Revised (SCL-90-R) (Derogatis, 1990)

The SCL-90-R evaluates a broad range of psychological problems and psychopathological symptoms. This questionnaire contains 90 items and measures nine primary symptom dimensions: somatization, obsession-compulsion, interpersonal sensitivity, depression, anxiety, hostility, phobic anxiety, paranoid ideation, and psychoticism. It also includes three global indices: (1) a global severity index (GSI), designed to measure overall psychological distress; (2) a positive symptom distress index (PSDI), to measure symptom intensity; and (3) a positive symptom total (PST), which reflects self-reported symptoms. The Spanish validation scale obtained good psychometrical indexes, with a mean internal consistency of 0.75 (Cronbach's alpha; Martínez-Azumendi et al., 2001). Cronbach's alpha (α) in the sample of this study is in the good to excellent range (indexes for each scale are included in **Table 2**).

Alcohol Use Disorders Identification Test (AUDIT) (Saunders et al., 1993)

This test was developed as a simple screening method for excessive alcohol consumption. AUDIT consists of 10 questions examining alcohol consumption levels, symptoms of alcohol dependence and alcohol-related consequences. Internal consistency has been found to be high, and rest-retest data have suggested high reliability (0.86) and sensitivity around 0.90; specificity in different settings and for different criteria averages 0.80 or more. Three categories were considered for this study, based on the ranges defined by Reinert and Allen (2002): null-low (raw scores under 6 for women and under 8 for men), abuse (raw scores between 6 and 20 for women and between 8 and 20 for men) and risk of dependence (raw scores above 20).

Additional Data

Demographic, clinical, and social/family variables related to gambling were measured using a semi-structured, face-to-face clinical interview described elsewhere (Jiménez-Murcia et al., 2006). Some of the CBB behavior variables covered were the age of CBB onset, the mean and maximum monetary investment in a single shopping episode, and the total amount of accumulated debts.

Procedure

The present study was carried out in accordance with the latest version of the Declaration of Helsinki. The University Hospital of Bellvitge Ethics Committee of Clinical Research approved the study, and signed consent was obtained from all participants. Experienced psychologists and psychiatrists conducted the two face-to-face clinical interviews.

Statistical Analysis

Statistical analysis was carried out with Stata13.1 for Windows. First, the comparison of the sociodemographical, clinical and personality measures between the derived empirical clusters was based on chi-square tests (χ^2) for categorical variables and analysis of variance (ANOVA) for quantitative measures. Cohen's-d measured the effect size of pairwise comparisons ($|d| >$

0.50 was considered moderate effect size and $|d| > 0.80$ high effect size). Bonferroni-Finner's correction controlled for Type-I error due to multiple statistical comparisons for variables measuring clinical state.

Second, a multinomial model valued the capacity of the participants' sex, age, age of onset, education level, civil status, and personality traits levels to discriminate the presence of CBB compared to the other behavioral addictions (gambling, Internet, IGD, and sexual addiction). This model constitutes a generalization of the logistic regression to multiclass-nominal-criteria (dependent variables with more than two categorical levels). Its parameters are estimated to predict the probability of the different categories compared to a reference category-level. In this study, with the aim of obtaining a discriminative model for the presence of CBB, this diagnostic subtype was defined as the reference level. In addition, the set of independent variables was simultaneously included into the model to determine the specific contribution of each variable in identifying CBB. The global predictive capacity of the model was assessed using the McFadden pseudo-R^2 coefficient.

Third, multiple regressions models valued the predictive capacity of the participants' sex, age, age of onset, and personality traits on the psychopathology symptom levels registered on the SCL-90-R depression, anxiety and GSI scales. The ENTER procedure was used to simultaneously include the set of predictors to obtain the specific contribution of each factor to symptom levels.

RESULTS

Evolution of the Prevalence of Consultations for Behavioral Addictions

Figure 1 shows the prevalence of patients attending the specialized unit for treatment because of CBB in comparison to other behavioral addictions (gambling disorder, sexual addiction, IGD, or Internet addiction). The prevalence of consultations due to CBB increased from 2.48% in 2005 to 5.53% in 2015, obtaining a significant linear trend ($\chi^2 = 17.3$, $df = 1$, $p =$

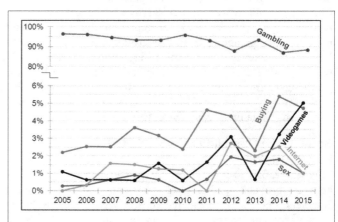

FIGURE 1 | Evolution of the prevalence of consultations due to different behavioral addictions.

0.006) and no statistically significant deviation from linearity ($\chi^2 = 7.27$, $df = 9$, $p = 0.609$). Our results demonstrate that the prevalence of gambling disorder was significantly higher compared to the other behavioral additions. As a whole, the prevalence of consultations was higher for CBB compared to IGD, Internet, and sexual addiction (except for IGD in 2015), but these differences were low.

Comparison between CBB and the Other Behavioral Additions

Table 1 contains the difference between diagnostic subtypes and the patients' sociodemographical variables, as well as data on substance abuse. The frequency of women in the CBB group (71.8%) was clearly higher when compared to the other diagnostic conditions (between 3.6% for sex addiction to 26.8% to Internet addiction). Considering other variables, CBB was characterized by: (a) a higher level of education compared to IGD and gambling addiction; (b) higher prevalence of being married

or living with a partner compared to the IGD and Internet addiction groups; (c) higher levels of employment compared to IGD; and (d) compared to gambling disorder, lower prevalence of smoking, and alcohol abuse and other drug use/abuse.

Table 2 includes mean comparisons between CBB and other diagnostic subtypes for the variables measuring clinical state: patients' age, age of onset, and duration of the problematic behaviors, psychopathological symptoms (SCL-90-R scales) and personality traits (TCI-R scales). No statistical differences emerged comparing CBB with the sexual addiction group. Compared to IGD, Internet addiction and gambling disorder, the CBB clinical profile was characterized by: (a) higher mean age and age of onset compared to IGD and Internet addiction; (b) as a whole, higher psychopathological symptoms (many SCL-90-R scales obtained higher mean scores); and (c) higher mean scores in the personality traits novelty seeking, harm avoidance (in comparison with gambling disorder), reward dependence (in comparison with IGD and gambling disorder),

TABLE 1 | Comparison between diagnostic subtypes for categorical variables: chi-square test and contrasts of buying subtype vs. the other diagnostic subtype.

| | Proportions (%) | | | | | Group | | | Contrasts: buying vs. other addictions | | | | | | | |
| | Buying | Sex | Internet/ gaming | Internet | Gambling | Chi-square tests | | | Sex | | Internet/gaming | | Internet | | Gambling | |
	$n = 110$	$n = 28$	$n = 51$	$n = 41$	$n = 3.094$	χ^2	df	p	p	|d|	P	|d|	p	|d|	p	|d|
SEX																
Female	71.8	3.6	5.9	26.8	10.1	387.15	4	**<0.001***	**0.001***	**1.98†**	**0.001***	**1.84†**	**0.001***	**1.01†**	**0.001***	**1.61†**
Male	28.2	96.4	94.1	73.2	89.9											
ORIGIN																
Immigrant	1.8	0	3.9	2.4	6.5	7.41	4	0.131	0.472	0.19	0.425	0.13	0.808	0.04	0.100	0.24
Spanish	98.2	100	96.1	97.6	93.5											
EDUCATION																
Primary	33.7	26.9	40.0	32.5	57.8	88.61	8	**<0.001***	0.778	0.15	**0.022***	0.13	0.291	0.02	**0.001***	**0.50†**
Secondary	43.3	50.0	55.6	55.0	36.3					0.14		0.25		**0.24**		0.14
University	23.1	23.1	4.4	12.5	5.9					0.00		**0.56†**		0.28		**0.50†**
CIVIL STATUS																
Single	35.5	22.2	91.8	65.0	35.4	84.98	8	**<0.001***	0.260	0.30	**0.001***	**1.44†**	**0.005***	**0.62†**	0.962	0.00
Married-couple	49.5	51.9	6.1	30.0	50.5					0.05		**1.11†**		0.41		0.02
Divorced	15.0	25.9	2.0	5.0	14.1					0.27		0.48		0.34		0.03
EMPLOYED																
No	50.0	35.7	79.6	56.1	43.5	30.00	4	**<0.001***	0.177	0.29	**0.001***	**0.65†**	0.506	0.12	0.183	0.13
Yes	50.0	64.3	20.4	43.9	56.5											
SMOKE USE																
No	62.7	67.9	76.5	75.6	38.7	83.36	4	**<0.001***	0.614	0.11	0.084	0.30	0.137	0.28	**0.001***	0.49
Yes	37.3	32.1	23.5	24.4	61.3											
AUDIT																
Low	95.4	85.7	98.0	95.1	85.0	19.19	8	**0.018***	0.065	0.34	0.415	0.15	0.940	0.01	**0.010***	0.36
Abuse	4.6	14.3	2.0	4.9	14.3					0.34		0.15		0.01		0.34
Risk dependence	0	0	0	0	0.7					0.00		0.00		0.00		0.12
OTHER DRUGS																
No	97.2	85.7	92.2	95.0	90.9	6.97	4	0.138	**0.014***	0.42	0.146	0.23	0.506	0.12	**0.024***	0.27
Yes	2.8	14.3	7.8	5.0	9.1											

*Bold, significant comparison (0.05 level). †Bold: effect size in the moderate (\|d\|> 0.50) to high (\|d\|> 0.80) range. p-values include Bonferroni-Finner correction.

TABLE 2 | Comparison of clinical profiles between diagnostic subtypes at baseline: ANOVA and effect size for pairwise comparisons.

		Means Buying	Sex	Internet/gaming	Internet	Gambling	ANOVA		Sex		Contrasts: buying vs. other addictions					
											Internet/gaming		Internet		Gambling	
		$n=110$	$n=28$	$n=51$	$n=41$	$n=3,094$	$F_{4;3319}$	p	p	$|d|$	p	$|d|$	p	$|d|$	p	$|d|$
Age (years)		43.3	41.3	22.0	31.7	42.9	38.03	<0.001*	0.909	0.17	0.001*	2.15†	0.001*	0.96†	0.997	0.03
Onset (years)		38.9	37.5	19.9	29.8	38.3	26.25	<0.001*	0.973	0.11	0.001*	1.81†	0.001*	0.72†	0.973	0.05
Duration (years)		4.4	4.3	2.5	2.4	4.9	3.82	0.013*	0.999	0.01	0.233	0.42	0.253	0.45	0.776	0.09
SCL-90-R: Somatization	$\alpha=0.89$	1.4	1.1	0.5	0.9	0.9	11.96	<0.001*	0.151	0.37	0.001*	1.03†	0.001*	0.62†	0.001*	0.52†
SCL-90-R: Obs./comp.	$\alpha=0.86$	1.8	1.5	1.1	1.5	1.1	16.99	<0.001*	0.406	0.25	0.001*	0.79†	0.193	0.31	0.001*	0.68†
SCL-90-R: Int. sensitivity	$\alpha=0.85$	1.4	1.3	1.1	1.1	1.0	6.63	<0.001*	0.880	0.14	0.135	0.30	0.138	0.35	0.001*	0.44
SCL-90-R: Depressive	$\alpha=0.90$	2.0	1.8	1.0	1.5	1.5	11.98	<0.001*	0.454	0.25	0.001*	0.99†	0.004*	0.56†	0.001*	0.53†
SCL-90-R: Anxiety	$\alpha=0.87$	1.5	1.3	0.8	1.0	1.0	9.81	<0.001*	0.776	0.16	0.001*	0.77†	0.006*	0.53†	0.001*	0.48
SCL-90-R: Hostility	$\alpha=0.82$	1.2	1.2	1.1	1.0	0.9	5.15	<0.001*	0.999	0.03	0.509	0.20	0.268	0.31	0.001*	0.37
SCL-90-R: Phobic	$\alpha=0.80$	0.8	0.6	0.3	0.5	0.5	6.93	<0.001*	0.168	0.36	0.001*	0.61†	0.018*	0.44	0.001*	0.42
SCL-90-R: Paranoid	$\alpha=0.77$	1.3	1.1	1.1	1.0	0.9	6.43	<0.001*	0.850	0.15	0.617	0.17	0.108	0.38	0.001*	0.43
SCL-90-R: Psychotic	$\alpha=0.83$	1.1	1.3	0.6	1.0	0.9	4.65	0.001*	0.512	0.23	0.004*	0.56†	0.855	0.14	0.065	0.22
SCL-90-R: GSI	$\alpha=0.98$	1.5	1.3	0.9	1.1	1.0	10.41	<0.001*	0.645	0.20	0.001*	0.78†	0.017*	0.49	0.001*	0.53†
SCL-90-R: PST	$\alpha=0.98$	54.0	50.7	37.2	48.0	46.3	5.53	<0.001*	0.895	0.14	0.001*	0.79†	0.416	0.28	0.002*	0.35
SCL-90-R: PSDI	$\alpha=0.98$	2.3	2.1	1.8	1.9	1.9	11.07	<0.001*	0.740	0.21	0.001*	0.63†	0.006*	0.59†	0.001*	0.60†
TCI-R: Novelty seeking	$\alpha=0.80$	114.4	108.2	103.0	101.5	108.8	8.13	<0.001*	0.154	0.42	0.001*	0.85†	0.001*	0.91†	0.001*	0.39
TCI-R: Harm avoidance	$\alpha=0.82$	109.7	103.7	102.8	105.8	101.3	6.05	<0.001*	0.341	0.32	0.089	0.34	0.617	0.20	0.001*	0.44
TCI-R: Reward depend.	$\alpha=0.77$	104.8	102.5	95.3	98.1	99.7	3.93	0.006*	0.902	0.14	0.002*	0.55†	0.073	0.39	0.005*	0.33
TCI-R: Persistence	$\alpha=0.87$	108.0	104.0	94.8	95.5	109.4	9.83	<0.001*	0.821	0.19	0.002*	0.65†	0.008*	0.68†	0.924	0.07
TCI-R: Self-directed.	$\alpha=0.85$	125.0	118.8	125.2	123.0	128.1	2.27	0.069	0.505	0.27	1.000	0.01	0.971	0.09	0.494	0.13
TCI-R: Cooperativen.	$\alpha=0.81$	137.1	128.3	128.6	132.4	132.0	2.76	0.037*	0.074	0.52†	0.025*	0.45	0.448	0.27	0.019*	0.30
TCI-R: Self-Trans.	$\alpha=0.83$	66.0	63.6	59.3	64.0	64.4	1.57	0.178	0.888	0.15	0.050	0.41	0.903	0.13	0.706	0.10

*Bold, significant comparison (0.05 level). †Bold: effect size in the moderate (|d|> 0.50) to high (|d|> 0.80) range. α: Cronbach's-alpha for the scale in the sample. p-values include Bonferroni-Finner correction.

persistence (in comparison with IGD and Internet addiction), and cooperativeness (in comparison with IGD and gambling disorder).

Figure 2 includes two radar-charts to graphically summarize the clinical and personality profiles for the different diagnostic subtypes in the most relevant variables of the study. The percentage of women was plotted for gender distribution and the z-standardized scores in the own sample for the quantitative clinical measures (standardization was made due to the different ranges –minimum to maximum values– of these variables).

Discriminative Model for the Presence of CBB Compared to other Behavioral Addictions

Table 3 contains the results of the multinomial model measuring the discriminative capacity of patients' sex, age, age of onset, education level, marital status, and personality profile. Compared to all the other diagnostic subtypes, the probability of CBB is clearly higher in women and individuals with higher scores in the personality traits novelty seeking, harm avoidance and self-directedness. However, it should be noted that scores on self-directedness were in the clinically low range for all groups when considering general population normative scores. The opposite pattern emerges in the case of harm avoidance, in that all diagnostic groups were in the clinically high range, with those with CBB scoring the highest. In addition, older age is predictive of CBB compared to Internet and IGD, higher education levels increased the probability of CBB compared to gambling disorder, and moderate levels of persistence (rather than low) are more likely in CBB compared to Internet and IGD.

Predictive Models of Psychopathology Symptoms for the CBB Group

Table 4 contains the three multiple regressions measuring the predictive capacity of the patients' sex, age, age of onset, and personality traits profile on levels of depression, anxiety, and GSI-index measured through the SCL-90-R for the CBB group ($n = 110$). High levels of depression were associated with women and patients with high scores in novelty seeking, harm avoidance, and cooperativeness, but low levels in reward dependence and self-directedness. High anxiety was registered for women, and

those patients with high scores in harm avoidance and low scores in self-directedness. High GSI scores were linked to women; obtaining high scores in novelty seeking, harm avoidance and self-transcendence; and low scores in self-directedness.

DISCUSSION

This study analyzed the specific characteristics of CBB compared to other behavioral addictions: gambling disorder, Internet gaming disorder, Internet addiction and sexual addiction. The results obtained in a large sample of treatment-seeking patients show that although CBB could likely be related to other addictive behaviors, significant differences in its phenomenology exist. CBB is characterized by a higher proportion of women, older age and age of onset, poorer general psychopathological state and higher levels of novelty seeking and harm avoidance and moderate levels of reward dependence, persistence, and cooperativeness. In this sense, CBB patients could be described as being curious, easily bored, impulsive and active seekers of new stimuli and reward, but at the same time showing pessimism and worry in anticipation of upcoming challenges. Several sociocultural contributors might also take part in the onset and maintenance of CBB, such as one's personal financial state, materialistic values, and the variety of goods available (Dittmar, 2005). One should also take into account the fact that in hoarding, one of the most commonly reported symptoms is acquiring behavior, and that other studies have identified numerous similarities between the two disorders (Frost et al., 2002). Clinical differences are lower compared to sex addiction and higher compared to gambling disorder, IGD, and Internet addiction.

Regarding gender, differences between diagnostic subtypes emerged in this study: the CBB group included a considerably higher proportion of women compared to other behavioral addictions. This result is consistent with other studies, which had also reported higher levels of compulsive buying in women (Fattore et al., 2014; Otero-López and Villardefrancos, 2014). Possible reasons for the elevated prevalence of women with CBB are most likely related to the higher frequency of shopping as a recreational activity in this group and other related socio-cultural factors (Maraz et al., 2015).

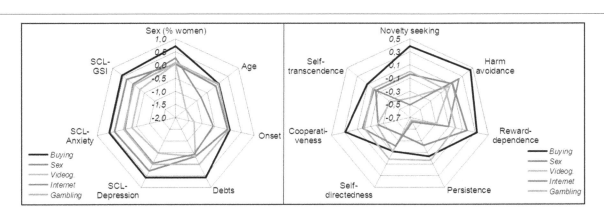

FIGURE 2 | Radar-charts for the main clinical variables in the study and personality traits.

TABLE 3 | Discriminative capacity of age, age of onset, studies level, civil status, and personality profile in the presence of a diagnostic subtype (n = 3.324).

| | Likelihood ratio tests | | Parameter estimates | | | | | | | | | | | |
| | | | Gambling vs. buying | | | Internet vs. buying | | | Internet/gaming vs. buying | | | Sex vs. buying | | |
	χ^2	p	p	OR	95%CI	p	OR	95%CI	p	OR	95%CI	p	OR	95%CI
Sex (male)	152.7	**<0.001**	**<0.001**	19.47	11.68 32.46	**0.005**	4.10	1.53 10.94	**0.001**	16.49	3.30 82.29	**<0.001**	77.04	9.25 641.4
Age (years-old)	80.54	**<0.001**	0.155	1.03	0.99 1.08	**0.004**	0.85	0.76 0.95	**<0.001**	0.78	0.70 0.88	0.972	1.00	0.91 1.09
Onset (years-old)	4.78	0.311	0.486	0.98	0.94 1.03	0.170	1.08	0.97 1.21	0.622	0.97	0.86 1.09	0.829	1.01	0.93 1.10
Studies (university)	23.66	**<0.001**	**<0.001**	0.28	0.15 0.51	0.403	0.59	0.17 2.04	0.195	0.32	0.06 1.79	0.579	1.37	0.45 4.21
Civil status (married)	3.37	0.498	0.144	0.71	0.45 1.12	0.392	0.68	0.28 1.64	0.152	0.37	0.09 1.44	0.633	0.80	0.31 2.03
TCI-R: Novelty seeking	56.44	**<0.001**	**<0.001**	0.96	0.95 0.98	**<0.001**	0.92	0.89 0.94	**<0.001**	0.90	0.87 0.93	**0.001**	0.95	0.92 0.98
TCI-R: Harm avoidance	16.04	**0.003**	**<0.001**	0.97	0.95 0.99	**0.002**	0.96	0.93 0.98	**0.008**	0.96	0.94 0.99	**0.028**	0.97	0.94 1.00
TCI-R: Reward dependence	5.78	0.217	0.521	0.99	0.98 1.01	0.515	0.99	0.96 1.02	0.432	0.99	0.96 1.02	0.106	1.03	0.99 1.07
TCI-R: Persistence	31.17	**<0.001**	0.733	1.00	0.98 1.01	**<0.001**	0.96	0.93 0.98	**0.002**	0.96	0.94 0.99	0.223	0.98	0.96 1.01
TCI-R: Self-directedness	12.17	**0.016**	**0.018**	0.98	0.97 1.00	**0.010**	0.97	0.95 0.99	**0.046**	0.97	0.95 1.00	**0.003**	0.96	0.93 0.99
TCI-R: Cooperativeness	3.29	0.511	0.740	1.00	0.98 1.01	0.340	1.02	0.98 1.05	0.504	1.01	0.98 1.04	0.445	0.99	0.95 1.02
TCI-R: Self-Transcendence	3.55	0.470	0.703	1.00	0.98 1.01	0.219	1.02	0.99 1.05	0.611	1.01	0.98 1.04	0.724	0.99	0.96 1.03

Bold, significant coefficient. Models obtained with multinomial regression entering simultaneously the set of predictors (ENTER procedure) (McFadden-R^2 = 0.283).

Results of this study also show that the proportion of patients attending our specialized unit for CBB treatment had a tendency to increase during the last decade, with a similar trend occurring for Internet, IGD and sexual addictions. However, these proportions of treatment-seeking patients were significantly lower compared to the number of consultations for gambling disorder. With regards to the evolution of the proportion of CBB consultations during the last decade, our results point to a drop between the years of 2010 and 2013, coinciding with the worst years of the economic crisis in Europe, and, more specifically, in Spain. Moreover, this decrease is consistent with results exploring other behavioral addictions requiring substantial amounts of money. In the case of gambling disorder, a significant drop in prevalence was also found during the European economic crisis (Jiménez-Murcia et al., 2014b), especially in 2010.

Patients' age and the mean age of onset of problematic addictive behaviors greatly differed between diagnostic subtypes, with older ages being found in CBB (mean age was 43.3 years and mean onset 38.9, nearly followed by gambling disorder and sex addiction) and younger ages for IGD (mean age 22.0 and mean onset 19.9 in this study). This finding dovetails with several studies reporting that young age is linked to problematic video game and Internet use (Griffiths and Meredith, 2009; Achab et al., 2011; Jiménez-Murcia et al., 2014a). Other variables, such as the endorsement of materialistic values among young people, should be considered in the scientific literature as an effective mediator of the young age of onset in some addictive behaviors, particularly in the case of compulsive buying (Dittmar, 2005).

Differences in the psychological state and personality traits between the diagnostic subtypes are also relevant: CBB and sexual addiction showed similar profiles, with their psychopathological symptoms and personality scores being clearly worse than for gambling, IGD, and Internet addictions. Although in behavioral addictions, impulsivity appears to be a core feature (Dell'Osso et al., 2006; Billieux et al., 2012; Lorains et al., 2014), multiple studies also show the existence of high levels of compulsivity (Blanco et al., 2009; Fineberg et al., 2010; Bottesi et al., 2015). Impulsivity and compulsivity seem to be characterized by deficits in self-control capacity. Nonetheless, a key distinction between impulsivity and compulsivity is that the former is associated with immediate gratification and reward seeking, while compulsion is aimed at finding relief from negative emotions.

Overall, the findings obtained in this study show that this combination of symptoms (impulsive/compulsive) is especially prominent in CBB and sexual addiction. This leads us to postulate the existence of phenotypical and possibly endophenotypical overlap across these disorders. This results support previous research that has found numerous shared features in CBB and sexual addiction (Müller et al., 2015a) and other behavior addictions (Lejoyeux et al., 2008; Villella et al., 2011). However, a notable difference in the sex prevalence of both disorders (higher proportion of women in CBB and of men in sex addiction) exists. This fact may partly explain why the similarities between these disorders have hardly been explored (Álvarez-Moya et al., 2007). Lastly and quite possibly due to higher awareness of this condition, the number of GD patients was vastly higher than

TABLE 4 | Predictive capacity of age, age of onset, and personality traits in the psychopathology symptom levels for the CBB group (n = 110).

Dependent variable →	SCL-90-R: depression (adjusted R^2 = 0.601)							SCL-90-R: anxiety (adjusted R^2 = 0.580)							SCL-90-R: GSI index (adjusted R^2 = 0.676)						
↓ Predictor	B	SE	Beta	t	p	95%CI(B)		B	SE	Beta	t	p	95%CI(B)		B	SE	Beta	t	p	95%CI(B)	
Constant	0.439	1.869		0.235	0.815	−3.28	4.16	−2.562	1.870		−1.370	0.174	−6.28	1.16	−1.900	1.339		−1.419	0.160	−4.56	0.76
Sex (male)	−0.692	0.172	−.289	−4.032	**<0.001**	−1.03	−0.35	−0.516	0.172	−0.221	−3.005	**0.003**	−0.86	−0.17	−0.469	0.123	−0.246	−3.817	**<0.001**	−0.71	−0.22
Age (years)	−0.004	0.016	−.041	−0.266	0.791	−0.04	0.03	−0.006	0.016	−0.059	−0.369	0.713	−0.04	0.03	−0.004	0.011	−0.047	−0.338	0.736	−0.03	0.02
Age of onset (years)	0.001	0.014	0.006	0.037	0.970	−0.03	0.03	0.010	0.014	0.114	0.718	0.474	−0.02	0.04	0.005	0.010	0.069	0.492	0.624	−0.02	0.03
TCI–R: Novelty seeking	0.014	0.006	0.180	2.167	**0.033**	0.00	0.03	0.012	0.006	0.167	1.959	0.053	0.00	0.02	0.013	0.004	0.210	2.809	**0.006**	0.00	0.02
TCI–R: Harm avoidance	0.019	0.006	0.356	3.436	**0.001**	0.01	0.03	0.025	0.006	0.479	4.504	**<0.001**	0.01	0.04	0.023	0.004	0.522	5.591	**<0.001**	0.01	0.03
TCI–R: Reward depend.	−0.012	0.005	−0.177	−2.193	**0.031**	−0.02	0.00	0.001	0.005	0.009	0.112	0.911	−0.01	0.01	−0.003	0.004	−0.052	−0.718	0.475	−0.01	0.01
TCI–R: Persistence	0.004	0.004	0.086	1.065	0.290	0.00	0.01	0.007	0.004	0.134	1.613	0.110	0.00	0.02	0.005	0.003	0.120	1.645	0.104	0.00	0.01
TCI–R: Self–directedness	−0.023	0.005	−0.503	−4.489	**<0.001**	−0.03	−0.01	−0.015	0.005	−0.333	−2.897	**0.005**	−0.02	0.00	−0.012	0.004	−0.332	−3.289	**0.001**	−0.02	0.00
TCI–R: Cooperateness	0.013	0.006	0.193	2.182	**0.032**	0.00	0.02	0.002	0.006	0.030	0.326	0.746	−0.01	0.01	0.002	0.004	0.040	0.495	0.622	−0.01	0.01
TCI–R: Self–Transcend.	0.002	0.005	0.037	0.464	0.644	−0.01	0.01	0.009	0.005	0.149	1.815	0.073	0.00	0.02	0.008	0.004	0.157	2.180	**0.032**	0.00	0.02

Models obtained with multiple regression entering simultaneously the set of predictors (ENTER procedure). Bold, significant coefficient.

the other behavioral addictions examined in this study. Future studies should aim to use larger, more diverse samples in order to overcome this drawback. The role of materialistic values and hoarding are also topics that should be considered. However, our findings should be considered in light of their limitations and we stress that the features of treatment-seeking patients in a single unit for behavioral addictions does not necessarily reflect the actual frequency of an addiction in the origin population. The lack of consensus regarding the diagnostic criteria for the behavioral additions examined in the study also limits the generalizability of our results.

CONCLUSION

The results of this study suggest that CBB should be considered as a behavioral addiction, in the same manner as other excessive behaviors (such as sexual addiction, gambling, IGD, or Internet addiction). At present, an integrative model for describing the underlying mechanisms which lead to the onset and development of the CBB is not available. Additional empirical evidence is needed to identify core contrasting factors so as to clarify whether CBB represents a distinct psychiatric entity or is better conceptualized as an epiphenomenon of other psychiatric disorders characterized by addictive and/or impulse control behaviors. As with most complex, multifaceted-multidimensional processes, these studies should cover different areas: neurobiological (to recognize implicated regions, networks, and executive/cognitive functions), clinical (to dispose of the complete patient phenotype and to identify distinct developmental trajectories of the condition), and psycho-socio-cultural (to clarify what consumer-culture and financial resources interact with psychological, individual, and personality traits to lead to an increase in buying behavior).

Ultimately, a detailed understanding of the CBB will allow for improving prevention and treatment efforts. New empirical studies are required to gain a better understanding of the etiology of CBB and to establish more effective intervention programs.

AUTHOR CONTRIBUTIONS

RG, FF, JM, ST, and SJ designed the experiment based on previous results and clinical experience of AD, MB, LM, NA, NM, and MG. RG, GM, TS, FF, and SJ conducted the experiment, analyzed the data, and provided a first draft of the manuscript. SJ, TS, GM, RG, and FF further modified the manuscript.

FUNDING

This manuscript and research was supported by grants from Instituto de Salud Carlos III (FIS PI11/00210, FIS14/00290, CIBERObn, CIBERsam, and Fondos FEDER) and PROMOSAM (PSI2014-56303-REDT). CIBERObn and CIBERSAM are both an initiative of ISCIII. This study was cofunded by FEDER funds/European Regional Development Fund (ERDF)—a way to build Europe and by a Ministerio de Economía y Competitividad grant (PSI2015-68701-R).

REFERENCES

Aboujaoude, E. (2014). Compulsive buying disorder: a review and update. *Curr. Pharm. Des.* 20, 4021–4025. doi: 10.2174/13816128113199990618

Achab, S., Nicolier, M., Mauny, F., Monnin, J., Trojak, B., Vandel, P., et al. (2011). Massively multiplayer online role-playing games: comparing characteristics of addict vs non-addict online recruited gamers in a French adult population. *BMC Psychiatry* 11:144. doi: 10.1186/1471-244X-11-144

American Psychiatric Association (1994). *Diagnostic and Statistical Manual of Mental Disorders, 4th Edn.* Washington, DC: American Psychiatric Association.

American Psychiatric Association (2000). *Diagnostic and Statistical Manual of Mental Disorders, 4th Edn, Text Revision (DSM-IV-TR).* Washington, DC: American Psychiatric Association.

American Psychiatric Association (2013). *Diagnostic and Statistical Manual of Mental Disorders, 5th Edn.* Washington, DC: American Psychiatric Association.

Álvarez-Moya, E. M., Jiménez-Murcia, S., Granero, R., Vallejo, J., Krug, I., Bulik, C. M., et al. (2007). Comparison of personality risk factors in bulimia nervosa and pathological gambling. *Compr. Psychiatry* 48, 452–457. doi: 10.1016/j.comppsych.2007.03.008

Ashley, L. L., and Boehlke, K. K. (2012). Pathological gambling: a general overview. *J. Psychoactive Drugs* 44, 27–37. doi: 10.1080/02791072.2012.662078

Baik, J.-H. (2013). Dopamine signaling in reward-related behaviors. *Front. Neural Circuits* 7:152. doi: 10.3389/fncir.2013.00152

Balogh, K. N., Mayes, L. C., and Potenza, M. N. (2013). Risk-taking and decision-making in youth: relationships to addiction vulnerability. *J. Behav. Addict.* 2, 1–9. doi: 10.1556/JBA.2.2013.1.1

Basu, B., Basu, S., and Basu, J. (2011). Compulsive buying: an overlooked entity. *J. Indian Med. Assoc.* 109, 582–585.

Billieux, J., Lagrange, G., Van der Linden, M., Lançon, C., Adida, M., and Jeanningros, R. (2012). Investigation of impulsivity in a sample of treatment-seeking pathological gamblers: a multidimensional perspective. *Psychiatry Res.* 198, 291–296. doi: 10.1016/j.psychres.2012.01.001

Black, D. W., Shaw, M., and Blum, N. (2010). Pathological gambling and compulsive buying: do they fall within an obsessive-compulsive spectrum? *Dialogues Clin. Neurosci.* 12, 175–185. doi: 10.1097/MJT.0b013e3181ed83b0

Black, D. W., Shaw, M., McCormick, B., Bayless, J. D., and Allen, J. (2012). Neuropsychological performance, impulsivity, ADHD symptoms, and novelty seeking in compulsive buying disorder. *Psychiatry Res.* 200, 581–587. doi: 10.1016/j.psychres.2012.06.003

Blanco, C., Potenza, M. N., Kim, S. W., Ibáñez, A., Zaninelli, R., Saiz-Ruiz, J., et al. (2009). A pilot study of impulsivity and compulsivity in pathological gambling. *Psychiatry Res.* 167, 161–168. doi: 10.1016/j.psychres.2008.04.023

Bottesi, G., Ghisi, M., Ouimet, A. J., Tira, M. D., and Sanavio, E. (2015). Compulsivity and impulsivity in pathological gambling: does a dimensional-transdiagnostic approach add clinical utility to DSM-5 classification? *J. Gambl. Stud.* 31, 825–847. doi: 10.1007/s10899-014-9470-5

Choi, S.-W., Kim, H. S., Kim, G.-Y., Jeon, Y., Park, S. M., Lee, J.-Y., et al. (2014). Similarities and differences in mental gaming disorder, gambling disorder and alcohol use disorder: a focus on impulsivity and compulsivity. *J. Behav. Addict.* 3, 246–253. doi: 10.1556/JBA.3.2014.4.6

Claes, L., Bijttebier, P., Van Den Eynde, F., Mitchell, J. E., Faber, R., de Zwaan, M., et al. (2010). Emotional reactivity and self-regulation in relation to compulsive buying. *Pers. Individ. Dif.* 49, 526–530. doi: 10.1016/j.paid.2010.05.020

Clark, L. (2014). Disordered gambling: the evolving concept of behavioral addiction. *Ann. N.Y. Acad. Sci.* 1327, 46–61. doi: 10.1111/nyas.12558

Cloninger, C. R. (1999). *The Temperament and Character Inventory-Revised.* St. Louis, MO: Washington University.

Davenport, K., Houston, J. E., and Griffiths, M. D. (2012). Excessive eating and compulsive buying behaviours in women: an empirical pilot study examining reward sensitivity, anxiety, impulsivity, self-esteem and social desirability. *Int. J. Ment. Health Addict.* 10, 474–489. doi: 10.1007/s11469-011-9332-7

Dayan, J., Bernard, A., Olliac, B., Mailhes, A. S., and Kermarrec, S. (2010). Adolescent brain development, risk-taking and vulnerability to addiction. *J. Physiol. Paris* 104, 279–286. doi: 10.1016/j.jphysparis.2010.08.007

Dell'Osso, B., Altamura, A. C., Allen, A., Marazziti, D., and Hollander, E. (2006). Epidemiologic and clinical updates on impulse control disorders: a critical review. *Eur. Arch. Psychiatry Clin. Neurosci.* 256, 464–475. doi: 10.1007/s00406-006-0668-0

Derbyshire, K. L., and Grant, J. E. (2015). Compulsive sexual behavior: a review of the literature. *J. Behav. Addict.* 4, 37–43. doi: 10.1556/2006.4.2015.003

Derogatis, L. (1990). *SCL-90-Administration, R., Scoring and Procedures Manual.* Baltimore, MD: Clinical Psychometric Research.

Di Nicola, M., Tedeschi, D., De Risio, L., Pettorruso, M., Martinotti, G., Ruggeri, F., et al. (2015). Co-occurrence of alcohol use disorder and behavioral addictions: relevance of impulsivity and craving. *Drug Alcohol Depend.* 148, 118–125. doi: 10.1016/j.drugalcdep.2014.12.028

Dittmar, H. (2005). Compulsive buying–a growing concern? An examination of gender, age, and endorsement of materialistic values as predictors. *Br. J. Psychol.* 96, 467–491. doi: 10.1348/000712605X53533

Echeburúa, E. (1999). *Adicciones Sin Drogas?. Las Nuevas Adicciones: Juego, Sexo, Comida, Compras, Trabajo, Internet.* Bilbao: Desclee de Brower.

Echeburúa, E., Báez, C., Fernández, J., and Páez, D. (1994). Cuestionario de juego patológico de South Oaks (SOGS): validación española. [South Oaks Gambling Screen (SOGS): Spanish validation]. *Anális Modif. Cond.* 20, 769–791.

El-Guebaly, N., Mudry, T., Zohar, J., Tavares, H., and Potenza, M. N. (2012). Compulsive features in behavioural addictions: the case of pathological gambling. *Addiction* 107, 1726–1734. doi: 10.1111/j.1360-0443.2011.03546.x

Engel, A., and Caceda, R. (2015). Can decision making research provide a better understanding of chemical and behavioral addictions? *Curr. Drug Abuse Rev.* 8, 75–85. doi: 10.2174/1874473708666150916113131

Farré, J. M., Fernández-Aranda, F., Granero, R., Aragay, N., Mallorquí-Bague, N., Ferrer, V., et al. (2015). Sex addiction and gambling disorder: similarities and differences. *Compr. Psychiatry* 56, 59–68. doi: 10.1016/j.comppsych.2014.10.002

Fattore, L., Melis, M., Fadda, P., and Fratta, W. (2014). Sex differences in addictive disorders. *Front. Neuroendocrinol.* 35:3. doi: 10.1016/j.yfrne.2014.04.003

Fernández-Aranda, F., Jiménez-Murcia, S., Alvarez-Moya, E. M., Granero, R., Vallejo, J., and Bulik, C. M. (2006). Impulse control disorders in eating disorders: clinical and therapeutic implications. *Compr. Psychiatry* 47, 482–488. doi: 10.1016/j.comppsych.2006.03.002

Fernández-Aranda, F., Pinheiro, A. P., Thornton, L. M., Berrettini, W. H., Crow, S., Fichter, M. M., et al. (2008). Impulse control disorders in women with eating disorders. *Psychiatry Res.* 157, 147–157. doi: 10.1016/j.psychres.2007.02.011

Fineberg, N. A., Potenza, M. N., Chamberlain, S. R., Berlin, H. A., Menzies, L., Bechara, A., et al. (2010). Probing compulsive and impulsive behaviors, from animal models to endophenotypes: a narrative review. *Neuropsychopharmacology* 35, 591–604. doi: 10.1038/npp.2009.185

First, M., Gibbon, M., Spitzer, R., and Williams, J. (1996). *Users Guide for the Structured Clinical Interview for DSM IV Axis I Disorders-Research Version (SCID-I, version 2.0).* New York, NY: New York State Psychiatric Institute.

Franken, I. H. A., Muris, P., and Georgieva, I. (2006). Gray's model of personality and addiction. *Addict. Behav.* 31, 399–403. doi: 10.1016/j.addbeh.2005.05.022

Frost, R. O., Steketee, G., and Williams, L. (2002). Compulsive buying, compulsive hoarding, and obsessive-compulsive disorder. *Behav. Ther.* 33, 201–214. doi: 10.1016/S0005-7894(02)80025-9

Grant, J. E., and Chamberlain, S. R. (2014). Impulsive action and impulsive choice across substance and behavioral addictions: cause or consequence? *Addict. Behav.* 39, 1632–1639. doi: 10.1016/j.addbeh.2014.04.022

Grant, J. E., Schreiber, L. R. N., and Odlaug, B. L. (2013). Phenomenology and treatment of behavioural addictions. *Can. J. Psychiatry* 58, 252–259.

Griffiths, M. D., and Hunt, N. (1995). Computer game playing in adolescence: prevalence and demographic indicators. *J. Community Appl. Soc. Psychol.* 5, 189–193. doi: 10.1002/casp.2450050307

Griffiths, M. D., and Hunt, N. (1998). Dependence on computer games by adolescents. *Psychol. Rep.* 82, 475–480. doi: 10.2466/pr0.1998.82.2.475

Griffiths, M. D., and Meredith, A. (2009). Videogame addiction and its treatment. *J. Contemp. Psychother.* 39, 247–253. doi: 10.1007/s10879-009-9118-4

Gutiérrez-Zotes, J. A., Bayón, C., Montserrat, J., Valero, J., Labad, A., Cloninger, C. R., et al. (2004). Inventario del Temperamento y el Carácter-Revisado (TCI-R). Baremación y datos normativos en una muestra de población general. *Actas Españolas Psiquiatr.* 32, 8–15.

Hartston, H. (2012). The case for compulsive shopping as an addiction. *J. Psychoactive Drugs* 44, 64–67. doi: 10.1080/02791072.2012.660110

Janiri, L., Martinotti, G., Dario, T., Schifano, F., and Bria, P. (2007). The Gamblers' Temperament and Character Inventory (TCI) personality profile. *Subst. Use Misuse* 42, 975–984. doi: 10.1080/10826080701202445

Jiménez-Murcia, S., Aymamí-Sanromà, M., Gómez-Peña, M., Álvarez-Moya, E., and Vallejo, J. (2006). *Protocols de Tractament Cognitivoconductual pel joc Patològic i D'altres Addiccions No Tòxiques.* Barcelona: Hospital Universitari de Bellvitge, Departament de Salut, Generalitat de Catalunya.

Jiménez-Murcia, S., Fernández-Aranda, F., Granero, R., Chóliz, M., La Verde, M., Aguglia, E., et al. (2014a). Video game addiction in gambling disorder: clinical, psychopathological, and personality correlates. *Biomed Res. Int.* 2014, 315062. doi: 10.1155/2014/315062

Jiménez-Murcia, S., Fernández-Aranda, F., Granero, R., and Menchón, J. M. (2014b). Gambling in Spain: update on experience, research and policy. *Addiction* 109, 1595–1601. doi: 10.1111/add.12232

Jiménez-Murcia, S., Fernández-Aranda, F., Kalapanidas, E., Konstantas, D., Ganchev, T., Kocsis, O., et al. (2009). Playmancer project: a serious videogame as an additional therapy tool for eating and impulse control disorders. *Stud. Health Technol. Inform.* 144, 163–166. doi: 10.3233/978-1-60750-017-9-16

Jiménez-Murcia, S., Granero, R., Moragas, L., Steiger, H., Israel, M., Aymamí, N., et al. (2015). Differences and similarities between bulimia nervosa, compulsive buying and gambling disorder. *Eur. Eat. Disord. Rev.* 23, 111–118. doi: 10.1002/erv.2340

Karim, R., and Chaudhri, P. (2012). Behavioral addictions: an overview. *J. Psychoactive Drugs* 44, 5–17. doi: 10.1080/02791072.2012.662859

Kellett, S., and Bolton, J., V (2009). Compulsive buying: a cognitive-behavioural model. *Clin. Psychol. Psychother.* 16, 83–99. doi: 10.1002/cpp.585

Konkolÿ Thege, B., Woodin, E. M., Hodgins, D. C., and Williams, R. J. (2015). Natural course of behavioral addictions: a 5-year longitudinal study. *BMC Psychiatry* 15:4. doi: 10.1186/s12888-015-0383-3

Leeman, R. F., and Potenza, M. N. (2013). A targeted review of the neurobiology and genetics of behavioural addictions: an emerging area of research. *Can. J. Psychiatry.* 58, 260–273. doi: 10.1016/j.biotechadv.2011.08.021

Lejoyeux, M., Avril, M., Richoux, C., Embouazza, H., and Nivoli, F. (2008). Prevalence of exercise dependence and other behavioral addictions among clients of a Parisian fitness room. *Compr. Psychiatry* 49, 353–358. doi: 10.1016/j.comppsych.2007.12.005

Lejoyeux, M., and Weinstein, A. (2010). Compulsive buying. *Am. J. Drug Alcohol Abuse* 36, 248–253. doi: 10.3109/00952990.2010.493590

Lesieur, H. R., and Blume, S. B. (1987). The South Oaks Gambling Screen (SOGS): a new instrument for the identification of pathological gamblers. *Am. J. Psychiatry* 144, 1184–1188. doi: 10.1176/ajp.144.9.1184

Lorains, F. K., Stout, J. C., Bradshaw, J. L., Dowling, N. A., and Enticott, P. G. (2014). Self-reported impulsivity and inhibitory control in problem gamblers. *J. Clin. Exp. Neuropsychol.* 36, 144–157. doi: 10.1080/13803395.2013.873773

Maraz, A., Griffiths, M. D., and Demetrovics, Z. (2015). The prevalence of compulsive buying: a meta-analysis. *Addiction.* 111, 408–419. doi: 10.1111/add.13223

Martínez-Azumendi, O., Fernández-Gómez, C., and Beitia-Fernández, M. (2001). [Factorial variance of the SCL-90-R in a Spanish out-patient psychiatric sample]. *Actas Españolas Psiquiatr.* 29, 95–102.

McElroy, S. L., Keck, P. E., Pope, H. G., Smith, J. M., and Strakowski, S. M. (1994). Compulsive buying: a report of 20 cases. *J. Clin. Psychiatry* 55, 242–248.

McQueen, P., Moulding, R., and Kyrios, M. (2014). Experimental evidence for the influence of cognitions on compulsive buying. *J. Behav. Ther. Exp. Psychiatry* 45, 496–501. doi: 10.1016/j.jbtep.2014.07.003

Mueller, A., Mitchell, J. E., Crosby, R. D., Gefeller, O., Faber, R. J., Martin, A., et al. (2010). Estimated prevalence of compulsive buying in Germany and its association with sociodemographic characteristics and depressive symptoms. *Psychiatry Res.* 180, 137–142. doi: 10.1016/j.psychres.2009.12.001

Müller, A., Claes, L., Georgiadou, E., Möllenkamp, M., Voth, E. M., Faber, R. J., et al. (2014). Is compulsive buying related to materialism, depression or temperament? Findings from a sample of treatment-seeking patients with CB. *Psychiatry Res.* 216, 103–107. doi: 10.1016/j.psychres.2014.01.012

Müller, A., Loeber, S., Söchtig, J., Te Wildt, B., and De Zwaan, M. (2015a). Risk for exercise dependence, eating disorder pathology, alcohol use disorder and addictive behaviors among clients of fitness centers. *J. Behav. Addict.* 4, 273–280. doi: 10.1556/2006.4.2015.044

Müller, A., Mitchell, J. E., and de Zwaan, M. (2015b). Compulsive buying. *Am. J. Addict.* 24, 132–137. doi: 10.1111/ajad.12111

Munno, D., Saroldi, M., Bechon, E., Sterpone, S. C. M., and Zullo, G. (2015). Addictive behaviors and personality traits in adolescents. *CNS Spectr.* 13, 1–7. doi: 10.1017/S1092852915000474

Otero-López, J. M., and Villardefrancos, E. (2014). Prevalence, sociodemographic factors, psychological distress, and coping strategies related to compulsive buying: a cross sectional study in Galicia, Spain. *BMC Psychiatry* 14:101. doi: 10.1186/1471-244X-14-101

Piquet-Pessôa, M., Ferreira, G. M., Melca, I. A., and Fontenelle, L. F. (2014). DSM-5 and the decision not to include sex, shopping or stealing as addictions. *Curr. Addict. Rep.* 1, 172–176. doi: 10.1007/s40429-014-0027-6

Potenza, M. N. (2014). Non-substance addictive behaviors in the context of DSM-5. *Addict. Behav.* 39, 1–2. doi: 10.1016/j.addbeh.2013.09.004

Probst, C. C., and van Eimeren, T. (2013). The functional anatomy of impulse control disorders. *Curr. Neurol. Neurosci. Rep.* 13, 386. doi: 10.1007/s11910-013-0386-8

Raab, G., Elger, C. E., Neuner, M., and Weber, B. (2011). A neurological study of compulsive buying behaviour. *J. Consum. Policy* 34, 401–413. doi: 10.1007/s10603-011-9168-3

Reinert, D. F., and Allen, J. P. (2002). The Alcohol Use Disorders Identification Test (AUDIT): a review of recent research. *Alcohol. Clin. Exp. Res.* 26, 272–279. doi: 10.1111/j.1530-0277.2002.tb02534.x

Robbins, T. W., and Clark, L. (2015). Behavioral addictions. *Curr. Opin. Neurobiol.* 30, 66–72. doi: 10.1016/j.conb.2014.09.005

Roberts, J. A., Manolis, C., and Pullig, C. (2014). Contingent self-esteem, self-presentational concerns, and compulsive buying. *Psychol. Mark.* 31, 147–160. doi: 10.1002/mar.20683

Rose, P., and Segrist, D. J. (2014). Negative and positive urgency may both be risk factors for compulsive buying. *J. Behav. Addict.* 3, 128–132. doi: 10.1556/JBA.3.2014.011

Saunders, J. B., Aasland, O. G., Babor, T. F., de la Fuente, J. R., and Grant, M. (1993). Development of the Alcohol Use Disorders Identification Test (AUDIT): who collaborative project on early detection of persons with harmful alcohol consumption–II. *Addiction* 88, 791–804. doi: 10.1111/j.1360-0443.1993.tb02093.x

Stinchfield, R. (2003). Reliability, validity, and classification accuracy of a measure of DSM-IV diagnostic criteria for pathological gambling. *Am. J. Psychiatry* 160, 180–182. doi: 10.1176/appi.ajp.160.1.180

Suissa, A. J. (2015). Cyber addictions: toward a psychosocial perspective. *Addict. Behav.* 43, 28–32. doi: 10.1016/j.addbeh.2014.09.020

Tárrega, S., Castro-Carreras, L., Fernández-Aranda, F., Granero, R., Giner-Bartolomé, C., Aymamí, N., et al. (2015). A serious videogame as an additional therapy tool for training emotional regulation and impulsivity control in severe gambling disorder. *Front. Psychol.* 6:1721. doi: 10.3389/fpsyg.2015.01721

Tavares, H., Lobo, D. S. S., Fuentes, D., and Black, D. W. (2008). [Compulsive buying disorder: a review and a case vignette]. *Rev. Bras. Psiquiatr.* 30(Suppl. 1) S16–S23. doi: 10.1590/S1516-44462008005000002

Trotzke, P., Starcke, K., Müller, A., and Brand, M. (2015). Pathological buying online as a specific form of internet addiction: a model-based experimental investigation. *PLoS ONE* 10:e0140296. doi: 10.1371/journal.pone.0140296

Unger, A., Papastamatelou, J., Yolbulan Okan, E., and Aytas, S. (2014). How the economic situation moderates the influence of available money on compulsive buying of students - A comparative study between Turkey and Greece. *J. Behav. Addict.* 3, 173–181. doi: 10.1556/JBA.3.2014.018

Vanderah, T., and Sandweiss, A. (2015). The pharmacology of neurokinin receptors in addiction: prospects for therapy. *Subst. Abuse Rehabil.* 6, 93–102. doi: 10.2147/SAR.S70350

Villella, C., Martinotti, G., Di Nicola, M., Cassano, M., La Torre, G., Gliubizzi, M. D., et al. (2011). Behavioural addictions in adolescents and young adults: results from a prevalence study. *J. Gambl. Stud.* 27, 203–214. doi: 10.1007/s10899-010-9206-0

Weinstein, A., Mezig, H., Mizrachi, S., and Lejoyeux, M. (2015). A study investigating the association between compulsive buying with measures of anxiety and obsessive-compulsive behavior among internet shoppers. *Compr. Psychiatry* 57, 46–50. doi: 10.1016/j.comppsych.2014.11.003

Williams, A. D., and Grisham, J. R. (2012). Impulsivity, emotion regulation, and mindful attentional focus in compulsive buying. *Cogn. Ther. Res.* 36, 451–457. doi: 10.1007/s10608-011-9384-9

Conflict of Interest Statement: The authors declare that the research was conducted in the absence of any commercial or financial relationships that could be construed as a potential conflict of interest.

17

Personalized Behavioral Feedback for Online Gamblers: A Real World Empirical Study

Michael M. Auer[1,2]* and Mark D. Griffiths[1,2]

[1] neccton Ltd, Lienz, Austria, [2] Psychology, Nottingham Trent University, Nottingham, UK

Responsible gambling tools (e.g., limit-setting tools, pop-up messages, and personalized feedback) have become increasingly popular as a way of facilitating players to gamble in a more responsible manner. However, relatively few studies have evaluated whether such tools actually work. The present study examined whether the use of three types of information (i.e., personalized feedback, normative feedback, and/or a recommendation) could enable players to gamble more responsibly as assessed using three measures of gambling behavior, i.e., theoretical loss (TL), amount of money wagered, and gross gaming revenue (GGR) (i.e., net win/loss). By manipulating the three forms of information, data from six different groups of players were analyzed. The participant sample drawn from the population were those that had played at least one game for money on the *Norsk Tipping* online platform (*Instaspill*) during April 2015. A total of 17,452 players were randomly selected from 69,631 players that fulfilled the selection criteria. Of these, 5,528 players participated in the experiment. Gambling activity among the control group (who received no personalized feedback, normative feedback or no recommendation) was also compared with the other five groups that received information of some kind (personalized feedback, normative feedback and/or a recommendation). Compared to the control group, all groups that received some kind of messaging significantly reduced their gambling behavior as assessed by TL, amount of money wagered, and GGR. The results support the hypothesis that personalized behavioral feedback can enable behavioral change in gambling but that normative feedback does not appear change behavior significantly more than personalized feedback.

Keywords: online gambling, responsible gambling, problem gambling, human–computer interaction, behavioral feedback, persuasive communication

Edited by:
Javier Jaen,
Polytechnic University of Valencia,
Spain

Reviewed by:
Luigi Janiri,
Università Cattolica del Sacro Cuore,
Italy
Elena Navarro,
University of Castilla-La Mancha,
Spain

*Correspondence:
Michael M. Auer
m.auer@neccton.com

Specialty section:
This article was submitted to
Human-Media Interaction,
a section of the journal
Frontiers in Psychology

INTRODUCTION

Gambling is a popular activity in many cultures. Surveys have reported that most people gamble but do so infrequently (e.g., Wardle et al., 2007). National surveys have also concluded that most people have engaged in gambling at some point during in their lives (Orford et al., 2003; Meyer et al., 2009). In Great Britain, the majority of the population (over two-thirds) engaged in at least one type of gambling in the previous 12 months (Wardle et al., 2012). This included offline and online gambling. A recent review by Gainsbury (2015) on internet gambling reported that in jurisdictions that have carried out studies, online gambling prevalence rates are still relatively low (8–16%). However, as internet gambling is accessible 24 h a day, potentially negative psychosocial impacts are an almost inevitable consequence for a small minority of individuals. This is because various structural and situational characteristics (e.g., accessibility, affordability, and anonymity) may increase the risk of developing a gambling problem among vulnerable and susceptible individuals (Griffiths, 2003; McCormack and Griffiths, 2013). Consequently, players need to be educated about how to gamble more responsibly and vulnerable groups need to be protected.

Responsible Gambling and Information Giving

Responsible gambling tools (e.g., limit-setting tools, pop-up messages, and personalized feedback) have become increasingly popular as a way of facilitating players to gamble in a more responsible manner (Griffiths et al., 2009; Auer and Griffiths, 2013). They are also given information about common misconceptions and erroneous perceptions concerning games of chance as these have been found to be important factors in the acquisition, development, and maintenance of problematic gambling (e.g., Gaboury and Ladouceur, 1989; Griffiths, 1994; McCusker and Gettings, 1997; Parke et al., 2007; Wohl et al., 2010). However, empirical evaluations demonstrating that providing gamblers with such information in an attempt to correct or change erroneous beliefs and misperceptions have been variable. For instance, some studies have supported the use of providing information in helping individuals gamble more responsibly (e.g., Dixon, 2000; Ladouceur and Sevigny, 2003), while other studies have reported no significant association between providing information and gambling responsibly (e.g., Hing, 2003; Focal Research, 2004; Williams and Connolly, 2006).

Responsible Gambling and Correcting Erroneous Beliefs

Some studies have successfully utilized educational programs as a way of correcting erroneous beliefs about gambling (e.g., Wulfert et al., 2006; Wohl et al., 2010). For example, animation-based educational videos have been developed that educate gamblers about how slot machines work (Wohl et al., 2010). After watching the animated video, gamblers said they intended to use strategies to (i) stay within their limits, and (ii) reduce the number of times they would exceed their limits. The same study also demonstrated that animated videos may be an effective tool for increasing the likelihood of gamblers setting financial spending limits.

Responsible Gambling Messaging and How it Is Presented

Research has also shown that the way information is presented can significantly influence behavior and thoughts. Several studies have investigated the effects of interactive vs. static pop-up messages during gambling sessions. Static messages do not appear to be particularly effective, whereas interactive pop-up messages and animated information have been shown to change irrational belief patterns and subsequent gambling behavior (e.g., Schellink and Schrans, 2002; Ladouceur and Sevigny, 2003;

Cloutier et al., 2006; Monaghan and Blaszczynski, 2007, 2010a; Monaghan et al., 2009).

It has also been recommended that warning signs containing information should utilize skills that facilitate self-regulation and self-appraisal rather than just simply providing information (Monaghan and Blaszczynski, 2010b). For instance, an experimental study on slot machine players by Monaghan and Blaszczynski (2010a) demonstrated pop-up messages that contained self-appraisal messages resulted in more self-reported thoughts and behavior while gambling compared to those that do not.

Responsible Gambling and Pop-Up Messaging

A study by Stewart and Wohl (2013) found that individuals were significantly more likely to stick to monetary limits while gambling if they received a pop-up reminder about monetary limits compared to those that did not. In a similar study, Wohl et al. (2013) examined the efficacy of two different responsible gambling tools (a pop-up message and an educational animated video) in relation to money limit adherence while gambling on a slot machine ($n = 72$). The authors reported that both tools were effective in helping gamblers keep within their predetermined financial spending limits. Munoz et al. (2013) conducted a study to examine whether graphic warning signs had greater efficacy than text-only warning signs. They reported that the graphic warnings were more successful than text warnings in getting gamblers to comply with the advice given, and more successful in getting participants to change their attitudes concerning gambling. While all of these studies have provided empirical support for the use of responsible gambling tools, they are limited by the small sample sizes and the lack of ecological validity (i.e., the studies were carried out in a laboratory situation).

More recently, a number of studies have been carried out in real world settings using real gamblers in real time. For instance, Auer et al. (2014) investigated the effect of a pop-up message that appeared after 1,000 consecutive online slot machine games had been played by individuals during a single gambling session. The study analyzed 800,000 gambling sessions (400,000 sessions before the pop-up had been introduced and 200,000 after the pop-up had been introduced comprising around 50,000 online gamblers). The study found that the pop-up message had a limited effect on a small percentage of players. More specifically, prior to the pop-up message being introduced, five gamblers ceased playing after 1,000 consecutive spins of the online slot machine within a single playing session (out of approximately 10,000 playing sessions). Following the introduction of the pop-up message, 45 gamblers ceased playing after 1,000 consecutive spins (i.e., a ninefold increase in session cessations). In the latter case, the number of gamblers ceasing play was less than 1% of the gamblers who played 1,000 games consecutively.

In a follow-up study, Auer and Griffiths (2015a) argued that the original pop-up message was very basic and that re-designing the message using normative feedback and self-appraisal feedback may increase the efficacy of gamblers ceasing play. As in the previous study, the new enhanced pop-up message that appeared within a single session after a gambler had played 1,000 consecutive slot games. In the follow-up study, Auer and Griffiths (2015a) examined 1.6 million playing sessions comprising two conditions [i.e., simple pop-up message (800,000 slot machine sessions) vs. an enhanced pop-up message (800,000 slot machine sessions)] with approximately 70,000 online gamblers. The study found that the message with enhanced content more than doubled the number of players who ceased playing (1.39% who received the enhanced pop-up compared to 0.67% who received the simple pop-up). However, as in Auer et al.'s (2014) previous study, the enhanced pop-up only influenced a small number of gamblers to cease playing after a long continuous playing session. At present, these two research studies (i.e., Auer et al., 2014; Auer and Griffiths, 2015a) are the only ones to examine the efficacy of pop-up messaging in a real world online gambling environment comprising actual online gamblers.

Responsible Gambling and Personalized Feedback via Behavioral Tracking Tools

Personalized feedback which informs players about their past behavior and incorporates a longer time period than just the current session has only been empirically researched in one real-world study to date. Auer and Griffiths (2015b) studied the behavior of 1,015 online gamblers in connection with their voluntary use of a responsible gaming behavioral tracking tool compared with 15,216 matched control group gamblers (that had not used the behavioral tracking tool) on the basis of age, gender, playing duration, and theoretical loss (TL) [i.e., the amount of money wagered multiplied by the payout percentage of a specific game played (Auer et al., 2012; Auer and Griffiths, 2014)]. The results showed that online gamblers receiving personalized feedback spent significantly less money and time gambling in comparison to those that did not receive personalized feedback (i.e., the matched controls). However, as gamblers who had used the behavioral tracking tool had volunteered to use it and had not been randomly assigned, this meant the effect might not only be due to the feedback but also to other factors not controllable by the researchers (for instance, those signing up to use the tool may have been more responsible gamblers to begin with).

Forsström et al. (2016) carried out a study on the use of the behavioral tracking tool *PlayScan*. The data from a total of 9,528 players who voluntarily used the system were analyzed. They found that the initial usage of the tool was high, but that repeated usage was low. Two groups of users (i.e., 'self-testers' and 'multi-function users') utilized the tool to a much greater extent than other groups. However, the study did not analyze changes in behavior as a consequence of using the tool. Wood and Wohl (2015) obtained data from 779 *Svenska Spel* online players who received behavioral feedback using *PlayScan*. Feedback to players took the form of a 'traffic-light' risk rating that was created via a proprietary algorithm (red = problematic gambling, yellow = at-risk gambling, and green = no gambling issues). In addition, expenditure data (i.e., amounts deposited and gambled) were collected at three time points (i) the week of *PlayScan* enrollment, (ii) the week following *PlayScan* enrollment, and 24 weeks after *PlayScan* enrollment. The findings indicated that those players at-risk (yellow gamblers) who used *PlayScan* significantly reduced the amounts of money both deposited and gambled compared to those who did not use *PlayScan*. This effect was also found the week following *PlayScan* enrollment as well as the 24-week mark. Overall, the authors concluded that informing at-risk gamblers about their gambling behavior appeared to have a desired impact on their subsequent monetary spending.

Personalized Feedback and Self-Efficacy

The focus of social cognitive theory is self-efficacy and is learned by observing other individuals' behavior (Bandura, 2001). Self-efficacy primarily concerns how capable an individual feels about performing a behavior and is at the heart of the health communication literature including the Health Belief Model (Maiman and Becker, 1974; Janz and Becker, 1984), Theory of Planned Behavior (Ajzen, 1985), Protection Motivation Theory (Rogers, 1983), and the Extended Parallel Process Model (Witte, 1992). All these theoretical perspectives assert that high levels of self-efficacy are highly likely to enable behavioral change. Consequently, it is important that to enable behavioral change, messages must include components of self-efficacy (i.e., belief that the person can carry out an action) and response efficacy (i.e., belief that the recommended action will lead to a desired outcome for the person; Witte et al., 2001; Perloff, 2008).

Another method of attempting to enable behavioral change in gambling is normative feedback. Studies researching smoking (Van den Putte et al., 2009), condom use (Yzer et al., 2000), and marijuana consumption (Yzer et al., 2007) have shown normative beliefs can play an important role in behavioral change. In a study of American college student gambling, Celio and Lisman (2014) demonstrated that personalized normative feedback decreased other students' perceptions of gambling and lowered risk-taking performance on two analog measures of gambling. They concluded that a standalone personalized normative feedback intervention may modify gambling behavior among college students. Miller and Rollnick (1991) have also emphasized that normative feedback is important in facilitating behavioral change in the use of motivational interviewing.

Outside of the gambling studies field, personalized behavioral feedback has been used to change other potentially addictive behaviors (e.g., cigarette smoking). Using a combination of both motivational interviewing and feedback from ultrasound was found as effective for reducing cigarette smoking among pregnant women (Stotts et al., 2009). Another study effectively delivered a smoking-cessation intervention via wireless text messages to college students using integrated internet/mobile phone technology (Obermayer et al., 2004). Another area where behavioral feedback has been investigated is in the area of sports and fitness. Buttussi et al. (2006) investigated the use of mobile phone guides in fitness activities using a Mobile Personal Trainer (MOPET) application. The mobile app gave verbal navigation assistance and also used a 3D-animated motivator. Evaluation of the results supported the use of mobile apps and embodied virtual trainers in outdoor fitness applications.

Many of the aforementioned approaches enabling behavioral change utilize the 'stages of change' model (Prochaska and DiClemente, 1983; Prochaska and Prochaska, 1991) and motivational interviewing (Miller and Rollnick, 1991). Based on these theoretical approaches, the present authors believe that to change an individual's gambling behavior, player feedback (utilizing behavioral tracking data) has to incorporate the stages of change model and be presented in a motivational way. More specifically, this means providing informational feedback to gamblers in a non-judgmental format along with normative information so that they can evaluate their gambling behavior compared to others like themselves. Transparent and non-judgmental feedback is important and has been emphasized by studies elsewhere. For instance, a study examining alcohol drinking by Lapham et al. (2012) advocated that feedback should be transparent and tailored to the individual (e.g., the extent to which individuals exceeded daily or weekly alcohol limits). This is because their participants explicitly wanted to know how they came to be specifically assigned to their alcohol drinking risk category.

Human–Computer Interaction and Persuasive System Design in Responsible Gambling

Given that the primary aim of gambling pre-commitment tools is to enable behavioral change, it is only recently that designs of such tools have utilized the principles of human–computer interaction (HCI) and persuasive system design (PSD). A recent study found that a monetary limit pop-up tool inspired by PSD and HCI principles was much more effective than tools not incorporating such principles (Wohl et al., 2014). As a research field, HCI examines the interaction of individuals with technology and attempts to facilitate usability and uptake. Persuasive Technology has been defined as interactive computing systems that attempt to change people's attitudes and behaviors (Fogg, 2003). Apart from user-feedback, HCI principles relevant for the design of pre-commitment measures are an aesthetic visual design, the incorporation of system-status updates, a sense of control over functionality, and the use of simple language (Hewett et al., 1992; Shneiderman et al., 2009; Preece et al., 2011). Apart from showing that messaging can effectively change thoughts about gambling and the gambling behavior itself, research has also suggested that the content of messages is important (Monaghan and Blaszczynski, 2010a,b; Auer and Griffiths, 2015b). The present authors take the view that the design of a feedback system for facilitating responsible gambling is paramount, and that HCI and PSD principles should be at the heart of such systems.

The Present Study and Hypotheses

This study goes beyond previous research as it applies an experimental approach in a real-world online gambling setting. This is in contrast to Auer and Griffiths' (2015b) study in which players voluntarily signed up for a service that provided

them with personalized spending information. In this study, players were randomly assigned to different types of interventions in order to investigate the effects of personalized feedback, normative feedback, and non-personalized recommendations. Additionally, a control group was drawn that allows for the causal inference of the different types of interventions. The main research questions (RQs) were: (RQ1) Does personalized information given to gamblers reduce their gambling behavior? (RQ2) Do different types of personalized information (i.e., personalized feedback, normative feedback, a recommendation to gamble responsibly) given to gamblers reduce their gambling behavior in different ways? (RQ3) Are gamblers' demographics and playing attributes associated with their gambling behavior in reaction to the various messaging interventions or do all gamblers react similarly to the specific interventions, regardless of the message attributes? It was hypothesized that compared to the control group, personalized feedback would impact positively on subsequent playing behavior as assessed by a reduction in time and money spent in the experimental groups (H1), and that the impact of personalized feedback and normative feedback would be larger compared to either a pure recommendation or no information at all (H2).

MATERIALS AND METHODS

Participants

The participant sample drawn from the population were those that had played at least one game for money on the *Norsk Tipping* online platform (*Instaspill*) during April 2015. A total of 17,452 players were randomly selected from 69,631 players that fulfilled the selection criteria (see next section for Sampling procedure). Ten players had won more money than they wagered over the time period and were thus excluded from analysis leaving 17,442 participants. Of these, 12,261 were males (69.1%) and 5,481 were females (30.9%). All but 40 participants were Norwegian. The mean average age was 40.52 years ($SD = 13.19$). Approximately 29% of the customers were younger than 30 years, and 22% were aged over 50 years. There is no significant age difference between males and females. Participants had been playing with *Norsk Tipping* for a mean average of 94 months (7.9 years; $SD = 38.31$).

Sampling

The participants only comprised players who had a net loss across all games in the past month before the study commenced (i.e., winners were excluded). Those who had self-excluded and/or taken a play break from gambling were also excluded from subsequent analysis. More specifically, the sample was drawn based on the amount lost across all games (online casino, sports betting, lottery, etc.) apart from scratchcards purchased offline (as these data were not fully available during the study period). The amount of money lost by each player was computed by simply subtracting the amount wagered from the amount won. The overwhelming majority of players lost only small amounts of money. Therefore, in order to examine the impact of messaging on high intensity players, there was an oversampling of high intensity gamblers.

Experimental Design

The study examined the effects of personalized messaging and manipulated the information given. **Table 1** contains the different permutations for the experimental design. The six groups were created based on three types of messaging intervention. These were:

1. Personalized information about the participant's gambling behavior (in the form of numbers and illustrations).
2. A recommendation (in the form of written information about using responsible gaming tools offered by *Norsk Tipping*).
3. Normative feedback (in the form of numbers and illustrations displaying the gambling intensity of the average active player at *Norsk Tipping* compared to their own).

Group 5 was designed to evaluate the effectiveness of non-personalized, purely informative recommendation. Group 6 served as the control group as participants did not receive any information at all. The distribution of high and low intensity players created by the sampling procedure was the same across all six groups. Each group contained approximately 2,957 participants. In this 2 × 2 × 2 design, only six groups were examined (rather than the normal eight) because normative feedback without personalized feedback would not make any theoretical sense. This is also the case with providing normative feedback and recommendations without personalized feedback.

The study was planned over the course of 1 year and executed during May and June, 2015. During the course of the study, players (excluding the control group) received information about their losses over the past 6-month period and/or, recommendations about existing responsible gaming tools, and/or normative information. It was hypothesized that personalized behavioral feedback would help players to gamble more responsibly (as assessed using the TL, the amount of money wagered in Norwegian Krone [NOK], and the gross gaming revenue (GGR) [NOK] – see 'Analysis' section below for more detail).

All players that received information were told (in writing) that *Norsk Tipping* was trying out new services and that the operator would be very grateful if they could participate in the study. Players were told that they would be receiving information that would help them become more aware of their personal gambling expenditure. They were also informed that a research

team had been asked to evaluate the effects of this service and that only anonymized data would be used for research purposes. Players had to press a 'Next' button to confirm that they agreed to participate and that their data would be used for research purposes. To not be included in the study, players were informed that they could simply close the message window. The demographic distribution was the same for all six groups (i.e., there were no significant differences across the six groups in terms of gender, age, and nationality). Of the 17,452 randomly selected players, 5,528 voluntarily participated in the study.

Personalized Feedback

A simple personalized message was sent to players in Groups 1–4 that said: "How much do you think you spent on gambling recently? Our records show that you lost [X] NOK last month." In addition, players were also presented with a line chart (see **Figure 1**) that contained the monthly values for their personal losses over the previous 6-month period. Players were also told that they could retrieve the information any time during the following month.

Normative Feedback

A simple message with normative feedback was sent to players in Groups 3 and 4 that said: *"It can be helpful to know about other peoples' expenditures to evaluate your own spending. For this reason we would like to let you know that the average Norsk Tipping player loses about 400 NOK per month."* The normative feedback about other players' losses was provided after the personalized feedback. Additionally, a line chart (see **Figure 2**) displaying their own losses compared with those of other players was also provided.

Recommendation

Groups 2, 3, and 5 received a helpful recommendation about responsible gambling tools and services that players could access via a hyperlink on the screen. Players could access tools provided by *Norsk Tipping* that helped players (i) manage their personal spending limits, (ii) activate a play break, (iii) take a diagnostic self-test about their gambling behavior, and (iv) see an overview of their recent spending. Players were also informed about the national gambling helpline if they wanted to speak to anyone about their gambling.

Analysis

Assessing whether personalized feedback results in the desired behavioral change means that behavioral change has to be assessed via specific variables and via specific time periods. In the present study it was decided that gambling behavior 7 days prior to the intervention would be compared with gambling behavior 7 days after the intervention message was read. This is because changes over a shorter time period would most likely only be due to chance and changes over longer time periods would not be expected based on the type of feedback.

The three measures of behavior that were used to assess gambling behavior were TL, amount of money wagered, and GGR (i.e., net win/loss). The TL statistic was computed as 'TL_after'

TABLE 1 | Experimental groups by type of feedback provided to gamblers.

	Personalized information	Recommendation	Normative feedback
Group 1	YES	NO	NO
Group 2	YES	YES	NO
Group 3	YES	YES	YES
Group 4	YES	NO	YES
Group 5	NO	YES	NO
Group 6	NO	NO	NO

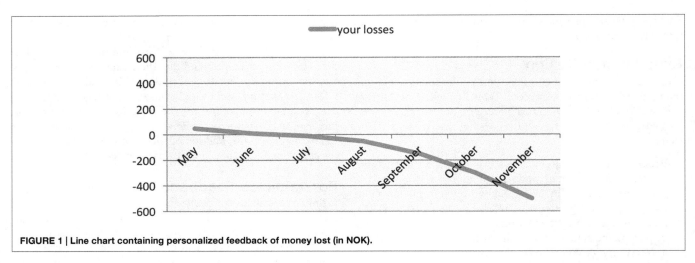

FIGURE 1 | Line chart containing personalized feedback of money lost (in NOK).

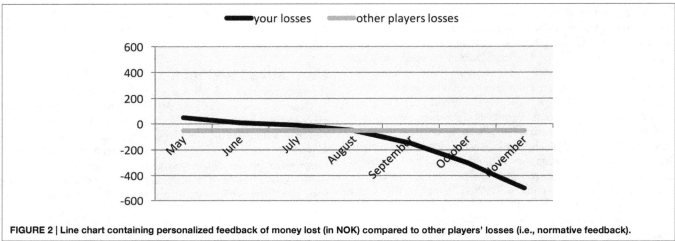

FIGURE 2 | Line chart containing personalized feedback of money lost (in NOK) compared to other players' losses (i.e., normative feedback).

minus 'TL_before' divided by 'TL_before.' This statistic reflects the change in behavior 7 days after the message was read as a percentage of the behavior 7 days before the message was read. This procedure helps assess the individual change as independent from the intensity of play as much as possible. A negative value indicates a decrease in gambling behavior and a positive value indicates an increase in gambling behavior. A value of 0 means that no change in gambling behavior occurred at all. A value of say −0.5 means that the gambling behavior decreased by 50% compared to 7 days before. The statistic ranges from −1 to +infinity. A value of −1 means that the player did not engage in gambling 7 days after the message was read. A value of +10 means that the gambling behavior increased 1000% in the 7 days after the message was read compared to 7 days before the message was read. Prior to analysis, data cleaning was performed. More specifically, it appeared that a few customers ($n = 28$) had negative TL values that led to negative change metrics. Consequently, these 28 customers were removed from the analysis. An outlier procedure was also performed which removed the 1% highest values in the change metric as this was naturally highly skewed. The comparisons across the groups were performed via Mann–Whitney U Tests due to the skewed

distribution of the metrics. Three statistical tests were carried out using chi-square analysis and using a Bonferroni correction, the significance level was determined to be 0.0167. The study was granted ethical approval by the research team's University Ethics Committee.

RESULTS

Theoretical Loss Analysis

Table 2 displays the statistics of the TL change variable after data cleaning. The largest values (top 1%) were discarded

TABLE 2 | Parametric (e.g., mean) and non-parametric (e.g., 1st quantile, median) statistics of the cleansed theoretical loss over a 7-day period.

Minimum	−1.00
1st Quantile	−0.87
Median	−0.42
Mean	0.06
3rd Quantile	0.15
Maximum	16.00

from further analyses as these extreme outliers would influence the results heavily. Very large values occur if players were gambling little before the intervention and heavily after as a consequence of the quotient which is computed. It can be safely assumed that those players who spend very little and received feedback are not the main target group for such interventions. The arithmetic mean demonstrated that the average player increased their gambling by about 6%. However, it is evident that the distribution is highly skewed as the median is much smaller. Half of the players (50%) decreased their gambling by about 42%. The non-normal distribution is of course due to the fact that there is a lower limit at −1 and a much higher limit at 16 (i.e., the maximum increase was 1600%).

Control Group Analysis

Players in the control group did not have a response date as there were no messages or recommendation sent to them. Players who received a message and read it had a specific response date on which they read the message. In order to do that they had to be online and be actively gambling. Given the missing response date in the control group, it is not easy to compare the computed change in gambling behavior 7 days after the message was read to a corresponding change in the control group. Simply looking at the gambling behavior in the same month as the other players received personalized messages is not valid as the responders in Groups 1–5 naturally showed some sort of activity and no such selection can be applied in the control group. Consequently, the level of monthly gambling across the responders is naturally higher than that of the control group. Therefore, an alternative procedure was chosen to analyze the data. In order to determine if the changes observed in Groups 1–5 were due to the message, it is important to find out how much players change on average when they do not receive a personalized message.

For each of the 2,958 control group members, every day on which they showed gambling activity was selected. This could be 1 day, a few days, or every day. For each and every control group player, a value between 0 and 30 with respect to active gambling days was calculated. For each and every player, and every active playing day, the gambling activity 7 days before that day and 7 days after that day was computed. Finally, the change statistic as used above was computed. Overall, it was assumed that all influences cancel each other out and that the average change statistic (across players and days) yields an average change in behavior.

Message Effect Analysis

Table 3 shows the distribution of the change in TL across five experimental groups and the control group. The control group statistics were computed across control group members and the respective days on which they were active. Examination of the median, mean, and maximum value clearly shows that the control group changed their gambling behavior less than the experimental groups. Whereas half of the players decreased their intensity by at least 42% (median) in the target groups, it was only 36% (median) in the control group.

TABLE 3 | Parametric (e.g., mean) and non-parametric (e.g., median, 1st quantile) statistics of the theoretical loss change variable by group mapping over a 7-day period).

	Target group	Control group
Minimum	−1	−1
1st Quantile	−0.87	−0.87
Median	−0.42	−0.36
Mean	0.06	0.58
3rd Quantile	0.15	0.37
Maximum	16.0	46.4

The average player (arithmetic mean) increased their play by 6% in the target group and 58% in the control group. Using a Mann–Whitney U Test, comparison of TLs after 7 days of receiving personalized messages between Groups 1 to 5 and the control group (Group 6) was significant ($X^2 = 32.208$, df = 5, $p < 0.0001$). Thus, personalized feedback appears to have had a significant impact on player behavior compared to those that had no such feedback (see **Table 4**).

Figure 3 shows the change in TL across all six groups, 7 days after the message was read. Again, this shows that the control group (Group 6) decreased the least in relation to TL (−36%) and that Group 2 had the largest decrease in play in relation to TL (−45%).

Data also showed that the most gambling-intense players often deplete their financial resources during the 1st week of the month. During this time they reach their spending limits and can only resume playing at the site at the beginning of the next month. For that reason, a further analysis was carried out on those players who responded to the messaging during the 1st week of the study. **Figure 4** (using TL) shows the change in behavior 7 days after the message was read for players who responded during the 1st week of the study. It is again evident that using the TL, players who did not receive any message and players who only received purely informational content decreased their play less than players who received personalized feedback.

It is also important to examine whether the control group changed their gambling behavior with respect to the GGR and the amount of money wagered. The median change in amount wagered over a period of 7 days was −34%, and is a smaller decrease compared to the experimental Groups 1–5 (see **Table 4**), and was significant ($X^2 = 26.66$, df = 5,

TABLE 4 | Differences between the experimental groups (EGs) and control group (CG) 7 days after gamblers had received personalized messages about their gambling behavior

	CG	EGs	X^2	d.f.	p
Theoretical loss	−36%	−42%	32.208	5	0.0001*
Amount wagered	−34%	−43%	26.66	5	0.0001*
Gross gaming	−48%	−58%	28.66	5	0.0001*

*Bonferroni correction significance level = 0.0167.

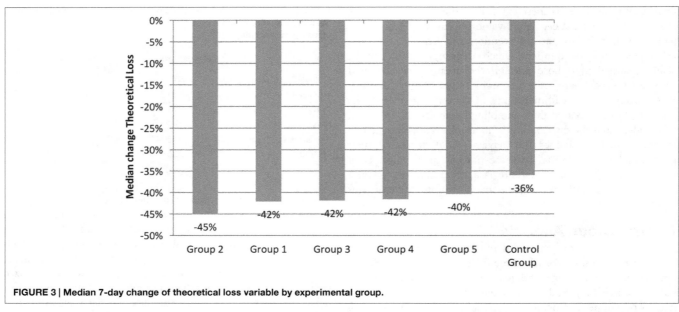

FIGURE 3 | Median 7-day change of theoretical loss variable by experimental group.

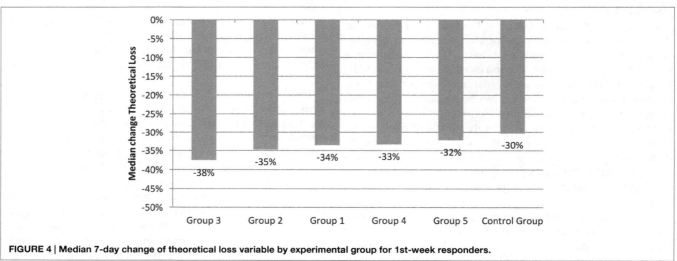

FIGURE 4 | Median 7-day change of theoretical loss variable by experimental group for 1st-week responders.

$p < 0.0001$). The median change in GGR over a period of 7 days was −48%, and is a smaller decrease compared to the experimental Groups 1–5 (see **Table 4**), and was also significant ($X^2 = 28.66$, df $= 5, p < 0.0001$).

Sub-Group Analysis by Game Type and Demographics

The previous section demonstrated that players who received personalized feedback changed more than those who only received a recommendation and more than those who did not receive any kind of information. For this reason, further analysis investigated whether gamblers' demographics and playing attributes were associated with their gambling behavior in reaction to the various messaging interventions. However, separating out all players into different clusters is difficult. In cluster analysis, statistical methods identify segments that are

different from each other whereas the members of a single segment are similar to each other.

In this case, the goal was slightly different. If the study population was randomly divided into clusters, each cluster would be made up of some players who received personalized feedback, some players who received normative feedback, etc. However, the clustering should occur according to a specific goal. Here, members of a specific cluster that received personalized feedback should be different with respect to the behavioral change from members of that cluster who received normative feedback, etc. This means that an algorithm should uncover different clusters, whereas each cluster is characterized by a maximum variance across the five different interventions with respect to behavioral change.

In order to delineate groupings that have a unique profile with respect to the five experimental groups, a two-step approach was chosen. This consisted of a k-means statistical procedure and a genetic algorithm. Genetic algorithms are machine-learning procedures that imitate evolutionary processes. Parameters are randomly chosen and are optimized due to the performance of the algorithm that is measured via a fitness function. In this case, the fitness function was defined via the profiles of the clusters that the *k*-means produced. The more distinct the members of a cluster with respect to the five experimental interventions, the higher the corresponding fitness function. The open source statistical package 'R' was used to analyze the data and perform the genetic algorithm. (Details about the procedure and the parameters used in the genetic algorithm are available from the first author). Finally different types of players were identified based on this two-step approach (all distinct with respect to their characteristics as well as the reaction toward the different messaging interventions). This led to five distinct groups of player whose profile is displayed in **Table 5**. The following descriptions are an attempt to capture the main aspects of the five profiles of players in relation to game preference and GGR: Profile 1 – Female scratchcard players with average GGR; Profile 2 – Lottery players with a low GGR; Profile 3 – At-risk lottery players with higher GGR; Profile 4 – At-risk casino players with past self-exclusions and a high GGR; Profile 5 – At-risk male sports bettors who recently won with a below average GGR.

The numbers in **Table 6** report the median 7-day change with respect to the theoretical loss in the five experimental groups for each player profile. For instance, players clustered in Profile 1 who were subject to Intervention 1 (personalized feedback only) reduced their gambling on average by 68% 7 days after they read the message. Players clustered in Profile 3 who were subject to Intervention 3 (personalized feedback, normative feedback, and a recommendation) reduced their gambling on average by 29% 7 days after they read the message. More specifically, the analysis demonstrated that:

- Profile 1: This group of players showed the largest decrease in play when presented with personalized feedback and a recommendation (i.e., a 68% reduction). The smallest decrease in play was when personalized and normative feedback were given together.
- Profile 2: This group of players showed the largest decrease in play when all three types of messaging were combined (personalized and normative feedback along with a recommendation). The smallest decrease in play was when they were given a recommendation only.
- Profile 3: This group of players showed the largest decrease in play when they were given personalized feedback and a recommendation or personalized and normative feedback. The smallest decrease in play was when they were given a recommendation only.
- Profile 4: This group of players showed the largest decrease in play when they were given a recommendation only. The smallest decrease in play was when they were given personalized feedback only.
- Profile 5: This group of players showed the largest decrease in play when they were given personalized feedback only. The combined intervention of personalized and normative feedback, and a recommendation appeared to increase play.

As shown in **Table 6**, in four of the five profiles, personalized feedback had a larger effect on gambling behavior (TL) than a sole recommendation. It was only in Profile 4 (highly involved at-risk casino players) where this did not hold true. Here, a sole recommendation had the largest effect on subsequent gambling behavior. The findings also suggest that although sports bettors benefit from personalized feedback, normative feedback plus a recommendation does not appear to make this group of players gamble less.

TABLE 5 | Profile of five groups that reacted differently toward messaging interventions.

Player group	Profile 1	Profile 2	Profile 3	Profile 4	Profile 5	Average
Number of participants	348	1,940	1,208	1,010	404	4,910
GGR	430	293	673	738	370	494
Total amount wagered (NOK)	732	634	1,552	16,839	3,926	4,471
Number of playing days	8	7	13	15	15	11
Other games	2%	3%	14%	1%	2%	5%
Lottery	21%	67%	50%	7%	13%	43%
Online casino	75%	23%	23%	75%	11%	36%
Sports betting	1%	4%	7%	5%	56%	9%
Sport	0%	1%	3%	1%	15%	3%
Slots (land-based)	0%	2%	3%	12%	2%	4%
Casino (land-based)	2%	7%	6%	67%	5%	19%
Scratchcards	73%	16%	16%	2%	5%	16%
Bingo	0%	0%	1%	6%	1%	2%
Mean age (years)	39	37	48	46	41	42
Tenure	94	93	113	106	100	101
Gender (female)	47%	33%	30%	24%	5%	29%
Self-exclusion	8%	7%	16%	62%	23%	22%
PlayScan risk	49%	13%	75%	79%	64%	49%

TABLE 6 | The effect of the different messaging interventions in each of the five experimental groups with respect to the change in theoretical loss.

	Profile 1	Profile 2	Profile 3	Profile 4	Profile 5
Intervention 1	−68%	−56%	−31%	−16%	−41%
Intervention 2	−87%	−53%	−35%	−27%	−21%
Intervention 3	−57%	−67%	−29%	−19%	18%
Intervention 4	0%	−57%	−35%	−22%	−17%
Intervention 5	−68%	−48%	−20%	−35%	−27%

DISCUSSION

The present study examined whether the use of three types of information (i.e., personalized feedback, normative feedback, and a recommendation to gamble more responsibly) could enable players to gamble more responsibly as assessed using three measures of behavior, i.e., TL, amount of money wagered, and GGR. By manipulating the three forms of information, data from six different groups of players were analyzed. The first hypothesis was that compared to the control group, personalized feedback would impact positively on subsequent playing behavior as assessed by a reduction in time and money spent in the experimental groups in terms of TL, amount of money wagered and GGR. On the whole, empirical support for H1 was confirmed. The second hypothesis was that that the impact of personalized feedback and normative feedback would be larger compared to either a pure recommendation or no information at all. H2 was also empirically supported although the difference in reduction of gambling behavior by viewing a recommendation only (compared to personalized and normative feedback) did not quite reach statistical significance.

The first research question (RQ1) the present study attempted to answer was whether personalized feedback given to gamblers reduces their gambling behavior? The findings presented here suggest that it does and supports previous real world studies showing that personalized feedback about gambling behavior can help some players to decrease the amount of time and/or money they spend gambling (Auer et al., 2014; Auer and Griffiths, 2015a,b). However, almost all previously published research that has examined player feedback to date has been conducted in laboratory settings and has not looked beyond a single gambling session. The present study is a significant advance on those studies as it was carried out in the real world and for a period longer than within a single gambling session. Given this, the present study makes both a novel and original addition to the literature.

The second research question (RQ2) was to investigate whether different types of personalized feedback given to gamblers reduce their gambling behavior in different ways? Players that received both personalized feedback and a recommendation (Group 2) decreased gambling behavior the most although this was not statistically significant compared to the other four experimental groups. Those players given a recommendation only (Group 5) had the least change in their gambling behavior but again this did not quite reach statistical significance compared to the other four experimental groups.

The other three groups (1, 3, and 4) showed equivalent decreases in gambling behavior. Findings suggest that the additional normative feedback received by Group 3 (who received all three types of message) did not have a more significant impact on gambling behavior than other groups. This may be due to a number of reasons. It could be due to the amount of information given (information overload – too many messages), or the fact that the types of gambler were diverse and that different messaging may impact more on different types of gambler. Furthermore, only one specific type of normative feedback was included in the present study (i.e., a comparison with the average player).

In relation to changes in GGR 7 days before and 7 days after the information was provided to players, gambling decreased more in Groups 1–4 (all of who received some kind of personalized feedback) compared to Group 5 (who received a recommendation only) supporting H1, although this did not quite reach statistical significance. This again tentatively supports the hypothesis that personalized feedback has a stronger effect in changing gambling behavior (as assessed using GGR) than pure informational content. In relation to changes in GGR 30 days before and 30 days after the information was provided, the findings were similar. Those groups that received some kind of personalized feedback (Groups 1–4) decreased their play (as assessed using GGR) after the message was provided. Those players that received a pure recommendation (Group 5) increased their play. Although across the groups as a whole the differences were not statistically significant, they are in line with H2.

In addition to TL and GGR, other studies (e.g., Broda et al., 2008; LaBrie et al., 2008; LaPlante et al., 2008, 2009; Nelson et al., 2008; Dragicevic et al., 2011; Braverman and Shaffer, 2012; Gray et al., 2012; Braverman et al., 2013) have frequently used the amount of money wagered as a proxy measure for gambling intensity. As with the findings above, the amount wagered by players 7 days after they had received personalized information was significantly less in the control group (supporting H1), and also less in players who only received a recommendation (supporting H2, although the finding was not statistically significant in the group that only received a recommendation compared to the other four experimental groups). After a period of 30 days, all groups tended to increase their play (as assessed using the amount wagered) after the information had been provided. Those that only received a recommendation (i.e., Group 5) showed the highest increase in amount wagered compared to the other four experimental group (supporting H2), although there was no significant difference across the five groups as a whole. Taken as a whole in relation to TL, GGR and amount wagered, the findings indicate that behavioral change is more intense in the days immediately after the information is provided to players, and also suggests that such information should be given more regularly.

The third research question (RQ3) investigated whether gamblers' demographics and playing attributes are associated with their gambling behavior in reaction to the various messaging interventions or whether all gamblers react similarly to the specific interventions, regardless of the message attributes? To supplement and refine the analysis in relation to RQ3, different types of player were delineated using a k-means procedure and which led to five different player profiles based on gender, game-type, and GGR. These were: (i) female scratchcard players with average GGR, (ii) lottery players with a low GGR, (iii) at-risk lottery players with higher GGR, (iv) at-risk casino players with past exclusions and a high GGR, and (v) at-risk male sports bettors who recently won with a below average GGR. Results showed that in all profiles (bar the at-risk casino players), personalized feedback had a larger effect on gambling behavior than providing a sole recommendation. Providing a sole recommendation to at-risk casino players led to the most significant reduction in gambling behavior. Such findings, although arguably tentative, suggest that operators will need to use their data to more specifically target specific types of players. However, the findings presented here need to be replicated using other datasets from other operators before more general recommendations can be made to online gamblers as a whole.

Based on these findings, normative feedback might have worked better if it had been tailored to the type of player (e.g., giving sports bettors normative information about other sports bettors rather than gamblers in general) and therefore perceived as more relevant for the recipient. The comparison of TL data 30 days before compared to 30 days after the information was provided showed a slight increase in gambling behavior. However, the smallest increase in gambling was amongst those receiving personalized feedback and a recommendation (Group 2) and the largest increase in gambling behavior occur was among those receiving a recommendation only (i.e., Group 5).

Limitations

Unlike the vast majority of studies carried out in the gambling studies field, the present study was a real world study using real online gamblers and carried out in real time. Furthermore, the sample size was relatively large and the dataset was robust. However, the study is not without its limitations. The players only comprised those that had gambled on the *Norsk Tipping* online platform during 1 month in 2015 and only evaluated the efficacy of viewing a single message on short-term behavior change in gambling (i.e., 1 week and 1 month after the message was viewed). Generalizations to other types of online gambler either in Norway or other countries cannot be assumed. Furthermore, players selectively retrieved the message and the information remained static, although the player behavior changed. It was also difficult to compare the players to the control group due to the fact that message retrieval was voluntary. Additionally it is not known if players read the message once or several times. Furthermore, the present study did not vary the display of the message content in terms of color or wording which may also have had a considerable impact on the message effect.

Future Research

Based on the findings presented here, there are many possible avenues for further research. Such research could investigate (i) the use of personalized messages more than once (for instance, the showing of messages once every month), (ii) the effects of recent wins on playing behavior and to what extent personalized messaging helps or hinders further gambling behavior, (iii) secondary data analysis of behavior connected to the retrieval of personalized spending information, (iv) varying the message content (e.g., emotional vs. warning vs. informative), (v) personalized messaging that addresses specific types of behavior (binge gambling, high loss gambling, high win gambling, etc.), (vi) the effects of regular personalized feedback compared to one-time feedback (e.g., weekly vs. monthly feedback), and (vii) long-term gambling behavior of samples rather than just over a 1-month period.

CONCLUSION

A number of conclusions based on the findings in the present study can be made. First, personalized behavioral feedback can enable behavioral change in gambling (based on data comparing those who received such messaging compared to those who did not). Second, additional normative feedback does not appear change behavior significantly more than personalized behavioral feedback. Third, patterns of gambling behavior associated with the effects of personalized messaging can be derived. Fourth, messages are most likely read during the 1st week after players have received them. Fifth, lottery players and female scratchcard players are more likely to read the message and act on messages than casino players. Sixth, lottery players (low and high spending) appear to benefit most from personalized feedback. Seventh, normative feedback does not appear to be beneficial for sports bettors, and high spending casino players do not appear to benefit from personalized feedback. In short, the data show that the effect of the three types of messaging (i.e., personalized feedback, normative feedback, and a recommendation) appears to depend upon players' gambling habits as well as demographic and game-type factors. This is especially important in practical terms because operators will also need to take into account player attributes and behaviors when presenting different kinds of messages. The present study demonstrates one way in which operators could use the big data that they routinely collect to help inform and encourage responsible gambling among its clientele. The study also demonstrates the positive way in which academic researchers can collaborate in innovative research initiatives that ultimately help relevant stakeholder groups.

AUTHOR CONTRIBUTIONS

MA: Co-designed the study, analyzed the data, and contributed to writing of the paper. MG: Co-designed the study and contributed to writing the paper.

FUNDING

This study was funded by *Norsk Tipping*. The second author was subcontracted by *neccton Ltd*.

REFERENCES

Ajzen, I. (1985). "From intentions to action: a theory of planned behavior," in *Action Control: from Cognitions to Behaviors*, eds J. Kuhl and J. Beckman (New York, NY: Springer), 11–39.

Auer, M., and Griffiths, M. D. (2013). Voluntary limit setting and player choice in most intense online gamblers: an empirical study of gambling behaviour. *J. Gambl. Stud.* 29, 647–660.

Auer, M., and Griffiths, M. D. (2014). An empirical investigation of theoretical loss and gambling intensity. *J. Gambl. Stud.* 30, 879–887. doi: 10.1007/s10899-013-9376-7

Auer, M., and Griffiths, M. D. (2015a). Testing normative and self-appraisal feedback in an online slot-machine pop-up message in a real-world setting. *Front. Psychol.* 6:339. doi: 10.3389/fpsyg.2015.00339

Auer, M., and Griffiths, M. D. (2015b). The use of personalized behavioral feedback for online gamblers: an empirical study. *Front. Psychol.* 6:1406. doi: 10.3389/fpsyg.2015.01406

Auer, M., Malischnig, D., and Griffiths, M. D. (2014). Is 'pop-up' messaging in online slot machine gambling effective as a responsible gambling strategy? An empirical re-search note. *J. Gambl. Issues* 29, 1–10. doi: 10.4309/jgi.2014.29.3

Auer, M., Schneeberger, A., and Griffiths, M. D. (2012). Theoretical loss and gambling intensity: a simulation study. *Gaming Law Rev. Econ.* 16, 269–273. doi: 10.1089/glre.2012.1655

Bandura, A. (2001). Social cognitive theory: an agentic perspective. *Annu. Rev. Psychol.* 52, 1–26. doi: 10.1146/annurev.psych.52.1.1

Braverman, J., LaPlante, D. A., Nelson, S. E., and Shaffer, H. J. (2013). Using cross-game behavioral markers for early identification if high-risk Internet gamblers. *Psychol. Addict. Behav.* 27, 868–877. doi: 10.1037/a0032818

Braverman, J., and Shaffer, H. J. (2012). How do gamblers start gambling: identifying behavioural markers of high-risk Internet gambling. *Eur. J. Public Health* 22, 273–278. doi: 10.1093/eurpub/ckp232

Broda, A., LaPlante, D. A., Nelson, S. E., LaBrie, R. A., Bosworth, L. B., and Shaffer, H. J. (2008). Virtual harm reduction efforts for Internet gambling: effects of deposit limits on actual Internet sports gambling behaviour. *Harm Reduct. J.* 5, 27–36. doi: 10.1186/1477-7517-5-27

Buttussi, F., Chittaro, L., and Nadalutti, D. (2006). "Bringing mobile guides and fitness activities together: a solution based on an embodied virtual trainer," in *Proceedings of MOBILE HCI 2006: 8th International Conference on Human-Computer Interaction with Mobile Devices and Services*, (New York, NY: ACM Press), 29–36.

Celio, M. A., and Lisman, S. A. (2014). Examining the efficacy of a personalized normative feedback intervention to reduce college student gambling. *J. Am. Coll. Health* 62, 154–164. doi: 10.1080/07448481.2013.865626

Cloutier, M., Ladouceur, R., and Sevigny, S. (2006). Responsible gambling tools: popup messages and pauses on video lottery terminals. *J. Psychol.* 140, 434–438. doi: 10.3200/JRLP.140.5.434-438

Dixon, M. (2000). Manipulating the illusion of control: variations in gambling as a function of perceived control over chance outcomes. *Psychol. Rec.* 50, 705–720.

Dragicevic, S., Tsogas, S. B., and Kudic, A. (2011). Analysis of casino online gambling data in relation to behavioural risk markers for high-risk gambling and player protection. *Int. Gambl. Stud.* 11, 377–391. doi: 10.1080/14459795.2011.629204

Focal Research (2004). *2003 NS VL Responsible Gaming Features Evaluation: Final Report*. Halifax, NS: Focal Research Consultants Ltd.

Fogg, B. J. (2003). *PSD: Using Computers to Change What We Think and Do*. San Francisco, CA: Morgan Kaufmann Publishers.

Forsström, D., Hesser, H., and Carlbring, P. (2016). Usage of a responsible gambling tool: a descpritive analysis of latent class analysis of user behavior. *J. Gambl. Stud.* 32, 889–904. doi: 10.1007/s10899-015-9590-6

Gaboury, A., and Ladouceur, R. (1989). Erroneous perceptions and gambling. *J. Soc. Behav. Pers.* 4, 411–420.

Gainsbury, S. M. (2015). Online gambling addiction: the relationship between internet gambling and disordered gambling. *Curr. Addict. Rep.* 2, 185–193. doi: 10.1007/s40429-015-0057-8

Gray, H. M., LaPlante, D. A., and Shaffer, H. J. (2012). Behavioral characteristics of Internet gamblers who trigger corporate responsible gambling interventions. *Psychol. Addict. Behav.* 26, 527–535. doi: 10.1037/a0028545

Griffiths, M. D. (1994). The role of cognitive bias and skill in fruit machine gambling. *Br. J. Psychol.* 85, 351–369. doi: 10.1111/j.2044-8295.1994.tb02529.x

Griffiths, M. D. (2003). Internet gambling: issues, concerns and recommendations. *Cyberpsychol. Behav.* 6, 557–568. doi: 10.1089/109493103322725333

Griffiths, M. D., Wood, R. T. A., and Parke, J. (2009). Social responsibility tools in online gambling: a survey of attitudes and behavior among Internet gamblers. *CyberPsychol. Behav.* 12, 413–421. doi: 10.1089/cpb.2009.0062

Hewett, T., Baecker, R., Card, S., Carey, T., Gasen, J., Mantei, M., et al. (1992). *Technical Report. ACM SIGCHI Curricula for Human-Computer Interaction*. New York, NY: ACM.

Hing, N. (2003). *An Assessment of Member Awareness, Perceived Adequacy and Perceived Effectiveness of Responsible Gambling Strategies in Sydney Clubs*. Lismore, NSW: Centre for Gambling Education and Research.

Janz, N. K., and Becker, M. H. (1984). The health belief model: a decade later. *Health Educ. Q.* 11, 1–47. doi: 10.1177/109019818401100101

LaBrie, R. A., Kaplan, S., LaPlante, D. A., Nelson, S. E., and Shaffer, H. J. (2008). Inside the virtual casino: a prospective longitudinal study of Internet casino gambling. *Eur. J. Public Health* 18, 410–416. doi: 10.1093/eurpub/ckn021

Ladouceur, R., and Sevigny, S. (2003). Interactive messages on video lottery terminals and persistence in gambling. *Gambl. Res.* 15, 45–50.

Lapham, G. T., Hawkins, E. J., Chavez, L. J., Achtmeyer, C. E., Williams, E. C., Bradley, K. A., et al. (2012). Feedback from recently returned veterans on an anonymous web-based brief alcohol intervention. *Addict. Sci. Clin. Pract.* 7:17. doi: 10.1186/1940-0640-7-17

LaPlante, D. A., Kleschinsky, J. H., LaBrie, R. A., Nelson, S. E., and Shaffer, H. J. (2009). Sitting at the virtual poker table: a prospective epidemiological study of actual Internet poker gambling behavior. *Comput. Hum. Behav.* 25, 711–717. doi: 10.1016/j.chb.2008.12.027

LaPlante, D. A., Schumann, A., LaBrie, R. A., and Shaffer, H. J. (2008). Population trends in Internet sports gambling. *Comput. Hum. Behav.* 24, 2399–2414. doi: 10.1016/j.chb.2008.02.015

Maiman, L. A., and Becker, M. H. (1974). The health belief model: origins and correlates in psychological theory. *Health Educ. Monogr.* 2, 336–353. doi: 10.1177/109019817400200404

McCormack, A., and Griffiths, M. D. (2013). A scoping study of the structural and situational characteristics of internet gambling. *Int. J. Cyber Behav. Psychol. Learn.* 3, 29–49. doi: 10.4018/ijcbpl.2013010104

McCusker, C., and Gettings, B. (1997). Automaticity of cognitive biases in addictive behaviors: further evidence with gamblers. *Br. J. Clin. Psychol.* 36, 543–554. doi: 10.1111/j.2044-8260.1997.tb01259.x

Meyer, G., Hayer, T., and Griffiths, M. D. (2009). *Problem Gambling in Europe: Challenges, Prevention, and Interventions*. New York, NY: Springer.

Miller, W. R., and Rollnick, S. (1991). *Motivational Interviewing: Preparing People to Change Addictive Behavior*. New York, NY: Guilford Press.

Monaghan, S. M., and Blaszczynski, A. (2007). Recall of electronic gaming machine signs: a static versus a dynamic mode of presentation. *J. Gambl. Issues* 20, 235–267. doi: 10.4309/jgi.2007.20.8

Monaghan, S. M., and Blaszczynski, A. (2010a). Impact of mode of display and message content of responsible gaming signs for electronic gaming machines on regular gamblers. *J. Gambl. Stud.* 26, 67–88. doi: 10.1007/s10899-009-9150-z

Monaghan, S. M., and Blaszczynski, A. (2010b). Electronic gaming machine warning messages: information versus self-evaluation. *J. Psychol.* 144, 83–96. doi: 10.1080/00223980903356081

Monaghan, S. M., Blaszczynski, A., and Nower, L. (2009). Do warning signs on electronic gaming machines influence irrational cognitions? *Psychol. Rep.* 105, 173–187. doi: 10.2466/PR0.105.1.173-187

Munoz, Y., Chebat, J. C., and Borges, A. (2013). Graphic gambling warning: how they affect emotions, cognitive responses and attitude change. *J. Gambl. Stud.* 29, 507–524. doi: 10.1007/s10899-012-9319-8

Nelson, S. E., LaPlante, D. A., Peller, A. J., Schumann, A., LaBrie, R. A., and Shaffer, H. J. (2008). Real limits in the virtual world: self-limiting behavior of Internet gamblers. *J. Gambl. Stud.* 24, 463–477. doi: 10.1007/s10899-008-9106-8

Obermayer, J. L., Riley, W. T., Asif, O., and Jean-Mary, J. (2004). College smoking-cessation using cell phone text messaging. *J. Am. Coll. Health* 53, 71–79. doi: 10.3200/JACH.53.2.71-78

Orford, J., Sproston, K., Erens, B., and Mitchell, L. (2003). *Gambling and Problem Gambling in Britain*. Hove: Brunner-Routledge.

Parke, J., Griffiths, M. D., and Parke, A. (2007). Positive thinking among slot machine gamblers: a case of maladaptive coping? *Int. J. Ment. Health Addict.* 5, 39–52. doi: 10.1007/s11469-006-9049-1

Perloff, R. M. (2008). *The Dynamics of Persuasion: Communication and Attitudes in the 21st Century*, 3rd Edn. New York, NY: Lawrence Erlbaum Associates.

Preece, J., Sharp, H., and Rogers, Y. (2011). *Interaction Design: Beyond Human Computer Interaction*, 3rd Edn. Chichester: John Wiley & Sons Ltd.

Prochaska, J. O., and DiClemente, C. C. (1983). Stages and processes of self-change of smoking: toward an integrative model of change. *J. Consult. Clin. Psychol.* 51, 390–395. doi: 10.1037/0022-006X.51.3.390

Prochaska, J. O., and Prochaska, J. M. (1991). Why don't people change? Why don't continents move? *J. Psychother. Integr.* 9, 83–102. doi: 10.1023/A:1023210911909

Rogers, R. W. (1983). "Cognitive and physiological processes in fear appeals and attitude change: a revised theory of protection motivation," in *Social Psychophysiology: A Sourcebook*, eds J. T. Cacioppo and R. E. Petty (New York, NY: Guildford Press), 153–176.

Schellink, T., and Schrans, T. (2002). *Atlantic Lottery Corporation Video Lottery Responsible Gaming Feature Research: Final report*. Halifax, NS: Focal Research Consultants.

Shneiderman, B., Plaisant, C., Cohen, M., and Jacobs, S. (2009). *Designing the User Interface: Strategies for Effective Human-Computer Interaction*, 5th Edn. Reading, MA: Peaerson Addison-Wesley.

Stewart, M. J., and Wohl, M. J. A. (2013). Pop-up messages, dissociation, and craving: how monetary limit reminders facilitate adherence in a session of slot machine gambling. *Psychol. Addict. Behav.* 27, 268–273. doi: 10.1037/a0029882

Stotts, A. L., Groff, J. Y., Velasquez, M. M., Benjamin-Garner, R., Green, C., Carbonari, J. P., et al. (2009). Ultrasound feedback and motivational interviewing targeting smoking cessation in the second and third trimesters of pregnancy. *Nicotine Tob. Res.* 11, 961–968. doi: 10.1093/ntr/ntp095

Van den Putte, B., Yzer, M., Willemsen, M., and de Bruijn, G. J. (2009). The effects of smoking self-identity and quitting self-identity on attempts to quit smoking. *Health Psychol.* 28, 535–544. doi: 10.1037/a0015199

Wardle, H., Griffiths, M. D., Orford, J., Moody, A., and Volberg, R. (2012). Gambling in britain: A time of change? Health implications from the British gambling prevalence survey 2010. *Int. J. Ment. Health Addict.* 10, 273–277. doi: 10.1016/j.jsat.2008.04.005

Wardle, H., Sproston, K., Orford, J., Erens, B., Griffiths, M. D., Constantine, R., et al. (2007). *The British Gambling Prevalence Survey 2007*. London: The Stationery Office.

Williams, R. J., and Connolly, D. (2006). Does learning about the mathematics of gambling change gambling behavior? *Psychol. Addict. Behav.* 20, 62–68. doi: 10.1037/0893-164X.20.1.62

Witte, K. (1992). Putting the fear back into fear appeal: the extended parallel process model (EPPM). *Commun. Monogr.* 61, 113–132. doi: 10.1080/10410236.2012.708633

Witte, K., Meyer, G., and Martell, D. (2001). *Effective Health Risk Messages: A Step-by-Step Guide*. Thousand Oaks, CA: Sage Publications.

Wohl, M. J., Christie, K. L., Matheson, C., and Anisman, H. (2010). Animation-based education as a gambling prevention tool: correcting erroneous cognitions and reducing the frequency of exceeding limits among slots players. *J. Gambl. Stud.* 26, 469–486. doi: 10.1007/s10899-009-9155-7

Wohl, M. J., Gainsbury, S., Stewart, M. J., and Sztainert, T. (2013). Facilitating responsible gambling: the relative effectiveness of education-based animation and monetary limit setting pop-up messages among electronic gaming machine players. *J. Gambl. Stud.* 29, 703–717. doi: 10.1007/s10899-012-9340-y

Wohl, M. J., Parush, A., Kim, H. S., and Warren, K. (2014). Building it better: applying human-computer interaction and persuasive system design principles to a monetary limit tool improves responsible gambling. *Comput. Hum. Behav.* 37, 124–132. doi: 10.1016/j.chb.2014.04.045

Wood, R. T. A., and Wohl, M. J. (2015). Assessing the effectiveness of a responsible gambling behavioural feedback tool for reducing the gambling expenditure of at-risk players. *Int. Gambl. Stud.* 15, 1–16. doi: 10.1080/14459795.2015.1049191

Wulfert, E., Blanchard, E. B., Freidenberg, B. M., and Martell, R. S. (2006). Retaining pathological gamblers in cognitive behavior therapy through motivational enhancement: a pilot study. *Behav. Modif.* 30, 315–340. doi: 10.1177/0145445503262578

Yzer, M. C., Fishbein, M., and Cappella, J. N. (2007). "Using behavioral theory to investigate routes to persuasion for segmented groups: a case study of adolescent drug use," in *Freiberger Beitraege zur Interkulturellen und Wirtschaftskommunikation: A Forum for General and Intercultural Business Communication*, Vol. 3, ed. M. B. Hinner (Frankfurt: Lang), 297–320.

Yzer, M. C., Siero, F. W., and Buunk, B. P. (2000). Can public campaigns effectively change psychological determinants of safer sex? An evaluation of three Dutch safer sex campaigns. *Health Educ. Res.* 15, 339–352.

Conflict of Interest Statement: The authors declare that the research was conducted in the absence of any commercial or financial relationships that could be construed as a potential conflict of interest.

Norsk Tipping provided access to the data and assisted in interpreting the results. However the writing of the paper, interpretation and conclusions reached were written in an independent capacity and not influenced.

Permissions

List of Contributors

Paul C. Quinn
Department of Psychological and Brain Sciences, University of Delaware, Newark, DE, USA

Kang Lee
Dr. Eric Jackman Institute of Child Study, University of Toronto, Toronto, ON, Canada

James W. Tanaka
Department of Psychology, University of Victoria, Victoria, BC, Canada

Laurie Bayet and Olivier Pascalis
Laboratoire de Psychologie et Neurocognition, University of Grenoble-Alps, Grenoble, France
Laboratoire de Psychologie et Neurocognition, Centre National de la Recherche Scientifique, Grenoble, France

Édouard Gentaz
Laboratoire de Psychologie et Neurocognition, University of Grenoble-Alps, Grenoble, France
Laboratoire de Psychologie et Neurocognition, Centre National de la Recherche Scientifique, Grenoble, France
Faculty of Psychology and Educational Sciences, University of Geneva, Geneva, Switzerland

Gwilym Lockwood
Neurobiology of Language Department, Max Planck Institute for Psycholinguistics, Nijmegen, Netherlands

Mark Dingemanse
Language and Cognition Department, Max Planck Institute for Psycholinguistics, Nijmegen, Netherlands

Ralf Brand
Sport and Exercise Psychology, University of Potsdam, Potsdam, Germany

Wanja Wolff
Department of Sport Science, Sport Psychology, University of Konstanz, Konstanz, Germany

Matthias Ziegler
Department of Psychology, Psychological Diagnostics, Humboldt Universität zu Berlin, Berlin, Germany

Milton Sousa
Leadership Knowledge Centre, Nova School of Business and Economics, Lisbon, Portugal

Dirk Van Dierendonck
Centre for Leadership Studies, Rotterdam School of Management, Erasmus University, Rotterdam, Netherlands

C. Philip Beaman
Centre for Cognition Research, School of Psychology and Clinical Language Sciences, University of Reading, Reading, UK

Dylan M. Jones
School of Psychology, Cardiff University, Cardiff, UK

Peishan Tan
Center for Studies of Psychological Application, School of Psychology, South China Normal University, Guangzhou, China

Lu Sun
Center for Studies of Psychological Application, School of Psychology, South China Normal University, Guangzhou, China
Primary School Affiliated to South China Normal University, Guangzhou, China

You Cheng
Center for Studies of Psychological Application, School of Psychology, South China Normal University, Guangzhou, China
Department of Psychological and Brain Sciences, Dartmouth College, Hanover, NH, USA

Chen Qu
Center for Studies of Psychological Application, School of Psychology, South China Normal University, Guangzhou, China
School of Economics and Management and Scientific Laboratory of Economics Behaviors, South China Normal University, Guangzhou, China

Edina Dóci and Joeri Hofmans
Faculty of Psychology and Educational Sciences, Vrije Universiteit Brussel, Brussel, Belgium

Jeroen Stouten
Department of Psychology, University of Leuven, Leuven, Belgium

Seth B. Agyei, F. R. (Ruud) van der Weel and Audrey L. H. van der Meer
Developmental Neuroscience Laboratory, Department of Psychology, Norwegian University of Science and Technology, Trondheim, Norway

Balazs Aczel, AbaSzollosi and Andrei Foldes
Institute of Psychology, Eotvos Lorand University, Budapest, Hungary

Bence Bago
Paris Descartes University, Paris, France

Bence Lukacs
Corvinus University of Budapest, Budapest, Hungary

Laura Mieth, Raoul Bell and Axel Buchner
Department of Experimental Psychology, Heinrich Heine University Düsseldorf, Düsseldorf, Germany

Helena L. Rohlf and Barbara Krahé
Department of Psychology, University of Potsdam, Potsdam, Germany

Bradly T. Stone, Kelly A. Correa, Maja Stikic, Robin R. Johnson and Chris Berka
Advanced Brain Monitoring, Inc., Carlsbad, CA, USA

Timothy L. Brown
National Advanced Driving Simulator, Center for Computer Aided Design, The University of Iowa, Iowa City, IA, USA

Andrew L. Spurgin
National Advanced Driving Simulator, Center for Computer Aided Design, The University of Iowa, Iowa City, IA, USA
College of Pharmacy, The University of Iowa, Iowa City, IA, USA

Stephen J. Rassenti
Economic Science Institute, Chapman University, Orange, CA, USA

Ellen P. Green
School for the Science of Health Care Delivery, Arizona State University, Phoenix, AZ, USA

Hernán D. Bejarano
Department of Economics, Center of Economic Research and Teaching, Aguascalientes, Mexico
Economic Science Institute, Chapman University, Orange, CA, USA

Jeroen Bommelé and Sebastian D. J. VandeVondele
Department of Social and Organizational Psychology, Utrecht University, Utrecht, Netherlands

E. A. Lind
Fuqua School of Business, Duke University, Durham, NC, USA

Kees van den Bos
Department of Social and Organizational Psychology, Utrecht University, Utrecht, Netherlands
School of Law, Utrecht University, Utrecht, Netherlands

Mowei Shen, JunYin, Xiaowei Ding, Rende Shui and Jifan Zhou
Department of Psychology and Behavioral Sciences, Zhejiang University, Hangzhou, China

Gemma Mestre-Bach, Laura Moragas, Neus Aymamí and Mónica Gómez-Peña
Pathological Gambling Unit, Department of Psychiatry, Bellvitge University Hospital-IDIBELL, Barcelona, Spain

Salomé Tárrega
Departament de Psicobiologia i Metodologia de les Ciències de la Salut, Universitat Autònoma de Barcelona, Barcelona, Spain

Amparo del Pino-Gutiérrez
Nursing Department of Mental Health, Public Health, Maternal and Child Health, Nursing School, University of Barcelona, Barcelona, Spain

Roser Granero
Ciber Fisiopatología Obesidad y Nutrición (CIBERObn), Instituto de Salud Carlos III, Barcelona, Spain
Departament de Psicobiologia i Metodologia de les Ciències de la Salut, Universitat Autònoma de Barcelona, Barcelona, Spain

Trevor Steward, Marta Baño and Núria Mallorquí-Bagué
Departament de Psicobiologia i Metodologia de les Ciències de la Salut, Universitat Autònoma de Barcelona, Barcelona, Spain
Pathological Gambling Unit, Department of Psychiatry, Bellvitge University Hospital-IDIBELL, Barcelona, Spain

Fernando Fernández-Aranda and Susana Jiménez-Murcia
Ciber Fisiopatología Obesidad y Nutrición (CIBERObn), Instituto de Salud Carlos III, Barcelona, Spain
Pathological Gambling Unit, Department of Psychiatry, Bellvitge University Hospital-IDIBELL, Barcelona, Spain
Department of Clinical Sciences, Faculty of Medicine, University of Barcelona, Barcelona, Spain

José M. Menchón
Pathological Gambling Unit, Department of Psychiatry, Bellvitge University Hospital-IDIBELL, Barcelona, Spain
Department of Clinical Sciences, Faculty of Medicine, University of Barcelona, Barcelona, Spain

Ciberde Salud Mental (CIBERSAM), Instituto de Salud Carlos III, Barcelona, Spain

Michael M. Auer and Mark D. Griffiths
neccton Ltd, Lienz, Austria
Psychology, Nottingham Trent University, Nottingham, UK

Index

A

Abstract Effort, 162

Altruistic Tendency, 67-71, 73, 75-77

Anger Reactivity, 134, 136-138, 140, 142-146

Anger Regulation, 134-147

Anger-eliciting Task, 134, 136-137, 144-145

Asch Paradigm, 178-179, 181, 183, 185, 187,189-191

Attentional Unit, 193, 195-197, 202

Auditory Cognition, 53

Auditory Scene Analysis, 53, 56-59, 64

B

Behavioral Addictions, 205-209, 211-215

Behavioral Affiliation, 178-181, 183-187, 189-191

Behavioral Disinhibition, 178-179, 181-192

Behavioral Feedback, 217, 219, 221, 223, 225,227-229

Behavioral Integration, 41-52

Behavioral Observation, 134-141, 143-145, 147

Behavioral Studies, 93, 95, 97, 99, 101, 103, 105

Behavioral Types, 162-163, 165, 167, 169-171, 173,175, 177

Belongingness Threat, 188

Benzodiazepine, 148-155, 157-161

C

Clinical Comparison, 205, 207, 209, 211, 213, 215

Cognitive Antecedents, 78-79, 81, 83, 85, 87, 89, 91

Cognitive Enhancement, 30-32, 39-40

Cognitive Performance, 30-34, 36-38, 160

Compulsive Buying Behavior, 205, 207, 209, 211,213, 215

Computational Evidence, 1, 3, 5, 7, 9, 11, 13, 15

Control Group, 23, 130, 217, 219-221, 223, 226-227

Cross-modal Correspondence, 16, 19

D

Decision Biases, 107, 109, 111, 113, 115-117, 119

Decision Making, 19, 41, 43-51, 75, 95, 107,116-119, 132, 175, 214

Demographics, 150, 159, 163, 171, 173, 177, 220,224, 226

Discriminant Function Analysis, 157

Driving Impairments, 148-151, 153, 155, 157-159,161

Drug Instrumentalization, 30-31, 33-35, 37-38

E

Expert Traits, 162-163, 165, 167, 169, 171, 173, 175,177

F

Face Perception, 1, 14

Facial Expressions, 1-3, 5, 7, 9, 11, 13-15, 203

Fatal Accidents, 148

G

Gambling Disorder, 205-209, 211-212, 214-215

Game Type, 224

Gaming Revenue, 217

Gender Categorization, 1-5, 7-13, 15

H

Handshakes, 193-195, 197, 199, 201, 203

Human-computer Interaction, 217, 220, 228-229

I

Ideophones, 16-18, 22-29

Individual Differences, 33, 39, 68, 75, 78-79, 82,90-91, 107-109, 111, 113-119, 136, 159, 188, 204

Individualized Scores, 108

M

Message Effect, 223, 227

Middle Childhood, 134-135, 137, 139, 141, 143-147

Mixture Modeling, 30, 37

Moral Dilemma, 162-165, 167, 169, 171-175, 177

N

Neuroenhancement, 30-33, 35-37, 39-40

Neuroimaging, 16-17, 19, 21, 23, 25-27, 29

Neurophysiological Signatures, 148-149, 151, 153,155, 157-159, 161

Non-addictive Behavior, 30

Non-social Paired Objects, 203

O

Online Gamblers, 217, 219, 221, 223, 225, 227-229

Operationalization, 42, 46-47, 50

Optic Flow Processing, 93, 95, 106

Optimal Distinctiveness, 178-179, 189

Overwriting, 53-61, 63-65

P

Passive Leadership, 78-89, 91

Persuasive Communication, 217

Phonotactics, 24

Pop-up Messaging, 219
Predicted Behavior, 166
Prescription Drugs, 30-32, 34-37, 39, 149
Problem Gambling, 116, 217, 228
Prospective Control, 93-103, 105-106
Psychoactive Drugs, 30-31, 214-215
Psycholinguistics, 16-17

R
Real Effort, 162, 169
Responsible Gambling, 217-221, 227-229

S
Self-evaluations, 78, 80, 82-84, 86-87, 89-91
Sense-making, 178, 180, 192
Servant Leadership, 41-52, 91
Shared Servant Leadership, 41-51
Short-term Memory, 53-54, 59, 63-66, 104, 152
Similarity-based Streaming, 63
Social Cooperation, 67, 120-123, 125, 127, 129,131-133
Social Processing, 203
Social Rejection, 134-140, 142-146, 190

Sound-symbolism, 16-29
Source Guessing, 125, 128-129, 132
Source Memory, 120-129, 131-133
Stereotyped-belief, 1
Synesthesia, 16, 21, 25, 28

T
Team Performance, 41-43, 45-52, 90
Third-party Punishment, 67-71, 73, 75-77
Transactional Leadership, 78, 81, 89
Transformational Leadership, 78-79, 81, 83, 85, 87,89-91

U
User Types, 30

V
Verbal Memory, 54, 56, 59, 61, 129
Virtual Stimuli, 99
Visual Motion Perception, 93-95, 97, 99, 101-103,105-106
Visual Organization, Attention, 193

W
Working Memory Load, 120

CPSIA information can be obtained
at www.ICGtesting.com
Printed in the USA
LVHW051620220519
618747LV00004B/22/P